FRENCH ARMOURED CRUISERS
1887–1932

FRENCH ARMOURED CRUISERS 1887–1932

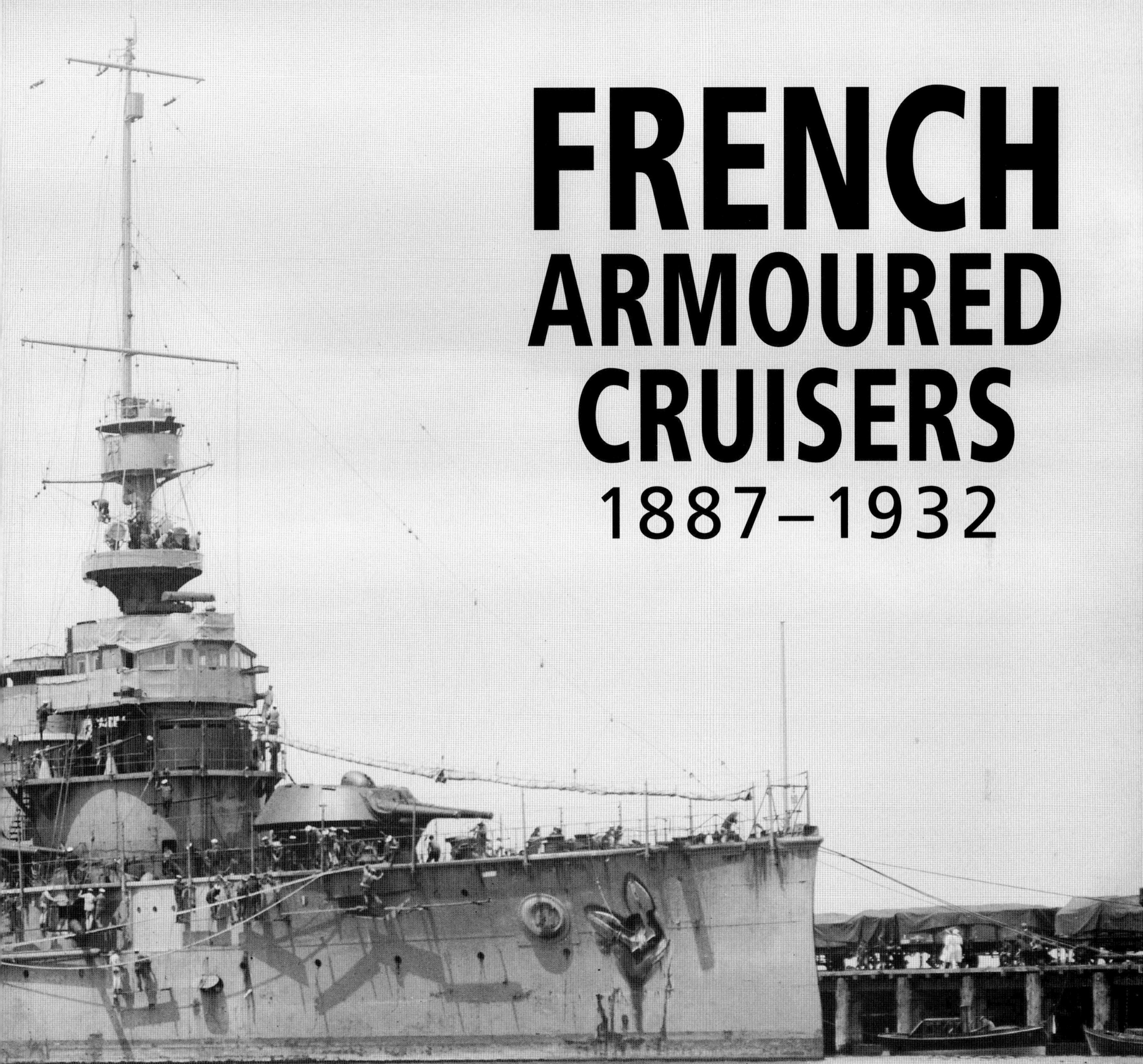

John Jordan & Philippe Caresse

Seaforth
PUBLISHING

Overleaf: The armoured cruiser *Victor Hugo* during a visit to Melbourne in January 1923. She accompanied the flagship *Jules Michelet* during her visit to Australia – see Chapter 12. *(Allan C Green collection, State Library of Victoria, H91_325_23)*

First published in Great Britain in 2019 by
Seaforth Publishing
An imprint of Pen & Sword Books Ltd
47 Church Street, Barnsley
S Yorkshire S70 2AS

www.seaforthpublishing.com
Email info@seaforthpublishing.com

British Library Cataloguing in Publication Data
A CIP data record for this book is available from the British Library

ISBN 978-1-5267-4118-9 (Hardback)

ISBN 978-1-5267-4120-2 (Kindle)

ISBN 978-1-5267-4119-6 (ePub)

Pen & Sword Books Limited incorporates the imprints of Atlas, Archaeology, Aviation, Discovery, Family History, Fiction, History, Maritime, Military, Military Classics, Politics, Select, Transport, True Crime, Air World, Frontline Publishing, Leo Cooper, Remember When, Seaforth Publishing, The Praetorian Press, Wharncliffe Local History, Wharncliffe Transport, Wharncliffe True Crime and White Owl.

Typeset and designed by Stephen Dent
Printed and bound in China

CONTENTS

PREFACE

This book is intended as a companion volume to *French Battleships of World War One*, published by Seaforth in 2017. Of the five books on the French Navy that I have coauthored (with Robert Dumas, Jean Moulin and now with Philippe Caresse) the present book has proved by far the most difficult to research. The other volumes all had firm foundations in the form of French-language monographs published by Marines Editions and Lela Presse. However, no book on the French armoured cruisers has ever been published in France. The only detailed coverage of their design and technical characteristics has been a series of articles on the early ships by Luc Feron published in a variety of journals including *Marines*, *Marines & Forces Navales*, and *Warship* (see Bibliography), and the original documentation relating to the design of the ships held in the archives at Vincennes, particularly for the later ships, is patchy and incomplete. I am therefore particularly grateful to Stephen Roberts, coauthor of a series of books on the French Navy in the Age of Sail,[1] for supplying copies of submissions and memoranda relating to cruiser design by the *Service Technique des Constructions Navales*, the *Conseil des Travaux* and the 4th Section of the Naval General Staff (EMG) during the key period in question, the years 1897 to 1900.

The principles which underpinned the design of the armoured cruisers were essentially the same as those which governed French battleships of the period, and the author has attempted to avoid excessive duplication between the two books, which are intended to complement one another. For a detailed account of technological developments in gunnery, steel and propulsion from the middle of the nineteenth century the reader is referred to the Introduction of *French Battleships*; the latter book also has comprehensive coverage of the developments in naval fire control which took place between 1890 and 1922. The present book focuses on the elements which were regarded as key to French armoured cruiser performance: the medium quick-firing (QF) and heavier 'semi-quick-firing' guns,[2] and propulsion machinery. The French were at the forefront of developments in both these aspects of cruiser design, principally through the early adoption of wing turrets in preference to side-mounted casemate guns, and through their experimentation with advanced small watertube boilers capable of generating high steam pressures (see Introduction). Much attention was also given to protection against the enemy's guns, and the graduated protection schemes of the French armoured cruisers, which were every bit as complex as those of the battleships, are covered in detail.

SOURCES

Luc Feron's series of articles on the earlier French armoured cruisers were invaluable, particularly for the discussions which preceded the approval of the designs and for the subsequent service careers of the ships. Theodore Ropp's superlative book *The Development of a European Navy*, written in 1937 and subsequently revised and edited for the US Naval Institute, provided a political and technical framework for the French Navy during the late nineteenth century. Ropp outlines the importance of the armoured cruiser for the *Marine Nationale* during the 1890s and the extent to which the projected strategic and tactical role of these ships figured in the disputes between the various factions.

Data on the guns are based on a set of tables produced by the French Navy, probably around 1914, and passed to the US naval *attaché*, Rear Admiral A T Long, in July 1919. Entitled *Bouches à Feu de l'Artillerie Navale de tous Calibres & Modèles*, it is extremely detailed with regard to the characteristics of the guns and their associated ammunition. However, it does not link a particular gun to a particular class of ship or provide figures for maximum range or for the firing cycle; this information has had to be pieced together using the plans of the ships and secondary French-language sources.

Construction dates have not always been easy to find, and there are often major disagreements between (and gaps in) secondary sources. Launch dates, which are usually well documented due to the degree of ceremony which accompanied the launch of a major vessel, are generally reliable. The date the ship was manned for trials (*armé pour essais*) is often recorded in the official documentation, as is the date the ship commissioned (*armement définitif*). However, determining the date a ship was laid down has been particularly problematic in the case of the armoured cruisers. Secondary sources often confuse the date the contract was signed (*date du marché*) – or, in the case of the naval dockyards, the date instructions were received from Paris – with the date that work on the frames and hull plating was begun (*mise en chantier*) or the date the keel was laid (*mise en cale*).

Machinery trials data are from documents, many handwritten and therefore difficult to read, held at the Centre d'Archives de l'Armement at Châtellerault. The published work of Emile Bertin, edited and translated by Leslie Robertson, and of J-M le Guilcher (see Bibliography), provided invaluable information on the technical characteristics of the marine boilers of the day.

The major source for the illustration of the technical chapters of the book is the extensive set of builders' plans of the ships published online by the Service Historique de la Défense (SHD). As in the earlier books the plans have been adapted and redrawn and, where appropriate, re-labelled in English at a scale suitable for reproduction on the page; the original plan(s) used have generally been referenced on the drawing. Data for dimensions and displacement are tabulated on the original Body Plan (*Plan des formes*) for each ship, and these have been used for the tables of characteristics. The Reports on Foreign Naval Affairs (RFNA), published by the British Admiralty from 1901 to 1908

[1] Rif Winfield and Stephen S Roberts, *French Warships in the Age of Sail 1526–1786* and *1786–1861* (Barnsley: Seaforth Publishing, 2017 and 2015 respectively).

[2] 240mm (9.45in) in *D'Entrecasteaux*, 194mm (7.6in) in the other ships.

and held in the Admiralty Library at Portsmouth, were useful for elucidating some of the technical issues surrounding the French armoured cruisers. These reports were drawn up following visits by Royal Navy intelligence officers to the French naval dockyards and other establishments, during which access was given to civil and naval engineers, and they often highlight aspects of French ship design and naval technology which differed from British practice.

ACKNOWLEDGEMENTS

Jean Moulin, co-author of two of the books on the French Navy of the interwar period, visited the Centre d'Archives de l'Armement at Châtellerault on a number of occasions to photograph plans and to conduct research on my behalf into particular aspects of these ships. The sections on propulsion and the data tables detailing the performance of individual ships during full-power trials are the result of Jean's invaluable work. Stephen Roberts supplied documentation on French cruiser design policy during the period 1897 to 1900 and copies of the tabular data for French guns.

Ian Sturton was kind enough to read through the technical and historical chapters and to provide detailed comments and advice. Jean Roche sent copies of articles published in French-language journals and provided documentation from a variety of sources, particularly *Le Yacht*. Alain Hérault of the Centre d'Archives responded promptly to my request for plans of the protection schemes of the cruisers *Léon Gambetta*, *Jules Michelet* and *Ernest Renan*, which had not previously been scanned and were not therefore available from the SHD website. Matthew Seligmann suggested the RFNA as a source of Royal Navy perceptions and intelligence.

This book would not have been possible without the collaboration of my co-author, Philippe Caresse. In addition to assisting with the research, Philippe made his extensive collection of contemporary photographs freely available and provided informative captions; other photographs were provided by Robert Dumas, Jean-Marie Gall and Conrad Waters. Images from known sources have been credited; for photographs from private collections or of unknown origin (credited 'DR') all rights are reserved. Finally, sincere thanks are extended to Rob Gardiner of Seaforth Publishing, who has offered his customary support and advice throughout the project, and to Stephen Dent, whose imaginative layouts have used the authors' material to best advantage.

John Jordan
January 2019

ACRONYMS AND ABBREVIATIONS

ORGANISATIONS

CAA Centre d'Archives de l'Armement (Châtellerault, SW France)
CSM *Conseil supérieur de la Marine* (Navy Board [advisory])
DNEO *Division navale de l'Extrême-Orient* (Far East Division)
DNL *Division navale du Levant* (Levant Division)
EMG *Etat-major général de la Marine* (Naval General Staff)
RFNA Reports on Foreign Naval Affairs
STCN *Service Technique des Constructions Navales* (Constructors' Department)

TECHNICAL

AP(C) armour-piercing (capped)
ATB anti-torpedo boat
B&S Barr & Stroud (British manufacturer of optical rangefinders)
BL breech-loading
BM (*poudre*) *Boulanger marine* (nitrocellulose propellant)
BR boiler room
cal calibre
CI cast iron (shell)
CV *chevaux* (horsepower: 1CV = 0.98632shp)
DL *Division légère* (Light Division)
DM *décision ministérielle* (ministerial directive)
ER engine room
FF French francs
GA general arrangement
HA high-angle (guns)
HE high-explosive (shell)
HP high pressure (cylinder)
HTE horizontal triple expansion (reciprocating engine)
IP intermediate pressure (cylinder)
kW kilowatts
LA low-angle (guns)
LD laid down
LP low pressure (cylinder)
Mle *Modèle* (model)
PBI *pont blindé inférieur* (lower armoured deck)
PBS *pont blindé supérieur* (upper armoured deck)
QF quick-firing
RF rangefinder
RFW reserve feedwater
rpg rounds per gun
rpm rounds per minute
SAP(C) semi-armour piercing (capped)
shp shaft horsepower
S/L searchlight (projector)
TT torpedo tube(s)
VTE vertical triple-expansion (reciprocating engine)
W/T wireless telegraphy

RANKS AND SPECIALIST PERSONNEL

CA *contre-amiral* (Rear Admiral)
CF *capitaine de frégate* (Commander)
CO commanding officer
CPO chief petty officer
CV *capitaine de vaisseau* (Captain)
C-in-C Commander in Chief
MO Medical Officer
PO petty officer
VA *vice-amiral* (Vice Admiral)

CONVERSION TABLES

DIMENSIONS

Length				Beam	
m	ft	m	ft	m	ft
100	328	145	476	15	49
105	345	150	492	16	52.5
110	361	155	509	17	55.5
115	377	160	525	18	59
120	394	165	541	19	62.5
125	410			20	65.5
130	427			21	69
135	443			22	72
140	459			23	75.5

Note:
Length to nearest 1ft, beam to nearest 0.5ft.

GUN CALIBRES

Main Guns		Medium Guns		ATB Guns	
mm (cm)	in	mm (cm)	in	mm	in
240 (24)	9.45	164.7 (16)	6.5	65	[9pdr]
194 (19)	7.64	138.6 (14)	5.46	47	[3pdr]
		100	3.9		

Nomenclature

Decks 1890-1900

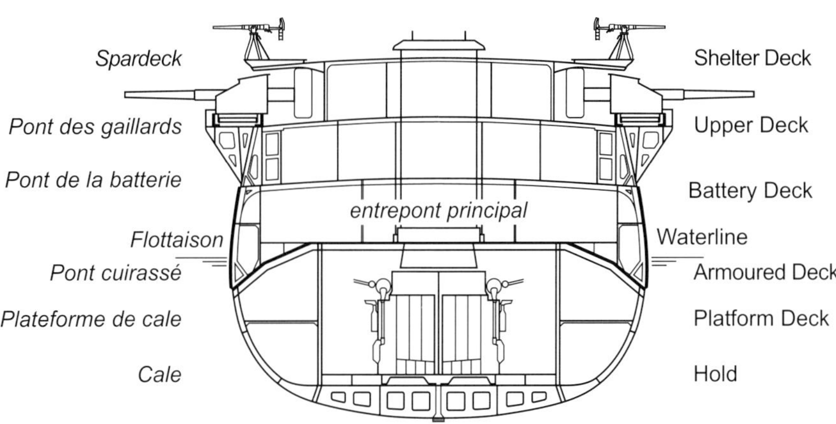

Decks 1900 onwards

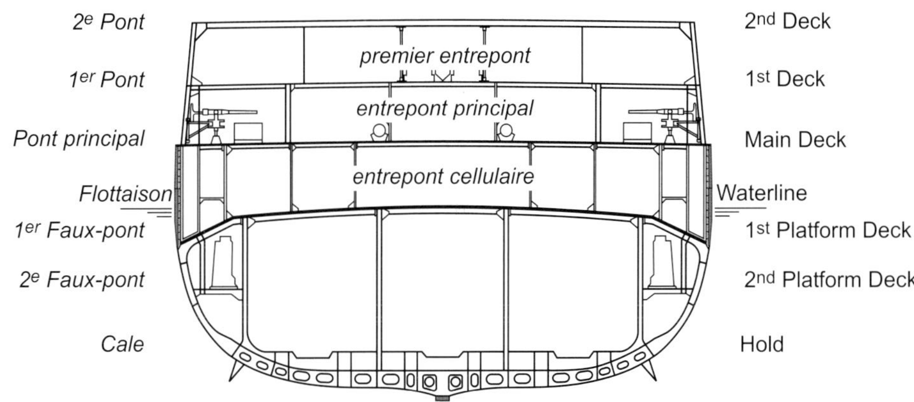

INTRODUCTION

I think this will work very well in practice. But will it work in theory?[1]

The French *Dupuy-de-Lôme*, designed by the distinguished naval architect Louis de Bussy, was the world's first modern armoured cruiser. Prior to the laying down of this revolutionary ship, cruisers with steel hulls had only horizontal protection in the form of a carapace over the ship's vitals. However, the advent of shell with a high-explosive bursting charge that could wreak havoc within the upper hull and superstructures changed perceptions. Fortunately the technology to resist the new shell was at hand in the form of lightweight armour plating of homogeneous nickel steel that could be applied to the ship's sides, and the resistance to penetration of this vertical armour would be enhanced during the 1890s by a 'face-hardening' process devised by the American Augustus Harvey and refined by the German armaments firm Krupp.

The *Marine Nationale* embraced the armoured cruiser concept with enthusiasm and remained at the forefront of development throughout the 1890s and the early 1900s. The fast cruiser was well-liked by the *Jeune Ecole* faction because of its commerce-raiding potential, despite its relatively high cost, while the more conservative elements of the Navy still wedded to the battleship quickly saw the value of a well-protected, powerfully-armed cruiser that could operate in the van of the battle fleet for scouting and screening. Whereas French battleship technology increasingly lagged behind that of the Royal Navy, the French armoured cruisers, which from the mid-1890s were designed by the innovative naval architect Louis-Emile Bertin and were ordered in numbers, were a major source of concern to the British. In the years 1903–04, the two years that preceded the *Entente Cordiale*, France completed no fewer than eleven of these ships, which were perceived as a major threat to Britain's trade.

Right: Louis-Emile Bertin was one of the world's most celebrated naval architects. During the period in question he was responsible for the design of all but one of the most modern and most powerful types of French armoured cruiser. *(SHD-M)*

THE DESIGN PROCESS

Technical advice on the design of French battleships and cruisers was initially the responsibility of the *Conseil des Travaux*, set up in 1831 to examine all projects relating to the construction of warships and dockyard infrastructure. Throughout its existence the *Conseil* normally comprised at least eighteen members: general and senior officers of the Navy and the engineering corps, generals of artillery, and inspectors of hydraulic works.

The process with regard to new warship proposals was as follows. The council considered the staff requirements drawn up by the *Conseil supérieur de la Marine* (a body of senior officers that advised the Minister of Marine on overall naval policy) and made its own observations. The project was then returned to the Minister, who commissioned design studies from the *Directeur du Matériel* (see below). These studies, which might involve competitive submissions by naval architects belonging to the corps of constructors (*Constructions Navales*), were then submitted to the *Conseil des Travaux* for further consideration. The council would approve some studies – usually with requests for modifications – and reject others, then pass the successful submission(s) back to the Minister for approval. *Constructions Navales* then completed the preliminary design work and followed every step of construction, supervised by the *Directeur du Matériel.*

The *Conseil des Travaux* had a preponderance of senior admirals, who during the 1890s came to be seen as exerting a conservative influence in a period of rapid transformation. During the period in question the *Conseil* did little beyond raising objections to the projects placed before it. Following the appointment of Emile Bertin as *Directeur du Matériel* in November 1895, a *Service Technique des Constructions Navales* (STCN) was established, with responsibility not only for drawing up design studies on the instructions of the Minister but for providing technical advice. Initial funding for the STCN was sufficient for only four naval architects, who were therefore able to submit only preliminary studies and general plans; much of the detailed design work was left to the architects attached

[1] Translation into English of the 'punch line' of a contemporary joke satirising the French mentality. The French 'Cartesian' approach to scientific and engineering problems is often contrasted unfavourably with the British 'pragmatic', experience-based approach.

Left: The starboard forward 164.7mm turret of the armoured cruiser *Condé*. The turret is a classic example of Bertin's *tourelle-barbette*, in which the lower part of the rotating gunhouse was housed within a ring of fixed armour. As can be seen from the men standing in front, the turret was relatively cramped. Note the hinged panels around the top edge of the gunhouse which provided natural ventilation when the gun was firing; the build-up of toxic gases within the turret was a major problem with QF guns. *(Private collection)*

to the dockyards and shipyards to whom contracts were awarded, leading to a lack of standardisation in equipment and machinery.

In philosophical terms the Navy had made lack of standardisation a virtue. In the wake of the block obsolescence of the fleet of ironclads designed by the distinguished naval architect Dupuy de Lôme, the Budgetary Committee chaired by Etienne Lamy in 1878 declared that 'as long as [France] builds her fleet in groups of identical ships, any progress in the naval art will weaken several elements of her naval strength at the same time'.[2] And throughout the 1880s all French battleships were 'custom built'; one of the less successful outcomes of this policy was the *Flotte d'échantillons* of the early 1890s, comprising five battleships with similar overall capabilities but designed by different naval architects.[3]

The principal problem with this approach was that developments in naval artillery, projectiles and propellant, armour steel and machinery were advancing so quickly during the period 1890–1900 that ships were becoming obsolescent almost before they were completed, and the differences between individual units, rather than facilitating conceptual progress, were simply complicating maintenance and the training of personnel. Also, the French predilection for incremental technical improvements between ships of the same basic design, together with constant tinkering with plans even after ships had been laid down, resulted in increased costs and prolonged building times. During the period in question the British Royal Navy forged ahead by adopting 'industrial' production techniques, building large classes of ships of almost identical design with standardised weapons, protection systems and machinery. It took five years for the French to complete a battleship or cruiser and at least another year to run trials. British building times were little more than half these figures, and the trials process was simplified because the uniformity of design meant that only the first ship of a class would need to undergo exhaustive trials; lessons learned would then be applied to the remaining units of the class. Thus in the time it took the *Marine Nationale* to get the five battleships of the 1890 programme into service the British were able to complete eight *Royal Sovereigns* and nine *Majestics*.

An example of the problems experienced as a result of non-standardisation of equipment and machinery was recounted in the contemporary journal *Le Yacht* in the issue of 2 March 1904. After the armoured cruiser *Léon Gambetta* struck a submerged rock in fog during her trials (see Chapter 7), it was found that the starboard propeller had stripped its blades, and the propeller on the centre shaft was also damaged beyond repair. The first thought was to use the propellers manufactured for *Léon Gambetta*'s sisters *Jules Ferry* and *Victor Hugo*, whose construction was less advanced. However, the propellers were found to be incompatible with the shafts, and an order for new propellers had to be placed with the builder of the machinery, Penhoët of Saint-Nazaire, resulting in a delay of four/five months before trials could be resumed. The author of the report made a plea for all ships of a series to have the same specifications, so that spares were interchangeable.

ARMAMENT

French guns were as good – if not better – than any in the world. Construction techniques were advanced, as

2 Quoted in Ropp, *The Development of a Modern Navy: French Naval Policy 1871–1904*, p 290.

3 See Jordan and Caresse, *French Battleships of World War One*, Chapter 1.

were breech mechanisms, and the Navy was well to the fore in the development of steel shell and smokeless propellant.[4] The one area where the French Navy initially lagged behind was in the development of the medium-calibre quick-firing (QF) gun. Quick-firing guns had their propellant charge in a single brass case and a modified breech. The Royal Navy had developed a 6in (152mm) QF gun capable of up to six rounds per minute in the late 1880s, and these guns constituted the secondary battery of the battleships of the *Royal Sovereign* and *Majestic* classes and the main battery of the British 1st class cruisers.[5] However, the French were slow to apply this principle to their 14cm and 16cm guns, and the latter calibre was in any case on the large size for a genuine QF gun. It was only during the mid-1890s that 16cm QF guns began to enter service with the *Marine Nationale*.

Moreover, the development of effective medium-calibre QF guns was not without its problems. The 138.6mm Mle 1891 and Mle 1893 guns that armed *Pothuau*, *D'Entrecasteaux* and *Jeanne d'Arc* employed a single propellant charge in a brass case with an overall weight of 7.28kg, while the 164.7mm Mle 1893 mounted in the battleship *Iéna* employed a similar cartridge weighing 13.10kg. However, later models of 164.7mm gun such as the Mle 1893–1896 featured a longer firing chamber better suited to the new slow-burning powders, and the heavier 18.3kg charge was divided into two for ease of stowage and handling: in addition to the main charge, which was in the standard brass cartridge case (*douille*), there was a smaller, lighter fore charge in a bag of serge or silk cloth (*gargousse*). There were a number of accidents involving these guns prior to the Great War, and these appear to have resulted from the ignition of the fore charge by burning powder residues remaining in the breech from the previous round. Larger, slower-firing guns generally had their breeches swabbed with water between rounds, but this was not possible with a QF gun, and these accidents generally occurred during gunnery exercises,[6] when a large numbers of rounds were fired over a short period and the barrel of the gun was already hot.

The second issue was the build-up of toxic gases from the combustion of the powder charge when the ship engaged in rapid fire. This was less of a problem when the QF guns were mounted in a battery, but in a small enclosed turret it could result in asphyxiation of the gun crew. Natural ventilation proved insufficient to resolve this problem.

PROTECTION SCHEMES

Dupuy-de-Lôme had a 100mm homogeneous steel belt that covered the entire upper part of the hull, together with a vaulted armoured deck over the machinery and magazines. The 2nd class cruisers of the *Amiral Charner* class that followed had a similar protection scheme, although the thickness of the side belt was slightly reduced and the top edge of the belt was one deck lower. The latter ships were designed by Jules Thibaudier, who was also responsible for the 1st class armoured cruiser *Pothuau*. *Pothuau* returned to the dimensions of *Dupuy-de-Lôme*, but the side belt was thinned in favour of a thicker armoured deck, which was no longer vaulted: instead there was a flat section on the ship's axis just above the waterline, with inclined sides that joined the lower edge of the belt. This was taken a stage further in *D'Entrecasteaux*, designed by Engineer Lagane of the La Seyne shipyard, which although initially classified as a *croiseur cuirassé* (armoured cruiser) was strictly a protected cruiser with light (internal) vertical protection.

The step change in French armoured cruiser protection schemes came with the appointment of Louis-Emile Bertin as *Directeur du Matériel*. Bertin favoured a high belt with a tightly-compartmented cellular layer behind it, sandwiched between two protected decks to create an armoured *caisson* above the ship's vitals. Directly behind the belt there was a cofferdam filled with water-excluding material, then a passageway approximately 1m wide subdivided at fixed intervals by transverse watertight bulkheads. Inboard of the passageway there were coal bunkers that provided additional protection against shell splinters. The early Bertin cruisers had a 'thick belt' (*cuirasse épaisse*) comprising a single strake of 150mm nickel steel, with a 'thin belt' (*cuirasse mince*) of 40–85mm special steel above;[7] the plates of the thick belt were secured to a teak backing, those of the upper belt directly to the shell. In the later Bertin cruisers the light upper belt was replaced by a second strake of 130mm nickel steel, again with a teak backing.

PROPULSION MACHINERY

One of the technical areas in which the French were considered to be preeminent was propulsion machinery, and in particular marine boilers. 'Locomotive'-type boilers, in which water in a large cylindrical drum was heated by hot gases from a coal-fired furnace located at one end of the cylinder passed through tubes, were still standard for major naval vessels in the early 1890s. However, from the end of the previous decade boilers of the Belleville or Niclausse type, in which large-diameter tubes filled with water were directly heated by the hot gases from a furnace below, were already being adopted for the latest battleships and cruisers of the *Marine Nationale*. Boilers of the Belleville type would subsequently be adopted by the Royal Navy, but serious technical problems were experienced for which differences in construction and deficiencies in the training of stokers were subsequently blamed.

By the late 1890s the French were opting for 'destroyer-type' small-tube boilers even for their armoured cruisers, largely at the prompting of Bertin, who considered that the adoption of small-tube boilers would result in improved power-to-weight ratios and greater flexibility of operation. The early small-tube boilers developed by Engineer Guyot at the Navy's Indret propulsion establishment were bulky and proved difficult to maintain, but Bertin's enthusiasm for this new technology was undiminished, and he was

[4] For a full account of development, see Jordan and Caresse, *French Battleships of World War One*, Introduction.

[5] The larger cruisers had two slow-firing 9.2in guns for support.

[6] Notably *Jules Michelet* in 1912, when she was serving with the Gunnery School (see Chapter 8).

[7] The 'station cruisers' of the *Dupleix* class, which had a sheathed hull, had a slightly different scheme (see Chapter 4).

Above: *Jules Ferry* was one of three French armoured cruisers – four if the reconstructed *Dupuy-de-Lôme* is included – equipped with Guyot–du Temple small-tube boilers. The boilers gave serious problems during trials, and the ship's entry into service was delayed by approximately two years before these issues were resolved. *(Private collection)*

confident that the problems experienced with the early models could be resolved with the right level of determination and investment.[8]

The British were so convinced of the significance of these developments that Bertin was persuaded to work up his lecture notes into an English-language book with the title *Marine Boilers*, edited by Leslie S Robinson with a Preface by the RN's Director of Naval Construction, Sir William White.[9] The following extracts from White's Preface to the 1898 edition demonstrate the high regard in which Bertin's ideas were held:

> M Bertin is the responsible designer of the latest and swiftest cruisers now building in France... .
>
> In the use of [tubulous] boilers for marine purposes the French engineers have shown remarkable *courage* and *enterprise*... [author's italics].
>
> English [*sic*] naval architects and marine engineers are happy to acknowledge the lead which their French colleagues have taken in this matter, and the benefit which they have obtained from French experiment and experience with tubulous boilers.[10]

However, although the French were in the forefront of boiler development they were slow to see the potential of marine turbines, and it would be the latter, allied to the all-big-gun concept, which would ultimately be responsible for the demise of the armoured cruiser as a type.

CONCLUSION

Although the armoured cruiser was obsolescent by 1914, having been overtaken in hitting power and speed by the all-big-gun, turbine-powered dreadnought 'battle cruiser', the French had invested a huge amount of money and effort into their own force of armoured cruisers, twenty-three of which remained in service at the outbreak of war. The seven powerful units that had entered service from 1905, the latest of which had been in service for little more than three years, constituted a key tactical element in the *Armée Navale* in the Mediterranean, while the cruisers of the *Gloire* and *Gueydon* classes were the workhorses of the French squadrons in the Channel and the Atlantic.

[8] Bertin was eventually to be proved right, although it was the 1920s before the Guyot–du Temple boiler became the standard model in French cruisers.

[9] DNC and Assistant Controller of the Navy 1885–1901.

[10] *Marine Boilers*, based on the work of L E Bertin, translated and edited by Leslie S Robertson (New York: Van Nostrand, 1906), pp ix–xi.

CHAPTER 1

FIRST STEPS: *DUPUY-DE-LÔME* AND THE *AMIRAL CHARNER* CLASS

IN THE SUMMER OF 1886 the French Ministry of Marine,[1] headed by Admiral Théophile Aube, had become concerned about the possible effect of shells containing the newly-developed high-explosive *mélinite* (picric acid) bursting charges on the current generation of 'protected' cruisers favoured by the *Jeune Ecole* for commerce raiding. The *Conseil des Travaux*[2] was asked for its views on the best means of protection against the new shell, and the unanimous view was that the only effective solution was side armour of the latest homogeneous steel over the entire length of the ship, extending from the upper deck to below the waterline. The Minister ordered that tests be carried out to assess the effect of the new projectiles on the old ironclad corvette *Belliqueuse*, and these took place early in 1887. The extent of the destruction wrought on

[1] The French Ministry of Marine, housed in an impressive colonnaded building on the Place de la Concorde on the east side of the Rue Royale, was responsible not only for the navy and its arsenals, but for the fisheries, the ports and the merchant marine. Responsibility for the colonies alternated between the Ministry of Marine and the Ministry of Commerce during the 1880s and the early 1890s, before becoming a separate ministry in 1894.

[2] The French Navy's advisory body on technical matters – see Jordan and Caresse, *French Battleships of World War One*, p 20.

Below: *Dupuy-de-Lôme* on trials in early 1895. Acclaimed by some, derided by others, *Dupuy-de-Lôme* was the first modern armoured cruiser designed and built for the French *Marine Nationale* and spawned a host of imitations abroad. *(DR)*

Dupuy-de-Lôme: Profile

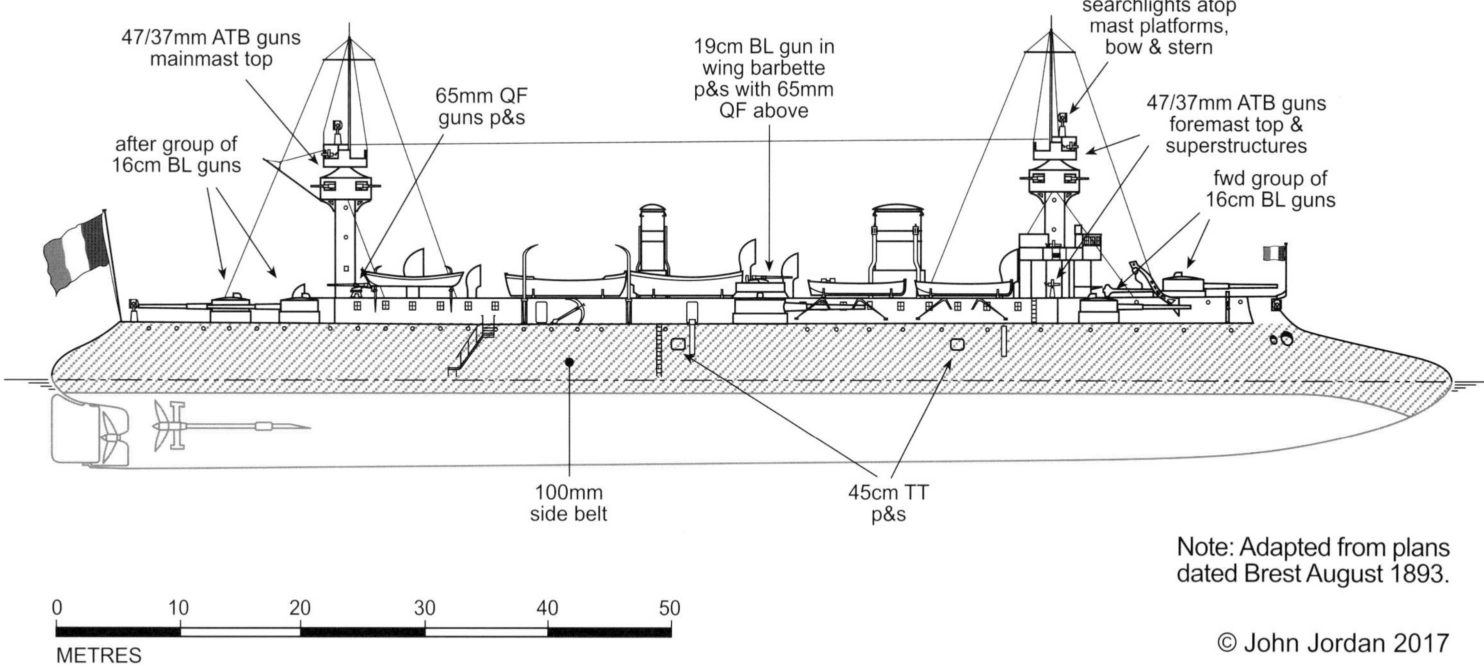

the interior of the old ship by 14cm and 16cm cast iron shells with relatively modest *mélinite* bursting charges was enough to convince both the Minister and the *Conseil* that there was an urgent need for larger, more powerful cruisers with armoured sides.

Accordingly, at its session of 20 July 1887, the *Conseil* set about defining suitable characteristics for both 1st class and 2nd class armoured cruisers. Its recommendations for a 1st class cruiser evolved into the *Dupuy-de-Lôme*; the 2nd class cruiser proposal would become the *Amiral Charner* (see below). The new cruiser programme would provide a political counterbalance to the resumption of work on the battleship *Brennus* (also agreed at the 20 July session), thereby appeasing the adherents of the *Jeune Ecole*, who continued to wield considerable influence both within and outside the *Marine Nationale*.

DUPUY-DE-LÔME

Selected naval architects were invited to submit design studies. The first to respond was Louis de Bussy, a well-respected architect who had been responsible for the design of France's first steel-framed battleship *Redoutable* (launched 1876). De Bussy had been appointed *Directeur des Contructions Navales* in 1880 and *Inspecteur Général des Contructions Navales* in 1885, and was an *ex officio* member of the *Conseil des Travaux*. His preliminary design study for the new 1st class cruiser was considered by the *Conseil* on 18 October; general characteristics were as follows:

- Displacement: 6000 tonnes.
- Dimensions: length pp 114m; beam 15.7m; draught 7.87m max.
- Armament: 2 x 19cm guns in wing barbette mountings; 6 x 16cm guns, also in barbette mountings, grouped in a triangular arrangement fore and aft; the two centreline guns to have a command of 7.5m, the wing-mounted guns 5.5m.
- Protection: 100mm belt extending from beneath the waterline to the upper deck; a 20mm vaulted protective deck joining the main belt at its lower edge, with an 8mm splinter deck over the machinery.
- Propulsion: triple-expansion engines on three shafts rated at 14,000CV for a maximum speed of 20 knots.

The characteristics of the ship were agreed, and Brest Naval Dockyard was instructed to lay down the ship, which was authorised as part of the 1887 Programme.

NOMENCLATURE

Arguably the most distinguished naval architect of his age, Stanislas-Charles-Henri-Laurent **Dupuy de Lôme** (1816–65) was primarily responsible for the powerful fleet of steam-powered ironclads built for the *Marine Nationale* during the 1850s and 1860s, of which the most famous was the first sea-going ironclad *Gloire* (launched 1859); he also designed the first operational submarine, *Gymnote*. In 1860 he was nominated Councillor of State and represented the French

BUILDING DATA

Name	Builder	Laid down	Launched	Trials[1]	Commissioned[2]
Dupuy-de-Lôme	Arsenal de Brest	4 Jul 1888	27 Oct 1890	1 Apr 1892	15 May 1895

Notes:
1 *Armée pour essais* (manned for trials)
2 *Armement définitif*

Above: The characteristic silhouette of *Dupuy-de-Lôme*, with her pronounced 'plough' bow incorporating a ram of forged steel. The photo was taken on 1 August 1905, shortly after her return from Kiel. Note the hinged funnel caps, which on the first funnel are in the lowered position. *(Musée de la Marine)*

Admiralty in Parliament. The following year he was appointed *Inspecteur Général du Matériel de la Marine*. At the beginning of the Franco-Prussian War, Dupuy de Lôme was appointed to the Committee for Defence. From 1869 to 1875 he was a *député* in the French parliament, and in 1877 was elected a Life Senator.

HULL AND SUPERSTRUCTURES

The hull-form adopted by de Bussy was the one currently in vogue, with the distinctive tumblehome sides (which favoured side-mounted guns on sponsons) and a pronounced 'plough bow' incorporating a ram of forged steel.

The hull was built of 50kg steel on the transverse principle, with a frame separation of 1.2m throughout. There was a double bottom from the bow to frame 76, but this was completely flat, and was not extended upwards at the sides as in the later armoured cruisers designed by Bertin; it constituted the hold and was used as the floor for the main magazines and shell rooms and for the machinery. Twelve watertight transverse bulkheads divided the hull below water into thirteen watertight compartments; they extended from the ship's bottom to the main deck.

The main deck was also the armoured deck (*pont cuirassé*). There were platform decks (*plateformes*) between the main deck and the hold for the steering gear and fresh water tanks (aft), the dynamos (forward) and coal bunkers (amidships, above the boiler rooms). Above the main deck were the 'battery' deck (*pont de la batterie*), on which the four above-water torpedo tubes were mounted, the upper deck (*pont des gaillards*), on which all but one of the main guns were mounted, and the shelter deck (*spardeck*), which not only carried the boats but was extended forward as a narrow forecastle into which the forward 16cm turret was set.

The ship was conned from a two-deck structure forward, with the compass platform and chart house on the upper level and a small, compact conning tower beneath which was linked to the *Poste Central* beneath the armoured deck by a cylindrical communications tube. There were two heavy 'military' masts that carried the platforms for the 47mm and 37mm anti-torpedo boat (ATB) guns and the main searchlight projectors. Each of the masts, which were seated on the main deck, comprised a cylindrical core 0.5m in diameter housing the ammunition hoists for the ATB guns, and an outer cylinder 1.72m in diameter with the spiral ladders that gave access to the platforms for the gun crews. The ATB gun platforms were 15m above the waterline, the tops 19.8m.

The anchor-handling arrangements adopted for *Dupuy-de-Lôme* were unusual. Because of the tumblehome sides and the proximity of the forward 16cm turret to the bow, the main anchors were stowed flat on the deck between the turret and the bridge, and were hoisted and lowered by hinged gantry-type cranes mounted on the sides of the narrow forecastle. The capstan and the cable lockers were between the bridge and the first funnel. This clumsy arrangement would be much criticised by successive commanding officers in their evaluations of the ship.

ARMAMENT

Main guns

Shortly after construction began there were proposals to revise the layout and protection of the main armament, and the Farcot Company submitted designs for

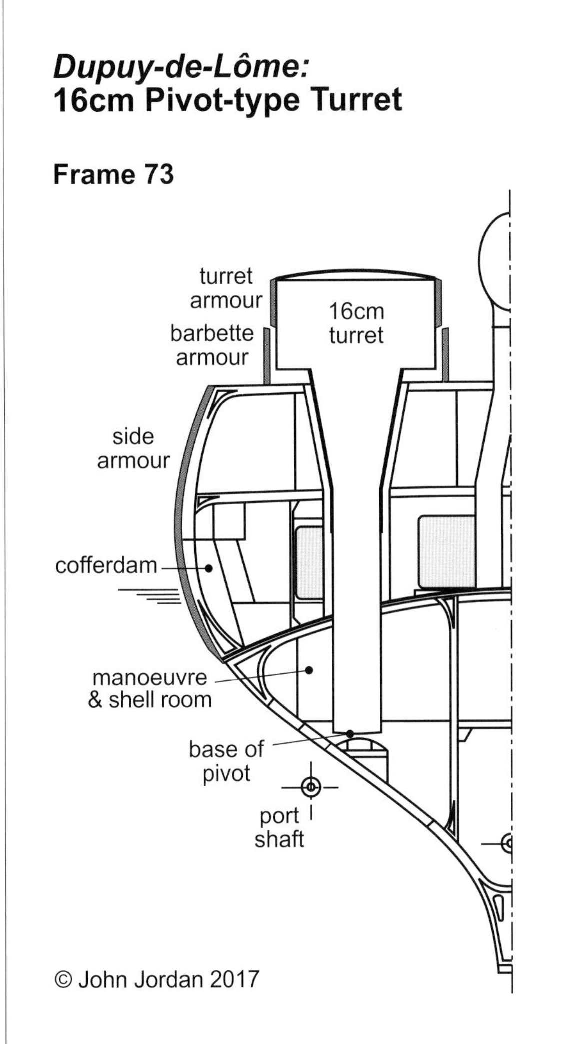

CHARACTERISTICS

Displacement:	6300 tonnes
Dimensions:	
Length	114.00m pp
Beam	15.70m wl
Draught	7.07m mean
Propulsion:	
Boilers	11 Amirauté cylindrical
Engines	3-shaft 3-cylinder VTE (centre shaft) / HTE (wing shafts)
Horsepower	14,000CV (designed)
Speed	20 knots (designed)
Coal	1080 tonnes full load
Endurance	4000nm at 10 knots
Armament:	
Main guns	2 x 19cm/45 Mle 1887 in single turrets
Medium guns	6 x 16cm/45 Mle 1887 in single turrets
	4 x 65mm/50 Mle 1891 QF in single mountings
ATB guns	8 x 47mm/40 Mle 1885 QF in single mountings
	6 x 37mm revolver cannon
Torpedo tubes	4 a/w tubes for 450mm torpedoes
	8 torpedoes Mle 1892
Protection:	
Main belt	100mm
Deck	20+10mm
19/14cm turrets	100mm
Conning tower	125mm
Boats:	1 x 12.5m steam launch (*vedette*)
	1 x 8.85m steam pinnace
	1 x 10m pulling pinnace
	4 x 8m pulling cutters
	2 x 8m whalers
	1 x 5m dinghy
Complement:	
As private ship	521 officers and men

fully-enclosed turrets in place of the original barbette mountings. In the design approved by the *Conseil des Travaux* on 6 April 1889, the gun turntable rested on a pivot shaft that extended down to the protective deck. The gun mountings and control levers were inside the gunhouse, and the ammunition hoists were within the shaft and turned with the gunhouse; the training mechanism, which was based on hydraulic rams, was at the base of the pivot shaft (see 16cm Turret drawing).

After further deliberation, Brest produced a revised design in which the 19cm and 16cm guns were all in single enclosed turrets, and the pivots of the 16cm turrets penetrated the armoured deck. The forward 16cm turret remained in its raised position – the gunhouse was countersunk into the raised forecastle. However, the three after 16cm turrets were now all at the same level – presumably to compensate for the additional topweight incurred by the adoption of turrets. This arrangement was approved by the *Conseil* on 15 October 1888. Unusually, the armoured barbette screens of the original design were retained; the broadly cylindrical gunhouses, which turned within them, were armoured only above the level of the barbettes (see Protection). The pivots housing the ammunition hoists, which were behind the armoured belt covering the upper part of the hull, were completely unprotected.

One curious anomaly of the new pivot-type turrets was that whereas the ammunition hoists for the 16cm guns rose directly from the shell rooms and powder magazines located in the hold (forward group) and on the platform deck (after group), the midship 19cm guns were separated longitudinally from their magazines, which were located two sections farther aft at hold level, abeam the forward engine room. The hoists for these magazines exited onto the *pont des gaillards*, at the same level as the turrets, and the projectiles and powder charges were then transported horizontally to the guns, presumably using overhead rails. This was a particularly unsatisfactory arrangement; it would not be repeated on later ships, in which the ammunition handing rooms were always directly beneath their respective guns

Both the 19cm and the 16cm guns belonged to the Modèle 1887 series, which was designed to exploit the new slow-burning powder known as *poudre B*, sometimes referred to as *poudre Boulanger marine* (named after the Minister of War of the day, General Georges-Ernest Boulanger). All the guns in this series except the large-calibre 34cm gun (42-cal) were 45 calibres long. Both the 19cm and the 16cm guns comprised a thick 'A' tube, reinforced over slightly more than half its length by a jacket and five hoops; a trunnion hoop was screwed on to the jacket. These and later French medium-calibre guns had an interrupted-screw

Below: A fine view of *Dupuy-de-Lôme* docked at Brest, showing the layout of the decks and the novel disposition of the main guns, all of which were in enclosed turrets. The three forward turrets for 16cm guns are nearest the camera, with the starboard-side wing turret for one of the two 19cm guns amidships. The foremost turret is countersunk into the forecastle so that only the upper part of armoured barbette protrudes. *(DR)*

breech with four threaded and four plain sectors.

The 19cm gun fired a 75kg cast iron (CI) shell with a 5kg black powder bursting charge; there was also a 90kg steel shell with a 4.3kg burster of *mélinite*, and this would soon be complemented by an armour-piercing shell (*obus de rupture*) with thicker walls and a smaller 1.6kg burster of *mélinite*. The 18.8kg propellant charge comprised two bags of BM9 powder. Muzzle velocity was 800m/sec with the CI shell, 770m/sec with the steel shell, and the theoretical firing cycle approximately one round per minute.

The 16cm gun fired a 45kg CI shell with a 2.1kg black powder burster; there was also a 53kg steel shell with a 3.1kg burster of *mélinite*, and later an armour piercing shell with a 1.0kg *mélinite* burster. The 13.1kg propellant charge comprised a single cartridge with BM9 powder. Muzzle velocity was as for the 19cm gun. Although the 16cm Mle 1887 used cartridge ammunition it was not a QF gun; the CI projectile had a weight comparable to that of the British 6in QF Mk I, but the steel shells were too heavy for one man to handle comfortably and the three-motion breech was slow to operate. In practice the rate of fire was probably little better than two rounds per minute. For *Dupuy-de-Lôme*'s immediate successors the lighter 14cm Mle 1891 gun would be preferred.

Light QF guns

For rapid fire against enemy surface ships *Dupuy-de-Lôme* was fitted with four of the newly-developed 65mm 50-calibre QF guns. Designed by Schneider, these hand-worked guns were on lightweight pivot mountings. Two were in tubs amidships immediately above the turrets for the 19cm guns, and two at the after end of the shelter deck, superfiring above the after wing 16cm mountings. The 65mm Mle 1891 gun was also fitted in the early battleships of the 1890 Programme (*'Flotte d'échantillons'*) – in the two later units of the series, *Masséna* and *Bouvet*, it was replaced by the heavier 100mm QF gun.

The 65mm Mle 1891 fired a 4kg cast iron projectile with a 0.2kg black powder burster or a 4.2kg steel projectile with a 0.1kg burster of *mélinite*. The 0.87kg BM3 propellant was in a single cartridge case. A sliding wedge breech ensured a fast firing cycle, up to 10 rounds per minute. The Mle 1891 gun was a handy, effective weapon against the upperworks of cruisers and as a counter to enemy torpedo boats, but its projectiles were incapable of penetrating even thin armour plating.

ATB guns

The weapon of choice against enemy torpedo craft was the 47mm/40 Mle 1885, which was designed by

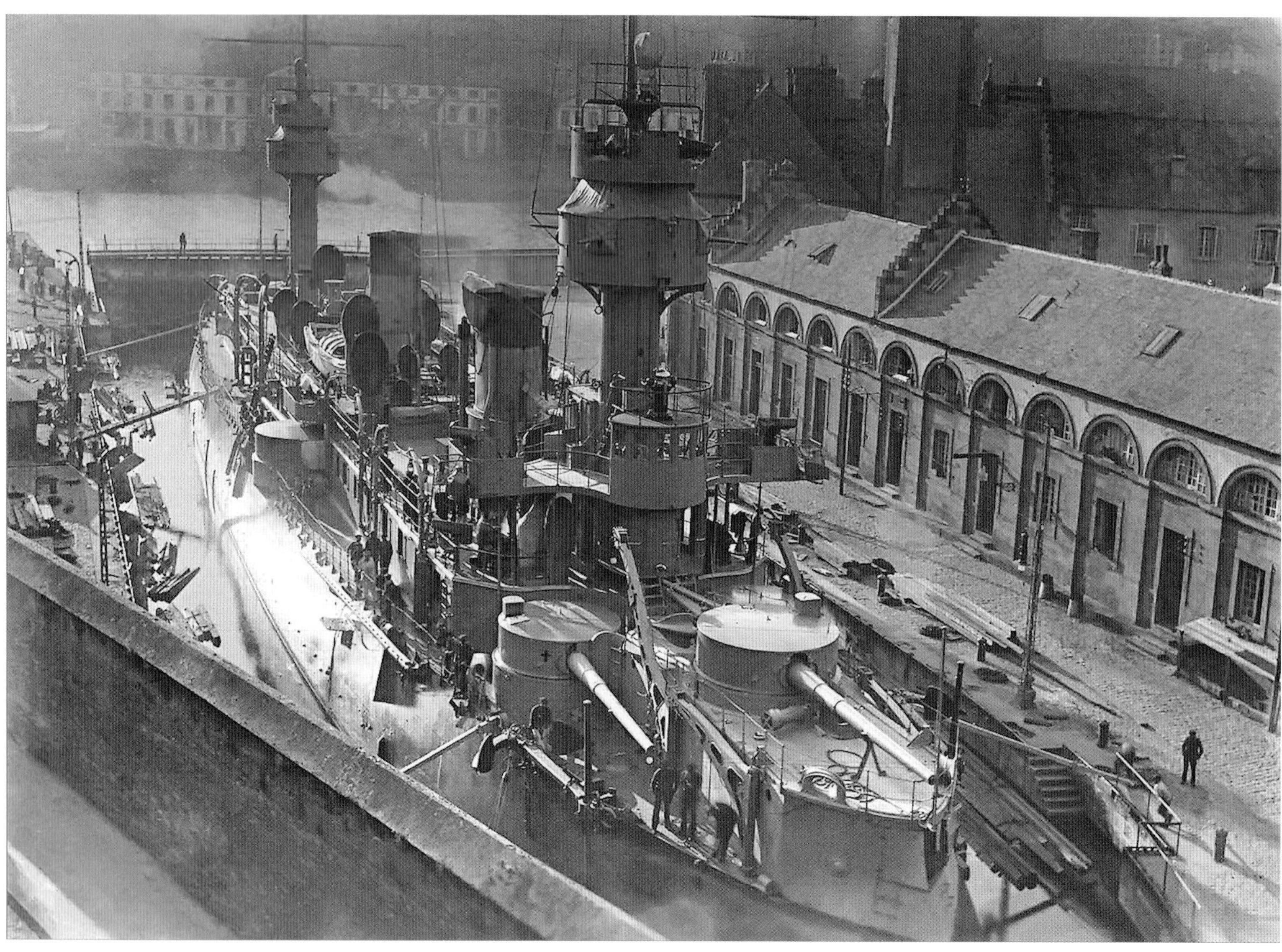

Hotchkiss and had been sold to (or manufactured under licence by) most of the major European navies.[3] When *Dupuy-de-Lôme* was first completed she was fitted with eight of these guns, which were mounted on the lower platforms of the two military masts. The 47mm guns were complemented by a similar number of 37mm revolver cannon, the primary role of which was to mow down the crews of attacking torpedo craft; two were mounted on each of the military masts, with a further four atop the forward superstructure. Both the 47mm and the 37mm guns had a particularly low angle of depression (in excess of -20°) to enable them to engage at close range. The composition of the ATB armament would later be modified.

Searchlight projectors

Given the comparatively short ranges of contemporary torpedoes, it was anticipated that attacks by small torpedo-carrying craft would take place under cover of darkness, either at sea or in an anchorage. Targets for the ATB guns were to be illuminated by searchlights powered by electricity. Six projectors with 60cm mirrors were fitted in *Dupuy-de-Lôme*: one on the upper platform of each of the two military masts (*ligne haute*), which could also be used for navigation in conditions of poor visibility, and four on the *pont des gaillards* (*ligne basse*). Of the latter two were at the extreme ends of the ship, and two were in the waist amidships on projecting platforms. The exposure of these lower searchlights to the elements tested the early electrics to their limits, and later ships had their searchlights arranged to give a higher level of protection when not in use.

Torpedoes

On 19 June 1890 it was decided to replace the planned fixed above-water torpedo tubes, which were slung on beams from the upper deck, by tubes on pivot mountings that could accommodate the new 45cm Mle 1892 torpedo. The tubes could be trained fore and aft of the beam using a semicircular rail set in the deck. Four were located behind watertight doors amidships on the battery deck (*pont de la batterie*).

The Mle 1892 torpedo was a Whitehead model initially purchased from that company's works at Fiume and subsequently manufactured under licence at Toulon Naval Dockyard. With a length of 5.05m and an all-up weight of 530kg (warhead: 75kg), the Mle 1892 had a maximum range of 800m at 27.5 knots. Two torpedoes were provided for each tube, for a total of eight.

PROTECTION

Hull

The sides of the hull were protected by a complete belt of 100mm homogeneous nickel steel that extended from 1.38m beneath the waterline to the upper deck. There were four strakes of armour plates secured directly by bolts to a double layer of 10mm hull plating. The plates were supplied by Marrel Frères and Schneider. After some initial quality-control issues, these were generally rated satisfactory.

A vaulted protective deck rose from the lower edge of the side belt (see Midship Half-section plan); its summit was just above the normal waterline. It was formed with 20mm of mild steel on 10mm plating. Beneath it and above the boiler and engine rooms there was a flat 8mm splinter deck. The space between the two decks was filled with coal; as this was a key part of the protection system (and not easily accessible) it was to be used last.

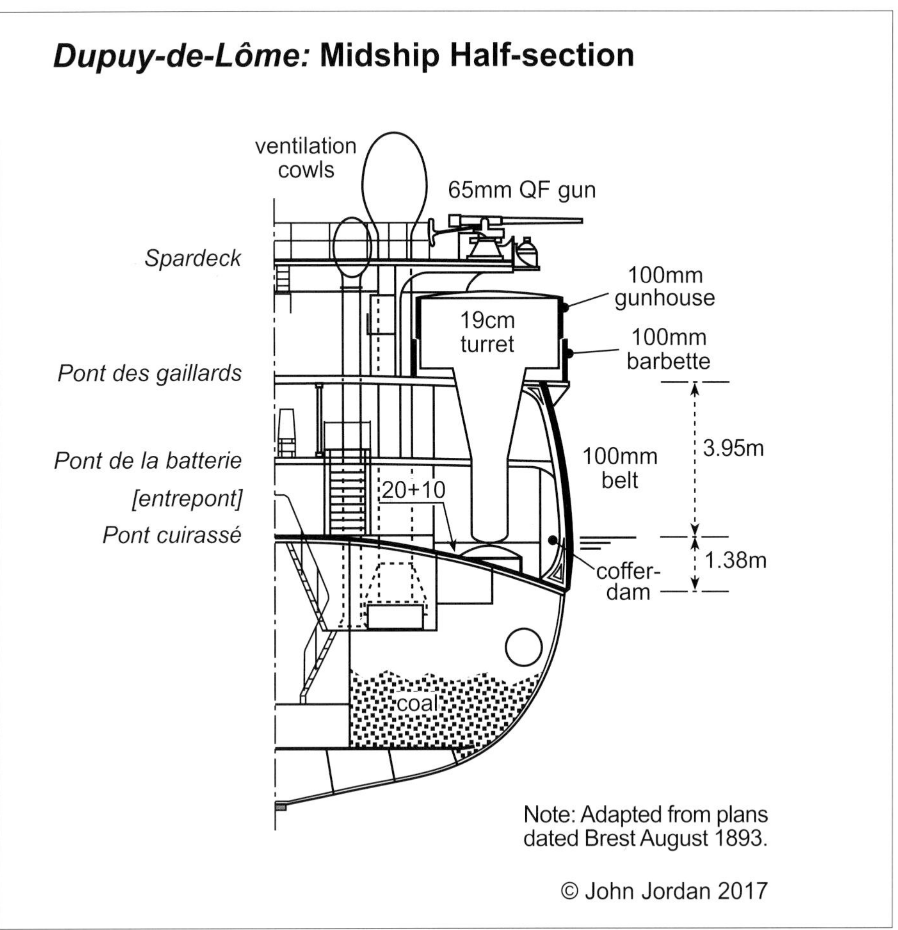

Directly behind the belt there was a cofferdam that ran the full length of the ship. The cofferdam was approximately 2m high (1m above the waterline) and was seated on the protective deck; its internal longitudinal bulkhead was 0.7–0.8m inboard of the hull plating. The cofferdam was tightly subdivided and filled with water-excluding material. Inboard of the cofferdam was a passageway 0.7m wide, subdivided at intervals by transverse bulkheads with watertight doors, to contain flooding.

Turrets

The circular barbettes of the original design were retained, and these were of 100mm homogeneous nickel steel. The section plans suggest that the sides of the turrets above the level of the barbettes had armour plates of a similar thickness (see Midship Half-section plan). The plates for the turrets were supplied by Fonderies, Forges & Aciéries de St-Etienne.

There is no information about the turret roofs, but these were probably formed using a double or triple layer of 10mm mild steel.[4]

[3] In Royal Navy service it was known as the 3-pounder.

[4] Contemporary ranges of engagement were 1500–2000m and trajectories were relatively flat, so enemy projectiles would strike only a glancing blow.

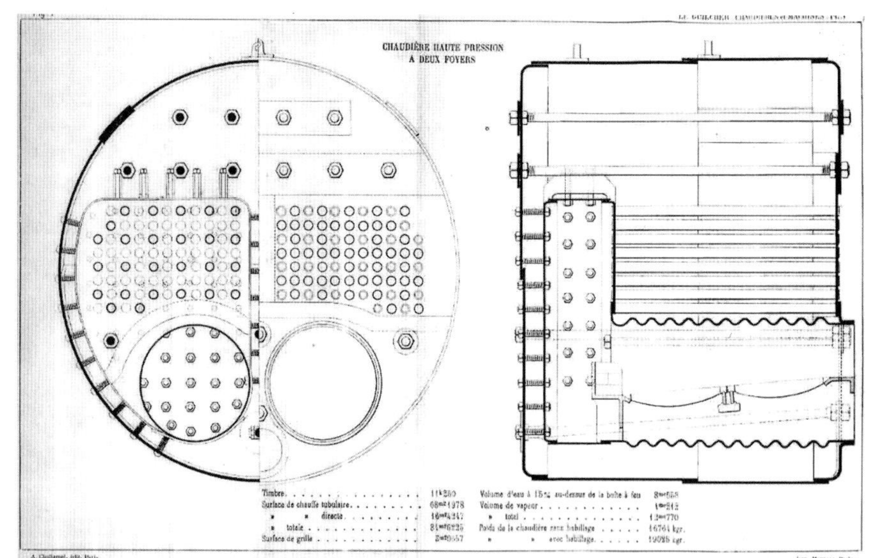

Face and internal profile drawing of a cylindrical 'fire-tube' boiler similar to the boiler mounted in *Dupuy-de-Lôme* on completion. This model has two furnaces with circular access doors. Coal was shovelled by the two stokers onto grates which sloped towards the rear of the boiler. The hot gases from the combustion chamber were channelled through banks of tubes surrounded by water, then exhausted through the funnel. The steam created by heating the water at high temperatures under pressure was collected and used to drive the pistons of the reciprocating engines.

The tubes were of brass, iron or steel; brass would be abandoned because of its higher cost and because it lost resistance at the high temperatures associated with higher pressures; however, brass tubes had the advantage of being longer-lasting and not subject to corrosion.

The cylindrical boilers in *Dupuy-de-Lôme* were 'single-ended'; those in the later *D'Entrecasteaux* (see Chapter 2) were 'double-ended', with furnaces at either end. The cylindrical 'loco' boiler was superseded by the large watertube boiler (see page 32) because of the limited pressures it could generate: 11.35kg/cm² in this model. (Le Guilcher, *op cit*)

Conning tower

The face and sides of the conning tower were protected by homogeneous armour 125mm thick; there is no information about the communications tube connecting the conning tower with the *Poste Central*, but as this was behind the hull plating it may have been unprotected.

MACHINERY

The machinery for *Dupuy-de-Lôme* was ordered from Ateliers & Chantiers de la Loire (ACL). Three engines of the triple-expansion type were necessary to provide the 14,000CV required for the designed maximum speed of 20 knots. Engines with horizontal cylinders were still standard in ships with limited deck-height, and these were used to power the two outer shafts. However, the third shaft required an engine with vertical cylinders, which could then be located in the aftermost engine room between the two outer shafts. Vertical triple-expansion (VTE) engines would become a standard feature of French cruisers, and would prove more reliable, as the horizontal engines were found to cause uneven wear on the piston rings. However, the latter type would be retained for the 2nd class armoured cruisers of the *Amiral Charner* class (qv), which had only two shafts.

The propellers on the wing shafts were of different design: 4.4m in diameter with a 5.1m pitch, compared with 4.2m diameter (5.3m pitch) for the propeller on the centre shaft.

Steam for the engines was supplied by eleven standard *Amirauté*-type cylindrical 'fire-tube' boilers, each with two 1.3m diameter furnaces. The boilers were distributed between three boiler rooms: the centre and after boiler rooms each housed four boilers side by

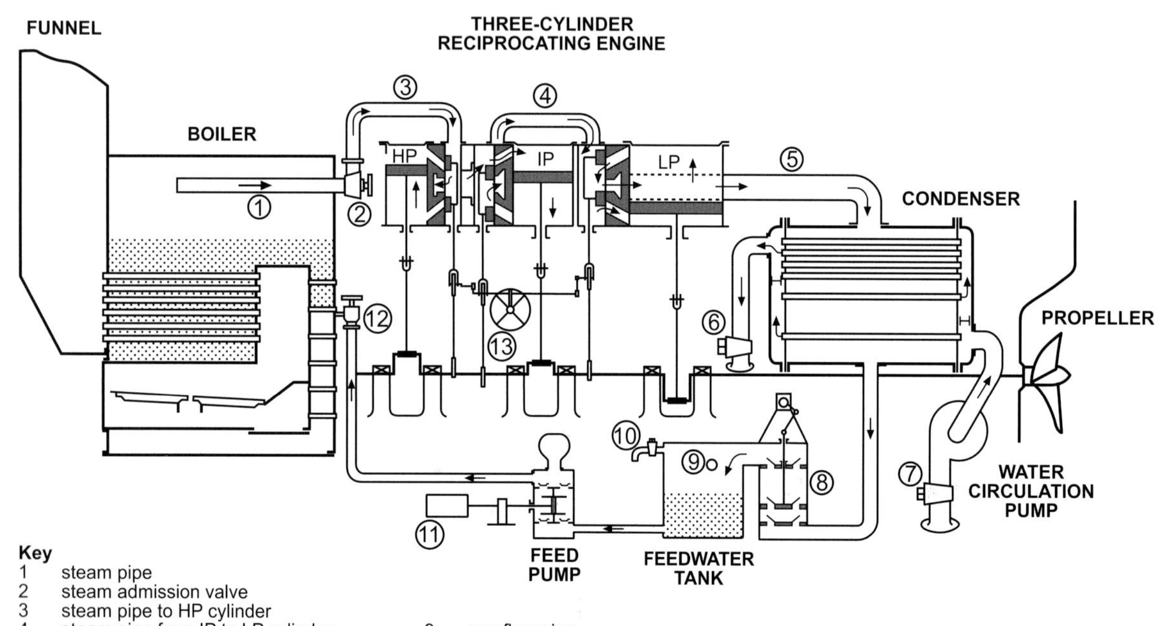

The schematic shows how a machinery installation based on a three-cylinder triple-expansion engine operated. The water used to produce the steam was in a closed circuit. Steam was admitted first to the high-pressure (HP) cylinder, then to the intermediate-pressure (IP) cylinder, and finally to the low-pressure (LP) cylinder; the steam was evacuated from the LP cylinder to the condenser. Later models of boiler often had an extra LP cylinder. The boiler depicted is the standard cylindrical 'loco'-type boiler of the day.

Key
1 steam pipe
2 steam admission valve
3 steam pipe to HP cylinder
4 steam pipe from IP to LP cylinder
5 steam evacuation pipe to condenser
6 stop valve
7 water admission valve
8 vertical air pump
9 overflow pipe
10 air release valve
11 feed pump motor
12 water feed regulator
13 wheel to reverse engine

© John Jordan 2017

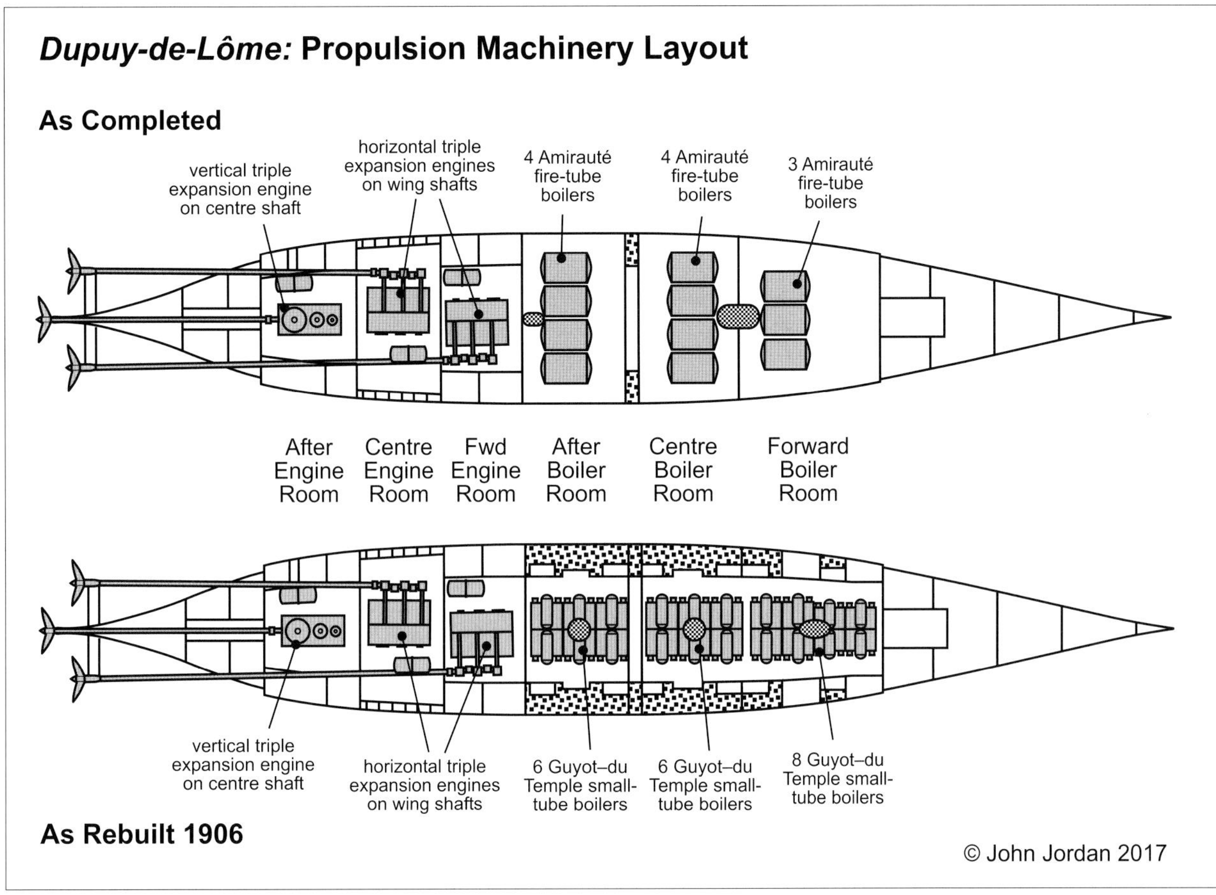

***Dupuy-de-Lôme:* Propulsion Machinery Layout**

As Completed

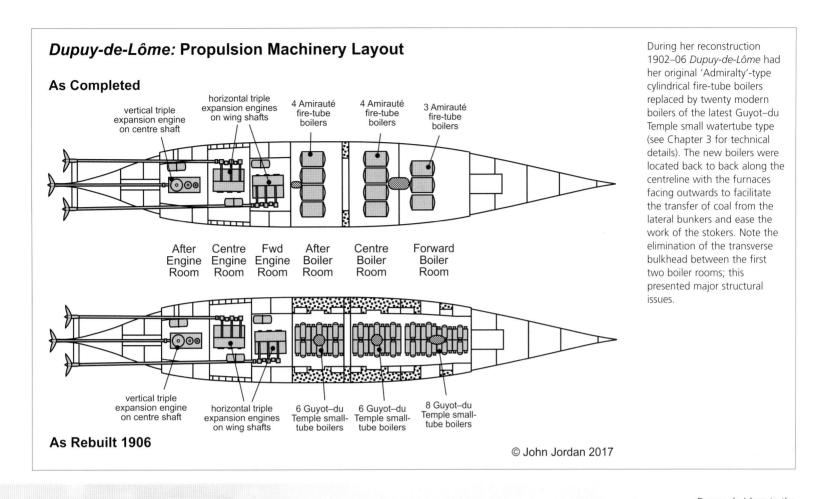

vertical triple expansion engine on centre shaft
horizontal triple expansion engines on wing shafts
4 Amirauté fire-tube boilers
4 Amirauté fire-tube boilers
3 Amirauté fire-tube boilers

After Engine Room
Centre Engine Room
Fwd Engine Room
After Boiler Room
Centre Boiler Room
Forward Boiler Room

vertical triple expansion engine on centre shaft
horizontal triple expansion engines on wing shafts
6 Guyot–du Temple small-tube boilers
6 Guyot–du Temple small-tube boilers
8 Guyot–du Temple small-tube boilers

As Rebuilt 1906

During her reconstruction 1902–06 *Dupuy-de-Lôme* had her original 'Admiralty'-type cylindrical fire-tube boilers replaced by twenty modern boilers of the latest Guyot–du Temple small watertube type (see Chapter 3 for technical details). The new boilers were located back to back along the centreline with the furnaces facing outwards to facilitate the transfer of coal from the lateral bunkers and ease the work of the stokers. Note the elimination of the transverse bulkhead between the first two boiler rooms; this presented major structural issues.

Dupuy-de-Lôme in the roadstead at Brest early in her career. The paint scheme was black hull, buff (*toile mouillé*) upperworks, and underside Schweinfurth green. *(DR)*

side, while the narrower forward boiler room had three. The broad fore-funnel housed the uptakes for the boilers in the first two boiler rooms, while the slim after funnel served the after boiler room.

CONSTRUCTION AND SERVICE

Dupuy-de-Lôme was laid down at Brest in July 1888 and launched on 27 October 1890. The ship's propulsion machinery gave problems from the outset. During preliminary trials on 20 June 1892 a boiler tube burst, causing a furnace blow-back and escape of steam that injured sixteen men. Despite modifications to the propellers, *Dupuy-de-Lôme* failed to make her designed speed, and during subsequent trials the furnace crowns of the cylindrical boilers were found to be sagging. Repairs and modifications to the boilers were made, and on 2 April 1895 the engines produced 13,186CV for a speed of 19.73 knots.

Dupuy-de-Lôme was finally commissioned on 15 May 1895 and assigned to the Northern Squadron. However, she was found to roll badly in a seaway, and measurements taken revealed a metacentric height of only 0.695m at her full-load displacement of 6,682 tonnes. The boilers continued to be a constant source of anxiety, and it was proposed that they be replaced by watertube boilers similar to those being installed in the latest cruisers.

After only seven years in service *Dupuy-de-Lôme* was taken in hand at Brest for a radical reconstruction.

Above: *Dupuy-de-Lôme* as completed. The boat booms are deployed and the boats are suspended from the davits (*poste de rade*). Note the pronounced tumblehome of the sides and the torpedo tubes protruding from their ports on the battery deck. *(Musée de la Marine)*

Right: *Dupuy-de-Lôme* making 18.6 knots on her post-reconstruction power trials in July 1906. Note the seas washing over the upper deck, evidence of the unsatisfactory hull form forward, which caused the ship to trim by the bow. *(DR)*

Above: *Dupuy-de-Lôme* at her moorings in 1909–10. The ship has been repainted in the new blue-grey livery decreed in January 1908, and the upper platform of the military foremast has been removed – compare with the previous photo. *(Musée de la Marine)*

The original fire-tube boilers would be replaced by sixteen large and four small boilers of the latest Guyot–du Temple small watertube type. The transverse bulkhead at frame 32 that separated the first two boiler rooms was removed, creating a single large space with ten large and four small boilers, which were disposed back to back along the centreline (see Propulsion Machinery Layout plan). The remaining six large boilers were mounted in the original after boiler room and were similarly disposed. The external appearance of the ship was radically altered, each of the three groups of boilers being served by a new funnel, the fore-funnel (serving eight boilers) being slightly broader than the second and third funnels (each serving six).

The new fore-funnel displaced the capstan, which was moved aft. As a result the path of the anchor cables changed direction twice, passing over two rollers: one against the forward ventilator and the other against the new fore-funnel. Finally, as a topweight reduction measure, the military mainmast was suppressed in favour of a simple pole, the 47mm ATB guns being mounted on a new platform at its base.

The reconstruction, which involved considerable strengthening of the structural members in the area of the boiler rooms, lasted from March 1902 until March 1906.

THE FINAL YEARS

The post-reconstruction trials were not a success. A two-hour full-power trial with forced draft produced only 12,888CV and a speed of 18.27 knots, and seakeeping was poor – a problem blamed on a restoration of the ship's designed trim[5] by the embarkation of 48 tonnes of iron bars in the forward part of the ship.

Dupuy-de-Lôme recommissioned on 3 October 1906, but was immediately placed in reserve, remaining largely inactive until late 1908. The ship was by now in poor condition, with extensive corrosion of the hull.[6] She was decommissioned on 20 March 1910 and stricken on 20 February 1911. She was subsequently reconditioned for sale to Peru as the *Comandante Elias*

5 As designed the ship should have trimmed 1.68m by the stern; however, when completed there would be a difference of fully 2.3m between the draughts forward and aft, and this was found to work well.

6 A thorough examination of the hull in late 1909 revealed corrosion and pitting over three-quarters of the ship's length. The plating had rusted through in some places, and these plates had to be cemented to keep them watertight; it was estimated that 320m^2 of plating needed replacement, and temporary repairs were effected by riveting on patches of plating and closing smaller holes with washers and a mastic compound held in place by a bolt.

Aguirre, but the deal for her purchase fell through. She remained at Lorient throughout the Great War, and in October 1918 was sold to Lloyd Royal Belge for conversion to a merchantman; she was renamed *Peruvier*. Her career in her new role was brief, and following a mid-Atlantic machinery breakdown and a coal fire in the hold in 1920, she was immobilised at Antwerp before being sold for scrap; she was broken up in Flushing from March 1923.

EVALUATION

Dupuy-de-Lôme was a poor ship, plagued throughout her career by machinery and structural defects. However, she had an impact well beyond her military value. She was the world's first modern armoured cruiser and spawned a host of imitations. Foreign powers were impressed by her heavy gun armament and her high speed, which made her a threat to commerce and in theory enabled her to stand in the line of battle – although she would have been vulnerable to the new armour-piercing (AP) shell. The next two decades would see the design and construction of ever-larger, more powerful and faster armoured cruisers for Britain, Germany, the USA, Russia, France and Japan.

AMIRAL CHARNER CLASS

For the 2nd class cruiser the *Conseil des Travaux* proposed a ship of lesser displacement with a main armament of two 16cm guns, six 14cm guns and two 65mm QF guns.[7] No dimensions were specified other than a maximum draught aft of 6.3m. Two-shaft propulsion was to give a speed of 17.5 knots with normal draught and 20 knots with forced draught; an economical speed of 12.5 knots was stipulated, and the ship was to be lit by electricity. Endurance was to be 4000nm at 12.5 knots and normal draught, and the complement was not to exceed 300 men, with provisions for 90 days and water for 20 days.

The protection system was to be similar to that of *Dupuy-de-Lôme* but at a reduced thickness. It was to comprise a full-length belt of 80mm steel, which was judged sufficient to resist penetration by the projectiles used against the *Belliqueuse*, reducing to 40mm at the ends and secured to a double thickness of 12mm construction steel; it would extend from the upper deck to 1.2m beneath the waterline. There would be similar protection for the turrets and for the conning tower. The vaulted protective deck would be of 18mm mild steel on a double layer of 9mm plating, and would be 0.5m above the waterline at its centre. Beneath it, 1.1m below the waterline, there would be a splinter deck 8mm thick over the machinery, as in *Dupuy-de-Lôme*. A cofferdam 0.8m wide would run the whole length of the ship, extending from the armoured deck to 1m above waterline level. There was to be a double bottom beneath the machinery spaces, and there were to be as many watertight compartments as possible.

The upper deck was to be of 10mm steel plate 'in all parts not protected by the forecastle and poop', the two latter structures being connected by a flying deck. The original proposal featured four steel masts, the foremast square-rigged carrying lower, top and topgallant sails, with the other three carrying fore-and-aft rig 'and staysails where possible'. In effect this was a classic 'colonial' cruiser, designed for overseas deployment rather than fleet use. The sails would have made the ships less dependent on coal supplies and would have reduced running costs, which remained relatively high for a steam-powered cruiser.

[7] The latest 2nd class protected cruisers of the *Alger* class, laid down in 1887, displaced 4300 tonnes and had an identical main armament; designed speed was 19 knots.

Right: *Amiral Charner* shortly after her completion. The design was a reduced version of *Dupuy-de-Lôme*, and had a similar arrangement of the main guns. Construction was protracted, and each of the four ships took 5–6 years to complete. *(Private collection)*

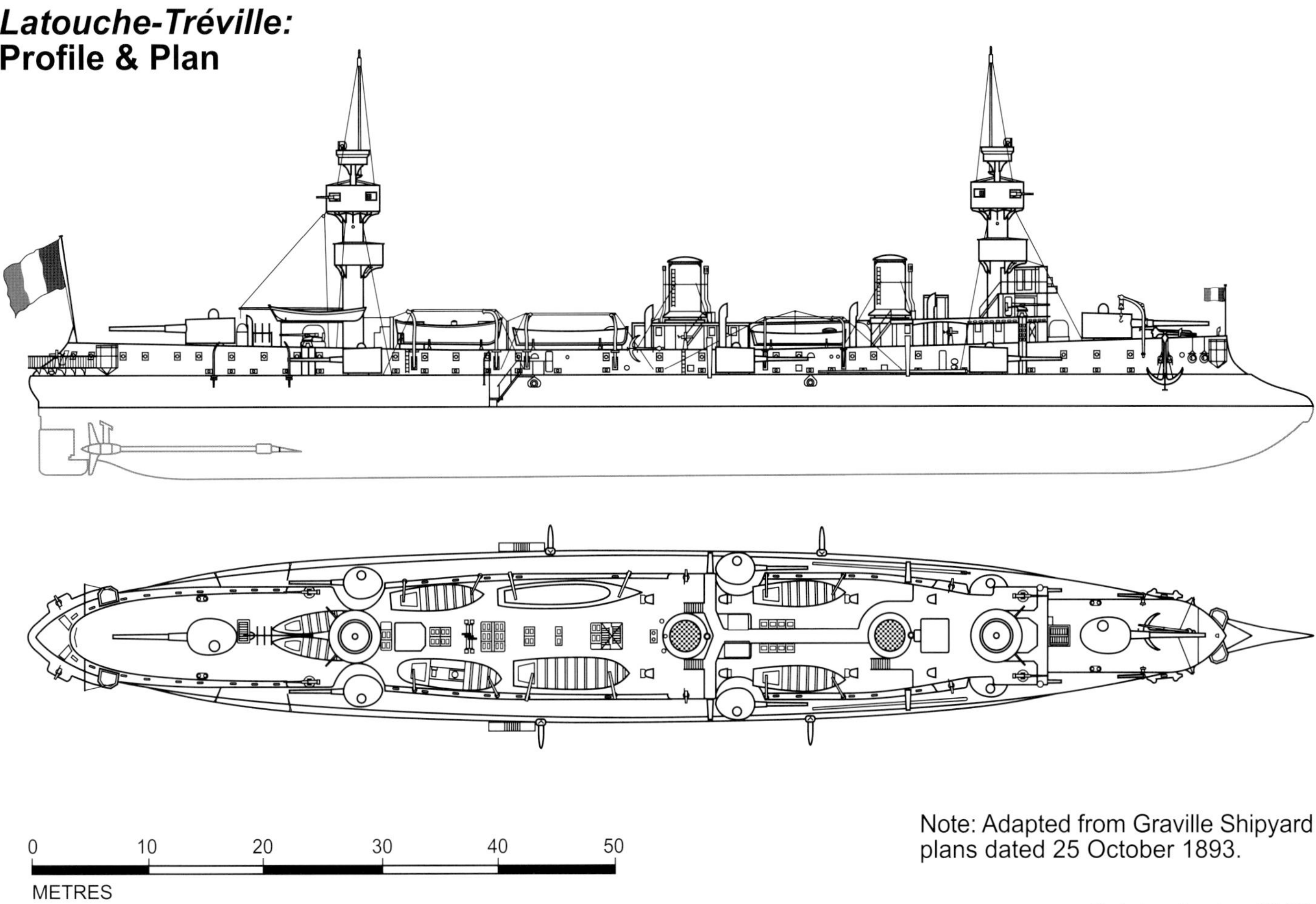

However, the Navy Ministry was concerned that the provision of sail, with all the attendant top hamper, would impact adversely on the fighting qualities of the ships. A year later, on 26 June 1888, under the heading '2nd class coast defence armoured cruiser', the *Conseil des Travaux* debated the role the ship was intended to play in wartime, 'in order that the design should provide the required qualities without resorting to an excessive displacement'. At the same time it pointed out that too restricted a displacement might put the ship at a disadvantage compared to the latest Italian cruisers. This appears to have evoked a prompt response, as on 31 July the *Conseil* submitted a revised set of requirements. The two 16cm guns of the original specification were upgraded to 19cm, and it was recommended that all the main guns be mounted in enclosed turrets, as in *Dupuy-de-Lôme*. The protective arrangements were similar to those of the earlier design but with thicker armour. The four rigged masts of the original proposal were suppressed in favour of two military masts. Displacement was to be around 4750 tonnes.

This proposal evidently met with ministerial approval, as on 10 August 1888 a programme of four 2nd class armoured cruisers was announced, and the *Conseil* called for suitable design studies. Of the six projects submitted, three were rejected because they failed to meet the requirements. The remaining three, by Engineers Thibaudier, Marchal and Guillaume, were retained for further examination, but it was the one by Thibaudier, for a ship of about 4700 tonnes displacement, that found favour with the *Conseil*.

The design was approved on 1 April 1889 and construction ordered on 4 June subject to the incorporation of some modifications that had been requested on 5 May. Four ships were authorised: two (*Charner*[8] and *Bruix*) were to be built at the Rochefort naval dockyard, and two by private yards: *Latouche-Tréville* was to be built at the Graville shipyard (Le Havre) of Forges & Chantiers de la Méditerranée (FCM), and *Chanzy* at Chantiers de la Gironde, Bordeaux; the contracts with the private shipyards were signed on 18 December 1889.

[8] *Charner* would subsequently be renamed *Amiral Charner*.

BUILDING DATA

Name	Builder	Laid down	Launched	Trials	Commissioned
Amiral Charner	Arsenal de Rochefort	15 Jun 1889	18 Mar 1893	18 Jan 1894	26 Aug 1895
Latouche-Tréville	FC Méditerranée (Le Havre)	26 Apr 1890	5 Nov 1892	16 Oct 1894	6 May 1895
Chanzy	Société de la Gironde	Jan 1890	24 Jan 1894	6 Feb 1894	20 Jul 1895
Bruix	Arsenal de Rochefort	9 Nov 1891	2 Aug 1894	15 Apr 1896	1 Dec 1896

NOMENCLATURE

Léopold-Victor-Joseph **Charner** (1797–1869) was a distinguished naval officer. Promoted rear admiral in 1852, he was recognised for his efficient organisation of troop transports during the Crimean War. He was promoted vice admiral in June 1855, and in 1860 he was appointed C-in-C of French naval forces in China, where he was involved in the Second Opium War. He left China for Vietnam in 1861 and relieved the siege of Saigon. Charner was made Admiral of France, the highest rank in the *Marine Nationale*, in 1864.

Etienne-Eustache **Bruix** (1759–1805) was an admiral during the French Revolutionary and Napoleonic Wars. He commanded a division that participated in the French invasion of Ireland in 1796. He was promoted rear admiral in 1797 and became Minister of Marine 1798–9. He was then promoted vice admiral in command of the squadron at Brest. Following various peregrinations and a failed pursuit by the British, Bruix returned to Brest. Napoleon appointed him admiral in 1801 and *conseiller d'état* in 1802. He was placed in command of the invasion flotilla at Boulogne but died in Paris of tuberculosis in 1805.

Antoine-Eugène-Alfred **Chanzy** (1823–83) was a general who distinguished himself in the Franco-Prussian War by his able tactical handling of the 2nd Army of the Loire. He was subsequently appointed Governor General of Algeria and Ambassador in St Petersburg. He died while commanding the VI Corps near the German frontier and received a state funeral.

Louis-René Levassor, comte de **La Touche-Tréville** (1745–1804) was a vice admiral who fought in the American War of Independence and became a prominent figure in the French Revolutionary and Napoleonic Wars. Promoted rear admiral in 1793, he was subsequently denounced as an aristocrat and imprisoned, but returned to active duty in 1799, being appointed to the command of the naval squadron at Rochefort. Promoted vice admiral in 1803, he was appointed Inspector General of the Mediterranean coasts, then C-in-C at Toulon. He died in 1804 on board his flagship *Bucentaure.*

HULL AND SUPERSTRUCTURES

The hull form and construction methods adopted for the *Amiral Charner* class were similar to those for *Dupuy-de-Lôme.* The two principal differences were that frame spacing was reduced from 1.2m to 1m, and there was only a single full-width deck above the armoured deck, the *pont des gaillards*; there was no 'battery deck' between them, which meant that both freeboard and the command of the guns in the wing turrets were reduced. This is turn resulted in substantial weight savings for the hull and the side protection; the height of the belt above the waterline was only 2.55m compared with 3.95m for *Dupuy-de-Lôme.*

Below: A fine view of *Chanzy* in Villefranche roads ca 1898. In the background are the battleships *Dévastation* and *Redoutable.* The relatively low command of the 16cm wing turrets made the guns difficult to work in heavy seas, and there was frequent ingress of water into the forward turrets. *(Jean Guiglini collection)*

ARMAMENT

Main guns

In contrast to *Dupuy-de-Lôme*, which had her main guns mounted on sponsons in the waist, in the *Amiral Charner* class the two 19cm gun turrets were mounted fore and aft and raised to the level of the forecastle (*spardeck*), which gave them a similar command to those in the earlier ship. The guns were the same model, the 19cm/45 Mle 1887, but the turrets differed in having a pivot that descended to the hold; the handing rooms were around the base of the pivots, and the shell rooms and powder magazines were adjacent to the handing rooms. This was a much more satisfactory arrangement that would be adopted for all the later French armoured cruisers.

In July 1890, shortly after the start of construction, *Latouche-Tréville*'s builders, Forges & Chantiers de la Méditerranée, put forward a proposal to equip her with electrically-operated turrets in place of the hydraulically-operated units specified in the original design. They provided a design for a turret that was balanced about the central pivot-shaft with the gun also balanced about its trunnions; it therefore required relatively little effort to rotate the turret or to elevate or depress the gun. In the event of failure of the electric motors, the training of the turret could easily be effected manually.

In order to achieve the weight distribution needed to balance the turret, the latter had to be elliptical in plan rather than circular. This had implications for the weight of protection, and a certain amount of redesign was necessary in order to achieve weights similar to those of the original specification.

The *Conseil des Travaux* was initially less than enthusiastic about electrically-powered turrets. However, it was conceded that, as the builders were working on secondary turrets with a similar power train for the battleship *Jauréguiberry*, which was at an earlier stage of construction at their La Seyne shipyard, the adoption of an electrical system in *Latouche-Tréville* would provide useful experience. *Latouche-Tréville* thus became the first French warship to have electrically-operated turrets. Power was supplied by two generators each delivering 20,080W at 80 volts DC. Each turret had electric motors from the Sautter-Harlé company[9] operating the ammunition hoist and the training mechanism, both of the latter being controlled by a device known as a *cartouche électrique*, which appears to have relied for its operation on a series of resistances brought into play in succession by a system of gears and linkages operated by a hand-lever.

Although these mechanisms seem to have functioned satisfactorily during trials, when the 19cm turrrets trained through 300° in 50 seconds, in service the defects of the *cartouche électrique* soon became apparent. The drive to the training mechanism included an electromagnetically-operated friction clutch whose windings overheated and tended to burn out at the normal operating voltage. Operation rapidly

[9] The Paris-based engineering company Sautter-Harlé & Cie, founded during the 1880s, would become the primary supplier of electric motors to the *Marine Nationale*. The only competitor in this field was Breguet, also of Paris, which supplied dynamos, searchlight projectors and mines.

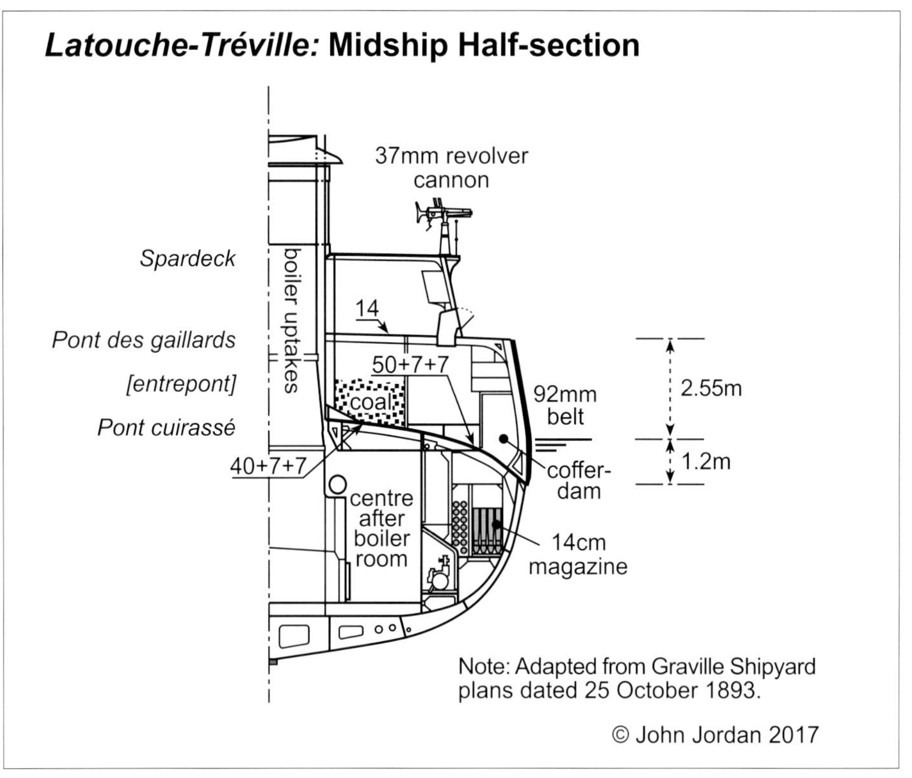

AMIRAL CHARNER CLASS: CHARACTERISTICS

Displacement:	4756 tonnes
Dimensions:	
Length	106.00m pp; 110.00m oa
Beam	13.98m wl
Draught	6.06m aft
Propulsion:	
Boilers	16 Belleville boilers, 17kg/cm^2
Engines	2-shaft 3-cylinder HTE
Horsepower	7600CV (designed)
Speed	19 knots (designed)
Coal	406 tonnes normal; 535 tonnes full load
Endurance	4000nm at 10 knots
Armament:	
Main guns	2 x 19cm/45 Mle 1887 in single turrets
Medium guns	6 x 14cm/45 Mle 1887 in single turrets
	4 x 65mm/50 Mle 1891 in single mountings
ATB guns	8 x 47mm/40 Mle 1885 in single mountings
	6 x 37mm revolver cannon
Torpedo tubes	4 a/w tubes for 450mm torpedoes
	8 torpedoes Mle 1892
Protection:	
Main belt	92mm
Decks	14mm PBS
	40/50 PBI
19/14cm turrets	92mm
Conning tower	92mm
Boats:	1 x 12.5m steam launch (*vedette*)
	1 x 8.85m steam pinnace
	1 x 10m pulling pinnace
	3 x 8m pulling cutters
	2 x 8m whalers
	1 x 5m dinghy
Complement:	
As private ship	36 officers, 378 men

Above: *Latouche-Tréville* moored in Toulon roads during the late 1890s. *(Musée de la Marine)*

became unreliable due to wear in the mechanical parts and, as the power supply was direct current, switching between the various resistances tended to cause arcing that quickly damaged the contacts, all of which interfered with the precision of aiming and risked immobilising the turret. Also, the device was susceptible to malfunction in the wet conditions that were the all-too-frequent result of water ingress into the turrets. In 1905 it was replaced by a more reliable system operated by relays. The other three ships all retained the hydraulically-trained turrets of the original design.

Medium guns

In place of the 16cm secondary guns of *Dupuy-de-Lôme* there were six 14cm guns, all in turrets mounted in the waist. The turrets were of the pivot type, and were broadly similar in conception to those of the battleships of the 1890 programme. The turrets in *Latouche-*

MAIN AND MEDIUM GUNS: *DUPUY-DE-LÔME* AND *CHARNER* CLASS

	19cm/45 Mle 1887			16cm/45 Mle 1887			14cm/45 Mle 1887		
Total length:	9046mm			7600mm			6450mm		
Chamber volume:	43.39dm^3			26.64dm^3			14.73dm^3		
Breech pressure:	2150kg/cm^2			2000kg/cm^2			2300kg/cm^2		
Shell:	CI	APC	SAPC	CI	APC	SAPC	CI	APC	SAPC
	75.0kg	90.3kg	89.5kg	45.0kg	54.9kg	52.6kg	30.0kg	35.0kg	35.0kg
Bursting charge:	5.07kg	1.59kg	4.33kg	2.10kg	0.97kg	3.10kg	1.30kg	0.58kg	1.69kg
	powder	*mélinite*	*mélinite*	powder	*mélinite*	*mélinite*	powder	powder	*mélinite*
Propellant:	18.8kg BM9 (2 x ½)			13.1kg BM9 (cartridge)			7.28kg BM7 (cartridge)		
Muzzle velocity (MV):	800m/sec (APC)			800m/sec (APC)			770m/sec (APC)		
Remaining V 2000m:	600m/sec (APC)			605m/sec (APC)			564m/sec (APC)		
Maximum range:	11,500m at 14.20°			11,500m at 15°			11,000m at 15°		
Firing cycle:	60 sec			30 sec			15 sec		

Tréville were elliptical in plan and were electrically operated; those in the other three ships were circular in plan and were trained using the conventional hydraulic rams.

The 14cm 45-calibre gun was likewise from the Mle 1887 series. The French were slow to apply quick-firing principles to medium-calibre guns, despite the early adoption of a cartridge case for the propellant, and the 14cm Mle 1887 was not a QF gun.[10] It fired a cast iron shell weighing 30kg with a 1.3kg bursting charge, or 35kg steel shells with bursters of 1.69kg *mélinite* (SAP) or 0.58kg black powder (AP). The 7.28kg BM 7 powder charge was in a single brass cartridge case.

Light QF guns

As in *Dupuy-de-Lôme* there were four 65mm/50 Mle 1891 guns on open pivot mountings. Two were mounted on the lower bridge deck at the forward end of the ship, the remaining two on the shelter deck aft, between the after turret and the mainmast.

ATB guns

The complement of ATB guns as completed appears to have varied slightly between the various units of the class, and was modified after completion. The plans of *Chanzy* show eight Hotchkiss 47mm/40 Mle 1885 guns on the lower platforms of the two military masts, and six 37mm revolver cannon: two on the shelter deck abeam the foremast, two on the same level abeam the second funnel, and two on the stern gallery.

Searchlight projectors

To provide illumination of targets at night for the ATB guns six Mangin 60cm searchlight projectors were fitted. The upper projectors (*ligne haute*) were located on the upper platforms of the military masts, as in *Dupuy-de-Lôme*, but the lower projectors (*ligne basse*), which were even more exposed to the elements due to the reduced freeboard of these ships, were mounted on 'bandstands' on either side of the bow and the stern, and were protected by hinged watertight covers when not in use.

[10] The first 6in QF guns were developed for the Royal Navy in the late 1880s. The first 14cm QF gun to enter service with the Marine Nationale was the Mle 1891.

Below: The two heavy military masts are prominent in this fine study of *Bruix*. The enclosed structures below the platforms for the 60cm searchlights each housed four Hotchkiss 47mm anti-torpedo boat guns. *(DR)*

Above: *Bruix* at her moorings at Brest during 1902, when she was serving with the Northern Squadron. She was flagship of the cruiser squadron until she was superseded in that role by more modern ships of the type. *(DR)*

Opposite: *Bruix* during her full-power trials on 15 September 1896, when she attained a maximum speed of 18.37 knots with 9107CV using forced draught. *(Private collection)*

Torpedoes

As in *Dupuy-de-Lôme* there were four 45mm above-water tubes for the Mle 1892 torpedo. The tubes were suspended from the *pont des gaillards*, and could be trained 35–40° either side of the beam; the port and starboard tubes were offset to enable them to be retracted to the centreline when not in use. The plans suggest that two torpedoes were provided for each of the four tubes.

PROTECTION

The protection system was similar to that of *Dupuy-de-Lôme*, albeit with a slight reduction in thicknesses. The side armour comprised plates of 92mm homogeneous nickel steel amidships reducing to 60mm at the bow and stern, secured to two layers of 9mm Siemens-Martin steel hull plating. It covered the full length of the hull to a height of 2.55m above the waterline and 1.2m below. The vaulted deck of mild steel, which at its sides joined the lower edge of the belt, was 40mm thick over the central section and 50mm at the sides, the protective plates being secured to a double layer of 7mm construction steel. As in *Dupuy-de-Lôme* there was a light splinter deck below over the boiler and engine rooms, and a full-length cofferdam above the protective deck behind the armour belt, which it was intended to fill with water-excluding cellulose.[11] The plating of the *pont des gaillards* had an enhanced thickness of 14mm, thereby forming a roof over the cellular layer of the *entrepont* (see Midship Half-section plan).

The turrets for the 19cm and 14cm guns had a similar thickness of protection to the hull, 92mm, as did the conning tower. Because the hull armour extended to the upper deck the pivots and hoists for the 14cm turrets in the waist were again unprotected, but those for the 19cm turrets had hoops of 92mm armour between the upper deck and the forecastle deck.

MACHINERY

The propulsion system adopted for the *Amiral Charner* class was less ambitious than for *Dupuy-de-Lôme*. There were only two shafts, which were driven by two horizontal-type triple-expansion engines in the first three ships. The three-cylinder engines of *Amiral Charner* and *Latouche-Tréville* were built by Forges & Chantiers de la Méditerranée at Le Havre, those of *Chanzy* by Schneider–Le Creusot. Those of *Latouche-Tréville* developed 7600CV with normal draught for 17 knots, and 8300CV with forced draught for 18.3 knots. The last ship, *Bruix*, had more powerful four-cylinder VTE engines (also built by Forges & Chantiers de la Méditerranée) mounted side by side, which delivered 9000CV with forced draught.

Steam was supplied by sixteen Belleville watertube boilers rated at 17kg/cm². The boilers were disposed back to back on the centreline in two identical boiler rooms with an auxiliary machinery room in between. The two elliptical funnels were placed in the centre of each of the boiler rooms, and were of similar height and configuration. The disposition and composition of

[11] This was not implemented in order to reduce weights when the compartmentation of the main deck was revised during building.

Amiral Charner Class: Machinery

The armoured cruisers of the *Charner* class were the first to have Belleville watertube boilers. The boilers were mounted back to back on the centreline so that the furnaces faced the lateral coal bunkers, thereby easing the work of the stokers who shovelled coal. The arrangement would be repeated in *Pothuau*. Note the very different arrangement of the auxiliary machinery in *Latouche-Tréville*, in which the turrets were trained using electrical motors rather than hydraulic rams.

Latouche-Tréville

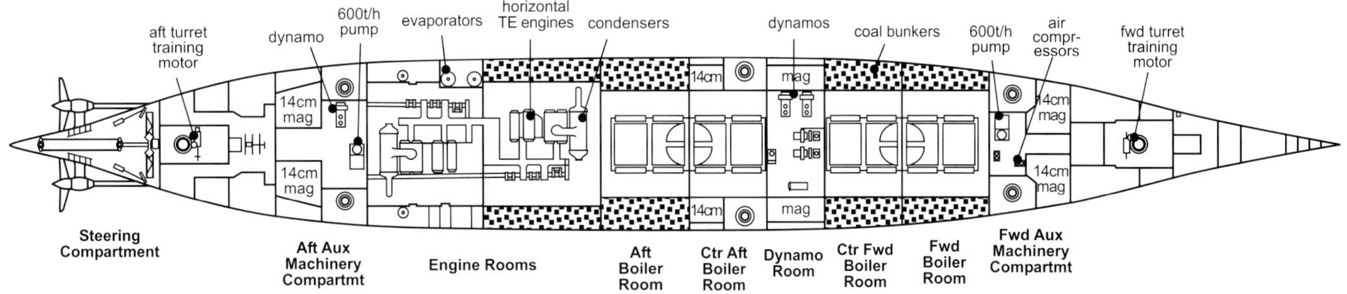

Chanzy

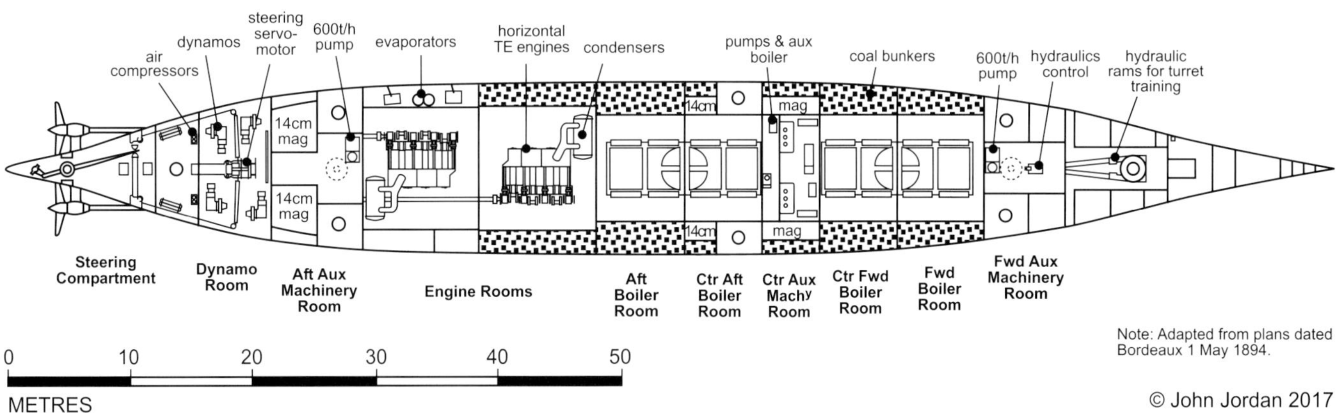

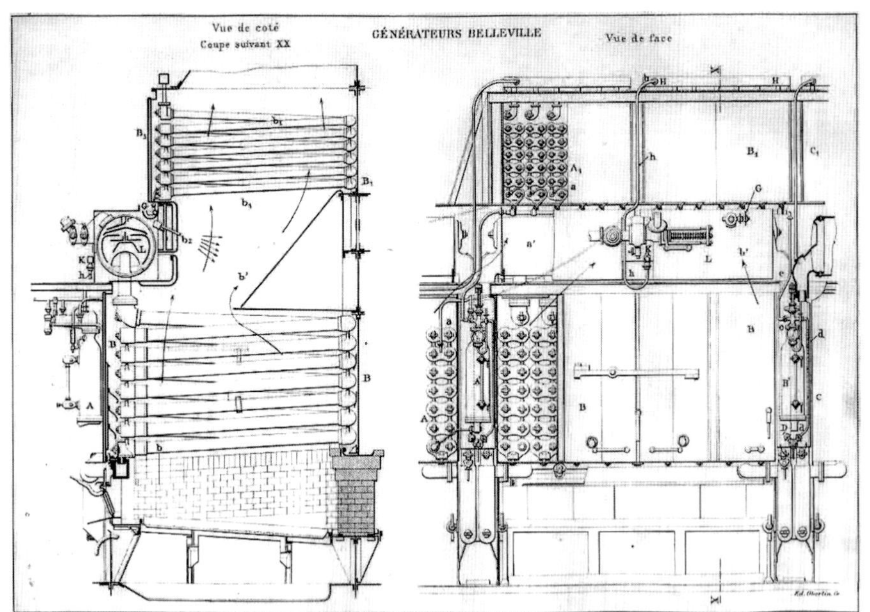

Internal profile and face of a Belleville large watertube boiler. The French were well to the fore in boiler development, and designs which entered service with the Navy from the late 1880s included the Belleville, which would become the standard type, the Niclausse and the Lagrafel & d'Allest. The great advantage of the watertube boiler was the higher pressures it could generate (in excess of 17kg/cm2) and its flexibility – the ability to change steam flow rapidly up or down. The large-diameter tubes in the Belleville boiler, which were around 80mm in diameter, passed backwards and forwards several times like a flattened spiral over the furnace; the tubes fed a cylindrical steam collector, seen top left on the profile drawing. (Le Guilcher, *op cit*)

the auxiliary machinery in *Latouche-Tréville*, which had electrically-powered turrets, differed markedly from those of her three sisters (see Machinery plan).

The Belleville boilers proved more reliable than the cylindrical boilers of *Dupuy-de-Lôme*, and the ships of this class seem to have experienced fewer problems with their propulsion systems over the course of their service lives, once initial defects had been resolved.

EARLY SERVICE

It is not clear at what point these four ships were reclassified as '1st class armoured cruisers'. Luc Feron states that this change of classification took place in 1891, shortly after they had been laid down. However, the official FC Méditerranée plans of *Latouche-Tréville*, which are dated 25 October 1893, still refer to her as *Croiseur cuirassé de 2e classe*. The Chantiers de la Gironde plans of *Chanzy* from the following year, 1 May 1894, confirm the new designation *de 1re classe*, suggesting that the ships were reclassified when three of them had been launched. French 2nd class cruisers were generally deployed as station cruisers to police France's overseas possessions, but during their early years the four ships of the *Charner* class were generally employed as 'fleet' cruisers in the light divisions (*divisions légères*).

All four units were built, launched and completed without any notable incident. However, all failed to reach their designed speed during trials; *Bruix* seems to have been the fastest, attaining 18.37 knots with 9107CV with forced draught on 15 September 1896. In *Latouche-Tréville* it was found that the engines were not developing their designed power due to an inefficient admixture of air with the gases in the furnaces, and the builders replaced the entire ventilation and boiler draught system with new compressors and fans. *Chanzy* had to be placed in 2nd class reserve shortly after her trials due to multiple machinery defects, and underwent extensive repairs. In August 1897 *Bruix* had to drop out of a planned visit to Kronstadt shortly after sailing when a piston rod fractured, damaging the medium-pressure cylinder of the port engine.

The four cruisers of the *Amiral Charner* class served as first-line units from their completion in 1895–6 until

Right: *Chanzy* in late 1906 in a white livery but with black funnel caps. She is about to deploy to the Far East. *(J Félix)*

Above: During her deployment to the Far East in 1907, on 20 May *Chanzy* struck an uncharted rock on Ballard Island in the Steep Strait, near the Chusan Archipelago. *(DR).*

Left: The half-demolished wreck of *Chanzy. (DR)*

Catastrophe du " LATOUCHE-TRÉVILLE "
Matelots nettoyant le pont après l'explosion

Right: The aftermath of the explosion in the after 19cm turret of *Latouche-Tréville* which took place in September 1898; the crew are swabbing the decks. *(DR)*

1904, being generally assigned to the light/cruiser divisions of the Mediterranean and Northern Squadrons (see table). In 1896 *Charner* and *Latouche-Tréville* served briefly with the *Ecole supérieure de guerre*, which was a sea-going staff college course in strategy and tactics devised by Rear Admiral Fournier; the course was repeated in 1899, again with *Amiral Charner* at the heart of a three-cruiser division.[12] There were also deployments to the Far East for *Bruix* (1898) and for *Amiral Charner* (1900–01).

By 1904 newer, more powerful armoured cruisers were becoming available in numbers to serve with the fleet. In November 1906 *Chanzy* and *Bruix* deployed to the Far East, but on 20 May of the following year *Chanzy* ran aground in heavy seas off Shanghai and was wrecked.

On 15 February 1907 *Latouche-Tréville* was recommissioned and attached to the gunnery school, and her activities were limited to gunnery exercises at Les Salins d'Hyères. Early in March her torpedo tubes were removed. On 22 September 1908 there was a serious accident in the after 194mm turret. According to a contemporary report the ship had been firing for two hours when she arrived at the end of the firing range, and had to suspend fire with the gun still loaded while she reversed course. It was decided to use this pause in firing to change the turret crew. Safety procedures to avoid accidental discharge outside the target area required that the breech be opened, and as the new crew embarked on this operation the propellant charge ignited.[13] The projectile was expelled harmlessly overboard but the explosion of the propellant swept through

Charner Class & *Pothuau*: Early Service

	Charner	Latouche-T	Chanzy	Bruix	Pothuau
1895	2nd Lt Div Med	1st Lt Div Med	1st Lt Div Med	Trials	Building
1896	School Ship	School Ship	4th Lt Div Med	Northern Squ	Trials
1897	2nd Lt Div Med	East Med	East Med	↓	Northern Squ
1898	↓	1st Lt Div Med	Reserve	Far East	Lt Squ Med (fl)
1899	Northern Squ		1st Lt Div Med	Northern Squ	
1900	Far East				
1901	↓			↓	
1902	3rd Arm Div			Atlantic Div	
1903	School Ship			Northern Squ	
1904		↓	↓	Reserve	
1905		Reserve	Reserve		↓
1906				↓	Reserve
1907		School Ship	FE – wrecked	Far East	School Ship
1908					
1909	↓			↓	
1910	Gd Ship Crete			Reserve	
1911		↓			
1912	↓	Reserve		Gd Ship Crete	
1913	Reserve	Bizerte/E Med			
1914	↓	↓		↓	↓

12 The third ship was the protected cruiser *Suchet*.

13 A commission of enquiry concluded that the probable cause of the accident was a failure to observe the regulations that stipulated that the priming tube be withdrawn and the firing bolt secured before the breech was opened; it is thought that the firing lanyard may have been accidentally snagged on an obstruction (reported in *Le Yacht*, 24 October 1908).

Left: *Bruix* at Toulon in the blue-grey livery introduced in 1908. The heavy military masts have been landed and replaced by simple pole masts. On the left of the photo can be seen the coast defence battleship *Amiral Tréhouart*. *(DR)*

the turret, killing everyone in its path and projecting the breech-block out through the turret door. The sighting hood, dislodged by the explosion, landed on the deck, killing another seaman. At the same time a jet of flame shot down the ammunition trunk, and a major catastrophe was only averted by an alert member of the handling party who closed the connecting hatch between the hoist and the magazine. It was particularly unfortunate that at the time of the accident both the original and the replacement crews were in the turret, resulting in fourteen men being killed and five wounded. Repairs to the turret took until the end of the year, and test firings were carried out on 4 January 1909. The cruiser then resumed her duties with the gunnery school until she was placed in reserve on 1 January 1912. On 1 October she was transferred to the Special Reserve, then recommissioned on 20 November for duty in Middle Eastern waters.

After a lengthy period in reserve, *Amiral Charner* and *Bruix* were reactivated as guard ships in the Eastern Mediterranean, based at Suda Bay in Crete, from 1910–12 and from 1912–14 respectively. The three surviving ships of the class would undoubtedly have paid off had it not been for the outbreak of war in August 1914, when they were reactivated for service in the Eastern Mediterranean. Despite their age, they gave much useful service in anti-submarine and blockade patrols and as convoy escorts, and their heavy guns proved useful for occasional coastal bombardments (see Chapter 11).

EVALUATION

The cruisers of the *Amiral Charner* class were considered reasonably good seaboats and handled well in most sea conditions. However, in all but the calmest conditions they were very wet forward, and their foreparts and bridges were constantly swamped and drenched in spray, causing water ingress into the forward turrets; in the case of *Latouche-Tréville* this resulted in frequent short-circuits in her electrical systems. In a long swell they had a tendency to roll heavily, which led to frequent requests for the fitting of bilge keels and the lightening of their upperworks.

As built all four ships were fitted with metal funnel covers that hinged to the sides when the funnel was in use. These heavy fittings were discarded early in *Latouche-Tréville*'s career (about 1896) after stability tests had revealed an inadequate metacentric height; they were replaced by a light metal framework over which a canvas cover could be fitted when the funnel was not in use. Further weight-saving measures included the replacement of the military masts by simple poles in 1910–14.

The design of these ships attracted criticism on account of their limited speed and endurance, and doubts were expressed as to their ability to use their armament effectively in any sort of a seaway. Service in tropical climates led to complaints that their internal ventilation was inadequate for such conditions. Despite this, most of their war service was in West or North Africa.

CHAPTER 2

THE CRUISER FLAGSHIPS *POTHUAU* AND *D'ENTRECASTEAUX*

POTHUAU

Designed from the outset as a '1st class fleet cruiser' (*croiseur d'escadre de 1re classe*), *Pothuau* was an enlarged *Amiral Charner*. She was intended to serve as a flagship for the Light Squadron (*Escadre légère*) in the Mediterranean, a role that required enhanced command spaces and accommodation for an admiral and his staff.

The role of the armoured 'fleet' cruiser was evolving during the 1890s as new ships entered service in increasing numbers. In a major fleet action the Navy viewed them as a reserve to finish off crippled enemy battleships; alternatively they could be put into the line of battle against older battleships vulnerable to steel shell with *mélinite* bursters.[1] These theories undoubtedly influenced the Imperial Japanese Navy, which employed its own armoured cruisers (purchased from British, French, German and Italian shipbuilders from 1897) in a similar role.[2]

The initial characteristics for the new ship were

[1] See Ropp, *The Development of a Modern Navy: French Naval Policy 1871–1904*, p 296.

[2] See Kathrin Milanovich, 'Armoured Cruisers of the Imperial Japanese Navy', *Warship 2014*, pp 70–92. When operating with the battle line at Tsushima in 1905, the IJN used its armoured cruisers as a 'fast wing'.

BUILDING DATA

Name	Builder	Laid down	Launched	Trials	Commissioned
Pothuau	FC Méditerranée (Le Havre)	25 May 1893	19 Sep 1895	17 Aug 1896	5 Jun 1897

Right: *Pothuau* shortly before her launch, on the slipway of the Le Havre Shipyard of FC Méditerranée. *(Private collection)*

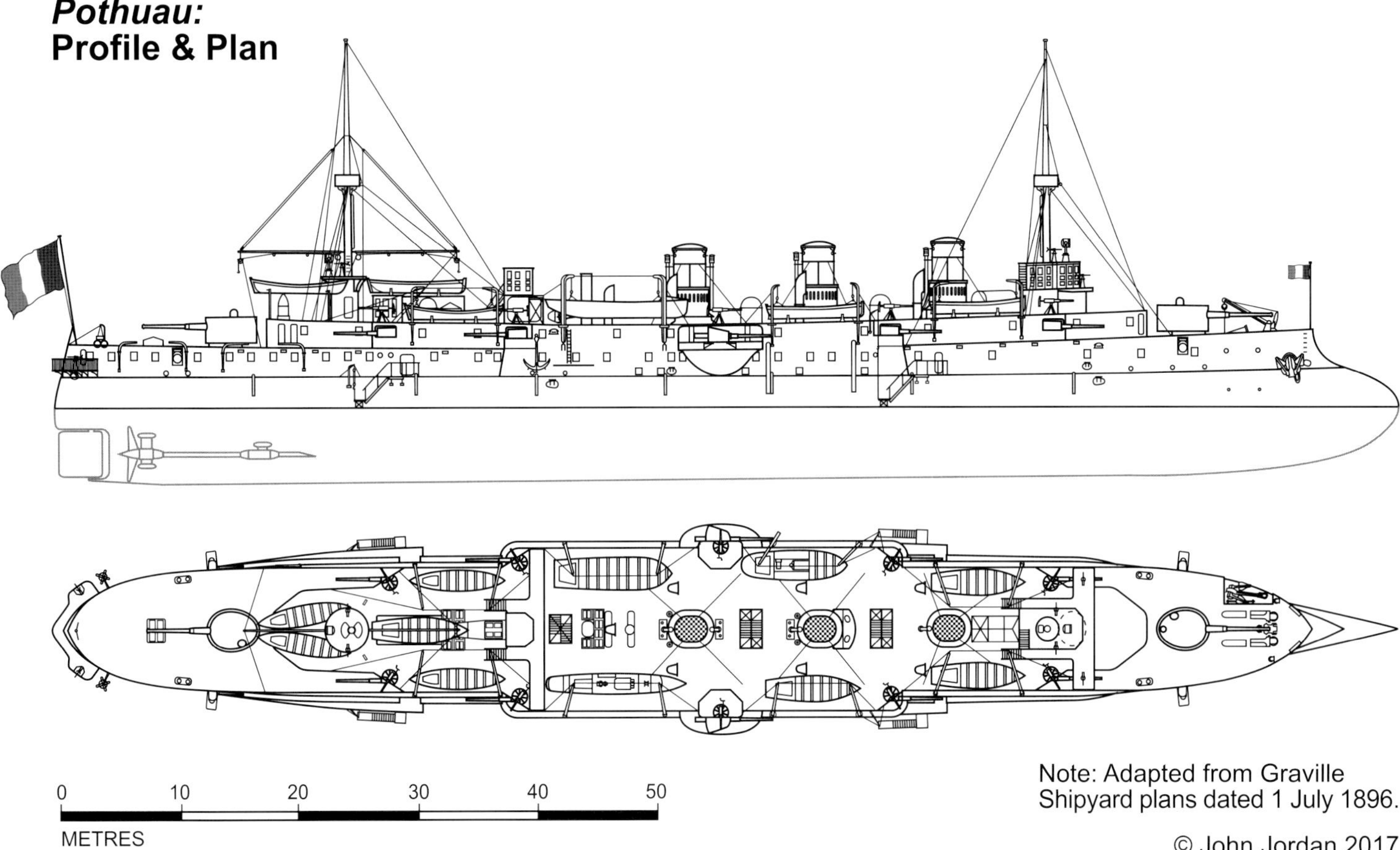

drawn up by the *Conseil des Travaux* during meetings that took place on 28–29 May 1891. Main armament was to be similar to that of the *Amiral Charner* class: two 19cm guns in single turrets fore and aft, and six 14cm guns in the waist. There was to be a protective deck 55mm thick (including plating) at the centreline and 100mm on the outer slopes where it joined the lower edge of the belt. The belt itself was to be in two strakes with a maximum thickness, including plating, of 100mm. There was to be a two-shaft propulsion system delivering a top speed of 19 knots, and endurance was to be 5000nm at 10 knots.

Jules Thibaudier, who was the Head of Naval Construction at Rochefort Naval Dockyard and had been responsible for the *Amiral Charner* class,[3] was commissioned to design the new ship. His proposal was reviewed by the *Conseil* on 15 March 1892. The design was approved, albeit with the customary requests for changes, and the ship was included in the new construction programme on 11 April 1893. The order was placed with the private shipbuilder Forges & Chantiers de la Méditerranée, Le Havre; cost was 11,156,433 French francs (FF).

NOMENCLATURE

Louis-Pierre-Alexis **Pothuau** (1815–82) was a French naval officer and politician. He took part in the bombardment of Mogador in 1844, and the bombardment of Odessa and the Siege of Sevastopol in 1854–5. Promoted rear admiral in 1864, he commanded the forts to the south of Paris during the siege of 1870–1. Promoted vice admiral and elected as a *député* for Paris, Pothuau was twice Minister of Marine (1871–3 and 1877–9), and ended his career as ambassador to the UK 1879–80.

HULL AND SUPERSTRUCTURES

The design drawn up by Thibaudier was for a larger ship than *Amiral Charner*, as the requirement for *Pothuau* to serve as a flagship implied a significant increase in internal volume: she displaced 5360 tonnes, an increase of 600 tonnes, and was 7m longer with 1.3m greater beam. The battery deck (*pont de la batterie*) that had been a feature of *Dupuy-de-Lôme* was reinstated to provide the necessary internal volume, and this had consequences for sea-keeping (higher freeboard), for gunnery (the guns in the waist had a higher command) and for protection (the side armour extended only as far as the battery deck, so there was no side protection between the latter and the 14cm QF battery).

The larger hull made possible a heavier armament, the number of 14cm QF guns in the waist being increased from six to ten. Their higher command (5.8m *vice* 4m) was a significant improvement from a gunnery point of view, particularly in heavy seas, but there was a cost in terms of both protection and topweight. Eight of the guns were mounted in casemates, while the centre pair were in shielded pivot mountings on sponsons. Further topweight was saved by replacing the heavy military masts of the *Amiral Charner* class with simple steel poles, the 47mm ATB guns being relocated from the lower mast platforms to the shelter deck (*spardeck*), directly above the 14cm guns.

The admiral's accommodation, which comprised a

[3] The first and last ships of the class, *Amiral Charner* and *Bruix*, had been built at Rochefort.

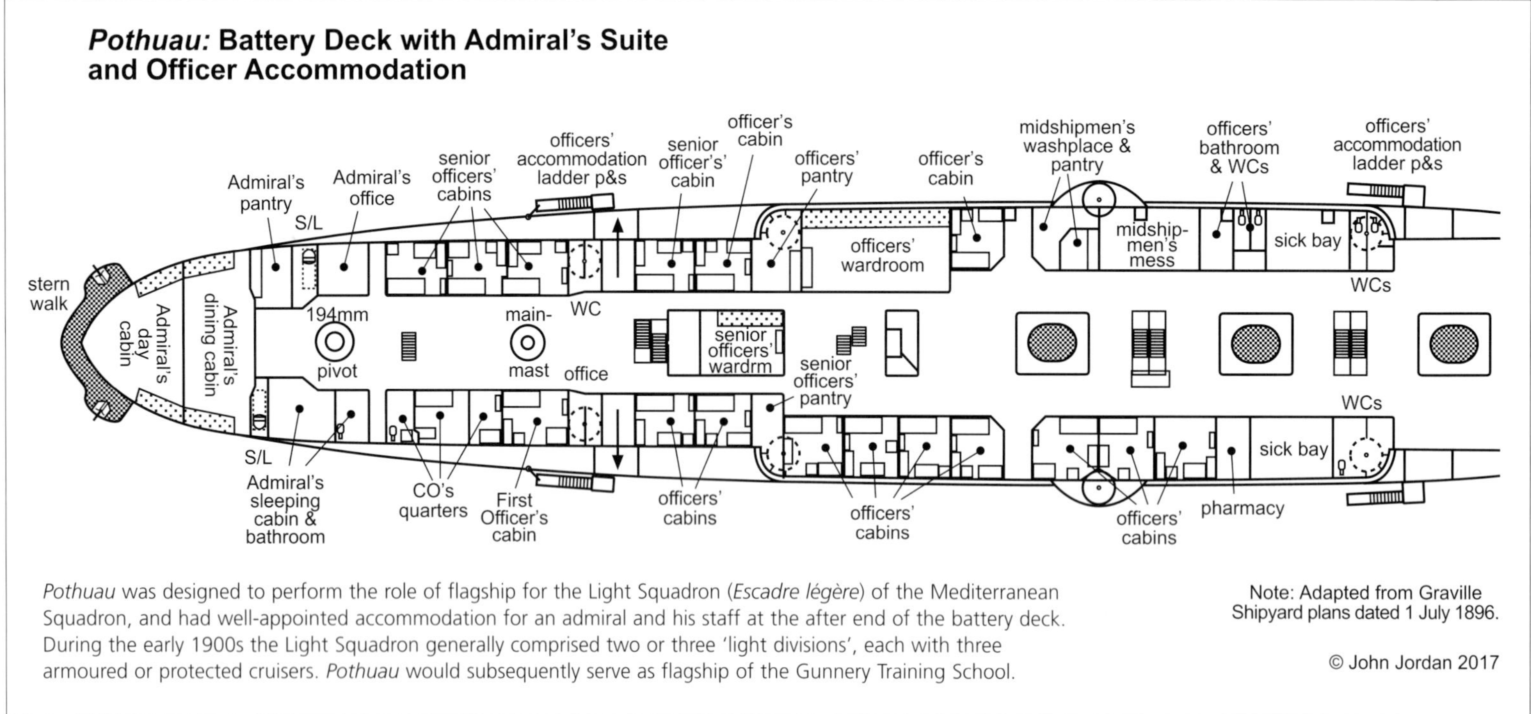

Pothuau was designed to perform the role of flagship for the Light Squadron (*Escadre légère*) of the Mediterranean Squadron, and had well-appointed accommodation for an admiral and his staff at the after end of the battery deck. During the early 1900s the Light Squadron generally comprised two or three 'light divisions', each with three armoured or protected cruisers. *Pothuau* would subsequently serve as flagship of the Gunnery Training School.

vast dining cabin with adjacent pantry, a spacious day cabin with access to the stern gallery, a sleeping cabin, office, bathroom and WC, occupied the entire after part of the battery deck from the stern to the pivot for the after 19cm gun (see Battery Deck plan). The cabins and offices for the flag staff and the ship's officers, together with wardrooms and bathrooms for the senior and junior officers, extended to the second funnel on the same deck on either side of the ship. Between the first and second funnels there was a large sick bay and pharmacy.

ARMAMENT

Main guns

The 194mm and six of the ten 138.6mm guns[4] mounted on *Pothuau* were Mle 1893; the remaining

4 From the mid-1890s gun calibres were designated in millimetres rather than centimetres in official documentation. This change is apparent in the labels on the official plans for *Pothuau*, which date from 1896; the plans of *Latouche-Tréville*, in which the guns are designated in centimetres, date from 1893.

Right: High freeboard meant that *Pothuau* was a better seaboat than her predecessors. It was made possible by mounting the guns in a battery rather than in enclosed turrets. *(Private collection)*

four 138.6mm guns, including the two sponson mountings, were Mle 1891.[5] The first guns of this series, including the 305mm and 274mm guns embarked in the battleships *Masséna* and *Bouvet* of the 1890 programme, were 45 calibres long, but it was found possible to obtain the same ballistics with 40 calibres without decreasing the factor of safety, and later guns were of this length. For the 194mm gun there was an A tube of uniform thickness except over the chamber, and the rear portion of the tube was supported by a single row of short hoops. The breech bush screwed onto the breech piece and abutted against the chamber hoops and rear end of the A tube.[6]

There would be a progressive increase in the volume of the firing chamber and the weight of the propellant between successive series of guns of the same calibre. For the 19cm Mle 1887 fitted in *Dupuy-de-Lôme* and the *Amiral Charner* class, chamber volume was 43.39dm³ and the propellant charge was 18.80kg of BM9 powder in two bags; for the 194mm Mle 1893 in *Pothuau* the respective figures were 49.03dm³ and 23.30kg of BM9, still in two powder bags. In theory this meant more accurate firing at longer ranges with the same shell; this would become more important as the anticipated range of engagement increased during the early 1900s.

Shell was likewise subject to development over the period. Powder-filled cast iron shell would be supplemented during the 1890s by high-capacity steel shell filled with the powerful new explosive *mélinite* (picric acid); there was also a steel shell with a thicker,

[5] These guns were very similar in construction and performance, and there are no visible differences on the plans.

[6] For a full description of the construction of this gun see Friedman, *Naval Weapons of World War One*, p 203.

POTHUAU: CHARACTERISTICS

Displacement:	5360 tonnes
Dimensions:	
Length	113.05m pp
Beam	15.30m wl
Draught	6.42m aft
Propulsion:	
Boilers	18 Belleville boilers, 17kg/cm²
Engines	2-shaft 4-cylinder VTE
Horsepower	10,000CV (designed)
Speed	19 knots (designed)
Coal	538 tonnes normal; 630 tonnes full load
Endurance	4500nm at 10 knots; 1150nm at 19 knots
Armament:	
Main guns	2 x 194mm/40 Mle 1893 in single turrets
Medium guns	10 x 138.6mm/45 Mle 1891/1893 QF in eight casemate and two shielded pivot mountings
ATB guns	10 x 47mm/40 Mle 1885 QF in single mountings 8 x 37mm in single mountings (see page 41)
Torpedo tubes	4 a/w tubes for 450mm torpedoes 8 torpedoes Mle 1892
Protection:	
Main belt	60mm
Deck	35/85mm
194 turrets	176mm
138 casemates	54mm
Conning tower	200mm
Boats:	1 x 11m steam launch 1 x 8.9m steam pinnace 1 x 10m pulling pinnace 2 x 8m pulling cutters 1 x 6m pulling cutter 4 x 8m whalers 1 x 5m dinghy
Complement:	
As private ship	21 officers, 434 men

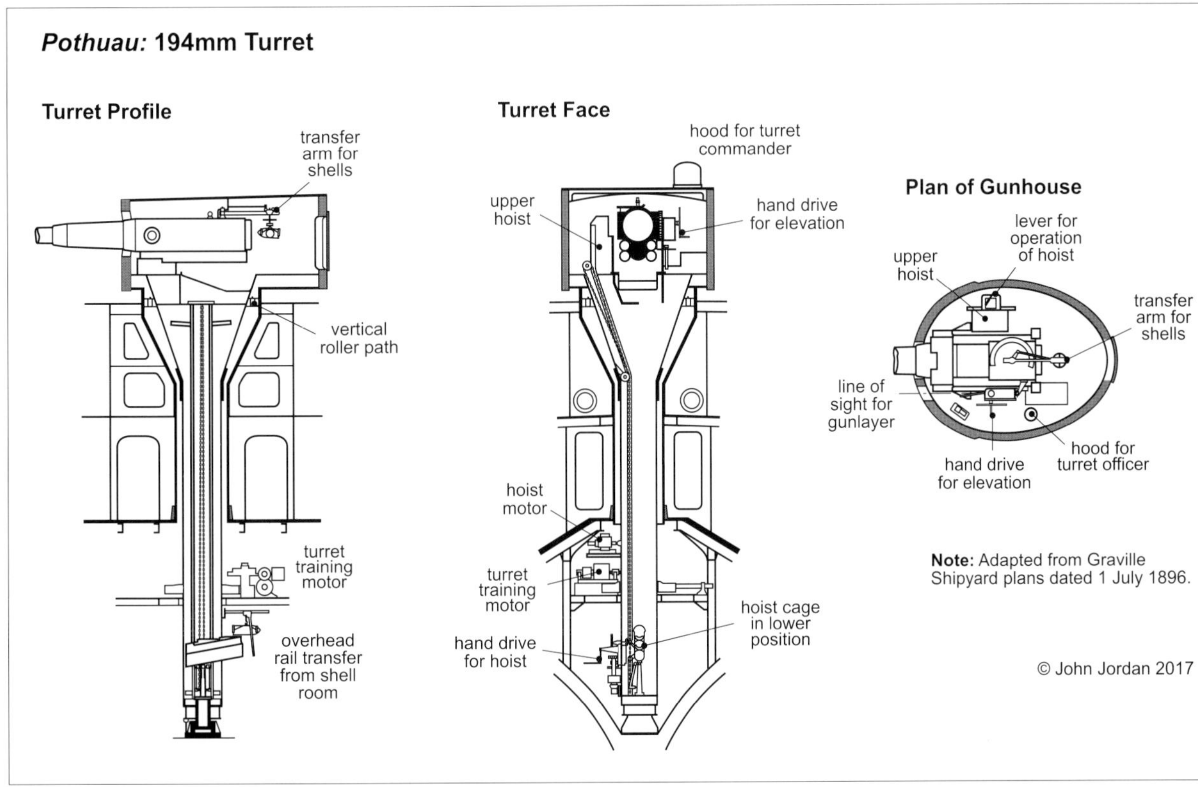

Three-view schematic of the 194mm turret. The turret and the single hoist were electrically powered with manual backup. The hoist cage held a projectile with two bagged half-charges below. When it arrived in the gunhouse, the 75/90kg projectile was lifted by a hinged arm mounted on the upper body of the gun onto the loading tray; the two half-charges, each weighing just over 11kg, were manhandled to the breech. The projectile, followed by the charges, was then rammed by hand with the gun depressed to -5°. The single armoured hood to the left of the gun was for the turret officer, who also operated the controls for training. The seat and the sights for the gunlayer were at the forward end of the gunhouse to the left of the gun, which was elevated manually using a hand wheel.

***Pothuau: Pont des Gaillards* Showing 138.6mm QF Guns and Hoists**

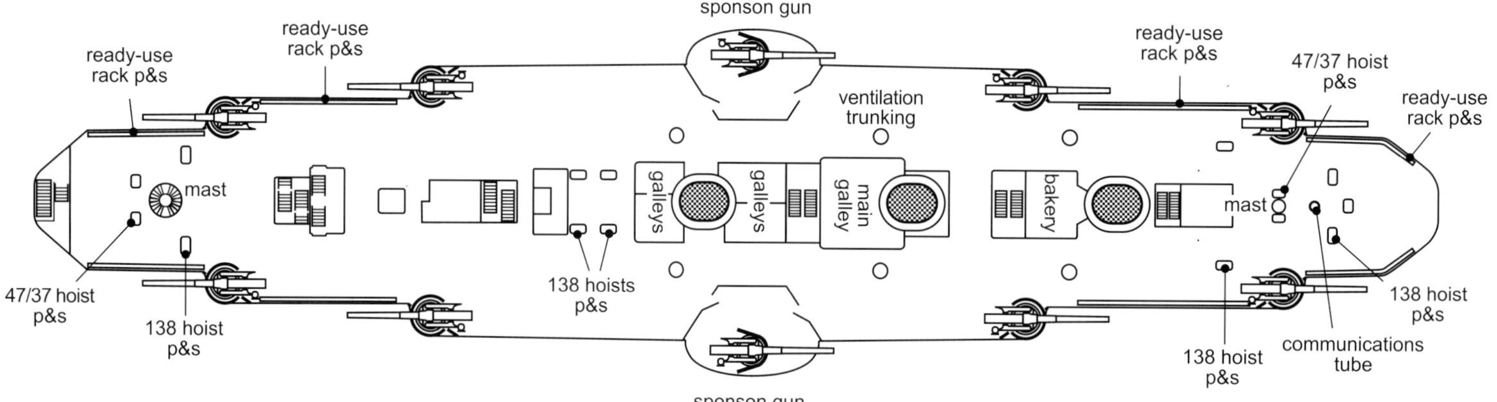

Note: Adapted from Graville Shipyard plans dated 1 July 1896.

In *Pothuau* all ten of the 138.6mm guns were mounted on the upper deck: eight in casemates and the two midship shielded mountings on sponsons. For the latter two guns the sides of the hull above the upper deck were angled inboard with access to the gun via watertight doors. In order to ensure a continuous supply of ammunition each gun had a designated hoist, although the open-plan layout meant that in practice any of the guns could be replenished by any of the hoists. Hoists for the 47mm and 37mm ATB guns passed through the upper deck fore and aft to the mountings on the shelter and superstructure decks.

stronger body and a smaller burster of black powder or *mélinite* intended to penetrate armour (*obus de rupture*). From around the turn of the century the steel shell would have a soft cap to aid penetration. New types of shell could be embarked with minimal modification to magazine stowage and handling arrangements provided that overall dimensions and configuration remained the same, so the complement of shells embarked in the magazines evolved over the service life of the ship. This has inevitably caused confusion in secondary sources, which often fail to give a precise date when recording the breakdown of shell types.

The 194mm turrets were similar in design and conception to those of *Latouche-Tréville*; they were elliptical in plan and were trained by electric motors. There were handing rooms at the base of the pivot with adjacent powder magazines and shell rooms. The single electrically-powered hoist came up to the right of the gun (see Turret plan). The projectile, which weighed 75–90kg, was transferred from the hoist to the breech by a hinged arm, and was then rammed by hand with the gun depressed to -5°, followed by the two bagged half-charges. Access to the gunhouse was by an armoured door in the rear wall.

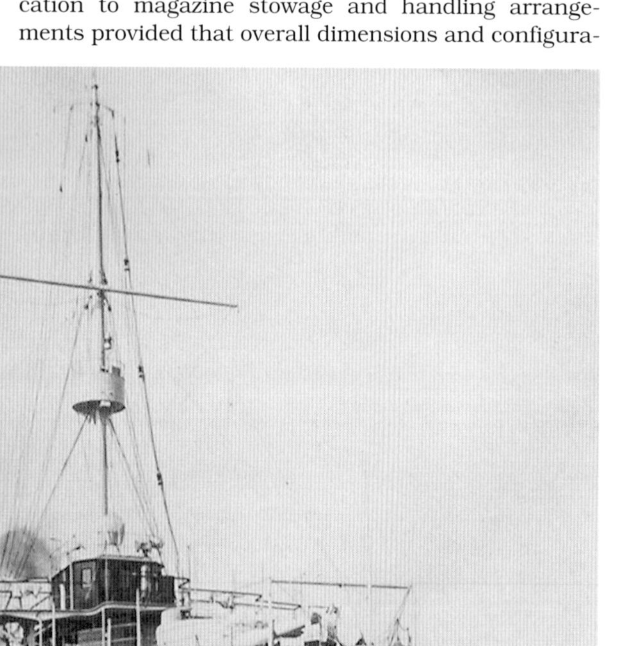

Below: *Pothuau* retained the hull form characteristic of the early French armoured cruisers, with pronounced tumblehome and a 'plough' bow. *(Private collection)*

QF guns

Eight of the ten 138.6mm guns were in casemates; the remaining two were in shielded pivot mountings on sponsons amidships. This arrangement was attractive primarily because of the considerable savings in weight. Long-trunk pivot-type turrets such as the ones adopted for the *Amiral Charner* class and the battleships of the 1890 programme were heavy, and the need to locate handing rooms and magazines around the base of the pivot imposed considerable constraints on the internal layout of the hull. The casemates required protection only for the circular shields of the gun mountings and the adjacent side plating, while the sponson guns had shields and armoured hoops to protect the base of the mounting.

Magazine arrangements could be far more flexible. In *Pothuau* there were just three double-sided combined shell/cartridge magazines: one forward at hold level, one aft at the level of the platform deck, and one amidships spanning both levels, between the after boiler room and the forward engine room. There were two hoists forward, two aft, and four amidships; these raised the shells and cartridges to the upper deck (*pont des gaillards*), where they were transferred to the guns by hand. The deck behind the casemate guns was open-plan; only the sponson guns had inner walls, with access via doors on either side. There were ready-use racks lining the outer walls of the deck (see plan).

ATB guns

Pothuau had a slightly enhanced ATB armament of ten 47mm Mle 1885 guns and eight 37mm guns. The 47mm guns were mounted on the shelter deck (*spardeck*) directly above the 138.6mm guns. Of the eight 37mm guns[7] four were mounted on the bridge platforms, two on a raised platform at the base of the mainmast, and two in the stern gallery.

Searchlight projectors

Six Mangin 60cm searchlight projectors were provided for target illumination at night, but their disposition was again modified. In the absence of military masts, the upper projectors were mounted atop the superstructures fore and aft, and the lower projectors at the four 'corners' of the ship as in the *Amiral Charner* class (though not as close to the bow and stern) behind watertight doors; the doors were hinged at the base, and were lowered to the horizontal and secured by iron stanchions; the projectors themselves were suspended from extending rails secured to the underside of the upper deck.

Torpedoes

As in the *Amiral Charner* class there were four above-water tubes for the Mle 1892 450mm torpedo. The tubes were suspended from the battery deck between frames 27 and 28, just forward of the bridge, and between frames 78 and 79, abaft the third funnel; the forward tubes could be trained 65° forward of the beam, 25° aft; the after tubes had arcs that mirrored those of the forward tubes. The forward tubes, which were more exposed to the seas when the ship was underway, could be retracted and stowed against the

[7] According to the *devis de campagne* of 1898, six of the eight 37mm guns were the QF model; the two atop the pilot house were revolver cannon. This is confirmed by the photograph below.

Below: In June 1897, shortly after her completion, *Pothuau* represented France at the review held at Spithead to mark Queen Victoria's Diamond Jubilee, and in August she embarked President Félix Faure for his subsequent visit to Kronstadt to cement the Franco-Russian Alliance signed in 1892. Assigned to the Mediterranean Squadron in September 1898, she became flagship of the Light Squadron. *(DR)*

Right: The historic turret of *Pothuau*, decorated to celebrate the Franco-Russian Alliance. The visit to Kronstadt took place in August 1897. *(Marius Bar)*

sides of the hull when not in use. The plans show racks for two or three reserve torpedoes directly beneath the tubes.

***Pothuau:* Midship Half-section**

47mm gun
Spardeck
138.6mm gun
Pont des gaillards
boiler uptakes
3
54
Pont de la batterie
7+7
[entrepont]
35+7+7
85+7+7
coal
60mm belt
2.5m
Pont cuirassé
coffer-dam
1.2m
Centre Boiler Room
coal

Note: Adapted from Graville Shipyard plans dated 1 July 1896.

PROTECTION

Hull

The system of protection in *Pothuau* was significantly modified compared to the earlier French armoured cruisers. The side armour extended only as far as the battery deck and was reduced in thickness. In compensation the protective deck directly behind it was considerably strengthened. The deck was not vaulted, as in the earlier ships, but comprised a flat section over the machinery spaces, with the slopes in two sections angled progressively downwards to meet the lower edge of the belt (see Midship Half-section plan).

The side armour was of homogeneous nickel steel 60cm thick; the plates were secured to a double thickness of 10mm hull plating. As in the *Amiral Charner* class, the belt was in two strakes and extended from 1.2m beneath the waterline to 2.5m above. The protective deck was of 35mm mild steel on the flat and 85mm on the slopes, the armour plates being secured to a double layer of 7mm 'construction' steel. Directly behind the armoured belt and seated on the protective deck there was the now-customary cofferdam, which for the first time appears to have been fitted with scuppers.[8] The roof of this cellular layer was formed by the battery deck, which was reinforced by a second layer of 7mm steel (total 14mm).

Turrets and conning tower

The main 194mm turrets were protected by plates of

[8] In the *Amiral Charner* class it was intended to fill the cofferdam with water-excluding cellulose, but this measure was rescinded to save weight (see Chapter 1). Once the ships entered service the crews found it difficult to remove water from the cofferdam in the event of flooding.

Left: The Mediterranean Squadron at anchor some time between 1904 and 1906. *Pothuau*, then flagship of the Light Squadron, is in the centre of the picture, bracketed by the battleships *Suffren* on the left and *Iéna* on the right. *(Private collection)*

Below: Part of the crew assembled on the shelter deck during one of the naval reviews held regularly before the Great War. Note the Hotchkiss 47mm Mle 1885 ATB guns on the shelter deck, and the 37mm QF guns on the lower mainmast platform. There is wooden planking on the shelter deck. *(Marius Bar)*

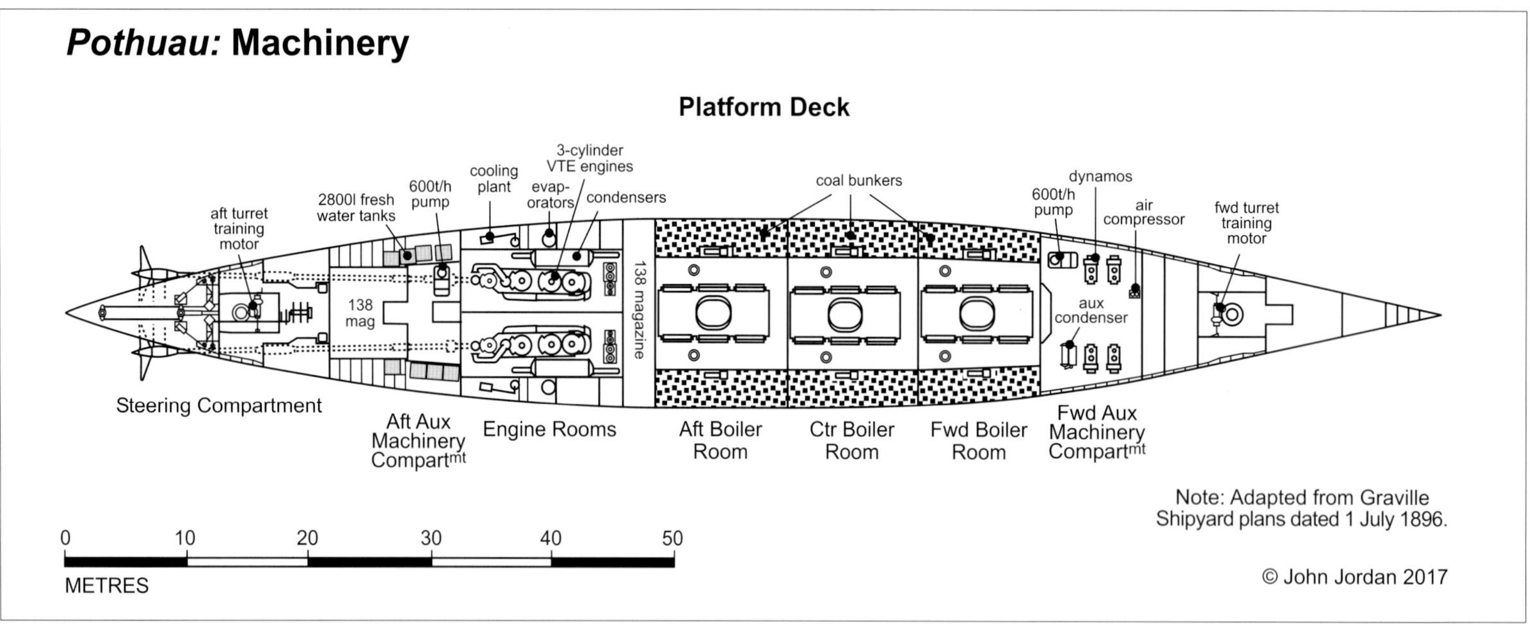

nickel steel with a maximum thickness of 176mm (turret face), and there was armour of reduced thickness in the form of a truncated cone over the pivots where they were exposed above the battery deck (see Turret plan). The thickness is not stated on the plans, but was probably 54mm as for the 138.6mm guns.

The casemate guns had circular shields of 54mm special steel, and there was similar protection for the walls of the hull around the embrasures. However, the battery deck behind the guns was open; there were no internal walls to enclose the casemates as in later ships. The two sponson mountings were given protective shields of similar thickness, and there was a hoop of 54mm plating around their bases.

The face and sides of the conning tower, which was elliptical in plan and larger than that of earlier ships in order to accommodate the admiral and personnel from his staff, were protected by armour plates 230mm thick.[9]

MACHINERY

The propulsion system adopted for *Pothuau* was similar in principle to that of the last ship of the *Amiral Charner* class, *Bruix*, but delivered more power to cope with the increase in dimensions and displacement. The two four-cylinder VTE engines, built by FCM Le Havre and mounted in twin engine rooms located side by side (see Machinery plan), were designed to deliver 10,000CV; they drove two shafts with propellers 4.4m in diameter.

Steam was supplied by eighteen Belleville boilers, which were disposed back-to-back in three identical boiler rooms separated by transverse watertight bulkheads and flanked by coal bunkers. *Pothuau* could be easily distinguished visually from the *Amiral Charner* class by her three equally-proportioned funnels, each of which served one of the three boiler rooms.

During trials on 25 December 1896 *Pothuau* attained a speed of 19.2 knots with 10,398CV. Endurance was calculated as 4500nm at 10 knots, and 1150nm at her top speed of 19 knots.

The four dynamos that provided the electrical power for the 194mm turrets and the lighting circuits were grouped together in an auxiliary machinery room forward of the boiler rooms, directly beneath the bridge.

CONSTRUCTION AND EARLY SERVICE

Pothuau was laid down at the Graville (Le Havre) shipyard of Forges & Chantiers de la Méditerranée on 25 May 1893. Attempted launches on 22 and 23 August 1895 failed due to insufficient lubrication on the slipway, and the hull was finally launched on 19 September. She was manned for trials on 17 August 1896 and commissioned on 5 June 1897.

[9] This figure probably includes a double layer of 15mm plating.

THE FRENCH FLEET JUNE 1900

Escadre de la Méditerranée (Toulon)

1re Division cuirassée:	*Brennus* (VA Fournier), *Gaulois*, *Charlemagne*
2e Division cuirassée:	*Charles Martel* (CA Roustan), *Jauréguiberry*, *Bouvet*
3e Division cuirassée:	*Bouvines* (CA Mallarmé), *Jemmapes*, *Amiral Tréhouart*, *Valmy*
Division légère:	*Pothuau* (CA Caillard), *Chanzy*, *Latouche-Tréville*

Escadre du Nord (Brest/Cherbourg)

1re Division cuirassée:	*Masséna* (CA Ménard), *Carnot*, *Amiral Baudin*
2e Division cuirassée:	*Formidable* (CA Duchaine d'Arbaud), *Amiral Duperré*, *Redoutable*
Division de croiseurs:	*Bruix* (CA Gourdon), *Dupuy-de-Lôme*

Note:
Following the summer grand manoeuvres, the division of coast defence battleships remained behind at Brest and was transferred to the Northern Squadron.

Little more than a week after commissioning *Pothuau* was despatched to represent France at Queen Victoria's Diamond Jubilee Review at Spithead, which took place on 26 June. The ship subsequently entered service with the Northern Squadron. On 23 August she embarked President Félix Faure at Dunkirk and took him to Kronstadt for a state visit to the Tsar, returning on the 27th.

In September 1898 *Pothuau* joined the Mediterranean Squadron as flagship of the Light Squadron (*Escadre légère*), serving in this role until mid-1905, when she was placed in reserve (see table page 34). Following modifications she recommissioned on 17 April 1907 as flagship of the Gunnery Training School. She was employed in this role until August 1914, trialling the prototype of the Le Prieur fire-control computer and time/range plot in 1913 prior to its installation on the battleships of the *Armée Navale*.[10] By early 1914 there were concerns about the pivot structure of the main guns, and it was envisaged that she would be replaced by *D'Entrecasteaux*. However, with the outbreak of war *Pothuau* would resume active service, being assigned to the *Division spéciale*.

[10] See Jordan and Caresse, *French Battleships of World War One*, pp 180–3.

EVALUATION

Pothuau was a distinct improvement on the *Amiral Charner* class: her higher freeboard made her a better seaboat, and she seems to have suffered few problems with her machinery. However, she quickly became obsolescent and served as a first-line unit for only eight years before being relegated to the training role. The extensive and well-appointed admiral's quarters made her popular as a flagship, and she served in this role as flagship of the Northern Squadron, the Light Squadron in the Mediterranean, and the Gunnery Training Squadron.

D'ENTRECASTEAUX

During the latter part of the nineteenth century the French established a colonial empire second only to that of Britain, with overseas territories that extended from the Caribbean to the South Pacific. The need to police these territories and to protect maritime communications with metropolitan France drove a large and ongoing programme of cruiser construction, with between two and six cruisers being laid down in any given year from 1886 (see table). These ships all had a protective deck over their machinery but no side armour, and had a maximum designed speed of 19–20 knots. Some of the early units had a sailing rig that enabled them to operate independently from ports

Below: *Pothuau* moored in front of the Mourillon slipways on the eastern side of Toulon dockyard, when she was serving as a gunnery training ship. She has been fitted with three 2m Barr & Stroud rangefinders atop the bridge. The photo probably dates from 1913–14, when *Pothuau* trialled the prototype installation of the Le Prieur time-range plot – see Jordan and Caresse, *French Battleships of World War One*, pp 180–1. *(DR)*

overseas without the need for an extensive network of coaling stations.

As the programme developed, two distinct categories of cruiser emerged: a ship of 3000–4000 tonnes with a main armament of four/six 16cm guns, backed up by 65mm, 100mm or 14cm QF guns; and a smaller ship of 2000–2400 tonnes with a main armament of two/four 14cm guns, complemented in the later ships by 100mm QF guns. The first type was classified '2nd class cruiser' (*croiseur de 2e classe*), the second '3rd class cruiser' (*croiseur de 3e classe*). In both types the main guns were in shielded upper-deck mountings or casemates, and the QF guns behind ports in the upper hull or in open mountings on the weather deck; there was no protection for the ammunition hoists above the protective deck.

France obtained control over northern Indochina following its victory over China in the Sino-French War of 1884–5. French Indochina was formed on 17 October 1887 from Annam, Tonkin, Cochinchina and the Kingdom of Cambodia; Laos was added after the Franco-Siamese War of 1893. The establishment of French hegemony over a large part of South-east Asia during this period created a requirement for a permanent naval presence in the form of a division of cruisers with supporting vessels. A standing squadron of this nature ideally required a larger flagship capable of impressing foreign dignitaries and the other colonial powers in the region, with extensive and well-appointed accommodation for an admiral and his staff, and the 8000-tonne cruiser *D'Entrecasteaux* was laid down in June 1894 to meet this requirement.

It could be argued that *D'Entrecasteaux* is out of place in a book that focuses on the French armoured cruisers, and she has generally been classified in English-language secondary sources as a 'protected cruiser'.[11] However, the placement of *Pothuau* in the 'armoured cruiser' category has likewise been questioned[12] due to the reduced thickness of the side armour (60mm) compared with the slopes of the armoured deck (85mm). Although a similar imbalance between the horizontal and the vertical protection is

[11] See, for example, Gardiner (ed), *Conway's All the World's Fighting Ships 1860–1905*.

[12] Ibid.

FRENCH PROTECTED CRUISERS 1887–1903

Name	Type	Built	Displ/Speed	Armament	Protection	Fate
Forbin[1]	3rd Class	Rochefort 1886–9	1950 tonnes	4 x 138[2]	30mm deck[3]	Collier 1913
Surcouf		Cherbourg 1886–90	20 knots	3 x 47		Stricken 1921
Coëtlogon		Penhoët 1887–94				Stricken 1906
Troude	3rd Class	Gironde 1886–91	1950 tonnes	4 x 138	30mm deck	Stricken 1908
Lalande		Gironde 1887–9	20.5 knots	4 x 47		Stricken 1912
Cosmao		Gironde 1887–9				Stricken 1922
Davout	2nd Class	Toulon 1887–91	3030 tonnes	6 x 164, 4 x 65	30/80mm deck	Stricken 1910
			20.5 knots	4 x 47		
Suchet	2nd Class	Toulon 1887–94	3360 tonnes	6 x 164, 4 x 100	30/80mm deck	Stricken 1906
			20.5 knots	8 x 37		
Linois	3rd Class	La Seyne 1892–5	2300 tonnes	4 x 138, 2 x 100	30mm deck	Stricken 1910
Galilée		Rochefort 1893–7	20.5 knots	8 x 47		Stricken 1911
Lavoisier						Stricken 1920
Alger	2nd Class	Cherbourg 1887–91	4300 tonnes	4 x 164, 6 x 138	30/80mm deck	Hulked 1911
Isly		Brest 1887–93	19 knots	2 x 65, 8/12 x 47		Stricken 1911
Jean Bart		Rochefort 1887–91				Wrecked 1907
Friant	2nd Class	Brest 1891–5	3900 tonnes	6 x 164, 4 x 100	30/80mm deck	Stricken 1920
Chasseloup-Laubat		Cherbourg 1891–5	18.5 knots	4 x 47		Hulked 1911
Bugeaud		Cherbourg 1891–6				Stricken 1907
Descartes	2nd Class	Loire 1892–6	3960 tonnes	4 x 164, 10 x 100	25/40mm deck	Stricken 1920
Pascal		Toulon 1893–7	19.5 knots	8 x 47		Stricken 1911
D'Assas	2nd Class	Loire 1894–8	3990 tonnes	6 x 164, 4 x 100	30/80mm deck	Stricken 1914
Du Chayla		Cherbourg 1894–8	20 knots	10 x 47		Stricken 1921
Cassard		Cherbourg 1894–8				Stricken 1924
Catinat	2nd Class	FC Méd 1894–8	4000 tonnes	4 x 164, 10 x 100	25/40mm deck	Stricken 1911
Protet		Gironde 1896–9	19.5 knots	10 x 47		Stricken 1910
D'Estrées	3rd Class	Rochefort 1897–9	2400 tonnes	2 x 138, 4 x 100	10/40mm deck	Stricken 1922
Infernet		Gironde 1896–1900	20 knots	8 x 47		Grounded 1910

Notes:

1 The nameship of the class is in ***bold italics.***

2 All gun calibres are in millimetres (mm).

3 The deck armour, which was generally of mild or hardened steel, was secured to two thicknesses of 10mm steel plating in the 2nd class cruisers and a single layer in the 3rd class ships, the sole exception being the two ships of the *D'Estrées* class, which had a double layer of 10mm steel on the flat and a double layer of 20mm steel on the slopes.

likewise apparent in *D'Entrecasteaux*, vertical protection remained a major consideration in the design of the latter ship (see below), and the FC Méditerranée plans of the ship are headed *Croiseur Cuirassé*, even though in service the ship would generally be referred to simply as a 'first class cruiser'. The decision to include *D'Entrecasteaux* in this account was primarily influenced by the important place this ship occupies in the development of the French armoured cruiser, constituting an intermediate step between the 5400-tonne *Pothuau* and the 11,000-tonne *Jeanne d'Arc*, the first of the modern French 'fleet' cruisers, and also providing the basis for the large 'station cruisers' (*croiseurs de station*) of the *Dupleix* class.

FIRST THOUGHTS

The design of *D'Entrecasteaux* went through a number of iterations. An early proposal by the Engineer Lagane of Forges & Chantiers de la Méditerranée for a *Croiseur protégé Chef de Station*, dating from 1891, was for a ship with a main armament of four 24cm guns mounted in single turrets and disposed in the 'lozenge' arrangement favoured for the contemporary battleships of the 1890 programme; the plans show a raised forecastle and poop deck, and three steel masts for a full sailing rig.[13] Given that FC Méditerranée was a private shipbuilder, the design may have been drawn up with a view to export, but it seems to have fed into an ongoing narrative in the *Marine Nationale*.

A meeting of the *Conseil des Travaux* was held on 7 July 1891 and discussed the desired characteristics for a large station cruiser. The *Conseil* wanted to hold displacement to a maximum of 8000 tonnes, but acknowledged that if the current proposed armament were retained and multitubular (ie Belleville-type) boilers adopted, it would be difficult to keep displacement below 8600 tonnes and length within 118m.

In addition to a main armament of four 24cm Mle 1887 guns, with 110 rounds per gun, the *Conseil* wanted eight 14cm QF guns on sponsons or in casemates on the upper deck with a complete shelter deck above for protection. The main turrets were to be trained using hydraulics, and the magazine arrangements for all guns (including the ATB guns) were to be

[13] See Luc Feron, article in *Marines*, p 66.

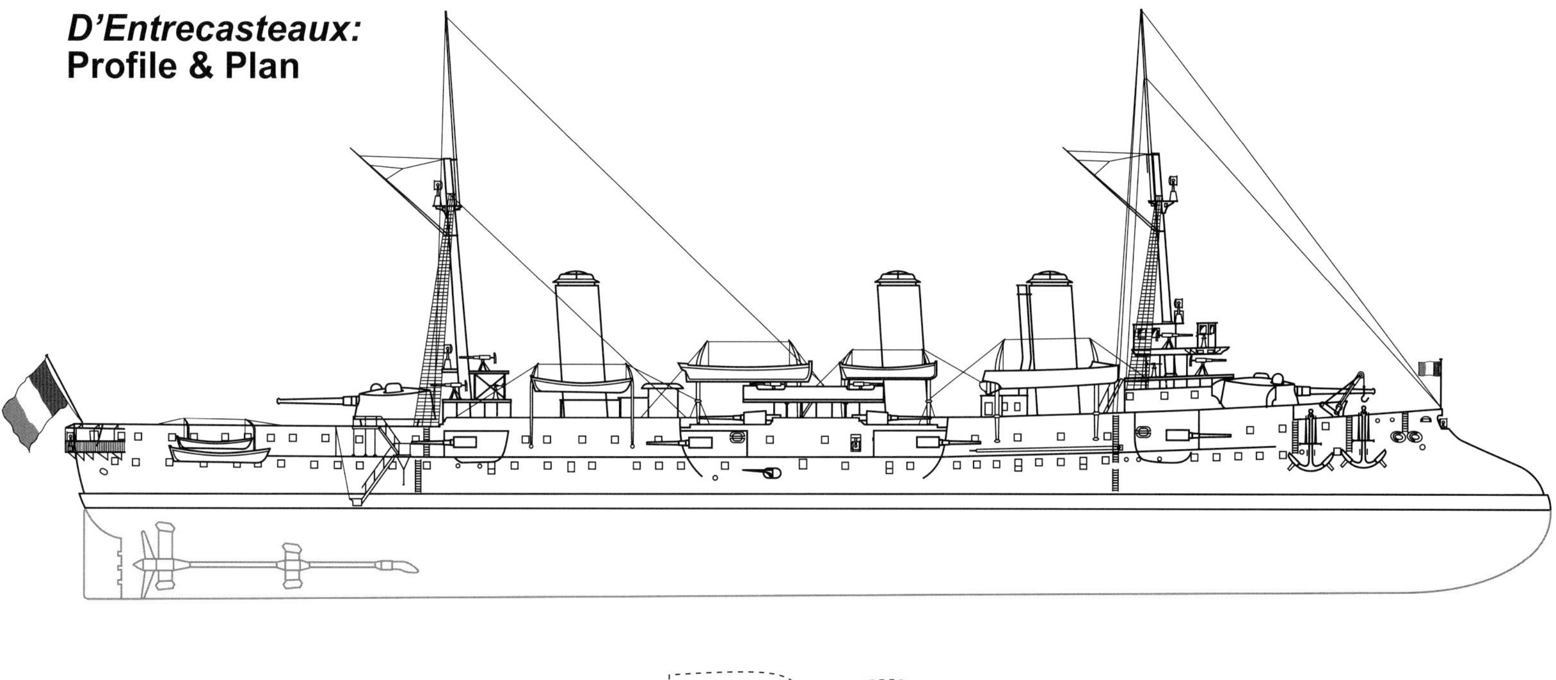

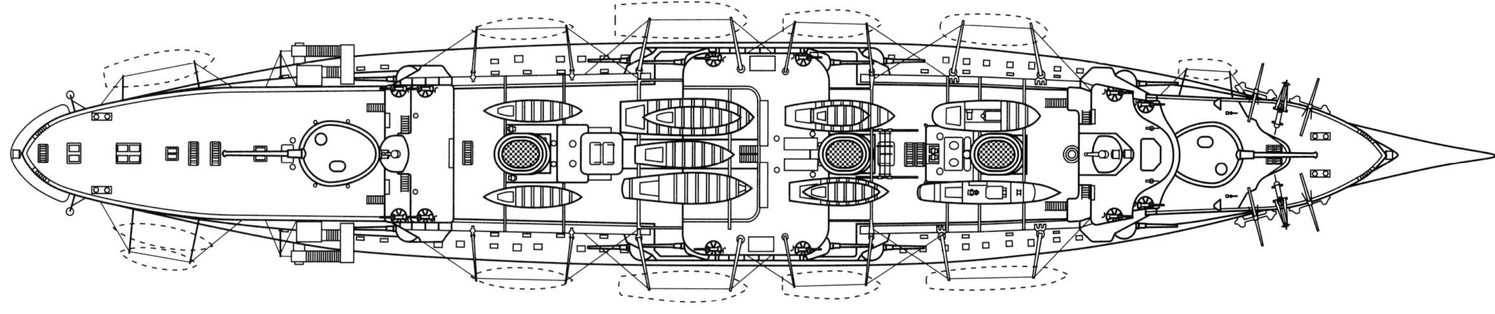

Note: Adapted from the FC Méditerranée Shipyard plans signed by Lagane.

optimised for rapid ammunition supply. There were to be five torpedo tubes with sights in the vertical plane above them.

Protection was to feature a complete protective deck, either vaulted or with a double angle (*à profil brisé*), as in *Pothuau*, with its outer edges 1.4m below the waterline. Thickness was to be 50mm (including plating) on the flat over the machinery spaces and 100mm on the slopes, with an 8mm splinter deck below. It was proposed to reinforce the inner bulkhead of the cofferdam with 40mm plating. However, if trials of this arrangement at the Gâvres proving ground were unsuccessful, the 40mm plating would be relocated to the outer shell of the hull (formed by a double thickness of 10mm steel) to give a total of 60mm.[14]

The turrets were to have 250mm armour on their faces and 210mm on their sides and rear. The relatively thin protection for the sides of the hull would have to be compensated by heavy (and deep) protection for the pivots of the turrrets: fixed armour was to be 200mm above the battery deck, and 140mm beneath it. The conning tower was to have a similar level of protection: 200mm.

The ship was to be capable of 18 knots with natural draught and 19 knots with forced draught. Power was to be provided by two reliable VTE engines, each located in its own watertight compartment, driving two shafts; steam was to be supplied by Belleville or Lagrafel & d'Allest[15] boilers. Endurance was set at 5500nm at 10 knots, with a 90-day supply of fresh water and ample stowage for provisions.

There were to be two 'semi-military' masts, each with platforms to support two ATB guns and a searchlight projector. The spars for the sailing rig were to be removable, and the masts were self-supporting.

THE *AVANT-PROJETS*

The *Conseil* recommended keeping displacement to 8000 tonnes by reducing either the weight of protection or the number/calibre of the main guns. It was subsequently decided to eliminate the 24cm mountings in the waist, which resulted in considerable weight savings. In their place would be four additional 14cm mountings, to be located behind shields on the upper deck, the remaining eight guns being lowered to the battery deck and housed in casemates. A ministerial directive dated 2 March 1892 re-designated the ship *croiseur de 1re classe* and decreed the suppression of sail. Design studies (*avant-projets*) were requested from four naval architects (Tréboul, Schwartz, Besson and Raymond) and three private shipyards (FC Méditerranée, AC Loire, and CA Gironde). These were considered on 29 March, when four were rejected; the three successful competitors were then asked to submit detailed proposals, taking in various requests for modifications.

On 31 January 1893 the *Conseil* met to consider the proposals, and approved those submitted by Tréboul and by Lagane (FC Méditerranée), expressing a preference for the former. The Minister gave his own approval, and Tréboul was invited to rework his proposal, which would finally emerge two years later in the form of a large protected cruiser to be named

14 Had this measure been adopted the designation of *croiseur cuirassé* would have been completely justified.

15 Boilers of the Lagrafel & d'Allest type had been adopted for four of the five contemporary battleships of the 1890 programme.

Right: The launch of the 'station cruiser' *D'Entrecasteaux* at La Seyne on 12 June 1896. The prominent plough bow is in evidence. *(Private collection)*

BUILDING DATA

Name	Builder	Laid down	Launched	Trials	Commissioned
D'Entrecasteaux	FC Méditerranée (La Seyne)	Sep 1894	12 Jun 1896	1 Jan 1898	4 Apr 1899

Jeanne d'Arc. However, in the interim, on 8 November 1893, a cruiser of 8400 tonnes (full load) to the plans of Lagane was ordered from FC Méditerranée; the ship would be named *D'Entrecasteaux*. Tréboul's revised *Jeanne d'Arc* design received ministerial approval on 21 August 1895, but funding was not forthcoming and the name *Jeanne d'Arc* would subsequently be re-allocated to a large 'fleet' cruiser designed by Emile Bertin (see Chapter 3).[16]

NOMENCLATURE

Joseph-Antoine Bruny **d'Entrecasteaux** (1737–93) was a naval officer, explorer and colonial governor, best known for his exploration of the Australian coast in 1792. He joined the Navy in 1754, and was on board the frigate *Minerve* when the Balearic Islands were secured for Spain. Appointed deputy director of ports and dockyards, he was then assigned to command the French Squadron in the East Indies. He opened up a new route to Canton by way of Sunda Strait, and was appointed Governor of Isle de France (Mauritius). Promoted rear admiral, he was put in command of an 1791 expedition to search for the naval officer and explorer La Pérouse in the area of Botany Bay. His exploration was beset by storms and difficulties, and d'Entrecasteaux died of scurvy in 1793.

[16] Luc Feron, *op cit*, has provided a full account of the Tréboul episode insofar as this is possible using the record available in the archives, and has published the plan and profile drawing produced by Tréboul and dated Cherbourg 2 July 1895.

HULL AND SUPERSTRUCTURES

As completed *D'Entrecasteaux* had the classic French cruiser hull form, with pronounced tumblehome and a prominent plough bow. The forecastle extended the full length of the ship, giving her a flush deck. *D'Entrecasteaux* was significantly larger than *Pothuau*, with a length between perpendiculars of 120m (*vice* 113m), a beam of 17.85m (*vice* 15.3m), and a displacement at normal load of 8123 tonnes. Construction was of steel, with a double layer of 10mm plating amidships over the cellular layer. The lower hull was clad with two layers of teak planking 80mm and 60mm thick with an external skin of 0.9mm copper sheathing. The cladding extended from the keel to just above the lower section of the cofferdam, and was intended to minimise marine growth in the tropical waters in which the ship was to operate.

Teak planking was also favoured for the weather decks of ships intended for overseas deployment. The shelter deck had teak planking 60mm thick, and there was 50mm planking on the bridge decks. The upper deck was lined with 7mm linoleum, and there was 4mm linoleum for the floors of the passageways and cabins. The magazine walls were lined with 15mm pine.

The spacious and well-appointed flag accommodation, designed to enable the ship to serve as the command ship for a major overseas squadron such as that based on Saigon, made *D'Entrecasteaux* a popular choice for successive rear admirals. The quarters for the general and senior officers were located high in the ship, on the upper deck (*pont des gaillards* – see plan). Accommodation for the junior officers was on the battery deck below.

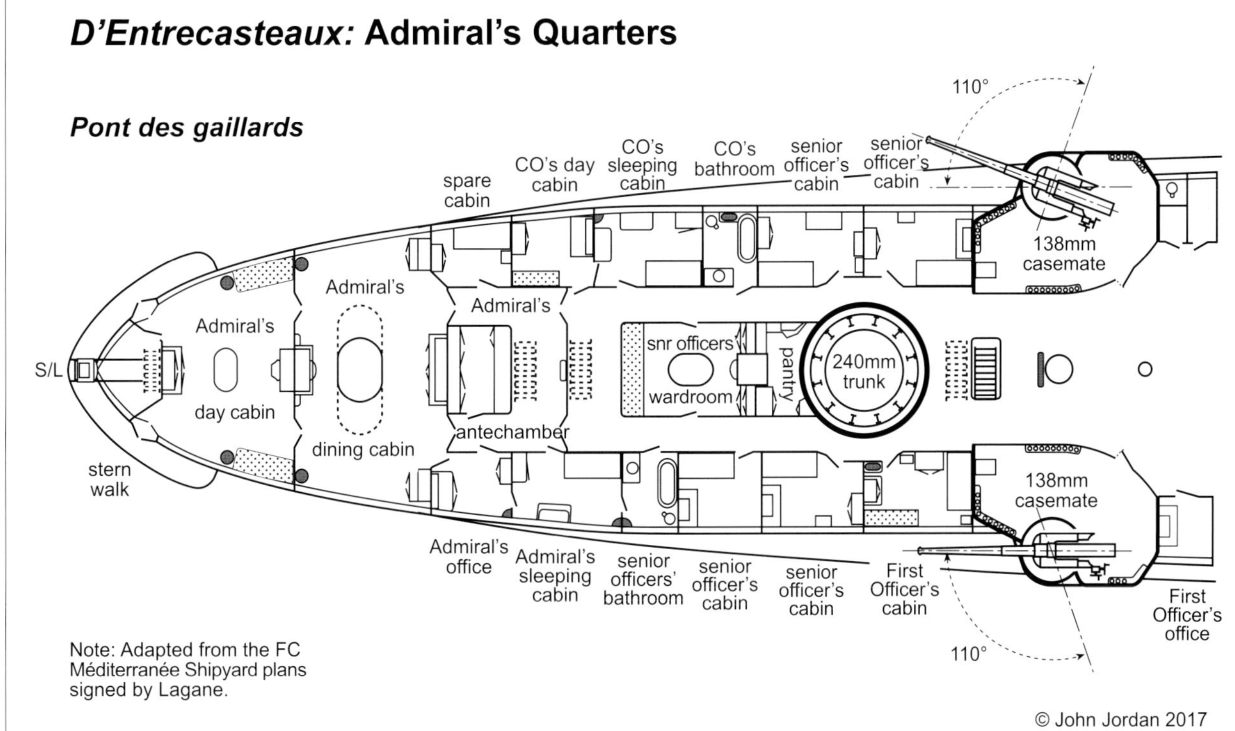

The admiral's and senior officers' quarters were located at the after end of the upper deck (*pont des gaillards*). The admiral's quarters were unusually spacious and well-appointed, making *D'Entrecasteaux* a popular choice as flagship when she served in the Far East.

There were two steel pole masts, angled slightly aft. They were fitted with a single high platform for a searchlight, but there were no lower platforms for the ATB guns, which were relocated to the bridge decks and the shelter deck. The three funnels, which were of uniform height and configuration, were raked like the masts. Unusually, the first two were close together but were separated by some distance from the third. Given the need to accommodate five double-ended cylindrical boilers, Lagane opted to locate the after boiler room (with only a single boiler) abaft the engine rooms, with a large coal bunker flanked by the magazines for the after QF guns outboard of the boiler room to port and starboard.

ARMAMENT

Main guns

The single turrets for the 240mm guns were disposed fore and aft on the forecastle deck. These were the largest guns installed in a French cruiser of the period. This was also to be the last installation of the heavy pivot-style turret, which would in future be retained only for battleships armed with 305mm guns, as the weight of the pivot and the fixed armour required to protect it meant that this type of turret could be accommodated only in a major vessel. The turret appears to have been specifically modified at the design stage to allow 20° elevation for the guns; French cruiser turrets of the period generally permitted a maximum elevation of 15°, suggesting that long-range fire (possibly against shore targets) was a major consideration in the design of *D'Entrecasteaux*.

The turrets were trained electrically, as in the battleship *Jauréguiberry* which was likewise designed by Lagane and built at La Seyne. Two dynamos (one to starboard, the other to port) powered servo-motors driving a toothed pinion with a continuous chain to rotate the pivot, and there was the customary manual backup at the front end of the gunhouse, using levers with a mechanical linkage to shafts from the dynamos. The turret could be trained though its maximum arc of 250° in 65 seconds; manual operation took three minutes. The first gunlayer's position had a commutator for 'coarse' training of the turret; four different speeds could be selected. A second position had push-buttons for fine tuning left or right, as in *Jauréguiberry*.

The gun was the 240/40 Mle 1893, which fired a 145kg CI shell and 170kg AP or semi-armour piercing (SAP) steel shell, the latter with a powerful bursting charge of *mélinite* (see the table and the caption for the drawing of the forward magazine for details). The 58kg BM13 powder charge was divided into two bagged half-charges.

QF guns

The eight 138.6mm guns mounted on the upper deck (*pont des gaillards*) were in individual casemates (*redoutes*), with armour of special steel on the face and the sides and a complete inner wall of mild steel.[17] The walls of each casemate were lined with racks for the vertical stowage of ready-use rounds. The casemates were well spaced so that two guns could not be disabled by a single hit. The four guns on the shelter deck were on shielded pivot mountings; the deck itself was cut away so that the sides of the upper hull protected the base of the mounting. All twelve guns were Mle 1893 (see *Pothuau* and the data table for characteristics).

The magazines for the 138.6mm guns were located fore and aft (inboard of the magazines and shell rooms for the 240mm guns), amidships (between the boiler rooms and the engine rooms), and outboard of the after boiler room. The twin ammunition hoists for the lower guns, each of which held three complete rounds, emerged directly into the casemate (see plan). The shells and cartridges were then transferred manually either to the breech of the gun or to ready-use stowage racks around the sides. There were two additional hoists serving the guns mounted on the shelter deck.

ATB guns

The number of 47mm Mle 1885 guns was increased to twelve. Four were mounted on the bridge decks, four on the after superstructure decks, and four on a raised

D'ENTRECASTEAUX: CHARACTERISTICS

Displacement:	8123 tonnes
Dimensions:	
Length	120.00m pp; 120.92m oa
Beam	17.85m wl
Draught	7.52m aft
Propulsion:	
Boilers	5 double-ended cylindrical
Engines	2-shaft 3-cylinder VTE
Horsepower	13,500CV (designed)
Speed	19 knots (designed)
Coal	980 tonnes normal
Endurance	5500nm at 10 knots
Armament:	
Main guns	2 x 240mm/40 Mle 1893 in single turrets
Medium guns	12 x 138.6mm/45 Mle 1893 QF in eight casemate and four shielded pivot mountings
ATB guns	12 x 47mm/40 Mle 1885 QF in single mountings 4 x 37mm QF in single mountings
Torpedo tubes	2 a/w, 2 sub tubes for 450mm torpedoes 12 torpedoes Mle 1892
Protection:	
Deck	30/80mm
194 turrets	230/190mm
138 casemates	52mm
Conning tower	230mm
Boats:	1 x 11m steam launch 1 x 8.9m steam pinnace 1 x 10.5m pulling pinnace 1 x 10m admiral's gig 1 x 9m pulling cutter 1 x 8m pulling cutter 3 x 8.5m whalers 1 x 6m whaler 1 x 5m dinghy
Complement:	
As private ship	559 officers and men
As flagship	+ 28

[17] Those in *Pothuau* are more correctly described as armoured gun ports; the guns were mounted in a widely-spaced battery, and the casemates were completely open to the sides and rear (see plan page 40).

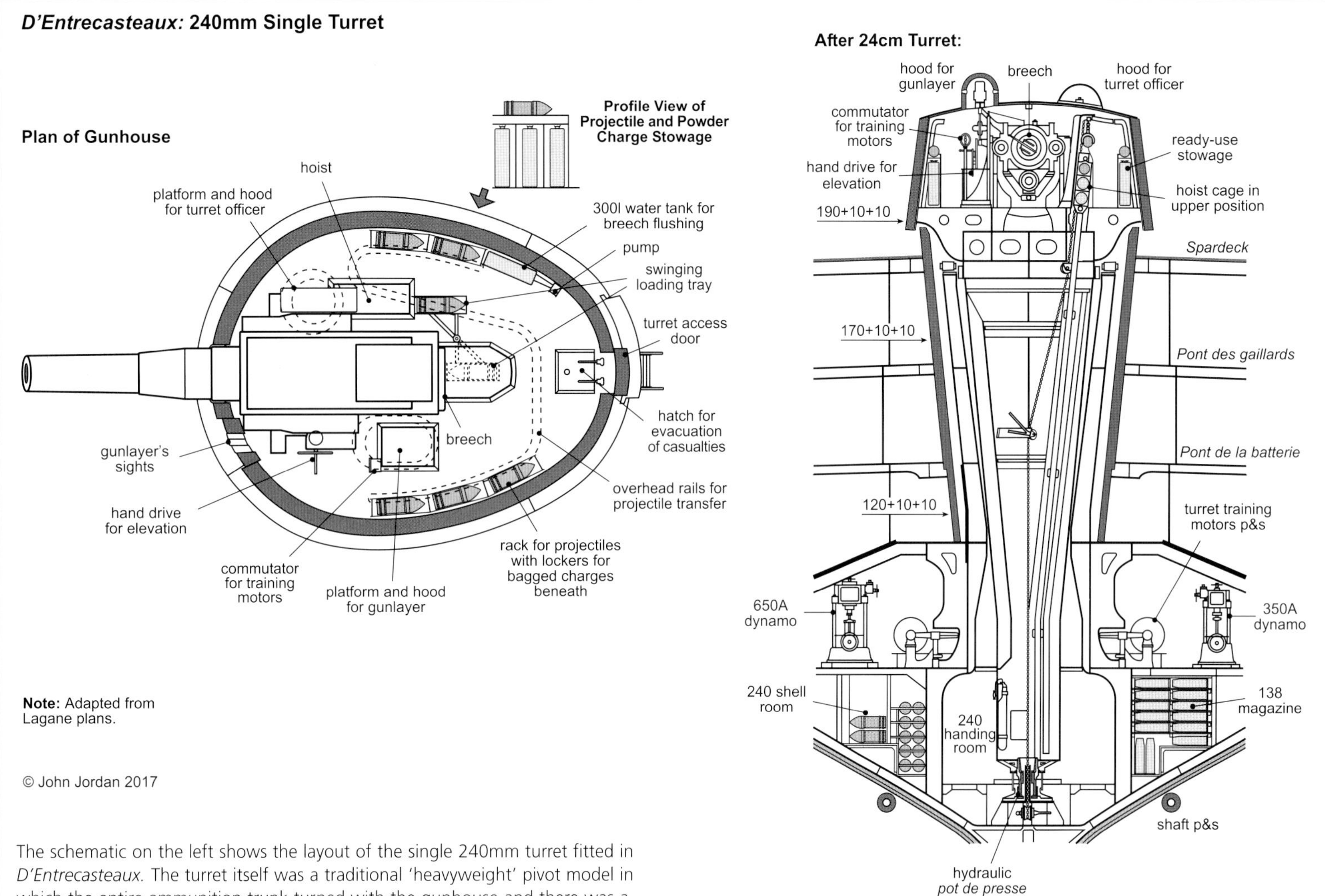

***D'Entrecasteaux:* 240mm Single Turret**

The schematic on the left shows the layout of the single 240mm turret fitted in *D'Entrecasteaux.* The turret itself was a traditional 'heavyweight' pivot model in which the entire ammunition trunk turned with the gunhouse and there was a single-stage hoist from the magazine and shell room. The pivot mounting had the customary hydraulic *pot de presse* at its base. The turret was slightly raised before training – there was a hand pump for backup.

Whereas earlier French cruiser turrets were generally circular in plan and had vertical walls, the configuration and layout of the 240mm gunhouse anticipate the 194mm and 164.7mm single turrets fitted in the later French armoured cruisers. The gunhouse was markedly broader at its forward end and had steeply inclined sides, the purpose of which was to deflect an enemy shell arriving with a horizontal trajectory upwards, while simultaneously increasing the theoretical thickness of the armour plating. (Some of the French turret plans give two separate thicknesses: one for the thickness of the plate and a second, higher figure showing 'horizontal' thickness taking into account the angle from the vertical at which the plate is mounted.)

Projectiles arriving in the gunhouse via the hoist, which was to the right of the gun, would either be shunted directly onto the loading tray or transferred using block and tackle suspended from an overhead rail to ready-use racks at the sides. Once the breech, which was hinged to the left, was opened and had been flushed out, the loading tray was swung 180° and the projectile was then rammed manually with the gun depressed to -5°, followed by the two powder bags, which were also rammed by hand; the breech was then closed and the gun was ready to fire.

Beneath the projectile racks were lockers in which the bagged half-charges were stowed vertically and secured; five complete ready-use rounds could be stowed. At the rear of the gunhouse there was a hinged door for access and a hatch in the floor for the evacuation of casualties. On the right-hand wall was a 300-litre water tank and pump for flushing out the breech after each firing.

There were separate positions for the turret officer and the turret trainer, who were seated on raised platforms beneath hoods to the right and left of the gun respectively. (In later models of turret both would be seated in tandem on an elongated platform with a single hood on the opposite side to the hoist, directly above the manual controls for training and elevation.) The gunlayer for elevation was seated at the forward end of the gunhouse, to the left of the gun, as in later models.

platform amidships, directly above the upper guns of the 138.6mm QF battery. There were also four 37mm QF guns, which were distributed between the forward and after superstructures.

Searchlight projectors

Eight Mangin 60cm searchlight projectors were fitted – an increase of two over earlier cruisers to take account of the enhanced battery of ATB guns. There were pedestal-mounted projectors at the base of the masts and on the upper mast platforms. The remaining four were mounted on rails in the upper hull in the traditional lozenge arrangement: one in the bow, one in the stern, and two between the midship casemates; they could be retracted within their embrasures for protection from the elements when the ship was at sea.

Torpedoes and mines

The original staff requirements for this ship featured five tubes for 450mm torpedoes. However, this figure was reduced to four in the final Lagane design: two above water and two submerged, the stern tube being eliminated.

The two above-water tubes were mounted on pivots

MAIN AND MEDIUM GUNS: *POTHUAU* AND *D'ENTRECASTEAUX*

	240/40 Mle 1893	194/40 Mle 1893	138.6/45 Mle 1893
Total weight:	20,750kg	10,340kg	4080kg
Total length:	10,045mm	8076mm	6445mm
Bore length:	9605mm	7760mm	6234mm
Chamber length:	1926.1mm	1306mm	761.22mm
Chamber volume:	112.87dm³	49.03dm³	14.73dm³
Breech pressure:	2400kg/cm²	2300kg/cm²	2300kg/cm²
Rifling:	72 grooves at 5°	58 grooves at 5°	42 grooves at 5°
Shell weight:	APC 170kg (2.77 cal) SAPC 170kg (3.13 cal) CI 144kg (3.164 cal)	APC 90.3kg (2.70 cal) SAPC 89.5kg (3.94 cal) CI 75.0kg (2.92 cal)	APC 35kg (2.98 cal) SAPC 35kg (3.20 cal) CI 30kg (3.37 cal)
Bursting charge:	APC 2.60kg powder (1.5%) SAPC 10.40kg *mélinite* (6.1%) CI 9.75kg powder (6.8%)	APC 1.59kg *mélinite* (1.8%) SAPC 4.33kg *mélinite* (4.8%) CI 5.07kg powder (5.8%)	APC 0.58kg powder (1.7%) SAPC 1.69kg *mélinite* (4.8%) CI 1.30kg powder (4.3%)
Propellant:	58.0kg BM 13 (2 x 1/2)	22.6kg BM9 (2 x 1/2)	7.28kg BM7 (cartridge)
Muzzle velocity (MV):	800m/sec (APC)	770m/sec (APC)	730m/sec (APC)
Remaining V 2000m:	671m/sec (APC)	619m/sec (APC)	543m/sec (APC)
Maximum range:	12,500m at 20°	11,500m at 15°	11,000m at 20°
Firing cycle:	30 secs	30 secs	15 sec

with semicircular guide rails on the battery deck amidships, at frame 68. They could be trained up to 18° forward of the beam and 55° abaft the beam. Torpedo bodies could be stowed close to the tubes, but the main torpedo stowage was one deck lower, on the armoured deck. The torpedo bodies were stowed on athwartship racks and were raised by block and tackle through a centreline hatch; the warheads were stowed separately on the armoured deck, just abaft the torpedo bodies.

TORPEDOES

450mm Torpedo Mle 1892

Length:	5.05m
Weight:	530kg
Propulsion:	piston engine/compressed air
Warhead:	75kg
Range:	800m at 27.5 knots

The underwater tubes were in a torpedo room that extended the full width of the hull between frames 26 and 29 on the platform deck, immediately abaft the pivot for the forward 240mm turret. The tubes fired at a fixed angle on the beam and were offset, with the

Right: *D'Entrecasteaux* in her colonial paint scheme of white hull, buff funnels and superstructures. *(Musée de la Marine)*

torpedo bodies on racks to the side and separate stowage for the warheads. Two reserve Mle 1892 torpedoes were provided for each of the two tubes.

There was stowage on the armoured deck abeam the ammunition trunk of the after 240mm turret for twenty mines (*torpilles automatiques*). These were a feature of all the cruisers built to serve on foreign stations during the 1890s, and would have been laid as a defensive measure to protect an otherwise open anchorage. There was no provision for minelaying on the cruisers. On *D'Entrecasteaux* the mines would have been raised by the hoists for the after pair of 138mm guns, which were adjacent, and would then have been embarked on smaller craft, including the ship's own boats.

PROTECTION

Hull

The protection system was broadly as in the early proposals. There was a thick protective deck with a horizontal section 60cm above the waterline with successive inclines at the sides at 22° and 36° to the

D'Entrecasteaux: Forward Magazines

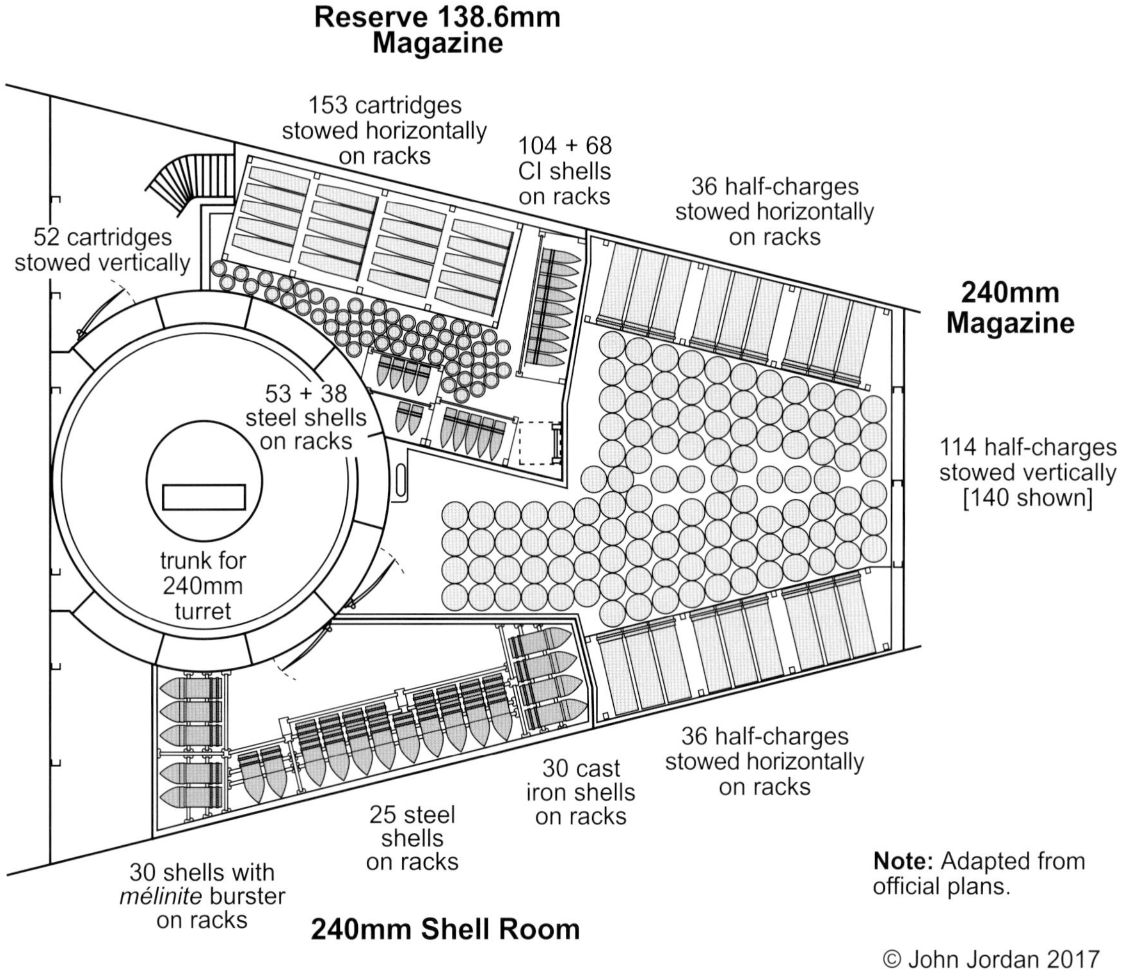

Note: Adapted from official plans.

© John Jordan 2017

This drawing is based on a detailed set of plans of the 240mm turrets and magazine handling arrangements by Lagane (chief engineer at La Seyne). The plans are undated, but show the state of play in the late 1890s, when *D'Entrecasteaux* was completed, at a time when technical advances in French projectile design and manufacture were beginning to take effect.

The plans show three basic types of 240mm shell: a CI powder-filled shell, a similarly-configured steel shell filled with the new, more powerful burster of picric acid (*mélinite*), and a shorter steel shell, probably with a black powder burster. While the former two shells were high-capacity models intended to devastate the unprotected upperworks of an enemy ship, the latter was designed for maximum penetration and was classified as an *obus de rupture* (AP shell); it would almost certainly have had a base fuse. All the shells were stowed horizontally on racks.

The bagged half-charges, which contained BM13 propellant, were stowed in cylindrical metal (tin?) cases with screw caps. A total of seventy-two were stowed horizontally in four-tier racks to the sides of the magazine, with the remainder stowed vertically on the magazine floor.

The plan also shows one of the 'reserve' magazines for the 138.6mm shell used by the ship's secondary QF battery. The plan shows 172 CI powder-filled shells, and 91 steel shells, all stowed horizontally on racks. The BM7 propellant for the 138.6mm Mle 1893 was in a single brass cartridge: 153 of these are stowed horizontally on racks, with a further 52 stowed vertically on the magazine floor.

The arrangement of shell rooms and magazine for the after turret was similar. In addition to the standard 240mm projectiles described above, the plans of the after shell room also feature three shrapnel rounds (*obus à mitraille*), which were intended for use at relatively close range against exposed members of the enemy ship's crew.

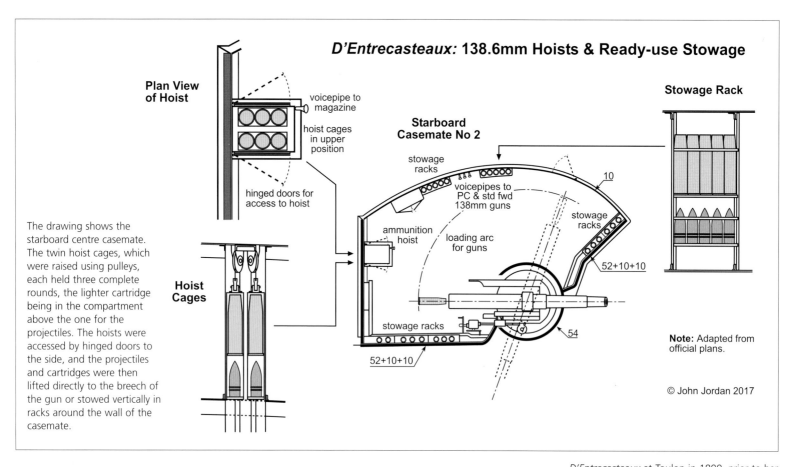

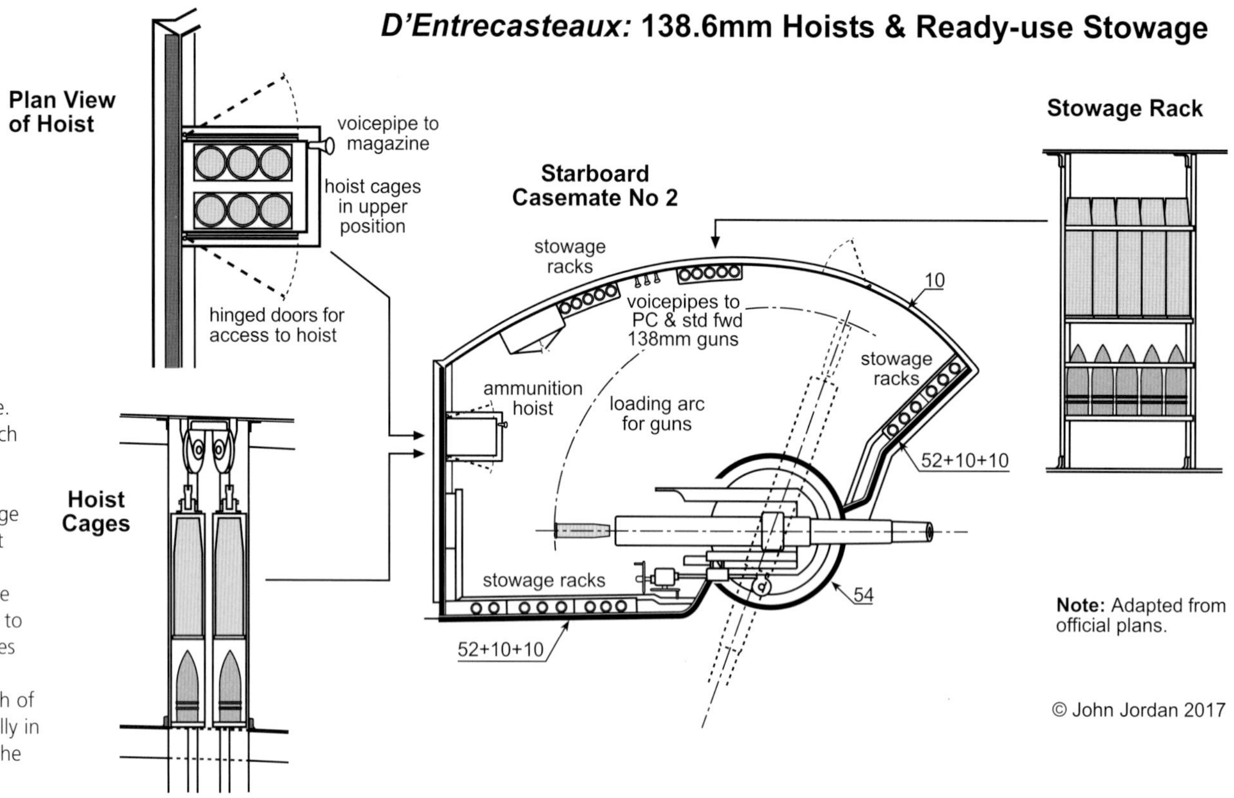

***D'Entrecasteaux:* 138.6mm Hoists & Ready-use Stowage**

The drawing shows the starboard centre casemate. The twin hoist cages, which were raised using pulleys, each held three complete rounds, the lighter cartridge being in the compartment above the one for the projectiles. The hoists were accessed by hinged doors to the side, and the projectiles and cartridges were then lifted directly to the breech of the gun or stowed vertically in racks around the wall of the casemate.

Note: Adapted from official plans.

© John Jordan 2017

D'Entrecasteaux at Toulon in 1899, prior to her first deployment to the Far East. She would arrive in Saigon on 12 May 1899, and would hoist the flag of the squadron commander, Rear Admiral de Courejolles, on 1 June. *(Marius Bar)*

horizontal respectively. The plates on the horizontal section were 30mm thick over the machinery spaces and 20mm fore and aft, those on the slopes 80mm over the machinery and 60mm fore and aft. Both thicknesses of plate were secured to a double layer of 10mm steel.

The cofferdam, which extended the full length of the ship, was 1.2m wide amidships. Boxes made of zinc were installed in the lower part of the cofferdam to a height of 20cm above the waterline, the boxes being enclosed from above by a steel roof (see Midship Half-section).[18] These boxes were devised with a view to increasing compartmentation and thereby restricting flooding, but there was a cost: each of the boxes weighed 170kg. The inner bulkhead of the cofferdam was reinforced by two layers of 20mm steel, and the battery deck above the cellular layer (and forming a roof) comprised a double layer of 10mm steel.

Turrets and conning tower

The main turrets had 230mm armour plates of nickel steel at the front end and 190mm on the sides and rear, all secured to a double layer of 10mm mild steel. The fixed (barbette) armour of the pivot was 170mm above the battery deck and 120mm below, where it was behind the 40mm inner wall of the cofferdam.

The casemate and sponson guns had 54mm shields, and the faces and sides of the casemates were of 52mm special steel on a double layer of 10mm plating.

[18] The first installation of these boxes was on the battleship *Brennus* during her reconstruction of 1893–4. In 1901 it was found that they had been eaten away by corrosion.

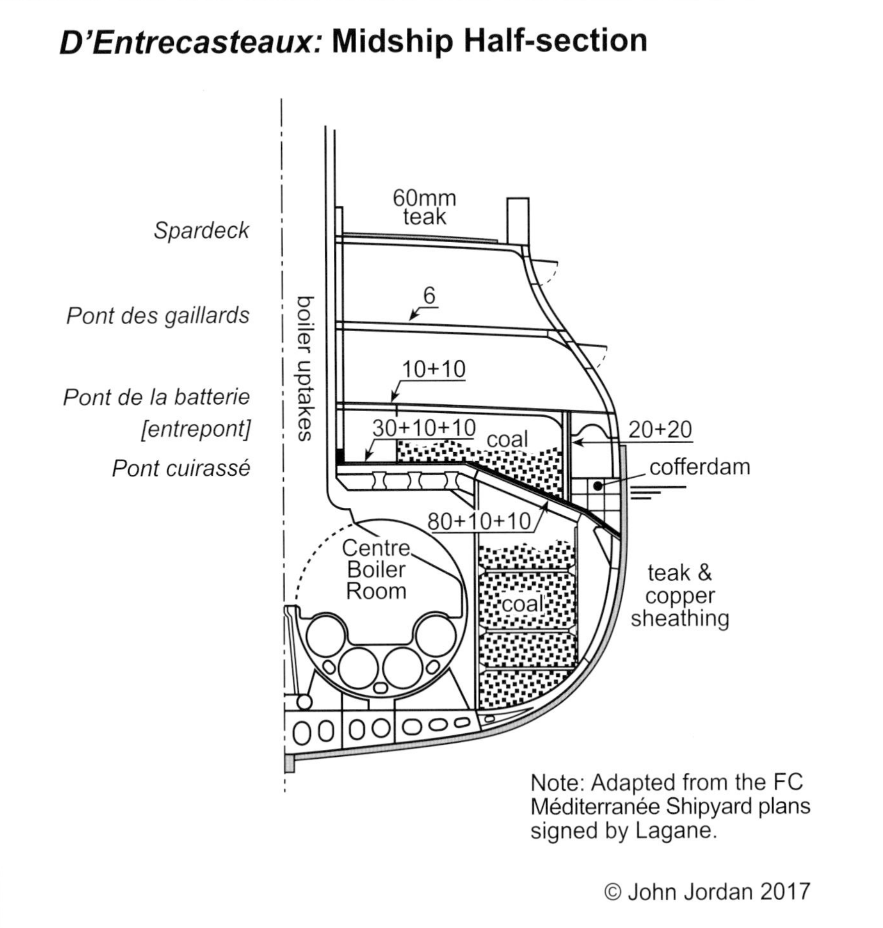

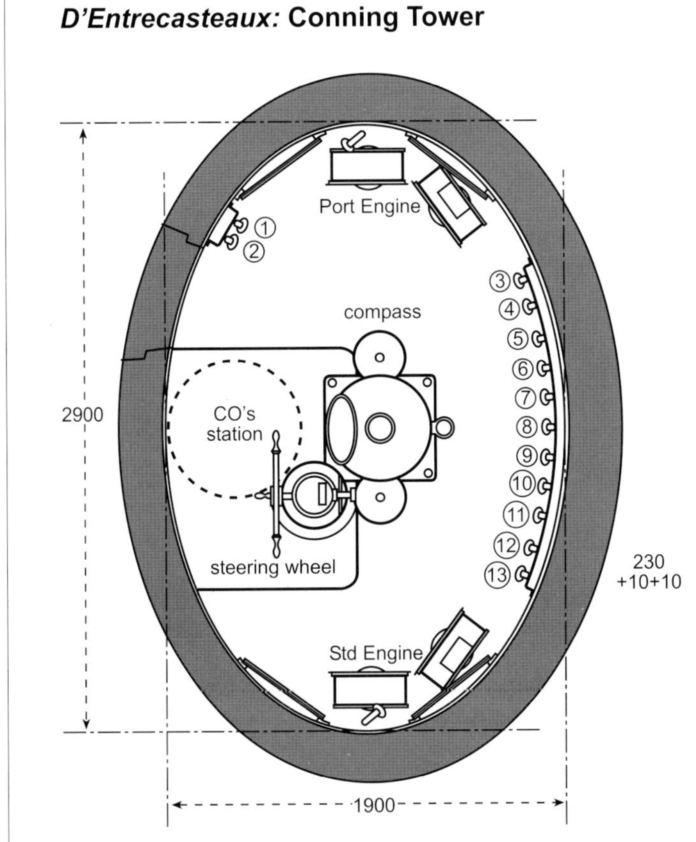

Key to Voicepipes
1 bridge
2 foremast platform
3 after bridge
4 138 port shelter deck
5 138 port fwd casemate
6 138 port mid aft casemate
7 240 after turret
8 *Poste Central*
9 after servo-motor
10 240 fwd turret
11 138 port mid fwd casemate
12 138 std mid aft casemate
13 138 std shelter deck

Note: Adapted from official plans.

© John Jordan 2017

Although the conning tower fitted in *D'Entrecasteaux* was larger and better protected than those of earlier cruisers, it remained small and cramped compared with those in later ships: internal dimension were approximately 2.9m wide by 1.9m deep. The commanding officer directed operations from a raised platform at the centre. Next to him was the helmsman, and to his right and left were control panels for order transmission to the port and starboard engines. Communication with the 240mm turrets, the 138.6mm casemates, the bridge and the *Poste Central* below the armoured deck was by voicepipe.

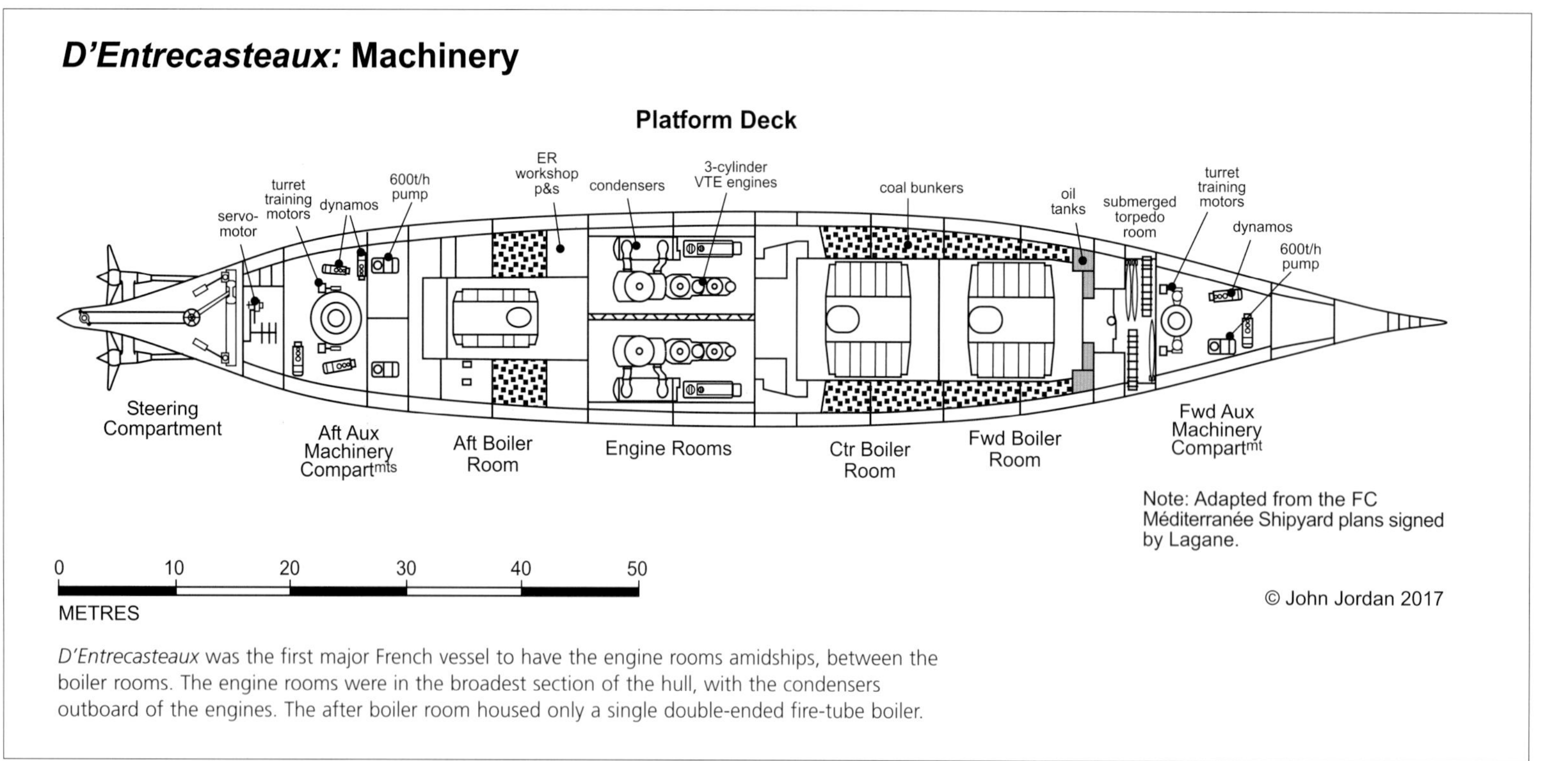

D'Entrecasteaux was the first major French vessel to have the engine rooms amidships, between the boiler rooms. The engine rooms were in the broadest section of the hull, with the condensers outboard of the engines. The after boiler room housed only a single double-ended fire-tube boiler.

The armour plates on the conning tower, which was elliptical in plan, were 230mm thick and were secured to a double layer of 10mm steel plating. The roof of the conning tower comprised a double layer of 25mm steel, and protection for the communications tube comprised hoops of 80mm special steel.

MACHINERY

The two large three-cylinder VTE engines, together with their associated pumps and condensers, were located side-by-side amidships in the broadest part of the hull, with a watertight longitudinal bulkhead on the centreline between them. Manufactured by the shipbuilder at their Marseille works, they were designed for a normal output of 8500CV using natural draught and 13,500CV with forced draught, the designed speed being 19 knots.

Steam was supplied by five double-ended cylindrical fire-tube boilers, each with four furnaces and rated at 10.5kg/cm^2. Two were located side-by-side in each of the two forward boiler rooms; the after boiler room had a single boiler on the centreline (see Machinery plan). The reversion to the fire-tube boiler has to be seen as a retrograde step. The four cruisers of the *Charner* class and *Pothuau* all received the more modern Belleville large watertube boiler, and these seem to have given fewer problems than the fire-tube boilers in *Dupuy-de-Lôme* and *D'Entrecasteaux*. During initial

Right: *D'Entrecasteaux* during her speed trials. On 28 April 1898, a boiler failure resulted in four stokers being seriously burned, and the completion of the trials was put back by six months. *(DR)*

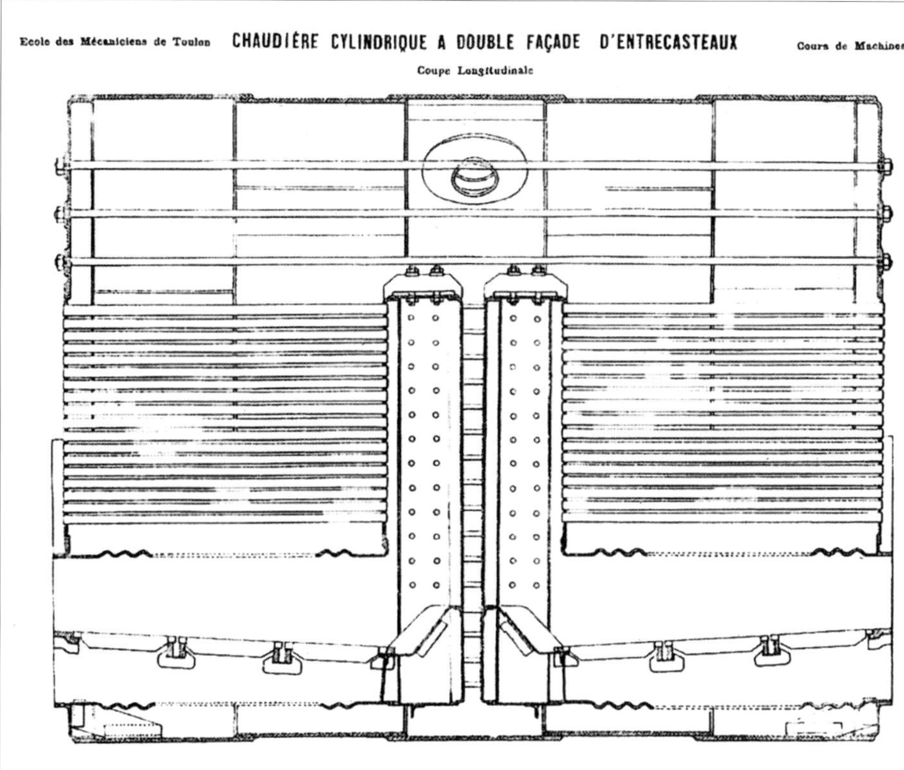

This cutaway profile drawing of the double-ended cylindrical boiler installed in *D'Entrecasteaux* was published in a contemporary instruction manual for the engineering school at Toulon. Note the back-to-back furnaces with their inclined grates and Fox-type corrugated walls (designed to allow expansion and contraction). The twin combustion chambers are at the centre of the boiler; there may have been a water layer between, although this is not clear from the drawing. (*Cours des machines, Ecole des mécaniciens de Toulon*)

sea trials on 28 April 1897 a number of tubes ruptured in the firebox of the starboard forward unit, seriously injuring four stokers and delaying full-power trials by six months.

In a full-power trial on 24 November 1898 *D'Entrecasteaux* attained a speed of only 18.8 knots on 13,500CV, earning the builder a penalty. The propellers were changed for a 4m model, and in a new trial on 23 December the ship attained 19.1 knots with 14,578CV. On the 24-hour trial 17.8 knots was sustained with 8893CV (natural draught).

EARLY SERVICE

D'Entrecasteaux commissioned on 15 February 1899, and was immediately assigned to the *Division navale d'Extrême-Orient et du Pacifique occidental*. She sailed for the Far East on 6 April and arrived in Saigon on 12 May, joining the protected cruisers *Descartes*, *Pascal* and *Jean Bart*. On 1 June Rear Admiral de Courejolles transferred his flag to *D'Entrecasteaux*, and she embarked on a lengthy cruise that took her as far as China.

During the Boxer Rebellion of 1900 she fired her main guns at Chinese forts. Problems were experienced with the breech screw and the locking mechanisms of the 240mm guns, and she was compelled to return to Toulon for repairs and modification during January to June 1901. She then left again for Saigon, arriving on 8 August. There were further cruises to Japan and China in 1901–02, before a return to Toulon for a major refit in 1903–05.

On 25 November 1905 *D'Entrecasteaux* left for a second deployment to the Far East via the Indian Ocean command. On 15 August Rear Admiral Boisse transferred his flag from the fast cruiser *Guichen*; *D'Entrecasteaux* now headed a force comprising the armoured cruisers *Dupetit-Thouars* and *Bruix*, the protected cruiser *Alger*, four gunboats and five destroyers. On 20 May 1907 she was involved in the attempted refloating of the cruiser *Chanzy* (see Chapter 1). *D'Entrecasteaux* finally left Saigon for Toulon on 25 October 1909.

A plan to modify the cruiser as a school ship for midshipmen (*école d'application*) to replace *Jeanne d'Arc* came to nothing, but *D'Entrecasteaux* underwent a major refit during which her hull and machinery were refurbished, cooling plant for the 14cm magazines was installed, the torpedo tubes (never used) were landed, and fire control and communications were upgraded: a Barr & Stroud rangefinder was fitted, the obsolete Eng order transmission system was replaced by the hydraulic Germain system, and a W/T office replaced the former admiral's galley.

On 1 January 1912 *D'Entrecasteaux* recommissioned as flagship of the Training Division of the Mediterranean Squadron; Rear Admiral Sourrieu transferred his flag from the old battleship *Brennus*. In early 1914 consideration was given to using the ship for gunnery training, replacing *Pothuau*, but the outbreak of war found her still in reserve at Toulon. She would subsequently be reactivated and assigned to the *Division spéciale*.

EVALUATION

D'Entrecasteaux was generally considered to be a good seaboat. However, she was overloaded at the ends and the weight of the forward turret, together with the pronounced ram bow, caused her to bury her head in a seaway when the wind was forward of the beam; speed had to be reduced or water flooded the forecastle, drenched the bridge and entered the forward casemates, which proved difficult to drain.

Once the problem with the breeches of the main guns had been resolved, the powerful main armament was well-regarded. However, protection was considered weak for such a major vessel, and the teak cladding

Above: *D'Entrecasteaux* in her overall blue-grey livery, moored in the Mourillon Basin at Toulon shortly before the First World War. *(DR)*

tended to act as a sponge. The engines were reliable, but the dated type of boiler was heavily criticised.

Ventilation of the accommodation, the magazines and the machinery spaces proved to be inadequate, which was a particular problem for a ship intended to operate in the tropics. Attempts to provide cooling for the magazines resulted in little improvement and by 1907, only eight years after her entry into service, *D'Entrecasteaux* was considered a second-line unit. She was retained largely because of her spacious command facilities, and in August 1914 she was re-activated for the Great War.

CHAPTER 3:

THE FAST ARMOURED CRUISER *JEANNE D'ARC*

IN 1890 EMILE BERTIN had returned from a four-year secondment to Japan, where he had overseen the development of the Sasebo and Kure naval dockyards, and was appointed deputy director of construction at Toulon. In 1892 he took over as *Directeur des Constructions Navales* at Rochefort, which was heavily involved in the construction of both armoured and protected cruisers for the *Marine Nationale*.[1] In late 1895 Bertin was appointed *Directeur du Matériel*. The situation he inherited from his predecessor was chaotic: there were ships whose design had been approved but for which there was no funding, and ships whose construction had been funded but for which there were no plans.[2]

The plans by the naval architect Tréboul for a large protected *croiseur de station* to be named *Jeanne d'Arc* (see Chapter 2 for details) had received ministerial approval on 21 August. However, funding for this ship was not authorised; instead, the Parliamentary Budgetary Commission had approved funding for a 'fleet' armoured cruiser of 11,000 tonnes. The preliminary design study, with the initial programme number D2, had been for a ship of 8500 tonnes, but had been heavily criticised by the *Conseil des Travaux*; there was now funding (2.25m FF for 1896) to begin construction at Toulon, which was currently desperately short of work, but no plans. On 28 December 1895 the new Minister of Marine, Edouard Lockroy,[3] instructed the Toulon dockyard to lay down a 1st class armoured cruiser of 11,000 tonnes to be named *Jeanne d'Arc*, 'to replace the one of the same name whose construction was suspended following a decision by the Budgetary Commission on 24 October'.

One of Bertin's first actions was to draw up plans for this ship (now designated C2). He would subsequently set about a complete reorganisation of the bodies responsible for naval design and construction. In late 1896 he was appointed head of the *Direction centrale des Constructions Navales*, and reformed it as the *Service Technique des Constructions Navales* (STCN). In addition to drawing up plans, the STCN under Bertin would provide technical advice to the Minister and to the *Conseil supérieur de la Marine* (CSM), the body charged with advising the Minister on future naval programmes and agreeing the military characteristics required in new designs.[4] The power and influence of the *Conseil des Travaux*, which Bertin deemed to be stuffed with elderly, conservative admirals, declined; its recommendations would increasingly be ignored or circumvented, and in 1905 it would be abolished altogether and replaced by a *Comité Technique*.

Initially, there was considerable resistance to Bertin's new ideas on ship design within the naval establishment. Renowned and respected naval architects such as De Bussy and Thibaudier bridled at Bertin's description of their battleships as '*chavirables*' (liable to capsize), and although successive Ministers were more receptive, Bertin did not get to design a first-line battleship (*cuirassé d'escadre*) until the *Patrie* class of 1901–02, being permitted only an experimental foray into battleship design with the small coast defence battleship *Henri IV* laid down in 1897.

Bertin's innovations were in protection and propulsion. For protection he favoured a high armour belt, with a well-developed cellular layer directly behind it sandwiched between upper and lower protective decks to form a 'citadel' (*caisson blindé*). He also favoured the latest developments in watertube boiler technology, which offered a combination of high speed and low machinery weights.

Ship design in the *Marine Nationale* during the 1870s and 1880s had been something of a 'closed shop'. Discussions in the two *Conseils* showed an awareness of developments abroad, but were principally focused on the calibre of the guns mounted (which needed to be matched) and the thicknesses of armour (which French guns needed to be able to penetrate); there was considerable resistance to radical solutions such as the partial belts of Royal Navy battleships of the period, and a deeply-entrenched predilection for traditional hull forms that featured a prominent ram bow and sides with pronounced tumblehome to provide a steady gunnery platform and to facilitate end-on fire. Bertin, who had a more 'international' outlook than his contemporaries due to his time in Japan, will have been aware of the large, fast British protected cruisers *Powerful* and *Terrible* laid down in 1894, and his initial proposal for *Jeanne d'Arc* was almost certainly influenced by what was known of their characteristics.

1 Rochefort had built the protected cruisers *Forbin* (LD 1886), *Galilée* (LD 1893), and *Lavoisier* (LD 1895); the dockyard had also been responsible for the first and last of the *Amiral Charner* class, *Amiral Charner* (LD 1889) and *Bruix* (LD 1890).

2 See Bertin's submission to the Minister dated 29 July 1896.

3 Lockroy was appointed on 1 November 1895; he replaced Admiral Armand Besnard.

4 The *Conseil supérieur* drew up the staff requirements including displacement, offensive/defensive qualities, speed and endurance – see Jordan and Caresse, *French Battleships of World War One*, p 20.

When completed *Powerful* and *Terrible* displaced 14,200 tons (virtually the same as contemporary RN battleships) and had a length between perpendiculars of 152.4m. They were powered by no fewer than forty-eight Belleville watertube boilers – a first for the Royal Navy[5] – and their two-shaft VTE engines had an output of 25,000ihp for a theoretical maximum speed of 22 knots.[6] They were armed with two single 9.2in/40 (234mm) guns in turrets and twelve 6in (152mm) QF guns in casemates. This was by no means an impressive armament for such large ships; their great length was effectively dictated by the need to accommodate the forty-eight boilers and powerful engines that gave them their high speed.

The adoption of the Belleville large watertube boiler in the Royal Navy was generally considered to have resulted in weight savings in excess of 20 per cent compared to the traditional cylindrical fire-tube boiler. The latest French small-tube boilers of the Normand and du Temple types, originally developed for torpedo boats,[7] promised even greater reductions in weight and volume for a given output of steam. They featured three collector drums in a triangular arrangement – the lower two for water and the upper drum for steam – connected by multiple 'vertical' tubes of much smaller diameter.

[5] The Belleville boiler was adopted by the Royal Navy following a visit to Toulon by the British DNC William White in 1892.

[6] Contemporary British battleships could steam at 15–16 knots using natural draught and 16–17 knots with forced draught (short periods only).

[7] The high-speed circulation boiler had been patented by the former naval officer and engineer Félix du Temple in 1876. It was subsequently developed by Jacques-Augustin Normand (to be installed in the torpedo boats built at his Le Havre shipyard), by Sigaudy of FC Méditerranée (Le Havre), and by *Ingénieur du génie maritime* Guyot of Indret. In trials that took place on 26 September 1895, only three months before the order for *Jeanne d'Arc* was notified to the Toulon Dockyard, Normand's experimental 'sea-going torpedo boat' (*torpilleur de haute mer*) *Forban* achieved an average speed of 31.03 knots – a world record that was not overtaken for some years. However, it was a huge jump from a torpedo boat of 127 tonnes to an 11,000-tonne cruiser, and Bertin's proposal was not without risk.

Below: Conceptually similar to *Jeanne d'Arc*, and possibly the inspiration for Bertin's design, HMS *Powerful* and her sister *Terrible* were the largest and fastest cruisers of the day and carried a similar armament. However, unlike *Jeanne d'Arc*, they were protected cruisers, with a 6in (150mm) deck over the machinery but no armour on their high, exposed sides. *(Allan C Green collection, State Library of Victoria)*

BUILDING DATA

Name	Builder	Laid down	Launched	Trials	Commissioned
Jeanne d'Arc	Arsenal de Toulon	24 Oct 1896	8 Jun 1899	1 Mar 1901	19 May 1903

BERTIN'S *JEANNE D'ARC*

To power *Jeanne d'Arc* Bertin initially opted for three VTE engines each rated at 9500CV (total horsepower: 28,500CV). Steam was to be supplied by an advanced type of small-tube boiler developed by engineer Guyot of Indret using the du Temple principle.[8] Initially a double-ended model was proposed: the steam generating plant was to comprise twenty-six boiler bodies paired back-to-back. The final design featured no fewer than thirty-six single-ended boilers of the Guyot–du Temple type, and each of the VTE engines had its power rating increased to 11,000CV (total horsepower: 33,000CV) to give the ships a designed speed of 23 knots. Both the boilers and the engines were to be built by the Navy's propulsion establishment at Indret.

The main armament was originally to comprise two 194mm guns in centreline turrets fore and aft, with eight 138.6mm QF guns in casemate/sponson mountings and between ten and twelve 100mm QF guns on the upper deck. This would subsequently be revised: the 100mm guns were replaced by six additional 138.6 mm guns in shielded upper-deck mountings, for a total of fourteen 138.6mm.

[8] Guyot lodged the patent for his boiler design on 5 December 1893.

NOMENCLATURE

Joan of Arc (**Jeanne d'Arc**, c1412–31) is a national heroine of France and a Catholic saint. A peasant girl born in eastern France who claimed divine guidance, she led the French army to several important victories during the Hundred Years War, which paved the way for the coronation of Charles VII as King of France. Tried and condemned in a French ecclesiastical court under English control, she was burned at the stake as a witch when she was 19 years old. The name *Jeanne d'Arc* had been borne by four previous French warships, and the armoured cruiser was later to become the first of a series of school ships for officer cadets that bore the same name.

HULL AND SUPERSTRUCTURES

The hull-form Bertin adopted for *Jeanne d'Arc* was altogether more 'modern', with sides that were vertical at the waterline amidships (see the comparative body plan with *Pothuau*). The prominent 'plough bow' that had been a constant feature of earlier French armoured cruisers was abandoned; in its place was a

***Jeanne d'Arc*: Profile & Plan**

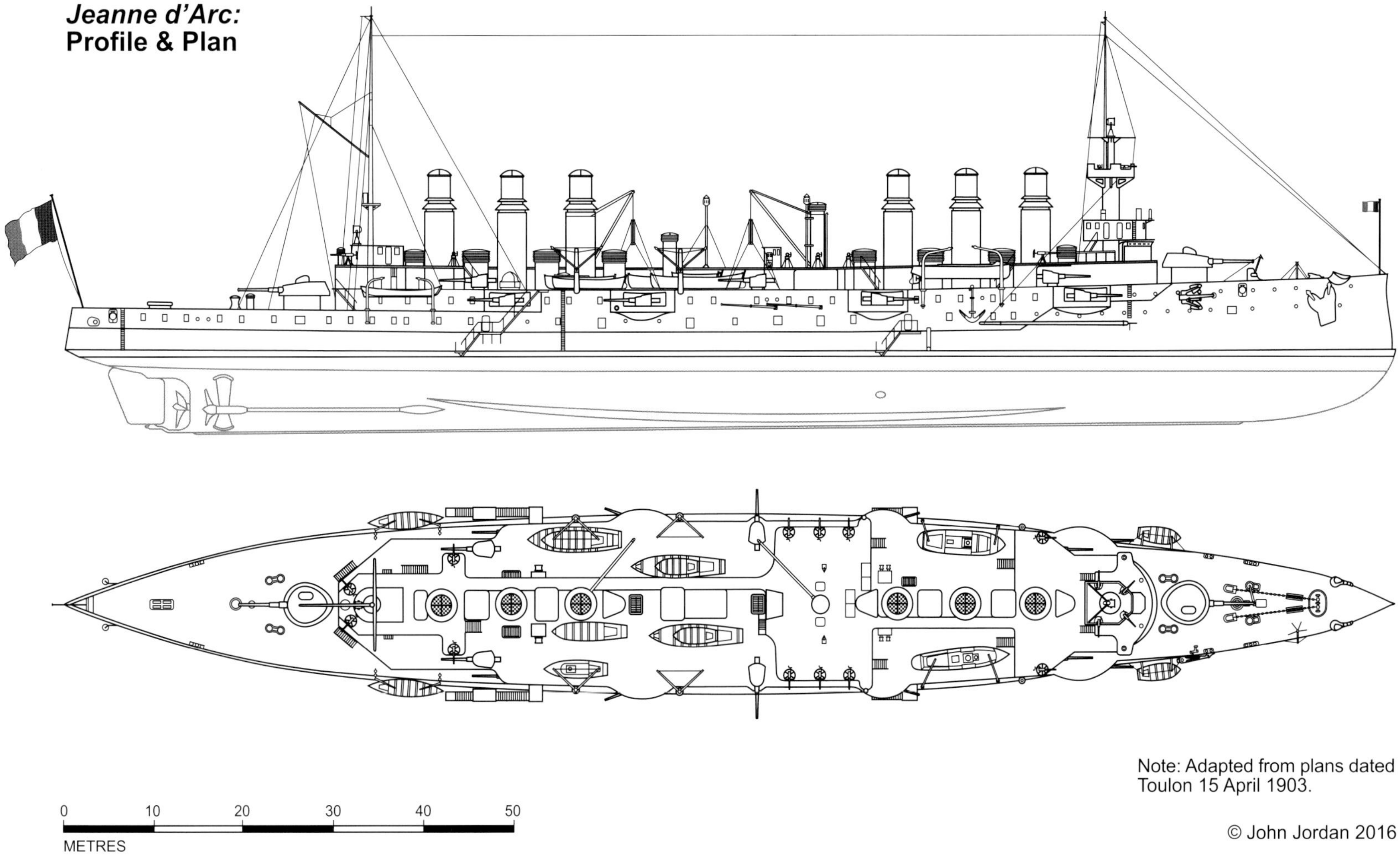

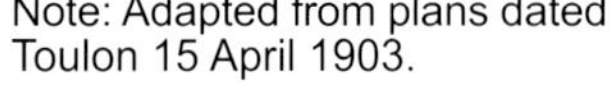

© John Jordan 2016

Jeanne d'Arc: GA Plans

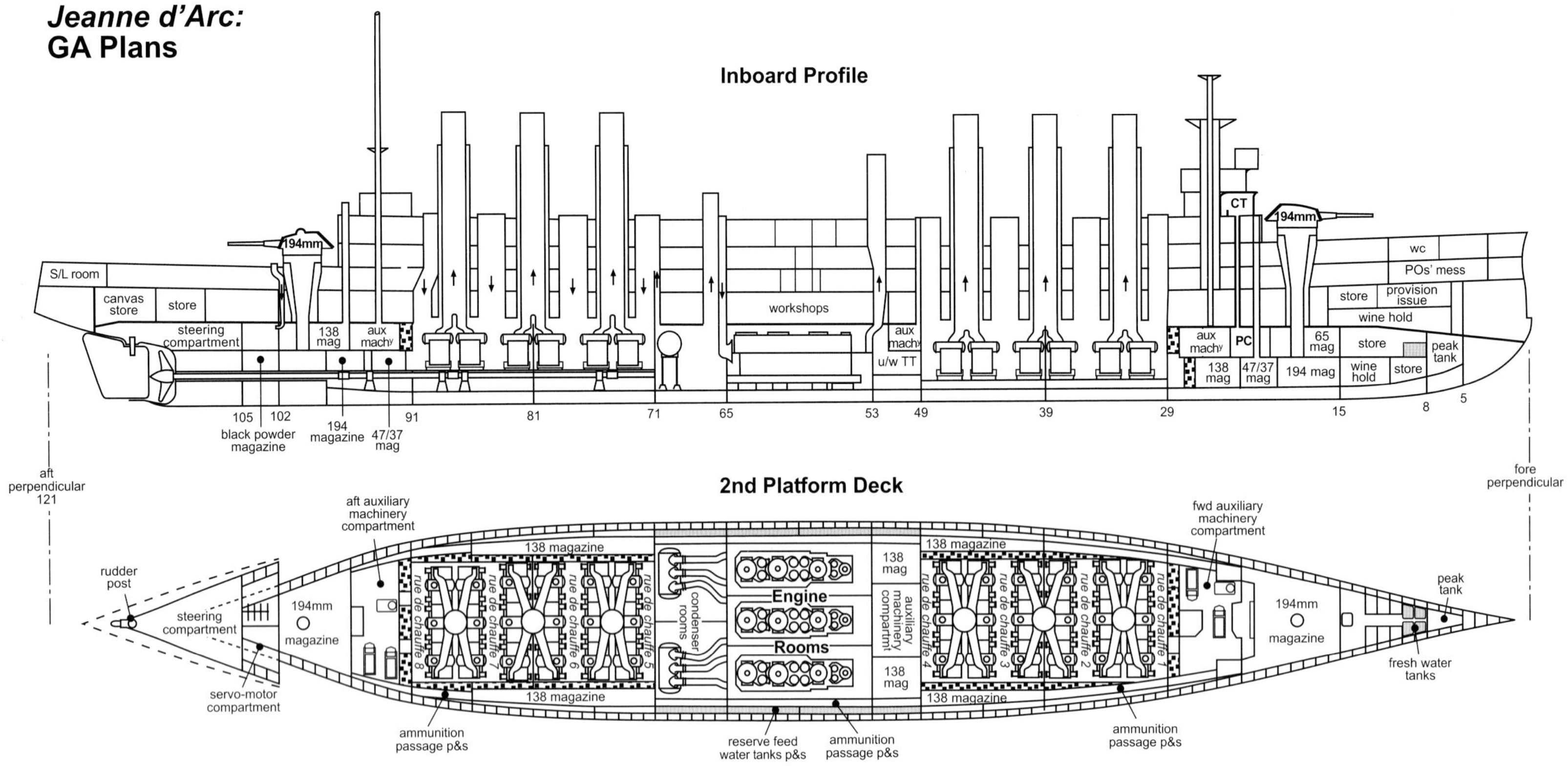

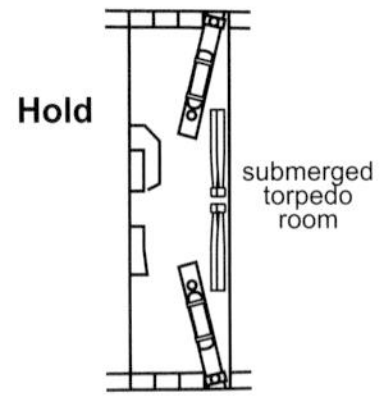

Inboard Profile

S/L room, canvas store, store, steering compartment, 138 mag, aux mach^y, workshops, aux mach^y, u/w TT, CT, 194mm, 194mm, wc, POs' mess, store, provision issue, wine hold, aux mach^y, PC, 65 mag, store, peak tank, 138 mag, 47/37 mag, 194 mag, wine hold, store

105 102 91 81 71 65 53 49 39 29 15 8 5

black powder magazine, 194 magazine, 47/37 mag

aft perpendicular 121

fore perpendicular

2nd Platform Deck

rudder post, steering compartment, servo-motor compartment, 194mm magazine, aft auxiliary machinery compartment, 138 magazine, rue de chauffe 8, rue de chauffe 7, rue de chauffe 6, rue de chauffe 5, condenser rooms, Engine Rooms, 138 mag, auxiliary machinery compartm^t, rue de chauffe 4, rue de chauffe 3, rue de chauffe 2, rue de chauffe 1, fwd auxiliary machinery compartment, 194mm magazine, peak tank, fresh water tanks, ammunition passage p&s, reserve feed water tanks p&s, ammunition passage p&s, ammunition passage p&s

Hold

submerged torpedo room

Note the narrow ammunition passages which ran along the sides of the ship and linked the magazines fore, aft and amidships. *Jeanne d'Arc* was the only French armoured cruiser to have this feature, although it was common in contemporary British ships.

Note: Adapted from plans dated Toulon 19 March 1903.

© John Jordan 2016

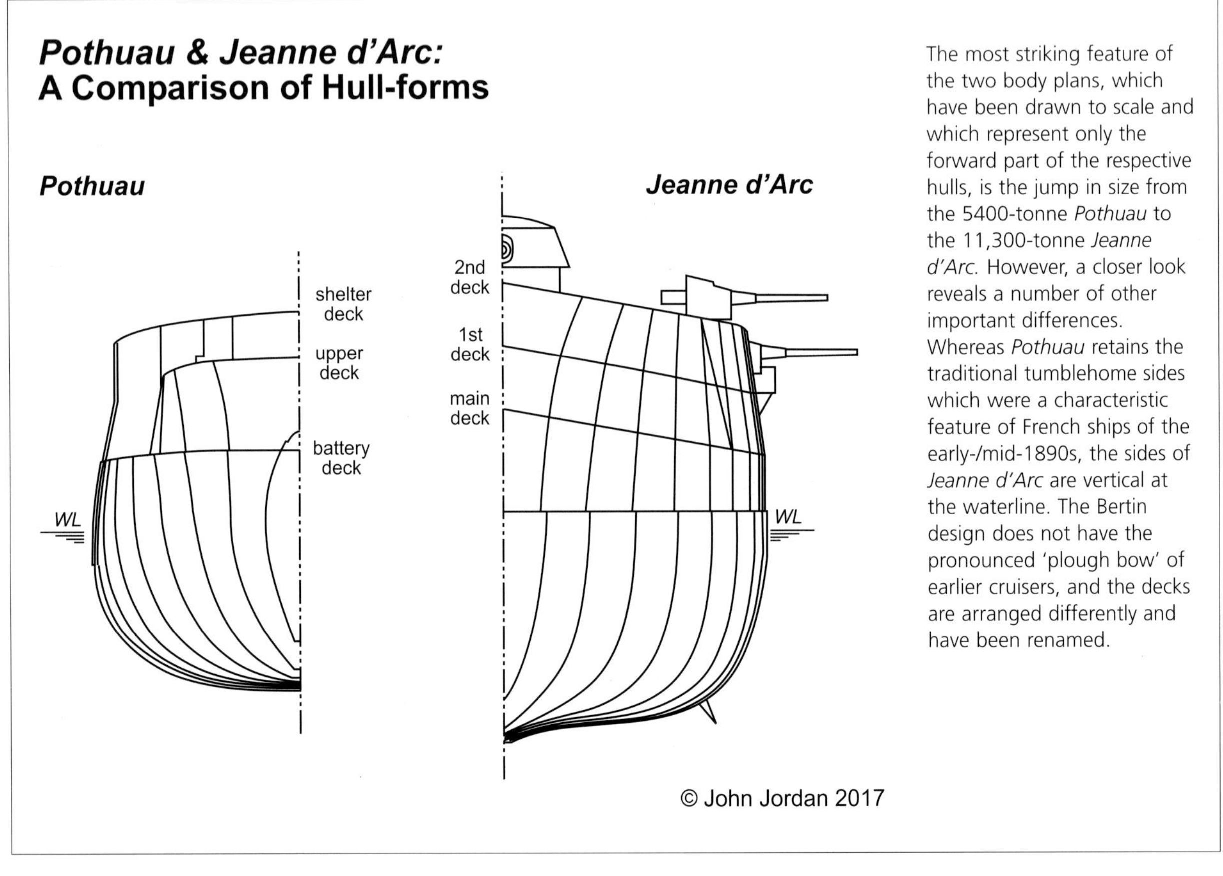

Pothuau & Jeanne d'Arc: A Comparison of Hull-forms

The most striking feature of the two body plans, which have been drawn to scale and which represent only the forward part of the respective hulls, is the jump in size from the 5400-tonne *Pothuau* to the 11,300-tonne *Jeanne d'Arc*. However, a closer look reveals a number of other important differences. Whereas *Pothuau* retains the traditional tumblehome sides which were a characteristic feature of French ships of the early-/mid-1890s, the sides of *Jeanne d'Arc* are vertical at the waterline. The Bertin design does not have the pronounced 'plough bow' of earlier cruisers, and the decks are arranged differently and have been renamed.

Above: The launch of *Jeanne d'Arc*, at the *Arsenal du Mourillon* at Toulon, on 8 June 1899. *(SHM Toulon)*

gently curved stem, still reinforced with forged steel but not a fully-fledged ram. There were three shafts with a single large semi-balanced rudder directly behind the propeller for the centre shaft. Frame spacing was 1.2m, as in contemporary battleships, and there were no fewer than fifteen watertight transverse bulkheads between the double bottom and the lower protective deck. In a break with previous cruiser practice, the double bottom was extended upwards at the sides as far as the lower armoured deck.

The protection system closely associated with Bertin comprised a high armoured belt with a closely-divided cellular layer behind it. The cellular layer was enclosed top and bottom by two protective decks, known respectively as the upper protective deck (*pont blindé supérieur* or PBS), and the lower protective deck (*pont blindé inférieur* or PBI). The height of the belt placed the upper protective deck, which was flat, well above the waterline. The lower protective deck, which was in effect the former 'armoured deck' (*pont cuirassé*), had its upper section roughly at the waterline; it was almost flat over the centreline and was sloped downwards at the sides to meet the bottom of the belt.

The new system prompted a complete renaming of the decks. The upper protective deck was now termed the main deck (*pont principal*), and housed the accommodation for the officers (aft), the petty officers (forward) and the mess decks for the crew (amidships); there was a large, well-equipped sick bay close to the bow. The lower protective deck was now the first platform deck (*premier faux-pont*), and below it were the former platform deck, now the *deuxième faux-pont*, and the hold (*cale*). The decks above the main deck were numbered and their traditional names discarded; the former battery deck (*pont de la batterie*) was now the first deck (*premier pont*), and the upper deck (*pont des gaillards*) became the second deck (*deuxième pont*). The QF battery and the accommodation for senior officers, including an admiral and his staff, were on the first deck. The superstructure deck above the second deck, formerly the *spardeck*, was now known as the 'bridge deck' (*pont passerelle*).

ARMAMENT

Main turrets

Some secondary sources state that the main 194mm gun in *Jeanne d'Arc* was Mle 1893–1896.[9] However, the timing of the order for the ship suggests that the gun was the Mle 1893, the same gun fitted in *Pothuau*, and this is borne out by the official plans of the turrets themselves. The major difference between these two guns was the length of the chamber, which was associated with a corresponding increase in the weight of the propellant charge: chamber length in the later gun was 2093mm in order to accommodate a 33.8kg BM10 propellant charge divided into three bags, whereas the earlier Mle 1893 had a chamber length of only 1306mm, and the 22.3kg charge of BM9 powder was in two halves: either two bagged half-charges (as in *Pothuau*), or a brass cartridge and a fore-charge in a bag of serge or silk cloth. The ammunition handling arrangements in the *Jeanne d'Arc* turret plans show paired charges in the lower and upper hoists, and a provision of two half-charges for each projectile in the ready-use stowage (see below).

Bertin adopted a distinctively novel solution for the single turret. The heavy pivot-shaft, which had been standard for French heavy and medium gun mountings since the battleship *Brennus* (LD 1889), was abandoned in favour of a turret supported on a horizontal roller path at the level of the weather deck. The upper part of the gunhouse (*coupole*) was elliptical in plan and had steeply inclined sides protected by thick plates of cemented armour; the lower part was

[9] Notably Campbell, *Conway's All the World's Fighting Ships 1860–1905*, and Friedman, *Naval Weapons of World War One*.

circular in plan and was unprotected (see Turret plan). A handing room for ready-use ammunition in the form of a bowl was suspended beneath the gunhouse and turned with it. The lower part of the gunhouse and the upper handing room (or working chamber) rotated within a fixed ring of heavy armour (*parapet*) that also provided protection for the horizontal and vertical roller paths and the training mechanism directly beneath the turret. The ammunition hoists from the shell room and magazine were fixed and did not rotate with the turret structure. Bertin designated this unusual arrangement a *tourelle-barbette*.

When Bertin first submitted his proposal, General Desbordes, the head of the ordnance department, in a note dated 9 March 1896, praised its simplicity and economy of weight. Given the command of the fore turret, it was calculated that the height of a pivot-shaft would have been 12.24m. However, in the design proposed by Bertin the axial tube would become no more than a vertical ammunition passage, thereby reducing substantially the rotating mass. On 24 June the construction department informed the ordnance department of its final approval of the new arrangement, and five companies (Schneider, Société des Batignolles, Châtillon & Commentry,

Opposite, top: *Jeanne d'Arc* fitting out at Toulon. *(Musée de la Marine)*

Opposite, bottom: *Jeanne d'Arc* departing Toulon shortly after she entered service. Her six funnels and minimal superstructures gave her a markedly modern silhouette for her time. The ship is in her original black and buff livery. *(Marius Bar)*

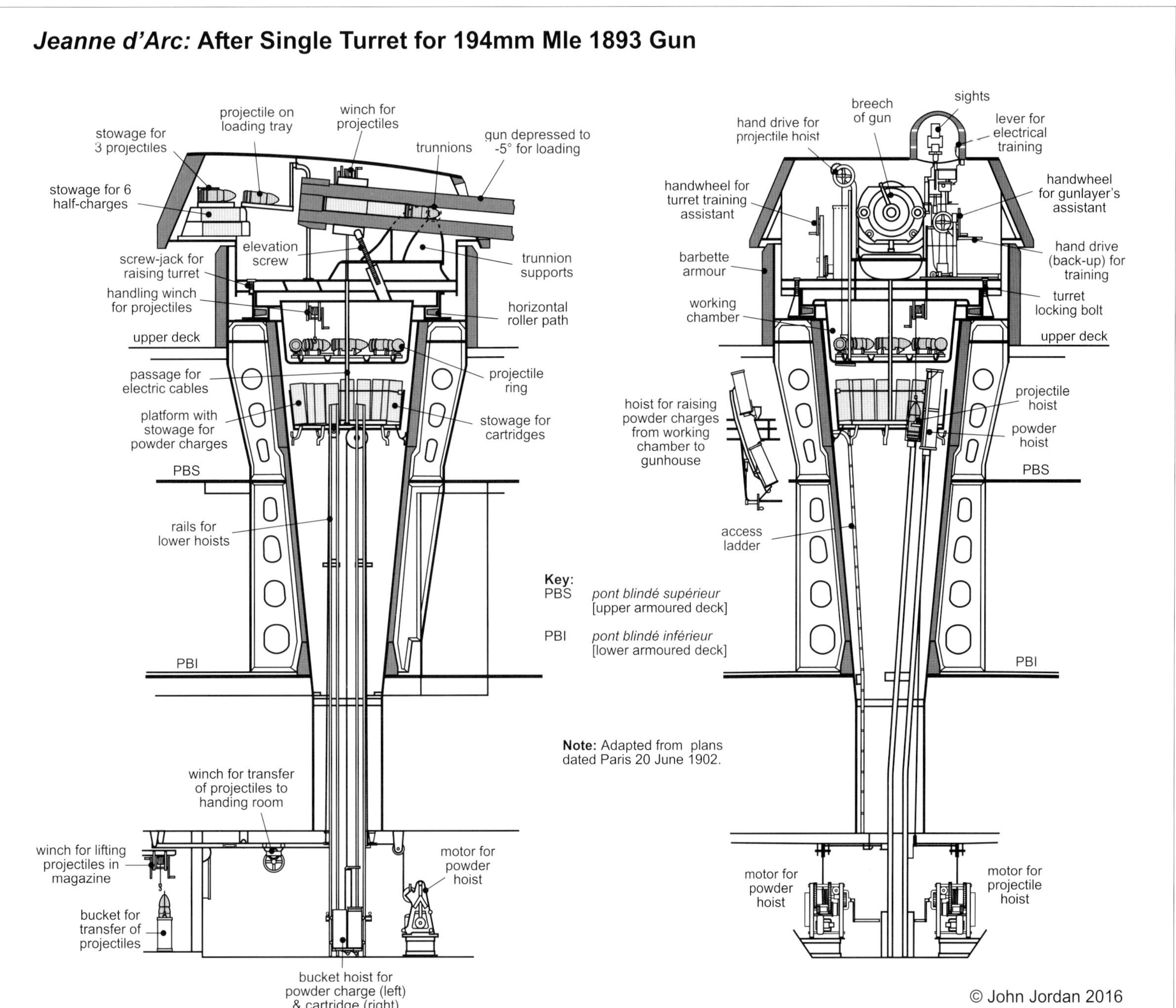

The design of the single turret for the main 194mm Mle 1893 gun incorporated a large number of new features which would be further developed. Note the cupola of the upper part of the rotating gunhouse, with its inclined armour, and the fixed barbette armour protecting the lower part. Note also the 'bowl' for the ready-use projectiles suspended beneath the gunhouse (and rotating with it), and the fixed platform below it for the ready-use propellant half-charges, which is secured to the fixed ammunition trunk with steel brackets. In later developments of the turret the 'bowl' would become a fully-fledged working chamber, deeper and cylindrical in plan, and would house not only the ready-use projectiles but the propellant charges (see Chapter 6, page 121).

Right: An early view of *Jeanne d'Arc* in Toulon roads. *(Private collection)*

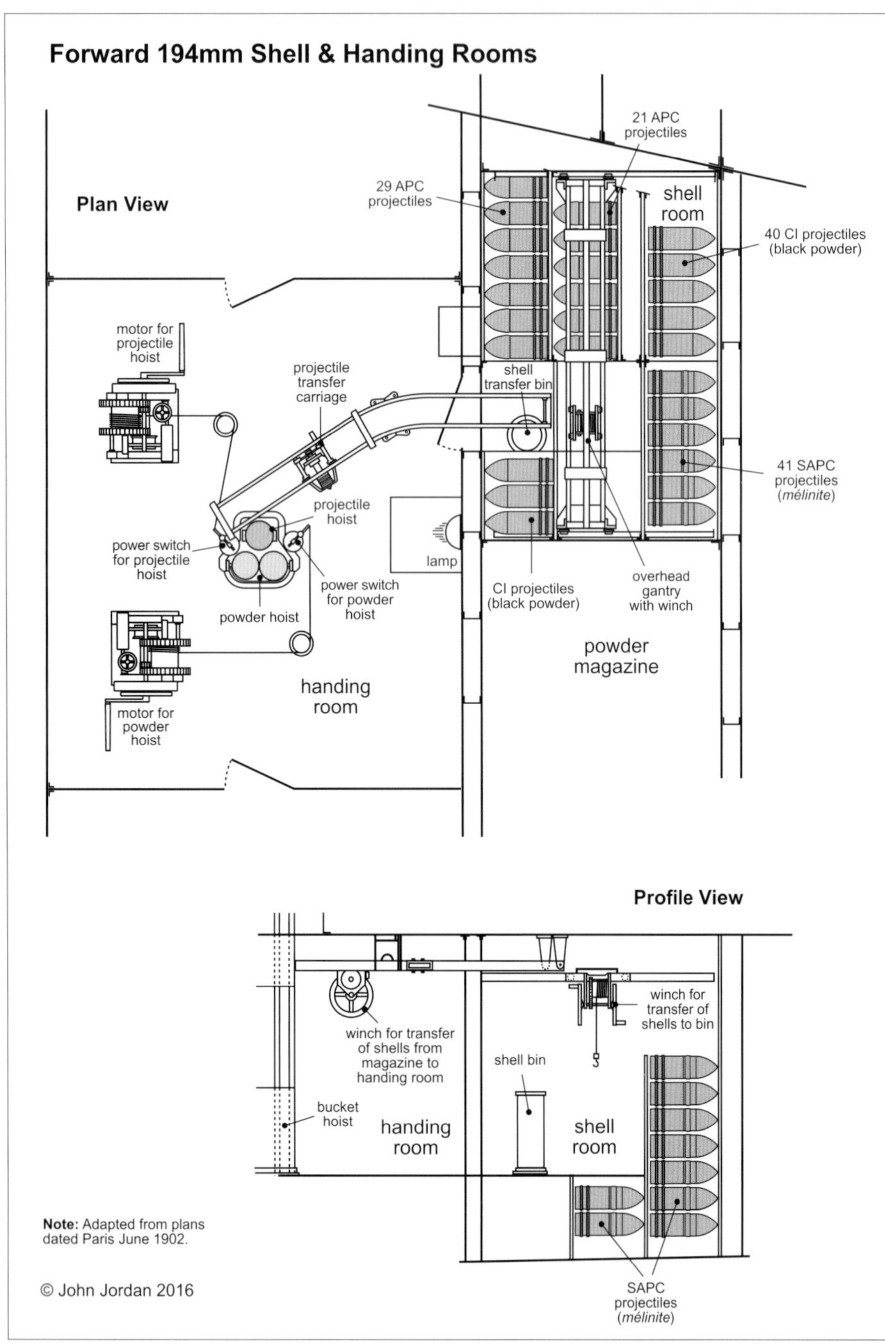

Saint-Chamond and FC Méditerranée) were invited to tender.

When the proposals were considered, the general view was that the design submitted by Saint-Chamond met all the requirements; it was also the least expensive. However, the ordnance department subsequently raised a number of objections to the design and it was concluded that, despite the higher quotation, the proposal from the Société des Batignolles should be accepted. The contract was duly placed on 18 March 1898.

In the final design, the separate electrically-powered hoists for the projectiles and powder charges emerged onto a fixed circular platform at the upper end of the ammunition shaft. The projectiles were raised from the hoist to the shell handing room suspended beneath the gunhouse using a hand winch, and were stowed on a horizontal ring that could hold up to eight shells; they were then lifted from the shell ring into the gunhouse by a second, manual hoist. The propellant charges were lifted from the hoist manually and stowed vertically around the outer edge of the platform; eight cartridges and eight bagged half-charges could be stowed in this way for a total of eight complete ready-use rounds. There was a separate, manual hoist with containers for two half-charges that emerged directly into the gunhouse; these were then lifted by hand and transferred to the breech. The charge stowage platform and the lower part of the shell handing room were protected by a fixed cone of heavy armour, and the cone was extended downwards at a reduced thickness as far as the lower protective deck (PBI).

The high freeboard of *Jeanne d'Arc* resulted in a favourable command for both 194mm guns: 10.2m for the gun in the forward turret, 7.1m for the after gun.

QF guns

The arrangements finally adopted for the secondary armament of fourteen 138.6mm QF guns were unusual. The eight hull-mounted guns (four per side) were mounted on projecting sponsons on the first deck rather than in casemates; the remaining six guns were mounted one deck higher on the second deck. All the guns, including the six weather-deck mountings, had full shields of 72mm steel, and 40mm screens at the top, bottom and sides of the sponsons provided a degree of splinter protection for the gun

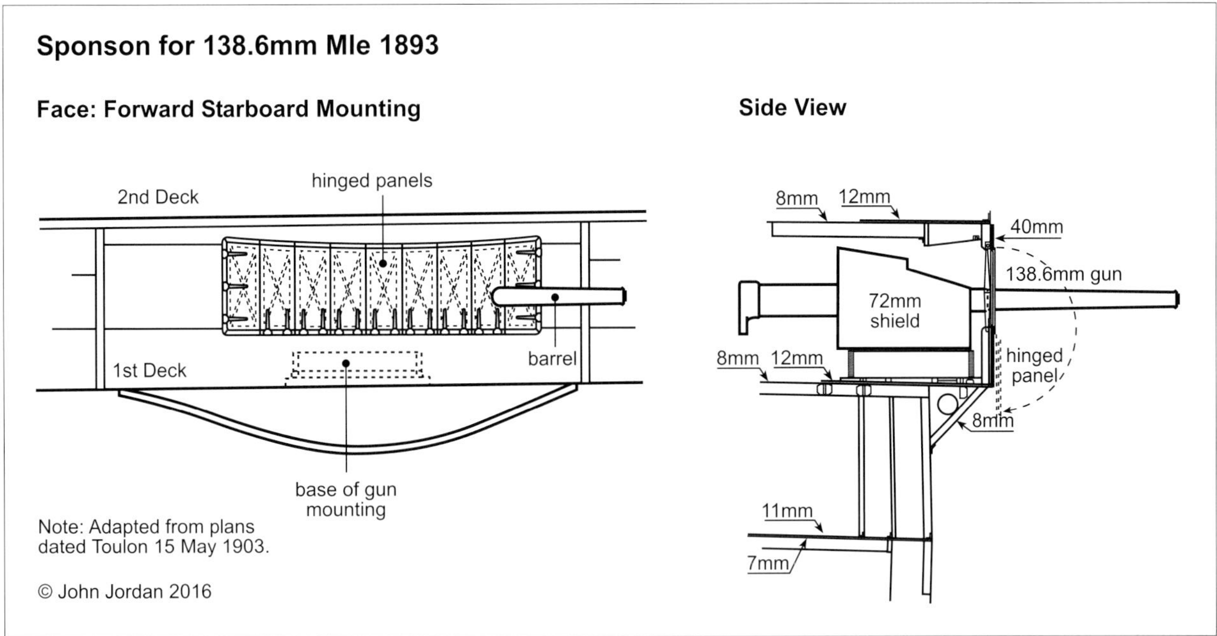

crews from shells striking the upper part of the hull. The second deck was shaped in such a way as to form a roof over the sponson guns, reinforced by 12mm plates of hardened steel, and the guns were protected from the elements by drop-down weatherproof hatches when the ship was at sea (see Sponson plan). The advantage of this arrangement over a conventional casemate was that the guns could be fired over exceptionally broad arcs: the arcs of the sponson guns mounted on the first deck were 150° compared to c110° for a casemate gun.

Magazine arrangements

With more than half the ship's length over the broadest part of the hull taken up by the machinery and boiler spaces, the location of *Jeanne d'Arc*'s magazines was problematic. Those for the 194mm guns were situated directly below the turrets at either end of the machinery spaces (see plan of the forward magazine and shell room for layout). Those for the medium and small-calibre guns were located in long, narrow spaces beneath the armoured deck, outboard of the boiler rooms and the coal bunkers and also above the torpedo flat amidships, between the forward group of boilers and the engine room. All the magazines (including the 194mm magazines fore and aft) were connected by ammunition passages that ran outboard of the internal bulkheads enclosing the machinery spaces[10] (see GA Plans and Midship Half-section). Overhead rails allowed the movement of projectiles and charges from one end of the ship to the other so that any gun could be supplied from any of the magazines.

ATB guns

The complement of ATB guns was enhanced to reflect the increase in size of the hull. *Jeanne d'Arc* was fitted with no fewer than sixteen Hotchkiss 47mm Mle 1885 guns: four on the lower platform of the light military

[10] Ammunition passages were also a feature of *Powerful* and *Terrible*, which introduced this feature to the Royal Navy.

CHARACTERISTICS

Displacement:	11,330 tonnes
Dimensions:	
Length	145.40m pp; 147.00m oa
Beam	19.42m wl
Draught	8.13m aft
Propulsion:	
Boilers	36 Guyot–du Temple boilers
Engines	3-shaft 4-cylinder VTE
Horsepower	33,000CV (designed)
Speed	23 knots (designed)
Coal	1400 tonnes normal; 2100 tonnes full load
Endurance	9000nm at 10 knots
Armament:	
Main guns	2 x 194mm/40 Mle 1893 in single turrets
Medium guns	14 x 138.6mm/45 Mle 1893 QF in shielded pivot mountings
ATB guns	16 x 47mm/40 Mle 1885 QF in single mountings
	6 x 37mm QF
Torpedo tubes	2 submerged tubes for 450mm torpedoes
	6 torpedoes Mle 1892
Protection:	
Main belt	150mm max
Upper belt	80–40mm
Decks	11mm PBS
	45/55mm PBI
194 turrets	176mm
138 shields	72mm
Conning tower	138mm
Boats:	1 x 11m steam launch
	1 x 10m steam pinnace
	1 x 7.65m White launch
	1 x 10.5m pulling pinnace
	2 x 10m pulling cutters
	1 x 8.5m pulling cutter
	1 x 8m pulling cutter
	2 x 8.5m whalers
	2 x 5m dinghies
Complement:	
As private ship	651 officers and men

Right: *Jeanne d'Arc* moored in Toulon roads between 1903 and 1908. Note the black-painted funnel caps. *(Private collection)*

foremast and twelve on the lower bridge deck (two forward, four aft and six amidships). This was a superior arrangement to contemporary battleships, in which a number of the ATB guns fired through ports in the hull and had restricted arcs in consequence; it also made it easier to coordinate fire against attacking torpedo boats.

Searchlight projectors

Six Mangin 60cm searchlight projectors were provided for target illumination at night, disposed as in *Pothuau*. The forward projector of the *ligne haute* was mounted on the upper platform of the military foremast, the after projector atop the superstructure deck at the base of the mainmast. The lower projectors

Right: In April 1903, shortly after her completion, *Jeanne d'Arc* embarked President Emile Loubet for an official visit to Algiers, escorted by the ships of the Mediterranean Squadron. The photo shows her spectacular arrival on the 15th, which was greeted by a 21-gun salute. A host of foreign warships was assembled for the occasion. On the left of the photo is the Italian battleship *Sicilia*, flagship of Vice Admiral Giovanni Frigerio, C-in-C of the Italian Mediterranean Squadron. In the distant haze can be seen the Russian cruiser *Bayan* with two British battleships of the *Majestic* class beyond; the British despatched the battleships *Magnificent* (Rear Admiral Curzon-Howe), *Mars*, *Jupiter* and *Prince George* from the Channel Fleet for the occasion. Other major foreign ships present included the Italian cruisers *Garibaldi* and *Varese*, the Russian turret ship *Imperator Nikolai I* and the Spanish barbette ship *Pelayo*. *(Private collection)*

(*ligne basse*) were set back in large rectangular embrasures at the four 'corners' of the ship, and were run out on rails suspended from the second deck (bow) and first deck (stern) respectively.

Torpedoes

Jeanne d'Arc was fitted with only two submerged torpedo tubes. These were in a special compartment amidships, between the forward boiler rooms and the engine room (see GA Plans), and were angled at 13° forward of the beam. Six 450mm Mle 1892 torpedoes were stowed on tiered racks against the forward transverse bulkhead. As *Jeanne d'Arc* was built as a 'fleet' cruiser, no mines were embarked.

PROTECTION

Hull

The side armour was arranged in two main strakes. The waterline belt (*cuirasse épaisse*), which was of homogenous nickel steel, was 2.2m high, with the upper edge 0.70m above the waterline. It was 150mm thick amidships, reducing to 100mm forward and 80mm aft, tapering to 50mm at its lower edge, and was secured to a 70mm teak backing. Above this was an upper belt (*cuirasse mince*) with a height of 1.92m amidships; it was 80mm thick at its lower edge tapering to 40mm at its upper edge, and was secured directly to the shell plating. Forward of the foremost 138.6mm gun sponson three more strakes of 40mm armour covered the entire bow section to the height of the forecastle. The sponsons themselves were protected by 40mm plating and had 20mm internal splinter screens.

Jeanne d'Arc had two protective decks. The upper protective deck was at main deck level; it comprised 11mm hardened steel on 7mm plating and rested on the top edge of the upper armour belt. The lower protective deck was at the level of the first platform deck: the plates over the horizontal central section were of 45mm mild steel on a double layer of 10mm plating; the outboard plating of this deck sloped downwards at an angle of 23° and joined the lower edge of the main belt 1.50m below the waterline (see Midship Half-section); the inboard strake of the slopes had 55mm 'super-soft' steel[11] in place of the 45mm plates, for a total thickness of 75mm.

The plating for the armour belt was supplied by Marrel Frères of Toulon, the armour plates for the decks by the Forges de la Chaussade at Guérigny.

The space enclosed by the two protective decks and the side armour contained the cellular layer that formed a key part of Bertin's protective system. Directly behind the side armour was a cofferdam comprising multiple cells a single frame in length (1.2m) and 0.5m deep partially filled with water-excluding cellulose. Inboard of the cofferdam there was a continuous passageway 1m wide, which was subdivided every four frames (4.8m) by a transverse bulkhead with a watertight door. The longitudinal bulkhead for the cofferdam was 7mm thick; that on the inboard side of the passageway was 8mm (see Protection plan). Between the floor of the passageway, which was just above the normal waterline, and the slope of the lower protective deck was a triangular space that provided access to allow inspection and repairs to be made to action damage to the cofferdam; scuppers in the floor allowed any flooding to drain directly into the bilges.

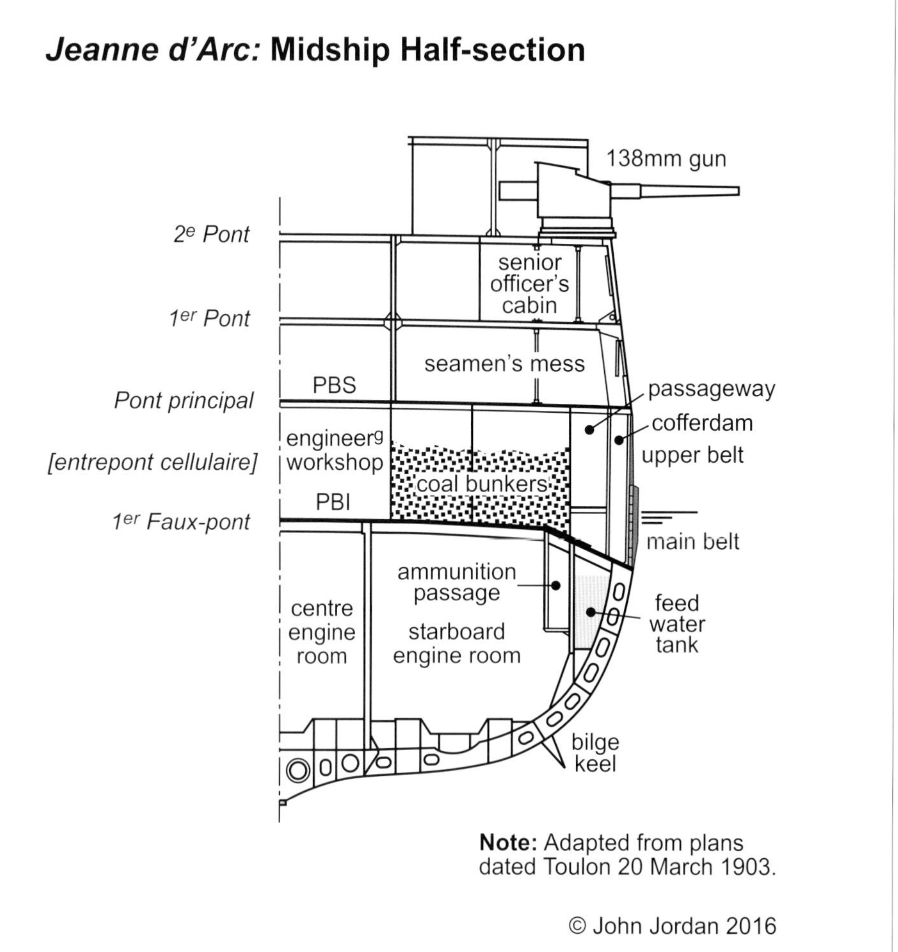

The space between the port and starboard longitudinal watertight bulkheads was closely subdivided: some of the compartments were left empty, others were used as coal bunkers – these were the last to be filled and the first to be emptied, and were used when the ship was at deep load. Where the ammunition hoists, boiler uptakes, ventilation trunks and access hatches passed vertically through this section they were enclosed in watertight casings with thick armoured coamings at their lower ends.

The 'citadel' formed by the belt and the upper and lower protective decks extended from the bow to frame 117, just short of the stern, where it was closed by a transverse bulkhead. The bulkhead was formed with two plates of special steel: the lower, which formed the end wall for the main belt, had a uniform thickness of 84mm; the upper, which closed off the upper belt, was graduated in thickness from 84mm at the bottom to 38mm at the top.

Turrets and conning tower

The cupola of the 194mm turrets was protected by six

[11] The term 'super-soft' is used here to translate the French *extra-doux*; this ductile steel was preferred to hardened steel for the reinforcing deck plates of the early armoured cruisers because when struck by shell it would deform rather than crack. Hardened steels were more likely to spray the stokers and engineering personnel below with splinters. Super-soft steel was also known as *métal de Saint-Jacques*.

Jeanne d'Arc: Protection

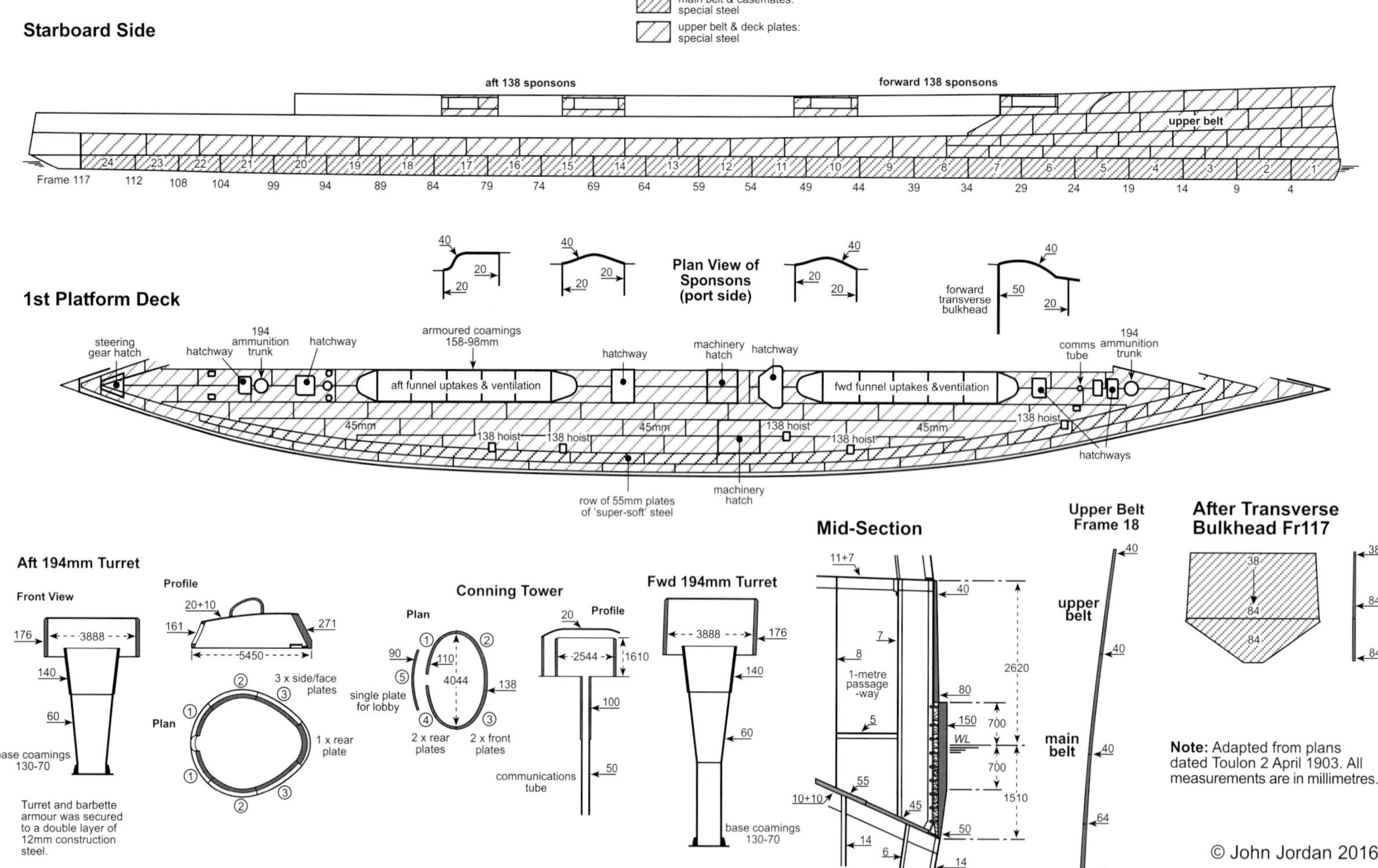

plates of 161mm cemented armour on the face and sides,[12] with a single 271mm 'balancing plate' of mild steel on the rear to stabilise the gunhouse and facilitate training; the armour plates were secured to a double layer of 12mm mild steel. The ring of the fixed parapet above the weather deck was of 176mm special steel and had a similar backing. The inverted cone protecting the shell-handling 'bowl' and the platform for ready-use charges had hoops of 140mm special steel, reducing to 60mm over the hoists; the protective plates were secured to a double thickness of 10mm mild steel.

The conning tower had special steel plating 138mm thick on its face and sides. This was reduced to 110mm on the rear wall, but there was a curved 90mm vertical bulkhead to protect access directly behind it – an arrangement that would become a characteristic feature of the conning tower on major vessels. The communications tube was formed by 100mm hoops of special steel above the second deck, reducing to 60mm behind the upper belt.

JEANNE D'ARC: ARMOUR PLATE THICKNESS MAIN BELT

Plate	Single Strake *upper/lower edge*
1-4	100/50
5	113/50
6	126/50
7	138/50
8-17	150/50
18	136/50
19	122/50
20	108/50
21	94/50
22-24	80/50

Notes:

1 All the protective side plating was of 'special' steel (*acier spécial*), hardened with nickel and chromium; the reinforcing plates on the lower protective deck were of 'super-soft' steel (*acier extra-doux*, otherwise known as *métal de Saint-Jacques*), which was intended to deform rather than crack when struck by enemy shell.

2 The upper belt was in four strakes over the bow section up to the foremast casemate. reducing to a single strake amidships. The latter tapered from 40mm at its upper edge to 80mm at its lower edge. The upper two strakes of the bow section were of 40mm special steel, the lower two were tapered from 40mm to 80mm through 63–65mm at the joint.

MACHINERY

The internal layout of *Jeanne d'Arc* was dominated by the machinery spaces, which occupied virtually the full width of the hull over more than 50 per cent of the ship's length, the hull being sharply tapered fore and aft

12 Note that because the plates were angled inwards at approximately 23° from the vertical, the thickness of plate that a shell striking with a horizontal trajectory would have to pass through was 175mm, approximately the same as for the armoured parapet.

Guyot–du Temple Boiler

Boiler Profile in Cross-section

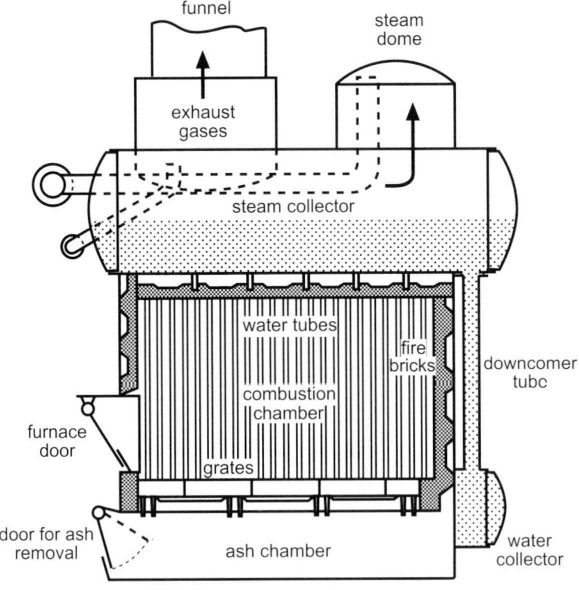

Boiler Facade & Cross-section

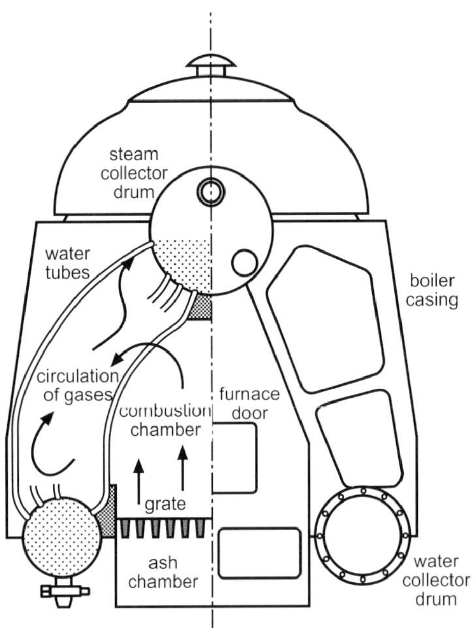

Schematic drawing of a Guyot–du Temple boiler. The du Temple boiler was an 'express' boiler (*à circulation accélérée*) which featured dense nests of tubes of much smaller diameter (30mm) than the Belleville and Niclausse boilers. The tubes were connected at either end to three drums in a triangular arrangement, and formed a vault over the combustion chamber – the tubes are sometimes referred to as 'vertical' tubes, to differentiate them from the tubes of the Belleville and Niclausse large watertube types. The lower two drums were water collectors; the drum at the apex was the steam collector, and was of significantly larger diameter. When the water in the tubes was heated it produced steam under pressure which was channelled from the upper part of the collector to the pistons of the reciprocating engines. The water which accumulated in the bottom of the steam drum was channelled down to the twin water collectors at the base by tubes of greater diameter (200mm) termed 'downcomers', which were located outside the boiler casing.

The tubes in the early du Temple boilers had a distinctive 'S' configuration to enable them to cope with the expansion which would occur at higher temperatures. However, it proved difficult to remove the deposits which accumulated in service, reducing the efficiency of the boiler. In later models the more extreme curves were replaced by a smooth-radiused bend to enable brushes on hinged rods to be passed through them.

(see GA Plans). The three powerful four-cylinder[13] VTE engines were mounted side by side amidships, at the widest part of the hull, and were in individual engine rooms separated by longitudinal watertight bulkheads. The propeller on the centre shaft had a diameter of 4.70m, the propellers for the wing shafts 5.00m.

The engines were served by two large condensers, which were located in a space abaft the engine rooms divided by a centreline bulkhead. Forward of the engine rooms were the midship magazines for the 138.6mm QF guns, with an auxiliary machinery room between and the submerged torpedo flat below. The lateral ammunition passages ran outboard of these spaces at the level of the second platform deck on either side of the ship, connecting the forward QF magazines to the after magazines. A second set of longitudinal compartments between the ammunition passage and the double hull contained reserve feed water for the boilers.

There were four boiler rooms to house the massive Guyot–du Temple small-tube boilers, which were disposed back-to-back in twelve rows of three. The forward boiler rooms were separated by a full-width transverse bulkhead; the after boiler rooms were similarly arranged, but the transverse bulkhead extended the full width of the ship only below the 2nd platform deck, which was potentially a threat to watertight integrity. There were no fewer than eight transverse stokehold platforms (*rues de chauffe*) from which the boilers were operated. The wide separation between the fore and after boiler rooms meant that the funnels were in two groups of three. The narrow forward and after magazines for the 138.6mm QF guns were located outboard of the boiler rooms and were connected by the lateral ammunition passages.

In order to provide electrical power for the turrets, ammunition hoists, searchlight projectors and internal lighting there were four 600A dynamos divided between auxiliary machinery rooms on the 2nd platform deck at either end of the main machinery spaces (see GA Plans). The fore and after auxiliary machinery rooms also housed a Thirion pump rated at 600 tonnes per hour for water evacuation and the auxiliary condensers. A third Thirion pump with a similar

13 One high-pressure (HP), one intermediate-pressure (IP) and two low-pressure (LP) cylinders.

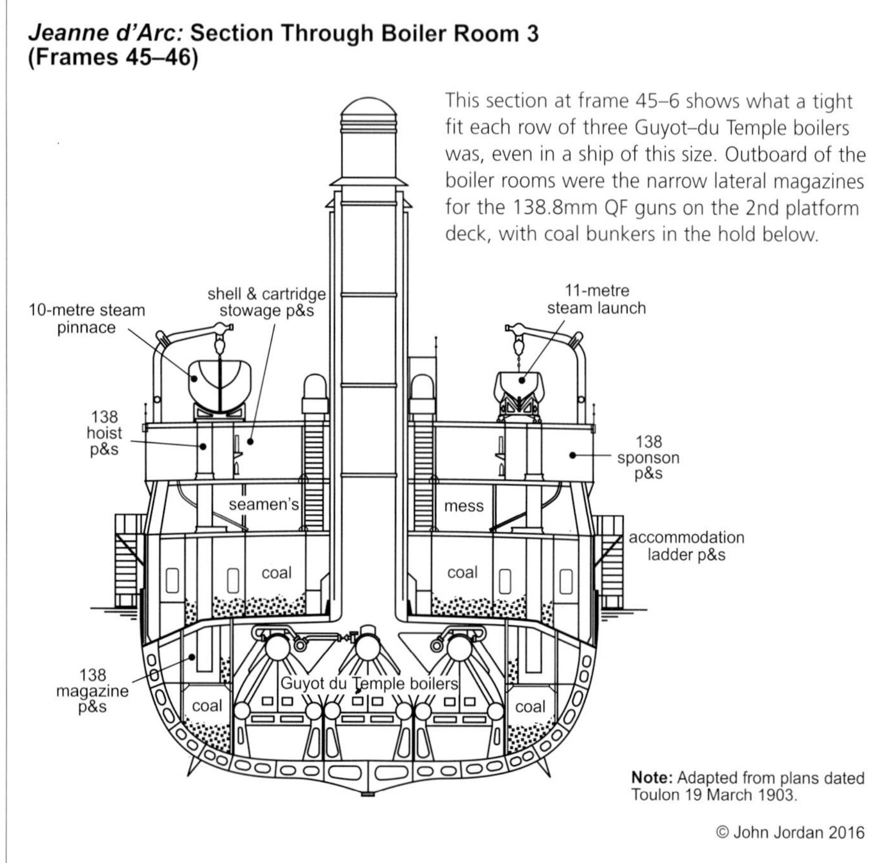

***Jeanne d'Arc:* Section Through Boiler Room 3 (Frames 45–46)**

This section at frame 45–6 shows what a tight fit each row of three Guyot–du Temple boilers was, even in a ship of this size. Outboard of the boiler rooms were the narrow lateral magazines for the 138.8mm QF guns on the 2nd platform deck, with coal bunkers in the hold below.

Note: Adapted from plans dated Toulon 19 March 1903.

capacity was mounted in the midship auxiliary machinery room on the same deck.

CONSTRUCTION AND TRIALS

The construction of *Jeanne d'Arc* was subject to lengthy delays. The ship was laid down at Toulon in October 1896, but little progress was made until the autumn of 1898. Friction between the naval administration and the construction department relating to errors in the stability calculations for the battleship *Carnot* led to the transfer to Brest of assistant engineer Maugas and a reprimand for the most senior constructors in the dockyard, including the director. Following the resumption of work, the cruiser was scheduled for launch in March 1899, but delays in the manufacture of the engines, which should have been installed while the hull was still on the slipway, meant that *Jeanne d'Arc* was launched three months later without them. There would be ongoing issues with the delivery of components of the machinery, which Indret had subcontracted to various private suppliers, causing further delays.

Jeanne d'Arc was manned for trials on 1 March 1901, and static trials of the machinery commenced later that month. Problems were experienced with excessively high temperatures of up to 65° Celsius on the stokehold platforms and a related failure of the feed pumps; these were found to be due to inadequate ventilation and poor insulation of the boiler lagging, and remedial measures were undertaken. Further problems with the Belleville feed pumps were experienced during sea trials in April 1902, leading to modifications to the piston rings of the main engines. Finally, during a full-power trial on 8 November 1902, the engines attained their designed rating of 33,000CV at the specified revolutions. However, the maximum speed attained was only 21.8 knots, and a subsequent inspection revealed that the propellers were thickly encrusted with marine growth. This was a great disappointment; on the other hand, no problems were experienced with the boiler feed, combustion was good, and the temperature on the stokehold platforms did not exceed 36° Celsius. Meanwhile, trials of the armament had been proceeding since 28 December 1901 and were completely satisfactory.

Acceptance trials were conducted from December 1902, and the functioning of the engines and steam plant was deemed to be completely satisfactory. However, the maximum speed attained was still only 21.72 knots with 29,596CV. Modifications were subsequently made to the propellers and the 'A' brackets supporting the shafts – a modification already applied to the fast cruiser *Guichen* – and a strip was removed from the bilge keels to reduce skin friction. In theory these modifications should have resulted in an increase in speed for a given horsepower, but in practice they made little difference.

EARLY SERVICE

Commissioned on 10 March 1903, *Jeanne d'Arc* embarked President Emile Loubet at Marseille on 14 April and left for Algiers. Following official visits to Algeria and Tunisia, the president reembarked at Bizerte for the return voyage.

On 20 May *Jeanne d'Arc* left Toulon for Brest, replacing the armoured cruiser *Bruix* as the flagship of Rear Admiral Bugard from 1 June. (For the composition of the Northern Squadron at that time see the accompanying table.) On 14 September, following serious problems with her boilers, *Jeanne d'Arc* was placed in normal reserve at Brest. Manned for further trials on 8 October she was decommissioned for repairs on 15 November. In May 1905 she was again manned for trials, only to return to the reserve on 6 August of that year.

On 26 May 1906 *Jeanne d'Arc* was assigned to the Mediterranean Light Squadron to replace *Marseillaise* as the flagship of Rear Admiral Campion; the other armoured cruisers in the squadron were *Condé* and *Kléber*. The cruiser left Brest on 5 June for Tangier, visiting Gibraltar in early July; she left Tangier on 12 July for Toulon. On 16 September she was present at a great naval review, attended by President Armand Fallières, which took place at Marseille to mark the laying of the first stone of the Rove canal.

On 23 January 1908 *Jeanne d'Arc* sailed from Morocco for Brest, calling at Gibraltar *en route*. Shortly after she put to sea a serious accident to boiler No 8 resulted in the deaths of five stokers; three others were badly burned. In reserve for repairs from 15 April 1908, *Jeanne d'Arc* was initially attached to the Northern Squadron's 2nd Cruiser Division – the other

Opposite: *Jeanne d'Arc* during her speed trials, when she attained a maximum of 21.8 knots instead of the hoped-for 23 knots. *(DR)*

Below: A fine stern view of the ship at her moorings. The photo was probably taken in 1904–05, when she was based at Brest. *(H Laurent)*

NORTHERN SQUADRON 1 JUNE 1903

1re Division cuirassée:	*Masséna* (VA Caillard), *Formidable, Dévastation*
2e Division cuirassée:	*Bouvines* (CA Stéphan), *Amiral-Tréhouart, Valmy*
Division de croiseurs:	*Jeanne d'Arc* (CA Bugard), *Guichen, Dupuy-de-Lôme*
Division navale de l'Atlantique:	*Tage* (CA Rivet), *Jurien-de-la-Gravière, Troude, D'Estrées*

ships in the division were *Marseillaise* (flag) and *Gueydon* – but was then taken out of service for modifications that would enable her to be used as a school ship for officer cadets from the naval college.

Recommissioned on 20 May 1911, the cruiser was attached to the 3rd Division of the Reserve Squadron but remained at Brest. On 1 May 1912 she was assigned to the Atlantic Training Division, then commanded by Rear Admiral Bouxin; the division included the protected cruisers *Châteaurenault* and *D'Estrées*. On 10 October 1912 *Jeanne d'Arc* sailed on her first world cruise, which took her to Bahía (Brazil), Fort-de-France (Martinique), Dakar, Toulon, Naples, Bizerte, La Pallice, Kronstadt, Bergen and Trondheim; she returned to Brest on 29 July 1913. Her second cruise, starting on 10 October, took her to the Indian Ocean, returning via the Suez Canal and arriving back at Brest on 27 July 1914. On the outbreak of war she was assigned to the 1st Division of the 2nd Light Squadron, serving with *Marseillaise* (flagship of CA Rouyer) and *Amiral Aube*.

EVALUATION

Jeanne d'Arc was a groundbreaking design in so many ways: hull-form, turret design, protection system and machinery installation all represented a major conceptual advance on earlier French armoured cruisers. However, she was essentially a 'technology demonstrator', and many of the design features she introduced were less successful than had been hoped. In particular, she never attained the high speed that was her *raison d'être* and to which many aspects of her design were subordinated, and the extreme length and relative fineness of the hull resulted in a lack of manoeuvrability; her turning circle on trials was c2000m. The light construction of her hull also made her subject to vibration, and the decks under the dynamos and steering engines had to be reinforced after completion in order to provide the necessary rigidity.

Jeanne d'Arc was significantly longer than contemporary battleships and had a similar displacement.[14] She was also expensive to build: unit cost was more than twice that of her predecessors and approximately

[14] The battleships of the *Charlemagne* class, laid down 1894–6, displaced 11,260 tonnes and had a length between perpendiculars of only 117.5m.

Below: *Jeanne d'Arc* in the mouth of the River Penfeld at Brest on 15 February 1908, following the boiler explosion off Gibraltar which killed five stokers and injured three more. She is still in her early livery of black hull and buff upperworks. *(H Laurent)*

Above: *Jeanne d'Arc* in the upper Penfeld at Brest between 1908 and 1911. She would be fitted out to serve as a school ship for officer cadets. *(Private collection)*

80 per cent that of a contemporary battleship of the *Charlemagne* class. Moreover, the extraordinary delays in construction at Toulon meant that she entered service much later than anticipated, thereby diminishing her impact on the international stage. Significantly, only one more large warship, the armoured cruiser *Dupetit-Thouars* of the *Gueydon* class (see Chapter 5), would be built at Toulon.[15]

Plagued by problems with her boilers and engines, *Jeanne d'Arc* would serve with the fleet for only five years before being relegated to a training role. Many of these problems would ultimately be resolved – or at least resolved sufficiently to be 'managed'. The ship would be reactivated to play her part in the Great War, and would even resume her role as school ship for officer cadets after the war.

Despite her technical limitations, *Jeanne d'Arc* provided the base-line for a new generation of armoured cruisers of more modest dimensions, all designed by Bertin, which showed a better balance between speed, armament and protection. The revolutionary *tourelle-barbette* would be further developed for later models of the 194mm gun and also for the 164.7mm guns of the same generation. Nor was the troublesome Guyot–du Temple small-tube boiler a technological dead end. On the contrary, newer, improved models would be installed in some of the later armoured cruisers, and the Guyot–du Temple boiler would come to be the standard type fitted in the generation of cruisers and destroyers designed and built during the 1920s.

THE C3 PROJECT

On 17 March 1897 the *Conseil des Travaux* met to discuss a proposed successor to *Jeanne d'Arc* designated C3. Characteristics were broadly similar except for a slight increase in dimensions (length 151m pp *vice* 145m, beam 20.24m *vice* 19.42m) and displacement (11,456 tonnes); speed and protection were unchanged.

The main difference concerned the armament. A new QF model of the 164.7mm gun was now available, and the fourteen 138.6mm guns of *Jeanne d'Arc* were to be replaced by ten 164.7mm Mle 1893–1896 guns (see Chapters 4 and 5), of which eight were in casemates and two in shielded upper-deck mountings, and four 100mm QF guns in open mountings, also on the upper deck. The casemate guns would have been mounted in a central battery (*redoute*) with armoured transverse bulkheads 60mm aft and 50mm forward; this 'redoubt' was to be divided into individual casemates by 20mm partition walls. The outer faces of the end casemates were to be 116mm (to include a double layer of 8mm plating), those of the central casemates 72mm.

The *Conseil des Travaux* was scathing about the project, which departed from the characteristics of future fleet cruisers outlined by the *Conseil supérieur* in its session of December 1896, and the tone of the report is a reflection of the antagonism developing between Bertin and the naval establishment.

[15] A second, *Victor Hugo*, was initially assigned to Toulon, but the order was subsequently transferred to Lorient (see Chapter 7).

Above: *Jeanne d'Arc* in a foreign port during one of her pre-war training cruises. The covers for the after funnels are rigged, suggesting that only the forward boilers are lit. The hinged covers for the sponsons are in the lowered position. *(Leo van Ginderen collection)*

Virtually all the detailed criticisms focused on the proposed speed of 23 knots. In the view of members of the *Conseil*, this was responsible for the extreme length of the proposed ship and the corresponding (and costly) increase in displacement; it contributed nothing to the offensive and defensive characteristics of the ship. A speed of 20 knots was considered sufficient for an armoured cruiser designed to operate with the fleet – a view supported by the CSM conclusions. A well-armed ship with good protection should be able to engage its counterparts successfully, so no speed margin was necessary, as a 20-knot ship could easily outrun a more powerful vessel (ie a battleship). The *Conseil* considered the proposed speed of 23 knots more appropriate to a smaller type of unarmoured dispatch cruiser deployed as a 'link ship' tasked with transmitting sighting data to the C-in-C with the battle squadron while the scouting force of armoured cruisers maintained contact with the enemy.

It was, moreover, inconceivable that the C3 design would be employed as a commerce raider. The *Conseil* considered the utility of such ships in any case problematic, but a commerce-raiding cruiser did not need to be armoured, and merchant ships were generally capable of only 12–13 knots. The exceptionally large coal bunkerage was no more justifiable than high speed. The figure of 5500nm at 10 knots was considered adequate even for the station cruiser proposal submitted to the *Conseil*; 9000nm with a full load of coal (*surcharge*) was deemed more than sufficient for a ship of this type.

Finally, the *Conseil* was unhappy with the level of protection accorded to the ship's vitals and guns, and also with the arrangement of the forward guns, for which the large casemate opening was incompletely closed by a mobile shield only 72mm thick.

The *Conseil des Travaux* made it abundantly clear that it was resolutely opposed to the project, and the current Minister of Marine, Armand Besnard, was less supportive of Bertin's ideas than his predecessor Lockroy. The ship was never laid down, and the next series of French armoured cruisers would be slower, with a designed speed of 21 knots, and would have more modest dimensions.

CHAPTER 4:

THE STATION CRUISERS OF THE *DUPLEIX* CLASS

IN HIS SEMINAL WORK *The Development of a Modern Navy*, written in 1937 but published only in 1987 by the US Naval Institute Press, the historian Theodore Ropp postulated that the confusion surrounding French cruiser policy during the mid-1890s was a consequence of the battles between three warring factions within the French Navy that took place in four key forums: the *Conseil supérieur de la Marine*, the *Conseil des Travaux*, the Ministry and the parliamentary Budgetary Committee. The three factions were: the *Jeune Ecole*, which favoured lightly-armed commerce-raiding cruisers with long range and high speed to enable them to evade pursuing enemy vessels; the older admirals, whose influence was a dead hand on both of the *Conseils* and who wanted, in addition to a squadron composed almost exclusively of battleships, cruising ships for foreign stations; and the officers with a more 'modern' outlook, who wanted armoured cruisers and small scouts to operate with the battle fleet.

The arguments were complicated by an unstable political situation, with frequent changes in administration that brought into office Ministers of Marine with their own personal enthusiasms and prejudices. The two Ministers during the period in question were Admiral Armand Besnard, a naval man of the 'old school', Minister from 17 January 1895 in 1 November 1895, then again from 29 April 1896 to 28 June 1898; and Edouard Lockroy, a radical politician and reformer, who served from 1 November 1895 to 29 April 1896 and again from 28 June 1898 to 22 June 1899. It was Lockroy who authorised the large, fast armoured cruiser *Jeanne d'Arc* shortly after his accession in November 1895 (see Chapter 3) in the face of opposition from the *Conseil des Travaux*.

On 29 April 1896, after only five months in the post, Lockroy was succeeded by Besnard. The latter wanted a smaller type of protected cruiser for foreign stations, and duly obtained approval by the *Chambre des Députés* in 1897, but the design was flatly rejected by the *Conseil des Travaux* (Meetings of 24 August, 1 September and 10 December) on the grounds that it could not stand up to the cruisers currently being built for commerce protection by the British Royal Navy. The *Conseil* was of the view that France already had too many protected cruisers and that what the Navy really required was 'ships that can deal out and withstand punishment'.[1]

Meanwhile, in 1896 the *Conseil supérieur* had drawn up a new naval programme that included three new armoured cruisers and three new protected cruisers for overseas service, together with five armoured 'fleet' cruisers for European waters (see table).

During this period Besnard's rival, Lockroy, was chairman of the Budget Committee. Lockroy was influenced by arguably the foremost naval theoretician of his generation, Vice Admiral François-Ernest Fournier,

[1] '... *il lui faut des bâtiments de combat, c'est-à-dire capable de donner des coups et d'en recevoir*' (Meeting of 10 December 1897).

STATUT NAVAL 1896 (PERIOD: 1897–1904)

	Total	New-build
European Waters		
Fleet battleships	28	8
Armoured cruisers	12	5
2nd class cruisers	12	1
3rd class cruisers	12	1
Torpedo boat destroyers (300t)	30	16
Fleet torpedo boats (150t)	30	29
Coast Defence – to be formed into third squadron		
Coast defence battleships	(9)	–
Armoured cruisers	3	3
2nd class cruisers	3	3
3rd class cruisers	3	3
Torpedo boat destroyers (300t)	9	9
Fleet torpedo boats (150t)	9	9
Coast Defence – assigned to defensive		
Coast defence battleships/Armoured gunboats	(14)	–
Torpedo sloops (400t)	20	10
1st class torpedo boats	200	62
Overseas Stations		
Armoured station cruisers	4	3
1st class station cruisers (raiders)	2	0
2nd class station cruisers	6	0
3rd class station cruisers	5	3
1st class sloops	7	3
Gunboats	10	4
Transport sloops	7	0

Notes:

1 The 1896 programme was a statement of intent, and had no legal force; funding for ships in the programme would have to be requested year on year. Not all of the planned ships would be authorised or built. The 1896 programme would effectively be superseded by the 1900 programme (see Chapter 6), which was statutory.

2 The coast defence battleships (numbers in brackets) were the existing ships, and were not to be replaced.

3 The three armoured cruisers to be built for station service overseas became the *Dupleix* class. The existing ship was *D'Entrecasteaux*, which was already authorised and building.

4 The seven armoured cruisers already built or building were: *Dupuy-de-Lôme*, the four ships of the *Amiral Charner* class, *Pothuau* and *Jeanne d'Arc*. In 1898 the number of armoured cruisers for European waters was increased from twelve to eighteen; the total number of armoured cruisers, including the seven for coast defence and overseas stations, was now to be twenty-five.

Source: Ropp, *The Development of a Modern Navy: French Naval Policy 1871–1904*, pp 365–6.

who favoured the construction of a large number of armoured cruisers smaller than *Jeanne d'Arc* capable both of operating with the fleet as strategic scouts (*croiseurs d'avant-garde*) and of commerce raiding. When in 1897 Besnard presented a proposal for the construction of a battleship, two armoured and two protected cruisers to be funded under the 1898 budget, the Budget committee struck out the battleship and offered 120 million FF for armoured cruisers and 60 million FF for torpedo boats and submarines.

Initially Besnard proposed an enlarged *Jeanne d'Arc* (C3 – see Chapter 3), but this was rejected by the *Conseil des Travaux* in its meeting of 17 March 1897. He then proposed three 7200-tonne station cruisers that became the *Dupleix* class, balancing this proposal with three 'fleet' armoured cruisers of the type favoured by Fournier, for service in European waters. The *Conseil* was unhappy with the creation of a 'special class of station cruiser'. However, Besnard's compromise proposal was welcomed by both the traditionalists and younger officers of the Fournier faction. It also dovetailed neatly with the programme of construction drawn up by the *Conseil supérieur* and with the requirements of the Budget Committee: each of the three cruisers of the *Dupleix* class would cost approximately 19 million FF, each of the three fleet cruisers 21 million FF (total 120 million FF).

THE ARMOURED STATION CRUISER

There was an irresistible logic behind the preference expressed by both the *Conseil supérieur* and the *Conseil des Travaux* in their respective meetings of December 1896 for a standard armoured cruiser that could serve both in home waters and overseas. French naval design during the early 1890s had been too disjointed, too experimental. The *Flotte d'échantillons* was the most obvious example, but in terms of armoured cruisers the period had produced only *Pothuau* and *D'Entrecasteaux*, very different ships designed for different theatres; even the smaller protected cruisers had been built in two and threes, and the three 'fast' cruisers laid down in 1894–6 differed markedly from one another despite being intended for the same commerce-raiding role. These ships all had different hulls and machinery; only the guns, which were designed and built at the Navy's establishment at Ruelle, had any sort of commonality. This greatly complicated the provision of spare parts and the training of personnel.

However, there was considerable resistance to this move towards uniformity. Flag officers who served in the Far East pointed out that the geographical and political demands of the theatre were very different to those in Europe. Ports and harbours were less well-developed, the prevailing weather and sea conditions could be more demanding, and the distances that needed to be covered in a normal deployment were of a completely different order. The pressure for ships designed to meet these different challenges is encapsulated in a submission to the Minister of Marine (Edouard Lockroy) from Vice Admiral Beaumont, C-in-C of the Far East Squadron, dated 5 October 1898. The memo is handwritten, and is a response to the proposal to lay down two armoured cruisers of 10,000 tons (*Gloire* class – see Chapter 6) for deployment to the Far East.

Beaumont expresses his opposition to the proposal. In his opinion, such a ship would be poorly suited to

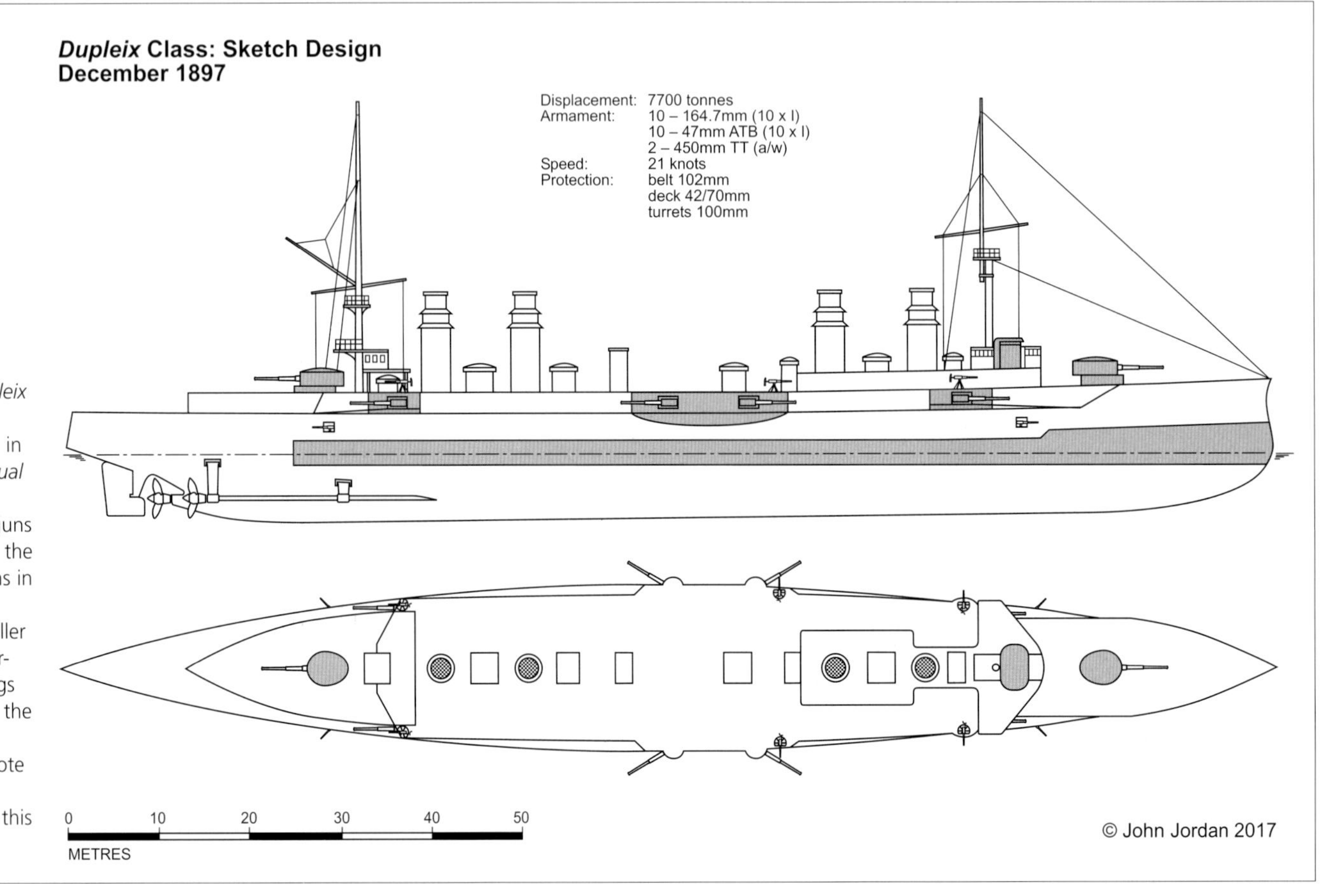

A re-working of the sketch plans of *Dupleix* with ten single 164.7mm published in *Brassey's Naval Annual* from 1899 to 1902. The fore and after guns are in single turrets, the remaining eight guns in individual armoured casemates. The smaller guns on open upper-deck pivot mountings and behind ports in the sides of the hull are 47mm ATB guns. Note that there were no 100mm QF guns at this stage of the plans.

Dupleix:
Profile & Plan

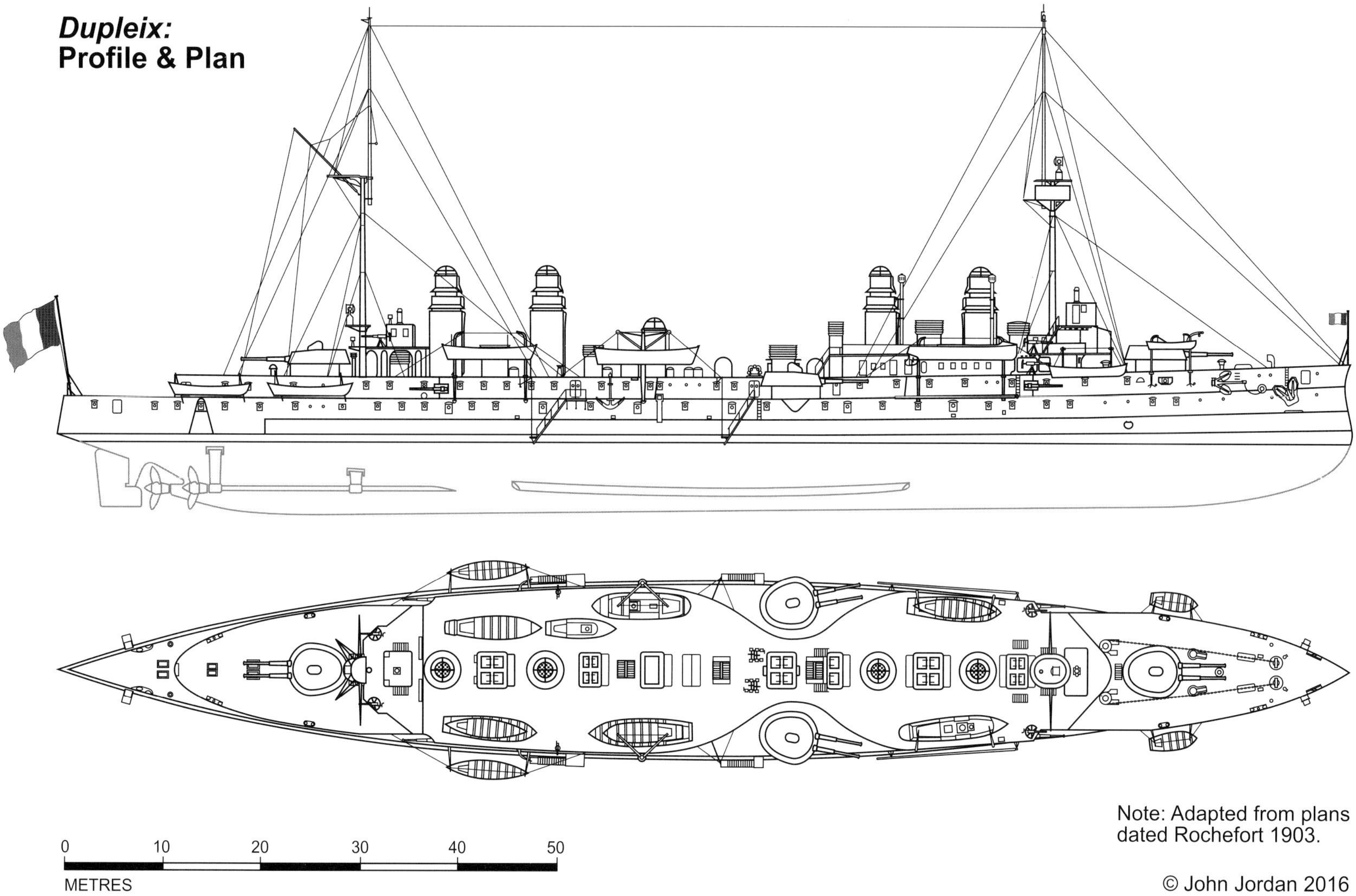

0 10 20 30 40 50
METRES

Note: Adapted from plans dated Rochefort 1903.

© John Jordan 2016

operations in the Eastern theatre. Its large size would be a hindrance when entering and berthing in many of the ports of China and the Philippines.[2] Beaumont's expressed preference was for three cruisers of 7500 tonnes (8000 tonnes maximum) with the following qualities: robust and seaworthy (high freeboard forward to cope with the Pacific swell) and a maximum draught of 7m (for easy access to ports on all tides); three shafts for a top speed of 19.5 knots, able to sustain 16 knots for several days; well-ventilated spaces with particular attention to the cooling of machinery rooms and magazines; no big, slow-firing guns but multiple 164.7mm QF, all-electric gun mechanisms (no hydraulics), and no above-water torpedo tubes; able to remain on station for long periods and to be maintained at Saigon.

Beaumont does not mention copper and wood hull sheathing, but this was generally a given for cruisers specifically designed for operations in tropical waters. It served to reduce marine growth on the underside of the hull, so dockings needed to be less frequent. The downside was that sheathing added to the cost of the ship and increased displacement by 300–500 tonnes. Other disadvantages that led to its eventual abandon-

Left: The launch of *Dupleix* at Rochefort Naval Dockyard on 28 April 1900. *(Private collection)*

[2] Beaumont cites the difficulties experienced by the British cruiser *Powerful* (14,200 tons, 152.4m pp – see Chapter 3) when deployed to the Far East.

ment were that the wood had a tendency to absorb water as it aged, further slowing the ship, and could not be secured to the face-hardened armour that was being fitted from the late 1890s.

THE *AVANT-PROJETS*

The first proposal by the *Service Technique* for the new station cruiser appears to have been drawn up in December 1896, and was approved by Minister Besnard. It was for a ship of 7300 tonnes. The three-shaft propulsion system was rated at 17,000CV for a maximum speed of 21 knots; endurance was 5000nm at 10 knots. The ship was to have a complement of 550 officers and men (including flag staff), and there was stowage for 75 days of provisions.

The main armament comprised ten 164.7mm QF guns, disposed in single enclosed turrets fore and aft with the remaining eight guns in casemates (see Preliminary Sketch). There were to be ten 47mm ATB guns and two 450mm above-water torpedo tubes.

Protection comprised a 70mm belt on a double layer of 8mm plating and a protective deck with 22mm armour plating on a double layer of 10mm mild steel over the horizontal section and 50mm plates of super-soft steel on the slopes. The turrets and the conning tower were to have 80mm armour on a double layer of 10mm plating, and the faces of the casemates 70mm armour on a double layer of 8mm. There were transverse bulkheads to close the after end of the belt (40mm) and to protect the casemates against enfilading fire (60–80mm), all secured to a double layer of 8mm steel. Masts were to be the plain poles specified for station cruisers, with a single platform on the foremast for rangefinding.

The *Conseil des Travaux* met on 31 December 1896, and requested a number of modifications. Members were unhappy with the coal bunkerage, which they considered insufficient for a station cruiser designed for overseas deployment. They were likewise unhappy with the level of protection afforded to the cellular layer. In order to address these issues it was thought that an increase in the displacement to 7600 tonnes would be necessary; failing this, additional coal bunkerage would have to be worked into the 7300-tonne design.

Bertin had similar concerns regarding the thickness of the side protection, and in a memo to the Minister dated 18 April pointed out that even an 84mm belt of special steel could be penetrated by all calibres down to 100mm at a range of 2000m. He duly produced a new design, which was considered by the *Conseil* at its meeting on 4 May 1897. The major changes were a significant increase in protection for the cellular layer and in endurance. The thickness of the armour plating on the belt, the turrets and the conning tower was now 100mm – the protective deck was unchanged – and the thickness of the plating on the faces of the casemates was increased from 72mm to 76–100mm. There was

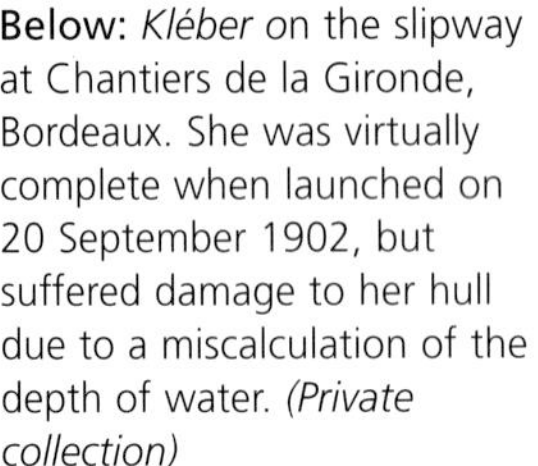

Below: *Kléber* on the slipway at Chantiers de la Gironde, Bordeaux. She was virtually complete when launched on 20 September 1902, but suffered damage to her hull due to a miscalculation of the depth of water. *(Private collection)*

Left: *Dupleix* passing under the Transporter Bridge at Rochefort shortly after her completion in 1903. *(Private collection)*

now sufficient bunkerage in the lower hull for 880 tonnes of coal, giving a theoretical radius of 6450nm at 10 knots. These measures, however, were at the cost of two of the 164.7mm casemate guns; there were now three guns in evenly-spaced casemates on either side of the ship.

The *Conseil* noted the improvements in protection and endurance while (typically) regretting the reduction in offensive power. It reiterated the view expressed in December that a special type of station cruiser was unnecessary, but considered the programme executable and generally well-developed. A few small modifications were recommended, including the reinstatement of the two casemate guns. In the definitive design displacement increased again to 7700 tonnes.

The order for *Dupleix* was placed with the Rochefort naval dockyard on 18 December 1897; it replaced an order for a protected cruiser of 5500 tonnes designated D3, which was cancelled. *Desaix* was ordered from the Société de la Loire and *Kléber* from the Société de la Gironde; the contracts for both of the ships built in private shipyards were signed on 28 December 1897, but it would be a further twelve months before keels were laid.

REARMAMENT

In the summer of 1898, by which time work had already begun on the plates and frames of *Dupleix*, the *Conseil des Travaux* proposed replacing the ten 164.7mm guns, currently disposed in single enclosed turrets fore and aft and in casemates, by eight 164.7mm in twin turrets disposed in a distinctive 'lozenge' arrangement, with the addition of four 100mm QF guns to be fitted at the 'corners' of the ship. This proposal received the support of the Minister, who asked the *Directeur du Matériel*, Jules Thibaudier, to consider suspending the construction of the ships and instructed the *Service Technique* to undertake the necessary studies.

Bertin was distinctly unhappy with the proposed changes. In a submission to the Minister dated 13 August, he reiterated his opposition to these ships, which he had voiced throughout the months May to October of the previous year, prior to their authorisation. He also pointed out the inherent problem with mounting two QF guns in a twin turret: the guns were necessarily mounted on either side of the axis, and the firing of the first gun resulted in oscillations that disturbed the loading and laying of the second, resulting in a lower rate of fire and a loss of accuracy. In support of his argument he cited recent trials in which one of the twin 138.6mm turrets of the battleship *Jauréguiberry* had been pitted against a single turret of the cruiser *Latouche-Tréville*.

The other problem for Bertin was that the STCN was currently fully occupied with plans for the new 10,000-tonne cruisers (*Gloire* class, see Chapter 6) and the 15,000-tonne battleships (*Patrie* class). He therefore proposed that responsibility for the redesign of the *Dupleix* class be devolved onto the engineers of Rochefort naval dockyard. However, by February 1899, Bertin was able to confirm that the new drawings would be with the Minister by early March, and that construction of *Desaix* and *Kléber*, which had been ordered from private shipyards, could proceed up to the armoured deck. The proposal received ministerial approval on 6 April and new drawings were issued.

Documentation held in the CAA for *Kléber* and

BUILDING DATA

Name	Builder	Laid down	Launched	Trials	Commissioned
Dupleix	Arsenal de Rochefort	18 Jan 1899	28 Apr 1900	15 Mar 1903	15 Sep 1903
Desaix	Société de la Loire	early 1899	21 Mar 1901	6 Aug 1902	5 Apr 1904
Kléber	Société de la Gironde	early 1899	20 Sep 1902	26 Sep 1902	4 Jul 1904

CHARACTERISTICS

Displacement:	7700 tonnes
Dimensions:	
Length	130.00m pp; 132.10m oa
Beam	17.8m wl
Draught	7.46m aft
Propulsion:	
Boilers	*Des & Dup:* 24 Belleville boilers, 20kg/cm^2
	K: 20 Niclausse boilers, 18kg/cm^2
Engines	*Des & Dup:* 3-shaft 4-cylinder VTE
	K: 3-shaft 3-cylinder VTE
Horsepower	17,100CV (designed)
Speed	21 knots (designed)
Coal	880 tonnes normal; 1200 tonnes full load
Endurance	6450nm at 10 knots; 1210nm at 21 knots
Armament:	
Main guns	8 x 164.7mm/45 Mle 1893–1896 in twin turrets
Medium guns	4 x 100mm/45 Mle 1893 QF in single mountings
ATB guns	10 x 47mm/40 Mle 1885 QF in single mountings
	2–4 x 37mm QF in single mountings
Torpedo tubes	2 a/w tubes for 450mm torpedoes
	6 torpedoes Mle 1892
Protection:	
Main belt	102mm max
Deck	22/50mm
164 turrets	110mm
Conning tower	120mm
Boats:	1 x 11m steam launch
	1 x 10m steam pinnace
	1 x 7.65m White launch
	1 x 10.5m pulling pinnace
	1 x 10m admiral's gig
	2 x 9.5m pulling cutters
	1 x 8m pulling cutter
	4 x 8.5m whalers
	2 x 5m dinghies
Complement:	
As private ship	19 officers, 550 men
As flagship	+ 5 officers, 33 men

Opposite: *Desaix* during her trials, which took place in 1902. Compared to French battleships of the day, these ships had a lean, uncluttered silhouette. *(Private collection)*

Desaix shows that the contracts were amended to specify a change in armament (*remaniement/changement de l'artillerie*) on 22 August and 3 September 1900 respectively.[3] The change appears to have resulted in major delays in the construction of the ships: building times from laying down to completion were between five and a half and six years. The order for the turrets for *Desaix* was placed with the Compagnie des Forges & Aciéries de la Marine et des Chemins de Fer at Saint-Chamond (Loire); data is lacking for the other two ships.

NOMENCLATURE

Joseph-François, marquis **Dupleix** (1697–1763) was a trader in the service of the Compagnie des Indes who made many voyages to America and India. In 1742, having worked to extend the influence of France in the Indies, he became Governor General of the French establishment in India and the rival of the British Major-General Robert Clive.

Louis-Charles-Antoine **Desaix** (1768–1800) was a prominent French general during the French Revolutionary Wars. He made his reputation during Napoleon Bonaparte's Egyptian campaign. He was killed by a musket ball at Marengo (Italy) while leading his three regiments against the enemy's centre.

Jean-Baptiste **Kléber** (1753–1800) was likewise a prominent French general during the French Revolutionary Wars. He served in the Rhineland during the War of the First Coalition then, following a brief retirement, returned to military service to accompany Napoleon in the Egyptian Campaign of 1798–9. On Napoleon's departure Kléber was appointed commander of the French forces there. He was assassinated by a student in Cairo in 1800.

HULL AND SUPERSTRUCTURES

In terms of their general hull design and layout the *Dupleix* class, like their 'fleet' counterparts of the *Gueydon* class (see Chapter 5), were classic Bertin three-shaft cruisers, both types being essentially scaled-down versions of *Jeanne d'Arc*. The engines were amidships, at the widest point of the hull, with the boiler rooms fore and aft and two widely-spaced pairs of funnels. The magazines for the wing turrets, which in the original design would have served the midship casemate guns, were between the forward boiler rooms and the engine rooms, and the condensers for the main engines in two side-by-side compartments directly abaft the engine rooms (see GA Plans)

The slightly larger *Gueydon* class had a light military foremast on the pattern of *Jeanne d'Arc*, the *Dupleix* class two simple steel poles. Both types had a forecastle deck that extended almost to the stern, so that the turrets fore and aft had a similar command. The wing turrets of *Dupleix* were one deck lower, and the forecastle deck was pinched in at the waist to enable the turrets to rotate through their designed arcs of 156° (78° fore and aft of the beam). The accommodation for the admiral, the flag staff and the ships' senior officers was in the after section of the forecastle deck.

Frame spacing was 1.2m, as in *Jeanne d'Arc*, and there was a double bottom that extended from the bow to the after magazines. The arrangement of the decks was likewise as in *Jeanne d'Arc*, and the nomenclature for the decks was similar except that the 'main deck' in the *Dupleix* class was the armoured deck: (from keel upwards) *Cale*, *Premier faux-pont*, *Pont principal*, *Premier pont*, *Deuxième pont*, *Troisième Pont*.[4]

ARMAMENT

Main guns

As with its larger companion, the 194mm gun, the 164.7mm/45 Mle 1893–1896 was distinguished from the earlier Mle 1893 principally in being designed for a more powerful propellant charge. The chamber length of the Mle 1893 was just over 950mm and chamber volume was 27dm^3; the respective figures

[3] No such amendment was necessary for *Dupleix*, which was building at Rochefort; any revision of the original armament would have been the subject of a Ministerial Directive.

[4] Interestingly, the turret plans from Saint-Chamond for *Desaix*, which are dated 1904, retain the older deck nomenclature (*Pont des gaillards*, etc), the only difference being that the former *Pont de la batterie* is designated *Pont intermédiaire*.

Desaix: GA Plans

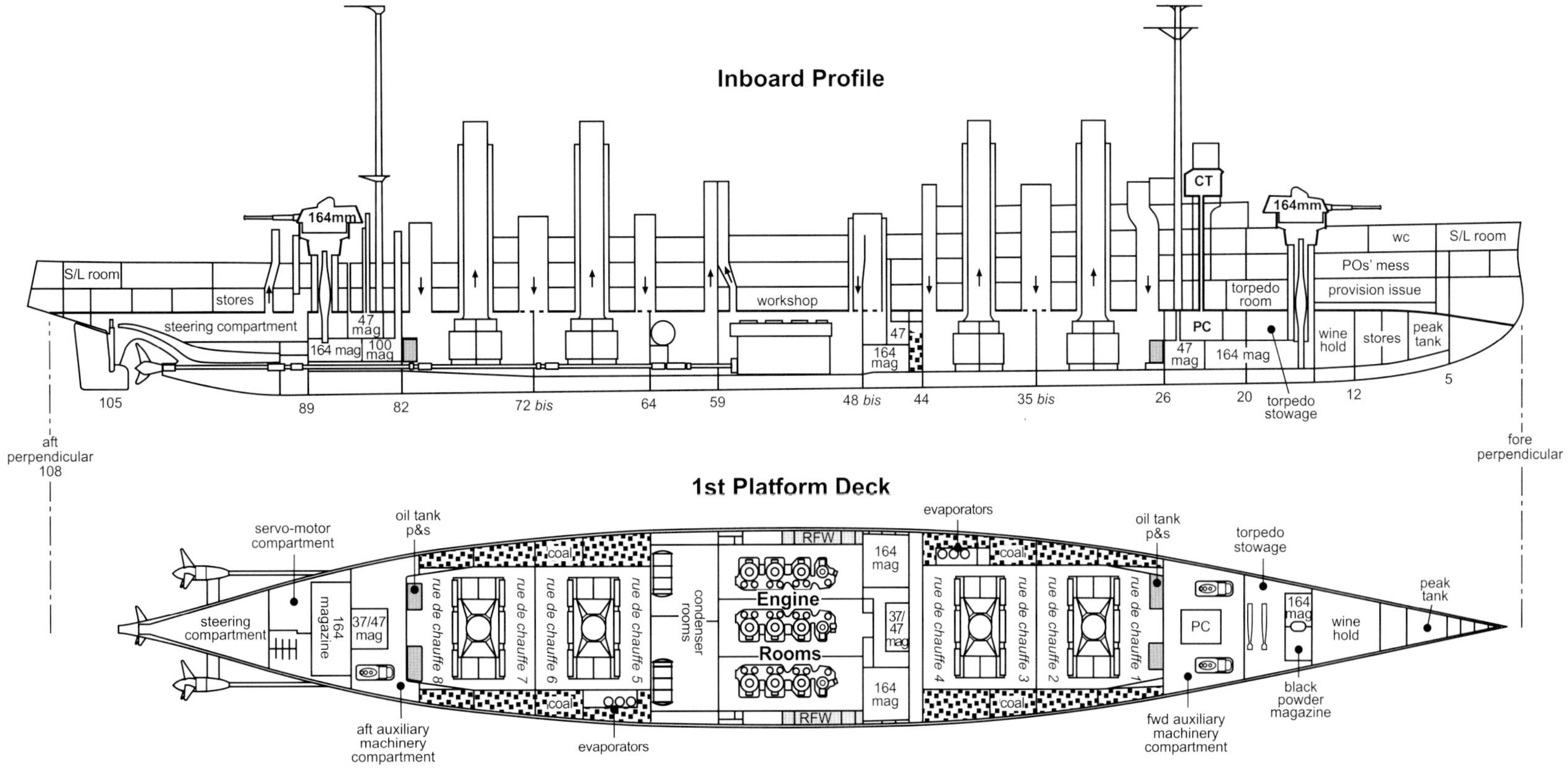

Inboard Profile

1st Platform Deck

Note: Adapted from plans dated Saint-Nazaire 28 September 1903.

for the Mle 1893–1896 were approximately 1300mm and 36.7dm^3. The Mle 1893,[5] which constituted the main armament of the latest French protected cruisers (including the 'fast' cruisers *Guichen*, *Châteaurenault* and *Jurien de la Gravière*) had its 13.1kg BM9 propellant in a single cartridge case. The propellant charge for the Mle 1893–1896, on the other hand, was not only significantly larger – 18.3kg of BM9 for the CI shell, 19.8kg BM10/11 for steel shell – but was divided into a fore charge in a bag of serge or silk cloth and a main cartridge with a brass case for ease of handling. The standard CI, AP and SAP shell could be fired to greater ranges, but at the expense of greater complexity in magazine stowage and ammunition supply.

The twin turret was similar in principle to that of the 194mm single turret mounted in *Jeanne d'Arc*, but with a number of significant improvements in layout, most of which concerned the stowage of ready-use ammunition and the ammunition supply to the guns. As in the 194mm *tourelle-barbette* of *Jeanne d'Arc*, the upper part of the gunhouse was an armoured cupola with inclined sides, while the lower part was protected by a fixed ring of vertical armour. The gunhouse itself needed to be broader in order to accommodate the two

[5] Designated '*à tir rapide*' or '*à T.R.*' (quick-firing or QF) on the plans.

Kléber: Sections

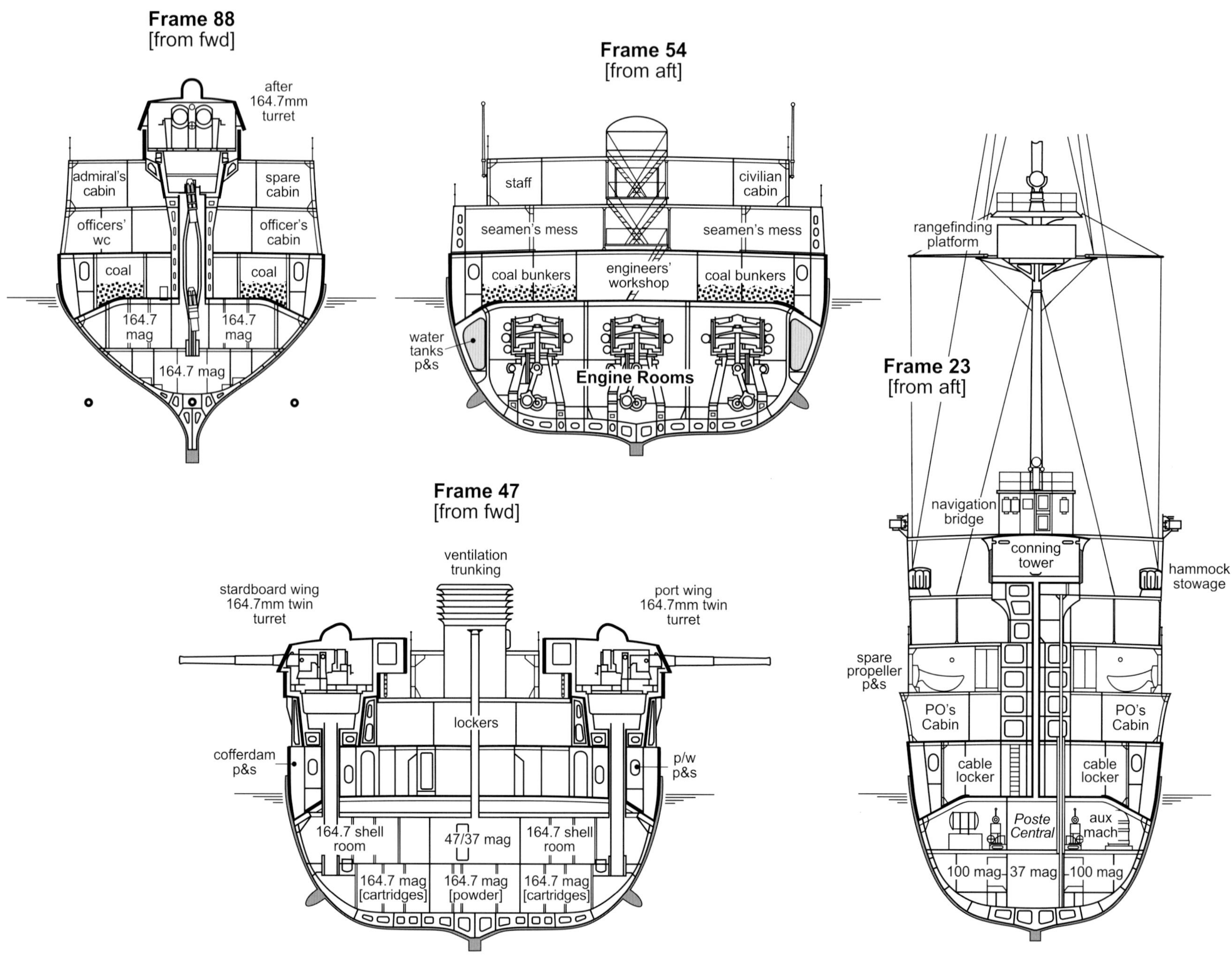

guns, and the internal layout was symmetrical, with the shell hoists emerging at the outer bracket of the gun cradles (see Turret plan), and the turret officer and turret trainer seated in tandem on a raised platform on the turret axis under a longer combined hood. An electric motor with manual backup was used for training; elevation was manual. When the ships were first completed the switch for the training motor was worked by hand from the sighting position, but the hand switch was subsequently replaced by a foot switch or pedal, leaving the gunlayer's hands free for elevating and firing the gun.

The principal innovation in terms of the general arrangement of the turret was a much deeper working chamber for the stowage and handling of the ready-use propellant charges. The working chamber was suspended beneath and rotated with the gunhouse, and was protected by a fixed truncated cone of armour. In the *Jeanne d'Arc* turret the revolving working chamber had been used only for the stowage of projectiles, and the powder charges had been stowed on a fixed platform served by a hoist that

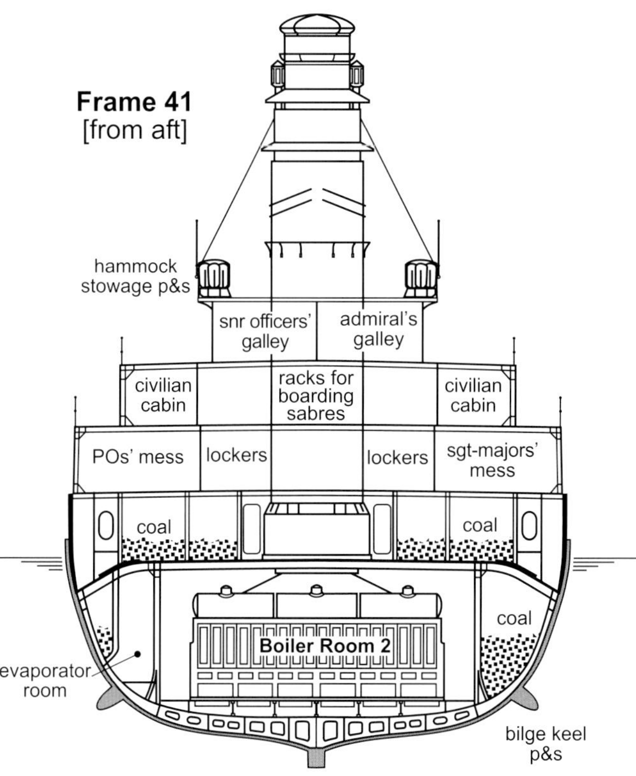

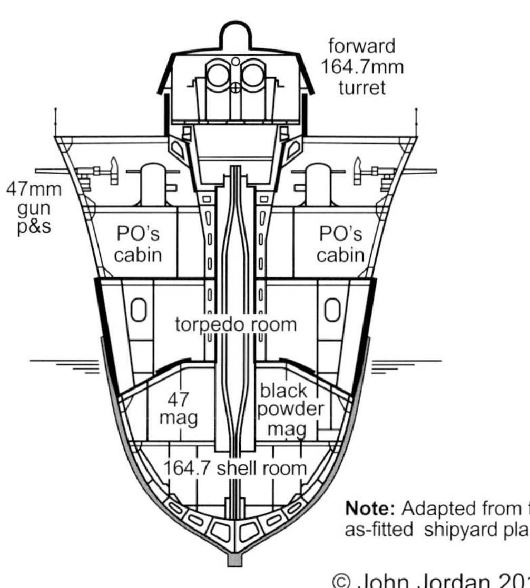

MAIN AND MEDIUM GUNS

	164.7/45 Mle 1893–1896	100/45 Mle 1893
Total weight:	8190kg	1700kg
Total length:	7742mm	4647mm
Bore length:	7420mm	4500mm
Chamber length:	1294.9mm	813mm
Chamber volume:	36.72dm^3	6.98dm^3
Breech pressure:	3100kg/cm^2	2400kg/cm^2
Rifling:	50 grooves at 4°	30 grooves at 5°
Shell weight:	APC 54.9kg (2.62 cal)	
	SAPC 52.3kg (2.94 cal)	SAPC 16kg (3.55 cal)
	CI 45.0kg (3.12 cal)	CI 14kg (4.10 cal)
Bursting charge:	APC 0.97kg *mélinite* (1.8%)	
	SAPC 3.10kg *mélinite* (5.9%)	SAPC 0.41kg powder (2.6%)
	CI 2.10kg powder (4.7%)	CI 0.69kg powder (4.9%)
Propellant:	19.8kg BM10/11 (bag + cartridge)	3.7kg BM7 (cartridge)
Muzzle velocity (MV):	865m/sec (APC)	710m/sec (SAPC)
Remaining V 2000m:	655m/sec (APC)	501m/sec (SAPC)
Maximum range:	10,800m at 15°	9000m at 20°
Firing cycle:	20 secs	10 secs

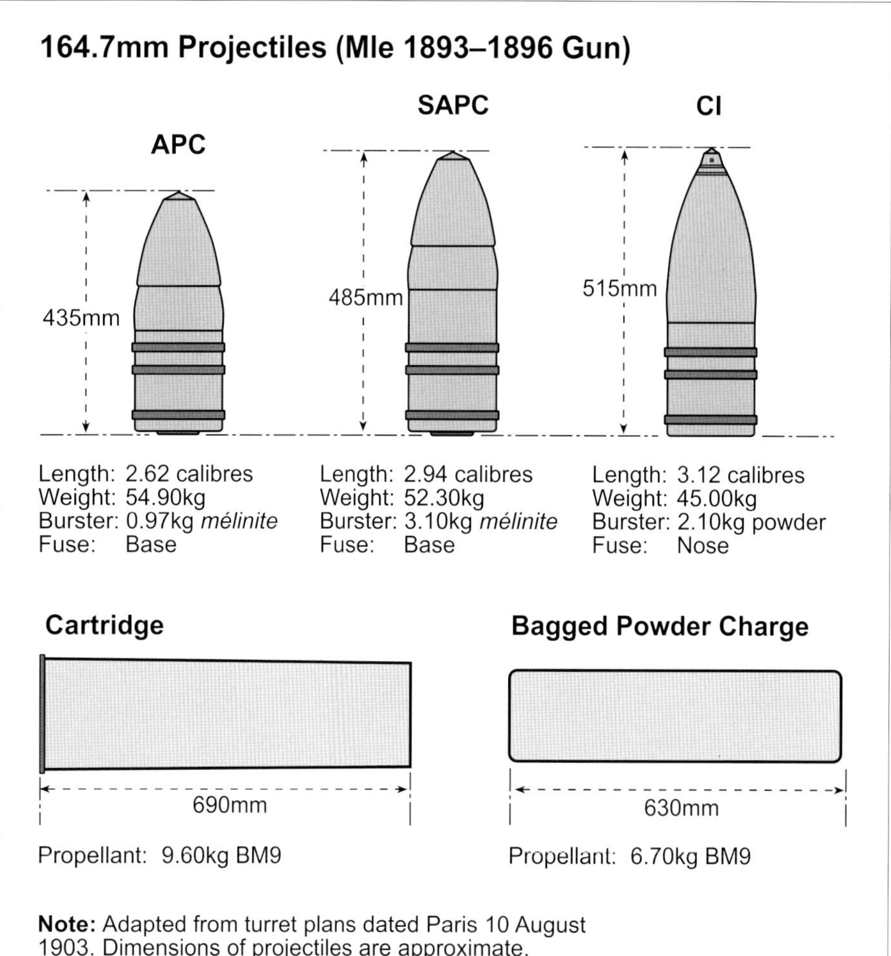

Twin turret for 164.7mm Mle 1893–1896

Profile View of Turret, Hoist and Magazine

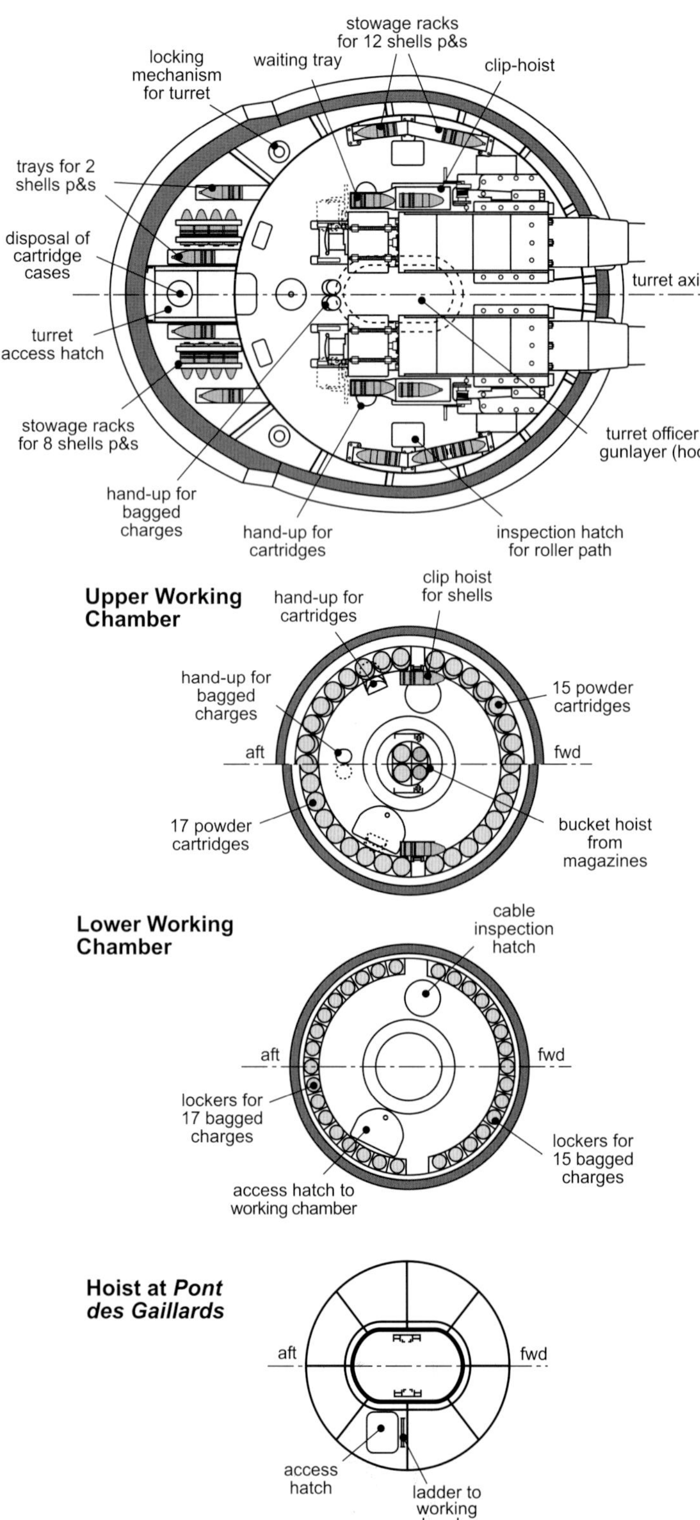

The *tourelle-barbette* ultimately adopted for the 164.7mm guns was the French Navy's first twin turret for guns of medium calibre. It differed from the 194mm single turret designed by Batignolles for *Jeanne d'Arc* in having a much deeper working chamber with almost vertical walls that was used to stow the two-part propellant charges. The bagged half-charges were stowed in lockers with flashproof doors around the base of the working chamber, with the cartridges above them, secured with flexible spiral springs to the chamber walls. Ready-use projectiles, which were less vulnerable to flash, were stowed on open racks around the sides and rear of the gunhouse.

Front View of Turret and Hoist

hood for turret officer & gunlayer
roller path
clip hoist for shells
2e Pont
basket in upper position
access hatch with ladder beneath
1er Pont
Pont principal
1er Faux-pont
2e Faux-pont
basket in loading position
Plancher de manoeuvre

Note: Adapted from plans dated Paris 10 August 1903.

© John Jordan 2016

emerged on the right side of the ammunition trunk (see page 65). In the new 164.7mm twin turret, ready-use projectile stowage was moved up to the gunhouse, which had racks to the sides for horizontal stowage of 2 x 12 shells of different types, and at the rear of the gunhouse, behind the guns, which could stow 2 x 10 shells, for a total of 44 projectiles (22 per gun). There was additional stowage in lockers at the rear of the turret for four bagged charges and four cartridges behind each gun, sufficient for eight rounds (see Turret plan). The bagged half-charges in the gunhouse plans are shorter than those shown in the working chamber, suggesting that these lockers were generally employed for the reduced charges used in exercise firings.

Because the working chamber for the powder charges revolved with the turret, the hoist, which was fixed, needed to be on the turret axis, emerging through the centre of the floor of the working chamber. The duplex hoist featured two linked baskets; when one was in the upper position, the other was in the loading position at the level of the magazines and shell rooms; the baskets ran on rails that enabled them to pass one another when half-way between the loading and off-loading positions. Each of the two basket frames held two complete rounds: the projectiles were above the bagged charges on the forward side of the hoist, the twin cartridges (which were longer than the bagged charges) on the after side.

The main hoist was powered by a Sautter-Harlé electric motor with alternative hand gear for backup. The motor was located on the 2nd platform deck just above the handing room, with control switches close to the motor and in the working chamber.

When the basket arrived in the working chamber the

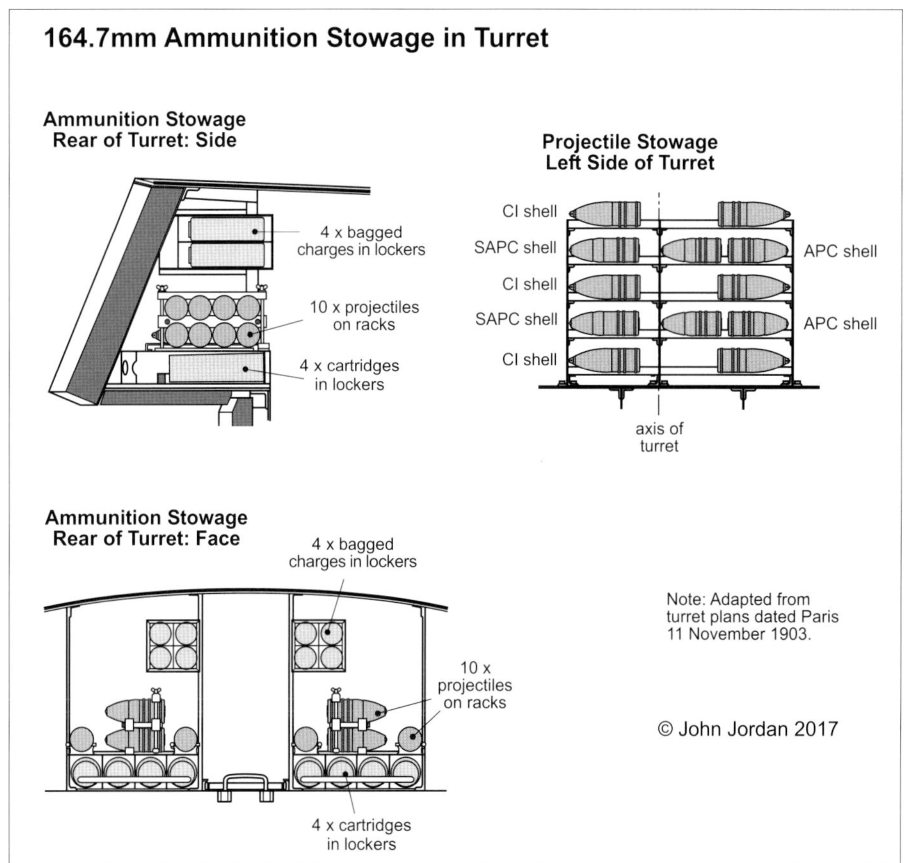

Right: *Kléber* in Toulon Roads. Designed as station cruisers, these ships had their hull sheathed with teak planking. *Kléber* has her original livery of black hull and buff upperworks. *(Private collection)*

Below: This view of *Kléber* undergoing maintenance at Brest highlights the unusual arrangement of her guns, disposed in twin turrets fore and aft and with a further pair of turrets in the waist amidships. The white (or light grey) paint scheme suggests a recent or future deployment with the Atlantic Division. *(Private collection)*

projectiles were lifted manually onto the horizontal cradle of one of two 'clip' hoists located at the sides. They were then raised directly to the gunhouse using a hand winch, emerging on either side of the guns; from there they were shunted onto the loading trays or stowed on the ready-use racks at the sides and rear of the gunhouse. The bagged charges were lifted manually from the basket and stowed vertically in bays with flash-proof steel doors around the sides of the working chamber, while the brass cartridges were stowed vertically above them and were secured by flexible spiral springs to the sides of the working chamber. The plans show stowage for a total of thirty-two bagged changes and thirty-two cartridges in the working chamber, sufficient for thirty-two rounds.

The major advantage of extending the working chamber downwards to accommodate the powder charges was that there was no need to provide a separate hoist as in *Jeanne d'Arc*; instead the charges were passed directly into the gunhouse via angled hand-up scuttles set in the floor between the guns. The hand-ups for the bagged charges were between the guns, close to the breech; those for the cartridges were outside the breech (see plan view of turret).

The forward and after turrets were mounted on the 3rd deck, and had a height of command of 8.8m and 8m respectively. The wing turrets were mounted one deck lower, on the 2nd deck, and had a command of 5.95m. Separate powder magazines and shell rooms were located around handing rooms forward, aft and amidships in the hold and on the 1st platform deck. The standard allocation of ammunition for the 164.7mm guns was 200 rounds per gun.[6]

The 164.7mm gun mounted in the *Dupleix* class does not seem to have been designated a QF gun by the *Marine Nationale*, in part because mounting the gun in a turret made it less easily manoeuvrable but also because the division of the propellant charge into two parts made loading more complex and time-consuming. However, these guns were in theory capable of firing three rounds per minute, particularly when using ready-use ammunition during the early part of an action (but see Chapter 7).

QF guns

The reduction from ten 164.7mm guns in single mountings to eight in twin turrets made it possible to accommodate four 100mm Mle 1893 QF guns, which were mounted behind ports with hinged watertight covers on the 1st deck at the four corners of the ship, effectively replacing the single 164.7mm end casemate mountings of the original design.

The 100mm/45 Mle 1893 was a dual-purpose gun, providing a useful supplement to the slower-firing 164.7mm against enemy cruisers at the relatively close battle ranges (*c*2000m) then anticipated, while being

[6] The figures given in the plans approved in April 1898 are: 219rpg for each of the end turrets and 165rpg for the wing turrets.

Below: The forward 164.7mm turret of *Desaix* photographed some time after 1908, when ships serving with the Northern Squadron and based at Brest wore an overall blue-grey paint scheme. Directly behind the turret can be seen the rounded walls of the conning tower; the navigation bridge, with its distinctive rectangular windows, is atop the conning tower. The pedestals in the bridge wings are for 37mm ATB guns. *(Private collection)*

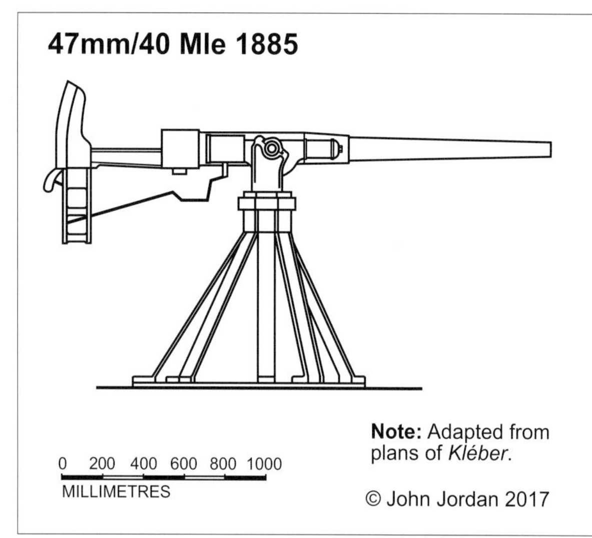

Below: An unusual aerial view of *Kléber* moored at Villefranche between 1904 and 1906, when she was serving with the Light Squadron in the Mediterranean. On 13 May 1905 she rescued the crew of the motor boat *Camille*, which sank during a race between Algiers and Toulon. *(Private collection)*

ANTI-TORPEDO BOAT GUNS

	47/40 Mle 1885
Total weight:	237kg
Total length:	2048mm
Bore length:	1878mm
Chamber length:	336.25mm
Chamber volume:	0.76dm^3
Breech pressure:	2000kg/cm^2
Rifling:	20 grooves at 7°10′
Shell:	1.50kg steel (3.2 cal) 1.50kg CI (3.7 cal)
Bursting charge:	0.022kg powder/*mélinite* 0.055kg powder (CI)
Propellant:	0.29kg BM2 (cartridge)
Muzzle velocity (MV):	650m/s
Remaining V 2000m:	306m/s
Maximum range:	5,000m at 20°
Firing cycle:	4–8 secs

able to engage and stop approaching torpedo craft attacking during the daylight hours. Its immediate predecessor, the Mle 1891, had been fitted in the battleships *Masséna* and *Bouvet*, and the Mle 1893 was mounted in the battleships of the *Charlemagne* class, which had eight guns in open, unshielded mountings on the lower superstructure decks. Both types of gun fired a 14kg CI shell or a 16kg steel shell, initially with a black powder burster. The propellant charge was 3.7kg of BM7 powder in a single cartridge case. The ammunition was 'semi-fixed': the cartridges and projectiles were stowed separately in the magazines and in the ready-use racks close to the guns but were assembled prior to insertion into the breech, which helped to speed the firing cycle – approximately six rounds per minute (four in sustained fire).

There was a magazine for each of the two forward guns, each served by its own hoist, forward of the machinery spaces, and a single athwartships magazine served by two hoists aft. Capacity was 250 rounds per gun. The 100mm gun was well-liked because of its versatility; application of the 'hail of fire' principle meant that at closer ranges it could pepper the unarmoured superstructures of an enemy ship, causing multiple fires and casualties.

ATB guns

The ATB battery of the *Dupleix* class was relatively weak and not particularly well sited. In the absence of a military foremast the ten 47mm Mle 1885 QF guns were distributed between the superstructure decks and the upper deck – four forward and two aft – and the upper hull,[7] with two mountings well forward on the 2nd deck and two aft on the 1st deck. There were also four 37mm QF guns:[8] two at the after end of the boat deck (3rd deck) and two on the quarterdeck (2nd deck) aft, beneath the after turret.

Searchlight projectors

The six 60cm searchlight projectors were disposed and mounted in the customary fashion: one atop the

[7] As with the 60cm searchlight projectors, the guns mounted on the masts and upper decks were termed *ligne haute*, those in the hull *ligne basse*.

[8] The 37mm QF gun was increasingly replacing the 37mm revolver cannon fitted in the earlier ships.

Above: *Desaix* moored in the Mourillon Basin at Toulon; in the background are the building ways. In 1907 the cruiser brought 400 mutineers of the 17th Infantry Regiment taken into custody at Gafsa to Sfax. *(Private collection)*

rangefinder platform on the foremast and one at the base of the mainmast (*ligne haute*), and four behind large rectangular ports at the outer corners of the hull (*ligne basse*).

Torpedoes and mines

The two above-water torpedo tubes were on the main deck forward, just abaft the ammunition trunk for the forward 164.7mm turret. The capacious torpedo room ran from frame 16 to frame 21*bis*. Because of the proximity of the tubes to the bow they were normally stowed against the rear wall of the torpedo room and moved on rails to the torpedo ports, which were fitted with watertight covers; once in place the tubes could be trained 50° forward of the beam and 20° abaft the beam. Two torpedo bodies were stowed to the sides of the compartment, and there was stowage on the deck below (1st platform deck) for four more with an athwartships hatch through which they could be lifted into the torpedo compartment; the torpedo warheads were stowed in vertical racks at the forward end of either the torpedo room or the stowage room. The above-water torpedo tubes were never liked, and *Kléber* had hers removed in 1908.

The plans of the ships show twenty mines (*torpilles automatiques*) stowed in the passageways inboard of the cofferdam on the main deck, abeam the after turret. The mines would have been laid by the ship's boats or by other craft.

PROTECTION

Hull

The protection system adopted by Bertin for the *Dupleix* class reverted to that employed in *Pothuau*, albeit with a well-developed cellular layer. There was a belt of uniform thickness allied to a single protective deck that was sloped downwards at the sides to meet the lower edge of the belt. Unusually, the main belt extended only as far as the after turret and its associated magazine and shell room, and was closed by a broad transverse armoured bulkhead at frame 92. The belt itself comprised two strakes of homogeneous nickel steel armour 102mm thick amidships, reducing to 84mm at the bow, forward of the 164.7mm shell room and magazine. There was no teak backing; as in the earlier French armoured cruisers, the armour plates were secured directly to the 10mm plating of the shell. The belt extended from the 1st deck, which was just under 2m above the waterline, to 1.2m below the waterline, and was tapered to 38mm at its lower edge.

There was teak cladding over the underside of the hull to a height of 60cm above the waterline; it was 60mm thick at its upper edge, increasing to a maximum of 180mm at the lower edge of the belt. The cladding extended over the bilge keels, but there was no copper sheathing.

The broad transverse bulkhead at frame 92 was composed of six plates of special steel with a uniform thickness of 84mm. Because the protective decks extended beyond frame 92 there was, unusually, a second, lighter transverse bulkhead at frame 105, comprising a single plate of 40mm steel, extending from the protective deck to the inner bottom.

Protection for the decks was relatively light. In contrast to other contemporary Bertin cruiser designs,

Desaix: Protection

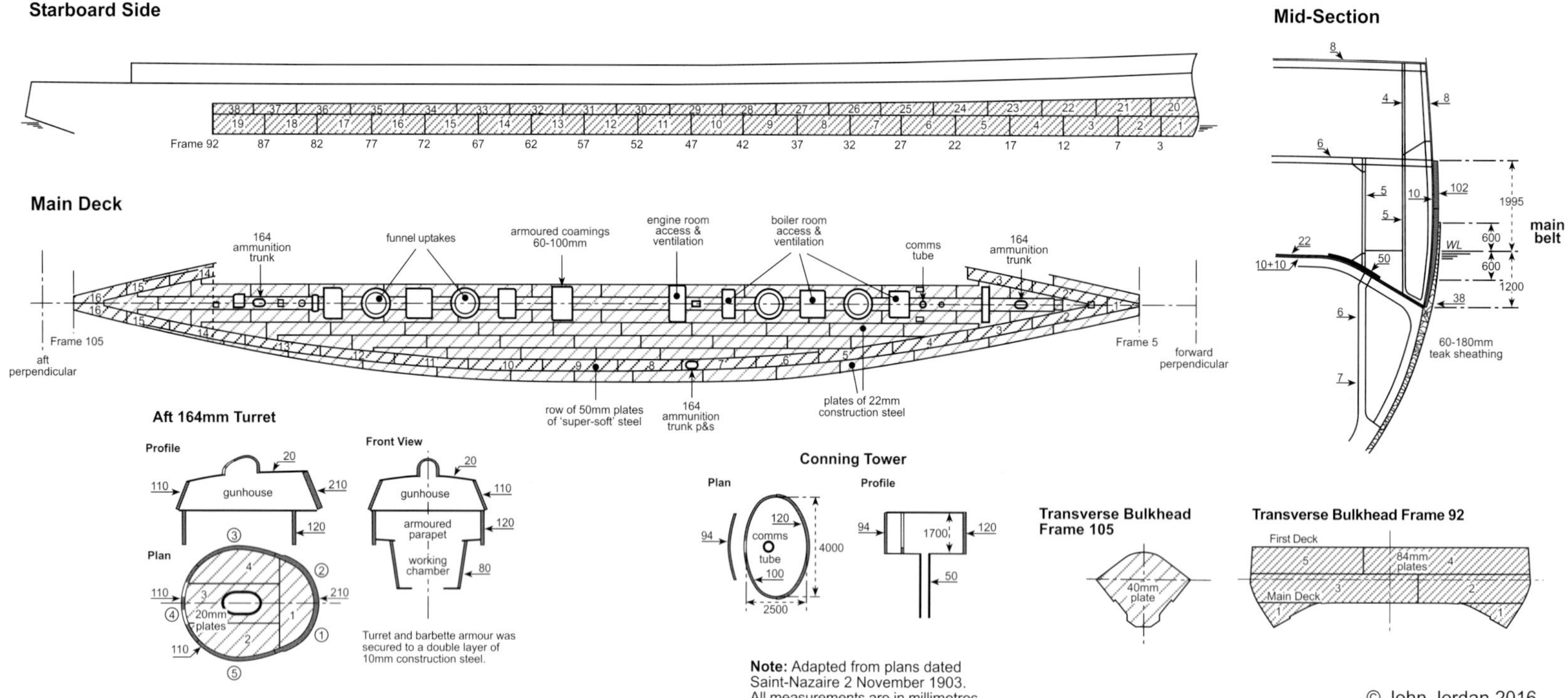

there was no upper protective deck to form the roof of the cellular layer. The main protective deck, which was just below the waterline and was inclined downwards at the sides to meet the bottom of the belt, was composed of 22mm plates of mild steel secured to a double layer of 10mm plating (total thickness 42mm). On the upper part of the slopes, just behind the cofferdam, the 22mm plates were replaced by plates of 50mm 'super-soft' steel (total thickness: 70mm).

The cofferdam and cellular layer were arranged as in other Bertin designs, with extensive use of coal bunkers on the main deck to provide protection for the machinery spaces and magazines.

WEIGHT OF PROTECTION (*DESAIX*)

	No of plates	Composition	Weight
Main belt	2 x 38 (p&s)	special steel	537t
Main deck (50mm plates)	32	super-soft steel	119t
Transverse b/head F92	5	special steel	15t
Transverse b/head F105	1	special steel	0.3t
164 turrets	4 x 5	cemented[1]	107t
164 barbettes	4 x 7	special steel	105t
Conning tower	5?	special steel	18.5t
Communications tube	n/a	special steel	5t
Armoured deck coamings	n/a	special steel	31.5t
		Total	938 tonnes

Notes:

1 The face and side plates were of Harvey cemented armour; the two rear plates were of 50kg mild steel to counter-balance the weight of the gun.

Source: Protection plans for *Desaix*, Saint-Nazaire, dated 2 November 1903. Note that these figures do not include the weight of the 22mm plates of 50kg mild steel used over the greater part of the armoured deck.

DESAIX: ARMOUR PLATE THICKNESS MAIN BELT

Plate	Upper Strake *upper/lower edge*	Lower Strake *upper/lower edge*
1-4/20-22	84	84/38
5-19/23-38	102	102/38

Notes:

1 The total weight of the plates in the main belt was **537 tonnes**; the heaviest plates weighed just under 10 tonnes. In contrast to other French armoured cruisers of the period, there was no light upper belt forward.

2 All the protective side plating was of homogeneous nickel ('special') steel.

Turrets and conning tower

The 164.7mm twin turrets had 110mm cemented armour on the inclined face and sides of the cupola secured to a double layer of 10mm mild steel; the 'balancing plates' at the rear of the turret were of mild steel and were 210mm thick. The armour for the turret face and sides was composed of three plates, with two thicker plates providing balance. The roof of the turret comprised four plates of hardened steel 20mm thick, secured to a single layer of 10mm plating.

The circular fixed barbette protecting the lower part of the gunhouse and the roller paths was of 120mm special steel, and the truncated cone over the working chamber 80mm; the fixed armour, like that of the gunhouse, was secured to a double layer of 10mm steel. The trunk for the ammunition hoists, which was elliptical in plan, comprised a double layer of 10mm steel with additional 20mm protection above the level of the 1st deck.

The conning tower was elliptical in plan, as in *Jeanne d'Arc*, and had the same dimensions and a similar system of protection, albeit at a reduced thickness; there was 120mm armour plating on the face and sides and 100mm plating on the rear, with a curved 90mm vertical bulkhead to protect access directly behind it. The communications tube was formed by 50mm hoops of special steel that extended down to the main deck.

MACHINERY

High tactical speed was not a priority for the station cruisers: a maximum speed of 21 knots was specified. Rather, the focus was on endurance and ease of maintenance in overseas dockyards. Of the French overseas territories only Martinique had a graving dock sufficiently large to accommodate a 1st class cruiser, and when deployed to the Far East station cruisers were generally docked in Japan.[9] The steam plant of the *Dupleix* class was therefore conservative in comparison with *Jeanne d'Arc*.

Dupleix and *Desaix* had four-cylinder VTE engines, which were built by FCM Le Havre and ACL Saint-Denis respectively; *Kléber* had a three-cylinder model from Schneider–Le Creusot. The engines were located side by side in three compartments amidships, the engine rooms being divided by longitudinal watertight bulkheads as in *Jeanne d'Arc*. They drove three shafts; the propellers on the wing shafts had a diameter of 4.3m, the propeller on the centre shaft 4.18m. The two large condensers were in a separate space directly abaft the engine rooms, divided by a centreline bulkhead as in *Jeanne d'Arc*.

Steam was supplied by twenty-four Belleville boilers rated at 20kg/cm² in *Dupleix* and *Desaix*, and by twenty Niclausse boilers rated at 18kg/cm² in *Kléber*. The boilers were arranged back-to-back in athwartship rows, with the stokehold platforms between – a pattern that would be replicated in all the later Bertin designs. The two Belleville ships had groups of six boilers in each of the four boiler rooms (see the GA Plans of *Desaix*), while *Kléber* had the same arrangement for the two inner boiler rooms, but groups of four boilers of a larger, more powerful model in the two outer rooms.

The Niclausse, like the Belleville, was a large water-tube boiler – the external diameter of the tubes was 84mm – but the tubes were concentric (see accompanying drawing and caption). The Niclausse and the Belleville would become established as the standard boilers for major French naval vessels during the late 1890s, and the choice would often be a matter of the preference of the shipbuilder rather than a requirement by the Navy.

During her preliminary trials on 22 August 1902, *Dupleix* had a serious incident involving boiler blowback in the 4th stokehold (forward centre boiler room) that resulted in seven stokers being badly burned, and had to return to the dockyard. On 30 September a 24-hour trial at normal power was interrupted when a crack developed in the HP cylinder of the port engine. The cylinder was replaced, but trials were put back by eight months pending further repairs and testing.

In service the Belleville boilers of *Desaix* were considered particularly successful; the only concern was the economisers, which required constant cleaning. The Niclausse boilers fitted in *Kléber* initially gave trouble due to the inefficiency of the air supply to the boilers; in her initial draft trial she attained only 13,000CV instead of the expected 14,000CV; however, these problems appear to have been resolved, as in 1905–06, in an interview with a British naval intelligence officer, her current CO claimed that during his time in command the Niclausse boilers had never given any trouble (RFNA 1906)

Machinery trials, however, were generally disappointing, and only one of the three ships (*Kléber*) made the designed speed of 21 knots; details of the results obtained in the three-hour full-power trial are given in the accompanying table. Endurance and fuel consumption were nevertheless considered satisfactory: endurance was estimated at 7600nm at 10 knots with a normal load of coal, and more than 4000nm at 16 knots.

In order to provide electrical power for the turrets,

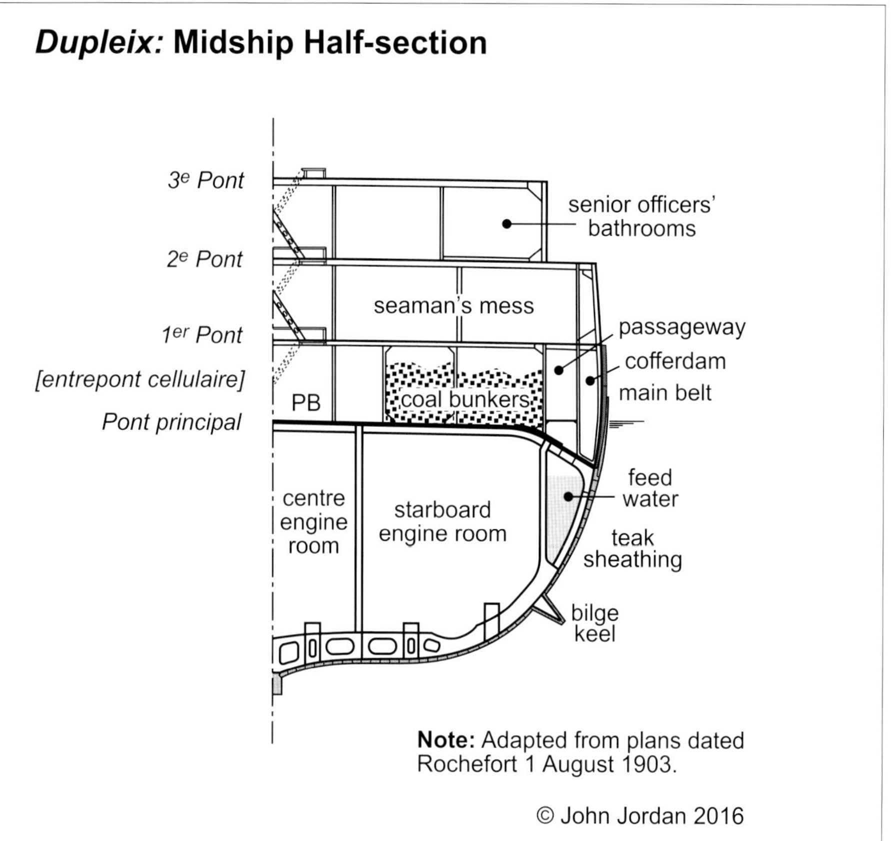

Above: *Kléber* during her trials. In a three-hour full-power trial on 14 October 1903 she recorded a maximum speed of 21.48 knots with 17,177CV. *(Private collection)*

[9] A new dock was authorised to be built at Saigon in 1896 at a cost of 3 million FF.

Niclausse Boiler

Boiler Profile in Cross-section

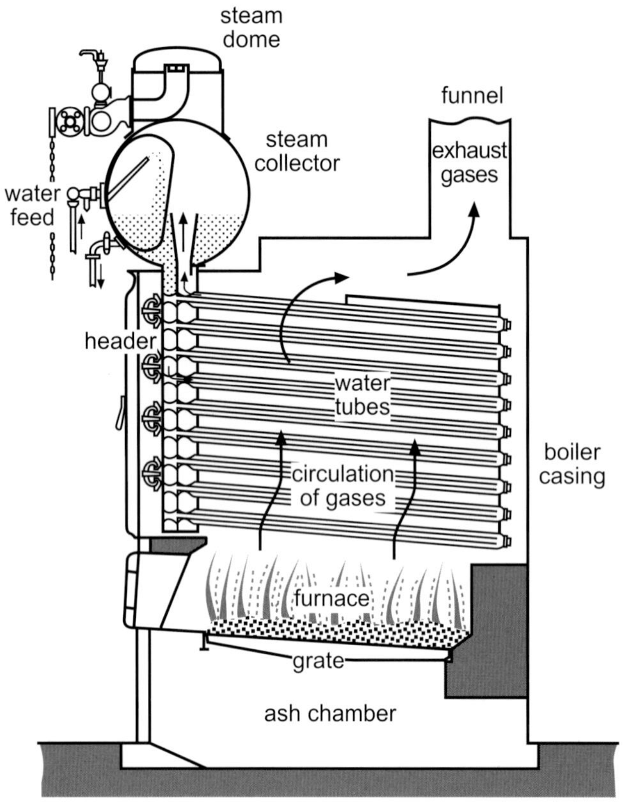

The large watertube boilers of the Niclausse type featured a vertical header tank separated by a diaphragm into inner and outer water-plates into which were set a series of concentric tubes set one inside the other. The outer tube was designated the 'generating tube' (*tube vaporisateur*) and the inner tube the 'circulating tube' (*tube directeur*). The outer tube, 82–84mm in diameter, was closed at either end by a threaded stopper. The inner 'circulating' tube, 40mm in diameter, was open at its lower end and ended several centimetres short of the stopper for the outer tube; it carried the feed water to the lower end of the generating tube where it was heated by direct contact with the combustion gases from the furnace. At the upper end of the inclined concentric tubes was a 'lantern' comprising two cones, which was joined to the corresponding water-plate of the header. There was a pipe inlet to supply feed water to the circulating tube and a riser for steam from the generating tube. Pressure was exerted from both the outside and the inside of the circulating tube, so there were no stresses.

The tubes of the Niclausse boiler were manufactured of 'super-soft' steel. The number of tubes was variable: 16, 18, 20, 22, 24, 26. The cylindrical collector (*récepteur*) was of cast or pressed mild steel; it extended the full length of the casing and was of sufficiently large diameter to minimise irregularity in the feed; baffles separated the currents of water and steam, and there was a steam dome atop the collector.

lighting, etc, there were three large 800A dynamos mounted in auxiliary machinery rooms on the 1st platform deck at either end of the main machinery spaces. Two were in the forward room and two in the after room, together with the high-capacity Thirion pumps and the auxiliary condensers.

The steering gear for *Desaix* was supplied by Duming & Bossière (Le Havre), the electrical appliances from Sautter-Harlé. The servomotor slide of the steam-powered steering engine was worked by an electric motor geared to it. The motor worked off the main electrical circuit of the ship, its movements being controlled by electric commutators worked by electric wheels or levers in alternative steering positions in the bridge, the *Poste Central* and the conning tower.

CONSTRUCTION AND EARLY SERVICE

Dupleix was laid down on 18 January 1899 at Rochefort naval dockyard on the same slipway from which *Bruix* had been launched in August 1894. However, the slipway was too short to accommodate her full length, which had now grown to 132m overall.[10] The Napoleon III Basin where she was due to be fitted out was also too small, and had to be partially demolished at one end in order to accommodate the hull after launch, which took place on 28 April 1900. Later French armoured cruisers would grow even further in size,[11] and *Dupleix* would be the last major vessel to be built at Rochefort, which would henceforth build only destroyers. She was manned for trials on 15 March 1903, and was commissioned in September of the same year.

Desaix, built by the Société de la Loire, was manned for trials in August 1902 but did not enter service until April 1904, more than five years after she was laid down. *Kléber* was even longer in build. Launched virtually complete on 20 September 1902 – even the turrets for the main guns had been installed – she struck the river bottom before she had completely left the slipway

10 Length overall for *Bruix* was 110m.

11 The cruisers of the *Gueydon* and *Gloire* classes had a length overall of just under 140m, their successors of the *Léon Gambetta* class more than 148m.

PERFORMANCE ON 3-HOUR FULL POWER TRIALS

	Date	Speed	Horsepower	Shaft Revs	Consumption	Boiler
Dupleix	13 Sep 1902	20.89kts	17,870CV	142.83rpm	0.807kg/h/cv	Belleville
Kléber	14 Oct 1903	21.48kts	17,177CV	146.91rpm	0.932kg/h/cv	Niclausse
Desaix	17 Nov 1903	20.61kts	17,861CV	148.75rpm	0.832kg/h/cv	Belleville

Source: CAAP: inventaire 432, sous-série 5I cartons 58 (*Du*), 105 (*Kl*), 54 (*De*).

due to the tide being lower than anticipated, and her hull was deformed. Repairs took some time, and trials took up most of the next 18 months; she was finally commissioned on 4 July 1904.

Once they entered service these ships were generally employed as initially intended, both in the Atlantic and the Far East. *Dupleix* initially served as flagship of the Atlantic Division (*Division de l'Atlantique*), visiting the Azores, West Africa and the Americas before handing over the role to *Desaix* in September 1905.

Following a spell in the Light Squadron in the Mediterranean, in December 1906 *Kléber* became flagship of the *Division des Antilles* then, in January 1908, flagship of the *Division du Maroc*.

After a lengthy spell in reserve at Cherbourg *Dupleix* was assigned to the Far East Naval Division, initially as flagship. She left Cherbourg on 12 November 1910 and was then based at Saigon until the outbreak of war in August 1914. In May 1911 she would be joined by her sister *Kléber*. Following a grounding in the Sea of Japan on an unmarked reef on 12 July 1912, *Kléber* underwent temporary repairs at Kobe and in January 1913 returned to Lorient, where she was placed in reserve; she would be replaced by the armoured cruiser *Montcalm*, which on arrival in Saigon assumed *Dupleix*'s role as flagship of the *Division navale de l'Extrême-Orient* (DNEO – Far East Division).

All three ships would play an active part in the Great War, being reactivated – or, in the case of *Dupleix*, recalled – to serve in the Eastern Mediterranean.

Dupleix Class: Early Service

	Dupleix	Desaix	Kléber
1903	Atlantic Div (fl)	Trials	Trials
1904	↓	Lt Squ Med	Lt Squ Med
1905	↓	Atlantic Div (fl)	↓
1906	Reserve	↓	↓
1907	↓	Lt Squ Med	Atlantic Div (fl)
1908	↓	Atlantic Div	↓
1909	↓	Reserve	Reserve
1910	Far East (fl)	↓	↓
1911	↓	↓	Far East
1912	↓	↓	↓
1913	Far East	↓	Reserve
1914	↓	↓	↓

EVALUATION

The *Dupleix* class was not well-liked. Successive commanding officers complained that the ships were undergunned for their size, and that their modest protection compared with their 'fleet' contemporaries of the *Gueydon* and *Gloire* classes meant that they were less able to sustain damage when in action with enemy ships of the same type. Of the three, only *Kléber* attained her designed speed on trials, and by

Below: *Kléber* at Lorient during 1907–08, when she was flagship of the Atlantic Division. Ships deployed to West Africa or the West Indies were painted white to reflect sunlight and make conditions on board tolerable for the crew. *(H Laurent)*

DUPLEIX vs *MONMOUTH* (GB)

	Dupleix	*Monmouth*[1]
No in class:	3	10
Built:	1897–1904	1899–1904
Displacement:	7600 tonnes	9800 tonnes
Dimensions:	130m x 17.8m	134m x 20.1m[2]
Propulsion:		
Engines	3-shaft VTE	2-shaft VTE
Horsepower	17,500CV	22,000CV
Speed	21 knots	22 knots
Armament:		
Main	8 x 164mm (4 x II)	14 x 152mm (2x II, 10 x I)
Medium guns	4 x 100mm (4 x I)	
ATB guns	10 x 47mm (10 x I)	10 x 76mm (10 x I)[3]
	4 x 37mm (4 x I)	3 x 47mm (3 x I)[3]
TT	2 x 450mm	2 x 450mm
Protection:		
Belt	102mm	100mm
Main turrets	110mm	125mm
Casemates	–	100mm
Conning tower	120mm	250mm
Deck	42/70mm[3]	30mm

Notes:
1. The *Monmouth* class was designed by White as a trade protection cruiser to counter the threat posed by the *Dupleix* class (see D K Brown, *Warrior to Dreadnought*, p 159).
2. Metric equivalents have been supplied for *Monmouth* in order to give a comparison. The equivalents for gun calibres are exact; those for armour thicknesses are to the nearest 5mm.
3. In RN service these guns were the 12pdr and 3pdr respectively.
4. For the protective deck, the first figure given relates to the flat, the second to the inclined section at the sides. The figures include a double layer of mild steel plating.

1914 they were regarded as slow. In service, fuel economy was less than anticipated: they burnt huge quantities of coal. The only high point noted by *Dupleix*'s new CO, Captain Daveluy, in 1913, was the spacious accommodation for the admiral's staff and for the crew. However, like other French ships of the period, magazine cooling was inadequate for a ship designed to operate mainly in tropical waters, and there was little insulation for the mess decks; in particular, the upper decks appear to have been of steel with linoleum rather than wooden cladding.

From purely a design point of view, the *Dupleix* class integrated successfully some of the new features introduced by Bertin in *Jeanne d'Arc*. The design of the twin 164.7mm *tourelle-barbette* was a major advance on the 194mm prototype by Batignolles, and anticipated the 194mm and 164.7mm twin turrets of the later French armoured cruisers.

Below: *Kléber* at Hampton Roads during a visit to Jamestown, Virginia, for the Tercentennial Exposition Naval Review of 1907. President Theodore Roosevelt presided over the review. The photo was probably taken on 12 June. *(US Naval History and Heritage Command)*

CHAPTER 5:

THE FLEET CRUISERS OF THE *GUEYDON* CLASS

A PROJECT FOR A 'FLEET' ARMOURED CRUISER (*croiseur cuirassé d'escadre*) to balance the 7700-tonne station cruiser design was drawn up by the *Service Technique* under the supervision of Emile Bertin in early April 1897 following an instruction from Minister Armand Besnard. Two *avant-projets* were produced: one of 20 knots, the other 21 knots; the 21-knot design was selected, and the Minister accepted the advice from the *Service Technique* that the wood and copper sheathing he personally favoured be suppressed.

The proposed design, which was for a ship with a displacement of 9500 tonnes and a length between perpendiculars of 138m, was the cruiser the Navy wanted, capable of inflicting and withstanding punishment. Armed with two 194mm and, in the initial design, ten 164.7mm[1] and four 100mm QF guns, it packed a similar offensive punch to *Jeanne d'Arc* and had a similar level of protection. The return to more modest dimensions was simply a function of reduced ambition regarding speed: the ships were designed for a maximum 21 knots.

The project was submitted to the *Conseil des Travaux* and was duly considered at its meeting of 27 July. In its report, the *Conseil* was quick to point out that the proposal was similar to the one it had put forward at its meeting on 30 December 1896. The members then proceeded to attack all the features introduced by Bertin, in particular the proposed speed of 21 knots, which they considered excessive, and the scheme of protection.

The December meeting of the *Conseil des Travaux* had proposed a maximum speed of 20 knots, and this had also been the recommendation of the *Conseil supérieur*. The main focus of criticism was, however, the thickness and disposition of the armour belt and the two protective decks. The *Conseil* had recommended a minimum thickness of 115mm (including plating) over the cellular layer, whereas the upper strake of Bertin's side belt was 120mm tapering to only 80mm at its upper edge. The recommendation of 115mm had been calculated on the basis of resistance to penetration by 164.7mm shell. Only the lower 0.2m of Bertin's proposed upper belt met this criterion, while the upper 1.5m of the belt could be easily penetrated. Moreover, the top edge of Bertin's thick main belt (170mm including plating) was only 0.6m above the waterline, and could easily be submerged when the ship rolled. This 'discontinuity' of the side belt was considered unacceptable.

The *Conseil* also pointed out that the upper protective deck which formed the roof of the cellular layer/'citadel' had a thickness of only 10mm over the central part of the ship, declining to 7mm at the ends. This barely qualified as a protective deck, although the *Conseil* conceded that 7mm was probably sufficient forward, where the deck was protected by the light 56mm upper belt which extended from the bow to the after end of the forward pair of casemates. It was suggested that the necessary weight of protection could be found by reducing speed to the recommended 20 knots(!). Members also considered the main protective deck, most of which was below the waterline, to be too low and requested that the *Service Technique* investigate the stability implications of raising it.

The *Conseil* was happy with the offensive armament, which was in line with its earlier recommendations. However, it wanted the ammunition provision for the 194mm guns to be increased from 63rpg to 105rpg, thereby extending fire from these guns from three to five hours.

The *Conseil*'s recommendations were a clear attack on Bertin's ideas, and showed little understanding of the design process. All the measures suggested would

Below: The hull framing is virtually complete in this early view of *Gueydon* under construction in the ship hall at Lorient. Note the railway tracks used to bring materials to the twin slipways. *(Private collection)*

[1] The report of the *Conseil* suggests that eight of the 164.7mm guns would have been in casemates, the remaining two in turrets (*tourelles*) on the upper deck. This may have been a misunderstanding of the STCN proposal, as early proposals for the 10,000-tonne cruiser (see Chapter 6) had these two guns in shielded pivot mountings amidships.

Above: The plating for the armoured deck is complete: the double layer of 10mm 'construction' steel would be topped by armour plates 30mm thick on the flat and 55mm on the upper slopes. *(Private collection)*

Below: *Gueydon* was launched at Lorient on 20 September 1899. *(Private collection)*

have increased weights high in the ship (greater protection for upper part of cellular layer/raising height of PBI) while at the same time reducing weights below the waterline (lighter machinery).

In typical style, Bertin responded to the *Conseil*'s concerns but without following its recommendations.[2] He increased the thickness of the upper strake of the belt over the cellular layer to a uniform 115mm (including plating), and increased the thickness of the upper protective deck (PBS) from 10mm to 16mm (6+10mm) over the central part of the ship and from 7mm to 10mm at the ends. The cost of these two measures in weight was 72 tonnes and 58 tonnes respectively (total: 130 tonnes). Bertin achieved this by reducing the height of the cellular layer (and hence the PBS) by 0.2m, by lowering the decks above by a comparable amount and by using 87 tonnes of the design margin. The designed speed remained 21 knots. Bertin was unable to find the necessary hull volume or weight (7 tonnes) to increase ammunition provision for the 194mm guns to 105rpg, but agreed to make the magazines as large as possible.

Bertin received the backing of the Minister for his new proposals. On 8 November 1897 Besnard replied to the *Conseil*'s submission stating that all the modifications it had requested which could be made *without altering displacement and speed* (author's italics) had been implemented, the solution to its concerns being a reduction in the height of the cellular layer and a corresponding increase in protection. He further stated: 'These are the only measures which the Minister intends to undertake to satisfy the wishes of the *Conseil*.'[3] He could hardly have been more dismissive.

The order for *Gueydon*, which was to become the name-ship of the class,[4] was placed with Lorient naval dockyard on 13 August 1897. *Dupetit-Thouars*, ordered on the same date, was allocated to Toulon, whose performance was to prove every bit as unimpressive as

[2] The Spanish Viceroys in South America during Spain's colonial rule used the expression: '*obedezco pero no cumplo*' ('I obey but do not comply'). This seems to have been very much Bertin's approach when dealing with the recommendations of the *Conseil des Travaux* during the late 1890s.

[3] '*Telles sont les seules mesures que le Ministre compte prendre pour donner satisfaction au voeu du conseil.*'

[4] Contemporary documents generally referred to the type as *croiseur de 9500 tonnes* or as the *Montcalm* class, after the first ship to be laid down.

Gueydon: Profile & Plan

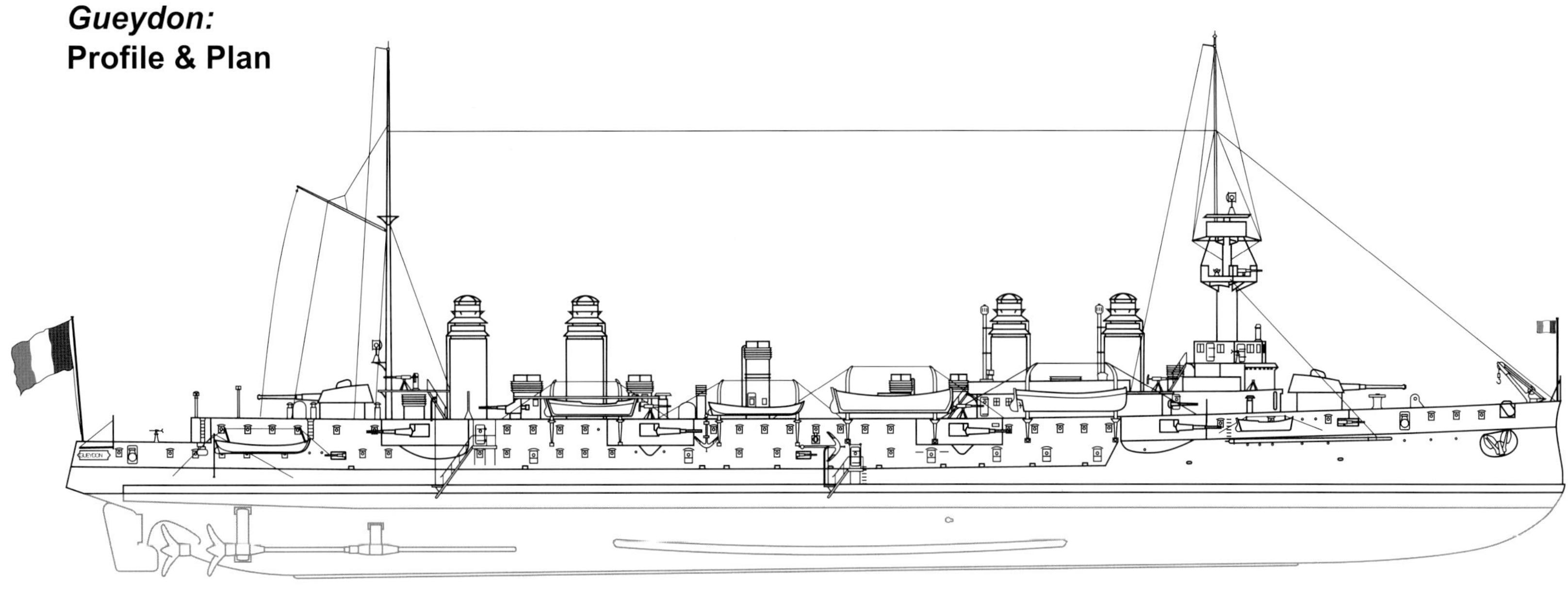

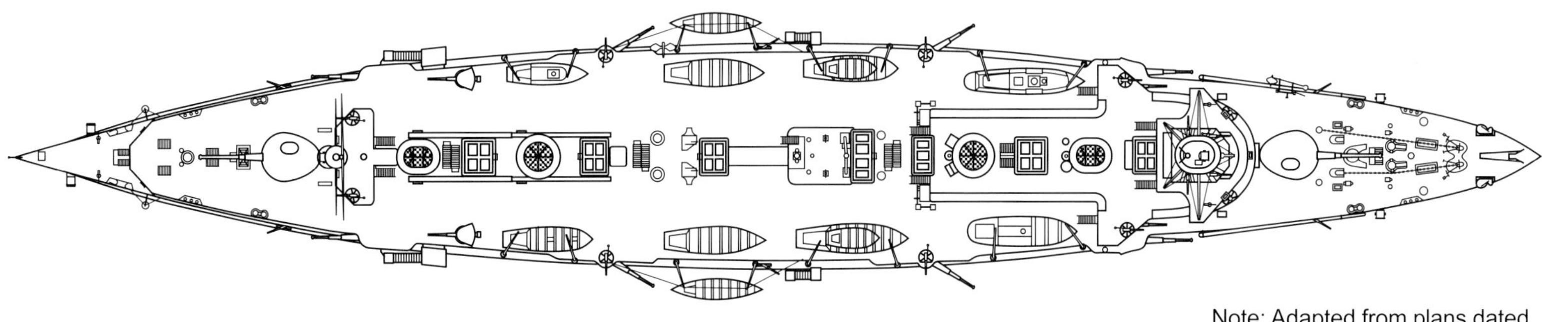

Note: Adapted from plans dated Lorient 23 December 1902.

with *Jeanne d'Arc*: *Dupetit-Thouars* would enter service only in 1905, three years after her sister *Gueydon* and six years after her keel was laid. The contract for the third ship, *Montcalm*, was placed with the private shipbuilder Forges & Chantiers de la Méditerranée, La Seyne, on 22 December 1897.

NOMENCLATURE

Louis Henri, comte de **Gueydon** (1809–86) was a vice admiral in the *Marine Nationale* and the first governor of Algeria under the Third Republic. He suppressed a long-running revolt of the indigenous Kabyles by declaring martial law, and allocated land to French colonists fleeing Alsace-Lorraine. He was elected to the National Assembly in 1885.

Louis-Joseph de **Montcalm**-Gozon, marquis de Saint-Veran (1712–59) was the commander of French forces in North America during the Seven Years' War. In 1756 Louis XV sent him to New France to lead its defence against the British. He met with notable successes in 1756, 1757 and 1758, but British

Above: *Dupetit-Thouars* is launched at Toulon on 5 July 1901. *(Private collection)*

BUILDING DATA

Name	Builder	Laid down	Launched	Trials	Commissioned
Gueydon	Arsenal de Lorient	13 Aug 1898	20 Sep 1899	15 Oct 1901	1 Sep 1903
Montcalm	FC Méditerranée (La Seyne)	27 Sep 1898	27 Mar 1900	22 Jul 1901	20 Mar 1902
Dupetit-Thouars	Arsenal de Toulon	17 Apr 1899	5 Jul 1901	1 Dec 1904	28 Aug 1905

Gueydon: GA Plans

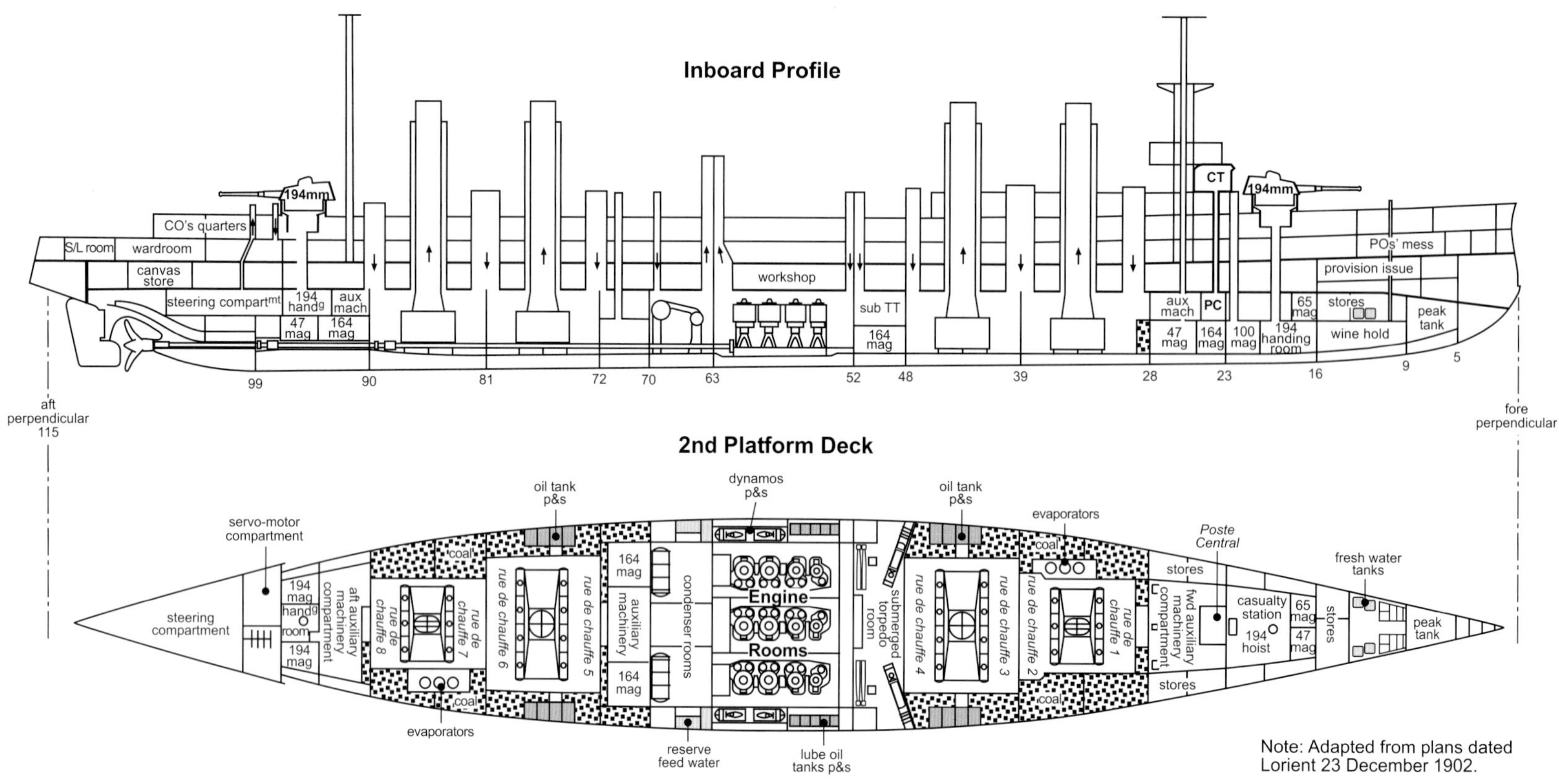

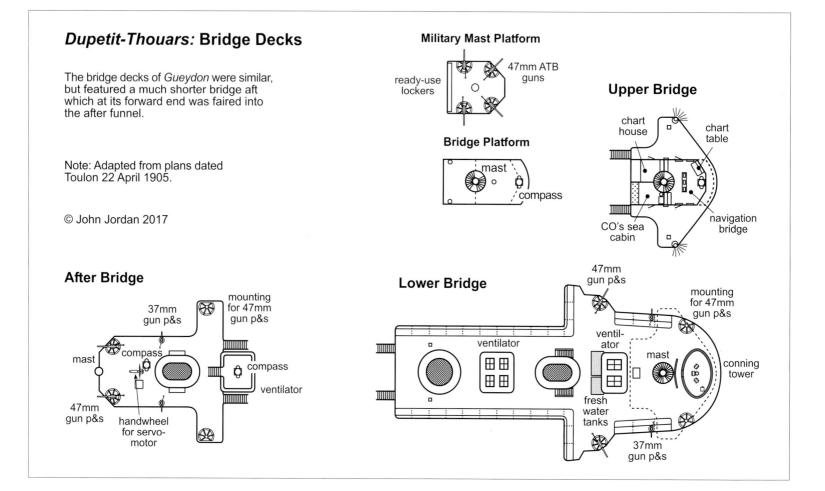

Dupetit-Thouars: Bridge Decks

The bridge decks of *Gueydon* were similar, but featured a much shorter bridge aft which at its forward end was faired into the after funnel.

Note: Adapted from plans dated Toulon 22 April 1905.

Military Mast Platform

ready-use lockers
47mm ATB guns

Bridge Platform

mast
compass

Upper Bridge

chart house
chart table
CO's sea cabin
navigation bridge

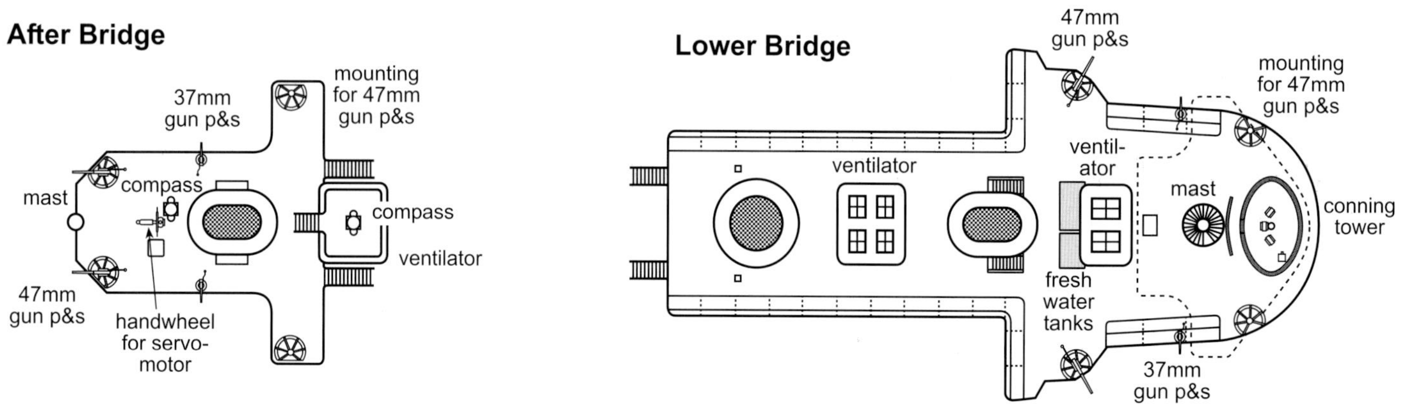

After Bridge

37mm gun p&s
mounting for 47mm gun p&s
mast
compass
compass
ventilator
47mm gun p&s
handwheel for servo-motor

Lower Bridge

47mm gun p&s
mounting for 47mm gun p&s
ventilator
ventil-ator
mast
conning tower
fresh water tanks
37mm gun p&s

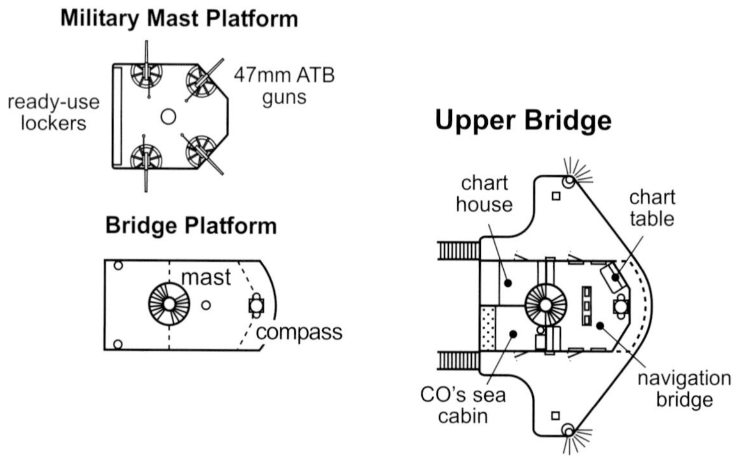

Above: *Montcalm*, still without her 194mm main guns, although the 164.7mm casemate guns are in place. She was laid down by Forges & Chantiers de la Méditerranée, La Seyne, in September 1898 and manned for trials on 22 July 1901. *(Private collection)*

Left: Due to internal problems at Toulon Naval Dockyard, *Dupetit-Thouars* entered service two/three years after her two sisters. She is seen here complete except for her topmasts. *(Private collection)*

mobilisation of large numbers of troops against New France led to military setbacks in 1758 and 1759, culminating in Montcalm's defeat and death at the Battle of Quebec and the French surrender at Montreal in 1760.

Aristide-Aubert **Du Petit Thouars** (1760–98) was a French naval officer and a hero of the Battle of the Nile (Aboukir). As commander of the *Tonnant* he forced HMS *Majestic* to break off combat, with heavy losses that included her captain. Having lost both legs and an arm, Du Petit Thouars continued to command from a barrel filled with wheat until he died.

HULL AND SUPERSTRUCTURES

The hull of the *Gueydon* class was a cut-down version of *Jeanne d'Arc*. Frame spacing was again 1.2m, and the internal decks were similarly arranged and given the same nomenclature. The principal difference was that the forecastle deck (2nd deck) was extended almost to the stern, as in the *Dupleix* class, so that both the two main turrets were on the same level with approximately the same command; in compensation the uppermost deck (3rd deck) was eliminated, making for a lower profile.

The 194mm guns were mounted in single *tourelles-*

***Dupetit-Thouars:* Sections**

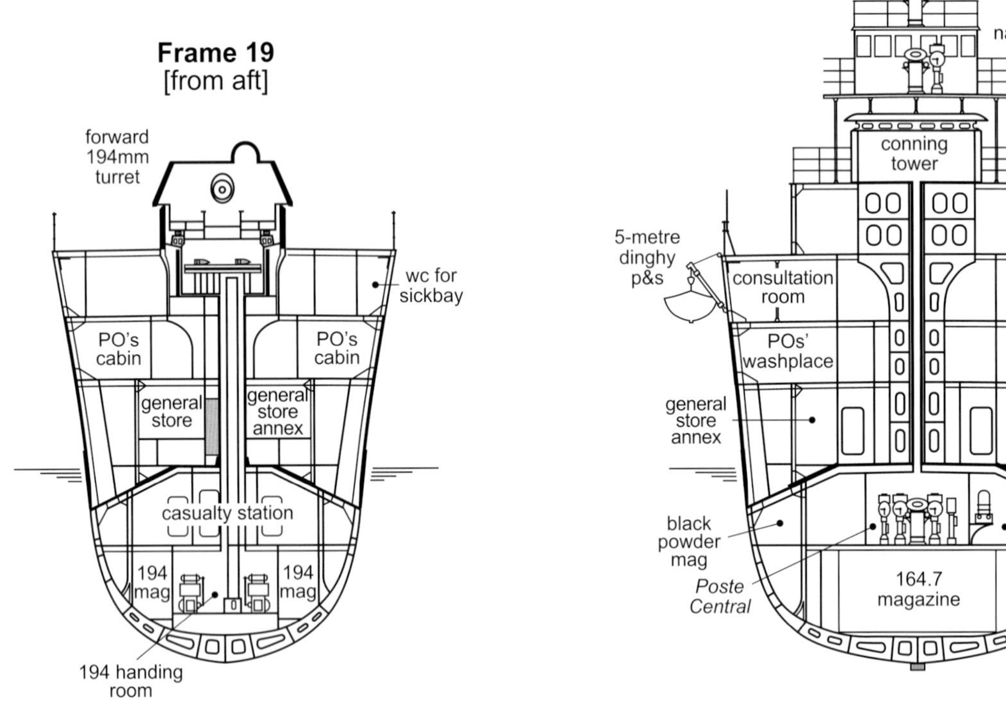

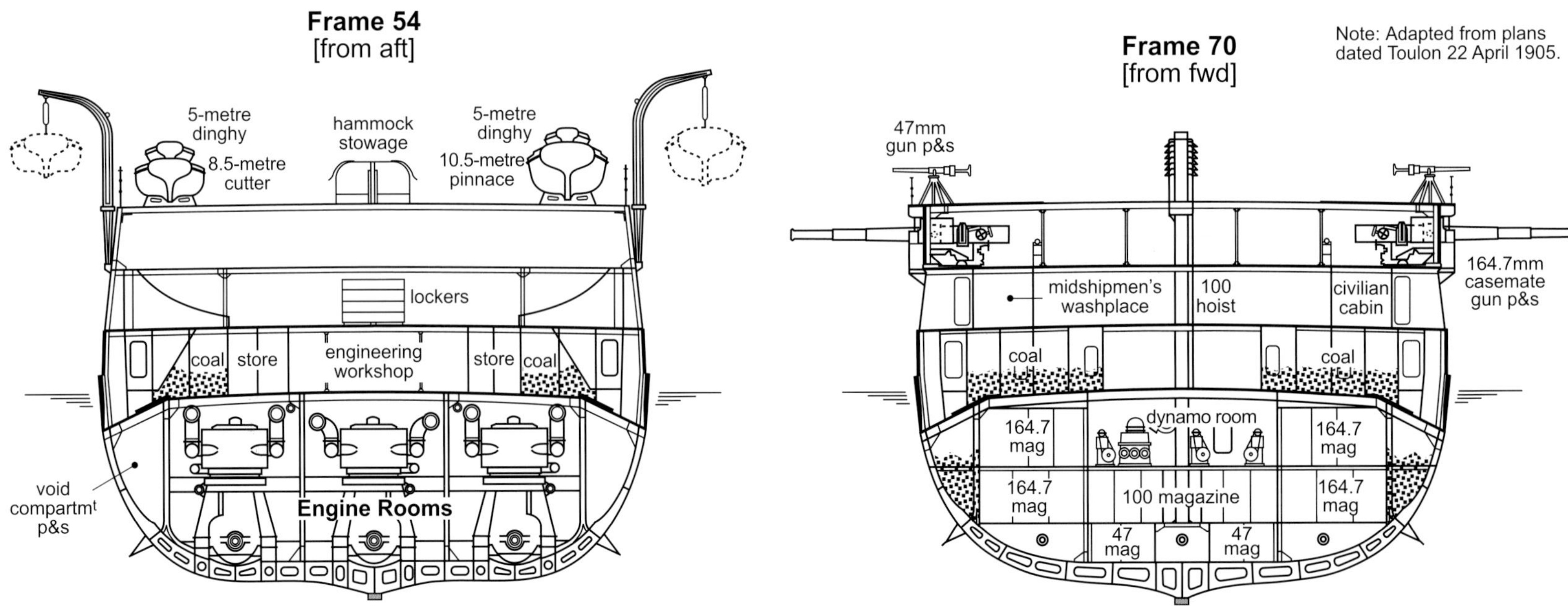

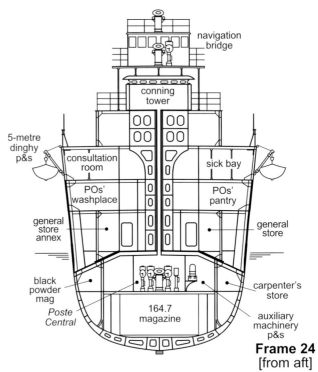

barbette fore and aft and the 164.7mm guns were in single widely-spaced individual casemates along the sides of the 1st deck – a similar layout to that originally envisaged for the *Dupleix* class (see drawing page 78). The 100mm QF guns were in single pivot mountings on the upper (2nd) deck at the four 'corners' of the ship.

The engines were amidships, as in *Jeanne d'Arc* and *Dupleix*, and the forward and after boiler rooms were widely spaced, with the funnels paired as in the *Dupleix* class. The unusually wide spacing of the boiler rooms and funnels reflected the requirement for magazines directly beneath the two pairs of midship casemate guns.

There was a superstructure deck forward that extended beyond the first two funnels, with a two-deck bridge structure above and a light military foremast similar to that in *Jeanne d'Arc*; as in the latter ship the mainmast was a simple steel pole.

Of the three ships of the class, only *Montcalm* was fitted as a flagship, a role in which she served throughout the pre-war period. The admiral's quarters were at the after end of the 1st deck, as in the *Dupleix* class. In *Gueydon* and *Dupetit-Thouars* these quarters were allocated to the ships' commanding officer.

Frame 44
[from aft]

hammock stowage p&s
midshipmen's galley
POs' galley
PO's cabin
PO's cabin
stokers' washplace p&s
scullery p&s
coal
coal
Boiler Room No 2
oil tank p&s

ARMAMENT

Main guns

The main armament adopted for the *Gueydon* class was significantly more powerful than that of the

CHARACTERISTICS

Displacement:	9500 tonnes
Dimensions:	
Length	138.00m pp; 139.68m oa
Beam	19.4m wl
Draught	7.5m aft
Propulsion:	
Boilers	*G:* 28 Niclausse boilers, 18kg/cm^2
	D-T: 28 Belleville boilers
	M: 8 double-ended & 4 single-ended Sigaudy–Normand boilers, 17kg/cm^2
Engines	*G & M:* 3-shaft 4-cylinder VTE
	D-T: 3-shaft 3-cylinder VTE
Horsepower	19,600CV (designed)
Speed	21 knots (designed)
Coal	1020 tonnes normal; 1600 tonnes full load
Endurance	6500nm at 10kts; 1230nm at 21kts at normal load
Armament:	
Main guns	2 x 194mm/40 Mle 1893–1896 in single turrets
Medium guns	8 x 164.7mm/40 Mle 1893–1896 QF in casemates
	4 x 100mm/45 Mle 1893 QF in single mountings
ATB guns	18 x 47mm/40 Mle 1885 QF in single mountings
	4 x 37mm QF in single mountings
Torpedo tubes	2 submerged tubes for 450mm torpedoes
	6 torpedoes Mle 1892
Protection:	
Main belt	150mm max
Decks	6+10mm PBS
	30/55mm PBI
194 turrets	161mm
164 casemates	102mm
Conning tower	174mm
Boats:	1 x 11m steam launch
	1 x 10m steam pinnace
	1 x 7.65m White launch
	1 x 10.5m pulling pinnace
	2 x 10m pulling cutters
	1 x 8.5m pulling cutter
	1 x 8m pulling cutter
	2 x 8.5m whalers
	2 x 5m dinghies
Complement:	
As private ship	26 officers, 569 men
As flagship	+ 9 officers, 64 men

Frame 95
[from fwd]

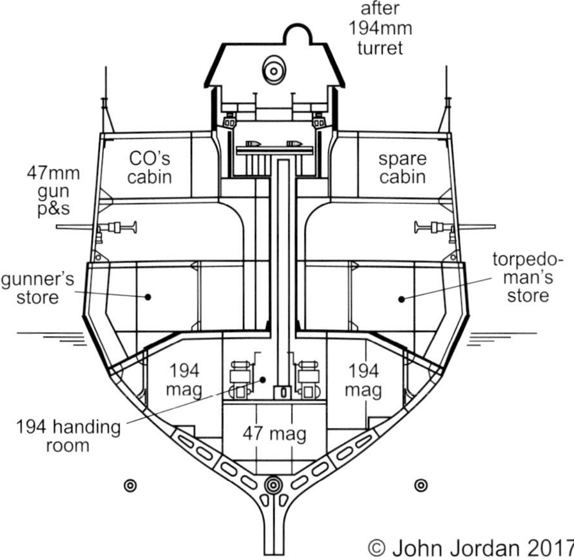

Dupleix class, and was on a par with that of the larger *Jeanne d'Arc*. The 194mm gun was the latest Mle 1893–1896 development of the Mle 1893. It had a longer firing chamber (2093mm *vice* 1306mm – an increase of 60 per cent) to accommodate a larger propellant charge (33.8kg *vice* 22.3kg – an increase of 51 per cent), which was divided into three bags; this had an impact on magazine stowage and arrangements for ammunition supply. Provision was *c*70rpg.

The single *tourelle-barbette* was broadly similar in configuration to that of *Jeanne d'Arc*, and the layout of the gunhouse was essentially unchanged. The major difference concerned the working chamber suspended beneath the gunhouse, which was deeper and had vertical sides. It housed not only a circular projectile ring, located in the upper part of the chamber, but also the ready-use bagged powder charges, which were stowed vertically in flash-proof lockers around the walls beneath the projectiles. Unusually, the basket-type hoist, which could lift two complete rounds, was offset slightly to the left of the turret (see Section plans); this arrangement would not be repeated in the succeeding *Gloire* class (see Chapter 6), which had the hoist on the turret axis.

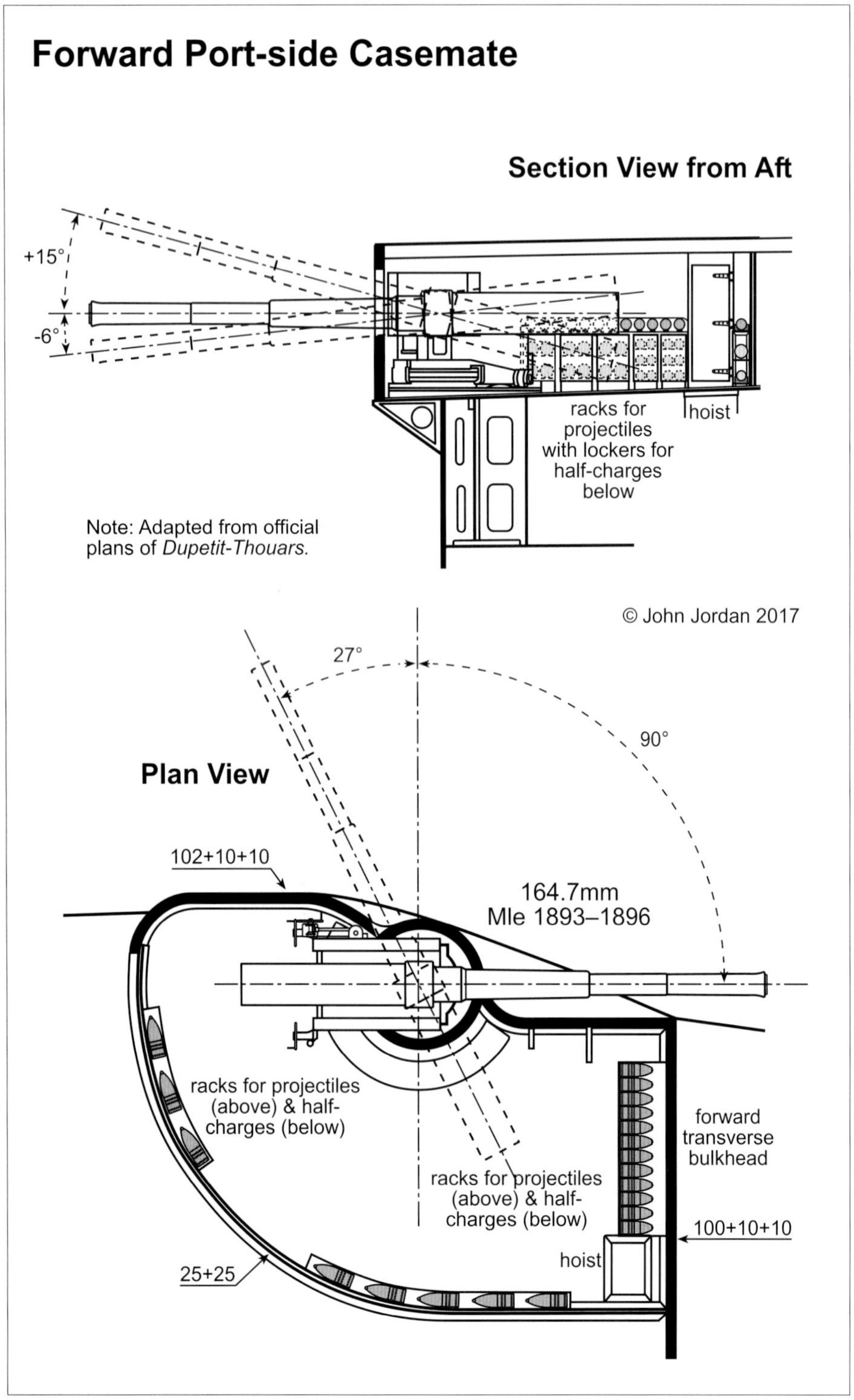

QF guns

The main QF battery of *Jeanne d'Arc* had been based on the 138.6mm Mle 1893 QF gun; as completed there were no fewer than fourteen guns distributed between the 1st and 2nd decks, with those mounted on the 1st deck on sponsons with screens and weatherproof hatches. The *Marine Nationale* had long aspired to a more powerful gun with a genuine quick-firing capability that could over-match the standard British 6in QF (152mm), and the 164.7mm Mle 1893–1896 was the result. Given that the *Gueydons* were smaller ships than *Jeanne d'Arc*, fewer guns could be accommodated, but these would be mounted in widely-spaced, fully-armoured single casemates (*redoutes*) on the 1st deck on either side of the ship. There were eight 164.7mm guns in casemates, complemented by four of the well-liked 100mm Mle 1893 QF gun, disposed in the customary fashion on the upper (2nd) deck at the four corners of the ship.[5] The 100mm guns were in shielded pivot mountings, and the two forward guns were incorporated into lateral extensions of the deckhouse that formed the lower bridge.

The 164.7mm casemate guns could elevate to 15° and could be depressed to -5/6°. The 100mm upper-deck guns could elevate to 20° and could be depressed to -10°. The technical data for both of these guns can be found in Chapter 4.

Each of the casemates was served by a single fixed

[5] Note that early plans of *Jeanne d'Arc* also featured a mixed QF battery of eight 138.6mm and ten 100mm guns (see page 61).

MAIN GUNS

	194/40 Mle 1893–1896
Total weight:	12,682kg
Total length:	8120mm
Bore length:	7760mm
Chamber length:	2093mm
Chamber volume:	71.85dm³
Breech pressure:	2800kg/cm²
Rifling:	58 grooves at 4°
Shell weight:	APC 90.3kg (2.71 cal) SAPC 89.5kg (3.04 cal) CI 75.0kg (2.92 cal)
Bursting charge:	APC 1.59kg *mélinite* (1.8%) SAPC 4.33kg *mélinite* (4.8%) CI 5.07kg powder (5.8%)
Propellant:	33.8kg BM10/11 (3 x ⅓)
Muzzle velocity (MV):	840m/sec (APC)
Remaining V 2000m:	679m/sec (APC)
Maximum range:	11,500m at 15°
Firing cycle:	30 sec

Left: *Gueydon* at Lorient shortly after she entered service. The bower anchors were stowed in recesses with hinged covers which, when closed, were flush with the hull; this served to reduce resistance and spray when the ship was operating at high speed in rough water. *(Private collection)*

Below: *Dupetit-Thouars* finally entered service on 28 August 1905. Following a deployment to the Far East, she returned to Brest and was assigned to the cruiser division of the Northern Squadron. Her two sisters are in the background in this photo. *(Private collection)*

Right: View of the forecastle of *Gueydon*, with the forward 194mm single turret in the foreground. Behind it is the navigation bridge, with its distinctive square windows. The armoured conning tower, with its narrow observation slits, is directly beneath. The guns on pedestals in the bridge wings are 37mm QF ATB guns. *(Private collection)*

Right: Stern view of *Dupetit-Thouars* at Saint-Nazaire in 1907. *(Private collection)*

Left: The 1st Deck of *Montcalm*, with the 8m cutter assigned to the ship's CO suspended from davits on the right. Note the Hotchkiss 47mm ATB gun mounted on the starboard wing of the after bridge. The photo was taken at Brest. *(Private collection)*

hoist. The inner walls of the casemates were lined with projectile racks with lockers for ready-use cartridges and bagged charges beneath. The plans of the port-side forward casemate of *Dupetit-Thouars* show ten projectiles on racks around the curved inner wall, each with a full propellant charge (one cartridge plus one powder bag) beneath, and a more substantial bank of racks on the forward transverse bulkhead for twelve full rounds (see Casemate plan).

The casemates were located directly above their respective magazines. The magazines for the two forward 164.7mm guns were immediately forward of boiler room No 1 at hold level, those for the two after guns immediately abaft boiler room No 4. The magazines for the midship guns were between the forward group of boiler rooms and the engine rooms, and between the after group of boiler rooms and the condenser rooms respectively (see GA Plans).

The magazines for the forward pair of 100mm guns were directly abaft the 194mm magazines, and those for the after guns between the magazines for 164.7mm guns Nos 5 and 6. Each of the magazines was served by a single centreline hoist. There were also ready-use racks for these guns, which used semi-fixed ammunition; the plans show stowage for twenty rounds on the rear wall of the deckhouse behind the two forward mountings, and around the after ventilator inboard of the two after mountings.

Magazine capacity was 200rpg for the 164.7mm guns and 250rpg for the 100mm guns.

ATB guns

The *Gueydon* class carried a more powerful battery of ATB guns than the *Dupleix* class. There were no fewer than eighteen 47mm Mle 1885 guns: four on the lower platform of the military foremast, four on the lower bridge deck and the flying deck around the mainmast, four on the upper deck (2nd deck) amidships, and six behind ports in the hull. Of the six hull guns, the forward pair was mounted on the 1st deck, the midship and after pairs on the main deck. There were also four 37mm QF guns: two in the wings of the bridge and two on the quarterdeck.[6]

The main magazine for the 47mm and 37mm ATB guns was on the ship's axis between the forward 164.7mm magazines, and was served by a single centreline hoist for the lower guns and a separate hoist for the guns mounted on the platform of the military foremast; there was a second magazine for the 47mm guns aft served by a single hoist. This was a less satisfactory arrangement than that of earlier ships, as ammunition supply for the after guns implied a significant level of horizontal transfer. These guns therefore relied heavily on the ammunition stowed in ready-use lockers close to the mountings. Magazine provision for the light guns was 750 rounds per gun.

Six 60cm searchlight projectors were fitted for target illumination, and these were disposed as in the *Dupleix* class.

Torpedoes

There were two submerged torpedo tubes for 450mm Mle 1892 torpedoes. The torpedo flat was on the 2nd platform deck amidships, immediately above the athwartship magazines for the second pair of 164.7mm guns (see GA Plans). The tubes were angled 20° forward of the beam, and there were four spare torpedo bodies stowed against the rear wall. No mines were embarked in these ships.

6 In *Dupetit-Thouars* the two after guns were on the forward extension of the after bridge deck (see drawing).

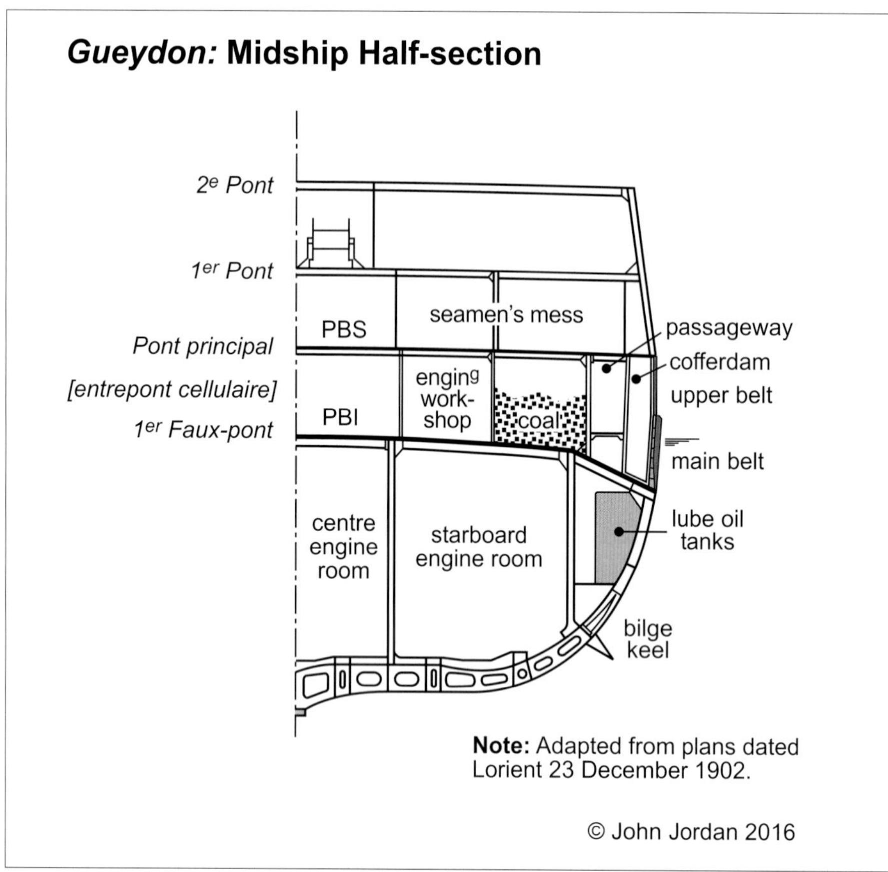

PROTECTION

Hull

The hull protection scheme adopted for the *Gueydon* class was almost identical to that of *Jeanne d'Arc*. There was a thick, single-strake waterline belt (*cuirasse épaisse*), topped by a light upper belt (*cuirasse mince*) that was increased in height at the forward end of the ship; the upper and lower belts extended from the bow almost to the stern, where they were closed by a transverse bulkhead of special steel. The main protective deck (PBI), which was inclined at the sides to meet the bottom of the belt, formed the floor of the cellular layer, while the upper protective deck (PBS) forming its roof was composed of lighter steel plating.

The main belt, which was secured to a 70mm teak backing, comprised twenty-four armour plates 1.95m high on either side of the ship; the length of each plate was 6m (ie five frames) amidships and 4.8m (four frames) at the ends. The plates were of homogeneous nickel-chrome steel and maximum thickness was 150mm amidships (plates 10–19), reducing progressively to 80/90mm at the bow and stern (see table). From 0.6m beneath the waterline the plates were tapered to 50mm at the bottom edge. The upper belt was secured directly to the hull plating (a double layer of 10mm steel amidships, reducing to 8mm fore and aft). Thickness was 85mm amidships,[7] declining to 75mm at the ends. At the bow it divided into two strakes, as in *Jeanne d'Arc*, and there was a thinner strake above it that tapered from 57mm to 40mm at its upper edge.

The after transverse bulkhead was composed of two separate plates (see Protection plan). The lower plate, which closed the main belt, had a uniform thickness of 84mm. The upper plate, which closed the light belt, was tapered from 84mm at its bottom edge to 40mm at the top edge.

The main protective deck (PBI) was the 1st platform deck. It comprised two layers of 10mm construction steel with an upper layer of 30mm mild steel plating (total thickness: 50mm). On the upper section of the slopes the 30mm plating was replaced by plates of 'super-soft' steel 55mm thick (total: 75mm). The upper protective deck (PBS), as in *Jeanne d'Arc*, was the main deck. It comprised a single layer of 10mm steel topped by reinforcing plates with a thickness of 6mm (total thickness: 16mm). Amidships, close to the centreline, there was a double layer of 10mm plating, still with a 6mm reinforcement.

Inside the armoured box formed by the two protective decks and the side belt there was the cellular layer introduced in *Jeanne d'Arc*, comprising a cofferdam, a longitudinal passageway 1m wide, subdivided by bulkheads with watertight doors every four frames (4.8m), and coal bunkers.

[7] Note that even with the double layer of 10mm plating this was less than the 115mm demanded by the *Conseil des Travaux*.

DUPETIT-THOUARS: ARMOUR PLATE THICKNESS MAIN AND UPPER BELTS

Plate	Main Belt *upper/lower edge*	Upper Belt *upper edge/joint(s)/lower edge*
1-6	90/50	40–57–66–75/70
7	105/50	40–57–75
8	120/50	40–57–75
9	135/50	40–57/75–85
10-19	150/50	85
20	135/50	85
21	120/50	75
22	105/50	75
23	90/50	75
24-26	80/50	75

Notes:

1. All the protective side plating was of special steel; the decks were of mild steel, while the 55mm reinforcing plates on the slopes were of 'super-soft' steel.
2. The total weight of the main belt was **430 tonnes**. The thickest plates of the main belt, which spanned five 1.2m frames, each weighed approximately 11.5 tonnes.
3. The upper belt was in three strakes, of which two covered the bow section up to the foremost casemate. The thickest (85mm) plates each weighed approximately 6.5 tonnes.

Dupetit-Thouars: Protection

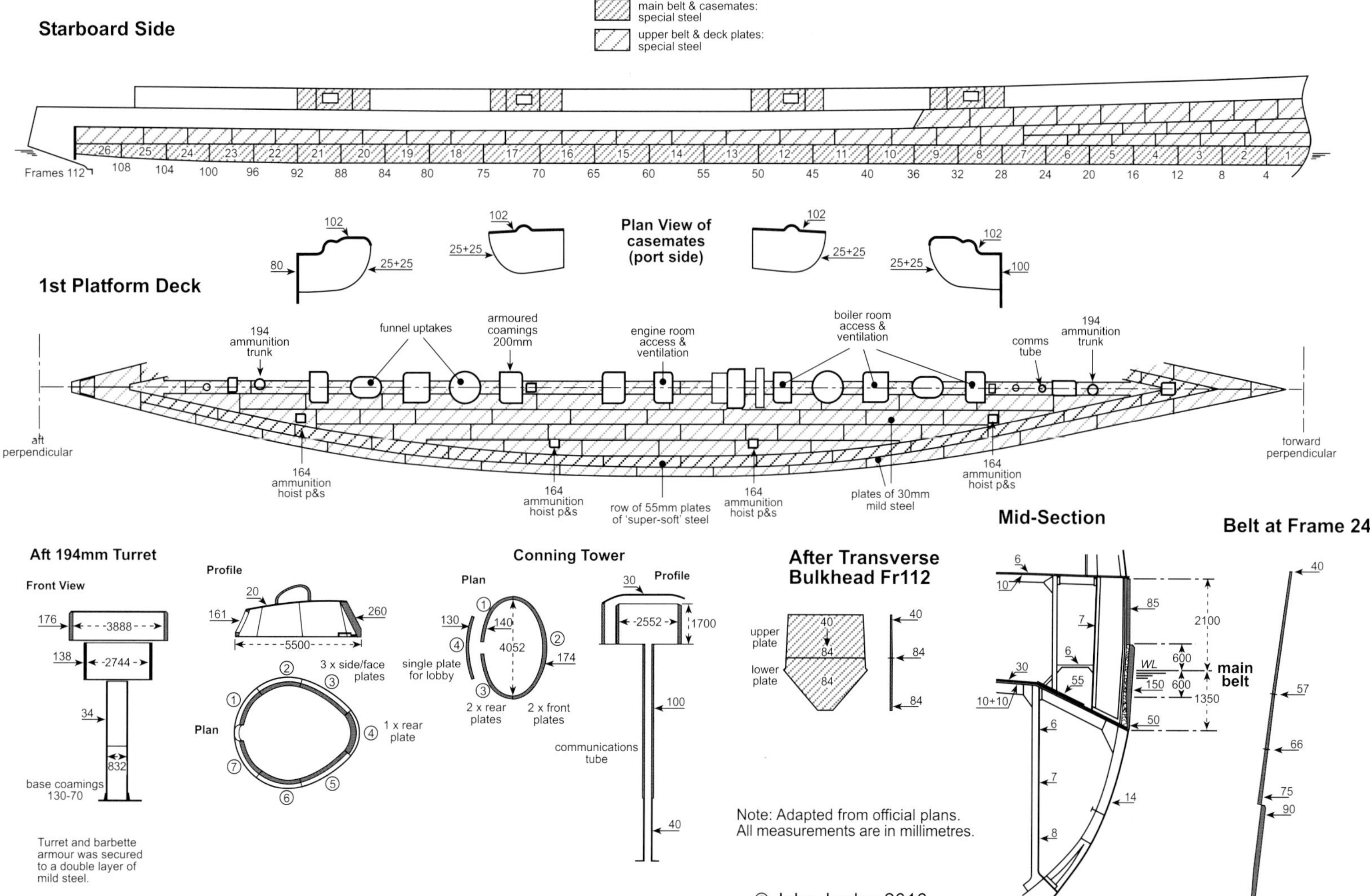

Turrets, casemates and conning tower

The 194mm turrets had a similar level of protection to those of *Jeanne d'Arc*. There were 161mm plates of special steel on the inclined face and sides of the cupola secured to a double layer of 13mm mild steel. The armour for the turret face and sides was composed of three plates on either side; the single 'balancing' plate at the rear of the turret was of mild steel and was 260mm thick. The roof of the turret was made up of plates of hardened steel 20mm thick, secured to a single layer of plating.

The circular fixed barbette protecting the lower part of the gunhouse and the roller paths was of 176mm special steel, and the ring over the working chamber was 138mm; the fixed armour, like that of the gunhouse, was secured to a double layer of 13/11mm steel. The trunk for the ammunition hoists, which was oval in plan, was of 34mm steel; the coamings at the base where the trunk penetrated the lower armoured deck were 130mm at their base tapering to 70mm.

The casemates were much more heavily protected than the sponson guns of the earlier ship. There was special steel plating 102mm thick on the faces, secured to a double layer of 10mm steel, and the forward and after casemates had end walls of special steel 100mm and 80mm thick respectively; the end walls were extended to the centreline and formed complete transverse bulkheads to protect against enfilading fire. The inner walls of the casemates comprised two layers of 25mm mild steel (total thickness 50mm)

The conning tower was elliptical in plan, as in *Jeanne d'Arc*, and had similar dimensions. However, the level of protection was increased, with 174mm armour plates on the face and sides and 140mm plating on the rear, and a curved 130mm vertical bulkhead to protect access directly behind it – for *Jeanne d'Arc* the respective figures were 138mm, 110mm and 90mm. The communications tube was formed by hoops of special steel 100mm thick above the upper protective deck and 50mm below, down to the main protective deck

MACHINERY

Despite attempts to standardise design in other areas, the *Marine Nationale* was still open to experimentation with propulsion machinery. Developments in engine and, in particular, boiler technology were at their peak during the mid-1890s, with prominent marine engineers such as Jacques-Augustin Normand, Sigaudy (FC Méditerranée, Le Havre) and Guyot (Indret) constantly advancing new proposals. The Navy was inclined to be conservative with regard to battleship design, but this was less true for cruisers, and the

Above: *Montcalm* during her speed trials in 1901 off the coast of Provence. She was the only ship of the three to have the Sigaudy–Normand small-tube boiler. *(Private collection)*

three ships of the *Gueydon* class all had different types of engine and steam-generating machinery.

Designed horsepower was 19,600CV. In *Gueydon*, built at Lorient naval dockyard, this was generated by four-cylinder VTE engines manufactured by the Société de la Loire in their works at Saint-Denis; *Montcalm*, ordered from the La Seyne shipyard of FC Méditerranée, had a four-cylinder model manufactured at their works in Marseille, *Dupetit-Thouars*, the last armoured cruiser to be built at Toulon, a three-cylinder model built by Schneider Le Creusot. The propellers on the outer shafts had a diameter of 4.6m, the propeller on the inner shaft 4.5m.

In *Gueydon* and *Dupetit-Thouars* steam was supplied by twenty-eight boilers: Niclausse in the former, Belleville in the latter. They were distributed between four boiler rooms, which were paired with an unusually wide separation between each pair due to the need to accommodate two athwartships magazines (for the centre 164.7mm casemate guns) between them in addition to the engine and condenser rooms. This meant that the end boiler rooms were at the point where the hull narrowed sharply: there were six boilers back-to-back in each of these spaces and eight in each of the broader centre boiler rooms (see GA Plans). The uptakes for each block of boilers were grouped together, and the funnels serving the end boiler rooms were narrower than the inboard pair, which were circular in plan – a feature that distinguished these ships from the contemporary *Dupleix* class.

Montcalm: Boiler Rooms

2nd Platform Deck
rue de chauffe 8
rue de chauffe 7
rue de chauffe 6
rue de chauffe 5
auxiliary machinery
condenser rooms
Engine Rooms
submerged torpedo room
rue de chauffe 4
rue de chauffe 3
rue de chauffe 2
Boiler Room 4 1 double-ended & 2 single-ended (port) Sigaudy–Normand boilers
Boiler Room 3 3 double-ended Sigaudy–Normand boilers
Boiler Room 2 3 double-ended Sigaudy–Normand boilers
Boiler Room 4 1 double-ended & 2 single-ended (std) Sigaudy–Normand boilers

The La Seyne-built *Montcalm* is generally credited in reference sources with twenty boilers of the Sigaudy–Normand small watertube type. The Normand boiler was more commonly fitted in torpedo boats, and there were initial concerns that it might not prove sufficiently robust or reliable for cruiser work. The Normand boiler as modified by engineer Sigaudy of FC Méditerranée was 'double-ended', and comprised two Normand-type boiler bodies mounted back-to-back with a common steam collector; the water drums at the base were generally bolted together rather than being shared. The theoretical advantage of such an arrangement was that there was some saving in space and weight compared to two independent boilers of the same type; the downside was that the steam collector was 6–7m long, so precautions were needed to prevent excessive changes in the water level when the ship was pitching. The only other installations of the Sigaudy–Normand boiler were in the fast cruiser *Châteaurenault*, which was building at the same La Seyne shipyard, and the two fleet torpedo boats of the *Dunois* class laid down at Cherbourg in 1896–7, although it was also initially considered for *Jeanne d'Arc* (see Chapter 3).

Châteaurenault had fourteen double-ended boilers to supply steam for engines that delivered 23,000CV, *Dunois* four for 7500CV. The latter ships are generally credited with eight boilers rather than four,[8] but this is clearly the number of boiler *bodies*, and this is also the case with *Montcalm*, which had a designed horsepower of 19,500CV. Plans of the machinery spaces of this ship[9] show a hybrid arrangement with three double-ended boilers of the Sigaudy–Normand type in each of the centre boiler rooms, and one double-ended plus two single-ended Sigaudy–Normand boilers in each of the outer boiler rooms (see schematic drawing).

The machinery trials of *Gueydon* were beset by problems. On 28 August 1902 a power trial was interrupted due to overheating, and on 31 October 1902 a full power trial had to be abandoned due to overheating of the head of a connecting rod. A 24-hour trial at normal power 10–11 January 1903 then had to be abandoned when the piston ring of the port HP cylinder gave way when the ship was steaming at 18 knots: seven of the nine bolts on the cover sheared and a serious accident was narrowly averted. In a full-power trial on 23 December 1902 *Gueydon* attained a speed of only 20.30 knots with 19,668CV, although this would be exceeded on 7 May 1903 when she made 21.05 knots.

The trials of *Montcalm* and *Dupetit-Thouars* ran more smoothly. A full-power trial for *Montcalm* on 30 October 1901 had to be abandoned but two weeks later, on 13 November, she made 21.14 knots with 19,735CV. On her own three-hour trial, run on 14 February 1905, *Dupetit-Thouars* attained

8 See, for example, Gardiner (ed), *Conway's All the World's Fighting Ships 1860–1905*, p 325.

9 The plans are held in the archives at Châtellerault and have not been made available online. The authors are grateful to Jean Moulin for this search.

PERFORMANCE ON THREE-HOUR FULL-POWER TRIALS

	Date	Speed	Horsepower	Shaft Revs	Consumption	Boiler
Montcalm	13 Nov 1901	21.14kts	19,735CV	135.97rpm	0.807kg/h/cv	Sigaudy-Normand
Gueydon	23 Dec 1902	20.30kts	19,668CV	135.23rpm	0.879kg/h/cv	Niclausse
Dupetit-Thouars	14 Feb 1905	22.02kts	22,031CV	139.07rpm	0.718kg/h/cv	Belleville

Source: CAAP: inventaire 432, sous-série 5I cartons 29620 (*Mo*), 83 (*Gu*), 58 (*DT*).

22.02 knots with 22,031CV, making her the fastest of the three. These ships were reportedly good steamers, with endurance for *Gueydon* calculated as 7030nm at 10 knots with a normal load of coal, and *Montcalm* 8500nm. The Sigaudy–Normand boilers of the latter ship apparently gave no trouble whatsoever during trials, and fuel consumption was estimated to be 8 per cent less than for the Niclausse boilers of *Gueydon* at full power, and 15 per cent less at 14,500CV. The Sigaudy–Normand boilers also proved more flexible, with a more rapid increase in power. For complete data on the power trials of these ships see the accompanying table.

One problem noted in relation to this class concerns the noise generated by the rattle and noise of the ash hoists. Coal-burning resulted in an accumulation of ash in the boiler grates that needed to be removed in order to maintain effective combustion. The ash was transferred into buckets that were then hoisted to the decks above and emptied over the sides. In the *Gueydon* class it was found that at full speed it was found necessary to keep all the ash hoists perpetually in operation, which prevented the men berthed in the vicinity from getting any sleep. Mechanical ash ejectors (*escarbilleurs*) were trialled in the stokeholds of some ships between 1895 and 1900, but the jaws used for crushing were perpetually breaking due to the fragments of hard minerals or iron mixed with the ashes.

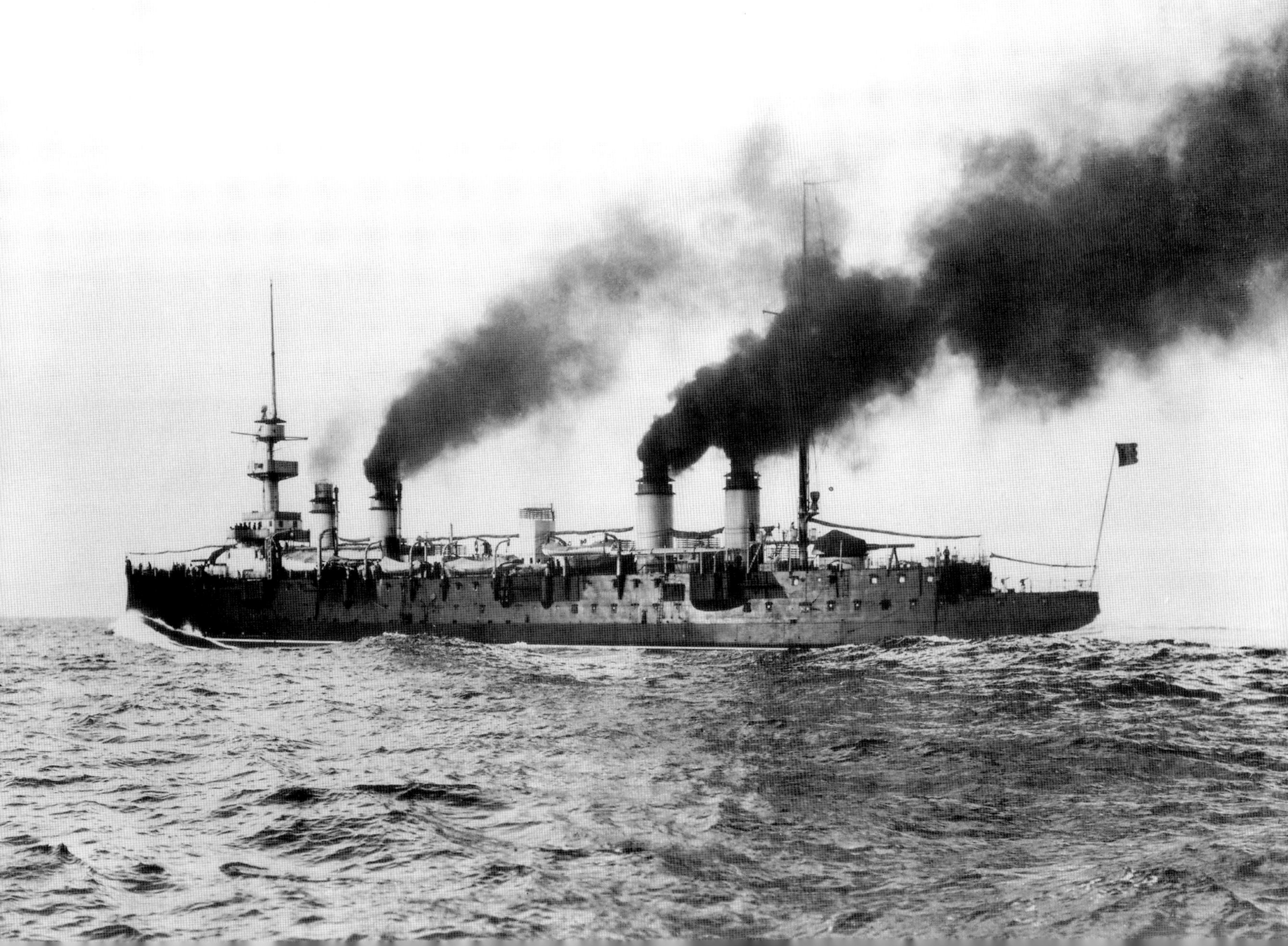

Below: *Gueydon* during her speed trials, probably in May 1903, when she made just over 21 knots with 17,500CV. *(Private collection)*

The problem would finally be resolved by the development of a new type of *escarbilleur* by Thirion & Fils, a well-known company of hydraulic engineers based in Paris that also provided bilge pumps to the Navy. The new model was first installed on the *Gambetta* class (see Chapter 7) and featured portable jaws that could be quickly changed in the event of damage.

Four 600A dynamos were provided to supply electrical power to the ship. Unusually, these were located not in the auxiliary machinery rooms, but in the wing compartments outboard of the engine rooms on the 2nd platform deck. The wing compartments were narrow and cramped, and both the dynamos themselves and the associated cabling were vulnerable to shock and water damage in the event of a torpedo hit, despite the provision of a longitudinal watertight bulkhead between the compartments and the side of the ship. There were auxiliary machinery rooms forward, aft and amidships, on the centreline between the magazines for 164.7mm guns Nos 5 and 6; each housed a large Thirion pump with a 600 tonnes/hour capacity, together with smaller pumps and the motors for the ammunition hoists for the QF guns.

CONSTRUCTION AND EARLY SERVICE

Montcalm was the first of the class to commission. Even before she officially entered service with the Northern Squadron, on 14 May 1902 she embarked President Emile Loubet for a state visit to Russia; the Tsar and Tsarina lunched on board at Kronstadt on 23 May, and the ship called in at Denmark, where she hosted the King, before returning to Dunkirk on 27 May. *Montcalm* was then despatched to Spithead, Portsmouth, flying the flag of Rear Admiral Richard, for a review to mark the coronation of King Edward VII. When she returned she was transferred, briefly, to the Mediterranean Squadron.

In 1903 both *Montcalm* and *Gueydon* were assigned to the naval squadron in the Far East, *Montcalm* serving as the flagship of Vice Admiral Maréchal from 22 March to 22 July, then Vice Admiral Bayle from 31 August. The presence of a powerful French squadron in the Far East was felt to be necessary during the hostilities between Russia and Japan, and in the autumn of 1905 *Montcalm* and *Gueydon* were joined by their newly-commissioned sister *Dupetit-Thouars*. All three ships returned to France in November of the

Below: *Dupetit-Thouars* moored in the roads at Le Havre. She is painted overall in the blue-grey livery adopted in January 1908. In October 1909 the 2nd Cruiser Division of the Northern Squadron would become the 2nd Light Division in the Mediterranean; the other two ships of the division were *Marseillaise* (flagship) and *Gloire*. *(Private collection)*

following year, arriving back in Brest in late December. During the transit *Montcalm* lost her port propeller and shaft in the Mediterranean, and had to undergo temporary repairs at Bizerte; on her return to Brest she was placed in reserve and underwent a major refit that lasted almost three years.

On completion of her repairs, *Montcalm* left for the Far East on 31 January 1910. She returned to Brest on 25 June 1911 to be placed in reserve, but was recommissioned in October of the following year and departed again for Saigon on 12 November 1912. She remained in the Far East with the cruiser *Dupleix* (see Chapter 4) until the outbreak of war, serving as the flagship of Rear Admirals Calloc'h de Kérillis and Huguet (24 December 1913 onwards).

In January 1907 *Gueydon* and *Dupetit-Thouars* were assigned to the 1st Cruiser Division of the Northern Squadron, with *Léon Gambetta* as flagship. On 12 June they were at Cherbourg to greet the Danish sovereigns. In October *Gueydon* was transferred to the newly-formed 2nd Cruiser Division, serving with *Gloire* (flag) and *Jeanne d'Arc*. Following manoeuvres in the Mediterranean, she returned to Cherbourg for a refit, and in October 1908 rejoined the Northern Squadron at Brest. On 27 July 1909, following the annual grand manoeuvres, ships of the Northern Squadron were at Cherbourg for a visit by the Tsar.

On 5 October 1909 *Dupetit-Thouars* was assigned to the 2nd Light Division of the Mediterranean Squadron, serving alongside *Marseillaise* (flag) and *Gloire*. With the entry into service of more modern cruisers in 1910, *Gueydon* and *Dupetit-Thouars* were placed in reserve. In November 1913 they were recommissioned to serve alongside *Gloire* (flag) in the Atlantic Training Division (*Division d'instruction de l'Océan*). With the outbreak of

Gueydon Class: Early Service

	Gueydon	Montcalm	Dupetit-Thouars
1902	Trials	Northern Squ (fl)	Building
1903	Far East	Far East (fl)	
1904			↓
1905			Trials
1906	↓	↓	Far East
1907	Northern Squ	Reserve	Northern Squ
1908			
1909	↓	↓	↓
1910	Reserve	Far East (fl)	Lt Squ Med
1911		↓	Reserve
1912		Reserve	
1913	↓	Far East (fl)	↓
1914	*Div d'instruction*	↓	*Div d'instruction*

Below: *Montcalm* in the white and buff livery of ships deployed to the DNEO. She would serve longer than any other French armoured cruiser in the Far East: from 1903 to 1906, from 1910 to 1911, and again from 1913 to 1915. In this photo she is flying the flag of a vice admiral from her foretopmast. *(Private collection)*

Right: *Montcalm* and *Gueydon* in Ha Long Bay, Indochina, between 1903 and 1906. *(Private collection).*

GUEYDON vs *CRESSY* (GB)

	Gueydon	*Cressy*[1]
No in class:	3	6
Built:	1898–1905	1898–1904
Displacement:	9500 tonnes	12,000 tonnes
Dimensions:	138m x 19.4m	134m x 21.2m[2]
Propulsion:		
Engines	3-shaft VTE	2-shaft VTE
Horsepower	19,500CV	21,000CV
Speed	21 knots	21 knots
Armament:		
Main guns	2 x 194mm (2 x I)	2 x 234mm (2 x I)
QF guns	8 x 164mm (8 x I) 4 x 100mm (4 x I)	12 x 152mm (12 x I)
ATB guns	18 x 47mm (18 x I) 4 x 37mm (4 x I)	12 x 76mm (12 x I)[3] 3 x 47mm (3 x I)[3]
TT	2 x 450mm	2 x 450mm
Protection:		
Belt	150mm	150mm
Main turrets	176mm	150mm
Casemates	102mm	125mm
Conning tower	174mm	300mm
Deck	50/75mm[2]	40mm

Notes:

1 The six armoured cruisers of the *Cressy* class were designed by White as a response to the cruisers of the *Gueydon* class (see D K Brown, *Warrior to Dreadnought*, p 157).

2 Metric equivalents have been supplied for *Cressy* in order to give a comparison. The equivalents for gun calibres are exact; those for armour thicknesses are to the nearest 5mm.

3 In RN service these guns were the 12pdr and 3pdr respectively.

4 For the protective deck, the first figure given relates to the flat, the second to the inclined section at the sides. The figures for *Gueydon* include a double layer of mild steel plating.

war they would be reactivated and assigned to the 2nd Division of the *Escadre légère* at Brest; the flagship of the division was *Gloire* (CA Le Cannellier).

EVALUATION

Following a period of experimentation, the three ships of the *Gueydon* class constituted France's first settled 'fleet' cruiser design. Although they had their faults, notably the lack of uniformity in their propulsion machinery, they were practical ships with a good balance between offensive and defensive capabilities and were good steamers. More importantly, the design would form the basis for a series of armoured cruisers with similar characteristics that would constitute the bulk of France's cruiser strength at the outbreak of war in 1914. The *Gueydon*s would be followed closely by the five improved ships of the *Gloire* class, and it was initially envisaged that their more powerful successors of the *Gambetta* class would be built in similar numbers.

Although worn out by August 1914, largely due to their extensive deployments to the Far East, they would be recommissioned to serve in the Channel, the Middle East and the Atlantic during the Great War.

CHAPTER 6:

THE FLEET CRUISERS OF THE *GLOIRE* CLASS

THE NAVAL PROGRAMME OF 1896 had stipulated the construction of five new armoured cruisers for the fleet. The immediate result was the authorisation of the three ships of the *Gueydon* class (9500-tonne type). This left two ships to be authorised, and in late 1897 the *Service Technique des Constructions Navales* (STCN) was instructed to undertake studies to see what could be achieved on 10,000 tonnes.

In the interests of continuity and uniformity Bertin was initially inclined to make minimal changes to the hull and machinery, particular if the ships were to be ordered from the same yards as the ships of the 9500-tonne type. He proposed simply adding two shielded 164.7mm mountings on the upper deck amidships with wide firing arcs (as featured in the original design for the 9500-tonne type) or, alternatively, two guns of the same calibre in turrets with 120mm protection. The open mountings of the first proposal would cost 100 tonnes, the turrets 220 tonnes. Both solutions would require adjustment in other weights, so displacement for the first ship would be 9840 tonnes, and for the second 10,150 tonnes. The study found that investing an extra 100+ tonnes in propulsion machinery would have little benefit, and that if greater endurance were required it would be preferable to return to the dimensions of the C3 proposal of 1897.

In 1898 the Navy's construction programme was amended to include a further six armoured cruisers, and it was planned to lay down three of these under the 1898 budget. The *Conseil des Travaux* duly met on 26 and 29 April and 3 May to advise on the best use of the additional 500 tonnes displacement. Minister Besnard wanted the hulls to be sheathed in wood, but the *Conseil* opposed this measure, which would have cost an estimated 350 tonnes, leaving only 150 tonnes available for improvements. The sheathing was also felt to be vulnerable to damage, and it could not easily be secured to the face-hardened armour plates now being introduced.

The STCN proposal for two additional shielded QF guns was considered, together with other options

Left: The armoured cruiser *Marseillaise* on the slipway at Brest. Note the temporary structure over the slipway to protect the work from the elements. *(Private collection)*

suggested by the 'Sections'. The principal modifications proposed by the *Conseil* were an increase from 63 to 105 rounds per gun (rpg) for the main 194mm guns (cost 10 tonnes), and an increase from 16mm to 30mm in the upper protective deck at the expense of the lower protective deck, for which 40–50mm was considered sufficient.

One radical solution offered for consideration was the replacement of the casemate guns by eight 164.7mm in twin turrets; this would give weight savings which could be invested in protection for the hull. Alternatively, there could be a mix of casemate guns and turrets – the solution finally adopted. The *Conseil* thought that this too would provide weight savings (125 tonnes) which could be invested in protection; however, this solution also implied the suppression of the additional two shielded guns proposed by the STCN, which it disliked.

The principal concern of the *Conseil* was to improve the protection of the armoured citadel by adopting a belt with a uniform thickness of 134mm (excluding plating), with upper and lower protective decks of 30mm and 40/70mm respectively.

Minister Besnard was compelled to accept the suppression of sheathing, which was opposed by all parties, and on 10 May instructed the STCN to draw up a new proposal. Bertin responded on 18 May with a project which, he claimed, differed from the recommendations of the *Conseil des Travaux* only in two respects: coal bunkerage was to remain the same as in the 9500-tonne type – the *Conseil* had wanted an additional 125 tonnes – and the height of the cellular layer had been increased from 2.1m to 2.35m. Ammunition stowage for the 194mm guns was increased from 63rpg to 100rpg, the four 164.7mm casemate guns amidships were now in single turrets,[1] and the number of 100mm QF guns had been increased from four to six. The after pair of 164.7mm casemates had been lowered by one deck as requested by the Council, so that the ammunition hoists were now protected by the cellular layer;[2] command was now 3.55m. These modifications cost 145 tonnes.

With regard to protection, the sides of the cellular layer were now protected by a second strake of Harveyised armour with a thickness (excluding plating) of 130mm, tapering slightly to 120mm at its upper edge, and the upper protective deck had been boosted to 30mm as requested by the *Conseil*; the thickness of the lower protective deck was

[1] The turret was to have been the enclosed turret (*tourelle fermée*) studied in connection with the original design for the 7700-tonne cruisers of the *Dupleix* class. It would subsequently be superseded by a new type of *tourelle-barbette*.

[2] There was less concern for the ammunition hoists for the forward pair of casemates, as these were protected by the 56mm upper belt.

Marseillaise: Profile & Plan

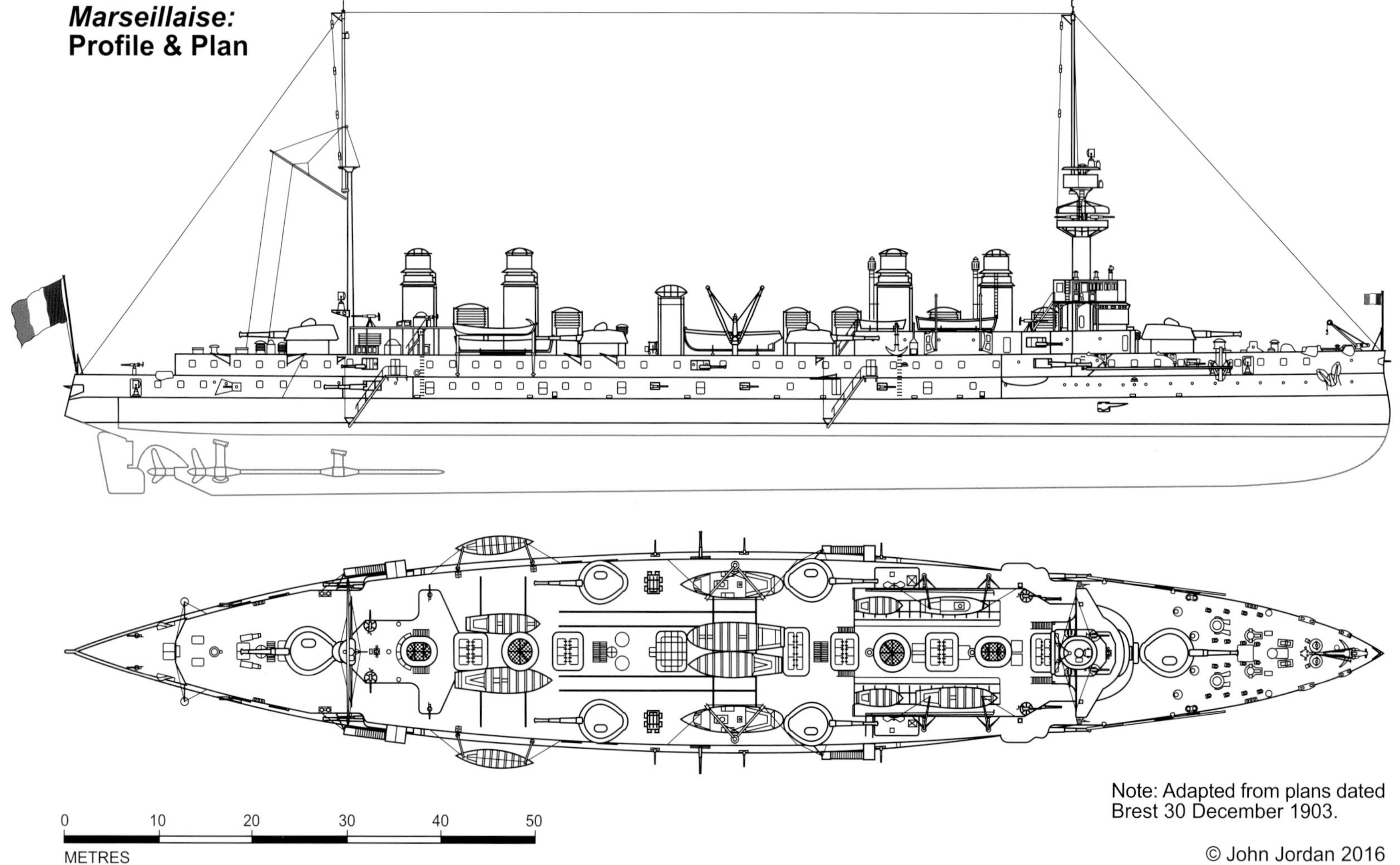

Note: Adapted from plans dated Brest 30 December 1903.

BUILDING DATA

Name	Builder	Laid down	Launched	Trials	Commissioned
Gloire	Arsenal de Lorient	5 Sep 1899	27 Jun 1900	2 Jan 1903	28 Apr 1904
Marseillaise	Arsenal de Brest	10 Jan 1900	14 Jul 1900	1 Feb 1903	Oct 1903
Sully	FC Méditerranée (La Seyne)	24 May 1899	4 Jun 1901	26 Jan 1903	Jan 1904
Amiral Aube	Société de la Loire	Feb 1901	9 May 1902	15 Apr 1903	1 Apr 1904
Condé	Arsenal de Lorient	29 Jan 1901	12 Mar 1902	15 Sep 1903	12 Aug 1904

unchanged. The cost of the additional hull protection was 214 tonnes.[3]

The modification to the distribution of weights compared with the 9500-tonne type was detailed as follows:

Hull	+117 tonnes
Artillery	+145.5 tonnes (incl protection)
Protection	+214.1 tonnes
Total	**+476.6 tonnes**

This gave projected displacements of 9516 tonnes (including a 115-tonne margin) for *Gueydon* and 9992.6 tonnes (including a 200-tonne margin) for the new ships.

Dimensions were to be 138m x 20.8m x 7.75m (aft). This represented an increase in beam of fully 1.4m (necessary to compensate for the increase in topweight), and Bertin warned that the width of the gates for the new Saigon graving dock, currently being manufactured at Le Creusot, would need to be increased by 1m if the new cruisers were to be docked there.[4] The machinery, which needed to be slightly uprated to deliver the designed 21 knots due to the increase in beam, was disposed as in the 9500-tonne type.

Bertin complained that the refusal by the *Conseil des Travaux* to consider speeds of 23 knots or more meant that French cruisers necessarily had to be more heavily armed and better protected than their foreign contemporaries. He claimed that higher speed would actually result in a cheaper ship, and proposed a return to the dimensions of *Jeanne d'Arc*. The Minister was willing to consider a ship of 11,500 tonnes, but only if the benefits extended to speed and radius. These ideas were rejected out of hand by the *Conseil* at

[3] Bertin was keen to point out that this represented an increase of 6 tonnes on the *Conseil*'s proposal, and that the distribution of weights was broadly in line with the principles laid down in the *Conseil*'s meetings of 11 and 15 February.

[4] Bertin also served notice that in the future docks overseas would need to accommodate cruisers with a beam of 25m.

Marseillaise: GA Plans

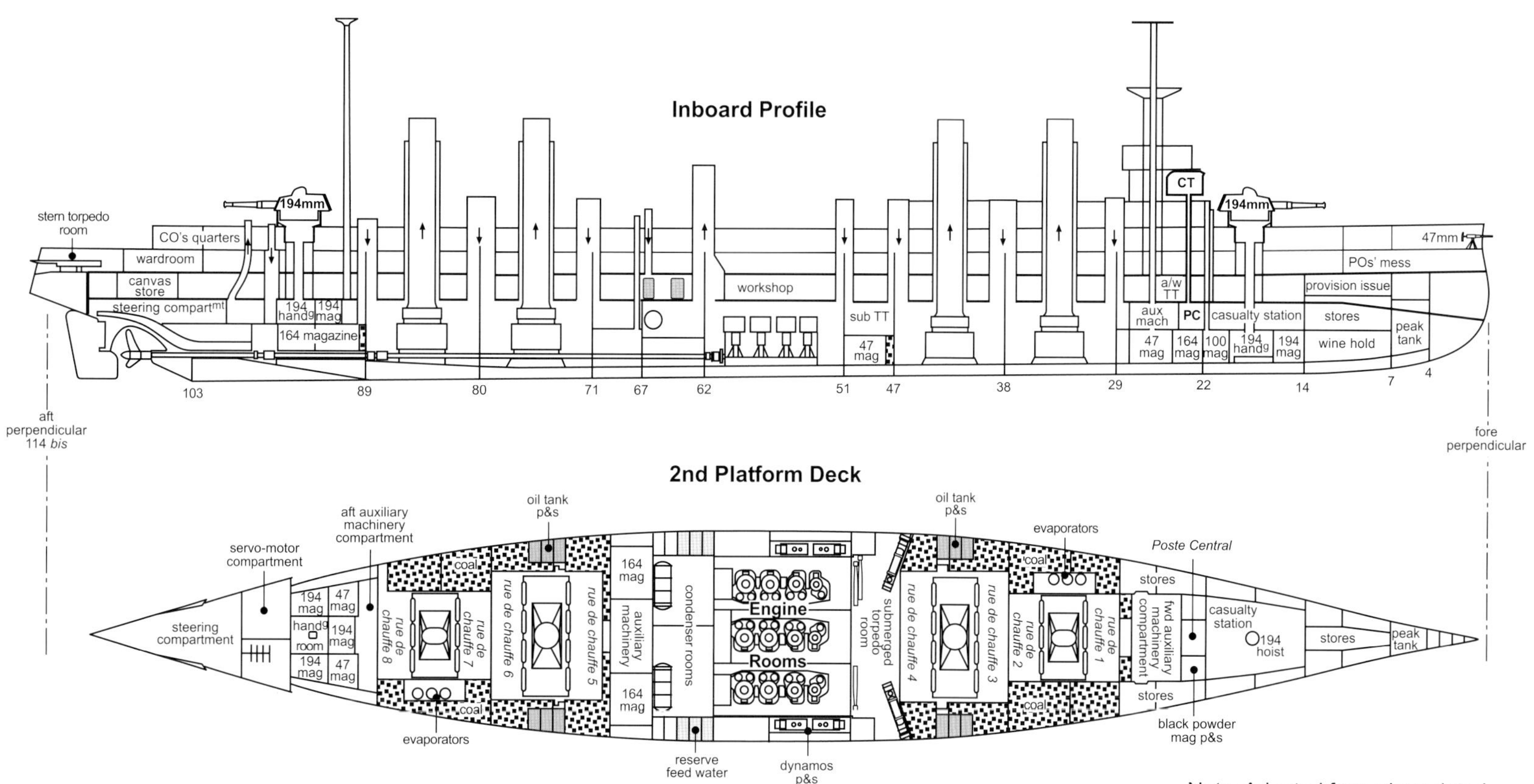

The bow 47mm ATB gun is present only in the plans of *Marseillaise* and *Sully*; it does not appear to have been fitted on completion.

Above: *Amiral Aube* shortly after she entered service in the black and buff livery worn until 1908. She was assigned, together with her sisters *Gloire* and *Condé*, to the 1st Cruiser Division of the Northern Squadron. *(Private collection)*

its meeting of 20 August, which recommended that only the 10,000-tonne project be retained. The *Conseil* also expressed its displeasure with the STCN's failure to implement its proposal to raise the height of the lower protective deck. However, by this time Besnard had again been superseded as Minister by Edouard Lockroy, who was more favourable towards Bertin's ideas, and the *Conseil*'s protests were ignored. Time being of the essence, on 17 September the new Minister authorised the construction of three cruisers of 10,000 tonnes to be based on the STCN plans. It was initially envisaged that *Condé* would be built at Cherbourg, *Gloire* at Lorient and *Sully* in a private shipyard. The orders for the two arsenal-built ships were placed on 17 September 1898, and a contract with FC Méditerranée (La Seyne) for Sully was signed on 24 May of the following year. Construction of *Condé* was subsequently transferred to Lorient (Ministerial Directive 8 April 1899), where she would follow *Gloire* onto the slipway. During 1899 two further ships were ordered: *Marseillaise* was to be built at Brest (ordered 19 June) and *Amiral Aube* by Société de la Loire (contract dated 9 August). The cost of each of the five ships, which was 22–24 million FF,[5] showed a slight increase over the *Gueydons*.

NOMENCLATURE

Gloire means 'Glory' and is one of the key tenets of the French Navy. The armoured cruiser *Gloire* was the fourteenth ship of the name; her most illustrious predecessor was the world's first ironclad, 1858–83.

La **Marseillaise** was a marching song written and composed by Claude-Joseph Rouget de Lisle in 1792. It was adopted in 1795 as the national anthem of the French Republic.

Hyacinthe-Laurent-Théophile **Aube** (1826–90) was a French admiral who held several important governmental positions during the Third Republic, and who developed the theories of the so-called *Jeune Ecole*, which favoured opposing an anticipated British naval blockade of French ports by a mass of cheap torpedo

[5] This compares with a figure of 28.5m FF for the contemporary battleship *Suffren*.

Above: *Sully* soon after she entered service. In early 1904 she would be assigned to the Far East Squadron, joining *Montcalm* (flagship) and *Gueydon*. In February the following year she would be lost following a grounding in Ha Long Bay – see page 132. *(Private collection)*

boats, allied to fast cruisers that would operate independently as blockade breakers to threaten British commerce. As Navy Minister 1886–7 Aube was responsible for a pause in the construction of battleships.

Maximilien de Béthune, duc de **Sully** (1560–1641), was a nobleman, soldier and statesman who became the right-hand man of Henri IV of France despite his Protestant faith. He built a strong, highly centralised administrative system using coercion and other highly effective techniques. He became a marshal of France in 1634.

Louis de Bourbon, Prince of **Condé** (1621–86) was a French general and the most famous representative of the Condé branch of the House of Bourbon. Known also as the Duc d'Enghien, he was appointed to command against the Spanish in Northern France during the Thirty Years War, and conceived and directed the decisive attack that won the Battle of Rocroi (May 1643). He subsequently fought with distinction in campaigns in the Low Countries and on the Rhine.

HULL AND SUPERSTRUCTURES

The hull of the *Gloire* class was similar in virtually every aspect of its construction and layout to that of the *Gueydon* class. Frame spacing was 1.2m, and the internal decks were similarly arranged and designated. Only the revised layout of the main guns impacted on the external configuration and the internal layout.

With the move to single turrets for the centre 164.7mm guns, the battery of 47mm ATB guns could no longer be partially mounted on the upper (2nd) deck. The four guns thereby displaced were moved down to the main deck and fired through open ports in the hull; there were now four pairs of guns disposed in this fashion. The ATB guns on the superstructure decks and on the lower platform of the military foremast remained in place.

Of the five ships of the class, only *Sully* appears to have been specially fitted as a flagship from the outset. She had a new type of conning tower with a floor area sufficient to accommodate an admiral and key personnel from his flag staff. As in *Montcalm* and the station cruisers of the *Dupleix* class, the admiral's quarters were at the after end of the 1st deck. In the other four ships these quarters were allocated to the ships' commanding officer. These arrangements were clearly flexible, and in 1904 *Marseillaise* was taken in hand at Toulon to undergo the necessary modifications that would allow her to serve as the flagship of Rear Admiral Campion (Light Division, Mediterranean Squadron). She and her sister *Gloire* would see extensive service as flagships both before and during the First World War.

ARMAMENT

Main guns

The main 194mm gun, mounted in single turrets fore and aft, was the same Mle 1893–1896 that equipped the *Gueydon* class. Height of command was 9.15m for the fore turret, and 8.8m for the after turret. The FC Méditerranée plans of *Sully* show that the turret was similar in conception to that fitted in the earlier ships but incorporated a number of improvements.

The deep working chamber suspended beneath the rotating gunhouse had vertical sides. Eight projectiles were stowed horizontally on a circular shell carrier, and twenty-four one-third (bagged) charges were

Right: The after 194mm turret of *Gloire*. Directly above the turret, on a platform projecting from the after side of the mainmast, is a 60cm searchlight projector under canvas. *(Private collection)*

Below: The forward 194mm gun turret of *Amiral Aube*. (Private Collection)

stowed in vertical bays around the sides of the working chamber beneath them.

Projectiles were moved from the shell room to the lower handing room in a steel crate via an overhead rail and dropped into a basket that had cells for a single projectile and three one-third charges (see schematic drawing). The duplex hoist had two linked baskets: when one ascended, the other descended. The basket was raised by the hoist, which was driven by a Sautter-Harlé electric motor with manual backup, from the handing room to the working chamber. As soon as the basket arrived at the top of the hoist it was automatically checked. The projectile, which weighed between 75kg (CI) and 90kg (APC/SAPC), was then lifted from the basket using a small hand winch and transferred to the circular shell carrier; the bagged charges were lifted out manually and stowed in the vertical bays.

The circular shell carrier could be rotated by hand to bring any desired shell under the hand-driven clip hoist. The selected projectile was raised into the gunhouse, emerging to the left of the gun; it was then lifted or shunted onto one of the three waiting trays or moved to the breech of the gun using an overhead rail. To the left of the breech three angled scuttles were set into the floor of the gunhouse, and the bagged charges passed through by hand. Three ready-use charges were stowed horizontally beneath the waiting trays close to the breech and there was vertical stowage for a further six charges on the left-hand wall of the turret.

Single Turret for 194mm Mle 1893–1896

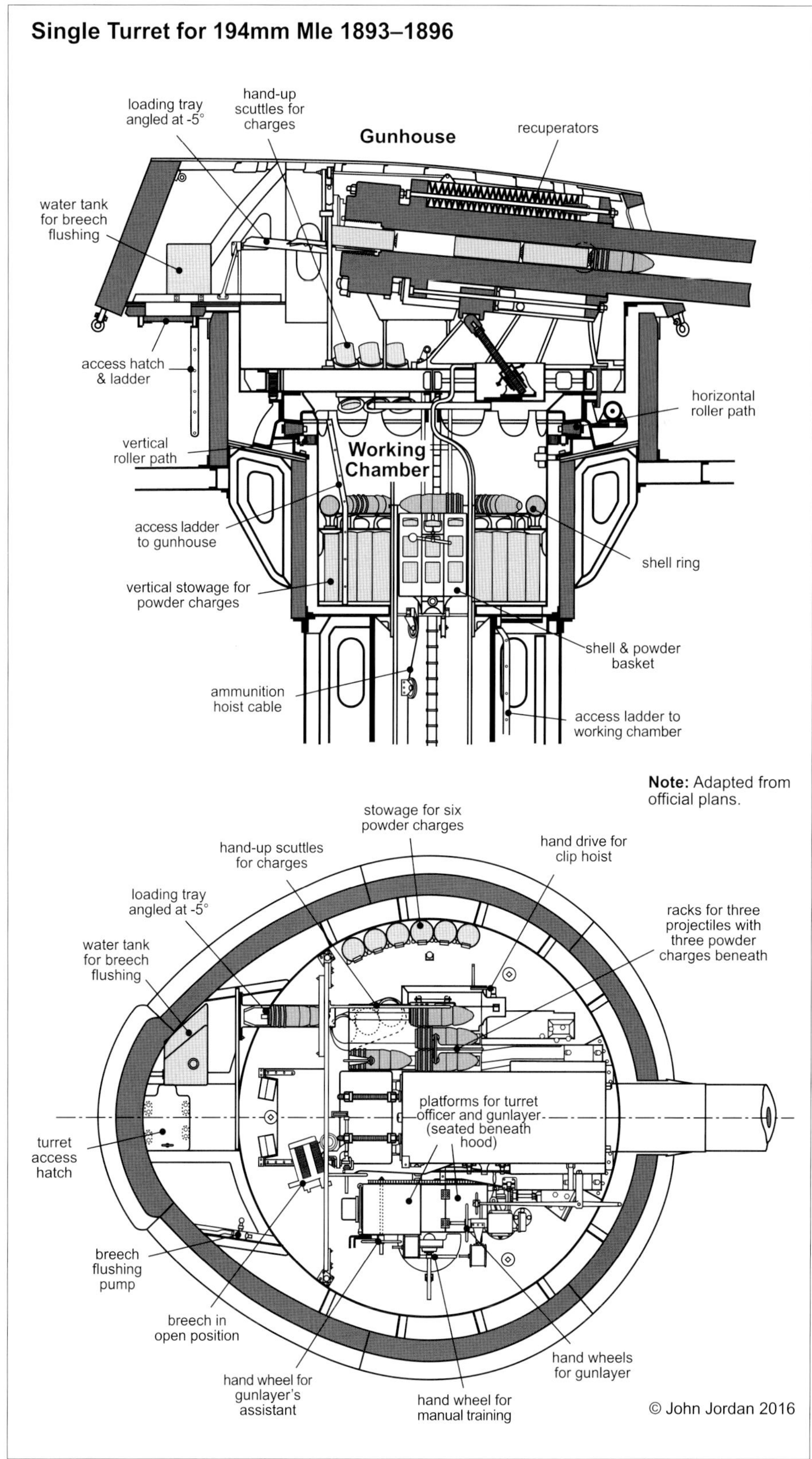

***Marseillaise:* Ammunition Supply for 194mm Guns (Schematic)**

Magazine Arrangements Aft

ammunition tube
overhead rail
shell room
hoist
magazine
164.7 magazine
handing room

Note: Adapted from sketches in Admiralty Reports on Foreign Naval Affairs 1904 Vol I.

Basket for Hoist

C1 C2 C3 Pr basket

C1–C3 are cells for powder bags. Pr is cell for projectile.

Steel Carrier for Projectile

mobile elements
fixed part of crate

Circular Shell Carrier

clip hoist
wall of working chamber
shell carrier

Clip Hoist

wire rope from local winch
inclined metal guides
securing clips

© John Jordan 2017

This gave a capacity of three complete ready-use rounds (each comprising one projectile plus three one-third charges) in the gunhouse, and eight in the working chamber.

In place of the rotating tray of earlier turrets there was a tray permanently angled at -5° that traversed laterally on a system of bars from a position just behind the waiting trays and was aligned with the breech when the gun was depressed for loading (see 194mm Turret plan). Ramming was done by hand, as with earlier guns.[6] The three bagged charges, each of which weighed approximately 11.25kg, were also loaded and rammed manually.

There was no stowage for projectiles or charges at the rear of the turret. This enabled the water tank and pump for breech-flushing to be mounted directly behind the breech.

6 Power loading and ramming in the *Marine Nationale* was a much later development.

164.7mm turrets

The single turrets for the secondary guns were similar in their conception and general layout to the 194mm turret, but there were a number of significant differences. The 164.7mm Mle 1893–1896 fired a projectile weighing 45–55kg that could be more easily manhandled than the 194mm shells, and had a propellant charge comprising a single brass cartridge and a single powder bag. This had an impact on loading procedures and on ammunition stowage and supply.

The *tourelle-barbette* had the same deep working chamber as the 194mm turret, but the projectiles were stowed not on a shell ring but in superimposed fixed

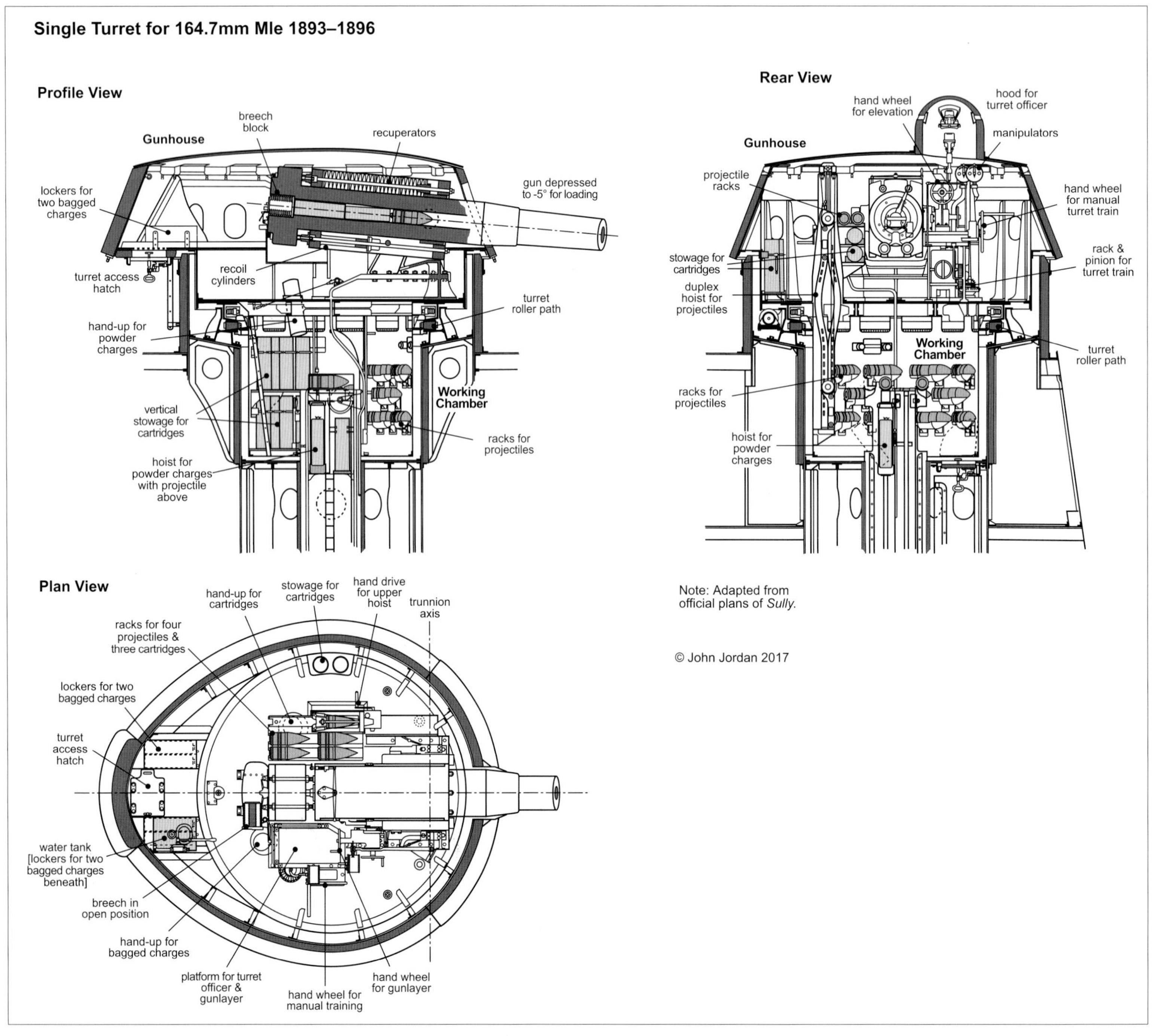

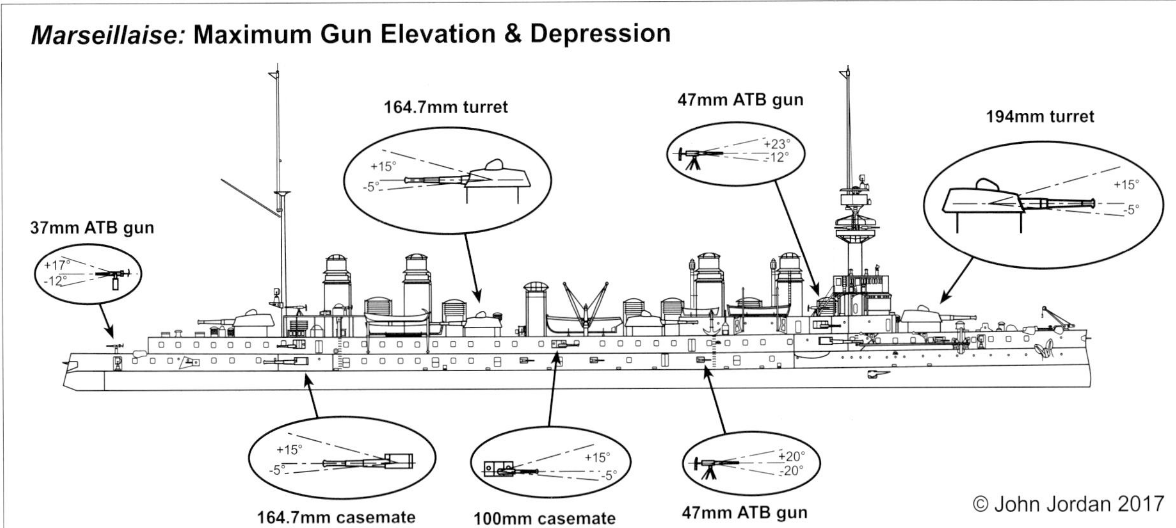

Note that for the 47mm ATB guns the angle of depression was more important than the angle of elevation, as it enabled the guns to fire against torpedo craft close-in. The angle of depression for each of the ATB guns varied according to its location.

racks on the front wall, with the charges stowed in a double tier on the rear wall. This increased shell stowage in the working chamber from eight to twelve. The capacity of the single hoist was likewise increased: the ammunition car carried two projectiles and two complete charges. The firing cycle of the 164.7mm gun was superior to the heavier 194mm gun, so the manually-driven hoist that raised projectiles from the working chamber to the gunhouse was a duplex model. There were separate hand-up scuttles in the gunhouse floor for cartridges and for the bagged charges – see 164.7mm Turret plan.

The projectiles were raised into the gunhouse by the customary manually-operated clip hoist and shunted onto waiting trays that could hold four shells. Beneath the waiting trays there were horizontal racks for two propellant cartridges, and there was vertical stowage for a further two cartridges against the left wall of the gunhouse. Flashproof lockers at the rear of the gunhouse could hold four bagged charges, making for four complete ready-use rounds in the gunhouse with a further twelve in the working chamber.

Both the 194mm and the 164.7mm single turrets allowed a maximum elevation of 15° and a maximum depression of 5° (see schematic drawing of *Marseillaise*). The 164.7mm and 100mm QF casemate guns were given the same angles of elevation/depression.

Casemate and 100mm QF guns

The armoured casemates for the forward pair of 164.7mm QF guns were on the 1st deck, as in the *Gueydon* class; the after pair of casemates was a deck lower, on the main deck. The height of command of the guns in the forward casemates was 5.9m; that of the after guns a mere 3.5m, making them difficult to work in heavy weather. The internal layout of the casemates varied from ship to ship. The plan of the starboard-side forward casemate of the last ship, *Condé*, shows a chute for projectiles running around the inner wall on either side of the access door (see Casemate plan). The ready-use shells were angled upwards on wooden blocks with lockers for vertical stowage of the cartridges and bagged charges beneath. In *Condé* the doors of these lockers were hinged so that when opened the charges were angled forwards to facilitate extraction. There was a rack for

CHARACTERISTICS

Displacement:	9996 tonnes
Dimensions:	
Length	138.00m pp; 139.78m oa
Beam	20.2m wl
Draught	7.55m aft
Propulsion:	
Boilers	*Gl & Con:* 28 Niclausse boilers others: 28 Belleville boilers
Engines	*Mar & AA*: 3-shaft 4-cylinder VTE others: 3-shaft 3-cylinder VTE
Horsepower	20,500CV (designed)
Speed	21 knots (designed)
Coal	1050 tonnes normal; 1660 tonnes full load
Endurance	6500nm at 10 knots
Armament:	
Main guns	2 x 194mm/40 Mle 1893–1896 in single turrets
Medium guns	8 x 164.7mm/45 Mle 1893–1896 QF in four single turrets and four casemates 6 x 100mm/45 Mle 1893 QF in single mountings
ATB guns	18 x 47mm/40 Mle 1885 QF in single mountings 4 x 37mm QF in single mountings
Torpedo tubes	3 a/w, 2 sub tubes for 450mm torpedoes 16 torpedoes Mle 1892
Protection:	
Main belt	150mm/130mm max
Decks	24mm PBS 25mm PBI
194 turrets	161mm
164 turrets	96mm
164 casemates	102mm
Conning tower	174mm
Boats:	1 x 11m steam launch 1 x 10m steam pinnace 1 x 7.65m White launch 1 x 10.5m pulling pinnace 2 x 10m pulling cutters 1 x 8.5m pulling cutter 1 x 8m pulling cutter 2 x 8.5m whalers 2 x 5m dinghies
Complement:	
As private ship	25 officers, 590 men

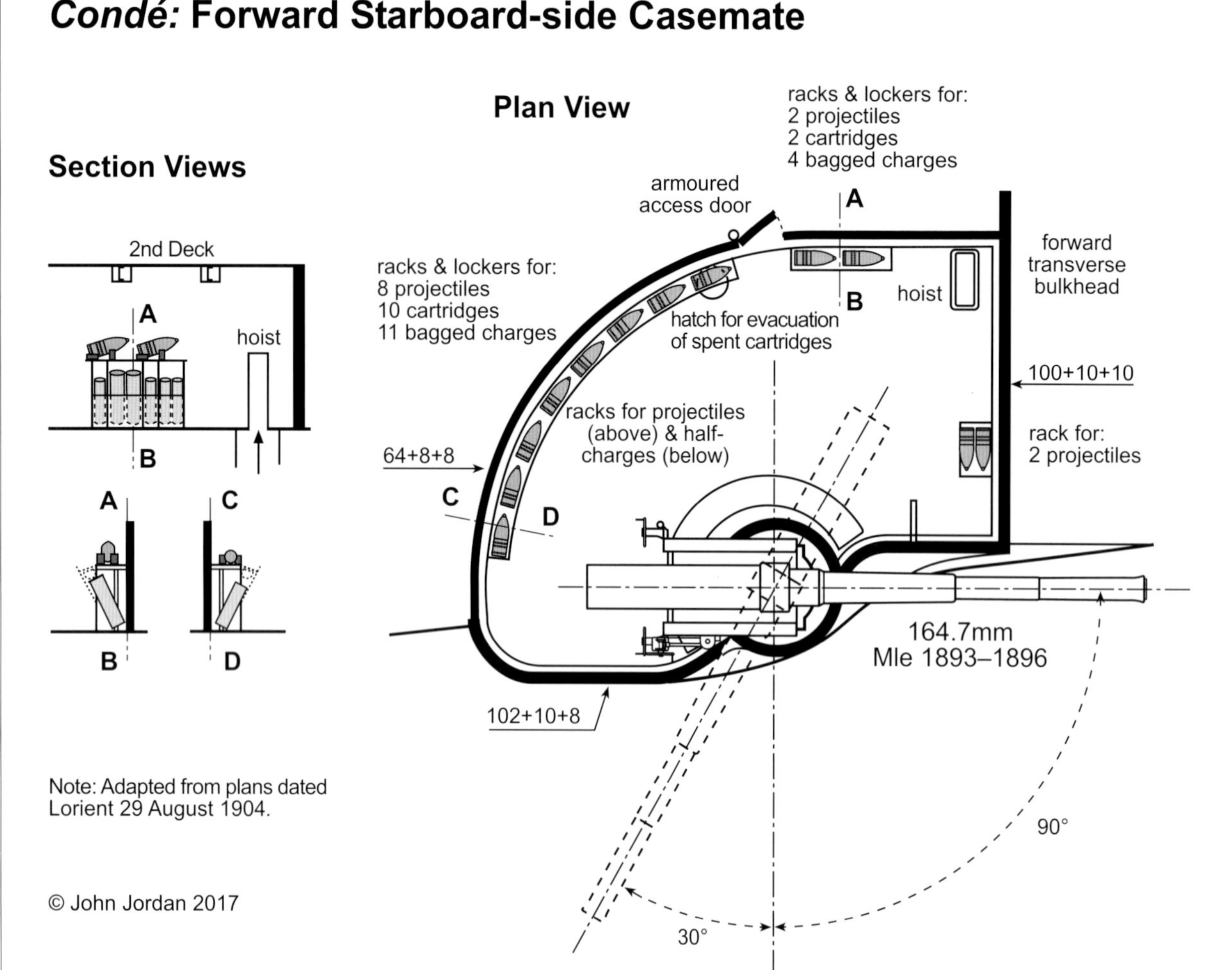

A comparison with the forward casemate of *Dupetit-Thouars* (see page 104) reveals that although it had a broadly similar configuration it was approximately 0.7m shorter at its forward end. The projectile racks around the inner wall had alternate paired lockers for cartridges and bagged charges, which were stowed vertically. The plans for *Condé* show locker doors which were hinged at half-height and when opened tilted the half-charge forward for easy access. Other ships of the class, including *Condé*'s Lorient-built sister *Gloire*, show different arrangements: *Gloire* had the same deep ready-use stowage rack on the forward bulkhead as *Dupetit-Thouars*, allied to an overhead rail system to transfer the projectiles to the breech of the gun. This highlights both the degree to which the engineer in charge of the construction of a particular ship could decide internal fittings and arrangements, and also the French predilection for incremental improvements even in ships of the same class built in the same yard.

two additional projectiles against the forward bulkhead; this made for a total of twelve complete ready-use rounds, as in the turrets.

Of the six 100mm QF guns the first pair was mounted within the wings of the lower bridge deck, as in the *Gueydons*. The remaining four guns were mounted in pairs amidships and aft on the 1st deck and fired through open ports in the hull; the after pair was directly above the after 164.7mm casemates. There was no protection for these guns, which were located in the intervals between the blocks of officer and petty officer cabins. Ready-use ammunition – generally twenty rounds – was stowed in racks against the outer walls of the cabins. The 100mm magazines were located as in the *Gueydon* class, all four of the after guns being served by the two hoists of the midship magazine.

New projectiles

Shells with steel or cast iron bodies filled with *mélinite* had been in service with the *Marine Nationale* since the late 1880s and had provided the rationale for the armoured cruiser as a type (see Chapter 1). *Mélinite* was a powerful explosive, but the shell needed to penetrate the sides of the ship's hull or superstructures in order to cause maximum damage and disseminate the potentially lethal fumes that accompanied combustion of the burster charge. The advent of lightweight homogenous steel armour, which was applied to the outer shell of the new cruisers, made penetration less likely.

Trials in 1896 against the old station battleship *La Galissonnière* demonstrated that against even thin armour black powder-filled shell was as effective as shells filled with *mélinite*; the latter was detonated by the armour plate and much of the force of the explosion was dissipated outside the target. While this served to confirm the conceptual superiority of the armoured cruiser over the protected cruiser in resisting damage, it also highlighted a potential weakness in the offensive power of the medium QF guns.

One consequence was the development and adoption of soft caps to aid penetration for both armour piercing and high-explosive shell. Experiments were carried out in 1900, one year after the first ship of the *Gloire* class, *Sully*, was laid down. The new projectiles, which were designated *obus de semi-rupture*, had a thicker, stronger steel body allied to a soft cap and a base fuse. Due to the delay in completing the new generation of armoured cruisers, the new APC and SAPC shell would be issued to all these ships when they entered service from 1902 onwards. Cast iron shell would be phased out from 1905.

ATB guns

The ATB battery was as in the *Gueydon* class, but the adoption of turrets for the centre 164.7mm guns precluded the mounting of 47mm guns on the upper

Above: *Gloire* in the port of Brest wearing the overall blue-grey livery introduced after January 1908. Beneath the transporter bridge, in No 4 Dock at Le Salou, can be seen the battleship *Saint-Louis*. *(Private collection)*

(2nd) deck. The guns were mounted as follows: four on the lower platform of the military foremast, four on the lower bridge deck and the flying deck around the mainmast, two in the forward part of the hull on the 1st deck, and eight amidships and aft on the main deck. There were also four 37mm QF guns: two in the wings of the bridge and two on the quarterdeck.

When the ship was at sea, the 47mm guns mounted on the 1st and the main decks were retracted fully and stowed against the internal bulkheads; the gun ports could then be closed flush with the hull, forming a watertight seal. In order to facilitate this there was a new type of mounting in which the gun was supported on a swinging arm and secured to a fixed 'fighting bolt' directly beneath the centre of the port for firing (see schematic drawing). Contemporary British intelligence reports state that this mounting was introduced in the last two units of the *Dupleix* class, *Desaix* and *Kléber*, but the swinging arms are visible only in the plans of the former.

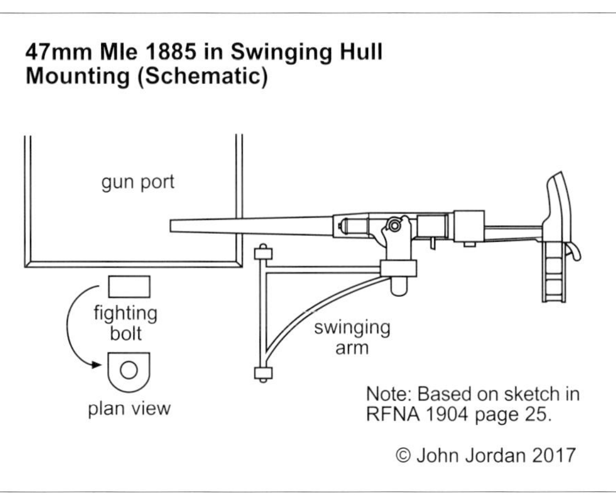

Searchlight projectors

Six 60cm searchlight projectors were fitted for target illumination, and were disposed as in the *Dupleix* and *Gueydon* classes. Earlier ships had the four hull-mounted searchlights (*ligne basse*) suspended from rails, but in the *Gloire* class they were mounted on wheeled trolleys that ran on rails mounted on the deck below. The watertight doors that covered the ports in the hull were hinged at their lower edge. When preparing the projectors for use, the doors were lowered to the horizontal position, in which they were rigidly held by stout folding iron supports. On the inner surface of the doors were prolongations of the deck rails on which the projectors ran. A small portable 'filling piece' was dropped down between the two sections of rail; the projectors were then run out and the portable electric cables connected. This arrangement was first trialled on *Dupetit-Thouars* and seems to have been successful, as it was adopted for successive classes of armoured cruiser.

Torpedoes and mines

There were two submerged torpedo tubes for 450mm Mle 1892 torpedoes located on the 2nd platform deck amidships, as in the *Gueydon* class. However, the *Gloire* design also featured three above-water torpedo tubes: two in a forward torpedo room between frames 22 and 28 on the 1st platform deck, and a third on the centreline at the stern on the main deck.

Above: *Condé* at her moorings. Note the fine lines of the stern, which favoured high speed. *(Private collection)*

The forward torpedo room had stowage racks for three torpedo bodies per tube. There was no stowage for torpedo bodies adjacent to the after tube; however, there was now a torpedo workshop amidships on the main deck with racks for four torpedo bodies that could be transferred forward or aft on overhead rails suspended from the deckhead. The total complement of torpedoes was now sixteen as compared to only six in the earlier Bertin cruisers.

The rationale for this marked increase in torpedo capacity is unclear, but it was almost certainly related to the 'fleet' role of these ships rather than their ancillary commerce-raiding mission. It was far cheaper to sink a merchantman with a gun than with a torpedo. On the other hand, torpedoes would have been particularly useful to despatch a crippled enemy battleship, whether by day or by night, as the relatively light guns of a cruiser would have little impact on a 300mm waterline belt. A similar complement of torpedoes was a feature of the original design for the cruisers of the *Léon Gambetta* class (see Chapter 7).

The *Gloire* class were the first French fleet cruisers to have mines (*torpilles automatiques*) embarked. Stowage varied from ship to ship: the plans for *Gloire* and *Condé* show twelve mines stowed in the forward above-water torpedo flat (1st platform deck), in the support for the conning tower; the plans for *Sully* and *Amiral Aube* show stowage for ten mines amidships and just forward of the ring bulkhead for the after turret respectively, while on *Marseillaise* the mines were distributed between this latter position (six) and the forward torpedo flat (eight).

Right: A close-up of the after part of *Condé*. The after 194mm single turret is hidden by the canvas awning, but the starboard after 164.7mm turret is clearly visible, as is the gun of the same calibre in the casemate, with a 100mm ATB gun directly above it. Note the proximity of the 164.7mm casemate gun to the waterline; this made it difficult to work the gun in heavy seas. *(Private collection)*

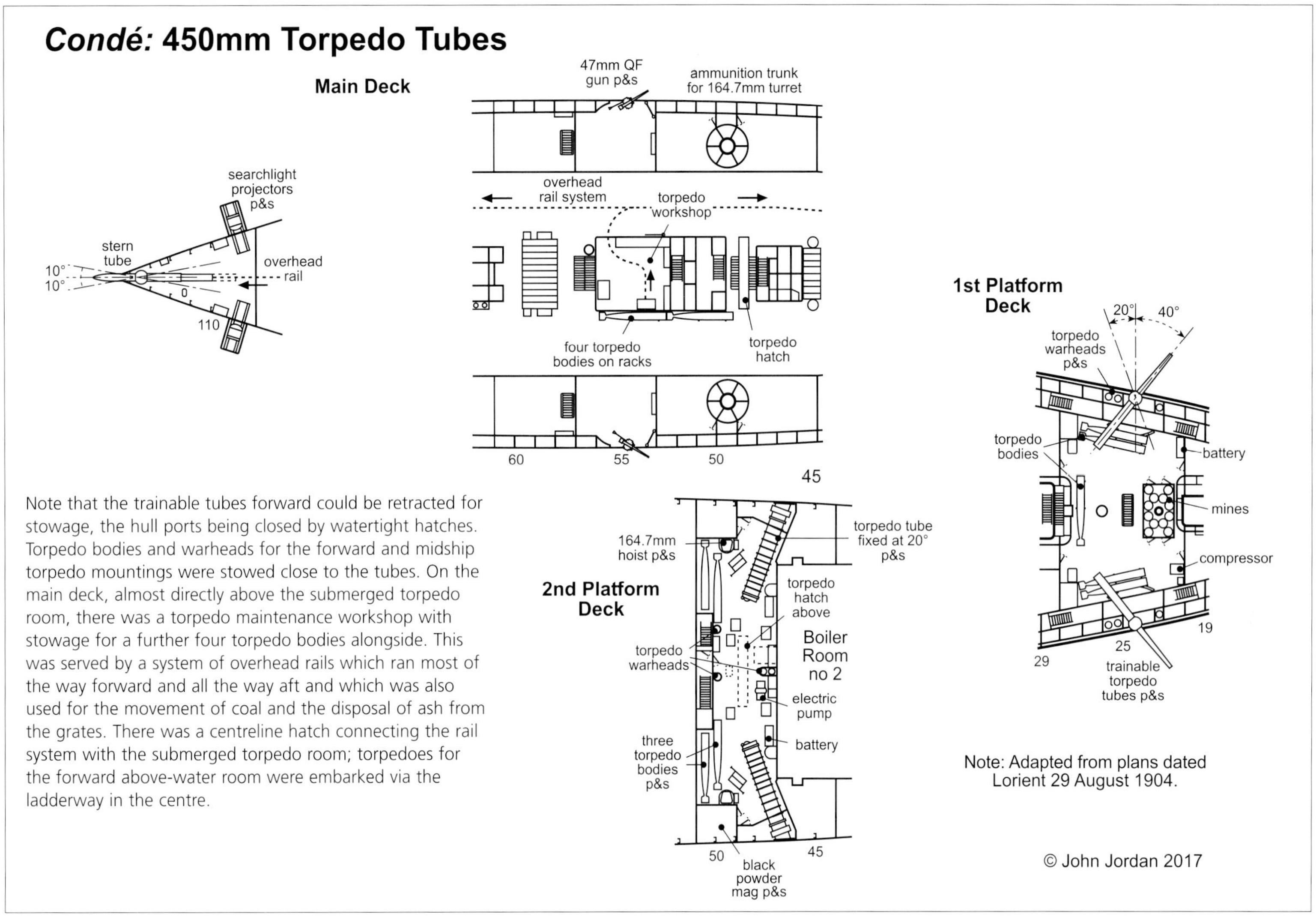

Condé: 450mm Torpedo Tubes

Main Deck

47mm QF gun p&s
ammunition trunk for 164.7mm turret
searchlight projectors p&s
stern tube
overhead rail
overhead rail system
torpedo workshop
four torpedo bodies on racks
torpedo hatch

2nd Platform Deck

164.7mm hoist p&s
torpedo tube fixed at 20° p&s
torpedo hatch above
Boiler Room no 2
torpedo warheads
electric pump
battery
three torpedo bodies p&s
black powder mag p&s

1st Platform Deck

torpedo warheads p&s
torpedo bodies
battery
mines
compressor
trainable torpedo tubes p&s

Note that the trainable tubes forward could be retracted for stowage, the hull ports being closed by watertight hatches. Torpedo bodies and warheads for the forward and midship torpedo mountings were stowed close to the tubes. On the main deck, almost directly above the submerged torpedo room, there was a torpedo maintenance workshop with stowage for a further four torpedo bodies alongside. This was served by a system of overhead rails which ran most of the way forward and all the way aft and which was also used for the movement of coal and the disposal of ash from the grates. There was a centreline hatch connecting the rail system with the submerged torpedo room; torpedoes for the forward above-water room were embarked via the ladderway in the centre.

Note: Adapted from plans dated Lorient 29 August 1904.

© John Jordan 2017

PROTECTION

Hull

The hull protection scheme adopted for the *Gloire* class marked a departure from *Jeanne d'Arc* and the *Gueydons*. The side belt of the latter two classes comprised a thick lower strake of homogeneous nickel steel covering the waterline and secured to a teak backing, with a light belt of special steel above it secured directly to the hull plating. The side belt of *Gloire*, on the other hand, comprised two strakes of cemented armour. The lower strake had a height of 2.00m amidships, and comprised twenty-eight plates each four frames (ie 4.8m) in length on either side of the ship; the upper strake comprised twenty-seven plates four frames in length – the end plates were longer – with a height of 1.625m amidships. The plates in the lower strake had a maximum thickness of 150mm, declining progressively to 80–90mm at the ends, and were tapered beneath the waterline to 50mm. The plates in the upper strake had a maximum thickness of 130mm amidships, tapering slightly to 120mm at their top edge. The maximum thickness was reduced progressively to 80–90mm at the ends (see Protection plan and table).

The plates in the upper and lower armour strakes were secured by armour bolts to a 70/90mm teak backing, which was in turn secured to a double layer of 10mm hull plating. The plates that formed the thick

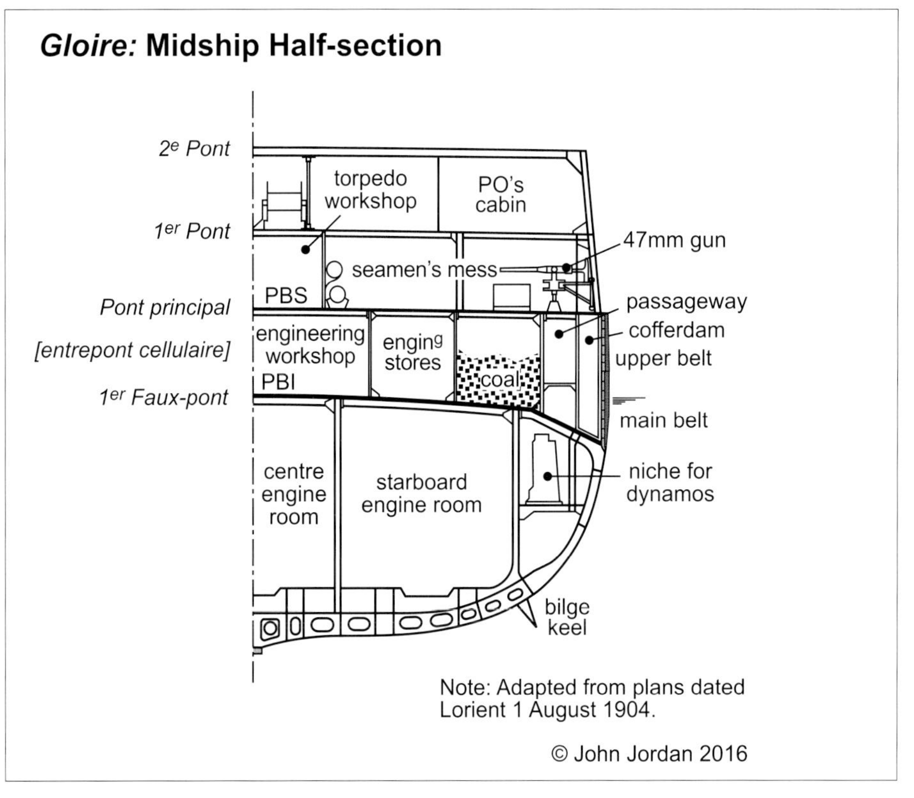

Amiral Aube: Protection

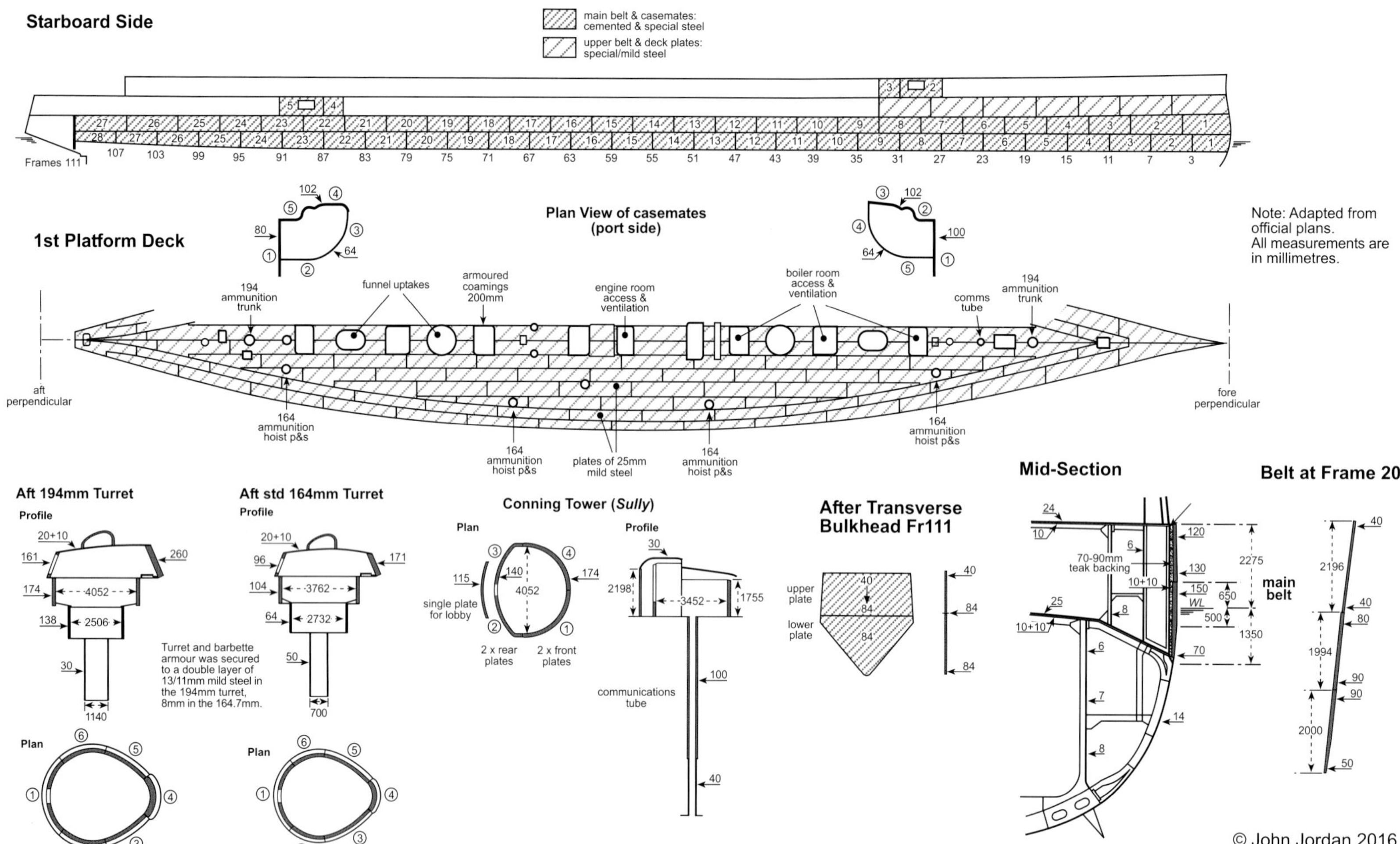

Opposite: *Gloire* in 1903 during her full-power trials; the highest speed she achieved was 21.58 knots with 21,334CV. *(Private collection)*

part of the belt amidships were of cemented armour, using the Harvey face-hardening process;[7] those at the ends were of homogeneous nickel steel.

The after transverse bulkhead was composed of two separate plates of special steel, as in the *Gueydon* class. The lower plate had a uniform thickness of 84mm, while the upper plate tapered from 84mm at its bottom edge to 40mm at the top edge.

There was a light upper belt (*cuirasse mince*) extending from the bow to the after end of the forward casemate. The plates were of special steel with a uniform thickness of 40mm and were secured directly to the shell plating.

The overall weight of protection accorded to the protective decks was reduced compared to *Jeanne d'Arc*, and the difference in thickness between them was less marked. The lower protective deck comprised two layers of 10mm construction steel with a uniform upper layer of 25mm mild steel plating (total thickness: 45mm); unusually, there were no reinforcing plates on the slopes. The upper protective deck comprised only a single layer of 10mm construction steel but was reinforced by a uniform layer of 24mm hardened steel for a total thickness of 34mm.

Inside the armoured box formed by the two protective decks and the side belt there was the customary cellular layer, comprising a cofferdam, a longitudinal passageway 1m wide, which was subdivided by bulkheads with watertight doors every four frames (4.8m), and coal bunkers.

Turrets, casemates and conning tower

The main 194mm turrets received an identical level of protection to those of the *Gueydon* class. However, the face, sides and *parapet* of the 194mm turrets, at least in *Amiral Aube*,[8] were of cemented armour, not special steel. This added to costs, and the experiment does not appear to have been repeated on later French armoured cruisers.

The protection scheme for the single 164.7mm turrets was similar in conception to that of the 194mm turrets, but with reduced thicknesses. There was a

[7] This was the first application in France of the face-hardening process to the belt armour of a cruiser, although cemented plates had previously been used for the main turrets. The first French battleship to have cemented belt armour was *Iéna*, laid down in January 1898. The Harvey process was time-consuming and expensive, and cemented armour added to the cost of the new ships. It could be used only for plates with a maximum width of 2m and a thickness greater than 120mm, hence the use of special steel for the end plates

[8] The plans for *Amiral Aube* have the most complete breakdown of the protective plating of this class. Data for the other four ships are less comprehensive.

single 96mm plate of special steel on the face of the turret with two plates on either side[9] and a single 171mm 'balancing' plate of mild steel at the rear; the armour plates were secured to a double layer of 8mm mild steel. The roof of the turret was made up of plates of hardened steel 20mm thick, secured to a 10mm layer of shell plating.

The circular fixed barbette protecting the lower part of the gunhouse and the roller paths was of 104mm special steel, and the ring over the working chamber was 64mm; the fixed armour, like that of the gunhouse, was secured to a double layer of 8mm steel. The trunk for the ammunition hoists was of 50mm steel.

Protection of the 164.7mm casemates was similar in principle to that of the *Gueydon* class, but whereas the inner wall of the casemates in the latter ships comprised a double layer of 25mm mild steel, in the

[9] Taking into account the inclination of the plates, 96mm was broadly equivalent to the 102mm vertical armour on the faces of the casemates – assuming enemy shell arrived with a horizontal trajectory.

AMIRAL AUBE: ARMOUR PLATE THICKNESS MAIN BELT

Plate	Upper Strake *upper/lower edge*	Lower Strake *upper/lower edge*
1–6	80/90	90/50
7	95/105	105/50
8	110/120	120/50
9	120/130	135/70
10–21	120/130	150/70
22	110/120	135/70
23	95/105	120/50
24	80/90	105/50
25	70/80	90/50
26	70/80	80/50
27	70/80	80/50
28	–	80/50

Notes:
1 Total weight of main belt: **842.60 tonnes**; plates 9–22 of the lower strake and 8–22 of the upper strake were of cemented armour; the end plates were of special steel.
2 Plates 1–7 of the upper belt forward were of 40mm special steel.
3 Plates 2–3 of the fwd casemate and plates 4–5 of the after casemate were of 102mm special steel.
4 For a list of armour plate manufacturers see page 130.

Gloire class the double layer was replaced by 64mm armour-quality (special steel) plating, secured to a double layer of 8mm mild steel plating (total thickness: 80mm). This involved a small increase in overall weight, and there was a slight reduction in the length of the casemate to compensate.

The conning tower for four of the five ships of the class had a similar configuration and level of protection to that of the *Gueydon* class. However, the conning tower of *Sully*, which was built from the outset as a flagship, was larger and had a completely new configuration (see Protection plan). It was no longer elliptical, but had an extension at the rear with a raised platform for the admiral; the new configuration would be adopted for the *Gambetta* class (see Chapter 7). Although the internal width of the conning tower remained the same at 4.05m, the depth was increased from 2.5m to 3.45m. Protection of the walls of the conning tower therefore implied a greater weight of armour and, in order to partially compensate for this, the thickness of the bulkhead protecting rear access was reduced from 130mm in the *Gueydons* to 115mm in *Sully*; in the other four ships it was increased to 190mm.

The communications tube was formed by hoops of special steel that were 100mm thick above the upper protective deck and 40mm below, down to the lower protective deck – the reduction from 50mm in *Gueydon* to 40mm in the *Gloire* class took into account the increase in thickness of the plating on the upper protective deck.

WEIGHT OF PROTECTION (*SULLY*)

	No of plates	Composition	Weight
Main belt	2 x 55 (p&s)	cemented/ special steel[1]	848t
Upper belt	2 x 7	special steel	56t
Armoured deck	89	mild steel	317t
Transverse b/head F111	2	special steel	5.5t
194 turrets + barbettes	2 x 6 (T)	cemented/ special steel[2]	145t
164 turrets + barbettes	4 x 6 (T)	special steel	140t
164 casemates	4 x 4	special steel	96.5t
Transverse b'heads (c/mates)	2 x 3	special steel	43t
Conning tower + comms tube	5	cemented/ special steel[3]	47.5t
Armoured deck coamings	n/a	special steel	73.5t
Torpedo tubes	n/a	special steel	3.0t
		Total	1,775t

Notes:

1 Only the thick plates of the upper/lower belt were cemented (see table for details).

2 The face, sides and parapet of the 194mm turrets were of cemented armour; the thick rear walls were of mild steel to counterbalance the turret; the turret hoods were of cast nickel steel.

3 The walls of the conning tower were cemented; the communications tube was of special steel.

Source: Official plans.

ARMOUR MANUFACTURERS: *AMIRAL AUBE* (AC LOIRE)

Main belt		
Cemented plates		
upper strake	Lot A	Marrel Frères
lower strake	Lot B	Schneider (Le Creusot)
Special steel plates		
lower strake	Lot C	Hauts Fourneaux/Forges & Aciéries de la Marine (St-Chamond)
upper strake	Lot D	Schneider (Le Creusot)
Upper belt		
Special steel plates	Lot E	Marrel Frères
Fore/Aft casemates		
Special steel plates	Lot F	Schneider (Le Creusot)
194 turrets		
Cemented plates	Lot G	Forges & Aciéries de la Marine (St Chamond)
Special steel plates	Lots H, I_1	ditto
164 turrets		
Special steel plates	Lots H, I_2	Forges & Aciéries de la Marine (St Chamond)
Mild steel c/b plates	Lot N	ditto
Armoured coamings		
Special steel plates	Lot J	Forges & Aciéries de St Etienne (Loire)
Conning tower		
Cemented plates (CT)	Lot K	Marrel Frères
Special steel plates (comms tube)	Lot L	ditto

Conditions of Acceptance (proving trials)

Plate thickness	Gun (weight of shell)
30–45mm	47mm (1kg)
46–75mm	65mm (4kg)
76–105mm	100mm (14kg)
106–149mm	138.6mm (30kg)
150-180mm	164.7mm (45kg)
181–220mm	194mm (75kg)
221–260mm	240mm (144kg)
261–340mm	274.4mm (216kg)

MACHINERY

The propulsion machinery was designed for a higher output (20,500CV *vice* 19,600CV) in order to compensate for the slight increases in weight and beam, but was arranged as in the *Gueydon* class. There was less inclination to experiment than with the cruisers designed in the mid-1890s: the two Lorient-built ships had Niclausse large watertube boilers, the others Bellevilles. These two types of boiler would now become standard for major vessels built for the *Marine Nationale*, although there would be some later experimentation in the cruisers. All five ships of the *Gloire* class had twenty-eight boilers, disposed as in *Gueydon* and *Dupetit-Thouars*.

The VTE engines were built by a variety of manufacturers. The engines in *Sully*, *Gloire* and *Condé* (the latter two ships built by Lorient) were three-cylinder models built by FCM Marseille, Schneider Le Creusot and FCM Le Havre respectively, while *Marseillaise* and *Amiral Aube* had a four-cylinder model manufactured by ACL Saint-Denis.

Machinery trials generally proceeded smoothly, although the power trials of *Gloire* and *Marseillaise* were interrupted on several occasions due to mechanical issues. The ships were rated as good steamers, and generally attained or exceeded their designed speed of 21 knots on trials. Results for the three-hour power trial are detailed in the accompanying table. Endurance was calculated as 7400nm at 10 knots.

The auxiliary machinery was arranged more economically than in the *Gueydon* class. The pumps were all-electric models of proven types, and the auxiliary condensers were located in the main condenser rooms, The four 600A dynamos were again in wing compartments outboard of the engine rooms on the 2nd platform deck, with a longitudinal bulkhead between the compartments and the side of the ship to mitigate the effect of leaks in the outer shell. There was now just one auxiliary machinery room for electrical distribution just forward of the foremost boiler room. The only steam-powered apparatus outside the main boiler rooms was the rudder servo-motor. This was served by pipework which ran above the armoured deck with a view to keeping temperatures in the magazines below 35°; a second steam line ran beneath the

Left: The central propeller of *Gloire*. Like all the Bertin cruisers, the *Gloire* class were powered by three triple-expansion reciprocating engines, each driving a single shaft. *(Private collection)*

armoured deck to provide redundancy in the event of damage. *Marseillaise* was fitted with a new, prototype system in which an electrically-powered wheel controlled the valve of a hydraulic engine that worked the tiller.

CONSTRUCTION AND EARLY SERVICE

The five ships of the class were laid down between May 1899 and March 2001 and began trials in 1903. *Marseillaise* was commissioned in October 1903, the others between January and August 1904. Times between keel laying and completion were 3.5 to 4.5 years, with *Condé*, the second of the two ships built by Lorient, completing in the shortest time.

Initially all five ships were assigned to the Northern Squadron; in April *Gloire* became flagship of the 1st Cruiser Division alongside her sisters *Amiral Aube* and *Condé*. Shortly after her commissioning *Sully* was detached to the Far East to join *Montcalm* (flag). On 2 February 1905 she grounded on an uncharted rock in Ha Long Bay (French Indochina), and foundered (see Box-out).

The fifth ship, *Marseillaise*, embarked President Emile Loubet for an official visit to Naples in April 1904, and was then assigned to the Light Division of the Mediterranean Squadron, serving alongside *Desaix* (flag) and *Kléber*. In October 1905 she became the flag-

PERFORMANCE ON THREE-HOUR FULL-POWER TRIALS

	Date	Speed	Horsepower	Shaft Revs	Consumption	Boiler
Sully	23 May 1903	21.41kts	20,110CV	138.58rpm	0.856kg/h/cv	Belleville
Marseillaise	5 Aug 1903	21.64kts	21,805CV	139.44rpm	0.860kg/h/cv	Belleville
Amiral Aube	12 Dec 1903	21.88kts	22,180CV	141.99rpm	0.831kg/h/cv	Belleville
Gloire	19 Jan 1904	21.27kts	21,334CV	139.56rpm	0.900kg/h/cv	Niclausse
Condé	11 May 1904	21.31kts	22,331CV	142.22rpm	0.859kg/h/cv	Niclausse

Source: CAAP: inventaire 432, sous-série 5I cartons 158 (*Su*), 120 (*Ma*), 5 (*AA*), 80 (*Gl*), 43 (*Co*).

Below: *Marseillaise* at Toulon in 1910–11, when she was serving with the Light Squadron in the Mediterreanean. *(Marius Bar)*

THE LOSS OF *SULLY*

[The following account is based on a report in the French Navy's in-house journal Le Yacht *dated 7 October 1905.]*

SHORTLY AFTER SHE COMMISSIONED, *SULLY* deployed to the Far East. On 8 February 1905 she was returning to her moorings in Ha Long Bay in northern Indochina following a torpedo-firing exercise. She was making 10 knots, and was approximately 120m inside the Canot Rock when, at 14.44, a succession of shocks were felt on board, then the ship came to an abrupt halt. Her commanding officer, CV Guibereau, who was on the bridge, ordered the engines full astern, but the ship was stuck fast. All watertight doors were sealed and the crew mustered on deck.

On 8 February 1905 *Sully* grounded on the Canot Rock in Ha Long Bay; she subsequently became a total loss. *(Private collection)*

Within five minutes the upper deck of *Sully* was 2m down to starboard and 3m to port. Water flooded the engine rooms and the forward compartments. The captain gave the order to abandon ship, the boats were lowered and the crew was evacuated onto the neighbouring rocks. The cruiser *Gueydon* was 400m away and, once alerted, took charge of the rescue; the protected cruiser *D'Assas* was likewise in attendance. Not a single member of the crew was lost.

The following morning the bow was underwater as far as the forward 194mm turret, with the stern and starboard propeller half out of the water. The hull of *Sully* was found to be balanced amidships on two rocky pinnacles 6.5m below the surface to starboard and 9.5m to port respectively; the ship was resting on her bilge keel against the latter. As the flooding progressed to the after magazines, the stern sank further and the fore part of the ship emerged to the height of the battery. A diver sent down to inspect the hull reported that a large part of the false keel had been carried away, and that there were two major holes forward. There were also gashes 25cm wide running parallel to the keel, the largest of which was, in a subsequent dive, found to be 80m long, and the double bottom had been breached over a considerable length.

Because the ship was held amidships by the two rocks, the fore part and the stern sagged at low tide. Guns were removed to lighten the ship, but by May rivets were shearing and the first major cracks appeared in the sides and the plating of the armoured deck. These cracks were progressive, and opened up further as time went on and the weather deteriorated.

Attempts at Salvage

Gueydon and *D'Assas* had begun their own salvage efforts on the evening of the grounding. The confidential documents and the personal effects of the officers, which were in the upper part of the stern, were rescued, but the petty officers' and seamen's messes forward were completely under water, and only a few of their belongings could be recovered.

On 8 February the Ministry authorised Vice Admiral Bayle, C-in-C of the Far East Squadron, to engage salvage contractors, most of which were foreign companies. The dockyard at Saigon sent tugs, pumps and lighters, and began the disembarkation of the after guns; the 100mm mountings and some of the 164mm guns were successfully removed. In March negotiations were undertaken with the Danish Company of Hong Kong, who sent their engineer, a Mr Jameson, to inspect the wreck. However, Jameson withdrew from the contract on 24 March, and the Navy was left to its own devices. The after part of the cellular layer was repaired and drained, but this proved insufficient to refloat the ship, as some of the transverse bulkheads were damaged and no longer watertight.

A plan was then devised to refloat the ship using two 4000-tonne floating docks. This was superseded by a proposal to use a 5600-tonne dock being built for an English company based in Hong Kong. The dock was launched on 6 May and arrived at Ha Long Bay on 13 May. However, weather conditions then deteriorated to such an extent that the attempt had to be abandoned. On

The heavy equipment, including the main guns, was progressively disembarked in an effort to lighten the ship. *(Private collection)*

The wreck of *Sully*, which broke her back in a storm in late September. The photo was taken in May 1906. *(Private collection)*

9 June an error by a tug led to the capsizing of a caisson due to be put in place the following day, and the dock had to be refloated. The services of a Norwegian salvage expert named Goundelius were now engaged. By this time *Gueydon*, aided by the dockyard personnel, had managed to recover all of *Sully* 's guns and turrets plus a large part of the ammunition.

After two and a half months' preparation everything was in place for a new salvage attempt when Ha Long Bay was struck by a typhoon. The dock was so badly damaged as to be unserviceable. On 30 September there was another severe storm, and the ship broke in two and sank.

The Enquiry

Sully was a brand-new ship which had cost the French taxpayer in excess of 24 million FF (just under £1 million sterling). Unsurprisingly, in late February there were questions in the Chamber of Deputies directed to the newly-appointed Minister of Marine, Gaston Thomson. Thomson defended both Admiral Bayle and Captain Guiberteau, praising their qualities and citing a similar grounding of the cruiser *Châteaurenault* on an uncharted rock in 1903.

Bayle's own Commission of Enquiry likewise cleared CV Guiberteau of all blame, the key evidence being that the submerged rock was not marked on the relevant chart (No 2277). However, the subsequent court martial (*Conseil de guerre*) held in France was unconvinced by this verdict: it was pointed out that local pilots recommended that ships keep at least 120m to the outside of Canot Rock, where the Hennette pass was 1800m wide. A campaign in the press questioned the capabilities of Guiberteau, claiming that he did not enjoy the confidence of his officers and was a personal appointee of the controversial former Minister Camille Pelletan, who had removed the well-respected CV Farret in his favour.

Le Yacht was by no means impartial in its account of the loss of *Sully* and the subsequent enquiry. It pointed out that the CO of the cruiser *Gueydon*, who witnessed the disaster and was a key member of the Commission of Enquiry, was none other than CV Ridoux, another Pelletan favourite. In December 1902 Ridoux had been given the command of the brand-new cruiser *Léon Gambetta* which, in late February 1904, he had grounded in the approaches to Brest during her trials. As if to confirm the internal battles still raging within the *Marine Nationale*, the author of the account in *Le Yacht* did not hesitate to blame Pelletan indirectly for both of these costly disasters.

Gloire Class: Early Service

	Gloire	Marseillaise	Amiral Aube	Sully	Condé
1904	Northern Squ	Northern Squ	Northern Squ	Far East	Northern Squ
1905		Lt Squ Med		wrecked	↓
1906					Lt Squ Med
1907		↓			
1908		Northern Squ			
1909	↓	↓			
1910	Lt Squ Med	Lt Squ Med			↓
1911	↓	↓	↓		Northern Squ
1912	Northern Squ	Northern Squ	Reserve		
1913	↓		↓		↓
1914	*Div d'instruction*	↓	Northern Squ		Atlantic Div

ship of the Light Division (CA Campion) and was joined by her sister *Condé*, which replaced *Desaix*. She served in this role until July 1907, when she was placed in reserve at Brest. She recommissioned as flagship of the 2nd Cruiser Division of the Northern Squadron in January 1908.

Following the entry into service of the six battleships of the *Patrie* class in 1908, the fleet was reorganised, and in October 1909 the former 2nd Cruiser Division of the Northern Squadron (now re-designated the 2nd Squadron) became the 2nd Light Division of the Mediterranean Squadron (renamed 1st Squadron): *Marseillaise* (flag), *Gloire* and *Dupetit-Thouars* were transferred to Toulon. They would shortly be joined by *Condé*; only *Amiral Aube* remained in the Atlantic.

Deployment to the Mediterranean was of relatively short duration. With the entry into service of the large, six-funnelled *Ernest Renan* and the two ships of the *Edgar Quinet* class, the more modern cruisers were concentrated in the Mediterranean and the four surviving units of the *Gloire* class returned to the Atlantic. In January 1911 the 1st Cruiser Division of the 2nd Squadron (Brest) comprised *Gloire* (CA Favereau), *Amiral Aube* and *Condé*. The completion of the battleships of the *Danton* class saw yet another complete reorganisation of the French fleet, and the cruiser division of the 2nd Squadron became the 3rd Light Division. The division, with *Marseillaise* replacing *Condé*, took part in the Great Naval Review of 4 September 1911 off Toulon, returning to Brest on 24 October.

On 20 September, just five days before the loss of the battleship *Liberté* to a magazine explosion, *Gloire* experienced a serious incident in one of her 194mm turrets. During a firing exercise at Les Salins d'Hyères a powder charge exploded prematurely, damaging the barrel of the gun; casualties were nine dead and five badly injured. The funeral rites were conducted hours after the catastrophic explosion on board *Liberté* and, as the coffins were lined up in the Gare de Toulon in readiness for repatriation to the families of the deceased in Brittany, the first officials and journalists were arriving from Paris to conduct their enquiry into the loss of the battleship.

From 1912 to 1914 a single division of three armoured cruisers was operational with the 2nd Light Squadron at Brest. The four surviving ships of the

Above: *Amiral Aube* in her overall blue-grey livery at Cherbourg. In reserve from 1912 to 1914, she was then re-assigned to the 1st Division of the 2nd Light Squadron. Note the hinged doors for the stern torpedo tube. *(Private collection)*

Gloire class were rotated, *Gueydon* and *Dupetit-Thouars* having by this time been placed in reserve. In November 1913 the latter two ships were recommissioned into a newly-formed *Division d'instruction de l'Océan* with *Gloire* (CA Cannellier) as flagship. They would be fully reactivated as the 2nd Division of the 2nd Light Squadron on the outbreak of war.

EVALUATION

The *Gloire* class was generally regarded as a successful design, and the four surviving ships remained first-line units up to the outbreak of the Great War, when they formed the bulwark of French naval defences in the Channel against the threat posed by the German High Seas Fleet.

The design of the *Gloire* class had a major impact on that of the battleships of the *Patrie* class, likewise designed by Bertin, the first of which would be laid down in December 1901. Not only was the protection scheme, with its high side belt and a tightly-divided cellular layer sandwiched between two protective decks of broadly equal thickness, similar in conception, but Bertin's preliminary sketch design for the new battleships, dated May 1898,[10] featured a similar disposition of the secondary 164.7mm battery: four guns in single turrets, with the remaining ten in casemates.

The next generation of French armoured cruisers would represent a quantum leap in size and power, and would in turn be influenced by the *Patrie* class in their final guise, with twin end turrets for the main guns and twin wing turrets for the 164.7mm QF guns. They would also be faster.

[10] See Jordan and Caresse, *French Battleships of World War One*, p 86.

CHAPTER 7:

THE LARGE FLEET CRUISERS OF THE *LÉON GAMBETTA* CLASS

THE YEAR 1898 proved to be a watershed both for France and for the *Marine Nationale*. The Fashoda Incident[1] highlighted the relative impotence of the Navy in the face of growing British naval power, while Admiral Tirpitz's First Naval Law of 1898 decreed the construction of no fewer than sixteen modern battleships (plus a flagship). The effect was to knock heads together: the bitter internal disputes and political see-sawing between the opposing factions would be laid aside, allowing the moderates to come to the fore. It was now universally recognised that against either Britain or Germany,[2] France would need a navy capable of protecting its growing maritime interests, which included an empire second in size only to that of Britain, and its own extensive coastline in the Atlantic and the Mediterranean. The problem was to devise a strategy and build a fleet that could deal with the two quite different threats posed by these potentially hostile powers.

In the event of conflict with Germany it was envisaged that the fleet would operate as a single unit and would adopt a Mahanian strategy of sea control. If France was opposed by Britain, however, the fleet would be dispersed and the Royal Navy drawn into a close blockade of the French ports; it would then be exposed to attrition by torpedo boats. The *Marine Nationale* would look to slip its fast cruisers past the blockading forces and cause havoc on the British trade routes, which would be only sparsely protected because of the large naval forces tied down by the blockade.

Armoured cruisers were seen as a key element in both strategies. Against Germany – and against Britain in the Mediterranean – they would have a 'fleet' role, providing scouting and screening, forming a fast wing of the battle fleet (much as the Japanese would do at Tsushima) and despatching crippled enemy stragglers with gun or torpedo. Against Britain their high speed, good endurance and powerful armament would make them formidable commerce raiders; they were to be coaled and supplied from a network of French overseas bases, some of which would now be fortified against enemy assault.

On 30 January 1900, no fewer than five separate bills were presented to the Chamber for approval with

Above: The French Naval General Staff wanted a cruiser which could match the British *Drake* class for firepower and protection. Emile Bertin would have preferred to match the 23-knot speed of these ships, even though the primary motivation for the high speed of the British cruisers was to counter the French *Jeanne d'Arc*. This is *Good Hope* in 1912; note the sixteen 6in QF guns in two-tier casemates. *(Leo van Ginderen)*

[1] The Fashoda Incident marked the climax of imperial territorial disputes between Britain and France. A French expedition to Fashoda on the White Nile sought to gain control of the Upper Nile River Basin and thereby exclude Britain from the Sudan. The French party and a British-Egyptian force (which outnumbered the French by ten to one) met on friendly terms, but the diplomatic confrontation between the two countries threatened war. Under heavy pressure the French withdrew, thereby securing Anglo-Egyptian control over the area. The *status quo* was recognised by an agreement between the two states acknowledging British control over Egypt, while France became the dominant power in Morocco.

[2] It was recognised that simultaneous conflict with Britain and Germany, while unlikely, was unsustainable. French foreign policy under Théophile Delcassé (Foreign Minister from June 1898 to June 1906) aimed to secure the neutrality of one or other of these two powers in the event of conflict with the other.

a view to securing a balanced maritime policy, including a Naval Law that specified future force strengths and the number and type of ships to be laid down. Besides the new *Statut Naval*, which was proposed by the new Minister of Marine, Jean-Marie de Lanessan (22 June 1899 – 7 June 1902), there was a bill to secure improvements to dockyard and port facilities, another for the improvement of coastal defences, a fourth to boost colonial defences to provide secure operational bases for ships deployed overseas, and a fifth to fund the extension of the undersea cable network to improve real-time communications. All but the third[3] and the fifth received approval.

STATUT NAVAL 1900 (PERIOD: 1900–1906)

	Total	New-build
First-line Fleet		
fleet battleships	28	6
armoured cruisers	24	5
torpedo boat destroyers	52	28
torpedo boats	263	112
submarines	38	26

Notes:

1 The Chamber of Deputies added 50 million FF to the government request, which added an estimated seventy-four torpedo boats and eighteen submarines to the above totals. At the end of the programme period, the Navy would still have numerous ships of types not included in the building programme, notably fourteen coast defence battleships and thirty-four protected cruisers.

2 The nineteen armoured cruisers built or building were: *Dupuy-de-Lôme*, the four *Charner* class, *Pothuau*, *D'Entrecasteaux*, *Jeanne d'Arc*, the three *Dupleix* class, the three *Gueydon* class, and the five *Gloire* class.

Source: Ropp, *The Development of a Modern Navy: French Naval Policy 1871–1904*, p 366.

THE *STATUT NAVAL*

The accompanying table shows the planned force strengths and the proposed construction programme, which once approved would have legal force.[4] France needed to build six new battleships, five armoured cruisers, 28 torpedo boat destroyers, 112 torpedo boats and 26 submarines in the next eight years. The Chamber not only approved the 477 million FF requested, but agreed a sum of 50m FF for additional torpedo boats and submarines – a proposal by future Minister of Marine and *Jeune Ecole* adherent Camille Pelletan – and reduced the term of the programme to seven years.

Bases

The dispersal of forces under the new strategy directed against Britain required a network of well-equipped

[3] The French Army retained overall responsibility for coast defence, although the Navy would deploy smaller-calibre guns (generally 75mm) close to the entrances of ports and harbours (*défenses des passes*) to protect the 'numbered' torpedo boats of the *défenses mobiles*.

[4] Earlier programmes drawn up by the Navy such as the programmes of 1896 and 1898 (see Chapters 5 and 6) were simply expressions of intent; funding for the ships had to be agreed and authorised by the Chamber on an annual basis.

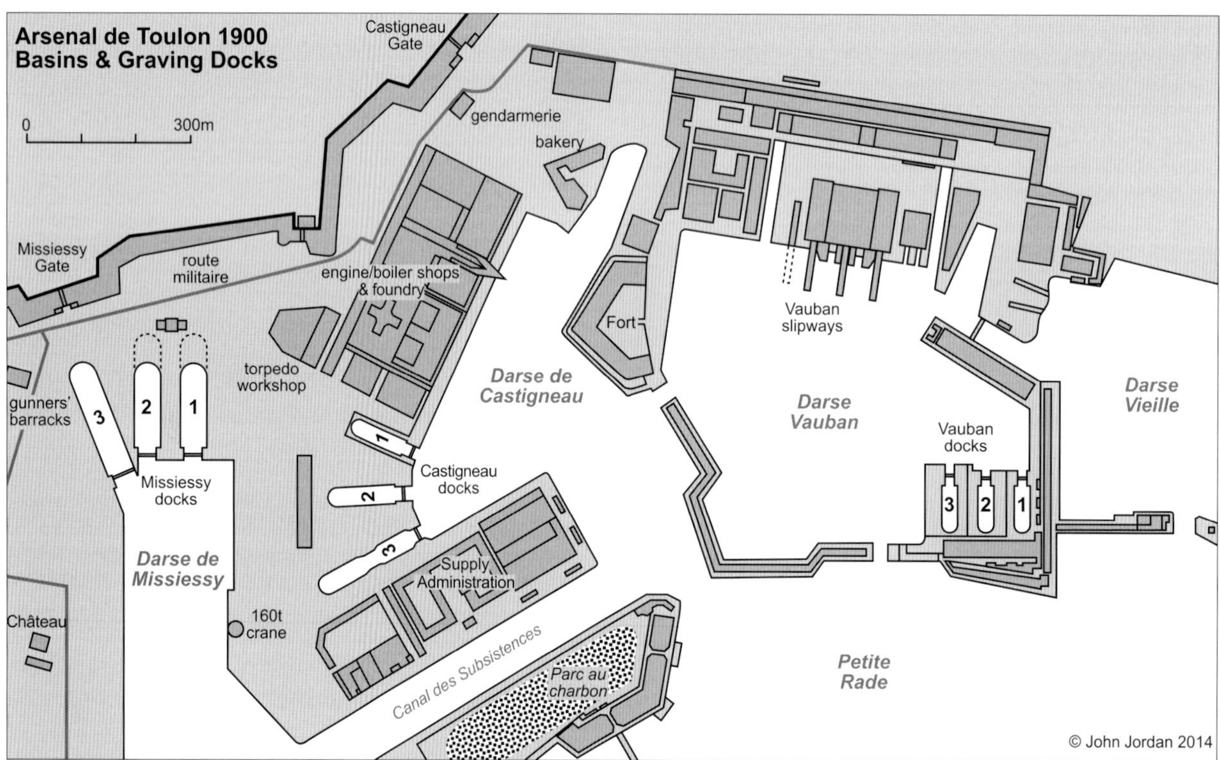

Toulon naval dockyard as it was in 1900. The Vauban Basin was the oldest in the dockyard, and the largest of its three graving docks, built 1841–6, was only 88m x 17.5m. The three docks in the Castigneau Basin, which had been built during the mid-nineteenth century, were larger: No 2 dock, completed in 1875, measured 114m x 22m; No 3 dock, completed in 1886, was enlarged to 156m x 24m during the early 1900s and could accommodate the latest armoured cruisers. To the west of Castigneau, the Missiessy Basin, on which work began during the 1860s, was designed to maintain the new generation of steel battleships. Dock No 3, which had only recently been completed, measured 179m x 30.5m. Docks Nos 1 and 2, which had a similar width but had been completed in 1880 and 1881 respectively, had a usable length of about 150m. They would be rebuilt from 1909 to 1913 to accommodate the new French dreadnoughts (see broken lines); when this work was completed their dimensions were 202m by 30.5m.

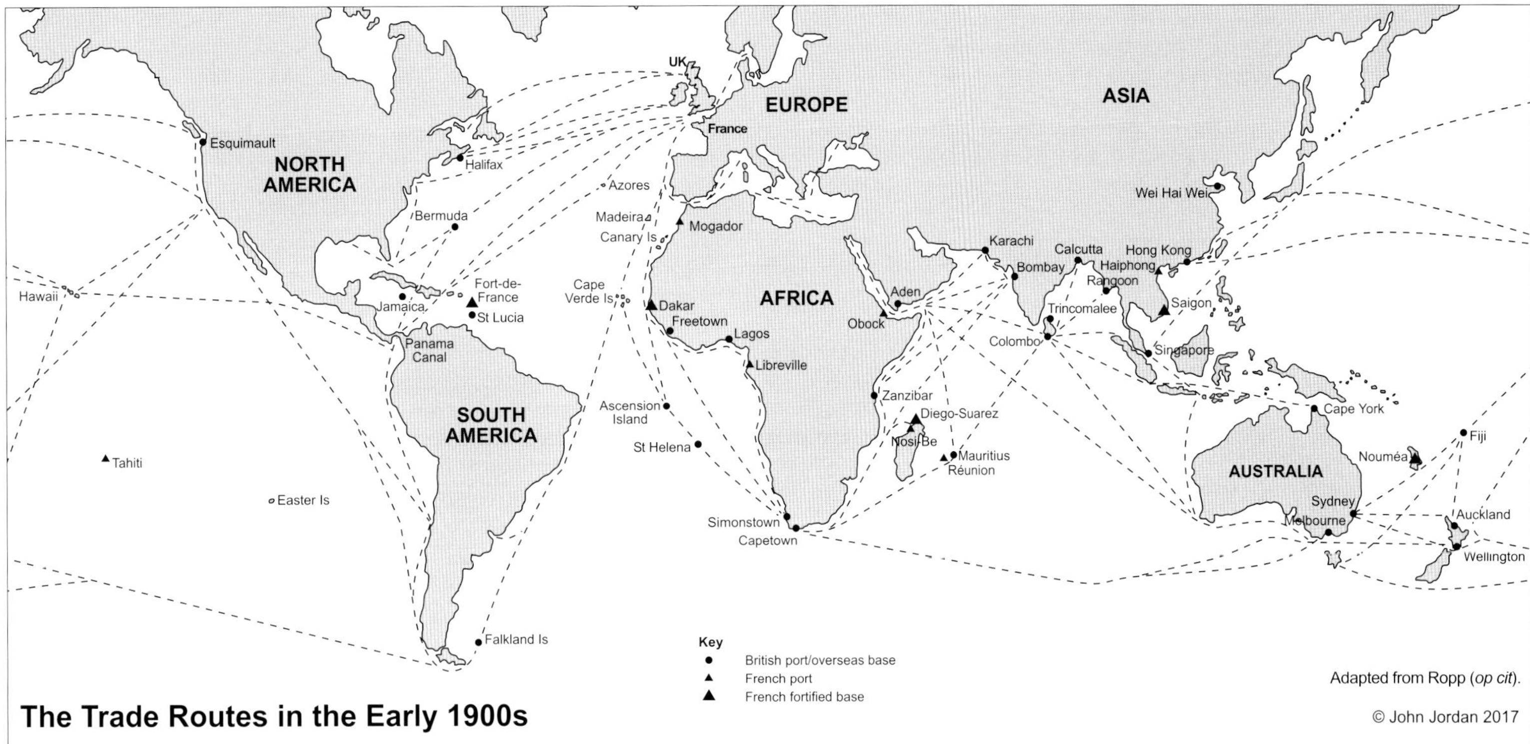

The Trade Routes in the Early 1900s

naval bases with modern facilities. Moreover, the scale of the proposed naval programme and the increased demands on maintenance, together with the larger dimensions of the ships themselves,[5] had implications for both the number and the dimensions of graving docks. Most of the larger docks at Toulon had been built during the time of Napoleon III to service first the ironclads (Castigneau Basin), then the new generation of steel battleships (Missiessy Basin). The French were particularly conscious at this time of the scale of infrastructure investment currently being made by Germany (the naval base at Wilhelmshaven and the Kiel Canal) to support its new fleet.

The new bill proposed improvements to bases in metropolitan France, North Africa and overseas. Funding of 170 million FF was duly approved; the only arguments in the Chamber concerned whether the Mediterranean or the Channel should be the focus in a war with Britain.

In the operational area of the Northern Squadron there were to be works at Brest and Rochefort (Atlantic), Cherbourg (Channel), and Dunkirk (North Sea); in the Mediterranean a new, well-equipped naval dockyard was to be built at Bizerte,[6] and there were to be improvements to Oran.[7]

Colonial and Commercial Warfare

A third bill, submitted by Minister for the Colonies Albert Decrais, proposed the construction of five fortified bases overseas to serve as strongpoints for territorial defence and as coaling/supply stations for commerce-raiding cruisers, at a cost of 61 million FF. These fortified bases were to be strong enough to resist attack – a new colonial army was in the process of being established.

The bases selected were at Dakar (West Africa/ South Atlantic), Diego-Suarez (Indian Ocean), Fort-de-France (Martinique/Caribbean), Saigon (Indochina) and Nouméa (South Pacific); the Chamber added some funding for the island of Réunion (Indian Ocean). There were to be small arsenals each equipped with a medium-sized graving dock at Dakar, Diego-Suarez and Fort-de-France. Saigon, which had an existing arsenal equipped with a dock large enough to accommodate a 10,000-tonne cruiser, was seen as important not only in a conflict against Britain but as a deterrent to a Japanese invasion of Indochina.

THE 12,550-TONNE ARMOURED CRUISER

The new *Statut Naval* released the funding for a new generation of armoured ships, some of which had been at the planning stage for two years. Already in 1898 Bertin had secured an agreement in principle for a battleship of 14,800 tonnes (future *Patrie* class), comparable in size and power to the latest British ships but significantly larger than the battleships authorised for the *Marine Nationale* during the 1890s, constrained as they were by the opposition of the *Jeune Ecole* and a national press that was implacably hostile to the ever-growing size and cost of these

5 An increase in displacement from the 12,400 tonnes of *Suffren* to 15,000 tonnes for the new battleships of the *Patrie* class had already been agreed in principle.

6 Bizerte, which had been relatively undeveloped prior to 1900, would have three (later four) large graving docks and, on the completion of the new dockyard at Sidi-Abdallah, would be referred to in the press as '*le Toulon africain*'.

7 Oran was preferred to Algiers, which was considered too 'open' from the sea. In the longer term it was envisaged that a third major base at Rachgoun (50 miles west of Oran) would be constructed, thereby creating a 'strategic triangle' bracketing the British trade route to India; this development was effectively pre-empted by the *Entente Cordiale* of 1904.

obsolescent 'mastodons'. The new battleships would be matched by armoured cruisers of comparable size and power.

On 12 August 1898 the Naval General Staff (*Etat-major général de la Marine* – EMG, *4e Section*) addressed the issue. Having already studied designs for a new *croiseur-estafette* – a fast, lightly-protected ship intended to liaise between the battle fleet and the detached strategic scouting forces – and the new *cuirassé d'escadre*, attention was turned to the armoured cruiser. In the view of the EMG the current types (*Dupleix*, *Gueydon* and *Gloire* classes) lacked the offensive power of the ships currently under construction abroad.

The EMG proposed a ship derived from *Gloire* with the same protection and speed – in order to maintain a high degree of uniformity in equipment and operational capability – but with a much more powerful armament of medium guns and greater endurance. The single 194mm turrets fore and aft were to be retained, but the number of 164.7mm guns was to be doubled from eight to sixteen at the expense of the six 100mm QF guns; endurance would be increased to 7500nm at 10 knots with a normal load of coal. Displacement would need to be increased to 11,700 tonnes, but the thicknesses of hull protection would be unchanged, and speed would remain at 21 knots. This equalled the speed of the British *Cressy* and the German *Fürst Bismarck*; it remained inferior to the 23-knot speed of the latest British armoured cruisers of the *Drake* class (which ironically had been designed to counter *Jeanne d'Arc*), but the EMG considered these ships a special case.

The Minister subsequently instructed the *Service Technique* to draw up plans for an *avant-projet*, and this was considered by the EMG at a meeting which took place on 20 June 1899. By this time the number of 194mm guns had been doubled from two to four (in twin turrets fore and aft), and displacement had risen to 12,416 tonnes. The medium 164.7mm guns were disposed in six twin turrets on the beam, as in the new battleships, with the remaining four guns in casemates, Horsepower was 24,000CV for 21 knots, an increase of 3500CV over *Gloire* to compensate for the increased size of the ship. The EMG found the STCN proposal 'completely satisfactory'.

The proposal was then submitted to the *Conseil des Travaux* for comment. The *Conseil* met on 18 July. It was unhappy with the reduction in the thickness of the upper protective deck from 40mm (as originally recommended) to 30mm, and wanted it increased to at least 35mm (25mm forward, behind the light upper belt). The layout of the 47mm ATB guns was also criticised, and the *Conseil* wanted the positions of the foremast platforms reversed – currently the ATB gun platform was above the rangefinder platform. On 31 August the *Service Technique* was instructed to make the necessary modification to the foremast; further modifications followed, and on 15 November the STCN was asked to draw up definitive plans for the new ships.

The previous day, on 14 November 1899, the *Conseil des Travaux* considered an STCN proposal for an even larger ship, with a length between perpendiculars of 155m and a displacement of 13,160 tonnes. The most striking features of this proposal was a uniform main armament comprising no fewer than eight 194mm guns in single turrets, disposed as in the final design for the *Gambettas* (see below), ten 100mm QF guns in a battery, and an increase in horsepower to 32,000CV for a designed speed of 23 knots. The *Conseil* was unenthusiastic: the 164.7mm was quite capable of penetrating the 150mm (6in) armour of the *Drakes* at 2000m and had a higher rate of fire, and the additional two knots was simply not worth the increase in size and cost.

Finally, the *Service Technique* produced two competing designs: one for a 22-knot cruiser of 12,550 tonnes based on the original proposal, the other for a 23-knot ship of 13,180 tonnes based on its second proposal but retaining the armament of the original project. In its session of 5 June 1900, the *Conseil des Travaux* again objected to the 23-knot design, which was more costly (+1.5 million FF) and less manoeuvrable, with a hull subject to greater stresses. It recommended the immediate approval of the 22-knot ship.

The Growth in Dimensions

147.0m x 19.4m
***Jeanne d'Arc* 1896**

122.3m x 20.8m
***Iéna* 1898**

132.1m x 17.8m
***Dupleix* 1898**

139.7m x 19.4m
***Gueydon* 1898**

125.9m x 21.4m
***Suffren* 1899**

139.8m x 20.2m
***Gloire* 1899**

135.3m x 24.3m
***Patrie* 1901**

148.4m x 21.4m
***Léon Gambetta* 1901**

The shaded rectangles are drawn to scale and represent maximum dimensions (length overall x beam at waterline). Note the differing hull ratios of the battleships (short and fat) and the cruisers (long and slim), the latter being designed for higher speeds. Following the laying down of the prototype fleet cruiser *Jeanne d'Arc* there was a return to more moderate dimensions. However, the new generation of battleships and cruisers built under the *Statut Naval* of 1900 would make greater demands on infrastructure, leading to the enlargement of existing graving docks at Brest and Toulon, and the construction of new docks after 1909. The development of the naval dockyard at Sidi-Abdallah, Bizerte, would relieve pressure on Toulon in the Mediterranean; it would have two graving docks each of 190m x 30m, each of which could easily accommodate the latest French armoured cruisers.

GAMBETTA AND HER FOREIGN CONTEMPORARIES

	Gambetta	*Drake* (GB)	*Fürst Bismarck* (Ger)
No in class:	3	4	1
Built:	1901–07	1899–1903	1896–1900
Displacement:	12,550t	14,150t	11,280t
Dimensions:	146.5m x 21.4m	152.4m x 21.74m[1]	125.7m x 20.4m
Propulsion:			
Engines	3-shaft VTE	2-shaft VTE	2-shaft TE
Horsepower	27,500CV	30,000CV	13,800CV
Speed	22 knots	23 knots	18.5 knots
Armament:			
Main guns	4 x 194mm (2 x II)	2 x 234mm (2 x I)	4 x 240mm (2 x II)
Medium guns	16 x 164mm (6 x II, 4 x I)	16 x 152mm (16 x I)	12 x 150mm (12 x I)
ATB guns	24 x 47mm (24 x I)	14 x 76mm (14 x I)	10 x 88mm (10 x I)
TT	5 x 450mm	2 x 450mm	6 x 450mm
Protection:			
Belt	150mm	150mm	200mm
Main turrets	138mm	150mm	200mm
2ndary guns	102mm	125mm	150mm
Conning tower	174mm	250mm	n/a
Decks	33mm + 45/65mm[3]	40mm	50mm

Notes:

1 Metric equivalents have been supplied for *Drake* in order to give a comparison. The equivalents for gun calibres are exact; those for armour thicknesses are to the nearest 5mm.

2 For the armoured decks, the first figure given relates to the upper protective deck, the second to the lower (flat/slopes).

Less than a month later, on 28 June and 2 July respectively, the Minister instructed Cherbourg and Brest naval dockyards to lay down two 12,550-ton cruisers to be named *Jules Ferry* and *Léon Gambetta*. A third ship, *Victor Hugo*, was initially allocated to Toulon (11 March 1901), but the order was transferred on 3 June 1902 from Toulon to Lorient, currently fully occupied with the construction of *Gloire* and her sister *Condé*. Due to the delays in laying down *Victor Hugo* at Toulon, the boilers, engines and armour plating were originally to have been reallocated to the fourth ship of the class, *Jules Michelet*, which was scheduled to be laid down at Lorient following the launch of *Condé*. However, when the order for *Victor Hugo* was transferred to Lorient this instruction was countermanded, and the construction of *Victor Hugo* was prioritised over that of *Jules Michelet*.[8] She was to be laid down on

8 *Jules Michelet* would eventually be laid down to a modified design, with a different armament and propulsion machinery derived from that of *Jules Ferry* (see Chapter 8).

Left: The launch of the armoured cruiser *Léon Gambetta* at Brest on 26 October 1902. *(Private collection)*

BUILDING DATA

Name	Builder	Laid down	Launched	Trials	Commissioned
Léon Gambetta	Arsenal de Brest	15 Jan 1901	26 Oct 1902	1 Dec 1903	21 Jul 1905
Jules Ferry	Arsenal de Cherbourg	19 Aug 1901	23 Aug 1903	23 Jun 1905	1 Jun 1907
Victor Hugo	Arsenal de Lorient	2 Mar 1903	30 Mar 1904	15 Jan 1907	16 Apr 1907

one of the two covered slipways at Caudan, and Toulon was instructed to despatch all material collected thus far to Lorient, either by ship or by heavy goods train.

The *Gambettas* were expensive ships: the average unit cost was 29–30 million FF, compared to around 22 million FF for each of the five ships of the *Gloire* class and 21 million FF for the *Gueydons*.[9]

NOMENCLATURE

In contrast to earlier French armoured cruisers, which were generally named – uncontroversially – after historical figures, the new ships were to bear the names of recently-deceased statesmen associated with the Third Republic that succeeded the Second Empire of Napoleon III in 1870. This confirmed a trend towards the elevation of republican values that can also be seen in the naming of the six contemporary battleships of the *Patrie* class.

Léon Gambetta (1838–82) was a French statesman prominent during and after the Franco-Prussian War, which he initially opposed. On 5 November 1871 he established a journal, *La République Française*, which

[9] Unit cost for the *Patrie* class was *c*40 million FF (up from 28 million FF for *Suffren*); the higher figures for the battleships compared to the cruisers reflected the inflated cost of armour-quality steel and the greater overall weight of protection. The total estimated cost of the six new battleships and the five armoured cruisers to be built under the *Statut Naval* accounted for around 390 million FF of the 477 million FF allocated for the entire programme. This serves to underline the financial attractiveness of the large fleet of unarmoured torpedo boats (*la poussière navale*) favoured by the adherents of the *Jeune Ecole* and many Deputies in the Chamber. Large armoured ships were expensive.

Below: When she entered service on 21 July 1905, *Léon Gambetta* became flagship of the 1st Cruiser Division of the Northern Squadron. Her *divisionnaires* were *Gueydon* and *Dupetit-Thouars*. *(Private collection)*

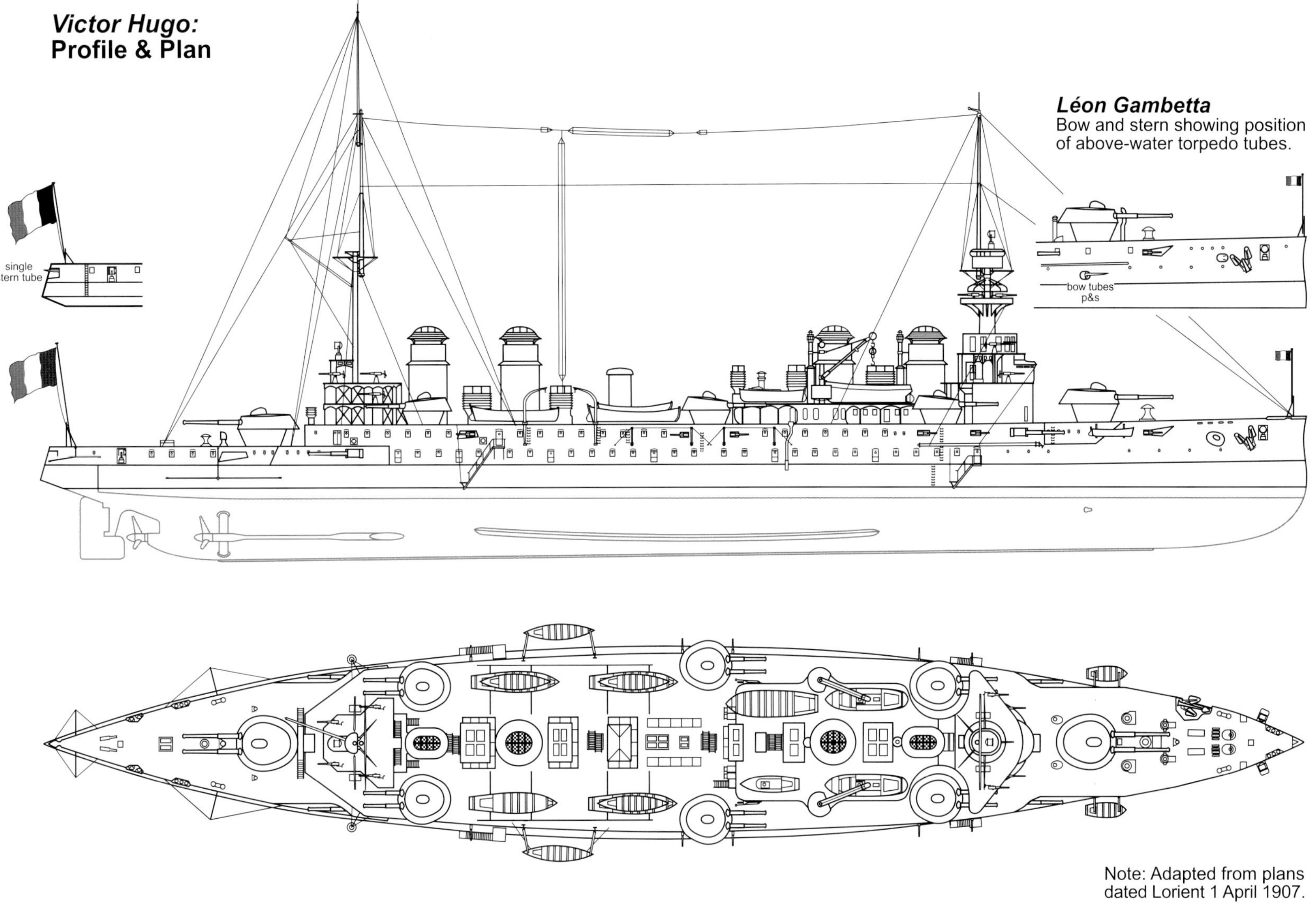

became the most influential in France, and he was instrumental in voting in the French Constitutional Laws of 1875.

Jules-François-Camille **Ferry** (1832–93) was likewise a prominent French statesman and republican. Following the military defeat by Prussia in 1870, Ferry promoted the acquisition of a great colonial empire, principally with the aim of economic exploitation. Ferry directed the negotiations that led to the establishment of a French protectorate in Tunis (1881), prepared the treaty for the occupation of Madagascar (1885), directed the exploration of the Congo and of the Niger region, and initiated the conquest of Annam and Tonkin in what became French Indochina.

Victor-Marie **Hugo** (1802–85) was a French poet, novelist and dramatist who opposed the accession of Napoleon III and took up exile in the Channel Islands. He finally returned to his homeland in 1870, and was promptly elected to the National Assembly and the Senate. Outside France, his best-known works are the novels *Notre-Dame de Paris* (*The Hunchback of Notre-Dame*) (1831), and *Les Misérables* (1862). As a politician he campaigned on social justice issues and for the abolition of capital punishment. Hugo was buried in the Panthéon, and his portrait featured on French banknotes.

HULL AND SUPERSTRUCTURES

The *Gambetta*s were broadly similar in their layout and configuration to the *Gueydon* and *Gloire* classes. The principal adjustment that needed to be made to the internal arrangements of the hull was the enlargement of the magazines for the twin 164.7mm guns in order to accommodate the required 200 rounds per gun, and the elimination of the athwartship magazine abaft the condenser room – there were now only three groupings of QF guns per side as opposed to four. This had the effect of compressing the space between the two pairs of funnels, which were notably broader to cope with the 35 per cent increase in the volume of exhaust gases from the larger boilers – the horsepower delivered by the more powerful engines was 27,500CV (up from 20,500CV in *Gloire*). These two measures combined to give the ships a more squat, compact appearance than their predecessors.

The other consequence of increasing the capacity of

Léon Gambetta: GA Plans

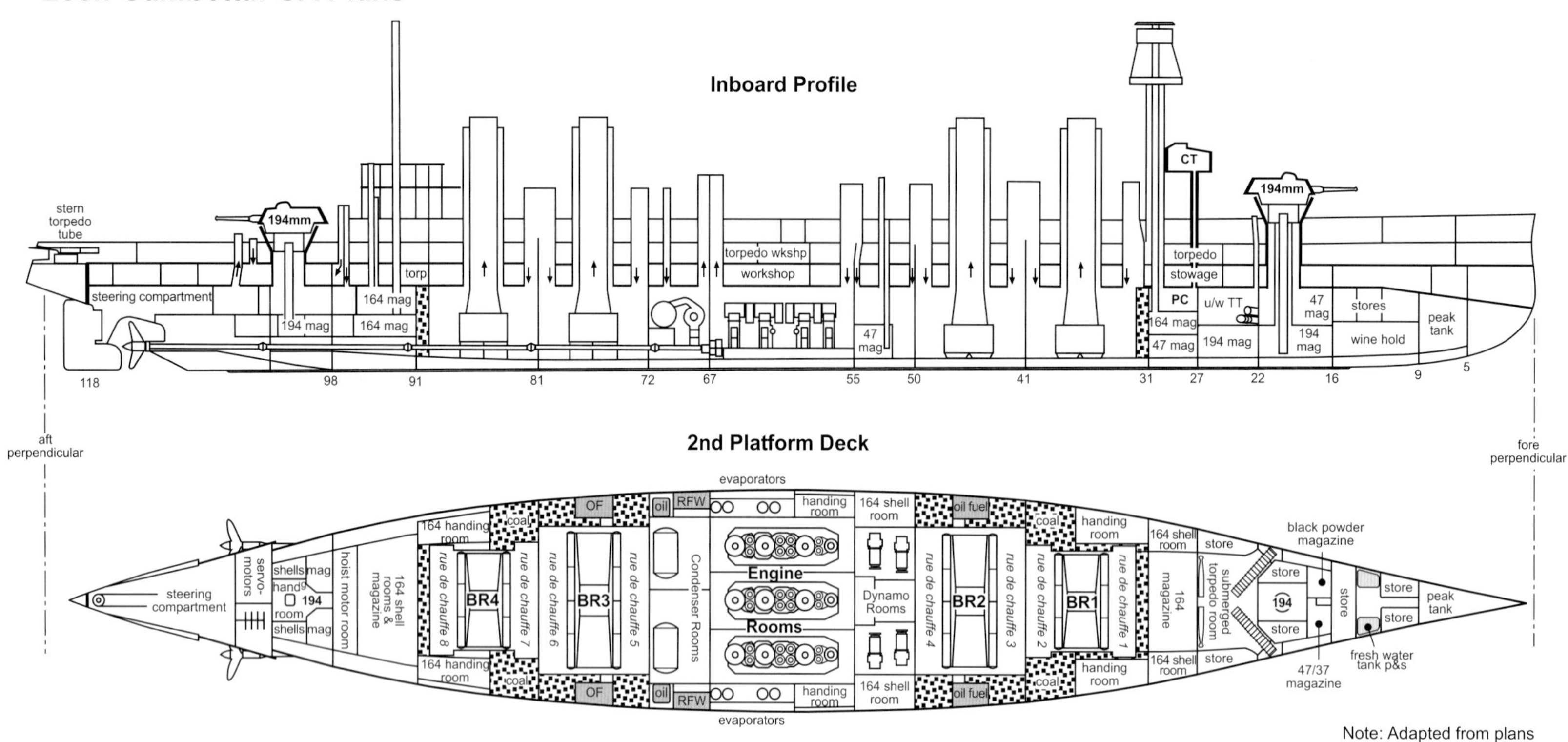

Note: Adapted from plans dated Brest 21 July 1905.

Note that *Léon Gambetta*'s sister *Victor Hugo*, laid down at Cherbourg nine months after work on *Gambetta* was begun at Brest, had a completely different arrangement of her machinery due to the adoption of the Guyot–du Temple boiler (see page 157).

Right: A senior officer's cabin on *Edgar Quinet*. Note the mirror wardrobe and the high-quality light fitting. *(Private collection)*

Jules Ferry: Accommodation

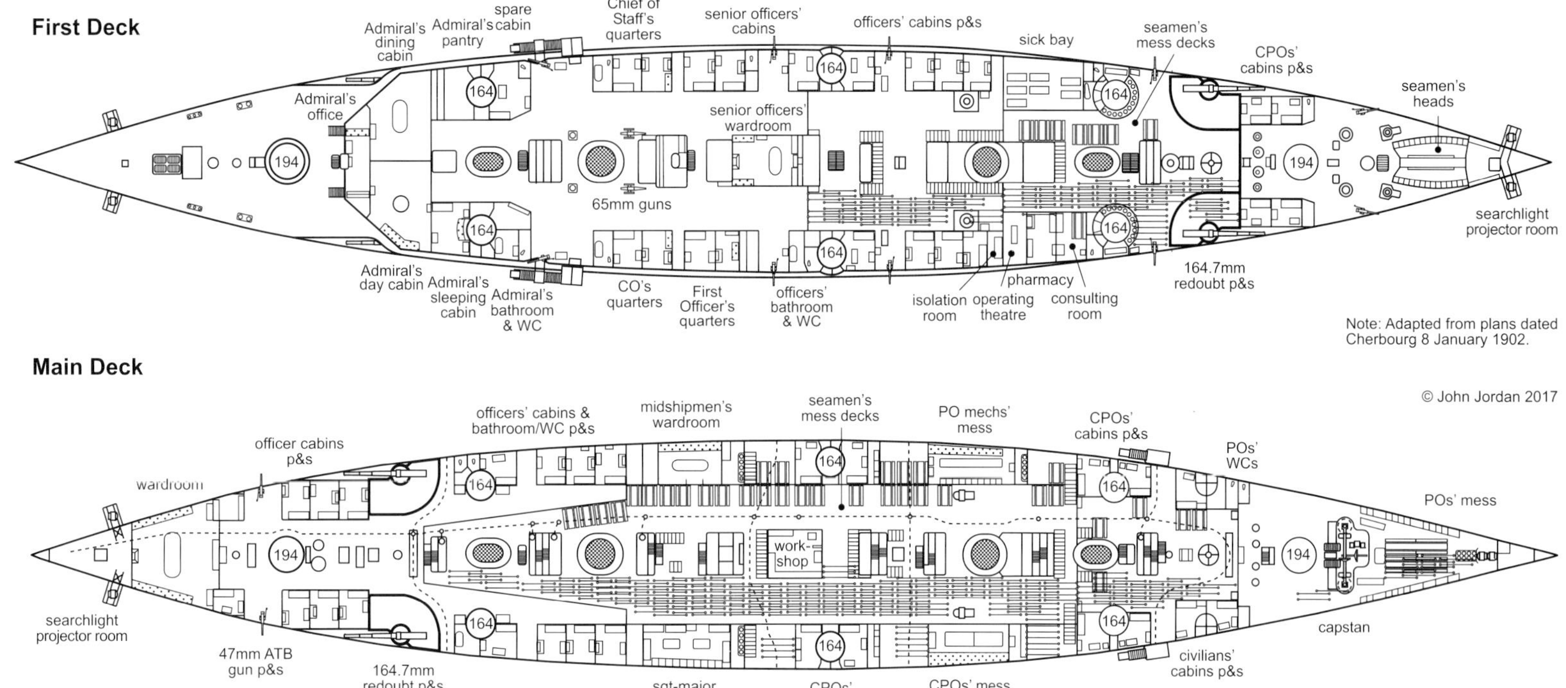

The official complement of the *Léon Gambetta* class as completed was 26 officers and 708 men; as a flagship there was a supplement of four officers and 41 men. The accommodation was on two decks. The admiral had a spacious and well-appointed suite of cabins at the after end of the 1st deck, the senior officers had smaller suites amidships on the same level, and the other officers had individual cabins on the first deck and on the main deck aft, each of which was fitted with a bunk, a wardrobe, a chest of drawers and a desk. The cabins located amidships and aft were less subject to pitching.

The chief petty officers (*maîtres*) had smaller individual cabins at the forward end of the ship on the two levels, with central messing, and the mess for the junior petty officers (*maîtres de 2e classe*) was in the bow on the main deck. The junior petty officers and the ordinary seamen slung hammocks, the seamen being accommodated in broad central messdecks on the first and main decks. The plans show the messing tables to port and the hooks for the hammocks to starboard. Note that sleeping arrangements for the men extended into the side bays and the forward redoubts. There was a large, well-equipped sick bay with a consultation room, operating theatre, pharmacy and isolation room on the 1st deck.

CHARACTERISTICS

Displacement:	12,550 tonnes
Dimensions:	
Length	146.50m pp; 148.35m oa (*VH:* 149.07m)
Beam	21.4m wl
Draught	8.18m aft
Propulsion:	
Boilers	*LG:* 28 Niclausse boilers *JF:* 20 Guyot-Du Temple boilers *VH:* 28 Belleville boilers
Engines	3-shaft 4-cylinder VTE
Horsepower	27,500CV
Speed	22 knots (designed)
Coal	1320 tonnes normal; 2100 tonnes full load
Endurance	7500nm at 10 knots; 2000nm at 22 knots
Armament:	
Main guns	4 x 194mm/40 Mle 1893–1896 in twin turrets
Medium guns	16 x 164.7mm/45 Mle 1893–1896M QF in six twin turrets and four casemate mountings
ATB guns	24 x 47mm/40 Mle 1885[1] QF in single mountings
Torpedo tubes	3 a/w,[2] 2 sub tubes for 450mm torpedoes 16/6 torpedoes Mle 1892 (*LG, JF*) or Mle 1904 (*VH*)

Protection:	
Main belt	150/130mm max
Decks	33mm PBS 45/65mm PBI
194 turrets	138mm
164 turrets	102mm
Casemates	102mm
Conning tower	174mm
Boats:	2 x 10m steam pinnaces 1 x 7.65m White launch 1 x 11m pulling pinnace 3 x 10.5m pulling cutters 1 x 10m admiral's gig 4 x 8.5m whalers 2 x 5m dinghies
Complement:	
As private ship	26 officers, 708 men
As flagship	+ 4 officers, 41 men

Notes:

1 *VH*: 47mm/50 Mle 1902.

2 *Gambetta* only – see text.

the magazines for the two centre turrets was that the submerged torpedo flat, which in *Gloire* had been located on the 2nd platform deck above this magazine, was displaced forward; it was now directly beneath the torpedo room for the above-water tubes, which in turn were moved from the 1st platform deck to the main deck.

In order to increase magazine capacity fore and aft there were three deck levels below the lower armoured (1st platform) deck between frames 27 and 41 and between frames 90 and 106*bis*: the extra deck, which was between the 2nd platform deck and the hold, was designated the 3rd platform deck

The twin 194mm turrets at the ends of the ships were significantly heavier than the singles in the *Gloire* and *Gueydon* classes, and the after turret was moved down to the quarterdeck (1st deck) to reduce topweight. All the other turrets were at forecastle (2nd) deck level, giving the guns an excellent command in all weathers. One new technical feature introduced was a modification to the protection of the *tourelles-barbettes*: whereas in earlier armoured cruisers the fixed barbette armour above the weather deck had been vertical, it was now inclined downwards and inwards at an angle of 20° (see Protection), and was continued down to cover the working chamber.

The British naval intelligence report of 1904 stated that slight modifications had been made to the drawings for the third ship, *Victor Hugo*, in order to improve the flow of water to the propellers by fining the lines aft. This ship, which was laid down two years after *Léon Gambetta* and 18 months after *Jules Ferry*, also featured a number of other small modifications, notably the models of torpedo and 47mm ATB gun embarked, and the disposition of the ATB guns mounted on the 1st deck (see Armament below).

All three ships of the class were fitted out as flagships. The capacious and well-appointed admiral's quarters were located at the after end of the 1st deck, just forward of the after 194mm turret (see Accommodation plan for *Jules Ferry*). The cabins for the senior officers of the flag staff and of the ship were amidships on the same deck; the accommodation for the junior officers was on the main deck below. The admiral had a chart house on the lower bridge deck and a signal house on the upper bridge deck. When the ship was in action his station was in the raised upper section at the rear end of the conning tower; the

Below: *Léon Gambetta* dressed overall during the visit of the Northern Squadron to Portsmouth in August 1905 to celebrate the signing of the *Entente Cordiale*. She is in her original livery of black hull and buff upperworks. *(Private collection)*

Above: *Jules Ferry* shortly after her completion, wearing the new blue-grey paint scheme overall. She spent most of her pre-war service with the Light Squadron in the Mediterranean. *(Private collection)*

captain occupied the forward section below, where the instrumentation for conning the ship (order transmitters for the engines and the rudder servo-motor, voice-pipes and telephones for internal communications) was located.

ARMAMENT

Main guns

The main 194mm gun, which was mounted in twin turrets fore and aft, was the same Mle 1893–1896 that equipped the *Gueydon* and *Gloire* classes. It fired an APC or SAPC steel projectile weighing 90kg.[10] The BM11 propellant charge was in three bags and weighed 33.8kg (see table for data). Command was 9.95m for the forward guns and 6.93m for the guns in the after turret. Range at the maximum elevation of 15° was around 11,500m.

As in the earlier ships, the turrets were trained electrically but the guns were elevated manually. The revolving working chamber beneath the turret floor was fed by a fixed hoist, which as in the *Gloire* class was of the duplex type: one basket ascended while the other descended, a guiderail down the centre of the hoist allowing them to pass. The hoist was powered by an electric motor with manual backup. When the basket arrived in the working chamber the bagged charges were lifted manually and stowed around the walls. The projectiles were raised into the gunhouse using clip hoists with manual drive that emerged on either side of the guns, and shunted onto waiting trays alongside the breech or stowed in ready-use racks at the rear of the turret. The bagged charges were handed up through the floor of the gunhouse via angled chutes. There was stowage for projectiles on racks at the after end of the gunhouse.

164.7mm turrets

The 164.7/45 Mle 1893–1896M was a modified version of the gun that equipped the *Gueydon* and *Gloire* classes. It fired a 55kg APC or a 52kg SAPC steel projectile using a two-part BM10/11 propellant charge (one cartridge plus one bag) with a total weight of 20.7kg. The firing cycle was three rounds per minute, and range was 10,800m for the turret-mounted guns and 9,000m for the guns in casemates at their maximum elevation of 15°.

10 Friedman, *Naval Weapons of World War One*, states that by the time *Léon Gambetta* entered service production of CI shell had been discontinued, except to top up the projectile complements of existing ships; however, the plans of *Victor Hugo* (dated April 1907) continue to show CI projectiles (*obus en fonte*) for the 164.7mm guns.

Léon Gambetta: Sections

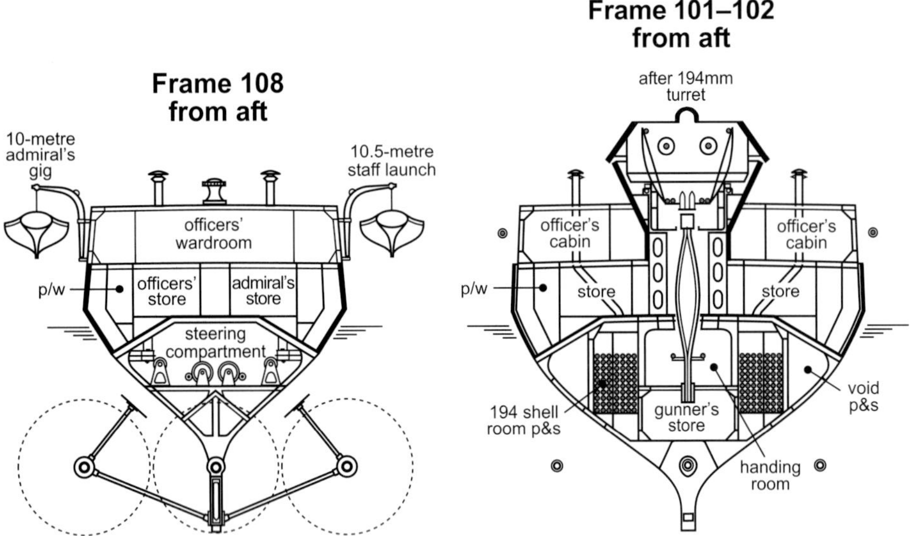

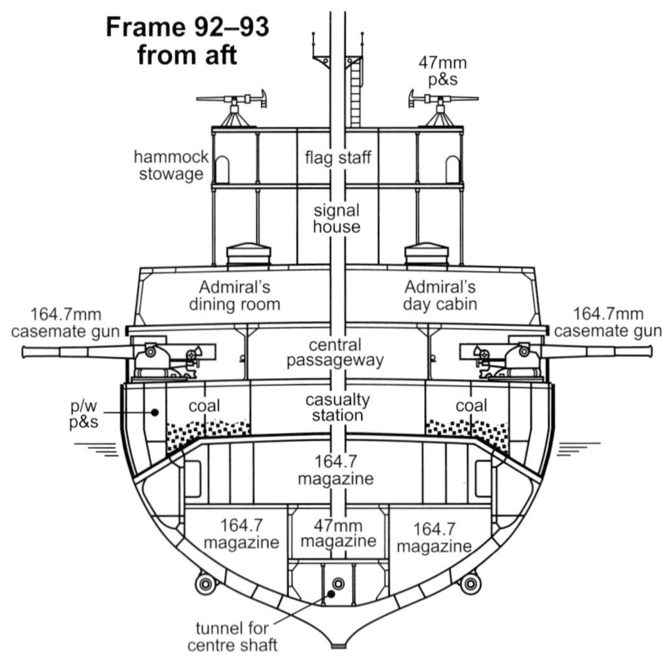

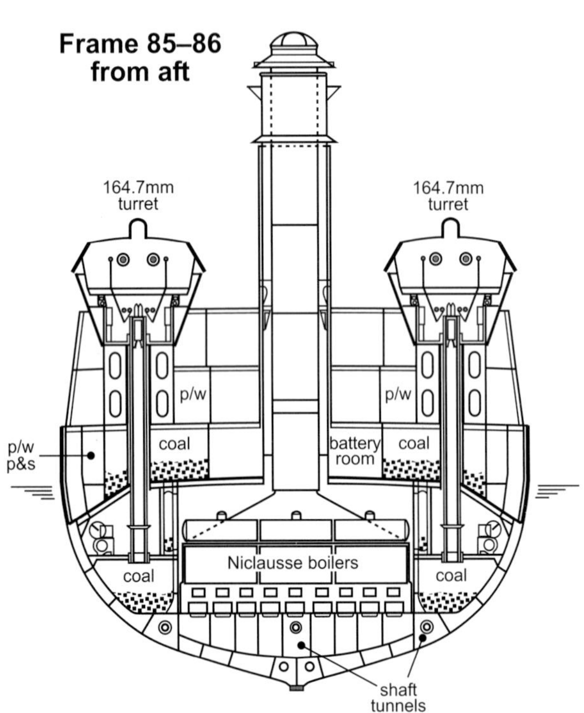

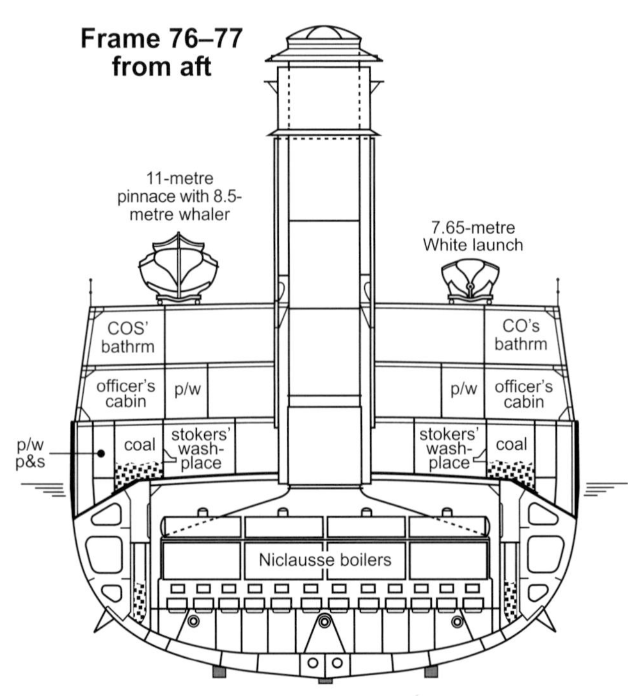

The twin turret was of identical design to the turrets adopted for the contemporary battleships of the *Patrie* class. Competing proposals from Schneider and from the *Direction de l'artillerie* were considered by the *Conseil des Travaux* on 23 December 1898, and the in-house proposal, which had independent loading for the guns and declutching for the individual guns in the event of damage, was approved. The turret was trained electrically using a single motor acting on a toothed wheel beneath the gunhouse. The training mechanism could cope with a 5° angle of heel, and there were three possible speeds, the slowest being 2.5°/sec and the fastest 6.3°/sec; as the turret was balanced, it could be turned at 1.7°/sec manually by only two men in the event of power failure. The guns were elevated by hand using an arc and pinion, and loading was possible at all angles of train and elevation.

The layout of the gunhouse was broadly symmetrical. Both the turret officer and the trainer/gunlayer were seated on a raised platform between the guns, beneath an armoured hood (see Plan drawing). The telescopic sights set elevation for the guns remotely, and the guns were fired together using a mechanical firing pin. The two gunlayers for elevation were seated at the forward end of the gunhouse, outboard of the guns.

Suspended beneath the gunhouse was a cylindrical working chamber that served as the reception post for

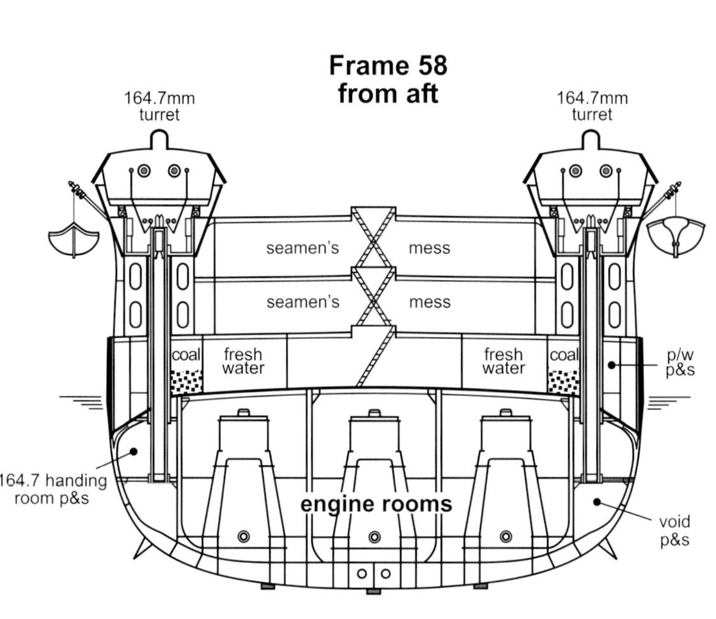

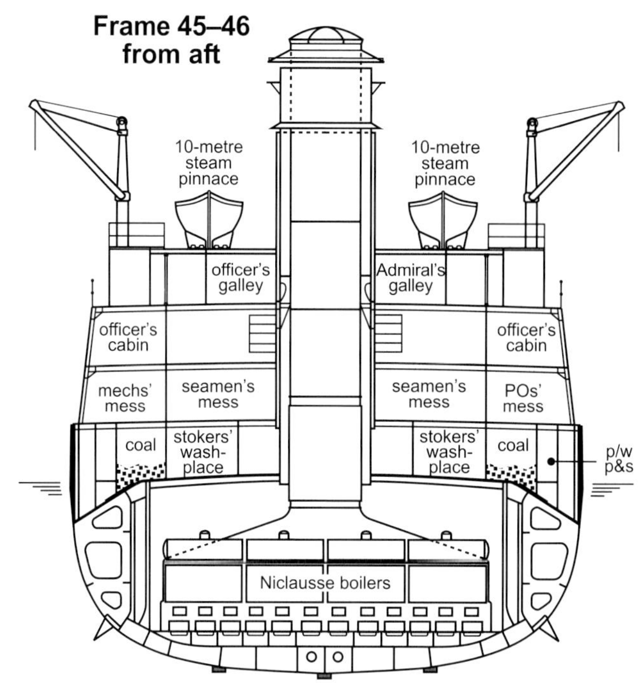

Note: Adapted from plans dated Brest 21 July 1905.

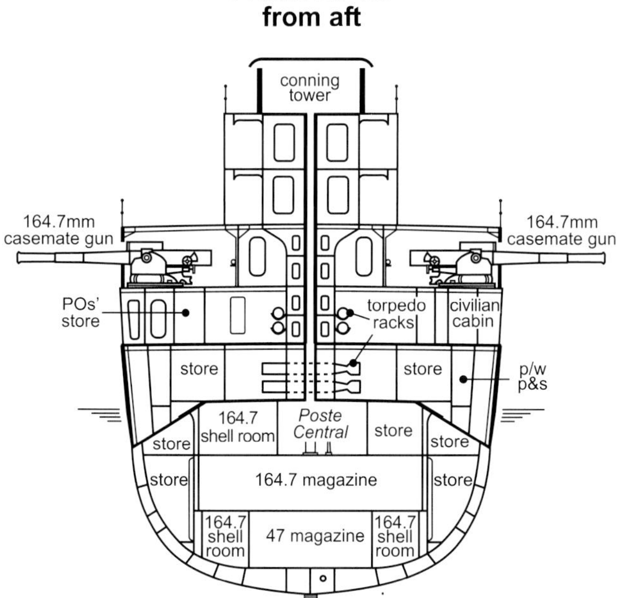

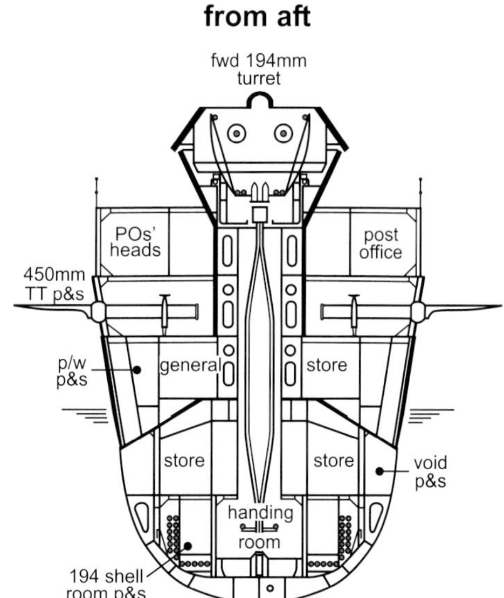

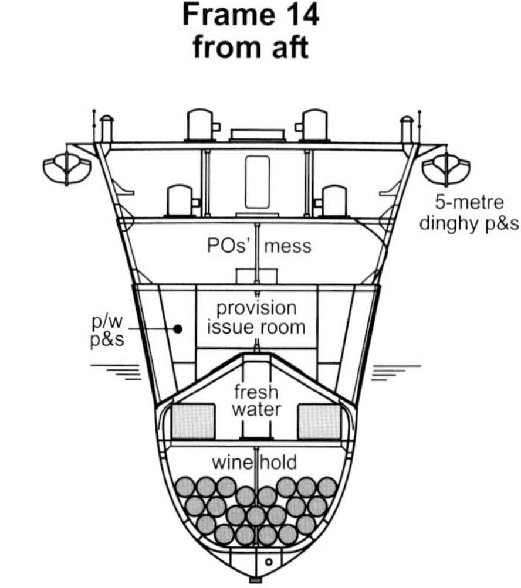

the fixed, electrically-powered duplex hoist. Each of the two linked baskets held two shells with four half-charges beneath (ie two complete rounds), stowed vertically. On arrival in the working chamber the shells were tipped onto waiting trays, and from there were raised to the gunhouse by manual clip hoists, each holding a single projectile. The hoists emerged outside the guns, and the shells were manhandled onto the rotating loading tray or onto stowage racks on the side and rear walls of the gunhouse (see Plan drawing). Cartridges and bagged charges were passed into the gunhouse manually via hand-up scuttles set into the gunhouse floor: the hand-ups for the cartridges were outboard of the breech, those for the bagged charges between the guns. Each turret had ready-use stowage for forty complete rounds (forty projectiles + sixteen half-charges in the gunhouse, sixty-four half-charges in the working chamber). In the event of a breakdown of the hoist motors, hand gear could supply two rounds per minute to the guns.

Casemate QF guns

The four casemate guns were disposed as in *Gloire*: the forward pair of armoured redoubts was on the 1st deck, the after pair on the main deck. Both were close to the end 164.7mm turrets and the guns were served by the same magazines. There were ready-use racks for 14–16 projectiles against the end bulkhead of each

MEDIUM GUNS

	164.7/45 Mle 1893–96M
Total weight:	8190kg
Total length:	7742mm
Bore length:	7408mm
Chamber length:	1210.6mm
Chamber volume:	36.74 dm^3
Breech pressure:	2800kg/cm^2
Rifling:	50 grooves at 4°
Shell weight:	APC 54.9kg (2.62 cal) SAPC 52.3kg (2.94 cal) CI 45.0kg (3.12 cal)
Bursting charge:	APC 0.97kg *mélinite* (1.8%) SAPC 3.10kg *mélinite* (5.9%) CI 2.10kg powder (4.7%)
Propellant:	20.70kg BM10–11 (2 x ½)
Muzzle velocity (MV):	900m/sec (APC)
Remaining V 2000m:	686m/sec (APC)
Maximum range:	10,800m at 15° (turrets) 9,000m at 15° (casemates)
Firing cycle:	20 sec

casemate with lockers for cartridges and bagged charges beneath. Chutes around the inner walls were used to transfer the projectiles to the breech at any angle of train.

Opposite: The forward 194mm turret of *Victor Hugo*. Note the distinctive inverted cone of the barbette, and the hinged covers over the three ventilation slots on either side of the gunhouse. *(Private collection)*

Magazines

There were three groups of magazines for the 164.7mm guns, the layout reflecting that of the turrets and casemates. The fore and after groups, each of which had to serve six guns (four in the turrets plus two casemate guns) were on three levels: 2nd platform deck, 3rd platform deck and hold. The magazines for the two centre turrets (four guns) were on two levels only, and at the level of the 2nd platform deck were interrupted by the port and starboard dynamo rooms and the electrical switchboards.

A report by British naval intelligence (RFNA 1905 Vol II) stated that the magazines were 'particularly spacious and well-ventilated'. The projectiles were stowed horizontally on racks, the cartridges either vertically or horizontally, and the bagged charges in lockers. Provision was 100rpg for the 194mm guns, and 200rpg for the 164.7mm guns. The magazines for the main guns were fitted with an air-cooling (*aéroréfrigérant*) system developed and manufactured by Fouché of Paris.

WEIGHT OF BROADSIDE

Number/Calibre of guns	Weight of projectile	Rate of fire	Weight of broadside
Condé[1]			
2 x 194mm	90kg	2rpm	360kg
4 x 164.7mm	55kg	3rpm	660kg
3 x 100mm	16kg	4rpm[2]	192kg
			1212kg
Suffren			
4 x 305mm	350kg	1rpm	1400kg
5 x 164.7mm	55kg	3rpm	825kg
4 x 100mm	16kg	4rpm	256kg
			2481kg
Gambetta			
4 x 194mm	90kg	2rpm	720kg
8 x 164.7mm	55kg	3rpm[3]	1320kg
			2040kg
Patrie			
4 x 305mm	350kg	1rpm	1400kg
9 x 164.7mm	55kg	3rpm[3]	1485kg
			2885kg

Notes:

1 The armoured cruiser *Condé* was a contemporary of the battleship *Suffren*, the *Gambetta* a contemporary of the *Patrie*. The table shows that *Condé* had only 50 per cent of the hitting power of *Suffren*, whereas *Gambetta* approached the hitting power of both battleship types due to the large number of 164.7mm QF guns embarked.

2 The official figure was 6rpm in *tirs accélérés*, using ready-use ammunition; once the ready-use ammunition was expended the gun would fire at a steady 3rpm (*tirs méthodiques*); the figure of 4rpm given here is therefore a compromise.

3 The 164.7mm gun had a theoretical rate of fire of 3rpm, but in practice problems with the accumulation of combustion gases in the twin turrets (see Chapter 8) restricted the turret guns to 2rpm. This affected the *Gambettas* and the early battleships of the *Patrie* class.

ATB guns

There were no 100mm QF guns, which served to reduce the number of different calibres of gun and to simplify magazine stowage and hoist arrangements. In their place were additional ATB guns, which were of uniform 47mm calibre; the 47mm guns in the first two ships were of the standard Hotchkiss 40-calibre Mle 1885, but those on the later *Victor Hugo* were a newer model designed and built by Schneider, the 50-calibre Mle 1902, which had longer range and improved penetration. Even the new model would attract criticism in view of the more powerful ATB guns fitted in contemporary British (12pdr/76mm) and German (88mm) battleships. In the battleships of the *Patrie* class the 47mm guns would be replaced by a lesser number of 65mm guns while the ships were building. Production problems with the new-model gun resulted in delays in installation on board *Victor Hugo*, which received her full complement of guns only in early May 1907.

There were no fewer than twenty-four 47mm guns in the *Gambettas*: four on the lower platform of the military foremast, four on the lower bridge decks forward, six on the after superstructure decks (*ligne haute*), and ten firing behind unarmoured ports in the upper hull on the 1st deck (*ligne basse*). All of the guns were capable of 20° elevation and -20° depression.

The fixed rounds were stowed in magazines forward, amidships and aft, each of which was served by a broad centreline hoist. The forward and after magazines were located immediately below the masts and superstructures in order to minimise the horizontal transfer of ammunition, and there was a separate circular hoist forward inside the military mast to serve the guns on the lower platform. There were the customary ready-use racks close to the guns.

Six 60cm searchlight projectors were fitted for target illumination, and these were disposed as in the earlier French armoured cruisers.

Torpedoes and mines

The arrangements for the torpedo tubes in the original design were similar to those of the *Gloire* class, with three above-water and two submerged tubes linked by a system of overhead rails fixed to the underside of the 1st deck; there was a torpedo maintenance shop amidships and a hatch to connect with the submerged torpedo flat. The major difference was that the compartment for the submerged tubes, which was amidships in *Gloire*, was displaced forward by the need to enlarge the magazine for the centre turrets, each of which now mounted two 164.7mm

164.7mm Twin Turret: Plan View

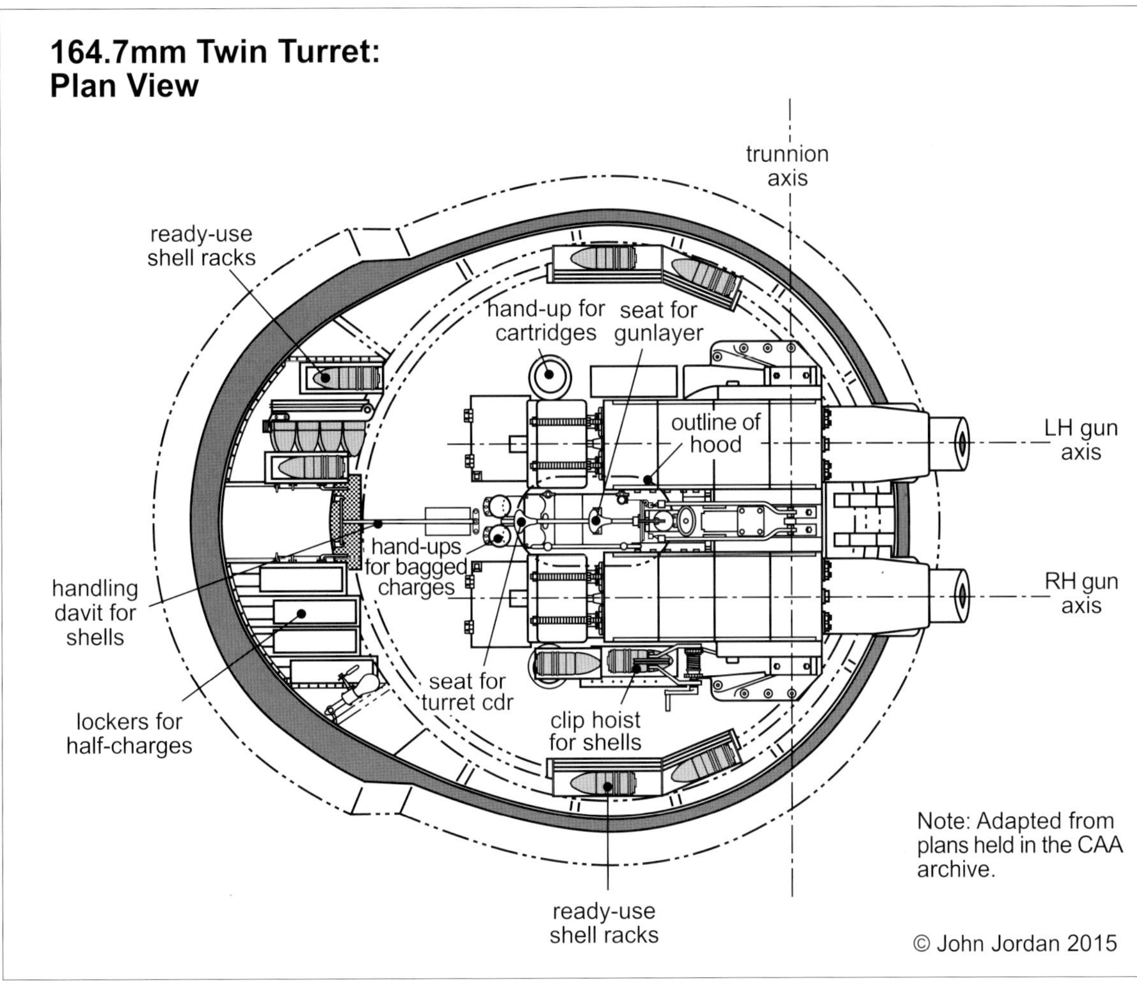

The twin 164.7mm turrets fitted in the *Gambetta*s had an identical configuration and layout to those in the *Patrie* class. In plan the layout was essentially symmetrical – the two sides of the drawing show two different levels for the gun and the stowage racks at the rear. There were racks at the side and rear of the gunhouse for twenty projectiles per gun, racks beneath the projectile waiting trays for four cartridges per gun, and flashproof lockers at the rear of the gunhouse for four bagged half-charges per gun. The remaining ready-use cartridges and powder bags were stowed around the walls of the working chamber below. Note the separate hand-up scuttles for the brass cartridges (outside the breech of the guns) and for the bagged charges (between the guns).

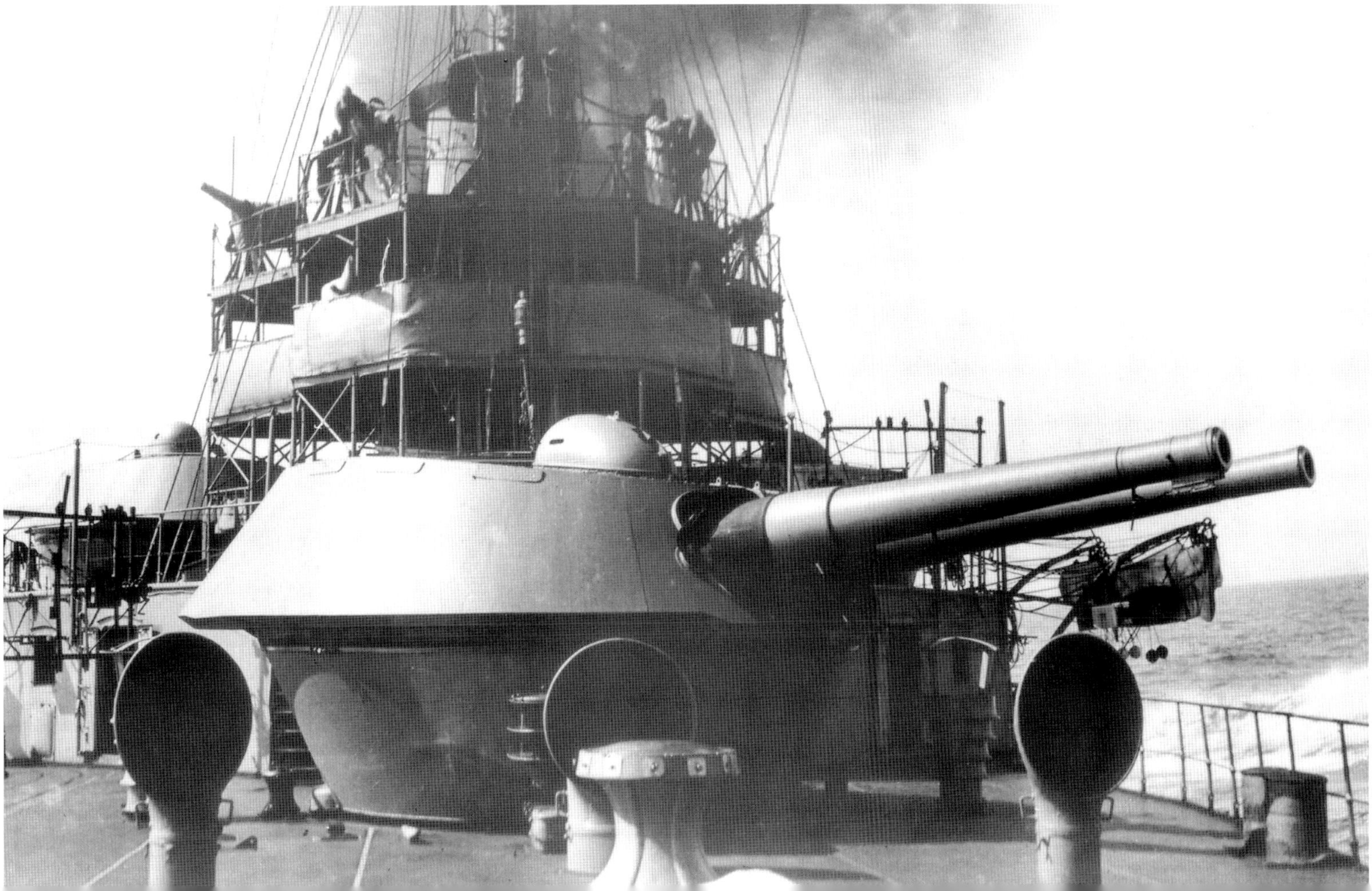

Right: The twin 164.7mm turrets of *Jules Ferry* seen from the military foremast. *(Private collection)*

guns. It was moved to a position immediately abaft the ammunition trunk for the forward 194mm turret, between frames 20 and 27, and the compartment for the paired above-water tubes was relocated from the 1st platform deck to the main deck, almost directly above, between frames 17 and 25. All three above-water tubes, together with the torpedo maintenance shop, were now on the main deck (see drawing). This was essentially the same arrangement as in the contemporary battleships of the *Patrie* class as designed,[11] although the latter ships were to have the above-water tubes suppressed while building, as would the two sister-ships of *Léon Gambetta*.

The plans of *Gambetta*, which are dated 21 July 1905, show four torpedo bodies stowed on racks in the seamen's mess aft, a further four on racks immediately abaft the above-water torpedo room, and two more on

[11] See Jordan and Caresse, *French Battleships of World War One*, Chapter 4.

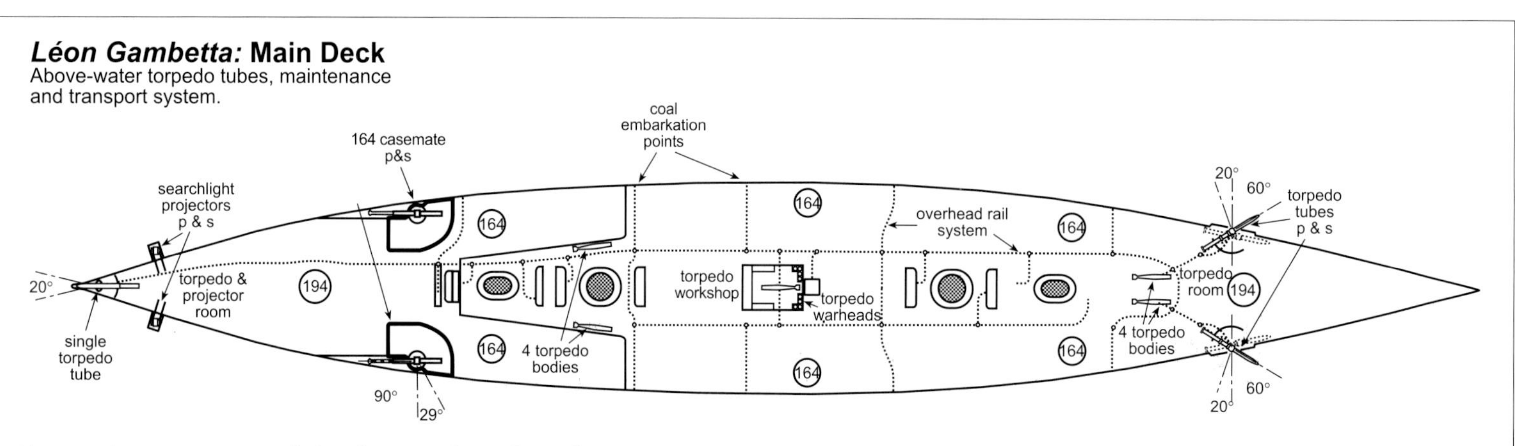

The torpedo arrangements as designed were similar to those of the *Gloire* class, with a central workshop and an overhead rail system to move the torpedo bodies around the main deck. The principal difference was that the submerged torpedo room was forward, abeam the ammunition trunk for the forward 194mm turret and directly beneath the two above-water tubes. However, the three above-water tubes and the torpedo workshop feature only on the plans of *Gambetta* (dated July 1905). The plans of *Jules Ferry* (dated January 1907) and *Victor Hugo* (April 1907) show only the submerged tubes and the overhead rail system and loading hatch; there are no above-water tubes and the former torpedo maintenance shop has become a general repair shop.

Above: The twin 164.7mm turrets of *Jules Ferry* seen from the military foremast. The two white bands on the third funnel mark her out as the third ship of the 2nd Light Division. *(Private collection)*

athwartship racks on the deck below, alongside the hatch serving the submerged torpedo flat. There was additional stowage in the submerged torpedo flat for six torpedo bodies and their associated warheads, so the total number of torpedoes embarked was as in *Gloire*: sixteen – a 17th is shown in the workshop on the main deck.

Gambetta appears to have been completed with her designed complement of torpedoes and tubes – the watertight hatch covering the axial stern tube is clearly visible in photographs. However, the plans of sister-ships *Jules Ferry* and *Victor Hugo*, dated January and April 1907 respectively, show only the underwater tubes, and the torpedo maintenance shop on the main deck has been converted into a general repair shop; it is labelled *atelier des mécaniciens* in *Jules Ferry* and *atelier de réparations* in *Victor Hugo* – although the latter plans do show two torpedo bodies being maintained.

The plans of *Léon Gambetta* and *Jules Ferry* show stowage for ten mines on the 1st platform deck aft, immediately forward of the ring bulkhead for the after 194mm turret. In the third ship, *Victor Hugo*, the complement of mines was doubled to twenty, stowed in racks in the same area.

TORPEDOES

450mm Torpedo Mle 1904

Length:	5.07m
Weight:	630kg
Propulsion:	piston engine/compressed air
Warhead:	100kg
Range:	1000m at 32.5 knots 2000m at 24.5 knots

PROTECTION

Hull

The vertical hull protection scheme replicated that of the *Gloire* class. There was a lower strake with a height of 2.05m amidships, comprising twenty-nine plates each four frames (ie 4.8m) in width except for the two bow plates, which were five frames (6m) wide. The plates had a maximum thickness of 150mm, declining progressively to 80–90mm at the ends, and were tapered beneath the waterline to 50mm. The upper strake likewise comprised twenty-nine plates four/five frames in length with a height of 1.625m amidships that increased slightly at the bow. The plates in the upper strake had a maximum thickness of 130mm amidships, tapering slightly to 120mm at their top edge. The maximum thickness was reduced progressively to 80–90mm at the ends (see Protection plan and table).

The plates in the upper and lower armour strakes

Victor Hugo moored at New York in May 1907, when she represented France at the Jamestown celebrations. *(Private collection)*

VICTOR HUGO

were secured by armour bolts to a teak backing 90/70mm thick, which was in turn secured to a double layer of 10mm hull plating. The plates that formed the thick part of the belt amidships were of cemented armour, using the Harvey face-hardening process; those at the ends were of homogeneous nickel steel. The heaviest plates in the lower belt weighed 10.2 tonnes, those in the upper belt just under 8 tonnes.

The after transverse bulkhead was composed of two separate plates of special steel, as in the *Gloire* and *Gueydon* classes (see Protection plan). However, the plates had a uniform thickness of 84mm throughout – in the earlier ships the upper of the two plates was tapered to 40mm.

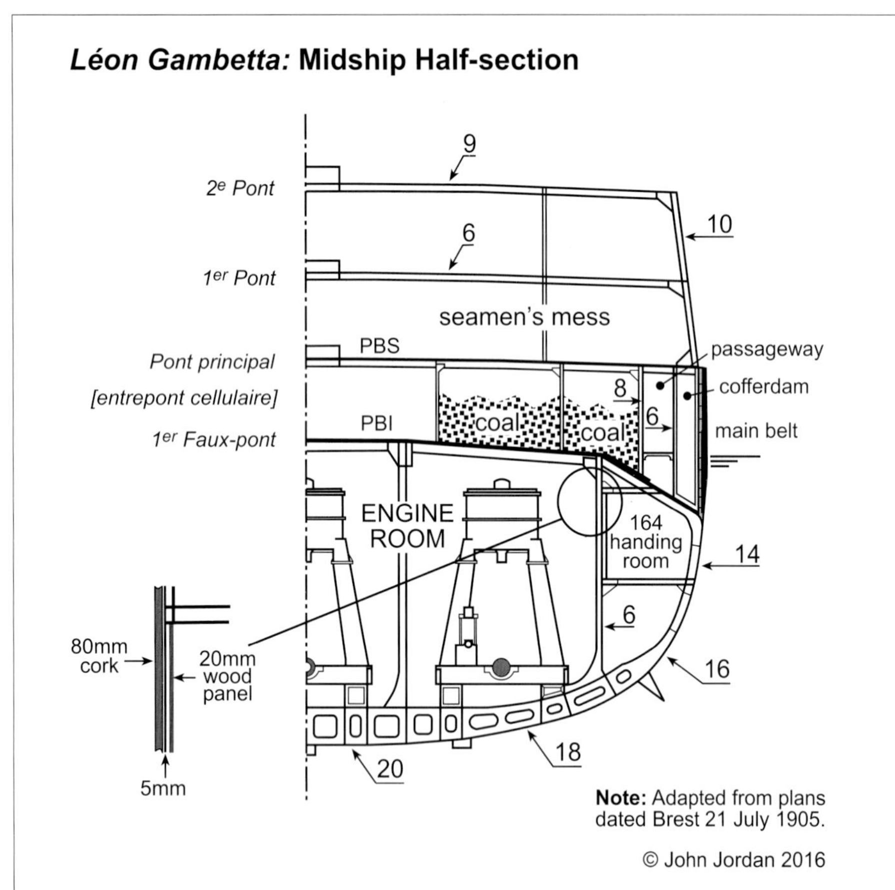

WEIGHT OF PROTECTION (*LÉON GAMBETTA*)

	No of plates	Composition	Weight
Main belt	2 x 58 (p&s)	cemented/ special steel[1]	918t
Upper belt	2 x 8 (p&s)	special steel	49t
PBS (upper 2 layers)		mild steel	313t
PBI (upper 2 layers)		mild steel	493t
35mm plates 1st Platform Deck	2 x 16 (p&s)	special steel	86t
Fwd transverse b/head	3	special steel	28t
Aft transverse b/head	2	special steel	7t
194 turrets + barbettes	2 x 5/6? (T)	cemented/ special steel[2]	312t
164.7 turrets + barbettes	4 x 7? (T)	special steel	520t
164.7 casemates	4 x 3 (faces)	special steel	102t
Hoists		special steel	22t
Conning tower + comms tube	5?	cemented/ special steel[3]	67t
Armoured deck coamings	n/a	special steel	95t
		Total	3011t

Notes:

1 Only the thick plates of the upper/lower belt were cemented (see table for details).

2 The thick rear walls of the 194mm turrets were of mild steel to counterbalance the turret; the turret hoods were of cast nickel steel.

3 The walls of the CT were cemented; the communications tube was of special steel.

Source: Official plans.

As in the *Gloire* class there was a light upper belt (*cuirasse mince*) extending from the bow to the after end of the forward casemate. The plates were of uniform 40mm special steel and were secured directly to the shell plating.

The horizontal protection scheme was a development of that adopted for the *Gloire* class, and was similar in principle to that of the battleships of the *Patrie* class: there were upper and lower protective decks (PBS/PBI) to provide a 'sandwich' for the cellular layer, but both comprised three layers of 50kg/mm^2 steel. Each of the three layers of steel forming the PBS was 11mm thick, for a total thickness of 33mm; each layer of the PBI was 15mm, for a total thickness of 45mm. The PBI had only two layers on the slopes, but the upper section was reinforced by plates of 35mm special steel (see drawing) for a total thickness of 65mm, and the lower section a row of 10mm plates (total: 40mm).

Inside the armoured box formed by the two protective decks and the side belt there was the customary cellular layer, comprising a cofferdam, a longitudinal passageway 1m wide, which was subdivided by bulkheads with watertight doors every four frames (4.8m), and coal bunkers.

Turrets, casemates and conning tower

The protection scheme for both the 194mm and 164.7mm turrets introduced a new feature: the *parapet tronconique*. The fixed armour for earlier variants of Bertin's *tourelle-barbette* had three elements: a ring of vertical armour above the weather deck to protect the lower part of the gunhouse, a ring of reduced diameter and thickness directly beneath the weather deck to protect the revolving working chamber, and a tube to protect the ammunition hoist between the working chamber and the upper armoured deck (PBS). For the *Gambetta* turrets the number of elements was reduced to two by combining the functions of the upper rings. In their place there was a single ring of armour in the shape of a truncated cone covering both the lower part of the gunhouse and the working chamber, its sides being angled inboard at 20°. The cone penetrated the weather deck, and in the larger 194mm turret was connected at its lower end to the ammunition tube.

The new arrangement saved weight and provided the same level of protection for the working chamber (which housed large numbers of ready-use propellant charges) as for the gunhouse itself. There was a cost: shells striking the inclined armour of the gunhouse cupola would tend to be deflected upwards; however, a shell striking the armoured *parapet* would inevitably be deflected downwards into the ship.

The main turrets of the *Gambetta* class were less heavily armoured than those of the *Gueydon* and *Gloire* classes. In the latter ships the plates on the cupola and the *parapet* had a thickness of 161–174mm; in the *Gambetta*s they were 138–140mm, secured to the customary double layer of 12/13mm mild steel plating. Only the plating on the sides of the cupola were of cemented armour. However, there was much thicker protection (100mm on a double layer of

Léon Gambetta: Protection

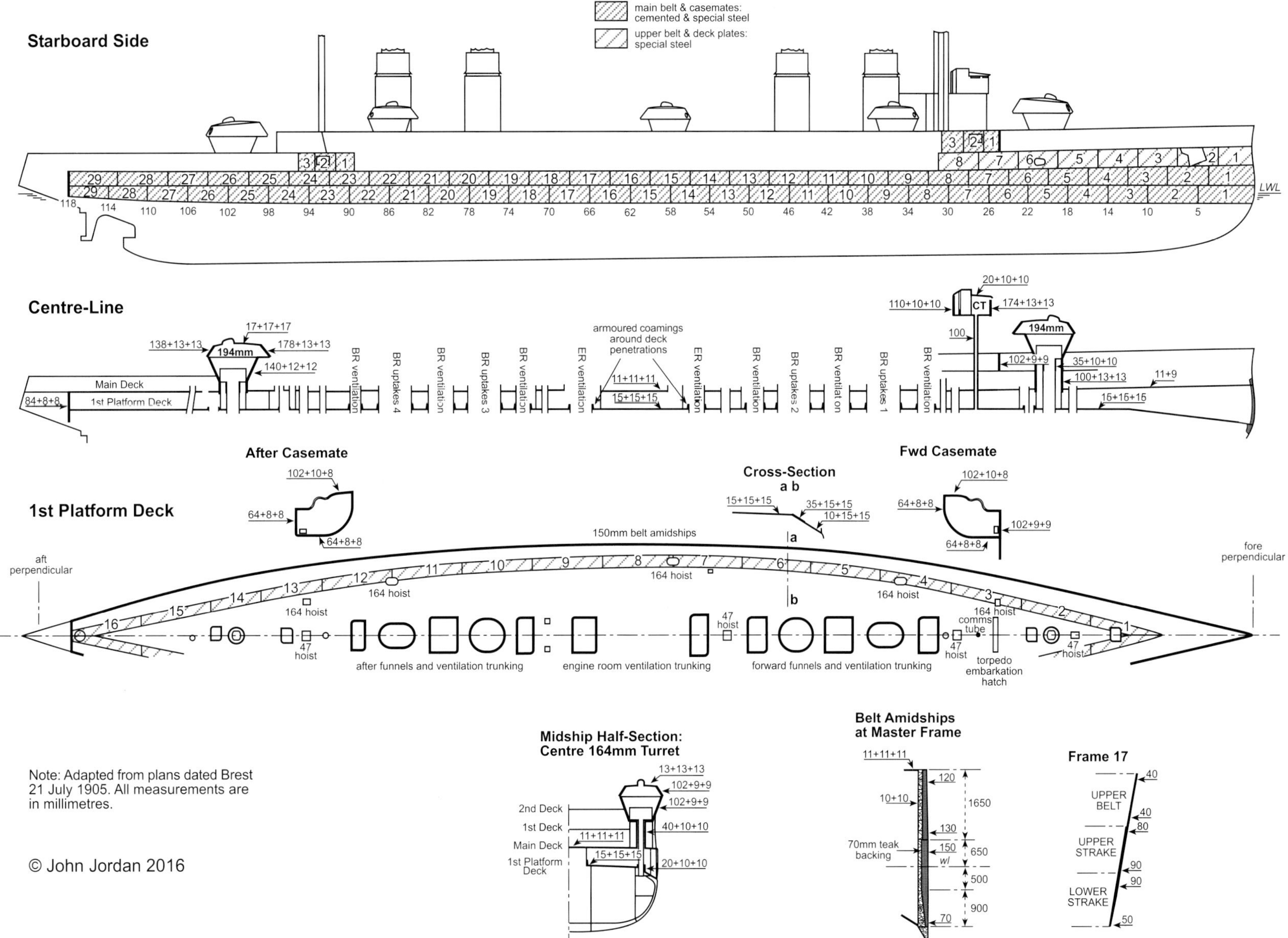

Note: Adapted from plans dated Brest 21 July 1905. All measurements are in millimetres.

13mm) for the ammunition trunk down to the upper protective deck (PBS), and 35mm on the upper part of the internal tube for the ammunition hoist (see Protection drawing). The level of protection accorded to the 164.7mm twin turrets was similar to that of the single turrets of the *Gloire* class, with 102mm plates of special steel for the cupola and the *parapet*.

The roofs of both the 194mm and the 164.7mm turrets were now composed of three layers of steel of equal thickness – in earlier turrets there was generally a thicker upper layer secured to a single layer of plating. The plates forming the roof of the 194mm turrets were of 17mm mild steel, those of the 164.7mm turrets were of 13mm steel; as with the decks, the upper of the three layers was hardened.

The protection of the 164.7mm casemates was similar to that of the *Gloire* classes, with 102mm special steel plating on the faces and 64mm special steel plating on the inner walls. The end walls of the forward casemates again formed part of a transverse bulkhead to protect against enfilading fire, and were of

LÉON GAMBETTA: ARMOUR PLATE THICKNESS MAIN BELT

Plate	Upper Strake *upper/lower edge*	Lower Strake *upper/lower edge*
1–4	80/90	90/50
5	80/90	105/50
6	80/90	120/50
7	95/105	135/70
8	110/120	150/70
9–22	120/130	150/70
23	120/130	135/70
24	110/120	120/50
25	95/105	105/50
26	80/90	90/50
27–29	70/80	80/50

Notes:

1 Total weight of main belt: **917.70 tonnes**; plates 7–23 of the lower strake and plates 8–24 of the upper strake were of cemented armour; the end plates were of special steel.

2 Plates 1–8 of the upper belt forward were of 40mm special steel.

3 Plates 1–3 of the fwd and after casemates were 102mm special steel.

Right: *Léon Gambetta* during her trials in April 1904, when she attained a speed of 23 knots with 29,029CV. *(Private collection)*

102mm special steel. However, there was no corresponding transverse bulkhead for the after casemates.

The conning tower was identical in size and layout to the one adopted for *Sully* and had a similar level of protection. The communications tube was formed by hoops of special steel 100mm thick and extended down to the upper protective deck (PBS).

MACHINERY

The propulsion machinery was significantly uprated compared with the *Gloire* class: designed horsepower was 27,500CV to deliver 22 knots, *vice* 20,500CV for 21 knots for the earlier ships. Despite this, the basic composition and layout of the plant was identical, at least for *Léon Gambetta* and *Victor Hugo*. There were three powerful four-cylinder VTE engines amidships, separated by longitudinal watertight bulkheads, with two condenser rooms immediately abaft the engine rooms. Steam was supplied by twenty-eight Niclausse large watertube boilers in *Gambetta* and twenty-eight Bellevilles in *Victor Hugo*, arranged as in the *Gloire* class: six boilers in BR1 (designated *Chaufferie*

Léon Gambetta: Operation of 'Y'-Frame for Boats

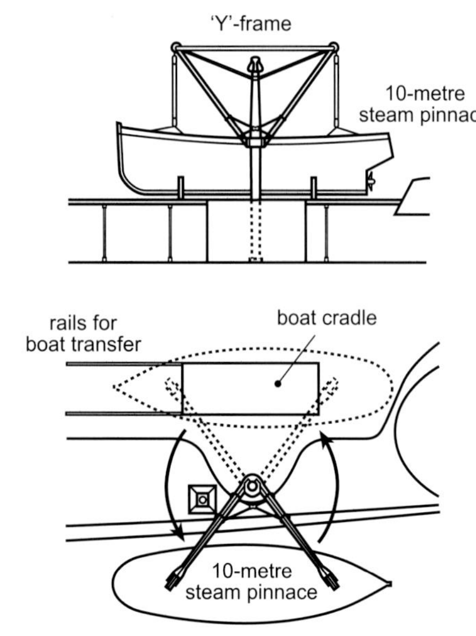

When the ship was at sea the boats were stowed on cradles which ran on rails (*poste de mer*).

The lighter boats were handled by davits. Once hoisted they were turned inboard and placed on the cradles.

The heavier boats were generally lifted by 'Y'-shaped cranes seated on the deck below which rotated through 180 degrees to the 'anchorage' position (*poste de rade*).

Of the three ships of the class, only *Léon Gambetta* was fitted with 'Y' frames, which were introduced for boat handling on the *Dupleix* class and were subsequently adopted for the five armoured cruisers of the *Gloire* class; *Gambetta*'s Lorient-built sister-ship *Jules Ferry* was fitted with 'goose-neck' cranes, while the third ship, *Victor Hugo*, had cranes of more modern design with an elevating boom. The cranes served as a prominent distinguishing feature between the ships.

A 'Y'-frame supporting an 8.5m whaler on the cruiser *Condé*. *(Private collection)*

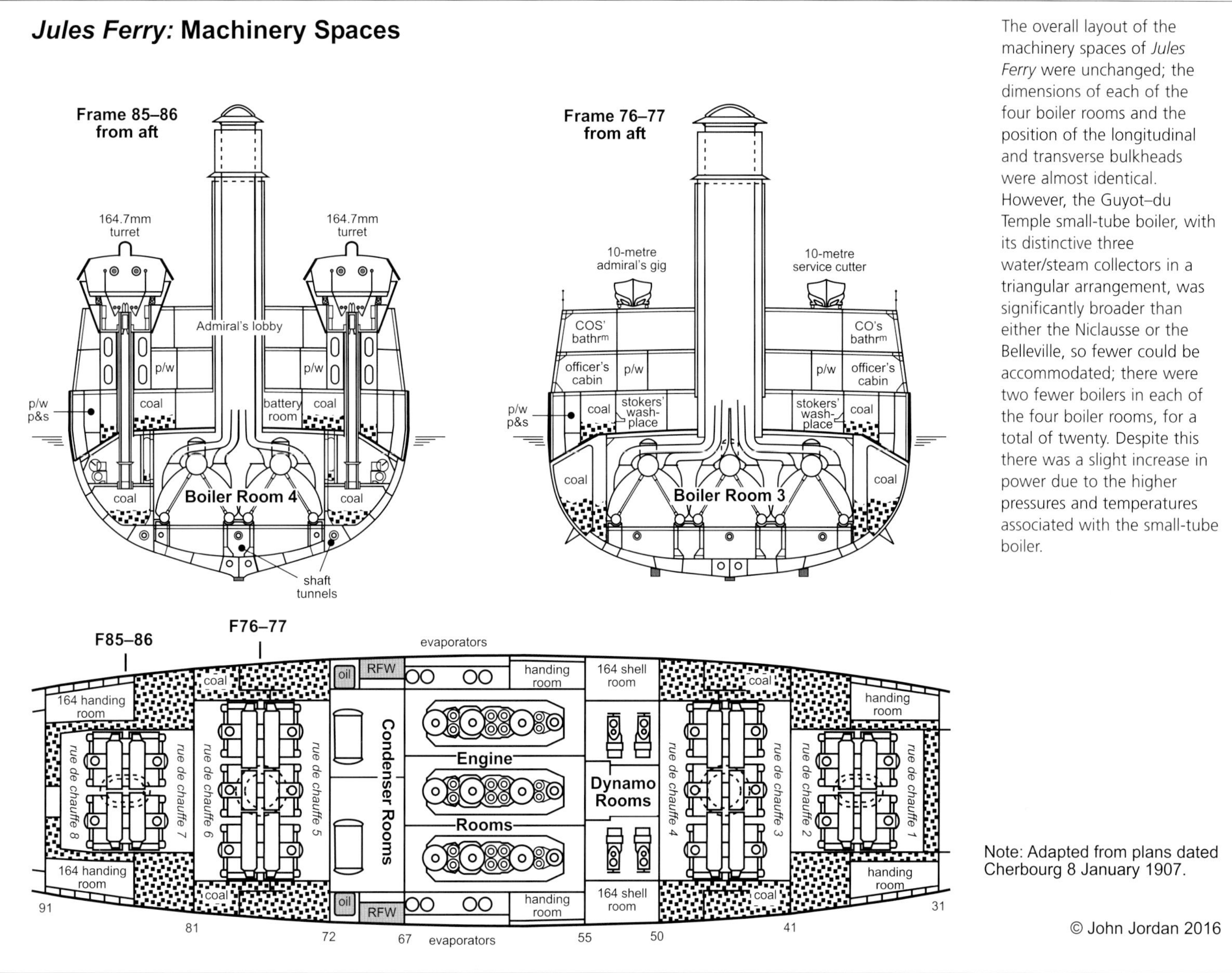

The overall layout of the machinery spaces of *Jules Ferry* were unchanged; the dimensions of each of the four boiler rooms and the position of the longitudinal and transverse bulkheads were almost identical. However, the Guyot–du Temple small-tube boiler, with its distinctive three water/steam collectors in a triangular arrangement, was significantly broader than either the Niclausse or the Belleville, so fewer could be accommodated; there were two fewer boilers in each of the four boiler rooms, for a total of twenty. Despite this there was a slight increase in power due to the higher pressures and temperatures associated with the small-tube boiler.

Avant), eight in BR2 (*Chaufferie Milieu Avant*), eight in BR3 (*Chaufferie Milieu Arrière*), and six in BR 4 (*Chaufferie Arrière*).

The engines for *Léon Gambetta* were contracted to the private shipbuilder Penhoët of Saint-Nazaire, and proved particularly successful; the Penhoët shipyard would subsequently be awarded the contract for *Ernest Renan* (see Chapter 8), which was originally to have been the fifth ship of the class. The engines for *Victor Hugo* were built by Indret; the propellers on the wing shafts were 5.25m in diameter, that on the centre shaft 5m. The total weight of the machinery was 1808 tonnes.

Jules Ferry, built by Cherbourg Naval Dockyard, had small-tube boilers of the Guyot–du Temple type. The Guyot–du Temple boiler, which had previously been adopted for *Jeanne d'Arc*, currently running trials, and which would also be selected for the modernisation of *Dupuy-de-Lôme*, had larger dimensions than either the Belleville or Niclausse type, and only twenty could be accommodated. There were six boilers back-to-back in each of the two larger boiler rooms, and four in each of the end rooms (see drawing). It was calculated that the small-tube boilers would provide an increase in horsepower to 29,000CV, although this figure was not quite attained on her power trials.

The propulsion machinery of *Jules Ferry* was built by Indret, and in service was found to be 'seriously defective' (see RFNA 1907). The boilers were found to be unreliable, and some of the condenser tubes were too short. Repairs and modifications were made during and following trials, but the problems experienced with the Guyot–du Temple boilers may have influenced decisions regarding the propulsion plants of the later French armoured cruisers.[12]

[12] In an interview with a British naval intelligence officer in mid-1903 (RFNA 1904 Vol I), engineer Guyot felt that opinion in the *Marine Nationale* was turning against the small-tube boiler. He ascribed the problems experienced with the earlier models to the excessively small diameter of their tubes (25mm), which led to overheating and made them difficult to maintain. Guyot stated that tubes with two to three times this diameter with stouter scantlings were now being employed.

Above: *Victor Hugo* at the Jamestown Tercentennial Exposition of 1907. The photo was taken on 12 June. *(NHHC 19-N-11-21-12)*

Like their predecessors of the *Gloire* class, the *Gambettas* were considered good steamers: endurance was calculated as 7500nm at 10 knots with a full load of coal, and almost 1950nm at 22kts. Results for the three-hour and ten-hour full power trials are detailed in the accompanying table.

The auxiliary machinery was arranged as in the *Patrie* class. Four powerful dynamos rated at 1200A (twice the rating of those in the earlier ships) were in compartments on either side of the centreline on the 2nd platform deck amidships, immediately above the magazine for the centre 164.7mm turrets, with the switchboard room between them (see GA Plans of *Gambetta* and Machinery Spaces plan of *Jules Ferry*). The dynamos for *Gambetta* and *Ferry* were from Breguet, Paris. The evaporators – eight *vice* six in the *Gloire* class – were relocated to the wing compartments outboard of the engines formerly occupied by the

dynamos except in the third ship, *Victor Hugo*, in which they were mounted outboard of the forward and after boiler rooms. *Victor Hugo* also had an all-electric rudder servo-motor installation; as with the experimental electric/hydraulic installation in *Marseillaise*, the purpose of this was the elimination of steam lines running from the boiler rooms to the stern, thereby reducing temperatures in the magazines and the accommodation spaces.

By the early 1900s all major French vessels had air cooling for their magazines, some of which were located in close proximity to the spaces occupied by the propulsion machinery and were therefore exposed to high ambient temperatures. All the magazines in the *Léon Gambetta* class were equipped with an air-cooling (*aéroréfrigérant*) system developed and manufactured by the prominent engineer Frédéric Fouché, whose company was based in Paris.

PERFORMANCE ON THREE-HOUR/TEN-HOUR FULL-POWER TRIALS[1]

	Date	Speed	Horsepower	Shaft Revs	Consumption	Boiler
Léon Gambetta	22 Apr 1905	23.00kts	29,029CV	126.11rpm	0.936kg/h/cv	Niclausse
Jules Ferry	7 Dec 1906	22.56kts	28,743CV	124.51rpm	0.831kg/h/cv	Guyot–du Temple
Victor Hugo	2 Mar 1907	22.26kts	28,344CV	127.00rpm	0.779kg/h/cv	Belleville
Jules Michelet[2]	17 Sep 1908	22.65kts	29,805CV	128.36rpm	0.844kg/h/cv	Guyot–du Temple

Notes:

1 *Léon Gambetta* and *Victor Hugo* underwent the traditional three-hour power trial; for *Jules Ferry*, *Jules Michelet* and their successors the trial was extended to ten hours.

2 *Jules Michelet* has been included here for comparison; she had the same hull form as the *Gambetta* class and a propulsion system comparable to that of *Jules Ferry*.

Source: CAAP: inventaire 432, sous-série 5i cartons 113 (*LG*), 102 (*JF*), 181 (*VH*), 103 (*JM*).

CONSTRUCTION AND EARLY SERVICE

Léon Gambetta was launched at Brest in October 1902; fitting-out was carried out promptly and efficiently and she was manned for trials just over one year later. However, the ship ran aground in fog in late February 1904; new propellers had to be ordered for the starboard and centre shafts (see Introduction), and hull plating was replaced between the forward 164.7mm turret and the bridge, and abeam the after funnels. Sea trials were resumed only in August 1904. There was then a minor grounding as the ship entered the River Penfeld at Brest in early September;[13] little damage was done to the plating, but the starboard bilge keel and blades of the propellers were bent, resulting in a further docking for repairs. Official trials finally took place off Brest between April and July 1905; the ship then entered service with the Northern Squadron as flagship of the 1st Cruiser Division, which initially comprised *Gueydon* and *Dupetit-Thouars*. *Léon Gambetta* would serve in this role until the autumn of 1909, when she transferred to the Mediterranean.

As France's most modern and powerful cruiser, *Gambetta* was assigned a number of prestigious showing-the-flag missions. In August 1905 the Northern Squadron visited Portsmouth to celebrate the conclusion of the *Entente Cordiale*; *Gambetta* was accompanied by the four ships of the *Gloire* class. In October 1905 she sailed for Lisbon, where she embarked President Emile Loubet. In May 1908 she embarked President Armand Fallières for a visit to Dover, and in July of the same year she was in Canada for the tercentenary of Quebec, returning to Brest on 17 August.

Jules Ferry, which was built by Cherbourg naval dockyard, embarked on her sea trials in July 1905, but serious problems with her boilers and condensers (see above) meant that official trials were delayed, and it was December 1906 before she underwent full-power trials. Trials then continued until May of the following year, when the ship joined the Light Squadron in the Mediterranean.

The third ship, *Victor Hugo*, was originally to have been built at Toulon. Construction was delayed by the need to transport the assembled materials to Lorient and by the latter dockyard's existing commitments,[14] and the ship was not laid down until March 1903. She was launched twelve months later, but fitting-out proceeded at a relatively slow pace, and *Hugo* was not manned for trials until 15 January 1907. The official trials proceeded relatively smoothly, with only the fuel consumption trial of 19 February being abandoned, and were concluded in early April. On 8 May *Victor Hugo* left Lorient and headed for New York, where she represented France at the Jamestown celebrations. When she returned in June she was assigned to the Light Squadron in the Mediterranean, embarking on further 'complementary' trials at Toulon in June 1908.

By January 1910 all three ships were based in the Mediterranean, where they formed the nucleus of an increasingly powerful Light Squadron. *Victor Hugo* was placed in reserve in 1911, but *Léon Gambetta* and *Jules Ferry* were both present at the Great Naval Review of 4 September (see Chapter 10), with the latter ship leading the line as flagship of Vice Admiral Jauréguiberry, Inspector General of the Navy and Vice President of the *Conseil supérieur*. In late 1911 the Light Squadron in the Mediterranean was reorganised as two three-ship divisions comprising the most modern armoured cruisers, and the three *Gambettas* were assigned to the 2nd Division. *Léon Gambetta* was the flagship first of Rear Admiral Dartige du Fournet, then of Rear Admiral Senès, serving in that role until her loss in late April 1915; *Victor Hugo* was the second ship in the division, and *Jules Ferry* the third.

Gambetta Class: Early Service

	Gambetta	Jules Ferry	Victor Hugo	Jules Michelet
1905	Northern Squ	Trials	Trials	Building
1906		↓	↓	
1907		Lt Squ Med	Lt Squ Med	↓
1908		↓	↓	Trials
1909		1st Lt Div Med	1st Lt Div Med	1st Lt Div Med
1910	↓		↓	↓
1911	1st Lt Div Med	↓	Reserve	Reserve
1912	2nd Lt Div Med	2nd Lt Div Med	2nd Lt Div Med	*Div des écoles*
1913				↓
1914	↓	↓	↓	1st Lt Div Med

13 *Jeanne d'Arc*, which had the same long, narrow hull form as *Gambetta*, had experienced similar difficulties in negotiating the narrow entrance to the River Penfeld (see Chapter 3), and these incidents gave new impetus to the need to develop facilities (new graving docks plus a new fitting-out quay) at Laninon, outside the Penfeld, to handle the larger vessels in service with the *Marine Nationale*.

14 The cruiser *Gloire* was manned for trials only in February 1903, and her sister *Condé* was still fitting out.

Left: A bow view of *Léon Gambetta* dressed overall, probably dating from the Grand Naval Review of September 1911 off Toulon. *(Private collection)*

EVALUATION

These powerful ships made a big impression abroad, particularly in Britain, where it was feared that with their powerful armament, high speed and good endurance they would pose a major threat to the trade routes. The Royal Navy responded by building a new generation of armoured cruisers that could match them; the result was the six ships of the *Duke of Edinburgh* and the *Warrior* classes, which were laid down between February 1903 and March 1904. However, shortly afterwards, on 8 April 1904, the *Entente Cordiale* was signed and British fears abated.

Once war was declared in 1914, the *Gambettas* would display the conceptual weaknesses characteristic of all armoured cruisers. They were vulnerable

Above: *Victor Hugo* leaving the anchorage at Toulon shortly before the Great War. The two white bands on the second funnel mark her out as the second ship of the 2nd Light Division of the Mediterranean Squadron. *(Marius Bar)*

Right: *Jules Ferry* before the Great War; the photo was probably taken in 1912. The two white bands on the third funnel mark her out as the third ship of the 2nd Light Division of the Mediterranean Squadron. *(Private collection)*

Above: Forward 194mm twin turret of *Victor Hugo*. The photo was taken at Toulon, probably shortly before the Great War. *(Private collection)*

both to the big gun, which made their deployment in direct support of the battle line a hazardous enterprise, and to the torpedo, against which they had no defence whatsoever. In the *Gambetta*s the magazines, shell rooms and handing rooms that lined the sides of the ship accounted for just under 60m of the 148m length (40 per cent). The consequences can be seen in the loss of *Léon Gambetta*, which sank with 680 men in ten minutes in April 1915 after being struck by two torpedoes from the Austrian submarine *U5* in the Strait of Otranto (see Chapter 11), and the sudden destruction in May of the following year of the British armoured cruisers *Black Prince* and *Defence*, both of which exploded under a hail of heavy shell at Jutland.

Even by the time the *Gambetta*s had been completed, their speed advantage over the battleship[15] had been eroded by the appearance of the turbine-powered HMS *Dreadnought*, which was capable of a sustained 21 knots. The advent of the turbine-powered armoured cruiser (later 'battle cruiser') would effectively nullify their theoretical speed advantage over other comparable vessels.

[15] The contemporary French battleships of the *Patrie* class and their British counterparts of the *Formidable* class had a maximum speed of 18 knots.

CHAPTER 8:

THE QUEST FOR SPEED: *JULES MICHELET* AND *ERNEST RENAN*

THE *STATUT NAVAL* OF 1900 had specified five new-build armoured cruisers. Following the authorisation of the three *Gambettas* this left two ships to be ordered. It was originally envisaged that these would also be of the *Gambetta* type, but the French vice of constant tinkering in favour of incremental improvements intervened, and the two ships that emerged from the design process differed not only from the *Gambettas* but from one another, thereby repeating the errors made with the *Flotte d'échantillons* of the earlier 1890 programme. This process, which was exacerbated by unstable government and by an unanticipated lurch into the past with the appointment to the post of Minister of Marine of the combative adherent of the *Jeune Ecole* Camille Pelletan in June 1902, was by no means limited to cruiser design. The laudable intention to build in rapid order a homogeneous class of six 15,000-tonne battleships (*Patrie* class) was quickly undermined by delaying tactics on the part of Pelletan, who attempted to cancel the later ships and gave the Navy the opportunity to decide on a fundamental revision of their main armament, leading to individual building times of five to six years.[1]

JULES MICHELET

The first of the two new cruisers had the same hull form and broadly the same internal layout as the *Gambettas* but a much-revised main armament. The 194mm gun, mounted in twin turrets fore and aft as in the earlier ships, was a new, more powerful 50-calibre model with greater penetration at the longer battle ranges now being contemplated.[2] It was the same gun that would be mounted in a mix of single

1 See Jordan and Caresse, *French Battleships of World War One*, Chapter 4.

2 By late 1903 it was anticipated that 'decisive' battle ranges might be in excess of 2500m, possibly as great as 4000–5000m.

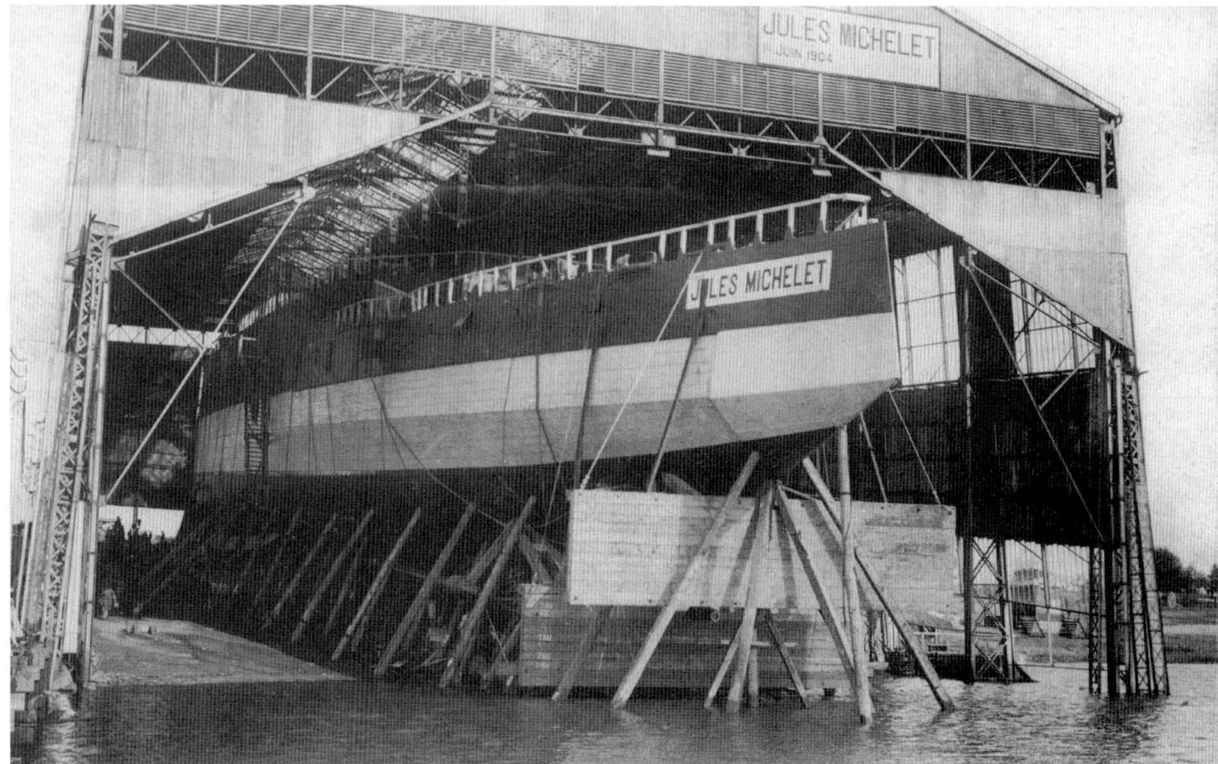

Right: *Jules Michelet* on the slipway at Lorient naval dockyard; she would be launched on 31 August 1905. Note the panel on the face of the covered building hall recording the date the keel was laid. *(Private collection)*

turrets and casemates in the *Démocratie* sub-group of the 15,000-tonne battleships – a decision taken only in October 1903.

The 164.7mm Mle 1893–1896M gun was to have been superseded by a new Model 1902; prototypes were built at Ruelle and trialled at the Gâvres proving ground in 1902–03. Like its 194mm contemporary the Mle 1902 was a 50-calibre weapon with longer range and greater penetration. It fired the same range of projectiles as the Mle 1893–1896M, but chamber length and volume were increased – the latter significantly[3] – in order to accommodate an enhanced combat charge of BM11 propellant. However, the decision to rearm the later ships of the *Patrie* class with 194mm guns meant that there were surplus guns of the earlier 164.7mm model available; the Mle 1893–1896M gun would therefore be retained for the medium QF battery.

The reversion to single turrets in *Michelet* and *Ernest Renan* is, on the face of it, surprising, as it meant a reduction from sixteen guns (twelve in twin turrets plus four in casemates) to twelve guns (eight in single turrets plus four in casemates). However, a trial during the late 1890s involving the battleship *Jauréguiberry* and the cruiser *Latouche-Tréville* had demonstrated that in rapid fire the number of rounds that could be fired by the twin turret was only 1.4 times that of the single (see also Bertin's comments on the proposal to rearm the station cruisers of the *Dupleix* class, Chapter 4). Concern had also been expressed regarding the possibility of a breakdown in the turret training mechanism due to mechanical/electrical failure or action damage; this would have less impact on the ship's overall fighting ability if the guns were in single mountings. The twin turret presented a larger target to the enemy guns, making such damage more likely.

Moreover, early trials of the new 164.7mm twin turret installed in the *Dupleix* class were not a conspicuous success. A problem highlighted in the British Admiralty's Reports of Foreign Naval Affairs (RFNA 1904, page 29), following a conversation between a British naval intelligence officer and a French engineer, was that the 'noxious gases given off on ignition of the powder form so serious a drawback that the limit of rapidity in practice is about four rounds per minute. At higher speeds than this the turret becomes so filled with gases as to asphixiate the men.'

Trials of the *Dupleix* class, which were the first to mount the twin turret, began in March (*Dupleix*), August (*Desaix*) and September (*Kléber*) of 1902

[3] Friedman, *Naval Weapons of World War One*, gives a chamber length of 1470mm (*vice* 1210mm) and a chamber volume of 52.95dm^3 (*vice* 36.74 dm^3).

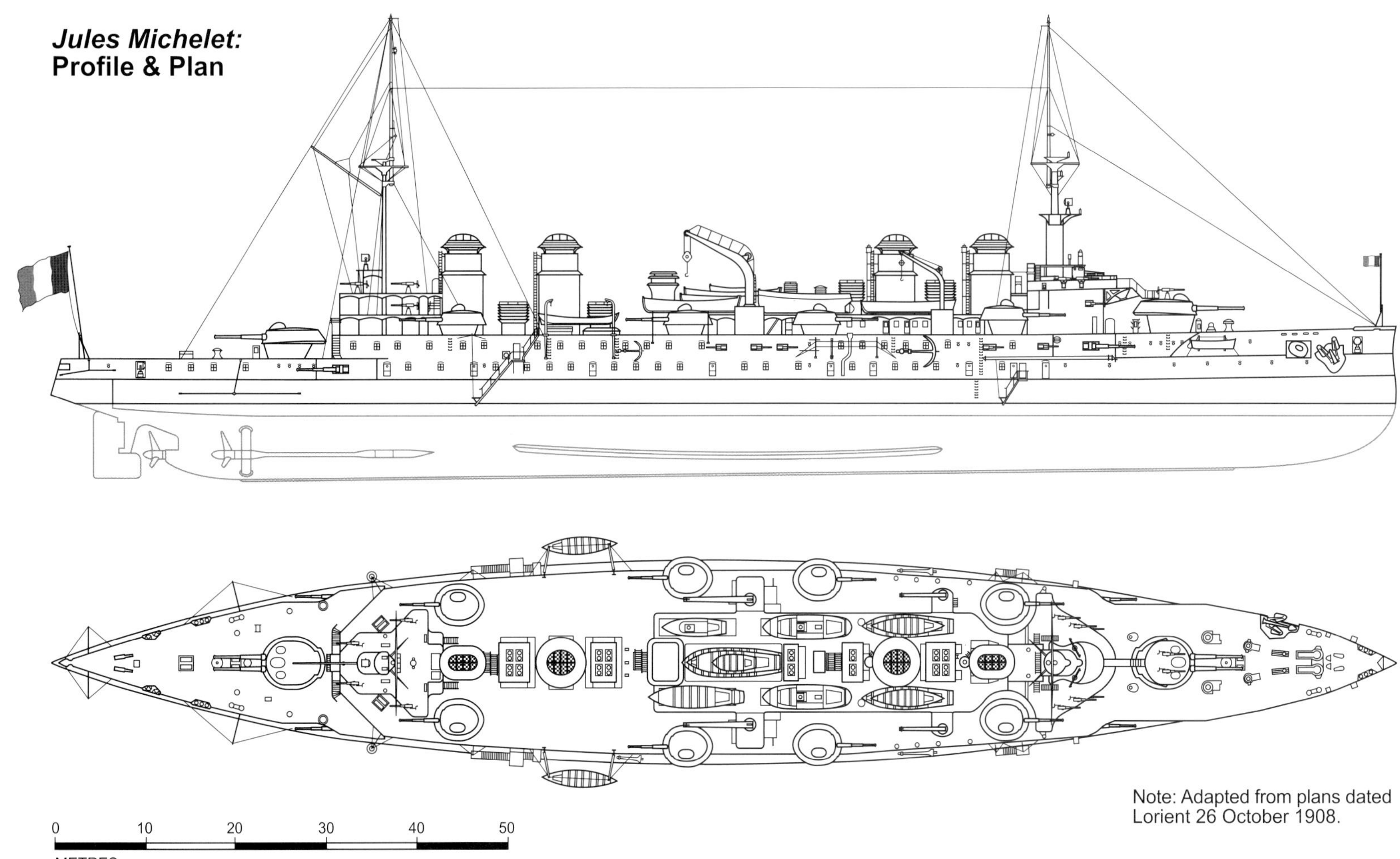

Jules Michelet was the first French armoured cruiser not to have a fully-developed military mast. The light ATB guns which had populated the lower platform in the *Gambetta*s were redistributed between the upper bridge and the forward 194mm turret. Note the unusual angled ladderway which gave access for the gun crew, and the distinctive 'goose-neck' crane for the boats amidships.

Right: An early view of *Jules Michelet* off Lorient. In the after 194mm turret the gun to starboard has been elevated close to its maximum 15°, while the port-side gun is depressed to its loading angle of -5°. *(Private collection)*

BUILDING DATA

Name	Builder	Laid down	Launched	Trials	Commissioned
Jules Michelet	Arsenal de Lorient	1 Jun 1904	31 Aug 1905	May 1908	10 Dec 1908

respectively, after the first two *Gambettas* had been laid down, so the twin turrets for the *Gambettas* may have been modified prior to installation. Combustion gases were evacuated via three slots at the top of the turret walls on either side, but this 'natural' ventilation proved unable to cope in a small cramped twin turret. The engineer's statement implies that each of the guns in these turrets was effectively limited to two rounds per minute, while the gun itself was capable of three, and it was this consideration that provided the rationale for the adoption of four single turrets in place of the three twins in *Jules Michelet* and *Ernest Renan*, which were laid down from mid-1904. Four guns in single turrets, each with a rate of fire of three rounds per minute (total: 12rpm), would in practice be equivalent to six guns in twin turrets each capable of two rounds per minute.

It proved possible to squeeze in an additional wing turret at forecastle (2nd) deck level on either side of the ship, but constraints on topweight, deck space and on the internal layout of the ship meant that the *Marine Nationale* was compelled to accept this theoretical reduction in firepower. Nevertheless, the reduction in the number of guns also provided the opportunity for increased magazine stowage per gun, so the ships' ability to conduct a sustained engagement was if anything enhanced.

High speed continued to be a major consideration, and the new ship, which would be named *Jules Michelet*, again adopted the Guyot–du Temple small-tube boiler built by the Navy's propulsion establishment at Indret. This advanced type of boiler had been fitted in the second of the *Gambettas*, *Jules Ferry*. *Ferry* had been built at Cherbourg Naval Dockyard, whereas the new ship would be ordered from Lorient, which was building the third unit of the class, *Victor Hugo*. She mounted twenty-eight Belleville boilers, so having completed a ship fitted with one type of boiler, the workforce at Lorient would now have to fit boilers of a completely different type. The French practice of building one-off units rather than in series had inevitable consequences for construction times, and it took Lorient Dockyard in excess of four years to complete *Michelet*.[4]

NOMENCLATURE

Jules Michelet (1798–1874) was a notable French historian. Born in Paris to a family with Huguenot traditions he was, like Gambetta, Ferry and Hugo, a committed republican with strong anti-clerical views. In 1867 he completed his greatest work, the *Histoire de France*. Covering the entire history of France from the earliest days up to the Revolution, it was published in nineteen volumes.

HULL AND SUPERSTRUCTURES

The hull of *Jules Michelet* was identical to that of the

4 Each of the three *Gambettas* took almost exactly four years to build, although *Gambetta*'s completion was delayed by repairs following her grounding during trials. One would have expected a 'follow-on' ship to be built within a shorter time-frame, whereas *Michelet* took three months longer to complete.

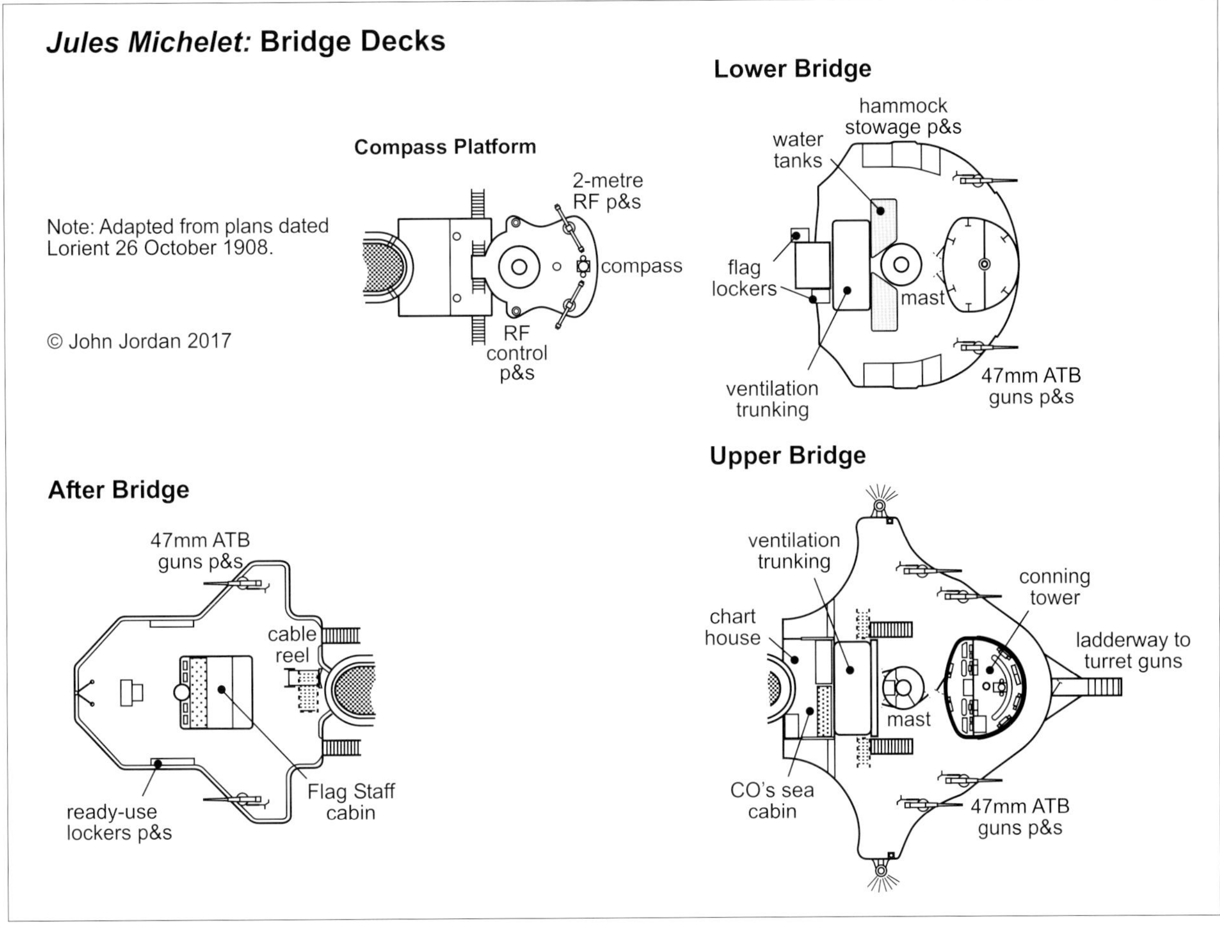

Gambettas except for modifications to the shaft brackets. However, there were a number of external features that served to distinguish her from her half-sisters. Most obvious is the number and configuration of the wing turrets for the 164.7mm guns, of which there were four singles in *Michelet* and three twins in the *Gambettas*. Other differences include the suppression of the lower platform on the military foremast for the 47mm ATB guns, and the mounting of two of the displaced guns atop the forward turret – a feature

Left: The armoured cruiser *Jules Michelet* leaving Lorient. The four single wing turrets are prominent in this view. Note that the position of the sighting hoods is reversed on the after turrets, so that the hood is always on the outboard side of the turret. This enabled the turret officer to have an unobstructed view during end-on fire. *(Private collection)*

common in contemporary foreign battleships but a first for the *Marine Nationale*. There was also a pair of 'goose-neck' cranes amidships, between the two centre gun turrets, to handle the larger boats, with a lighter crane of the same type abreast the forward funnels.

However, the major implications of these changes can be seen below decks. Each of the four wing turrets required an axial hoist, and in the *Gambetta*s there were only three groups of magazines: forward, aft and a magazine that extended for the full beam of the ship amidships, immediately forward of the engine rooms. There was no question of rearranging the magazines themselves, as this would have implied a complete revision of the machinery compartments and the internal subdivision of the ship. The answer was to group the two midship turrets together so that they could share the same magazines and shell rooms.

The end turrets and the redoubts for the four 164.7mm casemate guns were left in place. Although the magazines and shell rooms for the original centre turrets were forward of the engine rooms, between frames 50 and 55, the hoist and handing room for each of the turrets had been worked in abreast the forward part of the engine rooms, between frames 55 and 60, with the hoist centred on frame 58 (see GA Plans for *Léon Gambetta*, page 142). For *Jules Michelet* this handing room was lengthened by a single frame (it was now 7.2m long) and converted into a lateral ammunition passage. It was then extended aft to the rear bulkhead of the engine rooms (frames 61–67) to form a new handing room for the extra turret. In order to separate the two centre turrets from one another, the handing room for the first of the centre turrets was moved forward so that it occupied the outboard part of the main magazine. The hoists for the two centre turrets were now at frames 52.5 and 65 respectively (see plan of magazines and handing rooms page 169).

The eight evaporators, which in the first two *Gambetta*s had been in the compartment outboard of the engine rooms now occupied by the handing room for the fourth wing turret, were divided up and relocated in compartments outboard of the fore and after boiler rooms – *Victor Hugo* had a similar arrangement.

The suppression of the lower platform of the military foremast – which nevertheless retained its tubular structure, presumably for ease of access to the rangefinding platform via an internal spiral staircase – led to a complete reorganisation of the ATB guns, which were now more closely grouped for improved fire control (see Armament section). The forward searchlight was moved down to the new lower platform. Both measures served to reduce topweight, but critics were less than impressed. An article about the ship in *Le Yacht* dated 6 June 1908 pointed out that the upperworks of modern French warships were more cluttered than those of the latest IJN warships – which of course were influenced by British practice. The article also pointed out that once the ship was in action the ATB guns mounted on the upper decks and in the superstructures would quickly be eliminated: a group of four guns could easily be taken out by a single high-explosive shell.

Like the *Gambetta*s, *Jules Michelet* was fitted out as a flagship and saw extensive service in this role both before and during the First World War. The admiral's quarters were located at the after end of the 1st deck, just forward of the after 194mm turret, as in her half-sisters.

ARMAMENT

Main guns

The 194mm guns mounted in *Jules Michelet* belonged to the new Mle 1902 series of naval guns, which were 50 calibres in length and had an enlarged chamber to accommodate a more powerful propellant charge. They were also of more advanced construction than the 40-calibre guns of the Mle 1893 series.[5]

The 194mm Mle 1902, which was also mounted as the secondary gun in the contemporary battleships of the *Démocratie* sub-group, fired APC and SAPC steel projectiles weighing 88kg, both of which had a burster of *mélinite* (see table for data). The powerful charge of BM13 propellant was in three bags and weighed 38.5kg.

The twin turret in *Jules Michelet* was broadly similar in conception and configuration to the turret in the *Gambettas*,[6] but some modifications to the gunhouse and the balancing of the turret were necessary

CHARACTERISTICS

Displacement:	12,600 tonnes
Dimensions:	
Length	146.50m pp; 149.07m oa
Beam	21.4m wl
Draught	8.18m aft
Propulsion:	
Boilers	20 Guyot–Du Temple boilers
Engines	3-shaft 4-cylinder VTE
Horsepower	29,000CV
Speed	22.5 knots (designed)
Coal	1320 tonnes normal; 2070 tonnes full load
Endurance	7500nm at 10 knots
Armament:	
Main guns	4 x 194mm/50 Mle 1902 in twin turrets
Medium guns	12 x 164.7mm/45 Mle 1893–1896M QF in eight single turrets and four casemate mountings
ATB guns	24 x 47mm/50 Mle 1902 QF in single mountings
Torpedo tubes	2 submerged tubes for 450mm torpedoes 8 torpedoes Mle 1904
Protection:	
Main belt	150/130mm max
Decks	33mm PBS 45/65mm PBI
194 turrets	156mm
164 turrets	122mm
Casemates	138mm
Conning tower	174mm
Boats:	2 x 10m steam pinnaces 1 x 7.65m White launch 1 x 11m pulling pinnace 2 x 10.5m pulling cutters 1 x 10m admiral's gig 4 x 8.5m whalers 2 x 5m dinghies
Complement:	
As private ship	22 officers, 750 men

[5] See Friedman, *Naval Weapons of World War One*, p 203.

[6] The guns in the battleships were mounted in single turrets of different design.

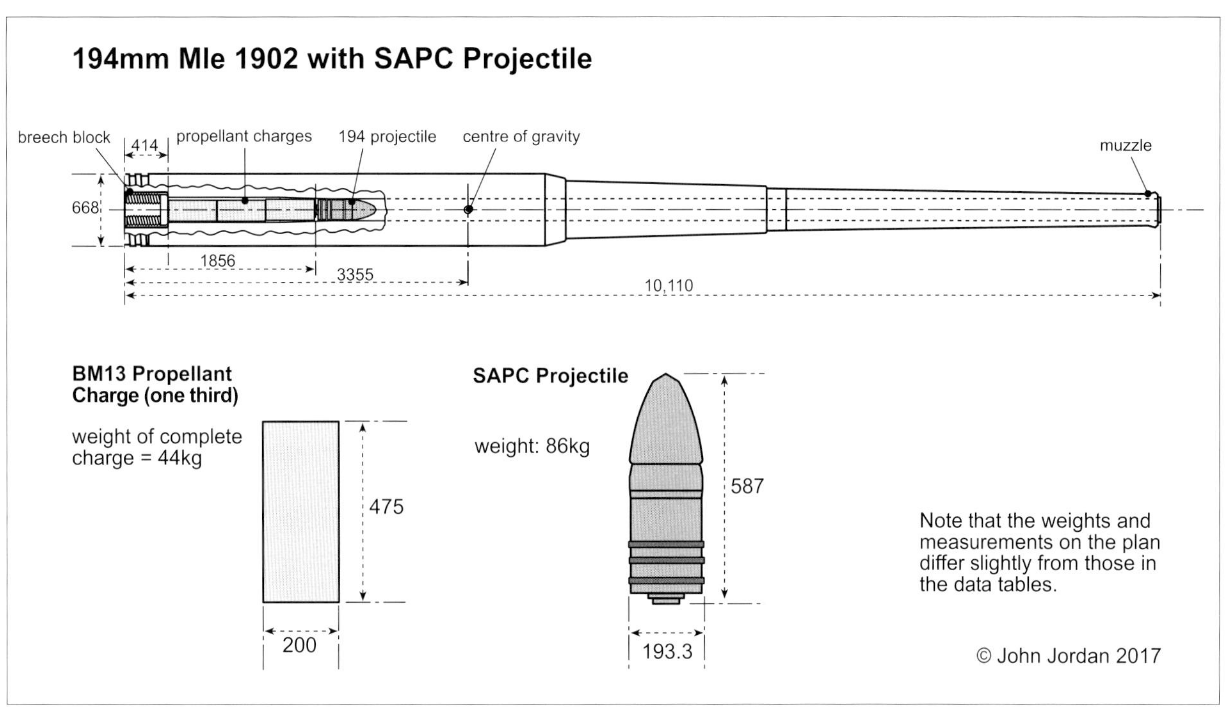

Jules Michelet: Layout of 164.7mm Magazines and Handing Rooms

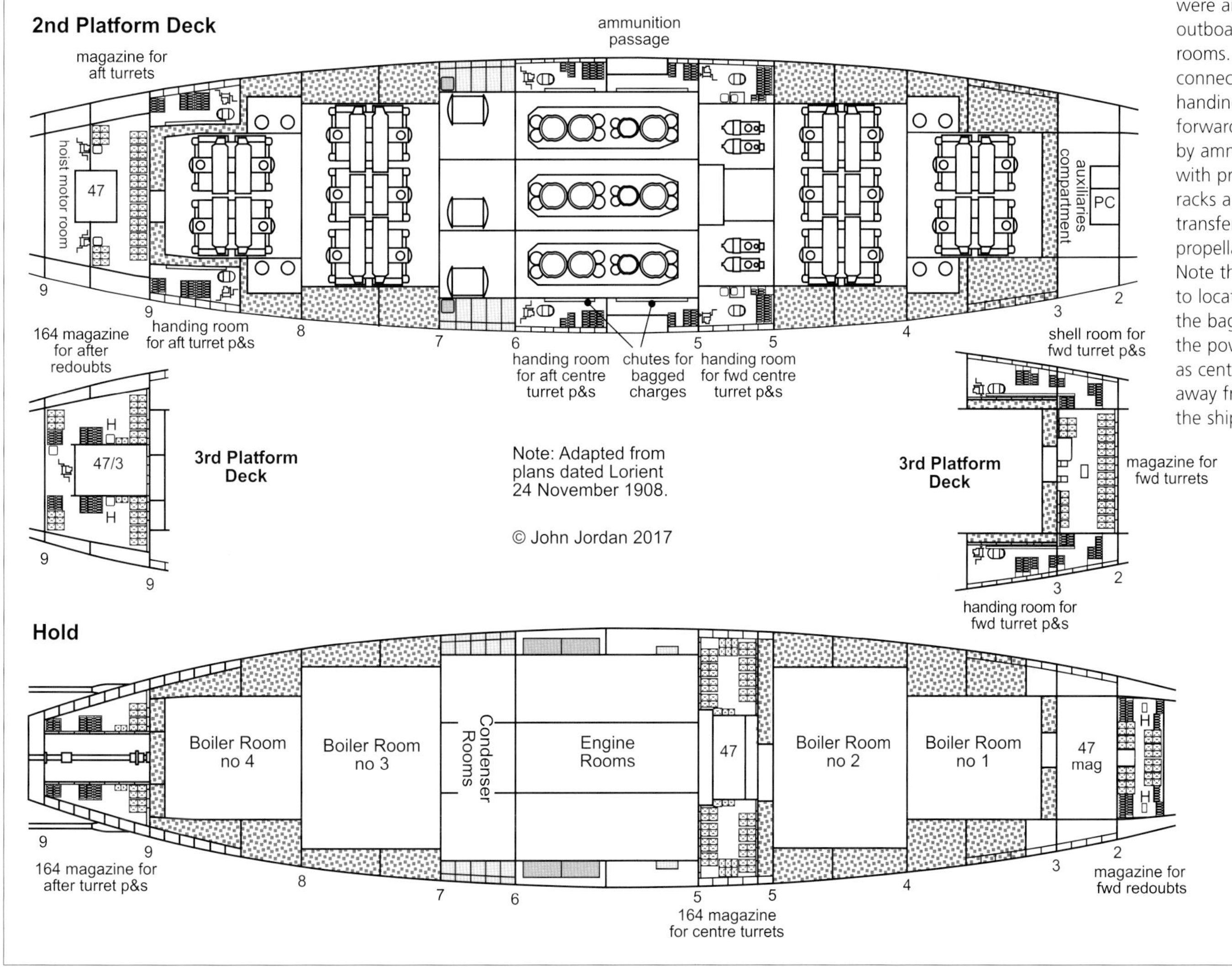

2nd Platform Deck

magazine for aft turrets

ammunition passage

hoist motor room

47

auxiliaries compartment

PC

9 9 8 7 6 5 5 4 3 2

164 magazine for after redoubts

handing room for aft turret p&s

handing room for aft centre turret p&s

chutes for bagged charges

handing room for fwd centre turret p&s

shell room for fwd turret p&s

3rd Platform Deck

47/3

H

Note: Adapted from plans dated Lorient 24 November 1908.

© John Jordan 2017

3rd Platform Deck

magazine for fwd turrets

handing room for fwd turret p&s

Hold

Boiler Room no 4

Boiler Room no 3

Condenser Rooms

Engine Rooms

47

Boiler Room no 2

Boiler Room no 1

47 mag

164 magazine for after turret p&s

164 magazine for centre turrets

magazine for fwd redoubts

The new handing rooms for the extra turrets were amidships, outboard of the engine rooms. They were connected to the handing rooms for the forward centre turrets by ammunition passages with projectile stowage racks and chutes for the transfer of bagged propellant charges. Note the efforts made to locate the lockers for the bagged charges in the powder magazines as centrally as possible, away from the sides of the ship.

MAIN GUNS

	194/50 Mle 1902
Total weight:	15,180kg
Total length:	10,110mm
Bore length:	9700mm
Chamber length:	1446mm
Chamber volume:	62.27dm^3
Breech pressure:	2700kg/cm^2
Rifling:	58 grooves at 4°
Shell weight:	APC 86kg (2.71 cal) SAPC 86kg (3.04 cal)
Bursting charge:	APC 1.40kg *mélinite* (1.6%) SAPC 4.30kg *mélinite* (4.9%)
Propellant:	38.52kg BM13 (3 x ⅓)
Muzzle velocity (MV):	950m/sec (APC)
Remaining V 2000m:	783m/sec (APC)
Maximum range:	12,000m at 15°
Firing cycle:	30 sec

because of the increased length and weight of the guns. The turret, which was also mounted in *Ernest Renan*, is described and illustrated on page 179.

164.7mm guns

Although the Mle 1893–1896M gun was retained for *Jules Michelet* and *Ernest Renan* and fired the same range of projectiles, the propellant charge, which previously comprised a bagged fore-charge and a longer brass cartridge, was now divided into two equal half-charges in serge bags; this simplified stowage and handling. The single turret, which was also a feature of *Ernest Renan*, is described and illustrated on page 180.

The magazines and shell rooms for the 164.7mm guns were on three levels. The handing rooms and shell rooms for the centre and after pairs of turrets were on the 2nd platform deck, as was the powder magazine for the after turrets (see plans). The handing rooms, shell rooms and powder magazine for the forward pair of turrets were on the 3rd platform deck, and the combined shell and powder magazine for the guns in the after redoubts was on the same level aft. The combined magazine for the guns in the forward redoubts was in the hold, as was the powder magazine for the centre turrets, and there was a combined shell/powder magazine for the after pair of turrets aft.

The rearrangement of the handing rooms to supply ammunition to the additional turrets amidships meant that the length of magazine spaces exposed to underwater damage was increased by 6m compared with the *Gambettas*. Bertin attempted to mitigate this by concentrating the powder magazines in relatively narrow spaces with stowage athwartships and as close to the ship's axis as possible. The two new handing rooms, together with the ammunition passages linking them with the existing handing rooms, had stowage only for projectiles, which were less vulnerable to an underwater explosion. Bagged powder charges for the centre turrets were transferred manually from the first handing room on either side to the second using a system of chutes (*glissoires*), prior to being loaded into the ammunition car of the hoist. Although this was less than ideal, it at least avoided the longitudinal ammunition passages that were a feature of *Jeanne d'Arc* and the later British armoured cruisers.[7]

7 The ammunition passages in the British ships have been implicated in the multiple explosions that took place on board *Warrior* and *Defence* at Jutland, resulting in the loss of both ships.

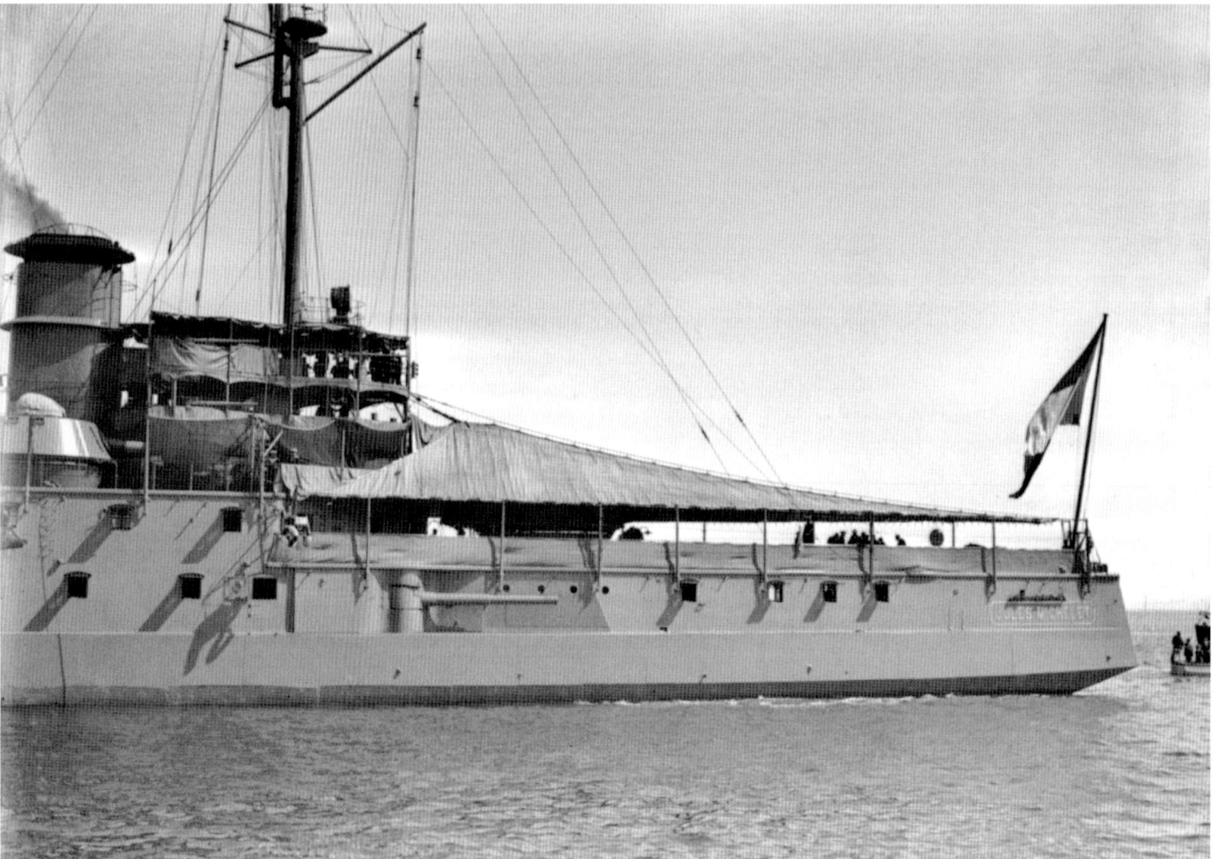

Right: A close-up of the after part of *Jules Michelet*, with the port-side after 164.7mm turret and casemate guns prominent. The 194mm main turret is concealed by the canvas awning over the quarterdeck. Three of the 47mm Mle 1902 ATB guns can be seen atop the after superstructure deck. *(Private collection)*

Although no information has been published regarding the provision of 164.7mm shell in *Michelet* and *Renan*, magazine capacity was similar to that of the *Gambetta*s while at the same time the number of guns was reduced from sixteen to twelve. This suggests that the number of rounds per gun was increased, perhaps to 250rpg.

Fire control

As in earlier ships, fire control was exercised from the conning tower by the gunnery officer (*Officier de tir* or OT), who was supported by an assistant (OTA) and the operators of the Germain order transmitters. The *Poste Central* below the armoured deck (also referred to as the *Poste de commande/de tir*) was still primarily a secondary conning position and damage control centre, and from a fire-control aspect functioned only as a relay for the transmission of range/bearing/deflection data and firing orders to the guns. The early Germain receivers had range dials that were scaled between 500m and 4500m. By 1907 they were being fitted with new faces that gave readings between 2000m and 6000m, reflecting the increased engagement ranges then being contemplated. In 1905 it was recommended that the standard 180mm-diameter dial be replaced by a 250mm model calibrated between 1500m and 7500m.

The gunnery officer and the gunnery section commanders received range data from a stadimeter operated by an observer stationed on the rangefinder platform (*hune de télémétrie*) on the upper foremast.[8] However, even the latest Ponthus & Therrode model still required successful identification of the target and a knowledge of enemy ship characteristics (including the height of the mast), and it was becoming increasingly evident that a rangefinder able to determine precise ranges quickly and independently, without reference to a database, was required. The French were aware of Barr & Stroud's optical rangefinders quite early on, but it was not until 1907 that the French adopted a 2m FQ2 model. Directives dated 11 July 1907 and 23 January 1908 decreed the fitting of

[8] See Jordan and Caresse, *French Battleships of World War One*, Chapter 4.

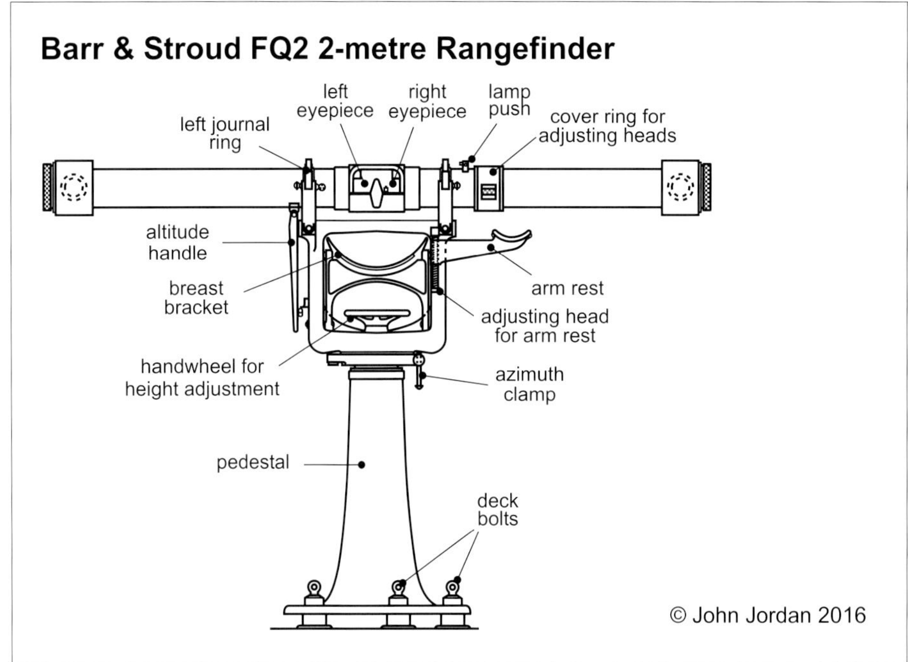

Below: A fine view of *Jules Michelet* leaving Toulon. The four single 164.7mm wing turrets on either side served to distinguish her from her three half-sisters of the *Léon Gambetta* class. Note the two 47mm Mle 1902 ATB guns mounted atop the main turret forward. *(Marius Bar)*

two of these rangefinders on pivot mountings atop the roof of the enclosed bridge in the latest battleships and armoured cruisers. The as-fitted plans of *Jules Michelet*, which are dated 26 October 1908, show two sided Barr & Stroud 2m rangefinders on the compass platform atop the conning tower.[9] The rangefinders are mounted in the open, and the photographs show only canvas screens around the guard rails; later installations would have screens of special steel around the rangefinder pedestals to protect the rangetaker from splinters.

Midship 47mm ATB Guns Frames 51–68

Léon Gambetta & Jules Ferry

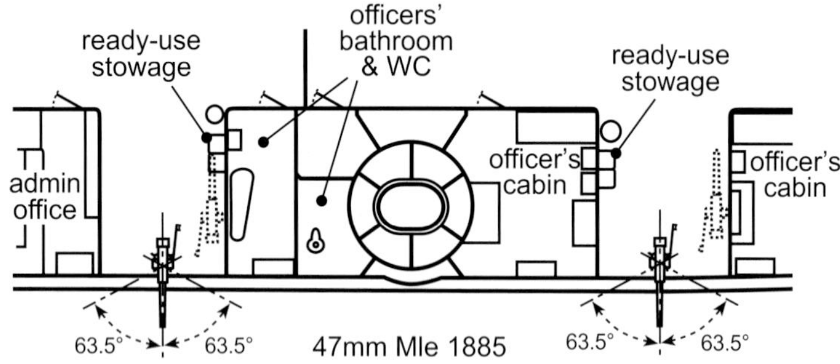

Victor Hugo

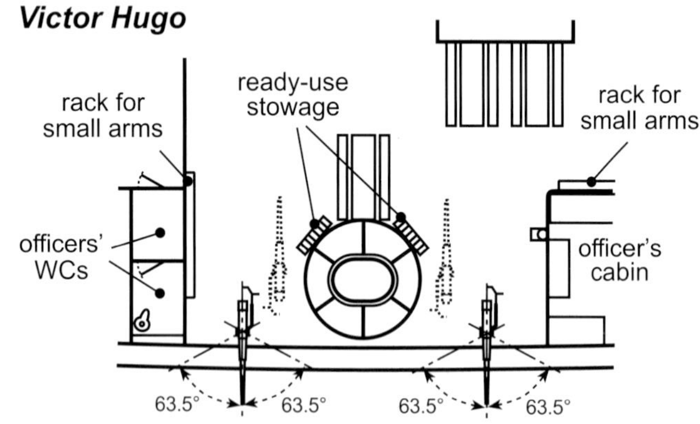

Note: Adapted from as-fitted plans.

Jules Michelet

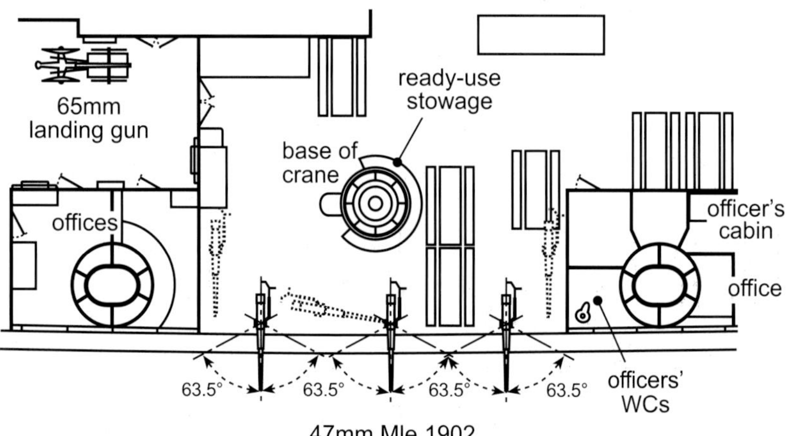

In *Léon Gambetta* and *Jules Ferry* the 47mm ATB guns in the upper hull were mounted individually, with adjacent ready-use stowage. In the two later ships the mountings were grouped together in twos and threes, with the stowage racks located around the bases for the 164.7mm turrets or, in the case of *Jules Michelet*, around the bases of the boat cranes.

ATB guns

The 47mm ATB gun fitted in *Jules Michelet* was the same 50-calibre Mle 1902 gun that equipped *Victor Hugo*. There were twenty-four guns in total – the same number as in the *Gambettas* – but the guns were mounted (and grouped) differently.

The lower ATB platform on the military mast was suppressed. Two of the four guns were relocated atop the forward 194mm turret; a prominent angled ladderway was constructed at the forward end of the upper bridge deck to provide access for the gun crews. The other two guns were grouped with the original pair of mountings on the upper bridge deck. The two mountings on the lower bridge deck were now enclosed and fired through ports, and this served to protect them from the blast of the forward 164.7mm turret guns. There were six guns on the after bridge decks, disposed as in *Victor Hugo*.

The remaining ten guns (*ligne basse*) were mounted in the upper part of the hull on the 1st deck, as in the *Gambettas*. However, whereas as in *Léon Gambetta* and *Jules Ferry* the five guns on either side were mounted independently at intervals between the officers' cabins, each with its own ready-use locker, in *Jules Michelet* they were grouped together, with common ready-use stowage. The forward pair of guns was mounted on either side of the ring bulkhead for the forward pair of 164.7mm turrets, and the stowage racks and lockers were on the rear side of the bulkhead. The after grouping of three guns port and starboard was located in the interval between the ring bulkheads for the two centre turrets, and the common ready-use stowage was fitted around the cylindrical base of the boat cranes (see accompanying plan). This arrangement had the advantage of locating the guns in close proximity to the forward and central magazine hoists, and also simplified fire control by allowing each group of guns to concentrate on a single target.

Although the Mle 1902 gun was an advance on the Mle 1885 in terms of range and penetration, it was now universally accepted that the 47mm calibre was inadequate to deal with torpedo boat attacks that were now as likely to be mounted on the high seas in broad daylight as at night in an anchorage. The contemporary battleships of the *Patrie* class would have the larger part of their 47mm battery – all except the guns mounted on the military foremast and bridge decks – replaced by the new 65mm Mle 1902 gun, the standard weapon of the latest destroyers. This decision was taken in 1905, and *Michelet* would be the last French armoured cruiser to have a uniform battery of 47mm ATB guns; her half-sister *Ernest Renan* (see below) would have the mixed battery of the battleships.

9 The 2m rangefinder (see accompanying plan) was designed for export, hence the metric base length. Other B&S models had imperial base-lengths; those that entered service with the *Marine Nationale* were referred to by the metric equivalent: 4ft 6in/1.37m, 9ft/2.74m, 12ft/3.66m and 15ft/4.57m.

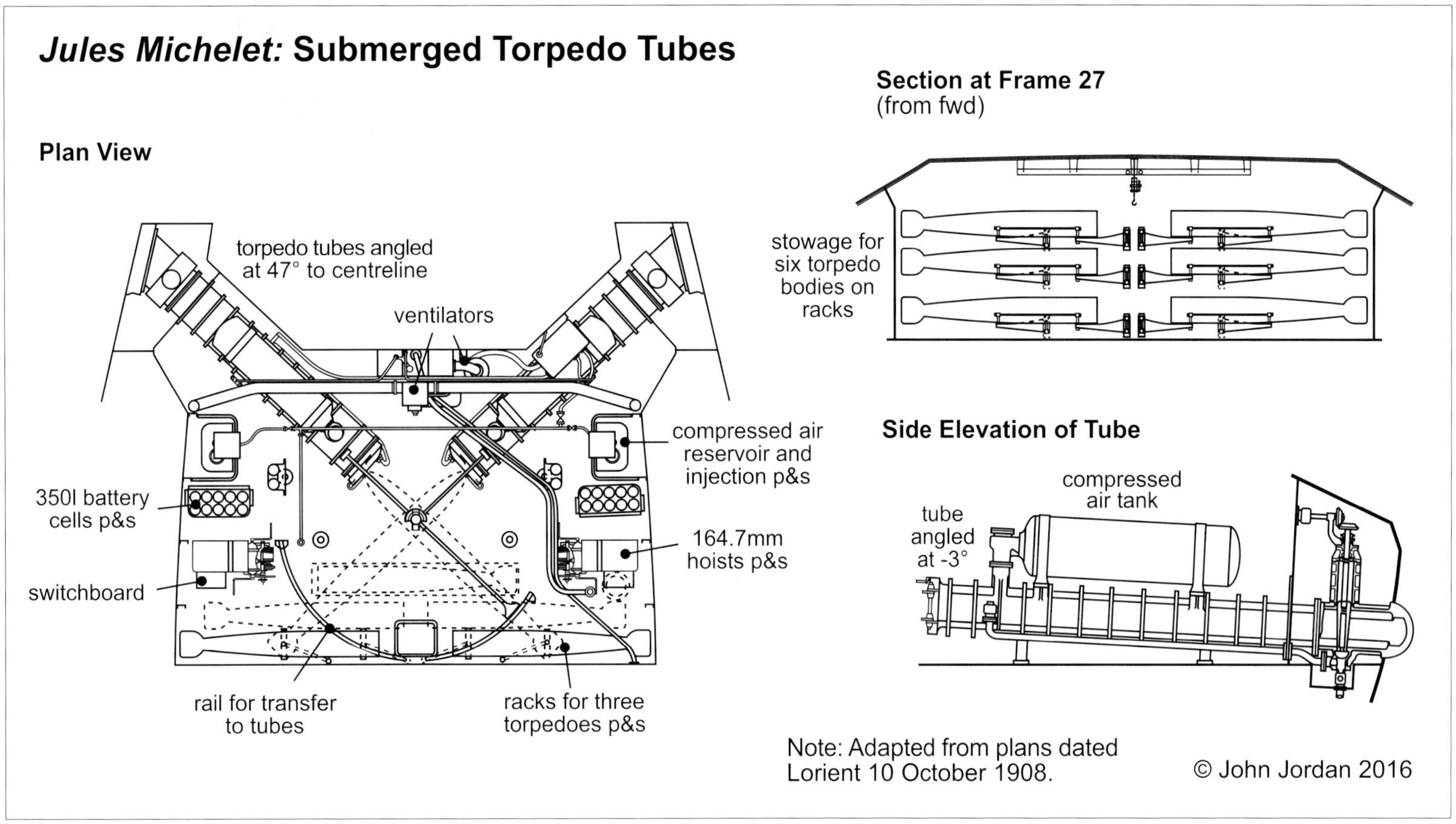

Jules Michelet: Submerged Torpedo Tubes

Plan View

torpedo tubes angled at 47° to centreline

ventilators

compressed air reservoir and injection p&s

350l battery cells p&s

164.7mm hoists p&s

switchboard

rail for transfer to tubes

racks for three torpedoes p&s

Section at Frame 27 (from fwd)

stowage for six torpedo bodies on racks

Side Elevation of Tube

compressed air tank

tube angled at -3°

Note: Adapted from plans dated Lorient 10 October 1908.

The searchlight arrangements for *Jules Michelet* were as in the earlier ships of the class.

Torpedoes and mines

Like the later ships of the *Gambetta* class, *Jules Michelet* had only two submerged torpedo tubes; the compartment was between frames 20 and 27 on the 2nd platform deck (see plans), and the two 450mm tubes were fixed at an angle of 47° to the ship's axis. There was a general maintenance shop amidships on the main deck served by a system of overhead rails, as in *Ferry* and *Hugo*, and two of the eight torpedo bodies were stowed at the forward end of this deck, close to the torpedo hatch.

Left: *Jules Michelet* leaving Toulon, probably in mid/late 1911. The island of Porquerolles can be seen in the background. The ship is flying the flag of Rear Admiral Ernest-Eugène Nicol, commanding the 2nd Light Division of the 2nd Squadron. *(Private collection)*

The plans of *Jules Michelet* show stowage for sixteen mines (*torpilles automatiques*) on the 1st platform deck aft, immediately forward of the ring bulkhead of the after 194mm turret.

PROTECTION

The hull protection scheme of *Jules Michelet* replicated that of the *Gambetta* class. However, the adoption of the longer Mle 1902 gun – it was approximately 2m longer and 2.5 tonnes heavier –required rebalancing of the twin 194mm turret, and advantage was taken of the reduction in the number of secondary guns to increase protection for the artillery.

The 194mm turrets mounted in the *Gambetta* class had 138mm plates on the face and sides of the cupola, and the 'balancing' plate at the rear was of 178mm mild steel; in *Jules Michelet* these figures were increased to 156mm and 344mm respectively, but the plates on the sides of the cupola were of special steel, not cemented armour. The armour plans of the ship show five 156mm plates on the face and sides, and a single 344mm plate on the rear of the turret to counterbalance the weight of the guns. The fixed armour of the *parapet* was of 147mm special steel (*vice* 140mm in the *Gambettas*) and there was 102mm on the ammunition trunk (*vice* 100mm).

Protection for the single 164.7mm turrets was similar to that of the twin turret of the earlier ships. The face of the turret comprised two plates of special steel 122mm thick, the two plates on either side were 102mm, and the single balancing plate at the rear was of 145mm mild steel. The fixed *parapet* was of 103mm special steel, and there was 40mm special steel to protect the ammunition hoists.

Protection for the casemate faces was increased from 102mm to 138mm – the inner walls remained at 64mm – and the transverse bulkhead that formed the forward wall of the first two redoubts on the 1st deck

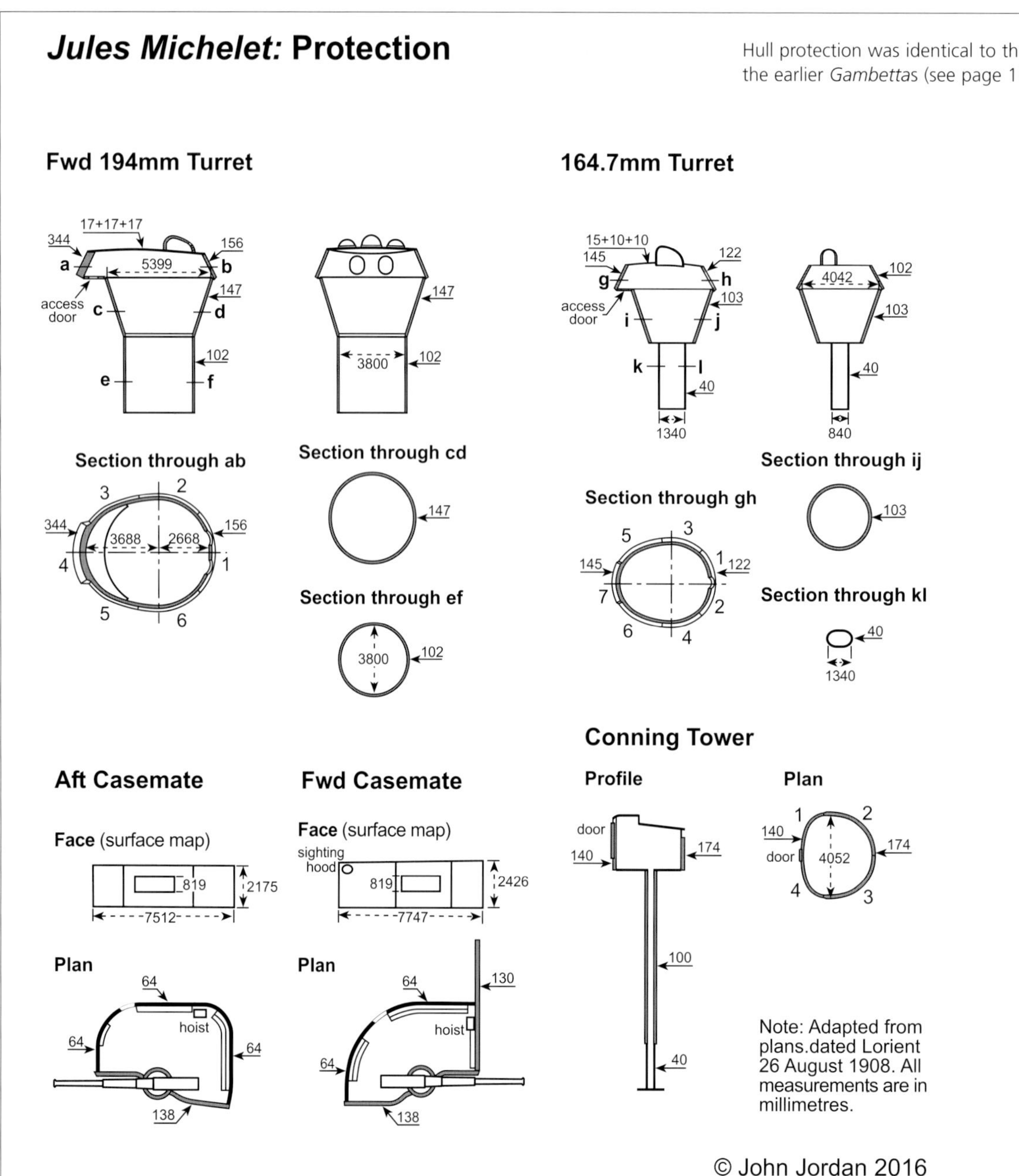

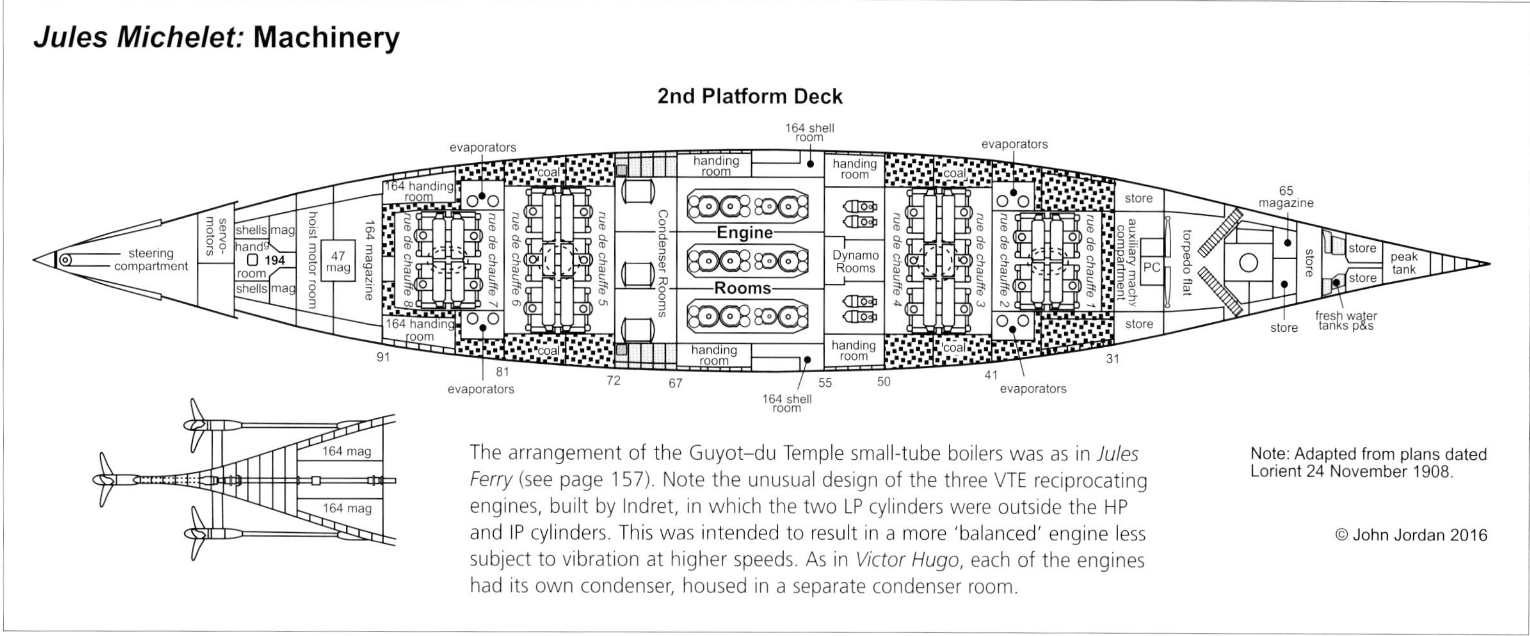

The arrangement of the Guyot–du Temple small-tube boilers was as in *Jules Ferry* (see page 157). Note the unusual design of the three VTE reciprocating engines, built by Indret, in which the two LP cylinders were outside the HP and IP cylinders. This was intended to result in a more 'balanced' engine less subject to vibration at higher speeds. As in *Victor Hugo*, each of the engines had its own condenser, housed in a separate condenser room.

to protect against enfilading fire was boosted from 102mm to 130mm.

The conning tower of *Jules Michelet* was similar to that of the three *Gambetta*s. Protection was identical, except that the curved 110mm bulkhead directly behind the access door at the rear of the tower was suppressed.

MACHINERY

Jules Michelet had essentially the same propulsion plant as *Jules Ferry*, with steam for her three four-cylinder engines supplied by twenty Guyot–du Temple boilers. Despite their early problems, Bertin was enthusiastic about the potential of the small-tube boiler to deliver higher speeds, and considered the reversion to the large-tube Belleville and Niclausse boilers in *Victor Hugo* and *Ernest Renan* (see below) to be a retrograde step. Designed speed and horsepower for *Jules Michelet* were on a par with *Jules Ferry*: 22.5 knots with 29,000CV.

The engines and boilers were built 'in house' at Indret. One significant innovation was the layout of the cylinders of the reciprocating engines: the two low-pressure (LP) cylinders were located at the ends, with the high-pressure (HP) and intermediate-pressure (IP) cylinders between. The order of the cylinders (from forward) was LP>HP>IP>LP, whereas the standard arrangement for a four-cylinder engine was HP>IP>LP>LP. In theory the new arrangement should have given better results and a better balanced engine; however, while it was repeated in *Ernest Renan*, ordered at around the same time and the fastest of all the French armoured cruisers, it was abandoned for *Edgar Quinet* and *Waldeck-Rousseau* in favour of the conventional cylinder layout.

During a ten-hour full-power trial that took place on 17 September 1908 *Jules Michelet* sustained an average speed of 22.65 knots with 29,805CV; the maximum speed attained was 22.86 knots with 30,438CV. Coal consumption was calculated at 0.77kg/h per unit of horsepower (see table page 160 for comparison with the *Léon Gambetta* class).

The auxiliary machinery was arranged as in *Victor Hugo*: the dynamos were paired in two compartments amidships on the 2nd deck with the main switchboard room between, and the evaporators were outboard of the forward and after boiler rooms.

CONSTRUCTION AND EARLY SERVICE

When the decision was made to transfer the construction of the cruiser *Victor Hugo* from Toulon to Lorient (see Chapter 7) on 3 June 1902, the construction of *Jules Michelet*, which had been awarded to Lorient barely two months earlier (5 April), was accorded a lesser priority. Initial assembly on the slipway at Caudan was begun only after the launch of *Victor Hugo* on 30 March 1904. *Jules Michelet* would be launched on 31 August 1905, little more than a year later, but fitting-out was relatively slow, and the ship did not begin her official trials until August 1908. These appear to have proceeded without incident, and she joined the Mediterranean Squadron in December of the same year, being assigned to the 1st Light Division with *Jules Ferry* (flag) and *Victor Hugo*. In January she was transferred to the *Division de réserve*, but she was reactivated for the Great Naval Review and manoeuvres of September 1911 (see Chapter 10), serving as flagship of the 2nd Light Division (CA Nicol).

From 1 March 1912 until 15 November 1913 *Jules Michelet* was attached to the Gunnery School at Toulon. During this period, on 26 June 1912, the ship experienced a powder explosion in a turret that killed five men. Following a short period in reserve she briefly replaced *Waldeck-Rousseau*, which was undergoing repairs, as flagship of the 1st Light Division (Rear Admiral Ramey de Sugny); she was them attached as fourth ship of the same division until the loss of *Léon Gambetta* on 27 April 1915, when she replaced her as flagship of the 2nd Light Division (Rear Admiral Charlier).

EVALUATION

Like her half-sisters of the *Léon Gambetta* class, *Jules Michelet* was a contemporary of the British armoured cruisers of the *Duke of Edinburgh* and *Warrior* classes, which were 1000 tonnes heavier and carried a more

JULES MICHELET VS *DUKE OF EDINBURGH* (GB)

	Jules Michelet	*Duke of Edinburgh*
No in class:	1	2
Built:	1904–08	1903–06
Displacement:	12,600t	13,750t
Dimensions:	146.5m x 21.4m	146m x 22.4m[1]
Propulsion:		
Engines	3-shaft VTE	2-shaft VTE
Horsepower	29,000CV	23,000CV
Speed	22.5 knots	22.3 knots
Armament:		
Main guns	4 x 194mm (2 x II)	6 x 234mm (6 x I)
Medium guns	12 x 164mm (12 x I)	10 x 152mm (10 x I)
ATB guns	24 x 47mm (24 x I)	22 x 47mm (22 x I)
TT	2 x 450mm	3 x 450mm
Protection:		
Belt	150mm	150mm
Main turrets	156mm	190mm
2ndary guns	122mm	150mm
Conning tower	174mm	250mm
Decks	33mm + 45/65mm[3]	25mm + 20m

Notes:

1 Metric equivalents have been supplied for *Duke of Edinburgh* in order to give a comparison. The equivalents for gun calibres are exact; those for armour thicknesses are to the nearest 5mm.

2 For the armoured decks, the first figure given relates to the upper protective deck, the second to the lower (flat/slopes).

powerful main armament of six 9.2in (234mm) guns. However, *Duke of Edinburgh* and her sister *Black Prince* suffered in comparison: their box battery of 6in QF guns was mounted so close to the waterline – command was only 3m – that the guns were notoriously difficult to work in even moderate seas.[10]

In the *Warrior* class the 6in battery was replaced by four single 7.5in guns in turrets. However, there was a cost: due to topweight concerns the eight wing turrets (four 9.2in and four 7.5in) were mounted one deck lower than the wing turrets in the *Gambettas* and *Jules Michelet*, which exposed them to water ingress in heavy seas. Command was 6m, compared to 8.8m for the wing 164.7mm turrets in *Jules Michelet*[11] and the *Gambettas*. The French considered that a favourable height of command was important not only to ensure that the guns could be fought under adverse sea and weather conditions, but also because the turret officer and the gunlayers had a consistently clearer view of the target.

Moreover, although the French 164.7mm fired a lighter shell than the British 7.5in and had inferior penetration characteristics, the high rate of fire of these guns, which were mounted in greater numbers, gave them considerable hitting power at moderate ranges, particularly against the unarmoured parts of the hull and superstructures of enemy cruisers. All of these relatively lightly-armoured vessels were vulnerable to the 'hail of fire' principle that continued to dominate French thinking, and the French ships could undoubtedly have held their own against the Royal Navy cruisers of the period.

ERNEST RENAN

Ernest Renan was originally intended as the fifth unit of the *Léon Gambetta* class. However, the design was subject to multiple revisions that delayed work on the ship until the autumn of 1904. She would emerge from the shipyard as a completely new type that constituted a stepping-stone between the *Gambettas* and the final pair of French armoured cruisers of the *Edgar Quinet* class.

The principal difference between *Ernest Renan* and her half-sister *Jules Michelet* lay in her propulsion machinery, which was significantly more powerful and in many respects marked a return to the principles that underpinned *Jeanne d'Arc*. The *Gambettas* represented a quantum leap in firepower compared to their predecessors of the *Gloire* class, but maximum designed speed increased by only one knot to 22 knots. They therefore had no speed advantage over the latest British armoured cruisers of the *Black Prince* and *Warrior* classes, which were laid down from 1903 and had a similar displacement and weight of armament. Emile Bertin, who again had overall responsibility for the design, wanted to increase speed in the new ship to 24–25 knots. This could only be achieved by returning to the long, slim hull-form and six groups of boilers that were features of *Jeanne d'Arc*; the hull of *Renan* therefore had to be completely redesigned. Overall dimensions and length-to-beam ratios of the three types were as follows:

Jeanne d'Arc	145m x 19.42m (L/B ratio: 7.47)
Léon Gambetta	146.5m x 21.4m (L/B ratio: 6.85)
Ernest Renan	157m x 21.36m (L/B ratio: 7.35)

Bertin was in favour of the more advanced Guyot–du Temple small-tube boiler, and when the ultimate decision was made in favour of the large-tube Niclausse accused the Navy of basing its decision on 'other than military' considerations.[12] While there may be some truth in this claim, it should be acknowledged that the installation of Guyot–du Temple boilers in *Jules Ferry* had not been a conspicuous success (see Chapter 7), and certain elements of the naval establishment were therefore in favour of a more 'conservative' solution – although commercial considerations may also have been a factor. Nevertheless, Bertin remained convinced that had *Ernest Renan* been equipped with Guyot–du Temple boilers she would have been even faster – as it was she achieved the highest speed on trials of any of the French armoured cruisers (see Machinery).

Having opted for a larger hull, the issue of the ship's main armament was revisited. A report in *Le Yacht* (7 March 1908) claimed that a uniform battery of 194mm guns, as in *Ernest Renan*'s successors *Edgar Quinet* and *Waldeck-Rousseau*, received serious consideration. However, given that the final armament of the latter two ships was decided upon in late January 1906 (see Chapter 9), when the hull of *Ernest Renan* was only a few months from launch, it was undoubtedly feared that any further changes to the plans would introduce further delays. *Ernest Renan* would therefore be completed with a main armament identical to that of *Jules Michelet*, with four 194mm guns in twin turrets fore and aft, and twelve 164.7mm guns in single turrets and casemates on the beam. The only modification to her armament was the replacement of the lightweight

10 During the First World War some guns would be relocated to the upper deck.

11 The forward pair of turrets in *Jules Michelet* had a command of 9.2m, the after pair 8.6m.

12 Campbell, *Conway's All the World's Fighting Ships 1860–1905*, p 307.

BUILDING DATA

Name	Builder	Laid down	Launched	Trials	Commissioned
Ernest Renan	Penhoët–St-Nazaire	1 Oct 1904	9 Apr 1906	15 Apr 1908	1 Feb 1909

47mm ATB gun by the heavier and more capable 65mm gun currently being fitted in the battleships.

The order for *Ernest Renan* was placed with the private shipyard Chantiers de Penhoët de Saint-Nazaire on 26 August 1903, although work on the ship would not begin for another twelve months due to revisions to the design. This was the first order for a major vessel to be awarded to this shipyard. Penhoët had been the contractor for the engines of *Léon Gambetta*, which had been particularly successful, and was one of the few shipyards with a slipway of the required length.[13] *Ernest Renan* would prove to be by far the most expensive of the French armoured cruisers – final cost was in excess of 35 million FF compared to 29–30 million FF for the *Gambetta*s and about 32.5 million FF for the following two ships. This was undoubtedly a consequence of the constant changes to the design.

NOMENCLATURE

Joseph-**Ernest Renan** (1823–92) was an expert on Semitic languages and civilisation. He is best known for his influential historical works on early Christianity and for his political theories concerning nationalism and national identity. Hugely influential in his lifetime, Renan was eulogised after his death as the embodiment of the progressive spirit in Western culture. However, his views on the determinism of racial characteristics and the supremacy of Western Europeans over Jews and Africans, which in his time were used to justify colonial expansion, have not withstood the test of time.

HULL AND SUPERSTRUCTURES

Although in her overall layout *Ernest Renan* resembled *Jules Michelet*, the hull had to be lengthened by 10.5m in order to accommodate the longer machinery spaces. Externally, the silhouette was much changed: in place of the four funnels of *Jules Michelet* and the *Gambetta*s, disposed as two widely spaced groups of two, there were six funnels in two groups of three, as in *Jeanne d'Arc*.

Other external features corresponded to the changes made in *Jules Michelet*: there was a light military foremast devoid of any platform for ATB guns, which were disposed (as in *Jules Michelet*) on the superstructure decks fore and aft. *Ernest Renan* also had the distinctive 'goose-neck' crane on either side amidships, between the two centre gun turrets, to handle the larger boats, with a lighter 'Y'-frame abreast the second and third funnels.

Unlike the *Gambetta*s and *Jules Michelet*, *Ernest Renan* was not fitted as a flagship. The apartments at the after end of the 1st deck, which in the other ships had been allocated to an admiral and his staff, were fitted out for the ship's CO and his senior officers.

ARMAMENT

Main guns

The gunhouse for the 194mm twin turret was symmetrical in layout, with the projectile hoists and the gunlayers' seats on the outboard side of the Mle 1902 guns, and the hand-up scuttles for the propellant charges and the controls for operation of the breech between them (see 194mm Turret plan). Directly above the breech operators, at the forward end of the gunhouse, was the platform for the turret officer and trainer, who were seated in tandem beneath a large armoured hood of cast nickel steel. The trainer's position was equipped with a telescopic sight, an axiometer

Below: *Ernest Renan* on the slipway at Saint-Nazaire prior to her launch. *(Private collection)*

[13] The hull of *Ernest Renan* was 23m longer than that of the battleships of the *Patrie* class, and 12m longer than that of the *Danton*s that followed them.

and the levers controlling the training motors for the turret. The gunlayers' positions were equipped with the customary handwheels for elevation and push-buttons for fine control.

The 194mm shell rooms and powder magazines for the forward turret were grouped around a central handing room at hold level; those for the after turret were divided between the 2nd and 3rd platform decks, with the handing room on the 2nd platform. Each of the twin baskets of the duplex hoist held a single

CHARACTERISTICS

Displacement:	13,650 tonnes
Dimensions:	
Length	157.00m pp; 159.00m oa
Beam	21.36m wl
Draught	8.18m aft
Propulsion:	
Boilers	42 Niclausse boilers, 21kg/cm^2
Engines	3-shaft 4-cylinder VTE
Horsepower	36,000CV
Speed	23 knots (designed)
Coal	1320 tonnes normal; 2260 tonnes full load
Endurance	7500nm at 10 knots
Armament:	
Main guns	4 x 194mm/50 Mle 1902 in twin turrets
Medium guns	12 x 164.7mm/45 Mle 1893–1896M QF in eight single turrets and four casemate mountings
ATB guns	16 x 65mm/50 Mle 1902 QF in single mountings 8 x 47mm/50 Mle 1902 QF in single mountings
Torpedo tubes	2 submerged tubes for 450mm torpedoes 6 torpedoes Mle 1904
Protection:	
Main belt	150/130mm max
Decks	33mm PBS 45/65mm PBI
194 turrets	156mm
164 turrets	122mm
Casemates	138mm
Conning tower	174mm
Boats:	2 x 10m steam pinnaces 1 x 7.65m White launch 1 x 11m pulling pinnace 3 x 10.5m pulling cutters 2 x 8.5m whalers 2 x 5m dinghies
Complement:	
As private ship	824 officers and men

Ernest Renan:
Profile & Plan

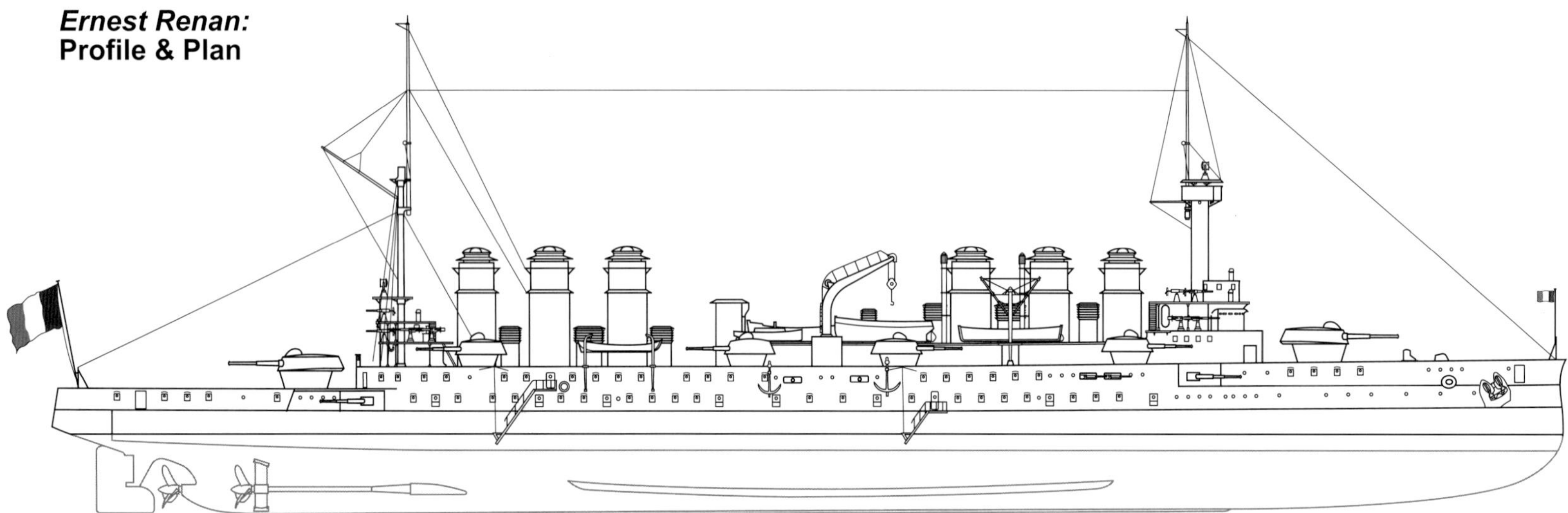

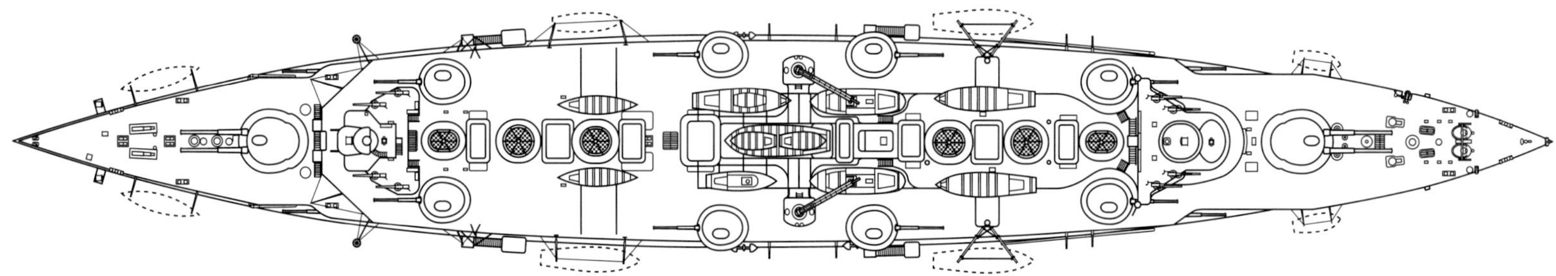

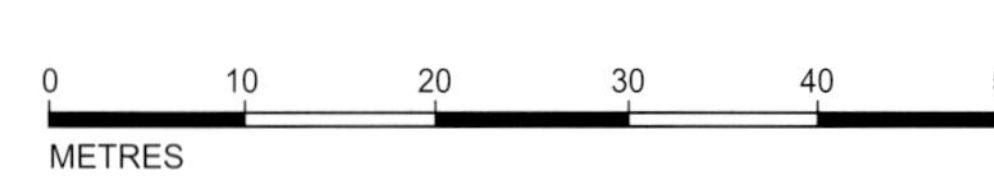

Among the features *Ernest Renan* shared with *Jules Michelet* were the large goose-neck cranes located between the two single 164.7mm turrets amidships. However, she retained the 'Y'-frame of *Léon Gambetta* to handle the forward boats, whereas *Michelet* had a second, smaller goose-neck crane. Note also the larger 65mm ATB guns and the higher position of the searchlight on the foremast.

Note: Adapted from plans of Penhoët–St-Nazaire.

projectile and three bagged charges, stowed vertically as in the *Gloire* class (see Chapter 6). When the basket arrived in the working chamber the projectile was lifted out of the basket by a mechanical arm, tipped over to the horizontal, and transferred to one of the two manual clip hoists located outside the guns, which raised it to the gunhouse. From there it was shunted onto one of the three waiting trays or transferred via a system of overhead rails to a ready-use rack at the after end of the gunhouse; eleven projectiles per gun could be stowed in the gunhouse. The bagged charges were lifted out by hand and stowed in lockers with flash-proof doors around the walls of the working chamber. There were additional lockers for ready-use charges beneath the projectile rack at the after end of the gunhouse.

The loading tray slid laterally on a supporting structure mounted on the gunhouse floor. Projectiles could be shunted onto it directly from the waiting trays at the side of the gun or from the ready-use rack. Once the breech was opened the loading tray, which was inclined at a fixed angle of -5°, was moved directly behind it and the shell was rammed by hand. The three propellant charges that completed the round were handed up using the scuttles set into the gunhouse floor, loaded by hand, then rammed.

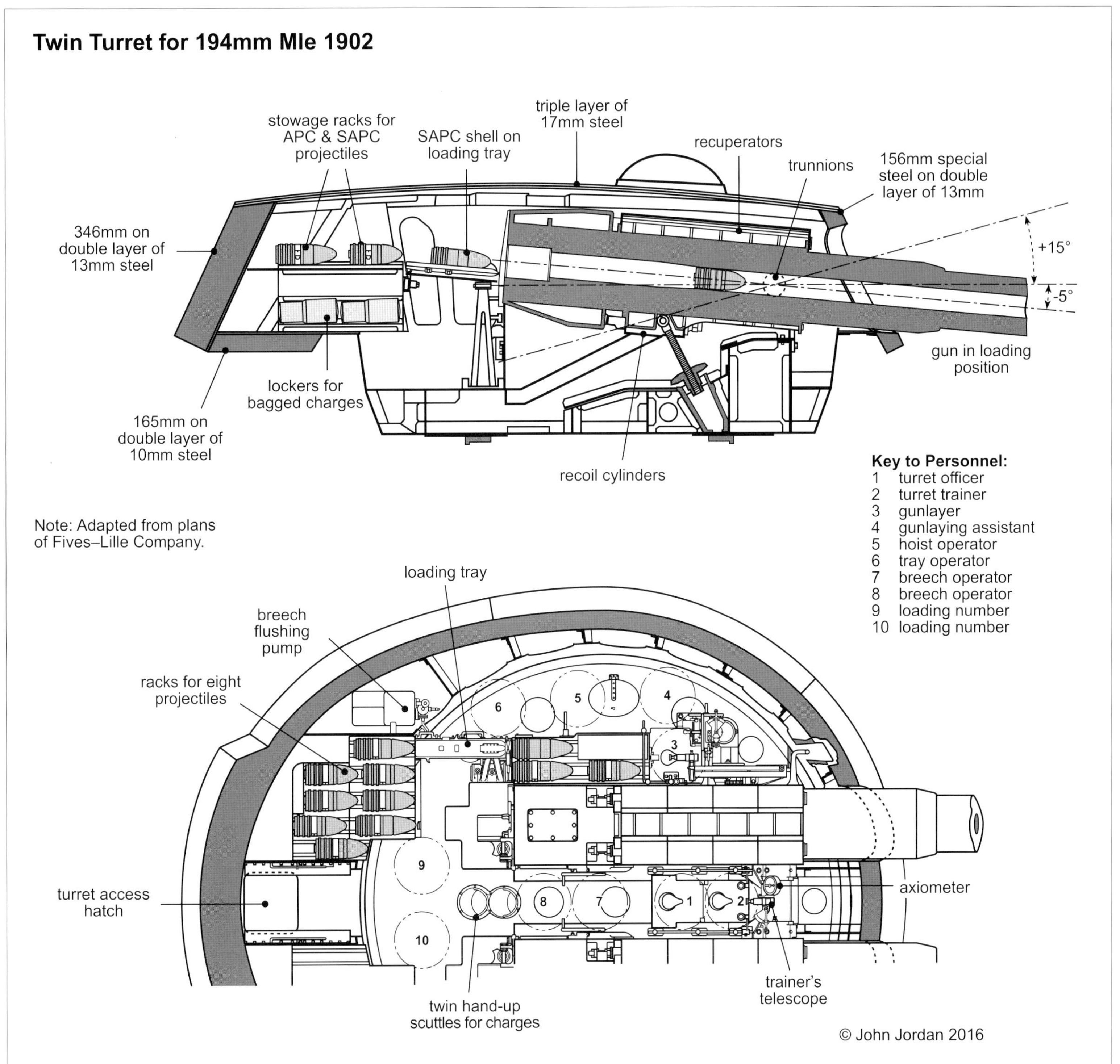

Single Turret for 164.7mm Mle 1893-1896M

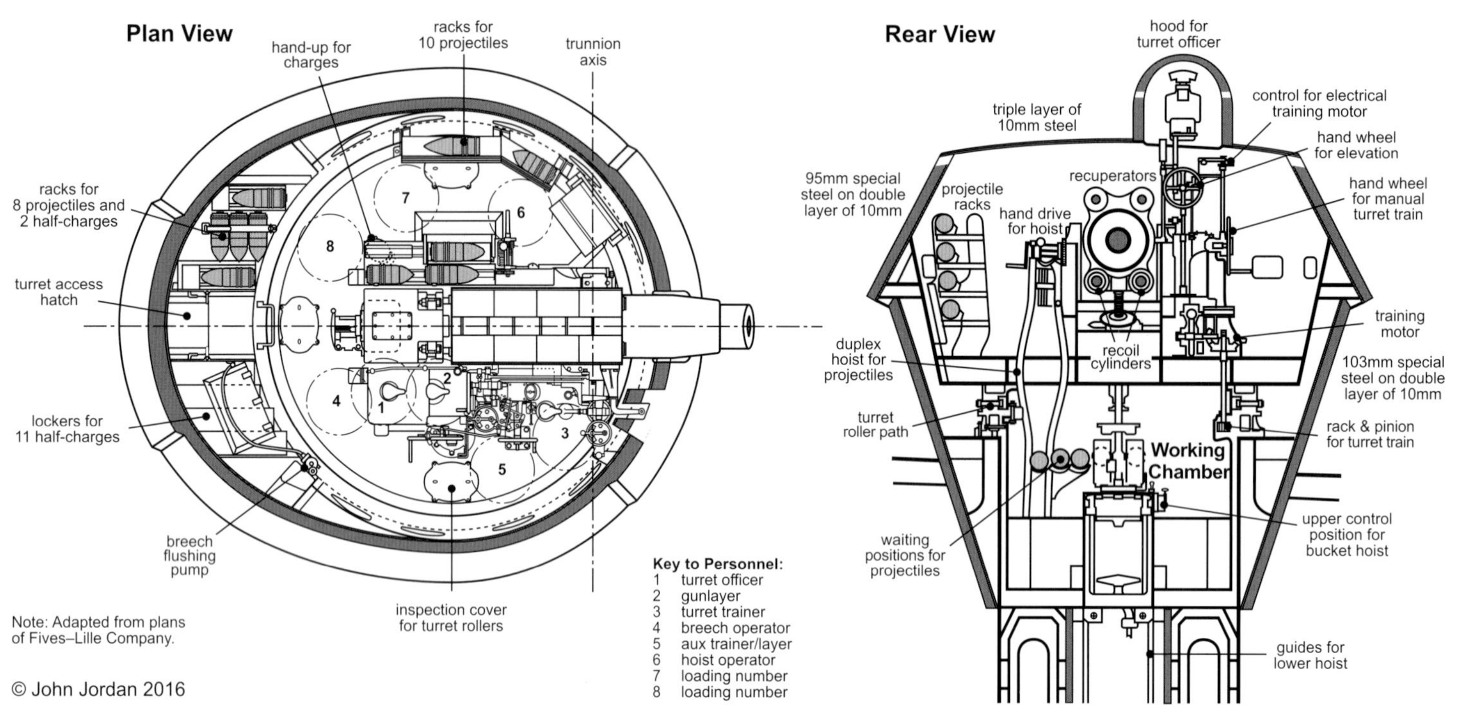

Plan View
hand-up for charges
racks for 10 projectiles
trunnion axis
racks for 8 projectiles and 2 half-charges
turret access hatch
lockers for 11 half-charges
breech flushing pump
inspection cover for turret rollers
Key to Personnel:
1 turret officer
2 gunlayer
3 turret trainer
4 breech operator
5 aux trainer/layer
6 hoist operator
7 loading number
8 loading number
Note: Adapted from plans of Fives–Lille Company.
© John Jordan 2016
Rear View
hood for turret officer
control for electrical training motor
triple layer of 10mm steel
hand wheel for elevation
hand wheel for manual turret train
95mm special steel on double layer of 10mm
projectile racks
recuperators
hand drive for hoist
training motor
duplex hoist for projectiles
recoil cylinders
103mm special steel on double layer of 10mm
turret roller path
rack & pinion for turret train
Working Chamber
waiting positions for projectiles
upper control position for bucket hoist
guides for lower hoist

Forward Casemate for 164.7mm Mle 1893-1896M

Side View
2nd Deck
hand wheel for elevation
hand wheel for train
trunnions
80mm
18mm on 8mm
6mm linoleum
156mm
1st Deck
Frame 35
34
33
31
30
29
28
Stowage for Bagged Half-Charges
Plan View
armoured access door
armoured access door
chutes for projectiles
hoist
forward transverse bulkhead
arc of recoil
arc of breech
collapsible chute
manhole
102mm special steel on double layer of 9mm
64mm special steel on double layer of 8mm
hand wheel for train
hand wheel for elevation
shield
head of section
30°
90°
138mm special steel on double layer of 8/10mm
Note: Adapted from plans of Penhoët–St-Nazaire.
© John Jordan 2016

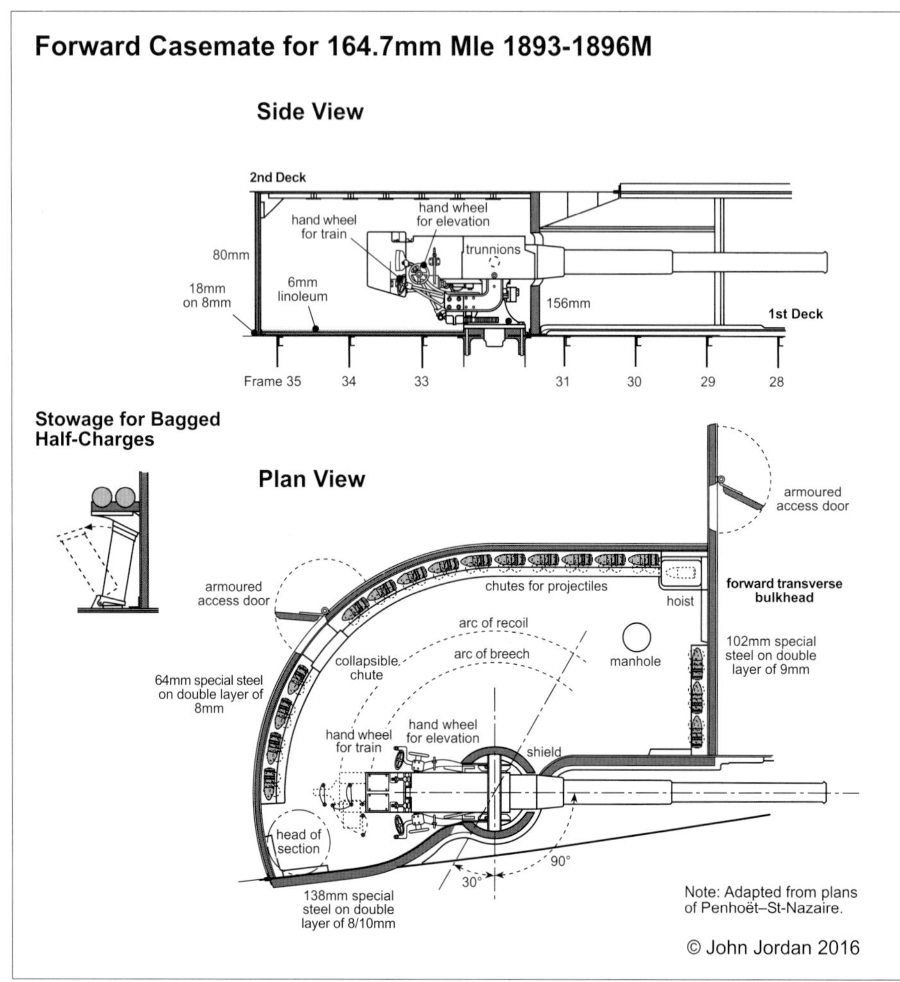

164.7mm turrets

The single turret for the 164.7mm guns which, like the twin 194mm turret described above, was manufactured by the engineering and armaments company Fives–Lille in northern France, was a development of the single turret mounted in the *Gloire* class (see page 122) and the battleship *Suffren*. The gunhouse was laid out in similar fashion, with the controls for the gun and the platform for the turret officer on the outboard side of the gun,[14] and the hoist, propellant hand-up scuttle and the ready-use projectile stowage on the inboard side (see 164.7mm Turret plan).

The principal difference in the handling, ammunition supply and stowage arrangements compared to the 194mm turret reflected differences in the weight of the projectile and the division of the propellant charge into two bags (*vice* three for the larger gun). The ammunition car for the main hoist held two complete rounds: two projectiles above and four bagged half-charges beneath. When it arrived in the working chamber the shells were offloaded onto horizontal waiting trays; from there they were transferred to a duplex manual hoist operated from the gunhouse. Once they arrived in the gunhouse they were shunted onto the waiting trays or lifted by hand onto ready-use

[14] The turrets were arranged to secure a maximum field of view for the turret officer and the gunlayers in end-on fire, so four were 'left-handed' and four 'right-handed'. In the forward turrets to starboard and the after turrets to port the gun controls and the platform for the turret officer were on the right-hand-side; in the forward turrets to port and the after turrets to starboard they were on the left. The plan depicts one of the former.

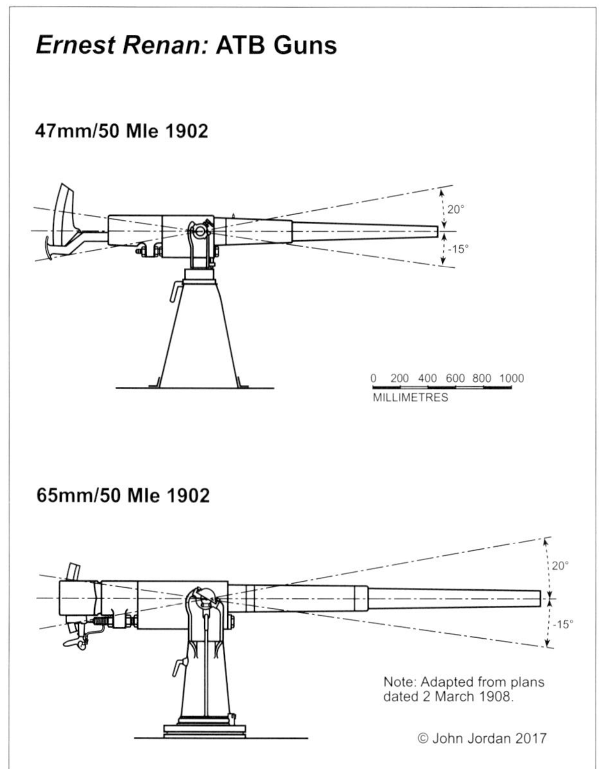

racks at the side and rear of the gunhouse. The bagged half-charges were lifted out and stowed vertically in bins with hinged lids located around the sides of the working chamber. There was a single hand-up scuttle set into the gunhouse floor on the inboard side of the gun, close to the breech. Ready-use lockers with flash-proof doors at the rear of the gunhouse could stow up to thirteen half-charges.

Both the 194mm and 164.7mm turrets allowed a maximum 15° of elevation, and the guns could be depressed to -5°. The casemate guns were capable of similar angles of elevation and depression.

164.7mm casemate guns

The two forward casemates were on the 1st deck and the two after casemates on the main deck, as in earlier French armoured cruisers. Height of command was 6.1m for the forward pair of guns, 3.6m for the after guns.

The internal arrangement of the casemate was similar in principle to that of *Condé* (see page 124); the adoption of bagged half-charges simplified stowage of the propellant. A chute for projectiles ran around the inner walls of the casemate, the projectiles being stowed horizontally on shaped wooden bases laminated with brass (see Casemate plan). The chute was continuous and was interrupted only by the single hoist (in the corner) and by the armoured door that gave access to the casemate. Beneath each projectile were twin bins for the bagged charges. These were hinged back towards the inner walls of the casemate when stowed, but could be tilted forward for access. Each shell was stowed above its charge, and each of the four casemates could accommodate seventeen complete ready-use rounds, compared to only twelve in *Condé*.

The plans of the casemate suggest that the hoist was similar to that of the turrets, except that only a single complete round could be lifted at a time.

Above: *Ernest Renan* manoeuvring in the port of Saint-Nazaire in April 1908; she is about to sail for her first trials. The 194mm guns of the main turrets have yet to be embarked. (*(Private collection)*

ATB guns

The main ATB gun was the new 65mm Mle 1902 designed and manufactured by Schneider; it superseded the 47mm Mle 1902, as in the battleships of the *Patrie* class, although the lighter gun was retained for the upper bridge decks.

The distribution of the ATB guns was slightly modified. Eight of the 65mm guns were on unshielded pivot mountings on the lower bridge decks fore and aft; the remaining eight were mounted in pairs behind ports on the 1st deck. Each of the pairs on the 1st deck was provided with ready-use racks, which were fitted around the ammunition trunks for the forward 164.7mm turrets and the cylindrical bases of the boat

ANTI-TORPEDO BOAT GUNS

	65/50 Mle 1902	47/50 Mle 1902
Total weight:	594kg	338kg
Total length:	3450mm	2538mm
Bore length:	3250mm	2350m
Chamber length:	674.3mm	336.3mm
Chamber volume:	2.25dm³	0.99dm³
Breech pressure:	2800kg/cm²	2200kg/cm²
Rifling:	26 grooves at 5°	20 grooves at 6°
Shell:	4.17kg steel (3.5 cal)	2.00kg steel (4 cal)
Bursting charge:	0.10kg *mélinite*	0.025kg *mélinite*
Propellant:	1.43kg BM5 (cartridge)	0.46kg BM3 (cartridge)
Muzzle velocity (MV):	870m/s	690m/s
Remaining V 2000m:	496m/s	356m/s
Maximum range:	8000m at 20°	6000m at 20°
Firing cycle:	15rpm	15rpm

ERNEST RENAN: ARMOUR PLATE THICKNESS MAIN BELT

Plate	Upper Strake *upper/lower edge*	Lower Strake *upper/lower edge*
1–5	80/90	90/50
6	80/90	105/50
7	80/90	120/50
8	95/105	135/70
9	110/120	150/70
10–25	120/130	150/70
26	110/120	135/70
27	95/105	120/50
28	80/90	105/50
29	70/80	90/50
30–32	70/80	80/50

Notes:

1 Total weight of main belt: **1007.51 tonnes**; thicker plates of cemented armour, end plates of special steel.

2 Plates 1–9 of the upper belt forward were of 40mm special steel.

3 The face plates of the fwd and after casemates were of 138mm special steel.

cranes amidships. The hoists for the guns on the lower bridge decks came up close to the guns; those for the guns on the 1st deck emerged on the centreline directly above the midship magazine.

There were eight 47mm (four forward, four aft) mounted on the upper bridge decks. The ATB guns on the fore and after bridge decks were grouped unusually close together on two levels, which facilitated fire control but meant that there were possibilities for mutual interference between the guns; the close grouping also exposed them to enemy fire.

The searchlight arrangements for *Ernest Renan* were as in the earlier ships of the class.

Torpedoes and mines

There were two underwater 450mm torpedo tubes, angled forward as in *Jules Michelet*. The spacious torpedo flat was moved slightly aft compared with the latter ship due to the narrower hull forward; it was between frames 23 and 30 (in *Jules Michelet* it was between frames 20 and 27). Three/four reloads for each of the tubes could be accommodated.

Stowage for mines was more extensive than in earlier ships of the class. The plans show stowage on the 1st platform deck for nine mines around the ring bulkhead for the after 194mm turret, and a for a further twelve in the casualty station between frames 99 and 107.

PROTECTION

The protection scheme of *Ernest Renan* replicated that of *Jules Michelet*. She had the same enhanced protection for the main turrets and the faces of the casemates. The hull protection was similar in conception, with a main belt comprising two strakes of 130/150mm Harvey cemented armour and a light upper belt of 40mm special steel from the forward casemate to the bow. However, the longer hull meant

Right: A fine bow quarter view of *Ernest Renan* at Toulon shortly after her completion. Built by Penhoët-Saint-Nazaire, she would spend all her service life in the Mediterranean. *(Private collection)*

that there were thirty-two plates in each of the two strakes in the main belt instead of twenty-nine, and nine plates (*vice* eight) in the upper belt; there was also an additional reinforcing plate on either side on the slope of the lower armoured deck (seventeen *vice* sixteen). These modifications added approximately 100 tonnes to the total weight of armour.

There were two other detail differences: the thickness of the forward transverse bulkhead against enfilading fire that formed the forward wall of the first two casemates reverted to the 102mm of the *Gambettas*, having been increased to 130mm in *Jules Michelet*; and the conning tower was similar in configuration to the original *Gloire* design, being perfectly elliptical in plan (see Protection plan). On the surface of it this was a retrograde step, as the conning tower fitted in the *Gloire* class proved to be cramped. The decision was related to *Ernest Renan*'s status as a private ship; the conning tower did not need to accommodate an admiral and his staff.

WEIGHT OF PROTECTION

	Composition	*Jules Michelet*	*Ernest Renan*
Main belt	cemented/special[1]	930t	1007.5t
Upper belt	special steel	53t	57t
Main & 1st platform decks	mild steel	??t	??t[2]
1st platform slopes	special steel	86t	94t
Transverse bulkheads	special steel	36.5t	15t
194 turrets & barbettes	special steel[3]	235t	251t
164.7 turrets & barbettes	special steel[3]	381.5t	373t
164.7 casemates	special steel	122t	151t
Hoists	special steel	??t	??t[2]
Conning tower	cemented	37t	27.5t
Communications tube	special steel	9.5t	9.5t
Armoured deck coamings	special steel	91t	116t
	Total	**1,981.5t**	**2,101.5t**

Notes:

1 Only the thick plates of the upper/lower belt were cemented (see table for details).

2 No figures are given on the plans for the weight of the protective decks or the hoists. In *Léon Gambetta* these accounted for c830 tonnes; the weight of the decks in *Jules Michelet* would have been similar, those in *Ernest Renan* slightly greater due to the greater length of the hull.

3 The thick rear walls of the 194mm and 164.7mm turrets were of mild steel to counterbalance the turret; the turret hoods were of cast nickel steel.

Source: Official plans.

Ernest Renan: Protection

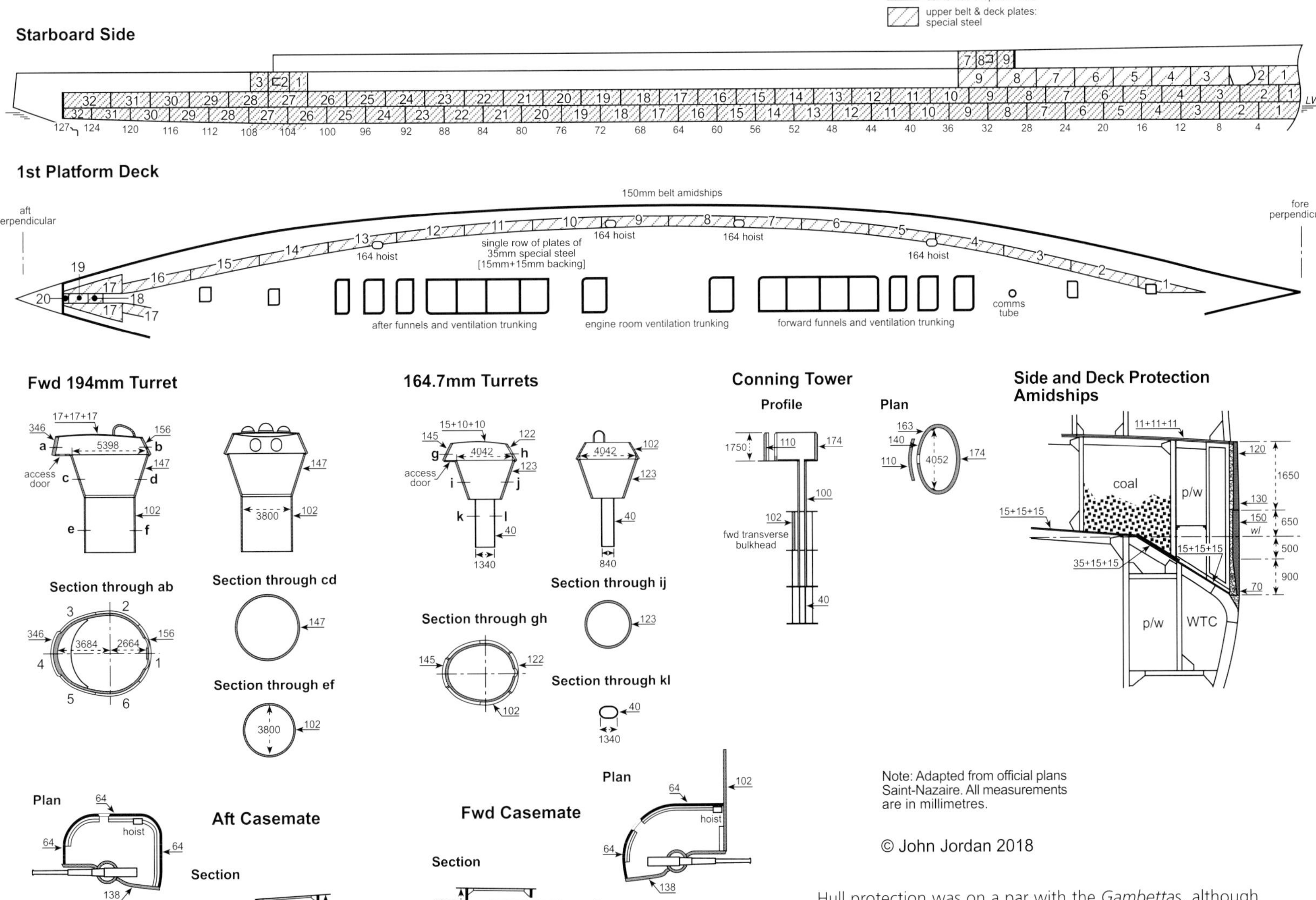

Hull protection was on a par with the *Gambettas*, although the longer hull meant additional plates on the main belt (+3 on either side), the light upper belt (+1) and the slopes of the lower protective deck (+1) – see text for details.

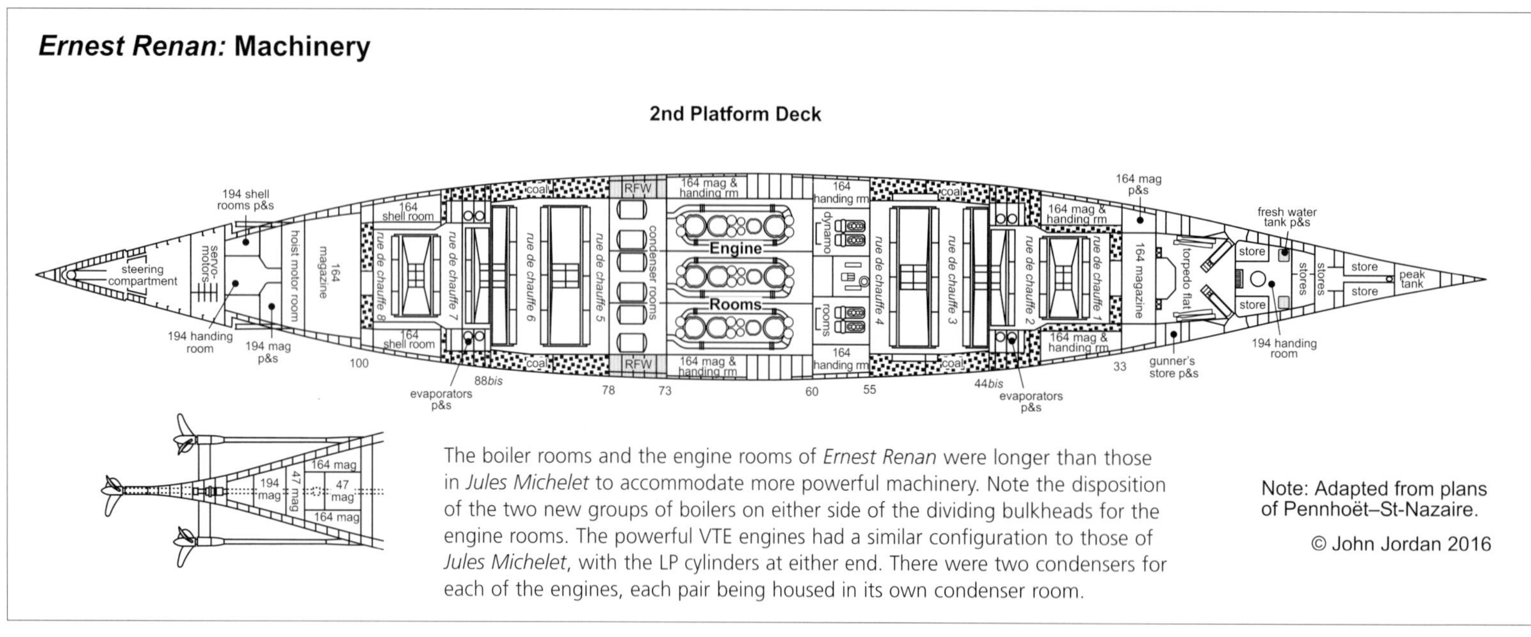

The boiler rooms and the engine rooms of *Ernest Renan* were longer than those in *Jules Michelet* to accommodate more powerful machinery. Note the disposition of the two new groups of boilers on either side of the dividing bulkheads for the engine rooms. The powerful VTE engines had a similar configuration to those of *Jules Michelet*, with the LP cylinders at either end. There were two condensers for each of the engines, each pair being housed in its own condenser room.

MACHINERY

The requirement for higher speed led to an increase in the number of boilers from twenty-eight in *Léon Gambetta* and *Victor Hugo* to an unprecedented forty-two in *Ernest Renan*. Had the Guyot–du Temple boiler favoured by Bertin been adopted, the figure would probably have been between twenty-eight and thirty, although each boiler would have had significantly larger dimensions (see the machinery plans of *Jules Ferry* and *Jules Michelet*).

In *Léon Gambetta* and *Victor Hugo* the boilers had been disposed in four boiler rooms in pairs separated by the midship magazines, engine rooms and condenser rooms (see GA Plans page 142). The boilers were arranged back-to-back in two groups of eight (inner boiler rooms) and two groups of six (outer boiler rooms), each of which was served by a single funnel. For *Jeanne d'Arc* Bertin had opted for six boiler rooms, but for *Ernest Renan* he retained the four boiler rooms of the *Gambetta*s but inserted two extra rows of boilers between the original groupings fore and aft, and located these two rows back-to-back with the dividing bulkhead between, so that the new funnels were directly above the dividing bulkheads (see Machinery plan). The inboard rows of the new groupings were of four boilers, those in the outer boiler rooms of three.

Below: *Ernest Renan* on her full-power trials, during which she attained a speed of 24.44 knots with 37,023CV; this was the highest speed ever recorded by a French armoured cruiser. *(Private collection)*

In order to make this work, each of the four boiler rooms had to be lengthened by 1.8m (=1.5 frames). The engine rooms likewise had to be lengthened, this time by a single frame, to accommodate the larger, more powerful engines. A comparison of *Ernest Renan* with *Jules Michelet* gives the following figures:

	BR1&2	ER+CR*	BR3&4
Jules Michelet	22.8m	20.4m	22.8m
Ernest Renan	26.4m	21.6m	26.4m

* Condenser Room

The total length of the machinery spaces was therefore 66m for *Jules Michelet* (45 per cent of length between perpendiculars) and 74.4m (47.4 per cent) for *Ernest Renan*. The changes to the machinery accounted for 8.4m of the 10.5m increase in the length of the hull.

The engines of *Ernest Renan* were manufactured by the shipbuilder, Penhoët–Saint-Nazaire, who had built the very successful engines fitted in *Léon Gambetta*. They show the same unusual arrangement of the cylinders as those in *Jules Michelet*, with the LP cylinders at either end. Each of the two LP cylinders had a diameter of 1.98m; the corresponding figures for the IP and HP cylinders were 1.73m and 1.18m respectively. Designed horsepower was 36,000CV, an increase of 30 per cent over the *Gambetta*s and 25 per cent over *Jules Michelet*. Steam from the engines in *Léon Gambetta* and *Jules Ferry* evacuated into two large condensers, while there were three condensers in the third ship of the class, *Victor Hugo*, and in *Jules Michelet*, housed in separate rooms directly abaft their respective engines. In *Ernest Renan* there were two smaller condensers for each of the three engines, again in three separate condenser rooms.

Trials of *Ernest Renan* appear to have been particularly successful: on her 10-hour full-power trials she achieved 24.44 knots with 37,023CV and all boilers lit. Coal consumption was calculated at 0.78kg/h per unit of horsepower (for a comparison with the two ships of the *Edgar Quinet* class see page 203).

Auxiliary machinery was as in the earlier units of

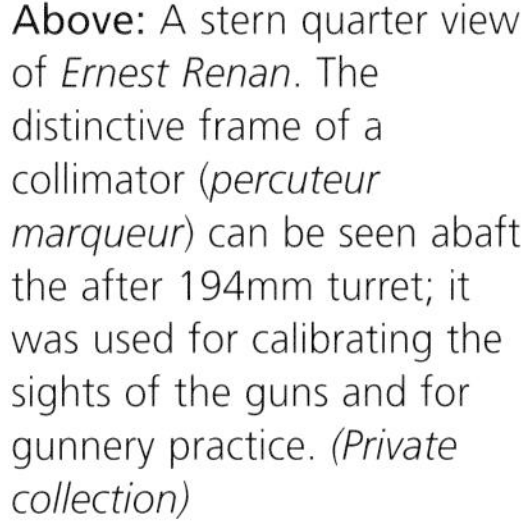

Above: A stern quarter view of *Ernest Renan*. The distinctive frame of a collimator (*percuteur marqueur*) can be seen abaft the after 194mm turret; it was used for calibrating the sights of the guns and for gunnery practice. *(Private collection)*

Left: This photo of *Ernest Renan* was taken when she took part in the Great Naval Review of 4 September 1911 – see Chapter 10. *(Private collection)*

the class, which had their three main bilge pumps uprated to 1000 litres per hour.

CONSTRUCTION AND EARLY SERVICE

Due to the constant revisions to the initial design, *Ernest Renan* was not laid down at the Penhoët shipyard until October 1904. Construction then proceeded relatively smoothly, and preliminary trials began on 21 May 1908. Official trials followed, beginning on 21 August of the same year. A trial on 8 September had to be abandoned as a result of overheating of an eccentric in one of the reciprocating engines, but the official trials were generally successful and *Ernest Renan* left Lorient for Toulon on 13 December 1908, arriving on the 17th. She entered service with the 1st Light Division of the Mediterranean Squadron in October 1909, serving alongside *Jules Ferry* (flag), *Jules Michelet* and *Victor Hugo*. She took part in the Great Naval Review of 4 September 1911 and the subsequent manoeuvres.

Following a major reorganisation of the fleet in late 1911 she was again assigned to the elite 1st Light Division, which now comprised the three most modern French armoured cruisers: *Waldeck-Rousseau* (flagship of Vice Admiral Auvert), *Ernest Renan* (2nd ship) and *Edgar Quinet* (3rd ship). This formation would remain largely intact, save for repairs to *Waldeck-Rousseau*, up to the outbreak of war.

EVALUATION

Ernest Renan was an impressive ship, and in terms of power, protection and speed was more than a match for the British *Warriors*. Had she been begun and completed on time she would undoubtedly have made a grander entrance on the world stage. However, constant tinkering with the design and the delays in construction meant that by the time she was completed in early 1909 that stage had been occupied by the three all-big-gun armoured cruisers of the *Invincible* class built for the Royal Navy. With a uniform armament of 12in (305mm) guns and a designed speed of 25.5 knots they were powered, like the revolutionary battleship *Dreadnought*, by steam turbines.

Turbines used less steam for a given power than traditional reciprocating engines, which meant that the number of (large-tube) boilers in the *Invincible*s could be kept to thirty-one, even though designed horsepower was 41,000shp – 5000shp more than in *Ernest Renan*. A rotary engine had fewer moving parts than a piston engine, required less lubrication, and was less subject to vibration and wear when run for extended periods at high speed; this favoured both pursuit of a less powerful vessel on the high seas, and escape from a more powerful opponent. A turbine installation made for significant savings in weight, volume and engineering personnel, allowing either a smaller hull or one that was better armed and protected. The disadvantages were a decline in the responsiveness and close-quarter manoeuvring capabilities of the ship due to the use of smaller-diameter propellers, and the poor fuel economy of direct-drive turbines at lower speeds. These problems were partially resolved by increasing the number of shafts (from two to four in the RN), and by the provision of separate astern and cruise turbines on two or all four shafts, but the increased weight and volume implicit in these measures served to erode one of the major advantages of the adoption of turbines.

It would be easy to criticise Emile Bertin for his focus on boiler technology as the solution to ever-higher speeds. However, he encountered resistance from the more conservative officers unhappy with the reliability and maintenance demands of the new, advanced small-tube boilers, and when eventually the French naval establishment came to consider the

Right: *Ernest Renan* at her moorings; ahead of her is the armoured cruiser *Edgar Quinet*. *(Private collection)*

turbine – not until mid-1906, more than 18 months after *Ernest Renan* had been laid down at Saint-Nazaire – particular concerns were expressed about its impact on manoeuvrability in formation and cruising range. It would be some years before the French mastered turbine technology. However, there can be little doubt that the advent of large cruisers powered by turbines hastened the end of the French armoured cruiser; *Ernest Renan*'s two successors, *Edgar Quinet* and *Waldeck-Rousseau*, laid down in November 1905 and June 1906 respectively, would be the last of the type

Above: A fine view of *Ernest Renan* departing Toulon for exercises. She would be the last armoured cruiser designed by Emile Bertin. *(Marius Bar)*

CHAPTER 9:

THE LAST ARMOURED CRUISERS: *EDGAR QUINET* AND *WALDECK-ROUSSEAU*

LOUIS-EMILE BERTIN took active retirement from his position as *Directeur du Génie Maritime* in March 1905. He was replaced by Albert Lhomme, a constructor with many years of service – he was 49 at the time of his appointment – who had been promoted *Ingénieur général de 2e classe* the previous year. As head of the *Service Technique* Lhomme would be personally responsible for the next (and in the event final) class of armoured cruisers and for the battleships of the *Danton* class that superseded the six ships of the *Patrie* class.

Judging from his work, Lhomme, who unlike Bertin and his successor Léon Lyasse does not even merit an entry in Etienne Taillemite's classic *Dictionnaire des marins français* (*op cit*), favoured an evolutionary approach that sat in marked contrast to that of Bertin, who fought against the French naval establishment for years before his ideas finally obtained acceptance. Lhomme had the misfortune to be responsible for French ship design during the period when the British Royal Navy introduced the all-big-gun battleship and the turbine-powered armoured cruiser to the world, thereby overturning 15 years of steady, evolutionary progress and casting established practice to the winds. Lyasse, who replaced him in November 1909, would be responsible for the first generation of French 'dreadnoughts'; the legacy of Lhomme, in contrast, comprised two costly classes of major warship[1] both of which became effectively obsolescent during their construction – a judgement underlined by their extraordinarily lengthy building times. The cruisers were laid down in 1905–06, but the first was not completed until early 1911; construction times for the battleships of the *Danton* class were shorter (3.5–4 years), but due to multiple design changes the first ship, *Voltaire*, would not be laid down until June 1907, when HMS *Dreadnought* had already been in service for six months.

Preliminary design work on the two new armoured cruisers that were to accompany the *Dantons*, designated C16 and C17, began towards the end of Bertin's

[1] *Edgar Quinet* and *Waldeck-Rousseau* would cost just under 33 million FF (= £1.3 million sterling) apiece; the battleship programme was initially costed at 36.7 million FF per ship, but the final unit cost was higher due to the constant revisions to the design: 56 million FF (= £2.2 million sterling).

EDGAR QUINET AND HER FOREIGN CONTEMPORARIES

	Edgar Quinet	*Minotaur* (GB)	*Scharnhorst* (Ger)
No in class:	2	3	2
Built:	1905–11	1905–09	1904–08
Displacement:	13,850t	14,850t	12,950t
Dimensions:	157m x 21.5m	149m x 22.7m[1]	143.8m x 21.6m
Propulsion:			
Engines	3-shaft VTE	2-shaft VTE	3-shaft VTE
Horsepower	36,000CV	27,000CV	26,000CV
Speed	23 knots	23 knots	22.5 knots
Armament:			
Main guns	14 x 194mm (2 x II, 10 x I)	4 x 234mm (2 x II)	8 x 210mm (2 x II, 4 x I)
Medium guns	–	10 x 190mm (10 x 1)	6 x 150mm (6 x I)
ATB guns	20 x 65mm (20 x I)	16 x 75mm (16 x I)	18 x 88mm (18 x I)
TT	2 x 450mm	5 x 450mm	4 x 450mm
Protection:			
Belt	150mm	150mm	150mm
Main turrets	174/144mm	200mm	170mm
Conning tower	174mm	250mm	200mm
Decks	30mm + 45/65mm[2]	20mm + 20m	30/60mm

Notes:

1 Metric equivalents have been supplied for *Minotaur* in order to give a comparison. The equivalents for gun calibres are exact; those for armour thicknesses are to the nearest 5mm.

2 For the armoured decks, the first figure given relates to the upper protective deck, the second to the lower (flat/slopes).

Above: The Royal Navy's counterparts to *Edgar Quinet* and *Waldeck-Rousseau* were the armoured cruisers of the *Warrior* and *Defence* classes. The *Warrior* class – *Natal* is seen here – was armed with six 9.2in guns (234mm) and four 7.5in (190mm) guns, the *Defence* class with only four 9.2in guns but no fewer than ten 7.5in guns. As with the French ships, all the wing guns were in single turrets, albeit mounted a deck lower. *(Allan C Green Collection, State Library of Victoria, H91_325_2121)*

tenure. In their overall dimensions, armament and internal layout the ships were to be virtually identical to *Ernest Renan*. According to documentation relating to *Edgar Quinet* held at the Centre d'Archives de l'Armement, Châtellerault, the initial characteristics of the ship as proposed under the 1904 budget were:

Displacement:	13,644 tonnes
Length pp:	157m
Speed:	23 knots
Main armament:	4 x 194mm, 12 x 164.7mm
ATB guns:	22 x 47mm QF, 2 x 37mm QF

However, before either ship had been laid down, a commission was set up by the newly-appointed Minister of Marine, Gaston Thomson (24 January 1905 to 22 October 1908), to review the design. It was composed of four senior Vice Admirals of the General Staff, de Maigret, Fournier, Richard and Touchard (chairman), and reported on 15 February 1905. The commission was unhappy about the extreme length of the new cruisers, which made them less manoeuvrable than the *Gambettas*, and considered them under-gunned for their size. Having considered all these issues at length, the commission recommended a ship derived from *Ernest Renan* but with the same armament as *Jules Ferry*. It was inclined towards the view that the problems currently being experienced with the twin 164.7mm turret could be resolved with the adoption of a turret of greater diameter.

A new, revised study was requested from the STCN, and on 22 April 1905 the dockyards were instructed to resume preparatory work. Characteristics were to be as follows:

Displacement:	14,100 tonnes
Main armament:	4 x 194mm, 16 x 164.7mm[2]
ATB guns:	14 x 65mm QF, 8 x 47mm QF

The orders for the two cruisers, to be named *Edgar Quinet* (C16) and *Waldeck-Rousseau* (C17), were placed with the naval dockyards of Brest and Lorient on 27 August 1904 and 31 July 1905 respectively; the ships were to be identical, and Brest was to be the lead yard with responsibility for all plans and other documentation. Lorient had built a number of the French 'fleet' cruisers, beginning with *Gueydon*, and was currently engaged in fitting out *Victor Hugo* and *Jules Michelet* (launched 31 August 1905). Brest's construction work had traditionally focused on battleships, although the dockyard had built both *Marseillaise* and *Léon Gambetta*. The existing slipway at Le Salou was barely

[2] The 164.7mm gun would almost certainly have been the longer, more advanced Mle 1902, probably in a new, more spacious twin turret.

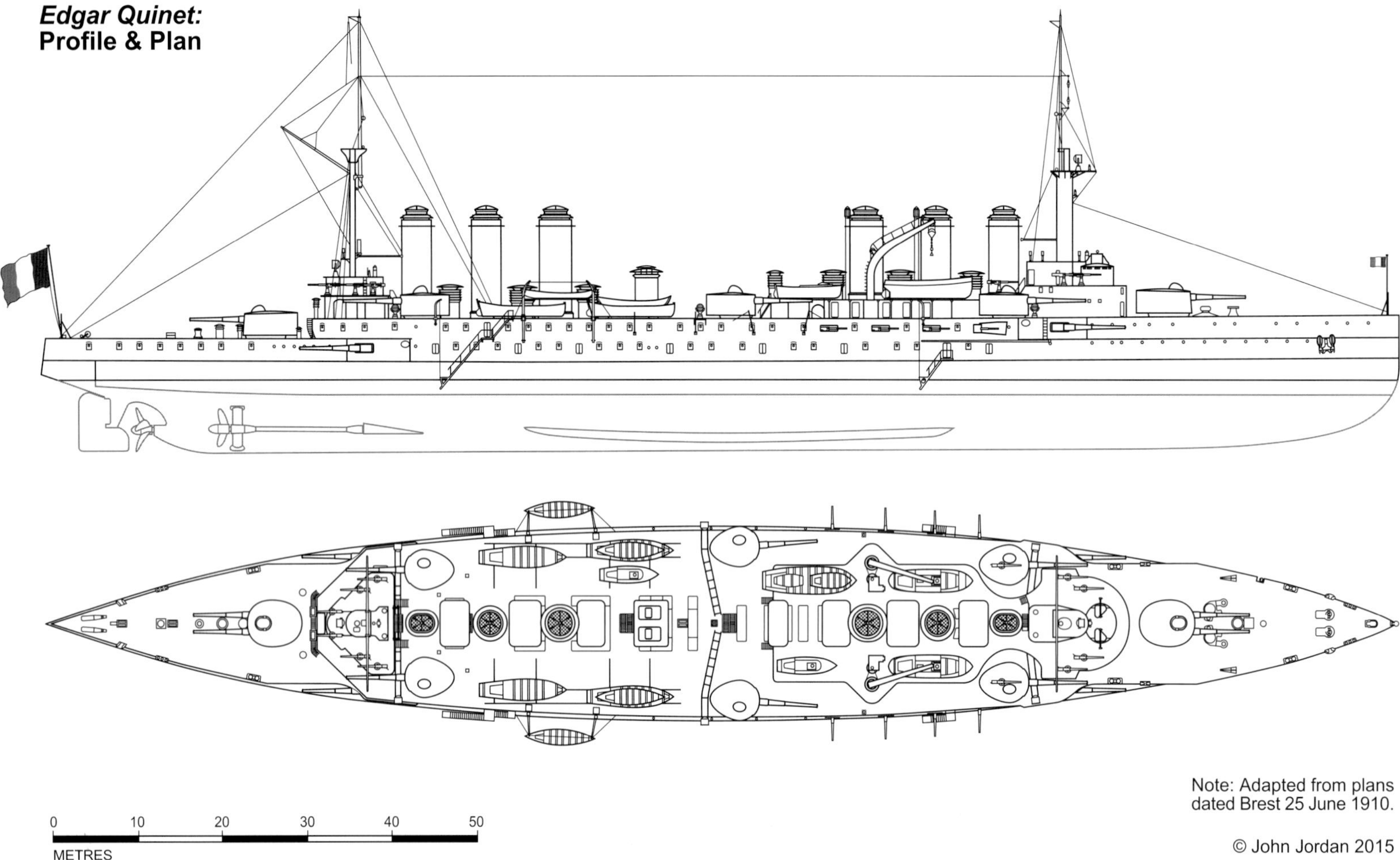

BUILDING DATA

Name	Builder	Laid down	Launched	Trials	Commissioned
Edgar Quinet	Arsenal de Brest	6 Nov 1905	21 Sep 1907	Apr 1909	15 Dec 1910
Waldeck-Rousseau	Arsenal de Lorient	16 Jun 1906	4 Mar 1908	13 Jan 1911	8 Aug 1911

long enough to cope with a hull the length of *Edgar Quinet* (158.9m overall), and it was planned to build a new covered slipway, to be named *Point-du-Jour*, to accommodate the name-ship of the *Danton* class (146.6m x 25.8m).

However, this was not to be the last of the changes. On 29 January 1906, when *Edgar Quinet* had already been laid down, it was decided to replace the 164.7mm medium guns by 194mm Mle 1902 guns, disposed in six single wing turrets and four casemates, giving the ships a uniform battery of fourteen 194mm guns. The rationale for this decision was the same which underpinned the rearming of the last four ships of the *Patrie* class: with the extended battle ranges now in prospect, the 164.7mm could no longer be expected to penetrate 6in/150mm of Krupp face-hardened armour.[3] The reduction in the number of guns and a corresponding decline in the rate of fire simply had to be accepted to ensure that the French cruisers were not outgunned by their foreign counterparts.

[3] The 194mm gun had a significant advantage in accuracy and penetration at ranges between 2500m and 3000m. By 1904 the Royal Navy was conducting long-range gunnery practices at 4000–6000 yards.

Further modifications while the ships were building were as follows:

9 May 1906:	to be fitted as flagship
6 May 1907:	18 x 65mm QF, 4 x 47mm QF
17 June 1907:	20 x 65mm QF

NOMENCLATURE

Edgar Quinet (1803–75) was a prominent French historian and a committed republican with strong anti-clerical views who, during the 1840s, was a close associate of Jules Michelet. Like Victor Hugo he went into exile on the accession on Napoleon III, fleeing to Switzerland, and returned only after the latter's fall from power in 1870. His book *Le siège de Paris et la défense nationale* appeared in 1871, and was followed by *La République* in 1872. His anti-German polemics and opposition to the peace terms following the Franco-Prussian War did much to cement his reputation in France.

Pierre-Marie-René-Ernest **Waldeck-Rousseau** (1846–1904) was a prominent French statesman. Born in Nantes, he studied Law and subsequently became a barrister. Elected to the *Chambre des Députés* in 1879, he championed the Third Republic and, despite

Opposite: The launch of *Edgar Quinet* at Brest naval dockyard on 21 September 1907. *(Private collection)*

Edgar Quinet: GA Plans

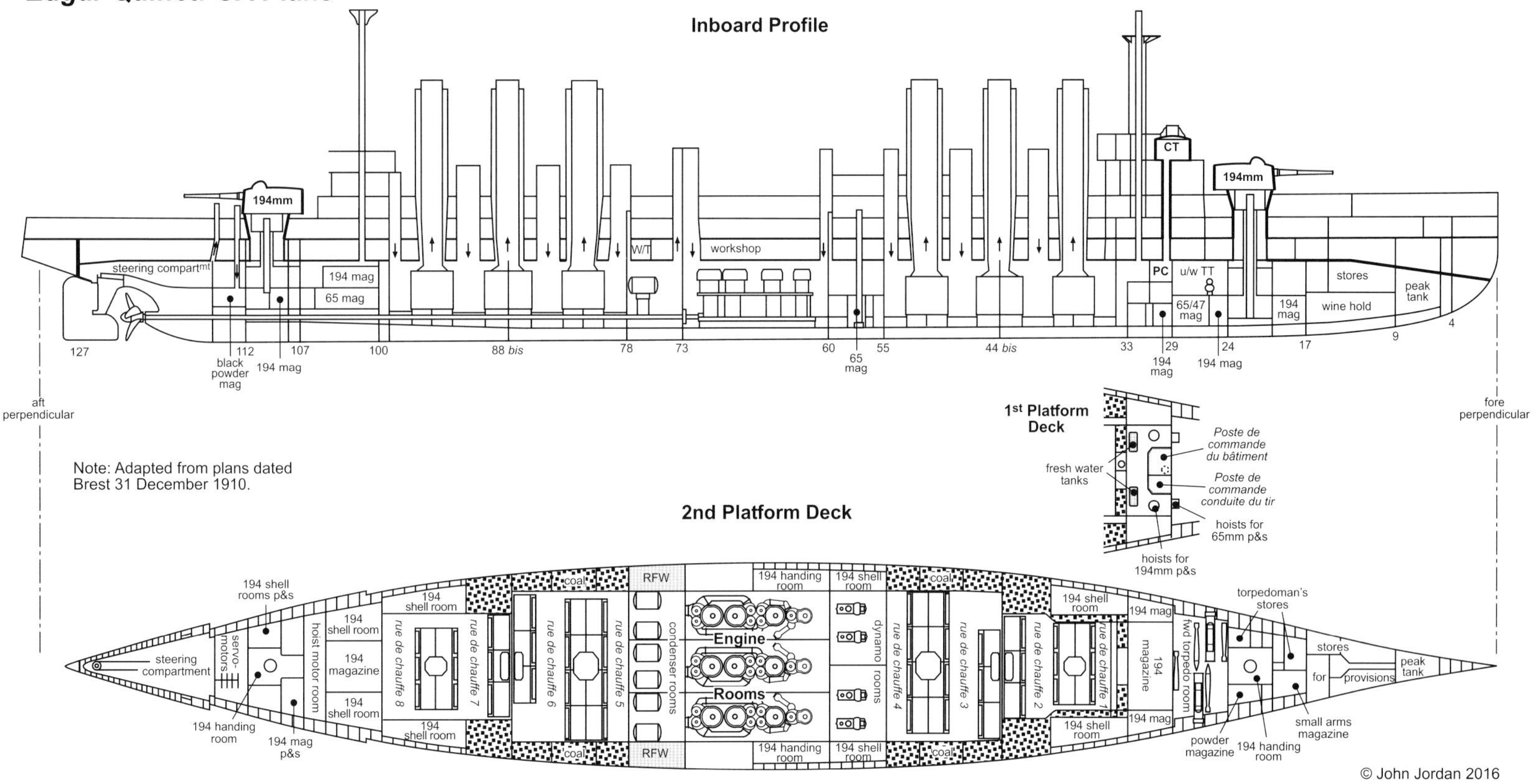

Inboard Profile

1st Platform Deck

2nd Platform Deck

Note: Adapted from plans dated Brest 31 December 1910.

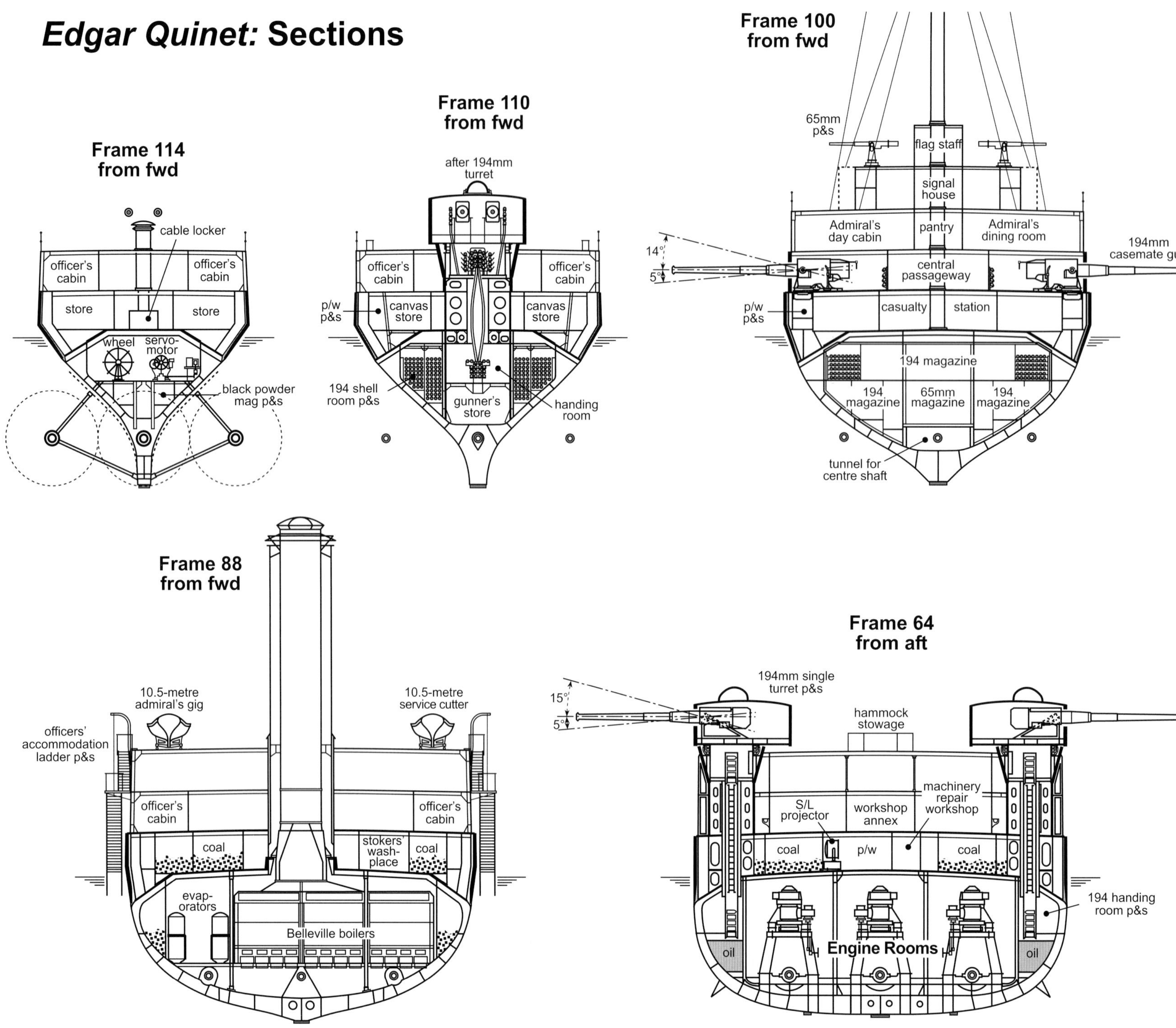

being from a Catholic family, supported the Jules Ferry laws (enacted 1881–2) establishing compulsory public secular education. Waldeck-Rousseau's primary focus was on the relationship between capital and labour, and he was instrumental in securing the recognition of trade unions in 1884. He died in 1904, shortly before the ship bearing his name was authorised.

HULL AND SUPERSTRUCTURES

The hull of *Edgar Quinet* and *Waldeck-Rousseau* had the same dimensions as that of *Ernest Renan*. Subdivision below the armoured decks was likewise the same, with the transverse watertight bulkheads for the magazines and machinery spaces identically spaced. The suppression of the fourth wing turret with its associated ammunition passage and handing room outboard of the engine rooms meant that magazine arrangements amidships were greatly simplified: *Edgar Quinet* and *Waldeck-Rousseau* effectively returned to the turret and magazine layout of the *Gambetta*s, albeit with single 194mm turrets replacing the 164.7mm twin turrets on the beam.

Externally the ships differed markedly in some aspects from their immediate predecessors. The *tourelle-barbette* favoured by Bertin was abandoned in favour of a more traditional enclosed turret (*tourelle fermée*) with vertical sides that extended almost down

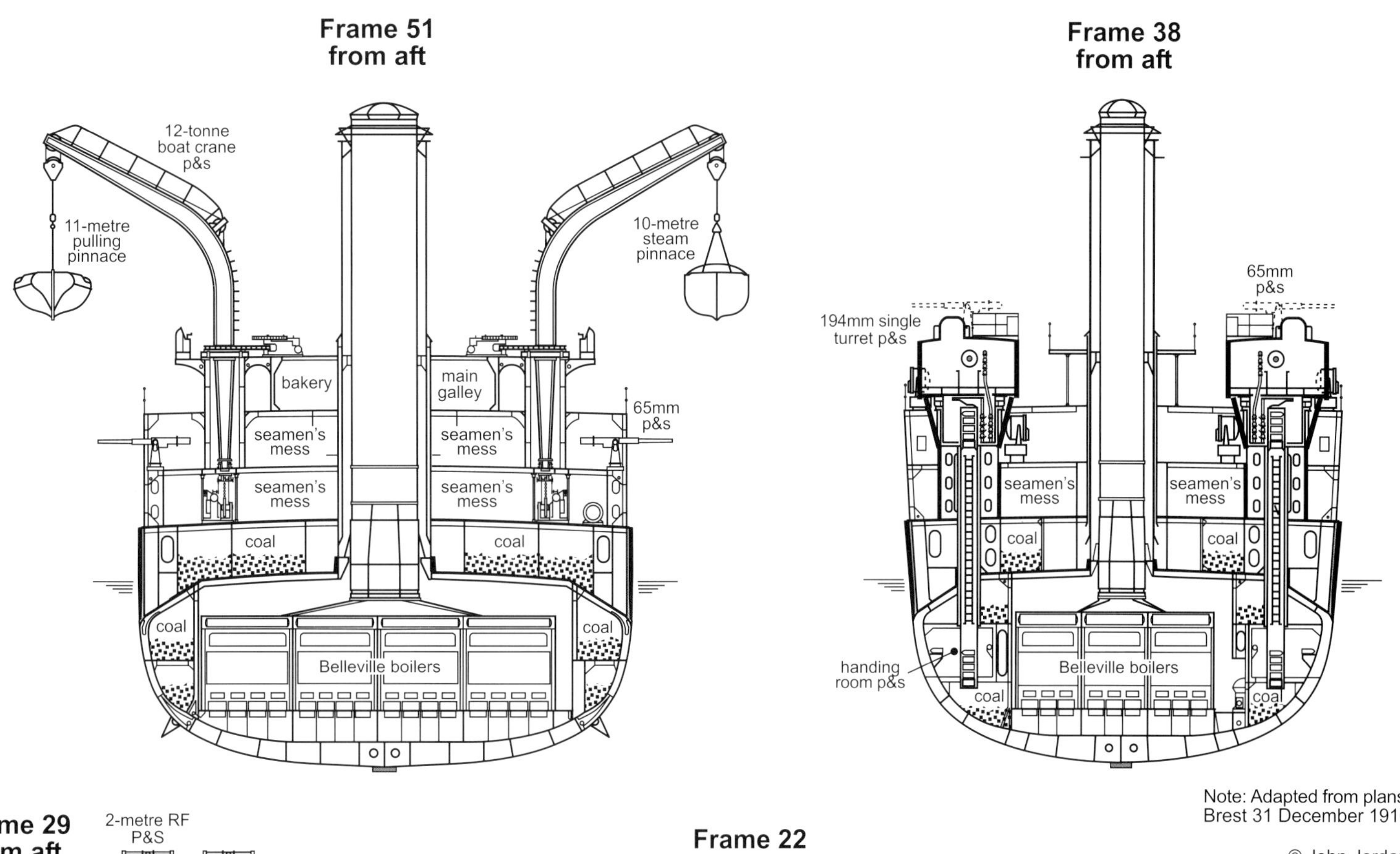

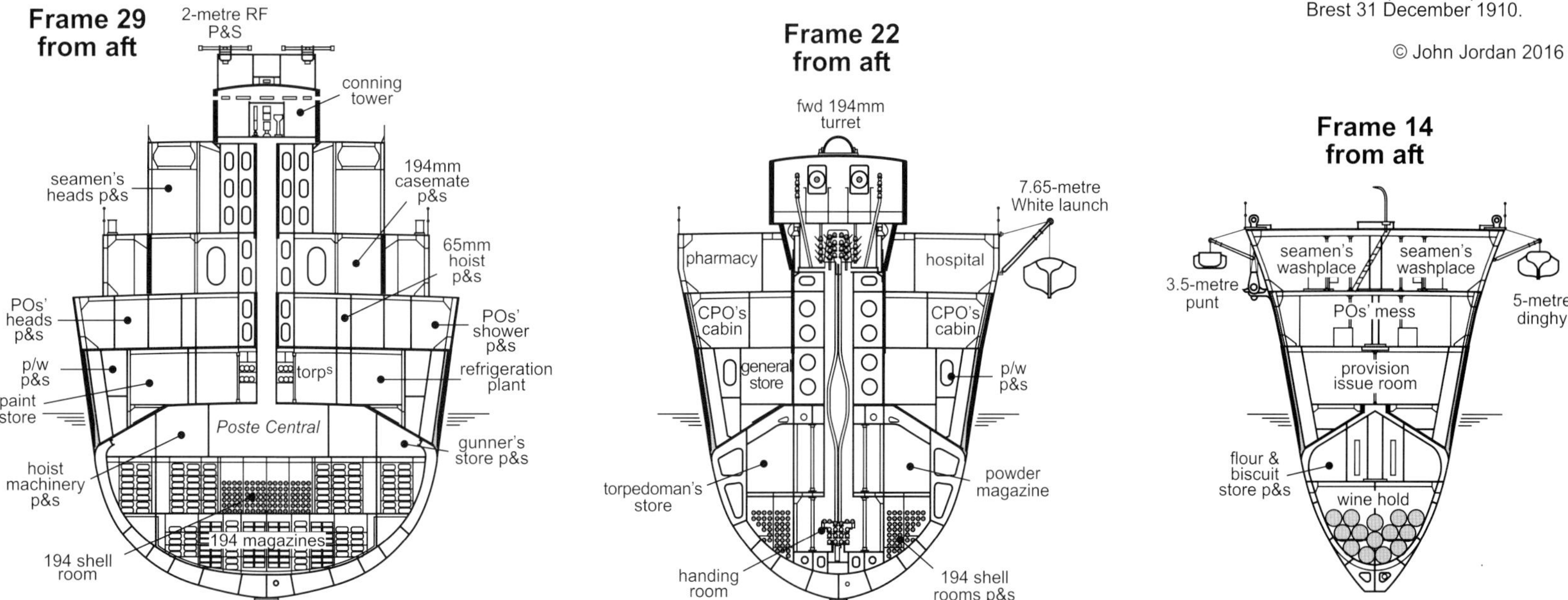

to the weather deck (see Armament below), and the funnels had outer casings that extended without a break up to the funnel cap – the armoured cruisers designed by Bertin all had a distinctive 'pagoda-style' outer casing. These two features made the ships instantly recognisable in bow and stern quarter views. Also, with the reversion to three wing turrets, the distinctive goose-neck cranes used to handle the heavier boats were moved forward to a position abreast the third funnel.

As in *Jules Michelet* and *Ernest Renan* there was only a light military foremast, with no lower platform for the light ATB guns. Instead, two of the forward group of ATB guns were located, not atop the fore turret as in *Jules Michelet*, but on the first pair of wing turrets.

Both ships were completed as flagships, with extensive accommodation for an admiral and his staff at the after end of the first deck. Following her entry into service *Waldeck-Rousseau* would serve briefly as flagship of the vice admiral commanding the prestigious Mediterranean Light Squadron (see Service).

ARMAMENT

Main guns

Edgar Quinet and *Waldeck-Rousseau* were armed with the same 194mm Mle 1902 gun that was mounted in the fore and after twin turrets of *Jules Michelet* and

CHARACTERISTICS

Displacement:	14,050 tonnes
Dimensions:	
Length	157.00m pp; 158.90m oa
Beam	21.50m wl
Draught	8.23m
Propulsion:	
Boilers	*EQ:* 40 Belleville boilers *W-R:* 40 Niclausse boilers, 21kg/cm^2
Engines	3-shaft 4-cylinder VTE
Horsepower	36,000CV (designed)
Speed	23 knots (designed)
Coal	1240 tonnes normal; 2260 tonnes full load
Endurance	7500nm at 10 knots, 1420nm at 23 knots
Armament:	
Main guns	14 x 194mm/50 Mle 1902 in two twin & six single turrets and four casemate mountings
ATB guns	20 x 65mm/50 Mle 1902 QF in single mountings
Torpedo tubes	2 submerged tubes for 450mm torpedoes 6 torpedoes Mle 1904
Protection:	
Main belt	150/130mm max
Decks	30mm PBS 45/65mm PBI
194 turrets	174/144mm
Casemates	164mm
Conning tower	174mm
Boats:	2 x 10m pinnaces 2 x 7.65m White launch 1 x 11.5m pulling pinnace 3 x 10.5m cutters 2 x 8.5m whalers 2 x 5m dinghies
Complement:	
As private ship	859 officers and men
As flagship	+ 11 officers, 72 men

Turret Design: Twin 194mm Turret

Ernest Renan

51
346
156
147
102

Note: Mobile parts of turret are black; fixed structure is grey.

Edgar Quinet

50
144
174
151
92

Ernest Renan; it also equipped the single wing turrets of the later ships of the *Patrie* class (*Démocratie* sub-group).[4] It fired APC and SAPC steel projectiles weighing 86kg, both of which had a burster of *mélinite* (see table page 170), and the BM13 propellant charge was in three bags and weighed 38.5kg. Muzzle velocity with the AP shell was 950m/sec.

[4] See Jordan and Caresse, *French Battleships of World War One*, pp 100–07.

Right: A gunner inspects the open breech of one of the 194mm Mle 1902 guns on board *Waldeck-Rousseau*. *(DR)*

The abandonment of the long-established *tourelle-barbette* in favour of an enclosed turret is in many respects surprising. The twin 194mm turrets of *Ernest Renan* and the single turrets of the battleships were both of the barbette type, with a turret cupola protected by steeply-angled plates of cemented steel above a truncated inverse cone of fixed barbette armour that protruded above the weather deck. However, both these ship-types were designed by Bertin, and it should be noted that Lhomme would also revert to a more conventional turret with vertical armoured sides for the 240mm secondary turrets of the contemporary battleships of the *Danton* class. The latter were twin turrets but, unlike the 305mm turrets of the same ships, were not of the pivot type and had the same ammunition supply arrangements as the standard French cruiser turret, with the working chamber suspended from the turret and a fixed ammunition hoist.

The problem with the prominent truncated cone of fixed armour, which in theory could deflect a shell down into the hull of the ship, has already been discussed (see page 154). However, it appears more likely that the rationale for the reversion to a turret with sides that extended down to the weather deck – a configuration last seen in *Pothuau* and *D'Entrecasteaux* – was that the internal volume of the

Edgar Quinet: Layout of Casemates

After Casemate: Main Deck

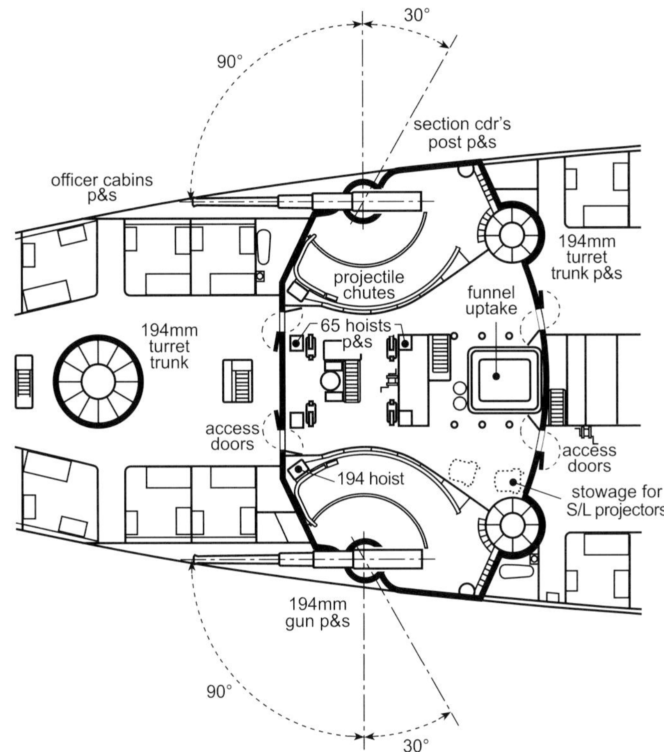

Forward Casemate: First Deck

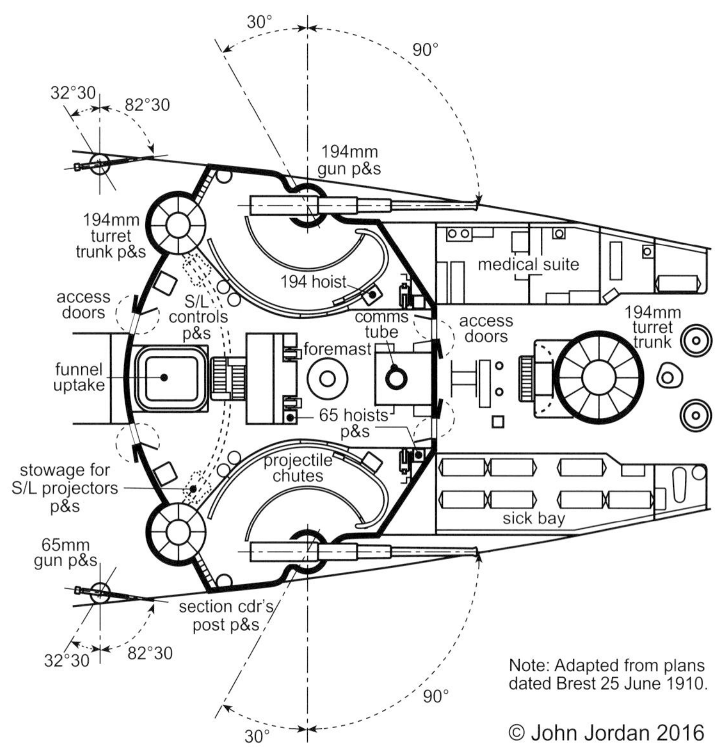

The grouping of the forward and after pairs of casemates into armoured redoubts which extended to the full beam of the ships had the advantage of eliminating the need for separate transverse armoured bulkheads to protect against enfilading fire, and for protection for the inner walls of the individual casemates, which now comprised simple curved bulkheads of 15mm mild steel.

The redoubts were shaped to incorporate the ammunition trunks for the forward and after wing turrets, and also provided protection for the hoists for the forward and after groups of 65mm ATB guns and for the searchlight projectors, which in their daytime 'action' position were stowed within the redoubts.

gunhouse was thereby increased and protection simplified. Moreover, at longer ranges the inclined armour of the cupola of the *tourelle-barbette* was less effective due to steeper shell descents.

The essential differences in the design of the twin turrets of *Ernest Renan* and *Edgar Quinet* are illustrated in the accompanying schematic drawing. Although no plans of the *Edgar Quinet* turrets have been published, ammunition supply arrangements and the internal arrangements in the working chamber and the upper part of the gunhouse would have been largely unchanged.

Command and elevation for the 194mm guns were as follows:

Edgar Quinet: Arcs for 194mm Turrets & Casemates

The layout of the main armament in these ships continued to be optimised for end-on fire. Six/eight guns could fire directly ahead and six/eight astern. The maximum number of guns able to fire on the broadside was nine, but the two casemate guns had arcs which were restricted to 30° forward/aft of the beam.

176° 120° 170° 170° 120° 135° 135° 135° 135° 120° 170° 170° 120° 176°

© John Jordan 2017

Right: Following some initial problems with her machinery, *Edgar Quinet* was commissioned on 15 December 1910; in late January 1911 she would be assigned to the Light Division of the 1st Squadron in the Mediterranean. *(Marius Bar)*

Below: *Waldeck-Rousseau* shortly after completion. Note the Barr & Stroud 4ft 6in (1.37m) rangefinders sided atop the bridge. There were similar rangefinders in each of the turret hoods. *(Private collection)*

Turret I (fwd twin)	9.95m (+15°/-5°)
Turrets II & III	9.00m (+15°/-5°)
Turrets IV & V	8.85m (+15°/-5°)
Turrets VI & VII	8.90m (+15°/-5°)
Turret VIII (aft twin)	6.85m (+15°/-5°)
Fwd casemates	5.95m (+14°/-5°)
Aft casemates	3.63m (+14°/-5°)

The relative proximity to the waterline of the after casemate guns remained a weakness. The 194mm Mle 1902 was the longest medium-calibre gun ever to be mounted in a lower casemate (see Section Views, frame 100).

The layout of the main turrets reflected a continuing preoccupation with end-on fire (see Arcs plan).

Although ramming was no longer envisaged – Bertin favoured a straight stem from a powering/sea-keeping point of view, and the battleships of the *Patrie* class would be the last to be fitted with a ram[5] – the principal role of the 'fleet cruiser' was to scout for the battle fleet. It was envisaged that the armoured cruiser divisions would be pushed on ahead of the main body. Cruisers screening the enemy battle fleet would most likely be encountered off the bow, so ahead fire continued to be important. Should the French armoured cruisers penetrate as far as the enemy's battleships they would then need to turn about and lead the enemy onto their own battle line, at which point they would be the leading ships in a stern chase and would engage the enemy with their

[5] Bertin's preliminary design for the *Patrie* class featured a straight stem; it was the *Conseil des Travaux* that insisted on a prominent ram for these ships (see Jordan and Caresse, *French Battleships of World War One*, p 87). Bertin was allowed far more latitude in his designs for cruisers.

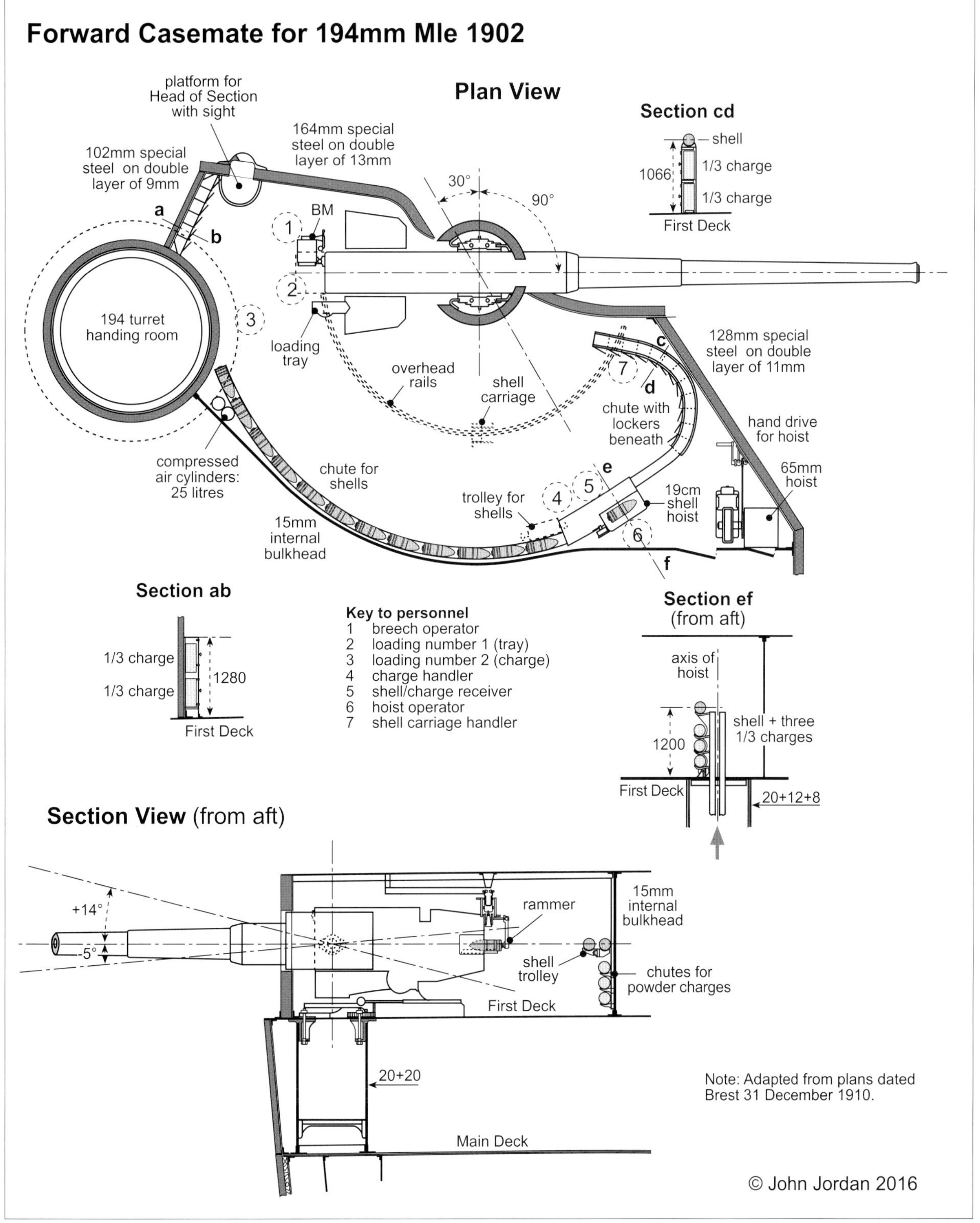

WEIGHT OF BROADSIDE

Number/Calibre of guns	Weight of projectile	Rounds per minute	Weight of broadside
HMS *Warrior*			
4 x 9.2in (234mm)	172kg	2rpm	1376kg
2 x 7.5in (190mm)	90kg	2rpm	360kg
			1736kg
Jules Michelet/ Ernest Renan			
4 x 194mm	90kg	2rpm	720kg
6 x 164.7mm	55kg	3rpm	990kg
			1710kg
HMS *Minotaur*			
4 x 9.2in (234mm)	172kg	2rpm	1376kg
5 x 7.5in (190mm)	90kg	2rpm	900kg
			2276kg
Edgar Quinet			
9 x 194mm	90kg	2rpm	1620kg
			1620kg

Note:
Rates of fire are approximate, but are consistent with what was achieved in battle practice.

after guns. During the main action between the fleets, the armoured cruisers would have insufficient protection to engage enemy battleships on the broadside, and manoeuvring as a 'fast wing' in the van of the main battle line would still tend to favour ahead or astern fire.

Fire control

Edgar Quinet and *Waldeck-Rousseau* were major warships; in size and cost they rivalled contemporary battleships, and they were equipped with similar state-of-the-art fire-control systems.

The conning tower was of a new type. It was designed to accommodate an admiral and his staff as well as the ship's CO and gunnery officer, but there was no raised platform aft for the admiral; instead the after section of the tower was given over to fire control. The tower was elliptical in plan, and the conning section at the forward end (*Poste de manoeuvre*) had stations for the admiral and the ship's commanding officer (see Conning Tower plan), who had good views forward and to the sides. In the centre of the conning tower floor, directly behind the CO, were the order transmitters for the three engines and the rudder servo-motors. The fire-control section (*Poste de tir*) was at the after end of the tower, where the gunnery officer supervised the operators for the Germain order transmitters mounted on the rear wall of the turret. There were dials for target-range, deflection, gun-range and bearing and for firing orders.[6] The fire control positions were duplicated port and starboard to enable the ship to engage targets on either beam. Two sided Barr & Stroud FQ2 rangefinders, initially of the 4ft 6in (1.37m type), later replaced by a 2m model, were

[6] See Jordan and Caresse, *French Battleships of World War One*, p 57.

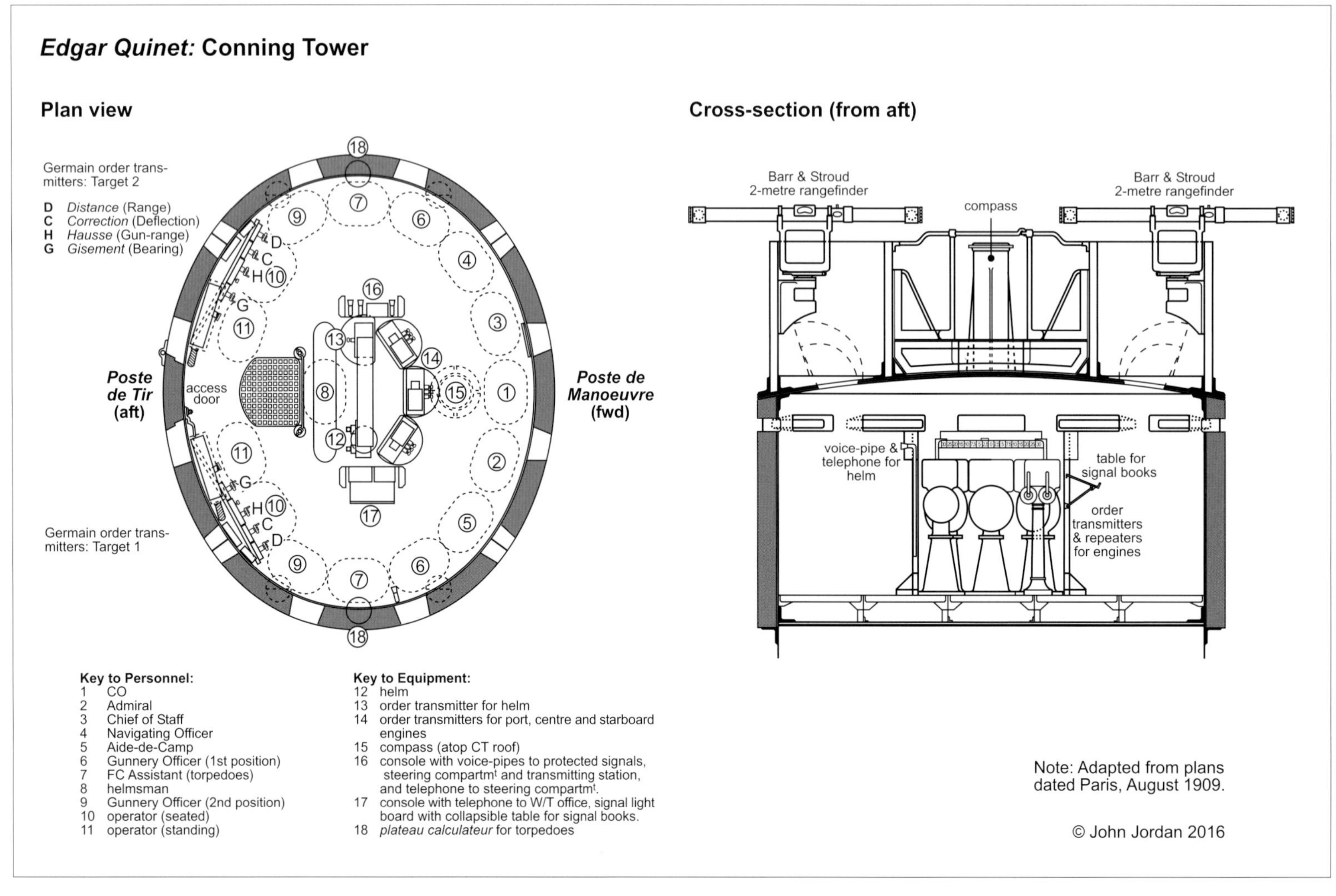

mounted atop the roof of the conning tower, the range-takers being protected by screens of special steel. The raw range data were entered by the operator directly onto the corresponding Germain dial below and then converted into gun-range by the control officer or his assistant using a hand-held *plateau calculateur* (similar in principle to the RN's Dumaresq) and a range clock (*pendule Lafrogne*).[7]

Fire-control orders were transmitted to a second set of dials located in the *Poste Central* below the main armoured deck, which like the conning tower was divided into a conning section (*Commande du bâtiment*) and a fire-control room (*Commande du tir*). In the Germain system the settings on the dials in the conning tower were transmitted directly to the dials in the *Poste Central* via hydraulic lines that ran down through the armoured communications tube. From the *Poste Central* deflection, gun-range data and firing orders were re-transmitted to each of the turrets, which were fitted with a set of receiver dials. The layout of the *Poste Central* of *Edgar Quinet* is shown in the accompanying plan.

Each of the main turrets fired independently, and the hoods of all the turrets were equipped with Barr & Stroud FQ2 4ft 6in (1.37m) rangefinders. In accordance with current practice, the two twin end turrets would have been fitted out as secondary fire-control positions.

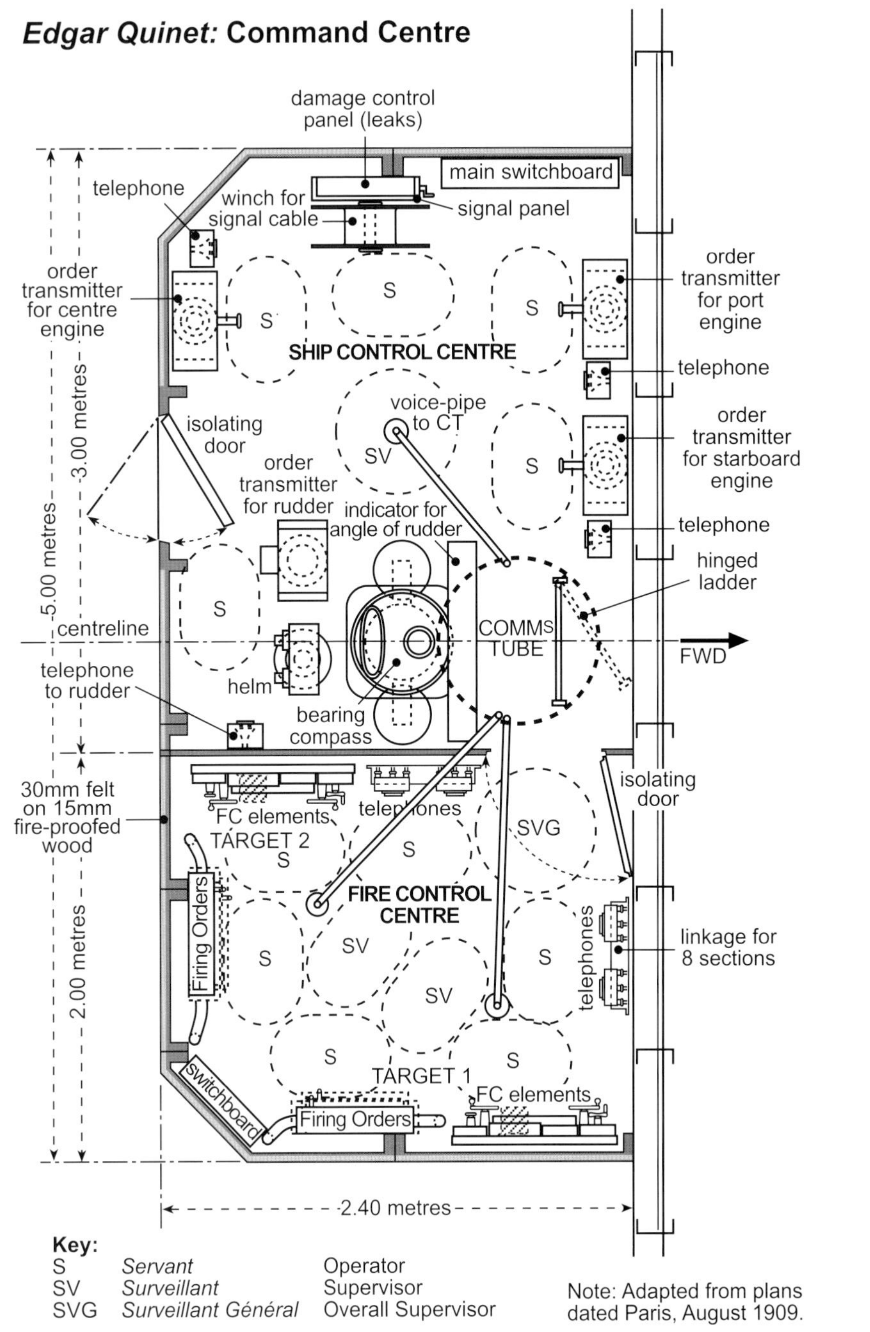

The *Poste Central* of *Edgar Quinet* was state-of-the-art for the period, and the fire-control equipment was on a par with the contemporary battleships of the *Danton* class.

The Ship Control Centre, labelled *Commande du bâtiment*, has a bearing compass plus the order transmitters for the rudder, and individual order transmitters for the three main engines; all four stations are equipped with a telephone, and operations are monitored by a supervisor (*surveillant*) stationed at the base of the voice pipe connecting the control room with the *Poste de manoeuvre* in the forward part of the conning tower, where the CO was stationed in combat.

The Fire Control Centre (*Commande du tir*) is equipped to engage two separate targets simultaneously, designated Targets 1 and 2 (*But 1/But 2*). Each set of equipment comprises order transmitters for the *Eléments du pointage* (Range, Deflection, etc), a separate order transmitter for *Ordres de feux* (Firing Orders), and a *Combinateur* to coordinate the individual gunnery 'sections' via a combat telephone system. There is an operator (*servant*) for each of the six panels, with a supervisor for each set of three panels; the supervisors are stationed at the base of a voicepipe connecting the control room with the *Poste de tir* in the after part of the conning tower, where the Gunnery Officer was stationed in combat. Operations in the Fire Control Centre are supervised by a *Surveillant général*, stationed close to the hinged 'isolating door' connecting it with the Ship Control Centre.

ATB guns

Edgar Quinet and *Waldeck-Rousseau* were given a uniform battery of 65mm ATB guns – *Ernest Renan* had retained some 47mm guns as part of a mix. The 65mm was a larger, heavier weapon than the 47mm Hotchkiss, so fewer could be mounted.

As in *Jules Michelet* and *Ernest Renan* the ATB guns were grouped together atop the bridge decks fore and aft (*ligne haute*), with another group firing through open ports on the 1st deck (*ligne basse*). The guns were disposed as follows: four on the lower bridge deck forward with a third pair atop the first wing turrets for the 194mm guns; six atop the bridge deck aft; and two groups each of four guns on either side of the hull between the forward and centre wing turrets, for a total of twenty. The latter guns were on fixed pedestals – not swinging frames as in earlier ships with the lighter 47mm gun – and could not therefore be retracted inside the hull. Each gun had adjacent ready-use ammunition stowage in a locker that backed onto the outer hull. The ready-use lockers were replenished from hoists that emerged onto the 1st deck inside the armoured walls of the forward redoubt (see above)

Searchlight projectors

The searchlight projectors, increased in number from six to eight, were of the new, more powerful 75cm/90A type introduced in the *Patrie* class; each was equipped with a Breguet remote-control system. Two were in the customary fixed positions on the masts (*ligne haute*), while the remaining six (*ligne basse*) were on rails on the upper (2nd) deck and could occupy one of three different positions:

– night action position: two port and starboard

7 See Jordan and Caresse, *French Battleships of World War One*, p 97.

Right: *Edgar Quinet* shortly after her completion. Ahead of her can be seen a battleship of the *Danton* class. *(DR)*

forward of the first two 194mm wing turrets (II and III); two immediately abaft the centre turrets (IV and V), and two abaft the after pair of 194mm wing turrets (VI and VII); in these positions the arcs covered were slightly greater than the firing arcs of the turrets

- sea position: the projectors were secured on the ship's axis, ready to be moved to their action positions on bronze rails
- daylight action position: the projectors were lowered via the adjacent ladderways to the 1st or main decks below and stowed in the armoured redoubts.

A similar arrangement was adopted for the contemporary battleships of the *Danton* class.[8] The remote power control mechanism proved to be fragile and unreliable, and was later discarded in favour of purely mechanical operation.

Right: *Edgar Quinet* at her moorings, with a battleship of the *Danton* class behind her. Flag 'M', hoisted to the foremast yardarm, signifies that she is currently serving as guard ship. *(Private collection)*

Edgar Quinet: Protection

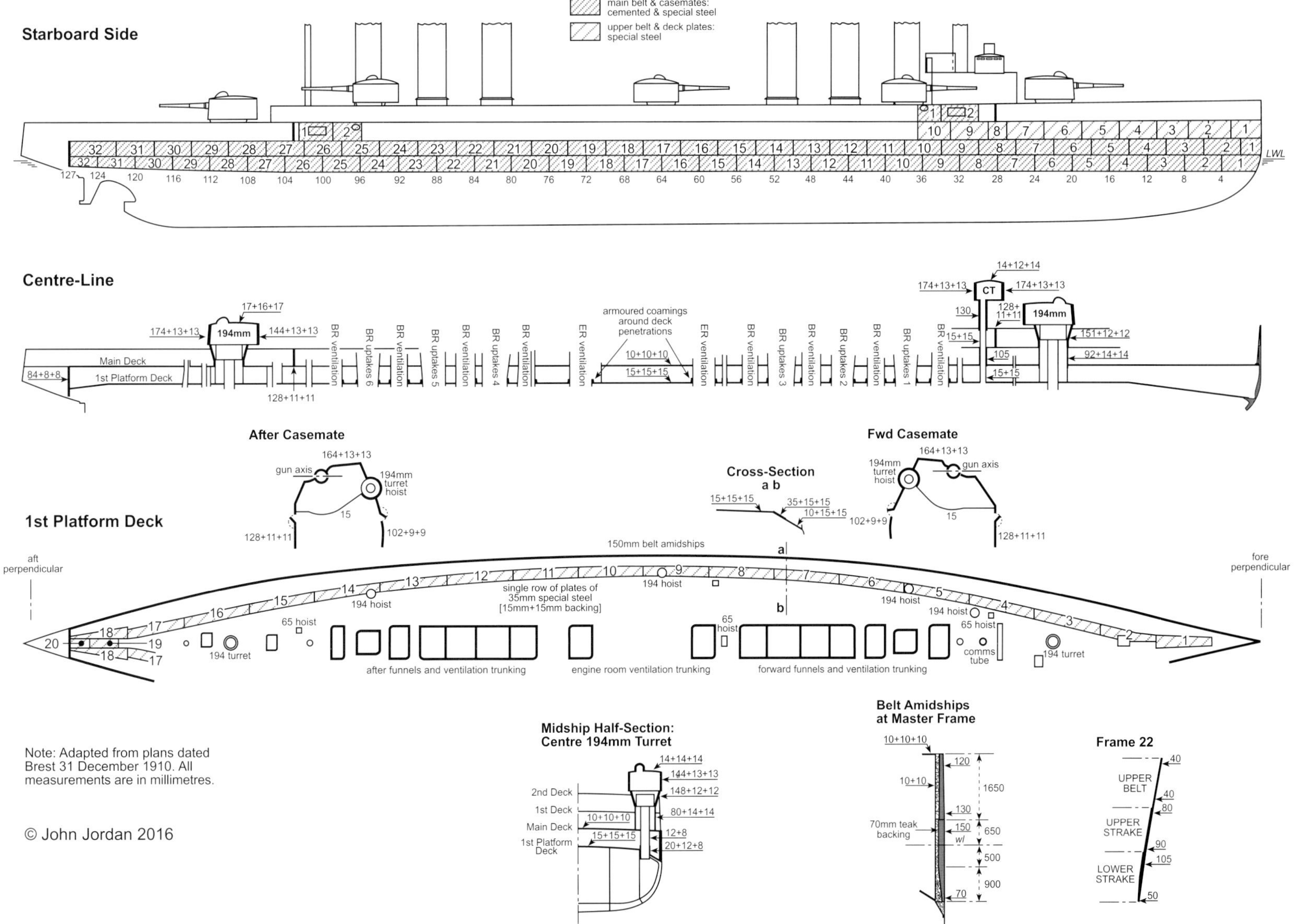

Torpedoes

The torpedo flat for the two underwater torpedo tubes was located forward on the 2nd platform deck, as in *Ernest Renan*. It was shorter (five frames *vice* seven) but extended the full width of the ship. Whereas in *Ernest Renan* the tubes had been angled forward at approximately 45° to the ship's axis, in *Edgar Quinet* and *Waldeck-Rousseau* they were aligned athwartships and fired on the beam. The tubes occupied the centre of the torpedo flat and were staggered port and starboard to facilitate reloading (see GA Plans page 191). There were racks each for three 450mm Mle 1904 torpedo bodies on the forward and after bulkheads of the compartment.

Ten of the latest Harlé moored mines were embarked. These were stowed around the communications tube on the platform deck. The Harlé mine replaced the older Mle 1892 mechanical mine, which was smaller and required less space.

8 See Jordan and Caresse, *French Battleships of World War One*, p 97.

EDGAR QUINET: ARMOUR PLATE THICKNESS MAIN BELT

Plate	Upper Strake *upper/lower edge*	Lower Strake *upper/lower edge*
1–5	80/90	90/50
6	80/90	105/50
7	90/100	120/50
8	100/110	135/70
9	110/120	150/70
10–25	120/130	150/70
26	110/120	135/70
27	95/105	120/50
28	80/90	105/50
29	70/80	90/50
30–32	70/80	80/50

Notes:

1 Total weight of main belt: **1010.88 tonnes**; thicker plates of cemented armour, end plates of special steel.

2 Plates 1–7 of the upper belt forward were of 40mm special steel; plate 8 40–90mm; plates 9–10 (beneath fwd casemate) 90mm.

3 Plates 1 and 2 of the fwd and after casemates were of 164mm special steel.

PROTECTION

Hull

Protection for the hull was virtually identical to that for *Ernest Renan*. The two-strake main belt, which was of cemented armour over the central part of the ship, was 3.7m high: 2.3m above the waterline at normal load, 1.4m below. The lower strake was composed of thirty-two plates with a maximum thickness of 150mm, and the upper strake by thirty-two plates with a maximum thickness of 130mm; both strakes were secured to a teak backing 70/90mm thick. The main belt was closed at the after end by a transverse bulkhead of 84mm special steel secured to a double thickness of 8mm mild steel, and there was a light upper belt of 40mm special steel secured directly to the hull plating that extended from the bow to the forward casemate. The latter comprised ten plates (*vice* eight in the *Gambettas*, nine in *Ernest Renan*) to take account of the different configuration of the 194mm casemates, the face of which extended farther aft than in the *Gambettas* and *Ernest Renan*.

The upper protective deck (PBS) was formed by three layers of 10mm mild steel (total 30mm), the lower protective deck (PBI) by three layers of 15mm mild steel (total 45mm). The reinforcing plates on the upper slopes of the PBI that replaced the top layer were of 35mm special steel (total 65mm). These figures were identical to those for the *Gambettas* and *Ernest Renan* except for a slight (1mm) reduction in the thickness of each of the layers of the upper protective deck.

WEIGHT OF PROTECTION (*EDGAR QUINET*)

	No of plates	Composition	Weight
Main belt	2 x 64 (p&s)	cemented/special steel[1]	1011t
Upper belt	2 x 10 (p&s)	special steel	78t
PBS (upper 2 layers)		mild steel	310t
PBI (upper 2 layers)		mild steel	493t
35mm plates 1st Platform Deck	2 x 18 (p&s) +1	special steel	96t
Aft transverse b/head	2	special steel	6t
194 turrets + barbettes	?	special steel[2]	956t
194 casemates	4 x 4 (outer walls)	special steel	201t
Hoists/RF screens		special steel	22t
Conning tower + comms tube	?	cemented/special steel[3]	49t
Armoured deck coamings	n/a	special steel	117t
		Total	3339t

Notes:

1 Only the thick plates of the upper/lower belt were cemented (see table for details).

2 The turret walls were of special steel throughout; the turrets were balanced, so there was no need for thick rear plates.

3 The face and side walls of the CT were cemented; the rear wall and the communications tube were of special steel.

Source: Official plans.

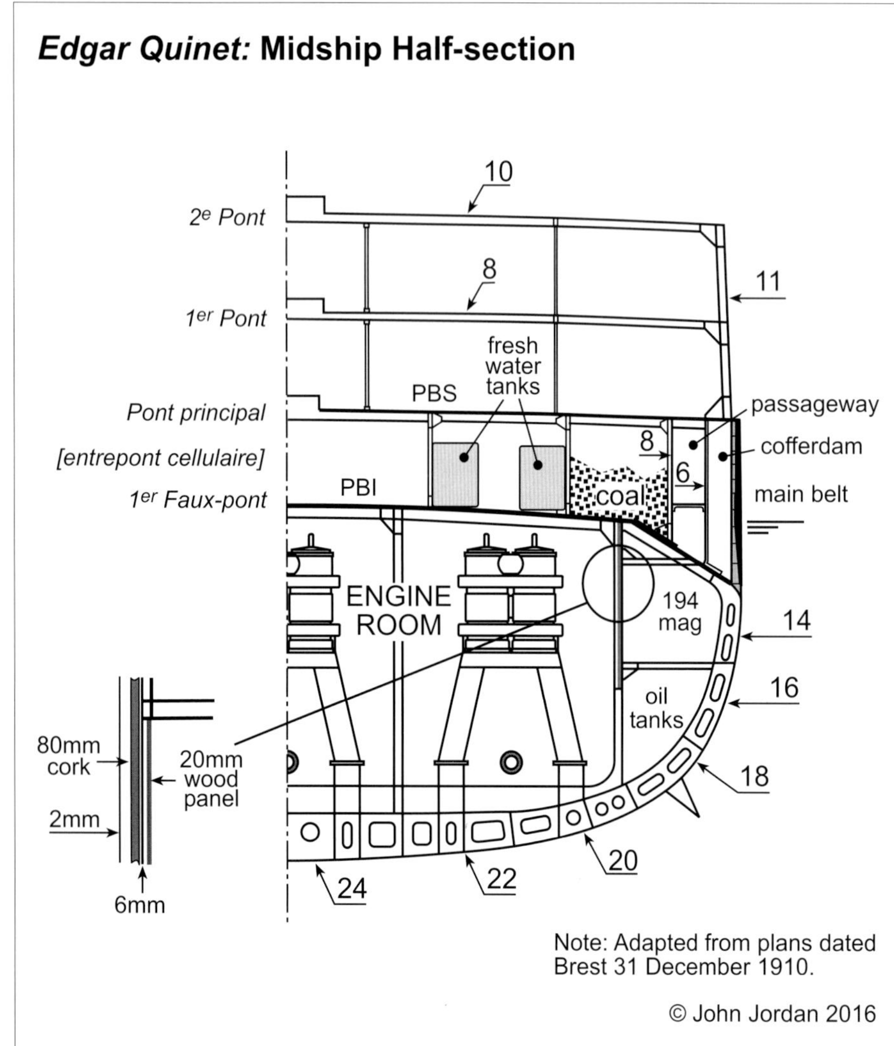

Turrets and casemates

Protection for the face and sides of the twin turrets was increased in thickness from 156mm in *Jules Michelet* and *Ernest Renan* to 174mm on the face and sides and 144mm on the rear. As the new turret had a more traditional configuration there was no need for a thick rear balancing plate, and special steel was used throughout. Protection for the single wing turrets was reduced in thickness to 144mm on the face and sides of the turret, likewise of special steel. The fixed *parapet* was of 151mm special steel for the twin turret and 148mm for the single, and the cylindrical hoops around the ammunition trunks were 92mm and 80mm respectively. The increase in armour thicknesses was in part compensated by the move from four to three wing turrets; nevertheless, overall weight of armour for the turrets and barbettes was 956 tonnes as against 624 tonnes for *Ernest Renan* – an increase of 332 tonnes or 53 per cent.

The incorporation of each pair of casemates into a single redoubt extending the full width of the ship likewise had a cost in weight, and the increase in the calibre of the casemate guns from 164.7mm to 194mm required a commensurate increase in armour thickness. The outer faces of the redoubts were of 164mm special steel (*vice* 138mm in *Ernest Renan*). The inboard walls of the redoubts were of 102mm special steel, and the end walls, which effectively replaced the transverse bulkheads for protection against enfilading fire, were of 128mm special steel. Total weight of armour for these redoubts was 201 tonnes, compared with a lesser figure of 151 tonnes for *Ernest Renan* (includes forward transverse bulkhead).

Conning tower

The walls of the conning tower were protected by plates of cemented armour of uniform 174mm thickness. The roof was composed of three plates with a combined thickness of 40mm, and the communications tube was formed with hoops of 130mm special steel above the

PERFORMANCE ON 10-HOUR FULL-POWER TRIALS

	Date	Speed	Horsepower	Shaft Revs	Consumption	Boiler
Ernest Renan[1]	12 Mar 1909	24.44kts	37,023CV	136.25rpm	0.778kg/h/cv	Niclausse
Edgar Quinet	6 Aug 1910	23.49kts	37,189CV	135.24rpm	0.759kg/h/cv	Belleville
Waldeck-Rousseau	8 Dec 1911	23.10kts	36,110CV	129.23rpm	0.871kg/h/cv	Niclausse

Note:

1 *Ernest Renan* has been included here for comparison; she had the same hull-form and a similar propulsion system to *Edgar Quinet* and *Waldeck-Rousseau*.

Source: CAAP: inventaire 432, sous-série 5i cartons 67 (*ER*), 63 (*EQ*), 183 (*WR*).

1st deck, and by a double layer of 15mm hardened steel below, where it passed through the forward redoubt; between the floor of the redoubt and the main deck there were hoops of 105mm special steel. The overall weight of armour on the conning tower was 32.9 tonnes; for the communications tube the corresponding figure was 15.9 tonnes.

MACHINERY

The propulsion machinery installed in *Edgar Quinet* and *Waldeck-Rousseau* broadly followed the pattern established by *Ernest Renan*. There were two fewer boilers (forty *vice* forty-two), but the position and relative size of the four boiler rooms was unchanged; in the middle group of boilers at the fore and after ends of the ship there were two rows of three, whereas in *Ernest Renan* there had been a row of four in the inboard boiler rooms and a row of three in the outer rooms (see GA Plans). There was no attempt to conduct further experiments with the advanced Guyot–du Temple small-watertube boiler. Instead the *Marine Nationale* took the 'safer' option, installing Belleville large-watertube boilers in *Edgar Quinet* and Niclausse in *Waldeck-Rousseau*. Although this had a small negative impact on initial performance, the Belleville and Niclausse boilers were now established in French naval service, and the same two types of boiler were being fitted in the contemporary battleships of the *Patrie* and *Danton* classes. This facilitated the training of personnel, and eased maintenance by

Below: *Edgar Quinet* with all boilers lit, departing Toulon. The white band on the third funnel marks her out as the third ship of the 1st Light Division. The photo was probably taken between 1912 and 1914. *(Private collection)*

As France's newest and most powerful armoured cruiser, *Edgar Quinet* was selected to take President Armand Fallières on a visit to Amsterdam in early July 1911. *(Private collection)*

ensuring that spare parts for the boilers were stocked in numbers.

The three powerful four-cylinder engines were designed for the same 36,000CV output as those of *Ernest Renan*. Those that powered *Waldeck-Rousseau* were built by Indret, while the engines mounted in *Edgar Quinet* were built by Schneider. The engines reverted to the traditional cylinder arrangement (HP>IP>LP>LP); the reasons for this are unclear, but it is possible that factory trials of the Indret-built engines installed in *Jules Michelet* and *Ernest Renan* failed to yield the hoped-for benefits. Cylinder diameters were: HP 1.18m, IP 1.73m and LP 1.98m, as in *Ernest Renan*.

During a ten-hour trial that took place on 6 August 1910, *Edgar Quinet* achieved a speed of 23.49 knots with 37,189CV. More than a year later, on 8 December 1911, *Waldeck-Rousseau* attained 23.10 knots with 36,110CV during a full-power trial with all boilers lit. The accompanying table has full details of the results of these trials.

The auxiliary machinery was as in *Ernest Renan*, with the dynamo rooms directly above the midships magazines.

CONSTRUCTION AND EARLY SERVICE

Laid down towards the end of 1905, *Edgar Quinet* was launched on 21 September 1907. Sea trials began on 2 June 1910, and these were followed by her official trials. A 24-hour trial on 17–18 August was abandoned at the request of the machinery contractor due to heavy expenditure of lubrication oil, but the problem was quickly resolved and a second 24-hour trial on 23–24 August was successful. The transfer of the ship to Toulon on 23–27 January 1911 (*traversée d'endurance*) was conducted at an average speed of 20.3 knots.

Completion of *Waldeck-Rousseau* took even longer. Launched on 4 March 1908, the ship began sea trials only in January 1911. On 2 February a ten-hour trial had to be abandoned when the port propeller struck an uncharted rock, bending two of the three blades and damaging the shaft. New propeller blades and shafts had to be ordered from Indret, and repairs took until July. Following further trials, the feed pumps had to be repaired and the baffle plates modified. The ship was assigned to the 1st Squadron while awaiting the delivery of the necessary parts. Full-power trials then

Below: *Waldeck-Rousseau* during her full-power trials, when she attained a speed of 23.1 knots with 36,110CV. *(DR)*

Left: *Edgar Quinet* in the Nordzeekanaal linking the North Sea port of Ijmuiden to Amsterdam, during the visit of President Fallières to the Netherlands in July 1911. Note the immaculate paintwork of the ship, which had only recently commissioned. *(Private collection)*

took place during December, and the machinery was finally signed off on 24 January 1912.

On completion both ships joined the Light Squadron of the 1st Squadron in the Mediterranean. In July 1911 President Armand Fallières embarked in *Edgar Quinet* for a visit to Amsterdam, and both ships took part in the Great Naval Review of 4 September 1911, with *Edgar Quinet* embarking the Minister of Marine, Théophile Delcassé. When the squadron was reorganised in January 1912, *Waldeck-Rousseau* became the first ship of the 1st Light Division, flying the flag of Vice Admiral Auvert (commanding the 1st Light Squadron), and *Edgar Quinet* the third ship; their consort was their half-sister *Ernest Renan*. However, on 22 February *Waldeck-Rousseau* ran aground at Golfe-Juan during a storm, causing serious damage to the hull. She was refloated and towed to Toulon, where she was docked for repairs that lasted until 9 August. She was recommissioned in early September and left on the 8th to rejoin the *Armée Navale* in the Adriatic (see Chapter 11). She would resume her role as flagship of the 1st Light Squadron.

Ernest Renan & Quinet Classes: Early Service

	Ernest Renan	Edgar Quinet	Waldeck-Rousseau
1909	1st Lt Div Med	Building	Building
1910		Trials	↓
1911		1st Lt Div Med	Trials
1912			1st Lt Div Med
1913			
1914	↓	↓	↓

EVALUATION

Edgar Quinet and *Waldeck-Rousseau* were to be the last French armoured cruisers. By the time the second ship was laid down in June 1906 it was already clear that the world had moved on: the first all-big-gun armoured cruisers powered by turbines had been laid down in Britain, and Germany would follow in early 1908 with the construction of *Von der Tann*. However, the conventional armoured cruiser armed with medium guns and powered by reciprocating engines did not become obsolete overnight. The last three RN armoured cruisers of the *Minotaur* class, which were comparable in size, firepower and speed to *Edgar Quinet* and her sister (and arguably less well protected), did not enter service until 1908, and it was only the five-year building times of the French ships that consigned them to a footnote of naval history.

'Battle cruisers' (as they were re-christened by the Royal Navy in 1911) would be built only by the two North Sea navies. In the Mediterranean neither the Italian nor the Austro-Hungarian fleets – France's potential opponents – possessed battle cruisers. Even Admiral Jellicoe saw a continuing fleet role for the armoured cruiser. At Jutland in May 1916 the battleships of the Grand Fleet, cruising in six columns each of four ships, were preceded by a scouting line comprising two four-ship squadrons of the latest armoured cruisers. The cruisers steamed in line abreast and within visual signalling distance of one another some distance ahead of the fleet,[9] with a linking ship between the scouting line and the main body to relay sighting information to the flagship. Had France been faced by the Italian fleet in the western Mediterranean, Admiral Boué de Lapeyrère would

[9] GFBO Cruiser Instructions specified a distance of 20 miles, but poor visibility on the day did not allow this.

Above: *Waldeck-Rousseau* as flagship of the elite 1st Light Division, with a single broad white band on the first funnel. *(Private collection)*

undoubtedly have employed similar tactics using his own two divisions of armoured cruisers;[10] the fleet organisation of 1914 even included a fast protected cruiser, *Jurien de la Gravière*, to serve as a dispatch vessel attached to the flagship, the brand-new dreadnought battleship *Courbet*. In the event the French fleet's opponent was the navy of Austria-Hungary, which never ventured outside the narrow waters of the Adriatic. The Adriatic favoured the deployment of light craft: light cruisers, destroyers and submarines. Battleships and armoured cruisers were vulnerable in these waters, as would be demonstrated by the torpedoing of *Jean Bart* in December 1914 and the loss of *Léon Gambetta* to the Austro-Hungarian submarine *U5* in April 1915 (see Chapter 11).

The problem for both Jellicoe and for Boué de Lapeyrère was the role the armoured cruisers would perform during the main action. Jellicoe envisaged the ships taking up position clear of the head and rear of the main battle line to engage the enemy's light craft. It is more likely that Boué de Lapeyrère, who had no battle cruisers, would have used his armoured cruisers as 'fast divisions' to outflank the enemy line and to put pressure on the enemy van (or rear) while the enemy's battleships were fully engaged with their opposite numbers. This had worked well enough for Togo at Tsushima – in part due to the inaccuracy of the Russian fire – but at Jutland the British armoured cruisers exposed themselves to the enemy's battle line while pursuing the crippled German light cruiser *Wiesbaden* and suffered heavily in consequence: the cruisers *Defence* and *Warrior* were disabled in quick succession with heavy loss of life. Armoured cruisers could simply not withstand the fire of battleships, and would never again be exposed in this way.

The problem for the armoured cruiser as a type was that it was neither fish nor fowl: armoured cruisers were too costly to perform the scouting role, for which light cruisers sufficed; on the other hand their guns were unable to penetrate battleship armour, and they were too vulnerable to the fire of the bigger guns to be able to stand in the line of battle. Inadequate protection would likewise become an issue for the lightly-armoured British 'battle cruisers', but their major-calibre guns did at least enable them to engage enemy battleships with a chance of success.

[10] The French did not have the option of using turbine-powered light cruisers, favoured by the British Battle Cruiser Fleet and its German counterpart for this role, as they had failed to build a single scout cruiser prior to 1914.

CHAPTER 10:

ORGANISATION

THE ADMINISTRATIVE STATUS OF SHIPS

After launch, a ship was manned ready to run her sea trials when fitting-out was well advanced. The Navy designated an officer – generally a *capitaine de vaisseau* (CV) for an armoured cruiser – to take command of the ship and supervise her progress to completion. The cruiser was from this point designated *armé pour essais*.[1] Preliminary trials began with static trials of the machinery (*essais au point fixe*), followed by trials in open waters (*essais en route libre*). These were followed by official trials which included a three-hour (later ten-hour) speed trial (*essai à puissance maximum*) and fuel-consumption trials (*essais de consommation*) at different shaft revolutions and power loadings. The ten-hour trial, which for ships built in the Atlantic was generally run on the Iles de Glenans/Ile de Groix range in Brittany, included a three-hour run at forced draught (*feux poussés*). Following official trials the ship's machinery was dismantled for inspection, and there was a final trial to check that everything was operating correctly (*essai de bon fonctionnement*).

The term *armement définitif* in practice corresponded to the physical completion of the ship.[2] The ship would now have her full peacetime complement and would have all consumables embarked. The term *clôture d'armement* signified that the ship and all its fittings and equipment had been accepted for service. The date of *admission au service actif* was the date the ship entered service. She was now in theory complete – although in practice late delivery of equipment meant that this was not always the case – and her crew had a reached a certain level of readiness. She was then generally incorporated into a division within a squadron.

Once in service, the ship was normally in a condition termed *armé* (in commission). Prior to 1914 each of the two main squadrons was allocated 'replacement ships' (*bâtiments de remplacement*) with a reduced crew (50–60 per cent) which could quickly be

[1] The terms *armé* and *armement* mean 'manned' and 'manning' respectively; this can be confusing to an English reader. The phrase *armé pour essais* literally means 'manned for trials'.

[2] Key items of equipment including guns were often mounted only after sea trials. If the ship was built in a private shipyard these items were generally installed at Brest or Lorient.

Left: The Great Naval Review of 4 September 1911, held off Toulon. The battleship *Masséna*, with President Armand Fallières on board, heads for the newly-completed battleships of the *Danton* class forming part of the right-hand column. *(Private collection)*

ARMOURED CRUISER DIVISIONS 1903–1914

Esc Nord	*Escadre du Nord*
Esc Méd	*Escadre de la Méditerranée*
Esc EO	*Escadre de l'Extrême-Orient*
EL	*Escadre légère*
DNEO	*Division navale de l'Extrême-Orient*
DL	*Division légère*
DC	*Division de croiseurs*
VA	*Vice-amiral*
CA	*Contre-amiral*

1903: Escadre du Nord – Escadre de la Méditerranée

Jan 1903	EL Esc Méd: *Montcalm* (CA Le Dô), *Chanzy*, *Latouche-Tréville*
20 Mar 1903	Esc EO: *Montcalm* (VA Bayle), *Châteaurenault* + *Gueydon* late 1903 + *Sully* early 1904
1 Jun 1903	DC Esc Nord: *Jeanne d'Arc* (CA Bugard), *Guichen*, *Dupuy-de-Lôme* (*Marseillaise* joined Oct)
4 Jul 1904	EL Esc Méd: *Desaix* (CA Antoine), *Kléber* + *Marseillaise* Oct 1904
Sep 1904	1st DC Esc Nord: *Gloire* (CA Bugard), *Amiral Aube*, *Condé* (replaced by *Jeanne d'Arc*)
4 Aug 1905	1st DC Esc Nord: *Léon Gambetta* (VA Gigon), *Gueydon*, *Dupetit-Thouars*
Sep 1905	EL Esc Méd: *Marseillaise* (CA Campion), *Condé*, *Kléber*
Oct 1905	Esc EO: *Montcalm* (VA Bayle), *Gueydon*, *Dupetit-Thouars*
Jul 1906	EL Esc Méd: *Jeanne d'Arc* (CA Campion), *Condé*, *Kléber* (replaced by *Desaix* Nov)
Jan 1907	1st DC Esc Nord: *Léon Gambetta* (VA Gigon), *Gueydon*, *Dupetit-Thouars* 2nd DC Esc Nord: *Gloire* (CA Decoux), *Amiral Aube*
Jun 1907	EL Esc Méd: *Jules Ferry* (CA Krantz), *Victor Hugo*, *Condé*, *Desaix*
Oct 1907	1st DC Esc Nord: *Léon Gambetta* (VA Jauréguiberry), *Amiral Aube*, *Dupetit-Thouars* 2nd DC Esc Nord: *Gloire* (CA Philibert), *Gueydon*, *Jeanne d'Arc*
Jan 1908	2nd DC Esc Nord: *Marseillaise* (CA Thierry)
Apr 1908	EL Esc Méd: *Jules Ferry* (CA Krantz), *Victor Hugo* DC Esc Nord: *Marseillaise* (CA Thierry), *Gueydon*, *Jeanne d'Arc*
1 Jan 1909	EL Esc Méd: *Jules Ferry* (CA Krantz), *Victor Hugo*, *Jules Michelet*, *Condé*
Jul 1909	1st DC Esc Nord: *Léon Gambetta* (VA Jauréguiberry), *Amiral Aube*, *Dupetit-Thouars* 2nd DC Esc Nord: *Marseillaise* (CA Auvert), *Gueydon*

5 Oct 1909: 2e Escadre (Brest) – 1re Escadre (Toulon)

Oct 1909	EL Esc Méd became 1st DL 1st Esc: *Jules Ferry* (CA Pivet), *Victor Hugo*, *Jules Michelet*, *Ernest Renan* 2nd DC Esc Nord became 2nd DL 1st Esc: *Marseillaise* (CA Auvert), *Gloire*, *Dupetit-Thouars*
Jan 1910	1st DL 1st Esc: *Jules Ferry* (CA Pivet), *Ernest Renan*, *Léon Gambetta* DNEO: *Montcalm* (CA De la Croix de Castries)

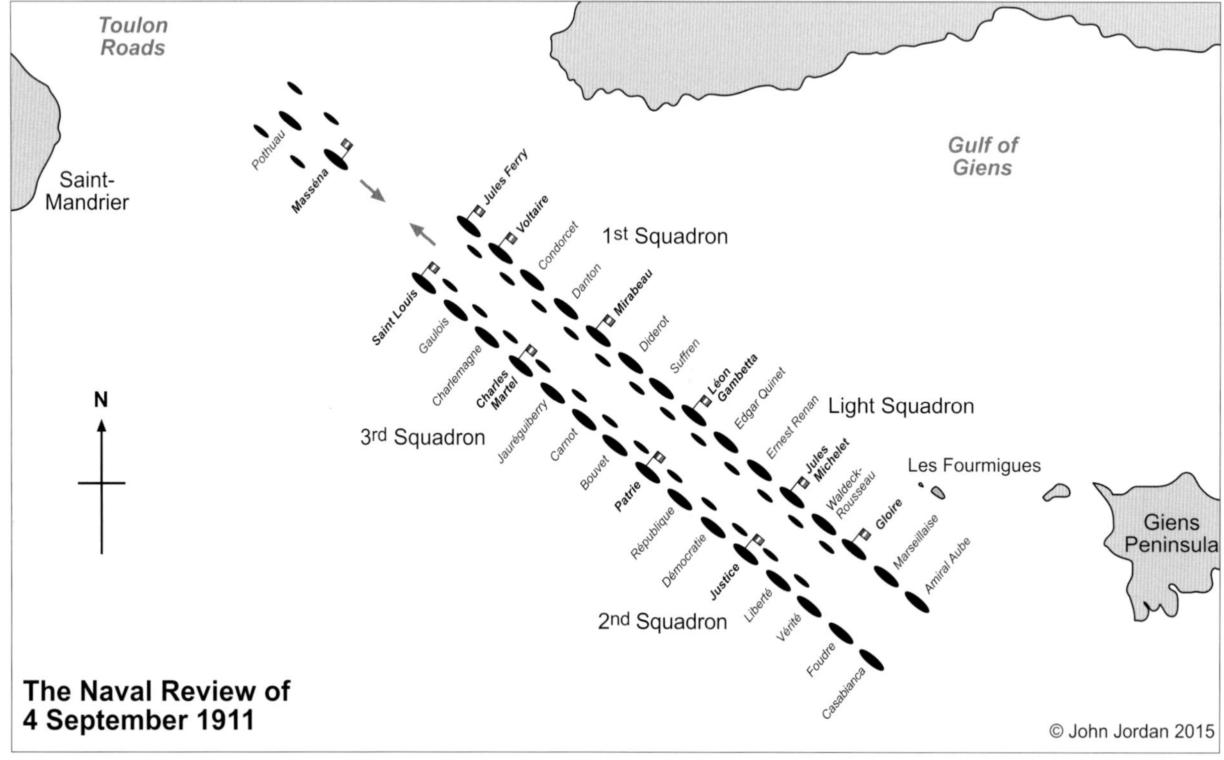

The Naval Review of 4 September 1911

© John Jordan 2015

Jun 1910	1st DL 1st Esc: *Jules Ferry* (CA Pivet), *Jules Michelet*, *Victor Hugo* 2nd DL 1st Esc: *Marseillaise* (CA Auvert), *Condé*, *Gloire*
Aug 1910	1st DL became 2nd DL: *Jules Ferry* (CA Pivet), *Jules Michelet*, *Ernest Renan*
Oct 1910	New 1st DL 1st Esc: *Léon Gambetta* (CA ??), *Ernest Renan*, *Edgar Quinet*
1 Nov 1910	DNEO: *Montcalm* (CA de la Croix de Castries), *Dupleix*
Jan 1911	DC 2nd Esc: *Gloire* (CA Dufaur de Lajarte), *Amiral Aube*, *Condé*
1911	Div de réserve 2nd Esc: *Gueydon*, *Dupetit-Thouars*, *Guichen*
4 Apr 1911	2nd DL 1st Esc: *Léon Gambetta* (CA Dartige du Fournet), *Jules Ferry*, *Victor Hugo*
21 Apr 1911	DNEO: *Dupleix* (CA de la Croix de Castries), *Kléber*

1 Aug 1911: 3e Escadre (Brest) – 1re & 2e Escadres (Toulon)

Aug 1911	[Entry into service *Danton* class] 2nd Esc became 3rd Esc; cruisers Brest became 3rd DL *Groupe de réserve*: *Amiral Aube*, *Gueydon*
4 Sep 1911	1st DL 1st Esc: *Léon Gambetta* (CA Dartige du Fournet), *Edgar Quinet*, *Ernest Renan* 2nd DL 2nd Esc: *Jules Michelet* (CA Nicol), *Waldeck-Rousseau*, *Jules Ferry* 3rd DL 3rd Esc: *Gloire* (CA Favereau), *Marseillaise*, *Amiral Aube*
Nov 1911	*2e Groupe de réserve* 3rd Esc: *Amiral Aube*, *Gueydon*, *Dupetit-Thouars*, *Guichen*
Jan/Feb 1912	1st DL 1st Esc: *Waldeck-Rousseau* (VA Auvert 10 Feb), *Ernest Renan*, *Edgar Quinet* 2nd DL 1st Esc: *Léon Gambetta* (CA Dartige du Fournet), *Victor Hugo*, *Jules Ferry* (Div formed 10 Feb) 3rd DL 3rd Esc: *Gloire* (CA Favereau), *Marseillaise*, *Condé*
1912	*Groupe de réserve* 3rd Esc: *Amiral Aube*, *Gueydon*

17 Oct 1912: 2e Escadre Légère (Brest) – Armée Navale with 1re/2e/3e Escadres de Ligne, 1re Escadre Légère (Toulon)

French Fleet concentrated in Mediterranean following Anglo-French agreement of 23 Jul 1912; Bizerte now operational. *Armée Navale* constituted day after departure of 3rd BS for Mediterranean.

Oct 1912	*Div de réserve* 2nd EL Brest: *Amiral Aube*, *Gueydon*, *Dupetit-Thouaurs*
Jan 1913	1st DC 2nd EL: Gloire (CA Favereau), *Marseillaise*, *Condé*
	DNEO: *Montcalm* (CA de Kérillis), *Dupleix*
Oct 1913	*2e Div de Réserve* 2nd EL: *Gueydon*, *Dupetit-Thouars*
10 Nov 1913	1st DC 2nd EL *Marseillaise* (CA Rouyer), *Condé*, *Amiral Aube* *Div d'instruction de l'Atlantique*: *Gloire* (CA Bouxin), *Gueydon*, *Dupetit-Thouars*
Jan 1914	1st DC 2nd EL: *Marseillaise* (CA Rouyer), *Condé*, *Amiral Aube*
20 Mar 1914	1st DL 1st EL: *Jules Michelet* (CA Ramey de Sugny), *Ernest Renan*, *Edgar Quinet* (*Waldeck-Rousseau* under repair until Oct)

Left: *Dupetit-Thouars* in the white livery of ships deployed to the Far East; the funnels and superstructures are painted yellow. *(Private collection)*

Right: *Condé* at Toulon in 1904–05. She has the paint scheme worn by major French units until January 1908: black hull, buff upperworks, underside of Schweinfurth green with a thin white band at the waterline. *(Bougault, NHHC 63908)*

Below: *Edgar Quinet* off the coast of Provence shortly before the Great War. The single white band on the third funnel marks her out as the third ship of the 1st Light Division. *(Private collection)*

reactivated to replace an operational vessel needing urgent repairs. For a major refit or repair ships were placed in 'normal' reserve (*réserve normale*), with a skeleton crew. Ships nearing the end of their service lives were placed in 'special' reserve (*réserve spéciale*). Although a ship in normal reserve could quickly be returned to service if assigned a full complement, a ship in special reserve could take a long time to become operational again, as she would require repairs and refurbishment. Special reserve was generally followed by striking the ship from the list (*rayé*) and then, unless the hull was to be used for accommodation, by sale for scrap.

ORGANISATION

During the period in question, French naval forces were distributed between two major formations based respectively at Toulon and Brest. Some vessels, mainly protected cruisers, sloops and gunboats, were deployed overseas to naval stations in the Antilles, West Africa, the Indian Ocean, and the Far East. Deployments to the Far East station, based at Saigon but with regular port visits to China, Singapore, Japan, and the French territories in the South Pacific, could last for two or even three years.

When serving with the fleet, cruisers were organised in divisions, in principle of three/four ships. From 1900 the most modern battleships were assigned to the Mediterranean Squadron (*Escadre de la Méditerranée*), based at Toulon, the older battleships to the Northern Squadron (*Escadre du Nord*), based at Brest. The few armoured cruisers available – *Dupuy-de-Lôme*, *Pothuau*, and the four units of the *Amiral Charner* class – were divided between the two squadrons. Each of the two squadrons was commanded by a vice admiral who devised his own tactical organisation independently of the other: the cruiser division in the Northern Squadron was generally designated *Division de croiseurs*, that of the Mediterranean Squadron the Light Division (*Division légère*).

During 1903–04 no fewer than eleven new armoured cruisers[3] entered service with the *Marine Nationale*. The older cruisers were placed in reserve, and a three-ship division was despatched to the Far East to provide a 'presence' during the Russo-Japanese War. When it returned to metropolitan France the Northern Squadron was expanded, in January 1907, to include

[3] *Jeanne d'Arc*, two ships of the *Gueydon* class, three of the *Dupleix* class and five of the *Gloire* class.

COST OF INDIVIDUAL SHIPS

Name	Prog No	Builder	Cost (sterling)	Cost (FF)[1]
Dupuy-de-Lôme		Brest	£652,354	16,308,850FF
Amiral Charner		Rochefort	£353,200	8,830,000FF
Chanzy		Ch Gironde	£360,000	9,000,000FF
Latouche-Tréville		Brest	ditto	ditto
Bruix		Rochefort	£409,622	10,240,550FF
Pothuau	D1>C1[2]	Le Havre (FC Med)	£384,000	9,600,000FF
D'Entrecasteaux	C1>D1	La Seyne	£667,740	16,693,500FF
Jeanne d'Arc	D2>C2	Toulon	£875,847	21,896,175FF
Dupleix	D3[3]	Rochefort	£652,354	16,308,850FF
Desaix	D4	Ch Loire	£762,759	19,068,975FF
Kléber	D5	Ch Gironde	£770,320	19,258,000FF
Gueydon	C5	Lorient	£817,994	20,449,850FF
Montcalm	C6	La Seyne	£902,809	22,570,225FF
Dupetit-Thouars	C3	Toulon	£831,839	20,795,975FF
Gloire	C7	Lorient	£883,269	22,081,725FF
Condé	C4[4]	Lorient	£863,799	21,594,975FF
Sully	C8	La Seyne	£954,536	23,863,400FF
Marseillaise	C9	Brest	£881,270	22,031,750FF
Amiral Aube	C10	Penhoët	£973,440	24,336,000FF
Léon Gambetta	C11	Brest	£1,169,940	29,248,500FF
Jules Ferry	C12	Cherbourg	£1,155,915	28,897,875FF
Victor Hugo	C13	Lorient	£1,229,932	30,748,300FF
Jules Michelet	C14	Lorient	£1,204,107	30,102,675FF
Ernest Renan	C15	Penhoët	£1,410,000	35,250,000FF
Edgar Quinet	C16	Brest	£1,307,536	32,688,400FF
Waldeck-Rousseau	C17	Lorient	£1,301,380	32,534,500FF

Notes:

1 Based on a rate of £1 = 25FF.

2 Prior to 1896 C = station cruiser (sheathed); D = fleet cruiser; in 1896 the letters were reversed.

3 D2 was the protected cruiser *Jurien de la Gravière*.

4 *Condé* was originally to have been funded alongside *Gueydon*) under the Extraordinary Budget of 1897 and was allocated to Cherbourg. The order for the ship was subsequently transferred to Lorient, by which time the 9500-tonne type had been superseded by the 10,000-tonne design; however, *Condé* retained her original programme number.

Source: *Brassey's Naval Annual*.

two cruiser divisions. Individual units – notably the 'station' cruisers of the *Dupleix* class – continued to be deployed to French overseas stations in the Atlantic (Fort-de-France in the West Indies and Dakar in West Africa), and one or two armoured cruisers were generally based at Saigon in the Far East.

In October 1909, following the entry into service of the six battleships of the *Patrie* class, there was a complete reorganisation of the fleet to reflect the new strategic situation and the enhanced naval forces available: the Mediterranean Squadron at Toulon became the 1st Squadron (*1re Escadre*), and the Northern Squadron at Brest the 2nd Squadron (*2e Escadre*). Taking advantage of the *Entente Cordiale* and the deterioration in relations between Britain and Germany, the bulk of the French fleet was now stationed in the Mediterranean,[4] and the 1st Squadron would be allocated the most modern and powerful ships. The 1st Light Division was formed at Toulon with the latest cruisers of the *Gambetta* class, and the 2nd Cruiser Division at Brest, comprising three modern ships of the *Gueydon* and *Gloire* classes, was transferred to the Mediterranean, becoming the 2nd Light Division.

When the six battleships of the *Danton* class and the two powerful armoured cruisers of the *Edgar Quinet* class entered service in 1911, this trend was accelerated. The 1st Squadron at Toulon would now comprise two squadrons each of six of the most modern battleships (*1re & 2e Escadres de ligne*) and a light squadron with the six latest armoured cruisers (*1re & 2e Divisions légères*); the 2nd Squadron at Brest would comprise a single six-ship squadron of the older battleships (*3e Escadre de ligne*) plus a three-ship division of armoured cruisers of the *Gloire* class (*3e Division légère*).

On October 1912, following the Anglo-French agreement of 23 July, the 3rd Battle Squadron was transferred from Brest to the Mediterranean,[5] and the naval force at Toulon became the *1re Armée Navale* under

[4] The major new base at Bizerte and its dockyard at Sidi-Abdallah were now operational.

[5] There was significant opposition to this move from local people and from their elected representatives, who took part in public protests. The Deputies and Senators justified their concerns by claiming that the French Atlantic coast would be overly exposed to attack from the powerful German High Seas Fleet in the absence of firm British guarantees. Local people were equally concerned about the loss of business the departure of the battleships represented; moreover, a large percentage of the sailors serving with the *Marine Nationale* came from Brittany, the region around Brest.

Below: Armoured cruisers of the 2nd Light Division at Toulon before the war. The flagship *Léon Gambetta* (two white bands on the first funnel) is photographed from her sister *Jules Ferry* (third ship – two white bands on the third funnel). Note the distinctive goose-neck cranes on *Jules Ferry* which served to distinguish her from her two sisters. *(Private collection)*

the command of Admiral Boué de Lapeyrère. The core of the *2e Escadre légère* at Brest was the 1st Cruiser Division comprising *Gloire* (CA Favereau), *Marseillaise* and *Condé*. The older armoured cruisers of the *Dupleix* and *Gueydon* classes were placed in reserve; they would be reactivated in August 1914 to form two additional cruiser divisions.

THE NAVAL YEAR

Training was undertaken according to an annual cycle termed the *année d'instruction*. The latter was derived traditionally from the French school year, and ran from October to July. A proportion of the crew of each ship, in part made up of conscripts, was renewed during the summer, with training recommencing in the Autumn. Training followed a logical progression: work-up with single ships, followed by exercises first with the division and then with the fleet. Most of these exercises, both for single ships and for groups, took place between the coast of southern France and Corsica in the Mediterranean, and off Brest and in the Bay of Biscay in the Atlantic. They were interrupted by short stays in the anchorages off the French coast (Villefranche, Les Salins and Golfe-Juan in the south of France, Quiberon or Douarnenez Bays in Brittany).[6]

In general, the training year ended with major exercises in which the squadrons based at Brest and Toulon were combined, generally during the summer months. These combined manoeuvres sometimes took place in the western Mediterranean and off the coasts of North Africa, sometimes in the Atlantic as far south as the coasts of West Africa, and often ended with a review of the fleet by the current Minister of Marine or the President of the Republic. The most important of these reviews took place on 4 September 1911 off Toulon, following the entry into service of the battleships of the *Danton* class. The fleet, led by the armoured cruiser *Jules Ferry* flying the flag of Vice Admiral Jauréguiberry, was reviewed by President Armand Fallières in the battleship *Masséna*, and Minister of Marine Théophile Delcassé was hosted by

[6] For a map of the Toulon environs and the Mediterranean ports of Provence see Jordan and Caresse, *French Battleships of World War One*, p 220.

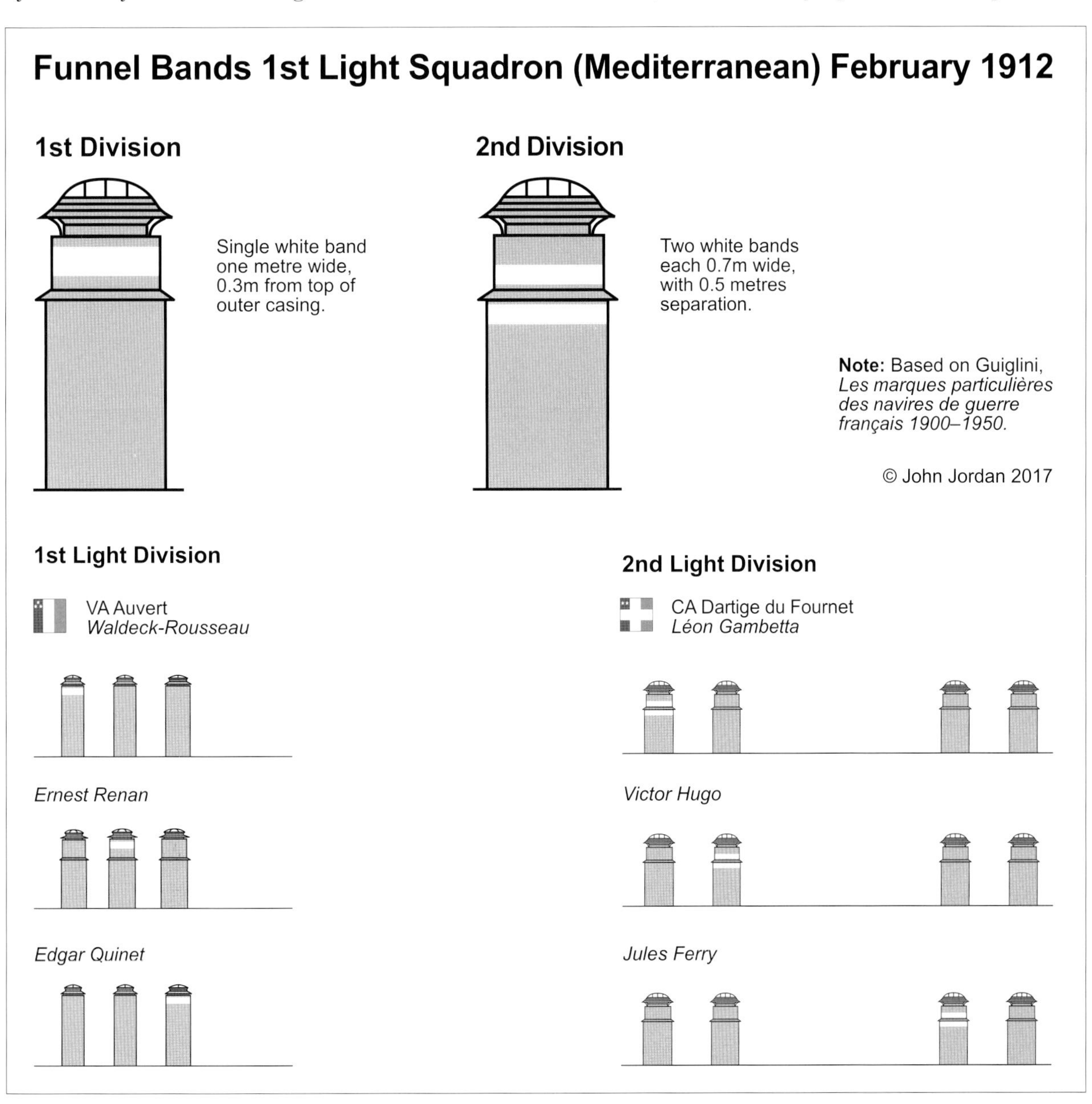

IDENTIFICATION MARKINGS 1912–1914

February 1912

1re Escadre légère (Toulon)

1re Division (VA Auvert)	2e Division (CA Dartige du Fournet)
Waldeck-Rousseau (1 white band on 1st)	*Léon Gambetta* (2 white bands on 1st)
Ernest Renan (1 white band on 2nd)	*Victor Hugo* (2 white bands on 2nd)
Edgar Quinet (1 white band on 3rd)	*Jules Ferry* (2 white bands on 3rd)

February 1914

1re Escadre légère (Toulon)

1re Division (RA Ramey de Sugny)	2e Division (CA Senès)
Jules Michelet (1 white band on 1st)	*Léon Gambetta* (2 white bands on 1st)
Ernest Renan (1 white band on 2nd)	*Victor Hugo* (2 white bands on 2nd)
Edgar Quinet (1 white band on 3rd)	*Jules Ferry* (2 white bands on 3rd)

2e Escadre légère (Brest)

1re Division (CA Rouyer)
Marseillaise (1 white band on 1st)
Condé (1 white band on 2nd)
Amiral Aube (1 white band on 3rd)

the brand-new cruiser *Edgar Quinet*. No fewer than fifty-four ships took part, of which nineteen were battleships (see accompanying map and photograph). The following day the fleet left for manoeuvres off the coasts of Provence under the direction of Admiral Jauréguiberry, returning to Toulon on the 16th.

PAINT SCHEMES

Until 1908 French battleships and cruisers had the following paint scheme: the underside was Schweinfurth green; the upper hull was black, and the dividing line at the waterline was marked by a white band approximately 0.25m wide (introduced in 1899); the funnels, masts and superstructures were a buff colour designated *toile mouillée claire* (literally 'light wet canvas'), with black-painted funnel caps. Decks were partially covered with a dark red linoleum secured by brass battens; major vessels often had wood planking on the weather decks. Ships deployed in tropical waters were painted white overall to lessen the effects of the heat; those deployed to the Far East generally had yellow upperworks.

A ministerial directive of 23 January 1908 stipulated a medium blue-grey livery overall for ships serving with the Northern and the Mediterranean Squadrons; the white band at the waterline was painted out. The changeover was gradual and took most of the year to implement.

During the Great War the linoleum, considered to be a fire risk, was stripped from the decks, which were now of bare steel. For similar reasons the paint was stripped from the gun turrets. In order to prevent oxidation these were coated with a mixture of grease and soot known informally as *bouchon gras*, which often makes them appear black in photographs.

During the 1920s the ships continued to be painted blue-grey. A ministerial directive of 30 November 1920 stipulated that a black band 1m wide was to be painted at the waterline.

TACTICAL MARKINGS[7]

On 5 October 1911 Admiral Boué de Lapeyrère introduced identification markings for the battleships and armoured cruisers of the Mediterranean Squadron. The Northern Squadron followed suit on 8 December, but the scheme was initially only implemented for the battleships; it was adopted for the armoured cruisers from the end of 1913.

From January 1912 ships belonging to the 1st Light Squadron were identified as follows:

First Division:

1st ship: single 1m band 0.3m from top of funnel casing on 1st funnel.
2nd ship: single 1m band 0.3m from top of funnel casing on 2nd funnel.
3rd ship: single 1m band 0.3m from top of funnel casing on 3rd funnel.

Second Division:

1st ship: two 0.7m bands with 0.5m separation on 1st funnel.
2nd ship: two 0.7m bands with 0.5m separation on 2nd funnel.
3rd ship: two 0.7m bands with 0.5m separation on 3rd funnel.

A similar system was adopted for the 2nd Light Squadron at Brest in November 1913. Initially there was only a single division with a single funnel band, but when the *Division d'instruction* was reactivated as the 2nd Division in July 1914 two bands were painted on the first/second/third funnel of *Gloire*, *Gueydon* and *Dupetit-Thouars* respectively. This system would remain in place until the end of 1915.

7 The source for this section is: Jean Guiglini, *Les marques particulières des navires de guerre français 1900–1950* (Vincennes: Service Historique de la Marine, 2002).

CHAPTER 11:

THE GREAT WAR 1914–1918 AND ITS AFTERMATH

THE GREAT WAR OF 1914–18 did not have the 'clean' start that many still imagine. The declarations of war between the major combatants were staggered over days and even weeks. France was at war with Germany by the evening of 3 August, but the British declaration of war on Germany did not take place until midnight (11pm GMT) of the following day. France and Britain did not declare war on Austria-Hungary before 12 August, and it was the end of October before Turkey entered the war on the side of Germany.

Moreover, wireless transmission was relatively undeveloped, and instructions to the naval commanders took time to draw up and transmit. The German declaration of war on France was timed at 18.45 on 3 August, but the C-in-C of the *Armée Navale*, Vice Admiral Boué de Lapeyrère, was not notified of hostilities until 01.15 the following morning. In the Far East Rear Admiral Huguet, who was on a Pacific cruise in his flagship *Montcalm*, received notification that France was at war only at 08.45 on 8 August.

Planned cooperation between the French and British navies had been agreed at the policy level, and a series of conventions drawn up between 1906 and August 1914. These agreements had been increasingly detailed and prescriptive. In broad terms, the British would have overall responsibility for the Channel and

Below: *Jules Michelet* at sea with battleships of the 1st Battle Squadron in mid-1914. She served as flagship of the 1st Light Division during repairs to *Waldeck-Rousseau*, hence the single white band on the first funnel. Behind her, with two white bands on her second funnel, is the *Danton*-class battleship *Mirabeau*; the flagship of the 2nd Division, seen here on the right, is *Voltaire*. *(Private collection)*

THE *1re ARMÉE NAVALE* 2 AUGUST 1914 (TOULON)

Hors rang:[1]	*Courbet* (VA Boué de Lapeyrère), *Jean Bart*[2] *Jurien de la Gravière*[3]
1re escadre de ligne:	
1re division:	*Diderot* (VA Chocheprat), *Danton*, *Vergniaud*
2e division:	*Voltaire* (CA Lacaze), *Mirabeau*, *Condorcet*
2e escadre de ligne:	
1re division:	*Vérité* (VA Le Bris), *République*, *Patrie*
2e division:	*Justice* (CA Tracou), *Démocratie*
Division de complément:	*Suffren* (CA Guépratte), *Saint Louis*, *Gaulois*, *Bouvet*
1re escadre légère:	
1re division légère:	*Jules Michelet* (CA R de Sugny), *Ernest Renan*, *Edgar Quinet*, *Waldeck-Rousseau*[5]
2e division légère:	*Léon Gambetta* (CA Senès), *Victor Hugo*, *Jules Ferry*
Division spéciale:	*Jauréguiberry* (CA Darrieus), *Charlemagne* *Pothuau*,[4] *D'Entrecasteaux*[4]
Groupe de mouilleurs de mines:	*Casabianca*, *Cassini*, *Lahire*
Flotille des torpilleurs d'escadre:	*Bouclier* (CA Lejay)
1re escadrille (800t):	*Casque*, *Dague*, *Boutefeu*, *Fourche*, *Faulx*, *Mangini*
2e escadrille (450t):	*Carabinier*, *Spahi*, *Asp Herber*, *Lansquenet*, *EV Henry*, *Mameluck*
3e escadrille (450t):	*Fantassin*, *Cavalier*, *Janissaire*, *Tirailleur*, *Voltigeur*, *Chasseur*[5]
4e escadrille (300t):	*Hussard*, *Sape*, *Pierrier*, *Mortier*, *Massue*, *Hache*
5e escadrille (300t):	*Poignard*, *Trident*, *Fanfare*, *Sabretache*, *Cognée*, *Coutelas*
6e escadrille (800t):	*Cdt Rivière*, *Bisson*,[5] *Magon*,[5] *Cimeterre*, *Renaudin*, *Cdt Bory*,[6] *Protet*[6]
Flotille des sous-marins:	*Dehorter* (CV Moullé)
1re escadrille:	[T/B] *Arbalète*, *Hallebarde* [S/M] *Ampère*, *Papin*, *Monge*, *Cugnot*, *Fresnel*, *Gay-Lussac*, *Messidor*
2e escadrille:[3]	[T/B] *Mousqueton*, *Sarbacane*, *Arc* [S/M] *Arago*, *Joule*, *Bemouilli*, *Coulomb*, *Curie*, *Circé*, *Faraday*, *Le Verrier*
Transport d'aviation:	*Foudre*
Pétrolier:	*Dordogne*
Transports:	*Vinh Long*, *Bien Hoa*

Notes:
1 *Hors rang* was the term used to denote that a ship outside the divisional structure.
2 *Jean Bart* arrived at Toulon on 7 August.
3 *Jurien de la Gravière* had left Toulon for Bizerte with the *2e escadrille des s/m* on 1 August.
4 Ready 31 August.
5 Under repair.
6 Trials.

the North Sea, the French for the Mediterranean. On 16 October 1912 the French 3rd Battle Squadron – the last major naval formation to be based at Brest – left for Toulon. In March 1913 a code of signals was agreed between the two navies and new signal books issued. However, cooperation at fleet level was patchy, despite the warm reception accorded to visiting British ships and their French counterparts at Portsmouth, Malta and Toulon during the years that preceded the outbreak of war.

The situation in the Mediterranean, where the French were to have overall command, was complicated by the fact that the C-in-C of the British Mediterranean Fleet, Sir Archibald Berkeley Milne, technically outranked his French counterpart.[1] Neither admiral made any effort to liaise with the other, despite an instruction from Paris to the French C-in-C at 10.00 on 3 August to do precisely that. On the following day, Boué de Lapeyrère failed to inform his British counterpart of the bombardment of French North African ports by the battle cruiser *Goeben* and her consort, the light cruiser *Breslau*, which made it difficult for the British hunting groups to locate the ships or to make an accurate assessment of the German Admiral Souchon's intentions.

THE FRENCH ARMOURED CRUISERS AT THE OUTBREAK OF WAR

When war was declared on 3 August 1914 the Navy was in the process of mobilising. Many of the older cruisers

[1] Milne had been made a full admiral in 1911; in the *Marine Nationale*, for historical reasons, vice admiral was the highest possible rank. This led to difficulties over 'seniority' that persisted into the 1930s: at the coronation of George VI in May 1937, then-Vice Admiral Darlan, the head of the French Navy, found himself 'behind a pillar and a Chinese admiral', according to his memoirs.

2e ESCADRE LÉGÈRE (CHERBOURG)

1re division légère:	*Marseillaise* (CA Rouyer), *Amiral Aube*, *Jeanne d'Arc*
2e division légère:[1]	*Gloire* (CA Le Cannellier), *Dupetit-Thouars*, *Gueydon*
3e division légère:[1]	*Desaix*, *Kléber* [no flag officer]
Croiseurs protégés:	*Guichen*, *Lavoisier*, *D'Estrées*
Groupe de mouilleurs de mines:	*Baliste*, *Flamberge*, *Pluton*, *Cerbère*
Flotilles:	Dunois (CV Lavenir)
Division de grands torpilleurs (800t):	*Francis Garnier*, *Capitaine Mehl*
1re escadrille (300t):	*Branlebas*, *Carquois*, *Oriflamme*, *Etendard*, *Obusier*, *Tromblon*
2e escadrille (300t):	*Glaive*, *Gabion*, *Fanion*, *Fleuret*, *Stylet*, *Claymore*
3e escadrille (300t):	*Catapulte*, *Bélier*, *Arquebuse*, *Rapière*, *Bombarde*, *Epieu*
Réserve:	*Sagaie*, *Harpon*
1re escadrille des s/m (Ch):	[T/B] *Francisque*, *Fauconneau*, *Sabre*
	[S/M] *Berthelot*, *Floréal*, *Fructidor*, *Germinal*, *Giffard*, *Pluviôse*, *Prairial*, *Ventôse*, *Watt*
2e escadrille des s/m (Ca):	[T/B] *Durandal*, *Escopette*
	[S/M] *Brumaire*, *Frimaire*, *Mariotte*, *Nivôse*, *Volta*, *Euler*, *Newton*?
3e escadrille des s/m (Ch):	[T/B] *Javeline*, *Epée*[2]
	[S/M] *Foucault*, *Montgolfier*, *Franklin*, *Amiral Bourgeois*,[2] *Archimède*,[2] *Thermidor*,[2] *Gustave Zédé*[2]

Notes:
1 Formed from Reserve.
2 In reserve or under repair.

Division Navale de l'Extrême Orient (Saigon)

Croiseurs:	*Montcalm* (CA Huguet), *Dupleix*
Torpilleurs:	*D'Iberville*, *Mousquet*, *Pistolet*, *Fronde*

Division de l'Atlantique (Caraïbes/Terre-Neuve)
Condé, *Descartes*, *Friant*

Division du Maroc (Casablanca)
Cosmao, *Cassard*

Division du Levant
Amiral Charner, *Bruix*, *Latouche-Tréville*

Note:
The Levant and Morocco divisions were merged to form the *Division spéciale de la Méditerranée*

had been deactivated and had reduced complements that would need to be completed by reservists.

Of the first-line ships, the seven most modern and most powerful cruisers (*Léon Gambetta* and *Edgar Quinet* classes, plus *Jules Michelet* and *Ernest Renan*) were serving with the Light Squadron of the *Armée Navale* based at Toulon. Of these, *Waldeck-Rousseau* was still being repaired after her grounding in February and would not recommission until early September, but the remaining six ships formed the 1st and 2nd Light Divisions. In the Channel, the three-ship division in full commission comprised the comparatively modern *Marseillaise* and *Amiral Aube* (*Gloire* class), together with the slightly older *Jeanne d'Arc*. Overseas deployments included the cruisers *Montcalm* and *Dupleix* in the Far East and *Condé* in the Caribbean. Of the three oldest surviving armoured cruisers of the *Amiral Charner* class, *Amiral Charner* was currently in reserve at Bizerte, while *Bruix* and *Latouche-Tréville* were serving on the Levant station.

Following mobilisation, some of the cruisers currently in reserve were hurriedly recommissioned. In the Channel, a second light division was formed with the armoured cruisers *Gloire* (CA Le Cannellier), *Dupetit-Thouars* and *Gueydon*, currently forming the *Division d'instruction de l'Océan*, and a third with the 'station' cruisers *Desaix* and *Kléber*. This left only *Pothuau* (currently a gunnery training ship) and *D'Entrecasteaux*, which were nominally assigned to the *Division spéciale* at Toulon, but which would require repair and refurbishment in the dockyard before they were fit for service; they would be ready for deployment by the end of August.

THE MEDITERRANEAN: THE PASSAGE OF XIX CORPS

The priority in the Mediterranean, which had been agreed between the Allies prior to the declarations of war, was the safe passage of the 25,000 men of the French XIX Corps from Algeria to metropolitan France.

The operation would require large numbers of requisitioned transports, with protection being provided by the French *Armée Navale* based at Toulon and the British Mediterranean Fleet at Malta. The principal threat, once Italy declared her neutrality on 1 August, was posed by the German fast squadron of Rear Admiral Wilhelm Souchon, comprising the battle cruiser *Goeben* and the light cruiser *Breslau*, which had been hosted by the Austro-Hungarians at their main fleet base of Pola in the northern Adriatic. This

Below: The *Armée Navale* at Algiers in 1914. In the foreground are the dreadnought battleships *Paris* and *Jean Bart*, with battleships of the *Danton* class and a six-funnelled cruiser of the *Edgar Quinet* class beyond them. The after part of *Jules Michelet*, identifiable by the broad flat-sided funnels and the distinctive goose-neck cranes, can be seen to the right of the first group of battleships. The presence and markings of the two dreadnoughts suggest that this photo may date from later than suggested in the original caption. *(Courtesy of Jean-Marie Gall)*

caused some confusion, with Milne apparently unclear as to whether his primary objective was the security of the French transport operation or the sinking of *Goeben*.[2]

The *Armée Navale* duly sailed from Toulon at 03.00 on 3 August, when war had yet to be declared. Boué de Lapeyrère divided his force into three independent groups, which were directed on Philippeville, Bougie and Algiers respectively (see map):

Group A: 1st Battle Squadron, 1st Light Division + 12 torpedo boats.
Group B: *Courbet* (flag), 2nd Battle Squadron, 2nd Light Division, seaplane carrier *Foudre* + 12 torpedo boats.
Group C: Older battleships (*Division de complément* + *Jauréguiberry*) + 4 torpedo boats.

[2] See Marder, *From the Dreadnought to Scapa Flow*, Vol II, p 22.

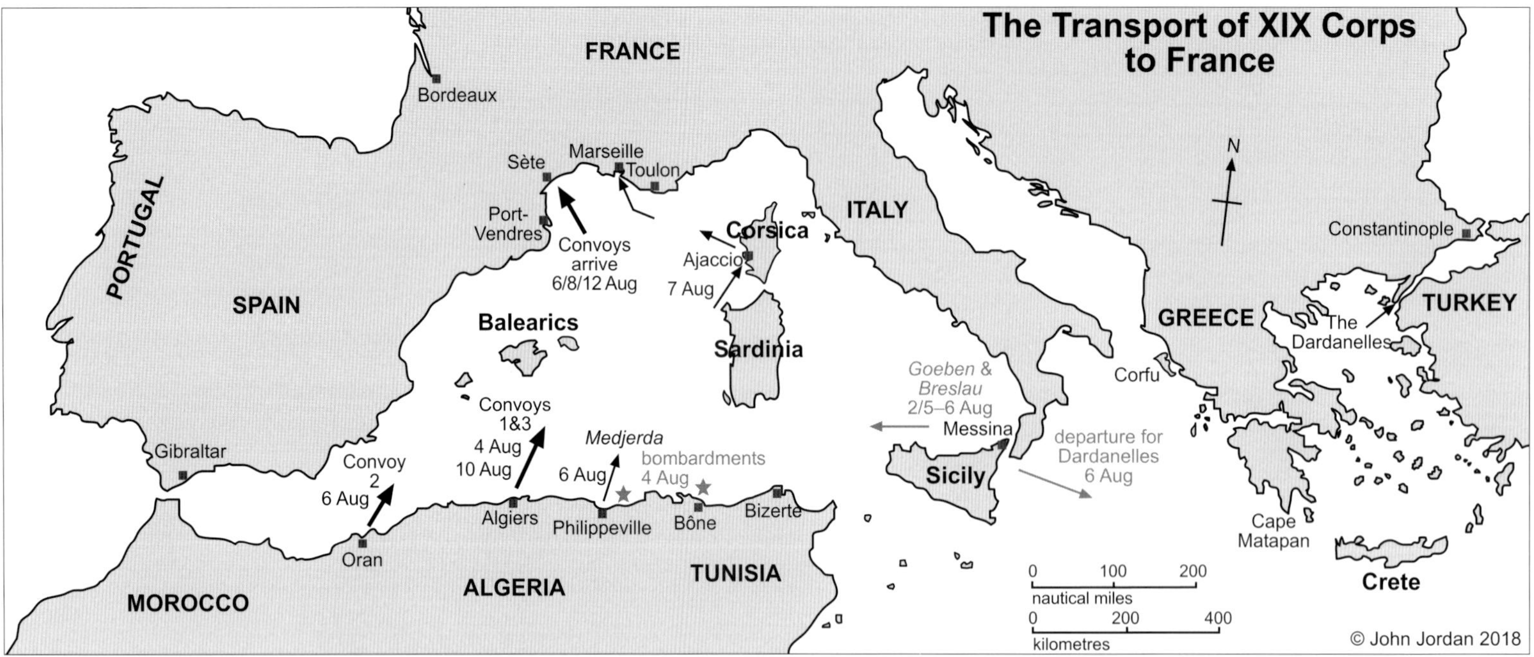

Each of these forces was sufficient to overpower the German squadron if it pressed home its attack, although only the armoured cruisers of the two light divisions were capable of speeds in excess of 19 knots.[3] No instructions were given beyond the route to be taken, and cruising speed was initially set at 12 knots. At 03.45 on 4 August, following notification of the declaration of war between Germany and France, the crews were ordered to Action Stations and speed increased to 14 knots.[4]

In anticipation of hostilities between Germany and France, Souchon had forward-deployed his two ships to the Sicilian port of Messina, and on the morning of 4 August they arrived off the coast of Algeria: *Breslau* fired some sixty rounds of 10.5cm shell at Bône, and *Goeben* forty-three rounds of 15cm shell at Philippeville. The bombardments caused little damage, but had a major impact on Allied perceptions and reactions. At one point the German ships passed within 50 miles of the *Armée Navale*, and they were shadowed for a time by Milne's battle cruisers, which were unable to engage because the British had yet to declare war on Germany. Souchon was able to return to Messina early on 5 August, and then surprised everyone by proceeding, in the late afternoon of 6 August, to the eastern Mediterranean rather than returning to the Adriatic.

The French high command had originally proposed that the troop transports for XIX Corps proceed independently to avoid delays. This was opposed by Boué de Lapeyrère, who wanted the transports to be assembled in two convoys in order to facilitate their protection by the *Armée Navale*. Following the German attacks on the North African coast on 4 August the views of the C-in-C prevailed. The first convoy, with seven ships, 7300 men and 1400 horses, left Algiers between 19.00 and 20.00 on 4 August, escorted by Force B with the 2nd Light Division (*Léon Gambetta*, *Victor Hugo* and *Jules Ferry*). The transports had no experience of convoy: some ships did not wait to be assembled and went on ahead; navigation lights were left on throughout the night by ships' masters who feared collision more than they feared enemy attack; and station-keeping was poor. Nevertheless, the convoy made a steady 10 knots and arrived without incident at Sète, where the troops were disembarked.

A second convoy (seven ships, 7250 men and 1400 horses) left Oran for Sète on 6 August, escorted by Group C. On the same day a single transport with 1750 men and 270 horses left Philippeville escorted by Group A with the 1st Light Division (*Jules Michelet*, *Ernest Renan* and *Edgar Quinet*). It was joined off Ajaccio by two more transports the following morning and made its way to Marseille.

By 8 August 16,900 men out of the 25,000-strong XIX Corps had arrived in France, but the *Armée Navale* was scattered all over the western Mediterranean. *Goeben* was now on her way to the Dardanelles, where she arrived on the 10th. On 8 August Paris ordered Boué de Lapeyrère to reassemble the *Armée Navale* at Bizerte and to join up with the British Mediterranean Fleet in Malta. The aim now was to prevent the Austro-Hungarian fleet from exiting the Adriatic and possibly joining the German and Turkish squadrons in the eastern Mediterranean. The C-in-C left Toulon with Group A at 08.30 on 9 August. The final convoy left Algiers with seven ships and 8100 men, escorted by the older battleships, and arrived at Sète on 12 August, the day that Boué de Lapeyrère entered Grand Harbour at Malta with the vanguard of the *Armée Navale*. On the same day Britain and France declared war on Austria-Hungary.

THE CHANNEL

Plans for operations in the Channel in the event of war had been drawn up in November 1912 and revised in December 1913. In the event of British neutrality, the C-in-C 2nd Light Squadron was to station half his submarines and two out of his three torpedo boat flotillas[5] in the Straits of Dover; they would be rein-

3 *Goeben* was theoretically capable of 27 knots, but due to ongoing problems with her boilers had a top speed of around 24 knots and a sustained speed of only 18 knots; the Allies, however, were unaware of this.

4 This was the maximum speed available to the 1st Battle Squadron due to engine problems in *Mirabeau*.

Left: *Gueydon* at her moorings shortly before the war; behind her is *Marseillaise*. The armoured cruisers of the *Gueydon* and *Gloire* classes would form the core of French naval forces in the Channel and the Atlantic throughout the war. *(Private collection)*

forced by the twenty torpedo boats of the *défenses mobiles* at Dunkirk. The remainder of the submarines and the 2nd Torpedo Boat Flotilla were to operate as part of a patrol line north of the Cotentin Peninsula. The cruisers were to act as flotilla leaders in support of the torpedo boats in the straits.

In the event of war with Britain as an ally – the Anglo-French agreement dated from 23 January 1913 – the Royal Navy was to defend the Dover Strait with a force of 20–24 destroyers plus two flotillas of submarines based at Dover, with four light cruisers in support. The French would provide two flotillas of submarines based at Calais and Boulogne plus the *défenses mobiles* at Dunkirk. Under a further agreement dated 10 February 1913 the French were also responsible for providing a barrier between the Cotentin Peninsula and the Isle of Wight, thereby sealing off the eastern part of the Channel from enemy incursions and allowing for the safe passage of the British Expeditionary Force.

On 26 July Rear Admiral Albert Rouyer, C-in-C of the 2nd Light Squadron, was at Quiberon in his flagship *Marseillaise*. He was ordered to concentrate his forces at Cherbourg. *Marseillaise* duly left on 28 July; the rest of his formation left Brest for Cherbourg on the evening of 1 August. At 01.40 on 3 August Rouyer was ordered to sail immediately and to prevent the passage of the German fleet through the straits.

Rouyer had under his command six armoured cruisers, two 800-tonne and twenty 300-tonne torpedo boats, fifteen submarines and two minelayers; it was a small but well-trained force. Rouyer arrived with his cruisers and fourteen torpedo boats in the Dover Strait at 16.00. The torpedo boats based at Dunkirk and the 2nd Submarine Flotilla (Calais) were already on station, while the torpedo gunboat *Dunois*, the 3rd Torpedo Boat Flotilla and half the 1st Submarine Flotilla were halfway between Le Havre and Portsmouth; the 3rd Submarine Flotilla was held in reserve at Cherbourg but ready to sail at a moment's notice. The cruisers patrolled just north of a line between Boulogne and the British coast by day; at night they retired just below Cape Gris-Nez and the submarines returned to Calais or Boulogne.

Much has been made in French secondary sources of the exposed position of this force, which was potentially faced by the might of the German High Seas Fleet. In reality on 2 August the French ambassador in London had received formal assurances from the British Foreign Secretary, Sir Edward Grey, that in the event of Britain not entering the war – a distinct possibility at this stage of events – the Royal Navy would not allow the Germans to attack the French Channel coast. However, all Anglo-French communications continued to be routed via London and Paris; a telegram was sent to Cherbourg, but Rouyer, by now headed for the Dover Strait, remained ignorant as to its contents, and there was naturally some trepidation among the ships' crews.

At 21.45 on 3 August Rouyer was authorised to liaise with the British, and at 03.30 the following day he was advised that France and Germany were now at war. One hour later he was instructed to implement the Anglo-French agreement of January 1913. Later that morning Rouyer headed west to join up with the 12th Cruiser Squadron of the British Rear Admiral Rosslyn Wemyss. Only the Dunkirk torpedo boats and the 2nd Submarine Flotilla (Calais) were left in the straits, and these would now liaise with the British destroyers and submarines of the Dover Patrol.

At 1630 on 4 August Rouyer informed Paris that the Anglo-French plans for protection of the Channel had been fully implemented.[6] Dispositions were as follows:

By day: two patrol lines of submarines (1st & 3rd ESM)

[5] The word 'flotilla' is used here to translate the French *escadrille*, although in strength it was closer to the German 'half-flotilla': an *escadrille* generally comprised six torpedo boats or submarines.

[6] Note that the British declaration of war on Germany was still some hours away.

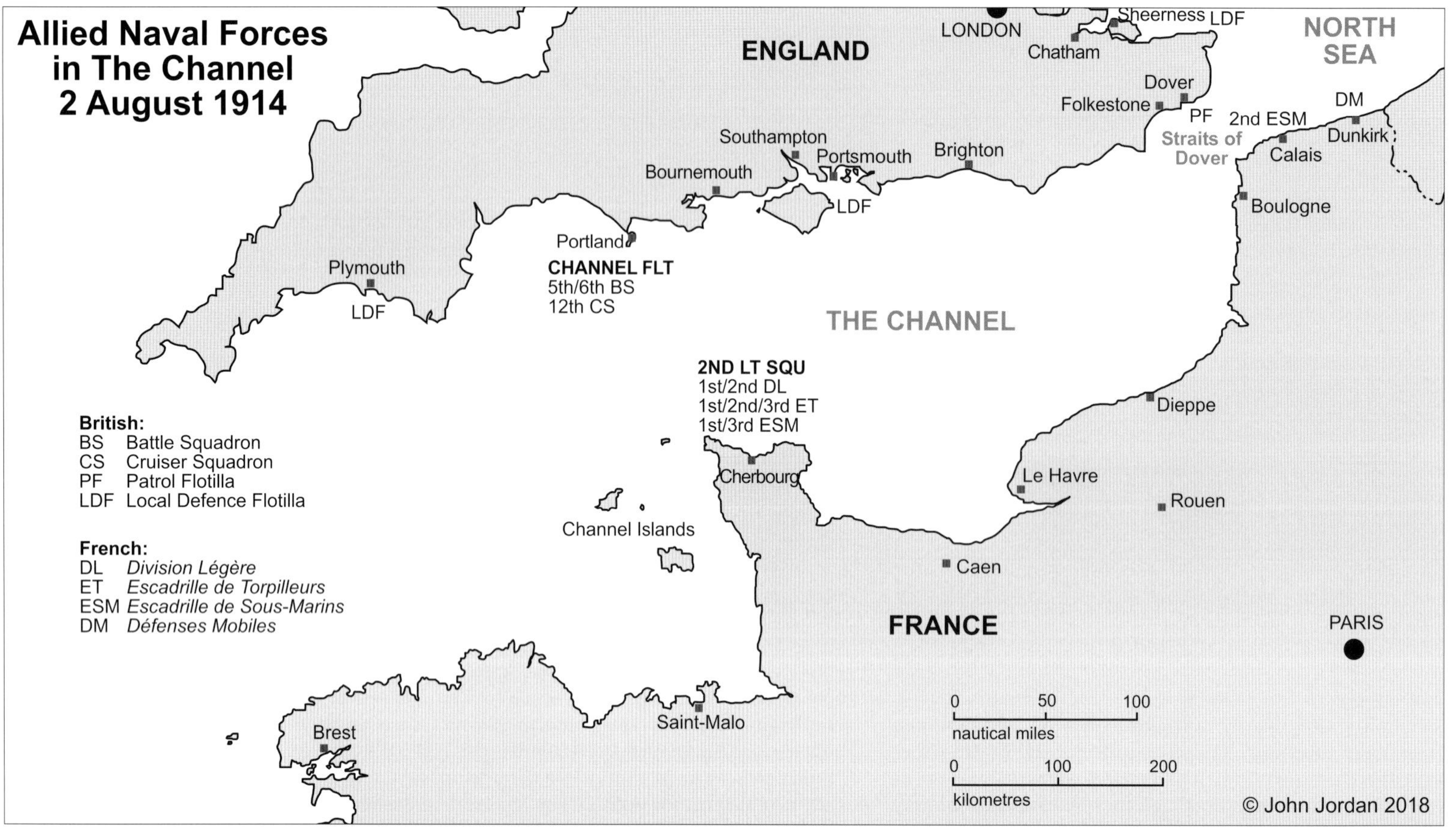

from La Hague to Portland and from Barfleur to the Isle of Wight.
By night: a patrol line of French torpedo boats between La Hague and Portland.

Permanent support for these patrol lines was provided by the five French armoured cruisers of the 2nd and 3rd Light Divisions of the 2nd Light Squadron plus the protected cruiser *D'Estrées* and the four cruisers of the British 12th Cruiser Squadron under Wemyss. These two groups operated with a separation of 8nm between Eddystone and Triagoz, and between Wolf Rock and Ushant. They were tasked with intercepting German shipping, which might include submarines and covert minelayers, and with monitoring mercantile traffic. Distant cover was provided 50nm to the east by the three armoured cruisers of the 1st Light Division, with Rouyer in *Marseillaise*.

SAFE PASSAGE FOR THE BEF

From 9 August the disposition of the Allied forces was adjusted to seal off the Channel and ensure the safe passage of the British Expeditionary Force (BEF): the cruisers of Rouyer and Wemyss continued to patrol to the west, while the Dover Patrol barricaded the straits in the east. Between Britain's south coast and Cherbourg were the battleships of the Channel Fleet under Vice Admiral Cecil Burney. North of the Dover Strait the British established a second patrol line with submarines of the Harwich Force of Commodore Roger Keyes.

The BEF as originally constituted comprised six infantry divisions and a single cavalry division. Fears of a German invasion led the British high command initially to hold back two infantry divisions, but the remainder of the force was embarked at Southampton from 9 August. The transports sailed singly or in pairs as soon as they were loaded, and the troops were disembarked at Le Havre or Rouen on the line of the River Seine; they were then formed into two army corps. A fifth infantry division arrived on 22–23 August to form the basis of III Corps.

On 24 August the 2nd Light Squadron was recalled to Cherbourg ready to be deployed in support of the northern ports and to support a possible landing at Ostend, and on 27 August the armoured cruisers in the western patrol line were replaced by protected and auxiliary cruisers.

On 29 August, in the face of a German military advance that threatened Boulogne and Le Havre, Field Marshal Sir John French ordered the operational base of the BEF to be moved south to Saint-Nazaire on the Loire. Le Havre was evacuated from 30 August to 6 September using British shipping escorted by French auxiliary cruisers, and a new maritime patrol line established off the River Loire between the Bay of Biscay, the island of Ushant and Cape Finisterre with the armoured cruisers *Gloire*, *Gueydon* and *Kléber*. The British High Command then despatched the 6th Infantry Division to stabilise the military situation in northern France; the men disembarked at Saint-Nazaire 9–10 September, with cover from Southampton to Ushant provided by the 1st Light Division led by *Marseillaise*.

None of the above operations was threatened by the German High Seas Fleet, which remained in its base at Wilhelmshaven, 260nm from the Dover Strait. The fleet was fully mobilised but inactive; the Kaiser decided it was not to be risked in offensive action. The German generals were confident they could wipe out Britain's 'contemptible little army' on land, and wanted the fleet to protect Army's flank and rear against British landings on the North Sea coasts. The first German submarine made its appearance in the Channel on 27 September, more than two weeks after the last elements of the BEF had disembarked.

On 15 October, claiming that Cherbourg was no longer safe from the depredations of the German U-boats, which were appearing in increasing numbers, Rouyer moved the 2nd Light Squadron to Brest, at precisely the moment that its presence was required to support the Flanders front. Instead, *Dunois* was duly despatched to Dunkirk with Rouyer's four biggest torpedo boats – the ex-Argentine *Aventurier* and *Intrépide* had now joined the fleet – and the minelayers *Pluton* and *Cerbère*; the admiral embarked in the destroyer *Francis Garnier*.

On 27 October Rouyer was replaced by Vice Admiral Charles-Eugène Favereau, who promptly reorganised the patrols in the Western Channel. The British cruisers of Wemyss patrolled the north, and the French cruisers the south. The latter force, which now comprised protected and auxiliary cruisers, had *Gloire* (CA Cannellier) as flagship and *Amiral Aube* as replacement. A new force formed with the remaining armoured cruisers, designated the *Division de combat* and commanded by Favereau in *Marseillaise*, was tasked with conducting patrols on the Ushant – Loire line and possible support/intervention in the Channel.

Patrols continued into 1915 but, with the stabilisation of the Flanders front and the expansion of Allied naval operations in the Aegean and the Levant, the armoured cruisers and the more modern protected cruisers of the 2nd Light Squadron were progressively transferred to the Eastern Mediterranean. *Kléber* was recalled by Favereau from an Atlantic cruise. In April, following maintenance periods at Brest, *Jeanne d'Arc* and the protected cruiser *Châteaurenault* sailed for the Mediterranean, followed in May by *Kléber*, *Dupetit-Thouars* and *Guichen*. A major anti-submarine barrage comprising nets and mines, backed up by destroyers and submarines, now sealed off the Dover Strait, and the cruisers on patrol in the western Channel were replaced by trawlers and armed merchant cruisers.

OVERSEAS THEATRES

The Pacific

In the Far East, faced with the threat from Germany's powerful East Asia Squadron under Vice Admiral Maximilian Graf von Spee, Anglo-French naval forces held joint exercises on 27 January 1913. On 6 February 1914, Vice Admiral Sir Thomas Jerram met with his French counterpart Rear Admiral Huguet to draw up a definitive memorandum that envisaged the incorporation of the two French armoured cruisers on station into the British China Squadron; it also covered coaling, the reciprocal use of ports, and communications.

The immediate implementation of this plan was preempted by the absence of Huguet's flagship *Montcalm*, which was on a cruise in the South Pacific when war was declared. Huguet learnt of the hostilities only on 8 August, when he received a telegram from Paris instructing him to join the Australian squadron in an attack on German Samoa. The other French armoured cruiser in the Far East, *Dupleix*, was in Japan at the time of the European crisis; she left for Hong Kong on 29 July, arriving on 5 August to be integrated into the British China Squadron.

On 9 September, following the entry of Japan into the war, *Dupleix* was sent to reinforce the torpedo gunboat *D'Iberville* and the French torpedo boats operating north of the Malacca Straits. On 27 September she was summoned to Colombo to escort a military convoy to Suez. The presence of the cruiser *Emden* was signalled in the Bay of Bengal, leading to a suspension of maritime traffic between Colombo and Singapore.

Left: *Dupleix* during a visit to Nagasaki in 1912. She left Cherbourg on 12 November 1910 and was then based at Saigon until the outbreak of war in August 1914, when she was integrated into the British China Squadron. *(Courtesy of Jean-Marie Gall)*

Right: *Montcalm*, the flagship of Rear Admiral Huguet (DNEO), was on a cruise in the South Pacific when war was declared, and was ordered to join the Australian squadron in an attack on German Samoa. This photo, taken from HMAS *Australia*, shows her operating with the protected cruiser *Encounter* in late 1914, during the occupation of German New Guinea. *(Norman Hill, courtesy of Jean-Marie Gall)*

The West Atlantic

In contrast to the Pacific, there was no pre-existing agreement on joint operations in the Atlantic Ocean, leading to some initial confusion.

On 30 July *Condé* and the protected cruiser *Descartes*, which constituted the *Division de l'Atlantique*, were at Veracruz in Mexico. They were recalled to France, but following the declaration of war *Condé* was informed of a sighting of the German light cruiser *Karlsruhe* off Havana, and remained in the area to ensure the security of maritime traffic. On 5 August the French agreed to the incorporation of their ships into the 4th Cruiser Squadron of Rear Admiral 'Kit' Craddock, and the French cruisers were despatched by him to join the light cruisers *Bristol* and *Berwick* in the hunt for *Karlsruhe* and *Dresden*. The Panama Canal opened on 15 August, leading to a large increase in the volume of traffic.

On 21 August *Condé* left Kingston for Fort-de-France, arriving on 28 August. There she replenished

Right: The armoured cruiser *Condé* was at Veracruz in Mexico when war was declared. From August 1914 until May 1916 she was would be deployed to the West Indies to hunt for German raiders. During this period she wore no funnel bands. *(Private collection)*

and her complement was brought up to full strength. The French cruisers were then left in charge of the zone while Cradock hurried south with his own cruisers to look for von Spee. On 16 October *Condé* joined HMS *Berwick* to hunt for *Karlsruhe* off the Brazilian coast. On 8 November, concerned that von Spee would pass through the Panama Canal, the Admiralty concentrated all available cruisers in the West Indies; however, five days later he was signalled off the coast of Chile. This chaotic situation stabilised following the elimination of von Spee's squadron at the Battle of the Falkland Islands on 8 December, and the cruisers resumed their search for *Karlsruhe*, unaware that she had been lost to an internal explosion on 4 November.

Condé and *Descartes* remained on the West Indies station until August 1915, by which time the British acknowledged that their presence was no longer required.

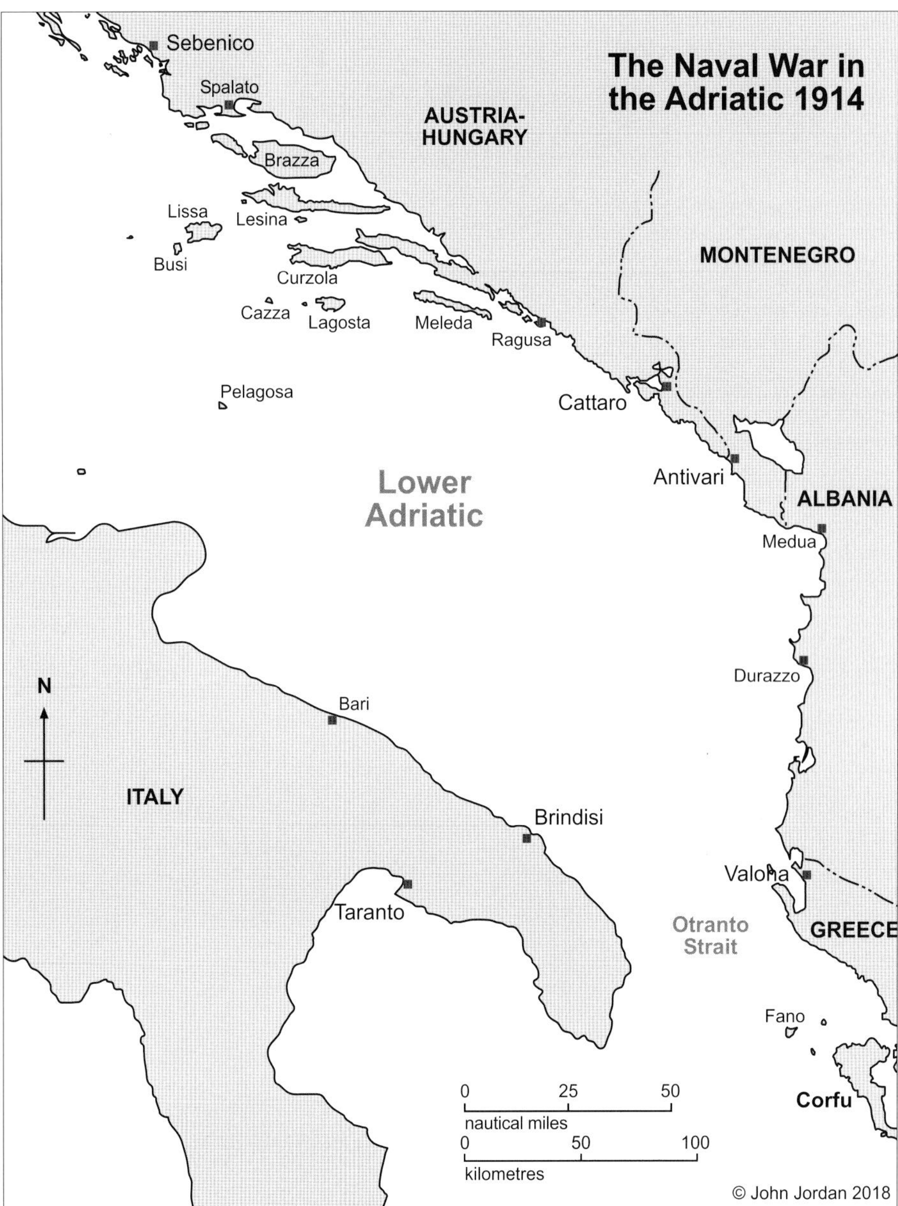

Africa

Following Souchon's raids on the coast of North Africa, the Minister ordered Boué de Lapeyrère to provide protection for convoys leaving Morocco. On 22 August the *Division du Maroc* was reconstituted with the protected cruisers *Cassard* and *Cosmao*, shortly joined by the elderly armoured cruisers *Amiral Charner*, *Bruix* and *Latouche-Tréville*. The cruisers were tasked with protecting the Mediterranean sea lanes off North Africa and between Gibraltar and Casablanca in the Atlantic; they were also to look for anchorages that might provide shelter for German submarines in the area of the Canaries. The ships were coaled at Oran. 27,000 troops were escorted in August, 15,800 in September. At the end of September the convoys ceased; in the absence of an enemy threat the force was reduced to the protected cruisers *Cassard*, *Cosmao* and *Friant*, tasked with the interception of illegal German arms shipments to Spain and Spanish Morocco.

In West Africa, operations were mounted against the German colonies. *Bruix* assisted British cruisers in operations against Cameroon. On 25 September *Bruix* was at Douala, where she landed troops and provided fire support; she bombarded Victoria on 13 November. *Pothuau* arrived to take command of the French naval forces in November; she put troops ashore on 2 December, and on the 15th her landing party occupied Kribi. After the capture of the German colonies, the French would keep a protected cruiser (*Friant*, then *Surcouf*) in the Gulf of Guinea until the end of the war.

THE *ARMÉE NAVALE* 1914–1915

Blockade of the Otranto Strait

On the morning of 13 August 1914, Boué de Lapeyrère, whom we left earlier with the *Armée Navale* at Malta, was informed of the French declaration of war on Austria-Hungary. He was instructed to gather up the available British forces and, passing in full view of the Italian coast, to conduct offensive operations against the Austro-Hungarian fleet. He was given complete freedom of action – in itself an admission that the Naval General Staff had failed to draw up any plans for this eventuality. The French C-in-C needed no second bidding, and sailed immediately for the southern Adriatic with the intention of relieving the blockade of the Montenegrin port of Antivari (see map) and engaging any Austro-Hungarian ships operating out of nearby Cattaro.

The *Armée Navale*, to which were added the British cruisers and destroyers of Rear Admiral Ernest Troubridge, were divided into two groups. The armoured cruisers of the 1st and 2nd Light Divisions, in company with the British ships, were to follow the Albanian coast, the two battle squadrons and the French torpedo boats the Italian side. The fleet set off at 19.00 on 15 August; the two groups were to join up off Cattaro and Antivari the following morning. Shortly before 09.00 the Austro-Hungarian cruiser *Zenta* and the destroyer *Uhlan* were sighted and engaged by the battleships, but the cruisers of the light divisions were too far off to intervene. In a chaotic and one-sided action that lasted only 18 minutes *Zenta* was sunk, but *Uhlan* escaped to Cattaro.

Boué de Lapeyrère had no intention of proceeding to Pola to give battle to the main Austro-Hungarian fleet, a decision that was subjected to unreasonable criticism from Paris. Pola was some 600km from the Otranto Strait, and while the Italian coast of the Adriatic was relatively flat and featureless, the eastern side was lined with inlets and islands that could shelter submarines and torpedo boats, and with

Right: A fine study of the cruiser *Victor Hugo* at Bizerte in 1914. She served as the 2nd ship of the 2nd Light Division (two white bands on the second funnel) until she was decommissioned in mid-1917. The 2nd Light Division was involved in all the major activities undertaken by the *Armée Navale* in 1914–15: the passage of XIX Corps from North Africa to metropolitan France; the blockade of the Austro-Hungarian fleet, the incursions into the Adriatic and the escort of convoys to the Montenegrin port of Antivari. *(Courtesy of Jean-Marie Gall)*

shallows that could be mined. A raid on Pola could have been conducted only at high speed, and coaling in these narrow waters was out of the question. The French torpedo boats were too short-ranged to accompany the bigger ships, and even the *Dantons*, which were powered by direct-drive turbines, would have had empty bunkers by the time they returned.

The only sensible course was to monitor the strait using a flotilla of torpedo boats, supported during the day by armoured cruisers, and to have the battle fleet patrolling to the south. However, it was quickly accepted that the blockade would lead to the consumption of vast quantities of coal, oil and fresh water; daily consumption for the *Armée Navale* was estimated at 5000 tons of coal and 1000 tons of oil. On 15 August twelve steamers of 300–4000 tons were chartered to carry coal from Cardiff to the Ionian islands, and thirteen French steamers were requisitioned to carry coal from Toulon, Bizerte and Ajaccio; capacity was 75,000 tons of coal per month. Four oilers were also needed to replenish the torpedo boats and submarines. The Otranto Strait was 600km from Malta, so coaling had to be performed alongside, either in open waters or in the shelter of islands, with the big ships underway.

Following her lengthy repairs *Waldeck-Rousseau* sailed from Toulon on 8 September to rejoin the *Armée Navale*, and with her arrival Rear Admiral Ramey de Sugny, commanding the Light Squadron, transferred his flag from *Jules Michelet*. The 1st Light Division now comprised the four most modern French armoured cruisers: *Waldeck-Rousseau*, *Ernest Renan*, *Edgar Quinet* and *Michelet*.

By 13 October it had become clear that the blockade was unsustainable in its current form due to the wear and tear of constant patrol: the battleships and cruisers were accorded rolling 10-day maintenance and leave periods in Malta, and the torpedo boat flotillas were despatched in sequence to Bizerte for repair and maintenance.

Incursions into the Adriatic

Following the destruction of *Zenta* Austria-Hungary abandoned its blockade of Montenegro, replacing its surface ships with mines and submarines while the torpedo boats conducted night raids.

The French General Staff wanted to take Cattaro and support Montenegro, and the *Armée Navale* was now tasked with protecting ships carrying supplies, men and materiel to Antivari. Ten further incursions in strength were made into the southern Adriatic before the end of 1914. These often involved a significant proportion of the *Armée Navale* escorting a single steamer with a few hundred tons of supplies. In late August equipment and personnel were landed at Antivari for a radio station to be set up on Mount Lovĉen, overlooking Cattaro, to inform the C-in-C of the movements of Austro-Hungarian naval forces, and the battleships engaged the Cattaro forts. In mid-September two siege batteries were disembarked at Antivari and the *Armée Navale* penetrated as far as the island of Lissa. The armoured cruisers provided support for the light forces: *Edgar Quinet* destroyed the Cazza lighthouse, and the 2nd Light Division took advantage of poor visibility to bombard Cattaro, but was driven off by the powerful coastal batteries. In mid-October the *Armée Navale* escorted the seaplane carrier *Foudre* to Antivari, where she disembarked two reconnaissance aircraft.

However, by October the *Armée Navale* was coming under increasing attack from Austro-Hungarian aircraft and submarines. Boué de Lapeyrère requested that two HA guns be fitted in each of the major ships – a measure that would take two years or more to implement. During the *Foudre* operation *Waldeck-Rousseau* was attacked by aircraft, then sighted approaching

Right: During an incursion into the Adriatic by the *Armée Navale* in September 1914, *Edgar Quinet* destroyed the Cazza lighthouse. The ship is seen here at anchor during 1912–13, with her boat boom and accommodation ladders deployed. *(Private collection)*

torpedo boats and the periscopes of two submarines. *U3* dived to escape attention, but *U4* passed between the 1st Light Division and the battle fleet, and was manoeuvring to fire torpedoes when the battleships turned away. On 2 November the 1st Light Division, which had penetrated as far as Lissa, was again attacked by aircraft, and the following day a torpedo attack by *U5* was thwarted only when the submarine was sighted by *Waldeck-Rousseau*. *U5* then manoeuvred to attack the 2nd Light Division, and launched a torpedo at the stern of *Jules Ferry* at a range of 700m; it missed by only 10m. Rear Admiral Senès, commanding the 2nd Light Division, warned the C-in-C that operating these large ships in the southern Adriatic was becoming hazardous.

The supply missions to Antivari continued, but while the *Armée Navale* was operating off Brindisi on the morning of 21 December, Boué de Lapeyrère's flagship, the dreadnought battleship *Jean Bart*, was struck in the bow by a torpedo from *U12*; a second torpedo passed only 50m away. The admiral transferred his flag to the battleship *France*, but *Jean Bart* would be under repair at Malta for the next five months. No one had expected a torpedo attack 90nm south of Cattaro, and the incident effectively ended incursions by the battle fleet into the southern Adriatic. The patrol line was now moved 60nm south of Otranto and a fleet anchorage established in Navarino Bay in late December.

The re-supply of Montenegro continued, but Boué de Lapeyrère now refused to risk his big ships. The merchantmen were escorted by torpedo boats, with distant support (20–50nm) provided by the armoured cruisers. By 1 March 1915 Antivari was no longer usable as a consequence of Austro-Hungarian raids, and the cargo ships had to unload at Medua in Albania. The last mission using neutral cargo ships took place on 20–21 April. However, the situation would be resolved by Italy's declaration of war on Austria-Hungary on 24 May.

A Distant Blockade

Following the torpedoing of *Jean Bart*, the patrol line of the *Armée Navale* was moved progressively south of the Otranto Strait: first to the Corfu parallel, then to a line off Zakynthos, then to Navarino. The strait itself was patrolled by four armoured cruisers of the 1st and 2nd Light Divisions.

On 10 January 1915 Boué de Lapeyrère was notified by Paris that the Austro-Hungarian fleet had sailed and was coming south. The C-in-C duly formed a line of battle and headed north at 10 knots, joined by the torpedo boats. The armoured cruisers *Waldeck-Rousseau*, *Ernest Renan*, *Jules Michelet* and *Léon Gambetta* assembled off Dukat, then patrolled off Corfu, while the battle fleet cruised on the Antipaxos parallel to the south. By 15.00 the following day there was still no sign of the Austro-Hungarian fleet, and the *Armée Navale* retired south. The British still feared a sortie by the Austro-Hungarian fleet to join up with Souchon's squadron and the Turkish fleet at Constantinople, so encouraged a continuation of the French blockade. Boué de Lapeyrère considered the anchorage at Navarino Bay ideal to intercept such a move, but he was increasingly concerned about the possibility of U-boats operating in Greek neutral waters, and on 13 March he ordered a further with-

Theatre of Operations of the *Armée Navale* 1915–1916

drawal to Suda Bay (Crete). However, the German and Austro-Hungarian consuls stirred up opposition among the local population, and the C-in-C decided coaling for the battleships would take place in Vatika Bay (at the southern tip of the Greek mainland), while Navarino was to be used as a coaling base for the armoured cruisers.

On 4 April Boué de Lapeyrère received a further report of the Austro-Hungarian fleet coming south and the *Armée Navale* headed for the Otranto Strait, but this again proved to be a false alarm. On 26 April the Allies persuaded Italy to declare war on Austria-Hungary, and a draft naval convention was drawn up. There were concerns about a pre-emptive attack on the southern Italian ports, so Boué de Lapeyrère moved the armoured cruisers of the 1st and 2nd Light Divisions, deploying in rotation, closer to the Otranto Strait.

On 26 April they were patrolling on a line between Leuca and Dukat (see map). The patrol line was divided into four sectors, each of 31nm. From west to east were: *Léon Gambetta* (sector 1), *Waldeck-Rousseau* (2), *Jules Ferry* (3) and *Victor Hugo* (4). At midnight *Léon Gambetta* was 15nm from Leuca, course NE, speed 6 knots. Ten minutes later she was sighted by the Austro-Hungarian submarine *U5*, which manoeuvred to take up a firing position, dived, and at 00.40 fired two torpedoes at 10-second intervals at a range of 500m. The first struck *Léon Gambetta* on the port side abeam the dynamo compartment; the second struck abreast the forward boiler room – the only room with boilers lit. The ship lost all power and immediately took on a 15° list, followed by a steady roll onto her side. The explosions had destroyed the W/T aerials and there were no torpedo boats in the vicinity. Three minutes after the impact the list had increased to 30°. The water was now only 1m from the upper deck; only two of the ship's boats could be launched, and one of these subsequently sank due to overloading. After nine minutes the ship was on her side with the keel exposed, sinking by the head. She capsized and sank at 00.50, leaving 500 men in water; all thirty-one of the admiral's staff perished, including Senès. The survivors were picked up by Italians. Fortunately Italy was still neutral, as *U5* had remained in the area in the hope of emulating the exploit of the German *U9* in September 1914;[7] however, there were only 137 survivors out of a crew of 821.

Following the loss of *Léon Gambetta*, the French armoured cruisers were pulled back from the Otranto Strait to the Gerogombos parallel (Kefalonia), and patrol speed was increased to 14 knots, resulting in further consumption of coal. On 1 May *Léon Gambetta* was replaced as flagship of the 2nd Light Division by *Jules Michelet* (CA Charlier), previously the fourth ship of the 1st Light Division.

On 8 and 10 May the *Armée Navale* coaled at sea, as this was considered safer than using unprotected anchorages. Following the appearance of the first German U-boat (*U21*) in the Mediterranean on 6 May, Boué de Lapeyrère decided to abandon Navarino and take the fleet to Malta. However, he was concerned that U-boats might be loitering in the waters off Malta, so the squadrons were given freedom of manoeuvre and sent to coal at Bizerte; they arrived on 14 May.

Italy Enters the War

Italy declared war on Austria-Hungary at midnight on 23 May 1915. The Italians, with naval bases at Taranto, Brindisi and Venice, immediately assumed responsibility for the blockade of the Austro-Hungarian fleet and the resupply of Montenegro. The French retained command south of a line between Cape Colonna and the island of Paxos. In response to an Italian request Boué de Lapeyrère sent twelve torpedo boats and six submarines of the *Armée Navale*, currently at Malta, to join the Italian 2nd Squadron based at Brindisi.

The Austro-Hungarian fleet sortied from its base at Pola on 24 May, and on 25 May the *Armée Navale* headed again for the Otranto Strait. However, following a bombardment of Ancona the Austro-Hungarians returned to harbour. This would be the last sortie by the *Armée Navale* as a unit. The harbour at Malta was now so over-crowded that the 1st Battle Squadron was sent to Bizerte, 600nm from the Otranto Strait.

Italy had declared war only on Austria-Hungary, so

[7] On 22 September 1914, *U9* had torpedoed and sunk in succession the British armoured cruisers *Aboukir*, *Cressy* and *Hogue*; the two last-named ships were sunk while attempting to rescue survivors from *Aboukir*.

Below: Artist's impression of the sinking of *Léon Gambetta* during the night of 26/27 April 1915. She was torpedoed by the Austro-Hungarian submarine *U5* while on patrol in the Otranto Strait, and was sunk with the loss of 684 officers and men. *(DR)*

surveillance of Italian ports to intercept German shipping was ongoing. Patrols began on 18 May; the armoured cruiser *Ernest Renan* was despatched to patrol first off Genoa, then Naples; *Amiral Charner* patrolled off Livorno, *Desaix* off Palermo. These patrols ceased on 6 June, when the Italians agreed to take over the surveillance.

The *Armée Navale* was now charged with monitoring the narrows between Malta and Bizerte. In June two patrol zones were set up: in the west, covering a sector from San Pietro (Sardinia) to Cape Colonna, was the 1st Light Division (*Waldeck-Rousseau*, *Ernest Renan* and *Edgar Quinet*), reinforced by *Guichen* and *Amiral Charner*; in the east, from Cape Colonna to the easternmost point of Crete, was the 2nd Light Division (*Jules Michelet*, *Jules Ferry* and *Victor Hugo*), with *Desaix* and (temporarily) *Dupetit-Thouars*. Both forces were based at Bizerte. The torpedo boats were likewise divided into two units, designated the *1re/2e Flotilles de l'Armée Navale*, and tasked with monitoring mercantile traffic, supported by the cruisers.

These patrols were reorganised at the end of July. From 1 August the 1st Light Division operated out of Algiers, and the 2nd Light Division was based at Alexandria and tasked with patrols in the southern part of the Ionian Sea. From September the 1st and 2nd Light Divisions were based at Malta, Bizerte and Alexandria.

THE EASTERN MEDITERRANEAN 1914–1915

The declaration of war on Turkey on 5 November 1914 opened up a huge maritime front. On 6 November the British requested replacements for the armoured cruisers *Black Prince* and *Warrior*, which were needed in the South Atlantic to pursue Von Spee's East Asia Squadron. The French despatched first the coast defence battleship *Requin* (Bizerte), which arrived at Port Said on 21 November, then the seaplane carrier *Foudre*, with France's only naval air squadron; the armoured cruiser *Amiral Charner* was already at Alexandria. These ships were placed under the command of Vice Admiral Peirse, C-in-C East Indies, and were tasked with preventing the resupply of the Turkish army in Asia Minor and Syria, and also with the protection of the Christian populations. On 29 November *Amiral Charner* was joined at Larnaca (Cyprus) by *D'Entrecasteaux*, despatched from the western Mediterranean, forming the *Division de Syrie*. These two ships would have to cover a 600km sector from Alexandretta to Jaffa.

The Turkish Assault on the Suez Canal

For Germany, Turkey was the key to action against the Suez Canal, through which maritime traffic from Persia, India and the Far East, including the transport of troops from India and Australasia, had to pass. A Turkish army of 25,000 men under Djemal Pacha was duly concentrated in Syria, and munitions and materiel assembled in Gaza and at Aqaba.

On 1 December five French Nieuport monoplanes were landed by *Foudre* at Port Said to fly reconnaissance missions, and on 20 January General Henry Maitland Wilson deployed 30,000 men in defensive positions on the African side of the Canal. In order to remedy his lack of artillery, British and French warships were moored at key points in the Canal itself. The old coast defence battleship *Requin* was moored south of Lake Timsah, and *D'Entrecasteaux* north of the Great Bitter Lake (she arrived 28 January).

Above: In December 1914 *D'Entrecasteaux* was assigned to the newly-formed *Division de Syrie*; she joined *Amiral Charner* at Port Said. She would subsequently play a key role in the defence of the Suez Canal against a major Turkish assault. *(DR)*

The attack on the Canal began on 3 February. *Requin* destroyed the Turkish heavy artillery, comprising two 15cm guns, and scattered the enemy columns; *D'Entrecasteaux* fired her 138mm guns at the advancing enemy columns at 6300–6700m, then her 240mm guns to break up the enemy attack. Fire ceased at 15.45, by which time *Requin* had fired sixteen 270mm and 152 100mm rounds, and *D'Entrecasteaux* five 240mm rounds and thirty-six 138mm rounds. By evening the enemy was in full retreat, having suffered 1000 dead and 1500 wounded; 700 prisoners were taken. Navigation in the Canal was suspended on 3 February, but was resumed on the 4th.

The 3rd Squadron

On 31 January French naval forces in the region were formed into the 3rd Squadron (*3e Escadre*) under the command of Vice Admiral Louis Dartige du Fournet, initially in *D'Entrecasteaux*, then in *Saint Louis* (5 February). Based at Port Said, the squadron was detached from Vice Admiral Peirse as an independent command; its zone of operations was from Port Said to Alexandretta. Initially the squadron comprised the battleships *Saint Louis* and *Jauréguiberry* and the cruiser *D'Entrecasteaux*, but there were constant changes in the composition of the force, and regular transfers between the 3rd Squadron and the French Dardanelles Squadron. The principal changes were as follows:

- 5 February: *Bruix* joined *Requin*, *D'Entrecasteaux* for the defence of the Canal.
- 16 February: *Desaix* arrived from Brest, and the coast defence battleship *Requin* was replaced by *Henri IV*.
- 15 March: *Montcalm* (CA Huguet) arrived from Singapore.
- 18 March: Huguet was placed in command of a division tasked with protecting the Canal and the Red Sea; the division comprised the armoured cruisers *Montcalm* and *Desaix* and the CD battleship *Requin*.

Following the abortive attempt to force the Dardanelles Straits on 18 March, the battleships *Henri IV*, *Jauréguiberry* (both March) and *Saint Louis* (April) were

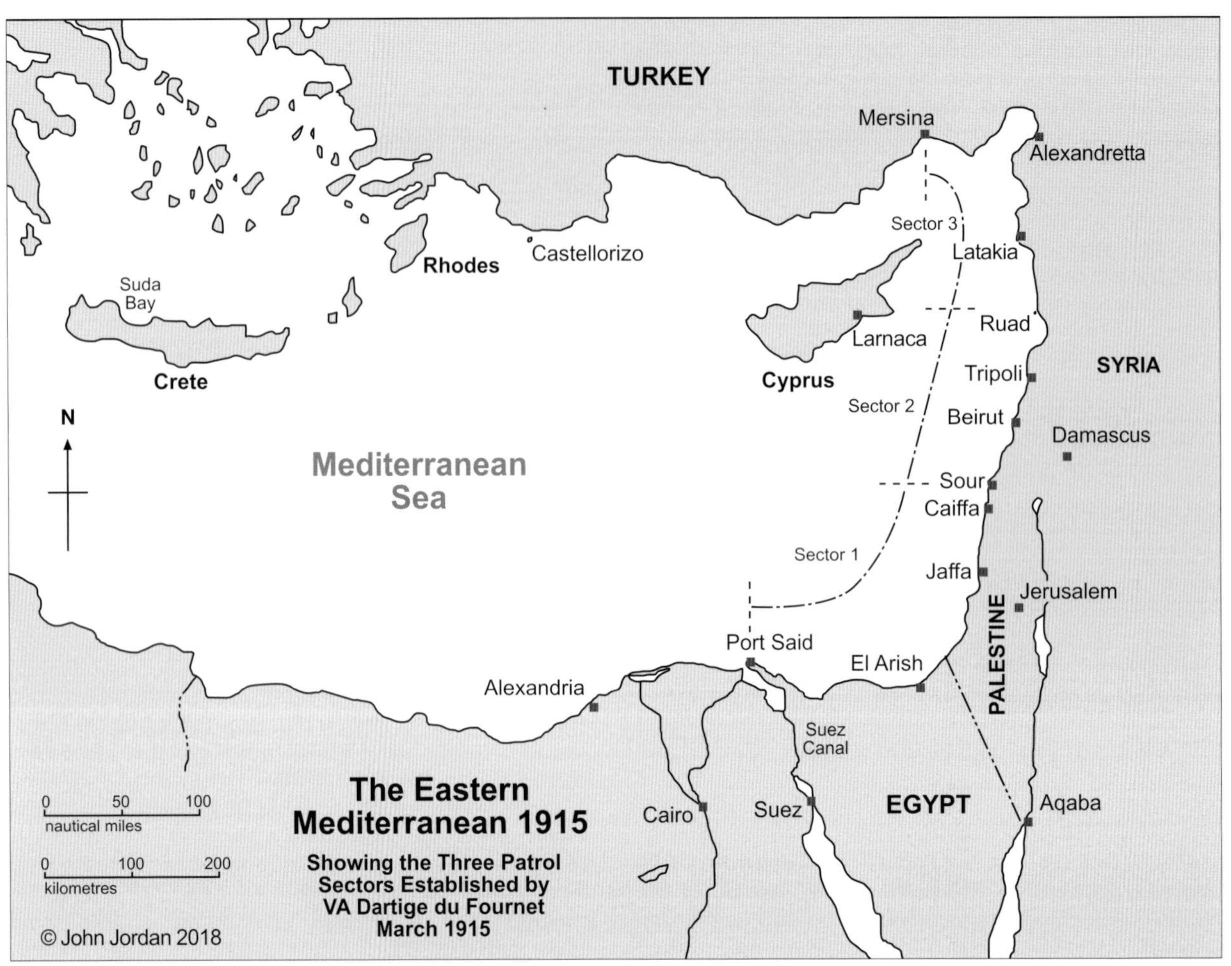

Right: When the *Division de Syrie* was renamed the 3rd Squadron on 31 January 1915, a number of the older cruisers formerly based in Morocco or the Channel were assigned to the formation. This is *Desaix*, which arrived from Brest on 16 February. *(Courtesy of Jean-Marie Gall)*

Above: *Jeanne d'Arc* arrived in the Eastern Mediterranean in April, and subsequently became the flagship of Vice Admiral Dartige du Fournet. She was particularly active in the bombardment and blockade of the coast of Syria. She is seen here moored at Port Said in December 1915, when she was the flagship of Vice Admiral Moreau. *(DR)*

transferred to the Dardanelles Squadron as replacements for *Bouvet* (sunk), *Suffren* and *Gaulois* (both damaged); they were replaced in the 3rd Squadron by the cruisers *D'Estrées*, *Latouche-Tréville* (both March) *Jeanne d'Arc* (April) and *Dupleix* (May).

Dartige du Fournet hoisted his flag in *Jeanne d'Arc* on 6 May, and established three patrol sectors: from Port Said to Sour; from Sour to the island of Ruad; and from Ruad to Mersina (see map). The ships were tasked with creating diversions to tie down enemy troops. Dartige wanted to take Syria to free the Christian populations, but three army corps would have been required, so activities were confined to the seizure of suspect ships and the bombardment of key facilities ashore. Some examples follow:

28 March: *D'Entrecasteaux* fired against enemy positions in Gaza.
15 April: *Latouche-Tréville* destroyed the railway bridge at Acre.
April/May: bombardments of the Turkish trenches at El Arish by *Saint Louis* and *Jeanne d'Arc*, using aerial spotting.
May: the destruction of fuel depots at Makry, Alexandretta, Mersina, and of the Wagner factory at Jaffa by *Jeanne d'Arc* and *D'Estrées*. The same ships also fired on the German consulates at Alexandretta, Mersina and Caiffa.

From 2 June the British imposed a blockade on the Turkish coast from Gallipoli to the island of Samos, and from the 25th the French imposed a similar blockade on the Syrian coast as far as Alexandretta. The 650km zone was divided by the C-in-C into four sectors: the first two, north of Latakia, were patrolled by *Desaix*, *Guichen* and *Foudre*, the other two, which extended as far as El Arish on the Sinai Peninsula, by *Jauréguiberry*, *Amiral Charner* and *D'Estrées*; Dartige du Fournet's flagship *Jeanne d'Arc* exercised overall control of operations. However, the blockade achieved little, as maritime traffic comprised mostly small sailing vessels.

On 12–13 September an operation was mounted to rescue 4000 Armenians who had been pursued by the Turks into the mountains. They were embarked in the Bay of Antioch by *Guichen*, *D'Estrées*, *Foudre*, *Amiral Charner*, *Desaix*, and the British seaplane carrier *Anne*.

These arduous patrols took a toll of the older cruisers, and Dartige du Fournet decided that harbours closer to the patrol sectors than Port Said were required. The island of Ruad was duly occupied on 1 September, and Castellorizo on 28 December; they provided moorings and facilitated replenishment.

On 12 September Dartige du Fournet was appointed C-in-C of French naval forces at the Dardanelles. He sailed from Port Said in *Jeanne d'Arc*, transferring his flag on arrival to the battleship *Saint Louis*; *Jeanne d'Arc* then proceeded to Malta for a docking.

In mid-October there were major changes in the French Mediterranean command. Following a request by Boué de Lapeyrère to be relieved from his post, Dartige du Fournet was appointed C-in-C of the *Armée*

Navale; he was replaced in command of the Dardanelles Squadron by Vice Admiral Dominique-Marie Gauchet. The latter embarked on *Jeanne d'Arc* following her docking at Malta and was taken to Salonika via Port Said and Mudros. Command of the 3rd Squadron was given temporarily to Rear Admiral Darrieus in *Jauréguiberry* pending the arrival of a new commander, Vice Admiral Frédéric Moreau, who hoisted his flag in *Jeanne d'Arc* on 8 November. From that date French naval forces in the Middle East were as follows:

3rd Squadron: *Jeanne d'Arc* (VA Moreau), *Amiral Charner*, *Jurien de la Gravière*, *D'Estrées*.
The Naval Division of Egypt: *Montcalm* (CA Huguet), *Jauréguiberry*, *Requin*.
Seaplane Squadron: at Port Said (integrated into the British Seaplane Squadron).

Moreau pointed out that the 3rd Squadron could also be called on to defend the Canal, and proposed the integration of the *Division navale d'Egypte* into a single independent command, and this was subsequently implemented. The 3rd Squadron now comprised two divisions:

1st Division: *Jeanne d'Arc* (VA Moreau), *Amiral Charner*, *Jurien de la Gravière*
2nd Division: *D'Entrecasteaux* (CA de Spitz – the ship arrived 20 December after a major refit Brest), *Amiral Aube* (arrived 24 December to replace *Montcalm*), *Jauréguiberry*, *Requin*

THE AEGEAN

The French armoured cruisers played no part in the bombardment of the Turkish forts in the Dardanelles in early 1915, but their involvement in operations in the Aegean increased following the decision to land troops. Troop convoys sailed from Egypt on 7 and 11 April, and *Jeanne d'Arc* and *Latouche-Tréville* sailed from Alexandria on 19 and 22 April respectively to provide cover.

During the landings *Jauréguiberry*, *Henri IV*, *Jeanne d'Arc* and the Russian cruiser *Askold* provided fire support for the troops at Kum Kaleh on 25 April. The following day *Jeanne d'Arc* was struck by two 15cm shells: one burst on the shield of the after sponson gun to starboard, the other passed through the hull plating and came to rest in a coal bunker. On the night of 4/5 May *Latouche-Tréville* was off the entrance of the Dardanelles to illuminate the forts for a bombardment; she was struck aft by a 15cm (possibly 21cm) shell that caused a small fire, which was nevertheless quickly mastered.

The increasing French commitment to the Aegean led to the formation of the *Escadre des Dardanelles* on 14 May, commanded by Vice Admiral Nicol in the battleship *Patrie*. The force initially comprised a newly-formed 3rd Battle Squadron and the armoured cruiser *Kléber*, later joined by *Bruix* and *Dupleix*; the force was no longer part of the *Armée Navale*, but under the British Rear Admiral John de Robeck.

Patrols off Asia Minor were extended after April. On 26 May *Dupleix* came under fire off Bodrum and bombarded the port: she suffered twenty-seven dead and eleven wounded. On 30 May *Kléber* grounded in Scala Nova Bay; she was engaged by shore batteries but was successfully refloated. A Franco-British naval blockade was now imposed on the coasts of Asia Minor: *Dupleix*, *Kléber*, *Bruix* and *Latouche-Tréville* operated out of Mytilene (Lesbos). The blockade forces were stretched, and the cruisers had to be supplemented by trawlers.

During May three British battleships were lost to enemy torpedo boats and submarines,[8] and the major French units were withdrawn to Mudros. Fire support for the troops ashore was generally provided by the torpedo boats, although *Latouche-Tréville* conducted a bombardment on 4 June. On 21 August the battleship *Charlemagne*, supported by the cruisers *Bruix* and *Dupleix*, created a diversion off Smyrna to facilitate the landings at Suvla Bay.

On 15 September Vice Admiral Dartige du Fournet took command of the squadron. However, by late September Salonika had become a greater priority than the Dardanelles. On 7 December a decision was taken in London to evacuate the peninsula, and this operation was completed by 9 January 1916.

Below: The damaged bow of *Kléber* following a collision with the British steamer *Bourara* east of the island of Skyros (Aegean) on 16 July 1915. *(Private collection)*

Salonika

Bulgaria mobilised against Serbia on 23 September 1915. The Greeks, who were signatories to the Treaty of Bucharest, mobilised the same day, but were willing to enter the conflict only if the Allies provided 150,000 men, to be disembarked at Salonika. The Allies saw the opportunity to use the extensive port facilities of Salonika to support their forces off the Dardanelles, and agreed to send an expeditionary corps of 18,000 men. The transports left Mudros escorted by *Latouche-Tréville* on 30 September, arriving on 5 October. Dartige du Fournet was appointed to command the detached naval forces, but on 16 October was appointed as C-in-C of the *Armée Navale*; he was replaced by Vice Admiral Gauchet.

On 9 October, while Allied troops were disembarking and organising at Salonika, an Austro-Hungarian Army under the German General August von

8 *Goliath* was sunk on the night of 12/13 May by enemy torpedo boats; *Triumph* and *Majestic* were sunk on 25 and 27 May, both torpedoed by the German *U21*.

Mackensen took Belgrade. Five days later the Bulgarians declared war on Serbia, leading the British, French and Italians to declare war on Bulgaria and impose a blockade on the Bulgarian coast. *Kléber, Askold* and four British ships bombarded Dedeagach and other ports. On 14 November a Special Squadron was put together under Vice Admiral Le Bris at Malta. It comprised three battleships of the *Patrie* class, the 1st Light Division (*Waldeck-Rousseau* and *Edgar Quinet*), and nine torpedo boats.

King Constantine of Greece, whose wife Sophia was German, inclined towards Germany and Austria-Hungary, and was unhappy with the concessions made to the Allies by First Minister Eleftherios Venizelos; in December he dismissed Venizelos and dissolved the Liberal-dominated parliament. The change of administration rendered the Allied occupation of Salonika precarious, and a blockade was imposed on the Greek ports; Constantine backed down and the Special Squadron was disbanded. Reinforcements were disembarked at Salonika, and by the end of December Allied forces in Salonika totalled 100,000 men, including 50,000 of the French *Armée d'Orient*.

U-BOATS IN THE MEDITERRANEAN

The first German U-boat to operate in the Mediterranean, *U21*, arrived at Pola on 13 May. At the end of the same month she sank the British battleships *Triumph* and *Majestic* and arrived in Constantinople. Other German U-boats followed: *U34* and *U35* on 23 August, *U33* and *U39* in September, and *U38* at the end of October. Smaller German submarines of the UB type were being assembled at Pola. An anti-submarine net barrage similar to the one in the Dover Strait was assembled and maintained by forty drifters in the Otranto Strait, and the focus of naval operations in the Mediterranean now shifted dramatically towards anti-submarine warfare. Losses to German and Austro-Hungarian submarines were 30,000 tons in September, 60,000 tons in October and 135,000 tons in November.

There were never enough torpedo boats or destroyers, so A/S forces had to be boosted by converted trawlers from Britain and from the French Atlantic coast. There was less call for the big ships, which were now used primarily for fire support of the troops ashore, for coastal bombardment and, in the case of the armoured cruisers, for escort and patrol in open waters. It was now considered too hazardous to use the big armoured cruisers for blockade, and the battleships of the *Armée Navale*, now generally lying idle at Malta and Bizerte, were raided for personnel and for light guns, to be embarked on merchantmen and subchasers.

Below: *Latouche-Tréville* at Toulon some time between 21 January and 9 February 1916; the Russian five-funnelled cruiser *Askold* (left background) is also present. In September/October 1915 *Latouche-Tréville* escorted the expeditionary corps of the French *Armée d'Orient* from Mudros to Salonika. Later in October the Russian cruiser joined *Kléber* and four British ships in a bombardment of the Bulgarian port of Dedeagach. *(DR)*

THE YEAR 1916

The Evacuation of the Serbian Army

Following the Austro-Hungarian assault on Belgrade and the declaration of war on Serbia by Bulgaria (see above) the Serbian Army, caught between two forces, retreated to the Albanian coast. The French attempted to re-supply from the outset. Following meetings on 11 and 13 November 1915, it was agreed that the British would re-supply the Serbian Army using Brindisi, and that the Italians would transport supplies with naval support from the British and French. As Antivari was now unavailable, the supplies were to be landed farther down the coast at Medua and Durazzo (Albania). By the end of the year the situation of the Serbian Army had become untenable, and the only solution was a complete evacuation. Vice Admiral Chocheprat was ordered to occupy Corfu, which was to be used to rebuild the Serbian Army. The armoured cruisers of the 1st and 2nd Light Divisions were committed to supporting the evacuation.

On 7 January 1916 *Jules Michelet* transported 700 men to Bizerte, and on 9 January Chocheprat left Bizerte with an occupation force for Corfu: the troops and engineers were transported in the cruisers *Waldeck-Rousseau*, *Ernest Renan*, *Edgar Quinet* and *Jules Ferry*, accompanied by the protected cruiser *Lavoisier* and five torpedo boats. They arrived on 11 January, and promptly set about securing the northern and southern ends of the anchorage with torpedo nets (see map). The approaches to Valona were guarded by Italian destroyers, French 800-tonne torpedo boats were stationed off and to the north of Durazzo; and a cruiser and torpedo boats were deployed off Cattaro to prevent interference from Austro-Hungarian light forces. The French provided ten transports (including a hospital ship), the Italians eleven, and the British a single transport. There were two groups of escorts, also provided by the French, each comprising four torpedo boats, and a covering force of seven torpedo boats and ten submarines.

Arrangements were in place by 15 January, and the transports began the evacuation on the 17th. By early February Corfu was receiving 1800 men per day. The transport operation ended on 20 February; within two months the Serbian Army was reconstituted and re-equipped at Corfu, ready to reinforce the Allied Expeditionary Force at Salonika.

Greece, having declared her neutrality, refused to let Allied forces cross her territory, so the Serbian Army had to be transported by sea around the Peloponnese, a voyage of 550nm that exposed the transports to enemy submarines. The transport operation began on 12 April, supervised by Rear Admiral de Gueydon in *Waldeck-Rousseau*, commanding the 1st Light Division at Corfu. It was a massive undertaking: 125,000 men, 20,000 horses and 5500 vehicles were to be ferried in relays by fourteen transports and five (unarmed) merchant cruisers; there were five ships for the horses, while the artillery was lifted by two naval transports. An additional 100,000 tons of supplies and materiel was carried in seventeen chartered vessels from Marseille, Toulon, Sète, and ports in Algeria.

The fast merchant cruisers made sixteen trips up to 15 June, the chartered steamers four. Transports sailed in pairs in fast convoys (14 knots plus) that took 47 hours, or in slow convoys that took 55 hours. Protection was provided by groups of torpedo boats, trawlers and drifters operating as a relay within fixed sectors, while distant cover was available from the 1st and 2nd Light Divisions at Corfu and the 1st and 2nd Battle Squadrons at Argostoli. On average 3000 men and horses were transported per day over 47 days; not

Right: *Ernest Renan* in a Mediterranean port during the war, looking a little worse for wear. During the night of 6 December 1916, while steaming at 20 knots towards Salonika, she collided with and sank the Italian steamer *Helvetia*. *(Private collection)*

Above: *Jules Ferry* docked at Toulon for maintenance during the Great War. On the left can be seen a battleship of the *Patrie* class. *(Private collection)*

a single man was lost. The operation was completed on 27 May, and from the 30th the Serbian Army was reconstituted at Salonika; it would subsequently play a key role in military operations in the Balkans.

The Reorganisation of the *Armée Navale*

At the beginning of 1916 the *Armée Navale* was at Malta and Bizerte. In the Aegean there were French ships at Salonika and Milos, while the British naval squadron was based at Mudros, watching for a sortie from the Dardanelles. The battleships *Justice* and *Démocratie* were despatched to bolster Admiral de Robeck, who had only three British battleships available. Following the evacuation of the Dardanelles in early January, on 6 February the *Escadre des Dardanelles* became the 4th Squadron (*4e Escadre*), at the request of Vice Admiral Gauchet.

From 2 to 9 March an Allied conference took place at Malta to reassess the situation in the Mediterranean and to agree the appropriate naval dispositions. It was decided that the *Armée Navale* should be regrouped at Bizerte, and that the Italians would counter any attempt by the Austro-Hungarian fleet to sortie from its bases in the Adriatic. The Greek island of Argostoli, south of Corfu, was to be occupied by the French to provide a base for the interception of the Austro-Hungarian fleet if it attempted a passage to the Black Sea.

With the entry into service of *Bretagne* class, the battle fleet was reorganised from 15 April as follows:

1st BS (VA Gauchet): the seven dreadnoughts of the *Courbet* and *Bretagne* classes.
2nd BS (VA Favereau, who had replaced Chocheprat on 30 March): the six battleships of the *Danton* class.
3rd BS (VA Moreau): the five battleships of the *Patrie* class + *Suffren*.
Division de complément (CA Salaün): the three battleships of the *Charlemagne* class + *Henri IV*.

On 27 April the 1st and 2nd Battle Squadrons duly moved to Argostoli, while the 3rd Battle Squadron and the *Division de complément* were at Salonika, tasked with intervention on the Macedonian coast against Bulgaria (and possibly Greece) in conjunction with British forces. The 1st and 2nd Light Divisions, the composition of which was unchanged, continued to be based at Corfu.

From June 1915 the battle fleet spent most of its time swinging at its moorings. The anchorage at Argostoli was well-protected but provided little oppor-

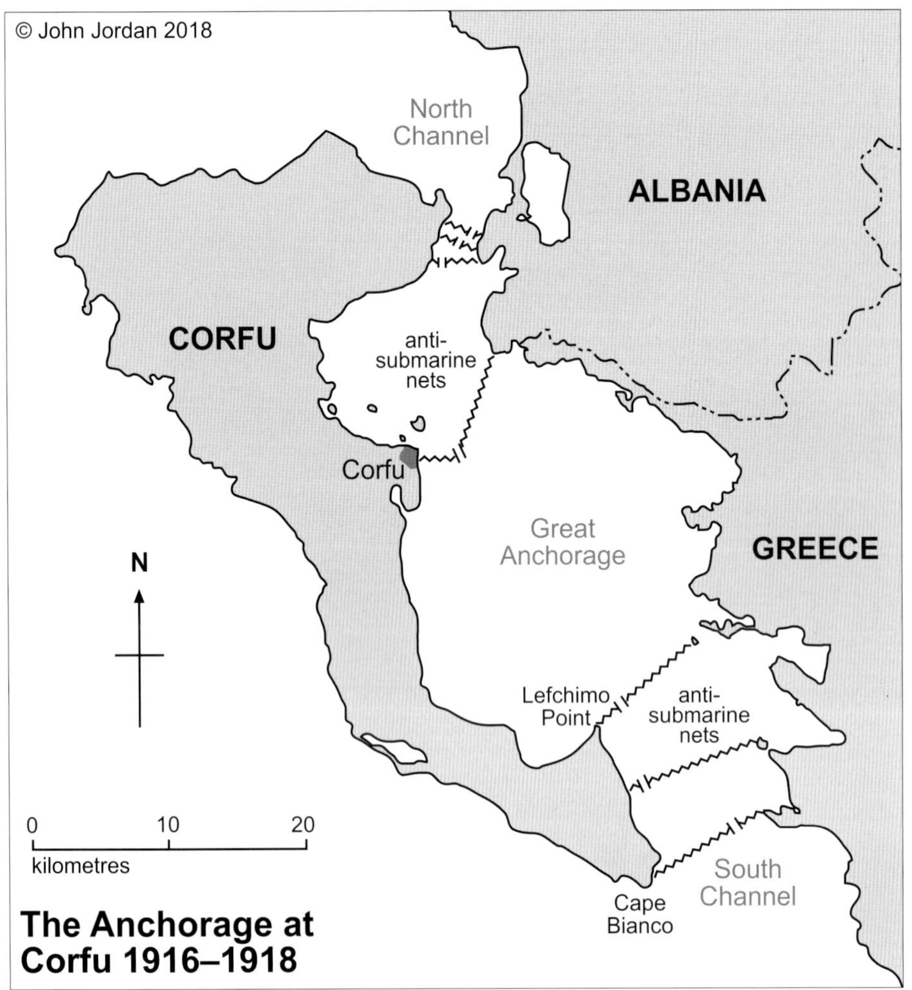

The Anchorage at Corfu 1916–1918

tunity for exercises, so the battle squadrons were detached in turn to Corfu, where the distance between the northern and southern net barrages was 12nm, making it possible to conduct basic manoeuvres, gunnery and torpedo exercises without interference from enemy submarines. The 3rd Battle Squadron at Salonika had the opportunity to use the firing range created by the British at Mudros, but returned to Argostoli in July.

The loss of the older battleships *Suffren* and *Gaulois* to enemy submarines in the space of a few days in late November served to emphasise the vulnerability of the big ships to the torpedo. Moreover, coal expenditure in the Mediterranean was now 50,000 tons per month. This led to fewer exercises, and the battleships were increasingly raided for personnel. Gauchet proposed reducing the *Armée Navale* to the 1st and 2nd Battle Squadrons, together with a handful of cruisers. By December the 1st Battle Squadron alone was short of 502 men, including 29 officers – 7 per cent of the regulation complements.

Syria and the Coastal Patrols

Wear and tear on the cruisers was making itself felt: *Amiral Aube* and the protected cruiser *Jurien de la Gravière* both suffered machinery breakdowns and had to undergo repairs. Vice Admiral Moreau questioned the continuing value of cruiser patrols, which were costing 8500 tons of coal per month, given that Turkish coastal traffic had all but ceased.

On 8 February *Amiral Charner* was torpedoed by *U21* 30nm off Beirut. The torpedo struck forward to starboard, and the old cruiser was quickly down by the head with her propellers out of water. She subsequently capsized and sank; only one survivor was found out of a crew of 427. Following her loss major ships were withdrawn from patrols, to be replaced by the torpedo boats of the 7th Flotilla from 15 February. The cruisers were now to be used only for defined missions of short duration.

In March the reorganisation of the forces at Salonika led to major changes in the composition of the 3rd Squadron. Moreau left with *Jeanne d'Arc* to take command of the 4th Squadron, *D'Entrecasteaux* and *Amiral Aube* departed for major refits at Brest, and the seaplane squadron was transferred to Argostoli to provide reconnaissance for the battle fleet. The 3rd Squadron now reverted to its former designation as the *Division de Syrie*. It comprised only the armoured cruiser *Pothuau* (CA de Spitz), the old battleships *Jauréguiberry* and *Requin*, and the 7th TB Flotilla.

A bombardment of the Whitehall factory at Mersina took place on 10 August with British participation, Alexandretta received the same treatment on 4 September, and Adalia on 16 September and 4 November. Results were mediocre due to a lack of worthwhile targets. Syria now became a secondary theatre, but the Foreign Ministry wanted a French presence maintained in the Red Sea. The protected cruiser *D'Estrées* was at Jeddah from 20 September, and trouble in Abyssinia led to the despatch of *Pothuau* and *D'Entrecasteaux* in October. However, there were British concerns that these ships would be used to extend French influence among the local Arab populations, and they were withdrawn.

The Precarious Situation in Greece

Following the evacuation of the Dardanelles, the French concentrated the 170,000 men of the *Armée d'Orient* at Salonika, which was now under a provisional government. They favoured putting pressure on Greece to join the Allied cause, but given the known inclinations of King Constantine and his German consort, Queen Sophia, the British and the Italians were reluctant to antagonise the Greeks and drive them into the arms of Germany and Austria-Hungary, and urged restraint.

In early May the Bulgarian Army entered Greek territory and on 26 May took Fort Rupel in eastern Macedonia, threatening Salonika. On 5 June the Minister ordered the C-in-C to have the 1st Light Division ready to go to the island of Milos at a moment's notice. On 8 June he was instructed to halt Greek maritime traffic and to prepare a new naval demonstration. The battleships *République* and *Démocratie* joined *Patrie* (VA Darrieus) and *Suffren* at Mudros. The French tried to pressure the Greeks into the demobilisation of their army and the dismissal of the pro-German First Minister Skouloudis. If the Greeks refused, 8000 men would occupy Piraeus, the port of Athens. Constantine conceded, and a new minister was appointed; the French operation was duly cancelled.

On 17 August a Bulgarian offensive was launched with the suspected collusion of Greek troops; Kavala was occupied on 11 September. A new display of force was planned by the French C-in-C: the battleships of Vice Admiral Darrieus were despatched to Salamina

Left: In March *Jeanne d'Arc* became the flagship of Vice Admiral Moreau commanding the 4th Squadron in the Aegean. *(DR)*

Bay, opposite the key port of Piraeus, and on 26 August Dartige du Fournet left Malta in his flagship to command the operation. On 28 August the cruiser *Bruix* was deployed to Piraeus to protect the French consulate, and plans were made to neutralise the Greek fleet. On the evening of 1 September the 1st Light Squadron (*Waldeck-Rousseau*, *Ernest Renan* and *Edgar Quinet*) arrived with the 2nd Torpedo Boat Flotilla in Salamina Bay.

Following an attack on the French consulate in Athens, Dartige du Fournet put landing parties ashore, and on 10 October ordered the decommissioning of the major units of the Greek fleet. The cruisers of the 1st Light Division at Piraeus were to prevent movement by the cruisers and torpedo boats. By the 13th Piraeus was under French control and the Greek fleet immobilised.

There followed a period of relative calm, but during November relations with the Greek government again deteriorated, and on the night of 30 November/ 1 December naval landing parties were put ashore to occupy the heights around Athens. The 1st Light

Left: *Amiral Charner* in her final configuration. She was lost on 8 February 1916, torpedoed by *U21* 35nm west of Beirut. There was only a single survivor. *(DR)*

Division provided four companies of 220 men out of the 2870 total. Fighting subsequently broke out on the Hill of the Nymphs, and despite fire support provided by the battleship *Mirabeau* the French parties lost 54 dead and 134 wounded. On 12 December Dartige du Fournet was relieved of his post as C-in-C of the *Armée Navale*; he was replaced by Vice Admiral Gauchet.

The Channel and the Atlantic

There were no big ships in the Channel in 1916. Anti-submarine patrols were conducted exclusively by torpedo boats and submarines, and extensive minefields laid across the Dover Strait and off the Belgian ports of Ostend and Zeebrugge. In the north the minefields were guarded by the four large French torpedo boats based at Dunkirk – five from March – and the light cruisers and destroyers of the British Dover Patrol, backed by monitors. The French armoured cruisers that had formerly operated from Brest and Cherbourg were redeployed either to the eastern Mediterranean or to the Atlantic.

The main concern in the early part of the year was the German commerce raiders, which were now armed merchantmen rather than regular naval units. In January the Allies were alerted to the presence of the raider *Möwe* in the area between the West Indies and the South Atlantic, and seven British cruisers were despatched to hunt her down. The French *Condé* and *Marseillaise* were still based at Fort-de-France, Martinique, and in February the 3rd Light Division (*Gloire*, *Gueydon* and *Dupetit-Thouars*) deployed to Dakar, to be joined by the protected cruiser *Château-renault*. The division returned in April and was replaced by *Desaix* and the protected cruiser *Guichen*. With the entry into service of the battleships of the *Bretagne* class, the Minister decreed a new organisation, and the armoured cruisers were assigned to seven light divisions, of which three were in the Atlantic, two (1st/2nd DL) with the battle fleet, and two (5th/7th DL) in the eastern Mediterranean. The new force structure took effect from May, and the composition of the Atlantic divisions was as follows:

3rd DL: *Gloire* (CA Etienne-Aubry), *Marseillaise*, *Amiral Aube*, *Condé*.
4th DL: *Jeanne d'Arc* (CA Grasset), *Gueydon*, *Montcalm*, *Dupetit-Thouars*.
6th DL: *Kléber* (CA Jaurès), *Desaix*, *Dupleix*.

One division was to be based at Fort-de-France and would operate in the West Indies under the British Vice Admiral North Atlantic, and a second based at Dakar was tasked with operations in the East Atlantic under the British rear admiral commanding the 9th Cruiser Squadron. On 24 April the 3rd Light Division was assigned to the West Indies, to be replaced in late September by the 4th DL. *Gloire* and *Amiral Aube* left Brest on 20 May, joining *Condé* and *Marseillaise* which were already on station. *Condé* returned in July for a refit at Chantiers de la Gironde (Bordeaux). *Kléber* (flagship of the 6th DL) left Brest on 20 July to join *Desaix* at Dakar; *Dupleix*, currently under repair, would join in September. However, the Germans steadily replaced surface raiders with submarines, against which the cruisers were of little use and vulnerable, and the cruiser divisions were withdrawn from the Atlantic by the end of the year.

THE YEAR 1917

The *Armée Navale*

In early 1917 Vice Admiral Gauchet undertook a reorganisation of the *Armée Navale*, the main body of which was to be based at Corfu from February. The fleet was still tasked primarily with the interception of the Austro-Hungarian fleet, but was hamstrung by the lack of torpedo boats: only three remained after their diversion to anti-submarine patrols. On 18 March the battleship *Danton* left Toulon for Corfu following a

Right: *Gloire* in 1916–17, with the single white band on her fore-funnel which marked her out as flagship of the 3rd Light Division (CA Etienne-Aubry). In March she deployed to Dakar, and in mid-May left Brest with *Amiral Aube* to join her sisters *Condé* and *Marseillaise* in the West Indies. *(Private collection)*

THE *ARMÉE NAVALE* 13 FEBRUARY 1917

1re escadre de ligne:	
1re division:	*Provence* (VA Gauchet), *Bretagne*, *Lorraine* (CA Sagot-Duvauroux), *France*
2e division:	*Paris* (CA de la Taste), *Courbet*, *Jean Bart*
2e escadre de ligne:	
1re division:	*Diderot* (VA Favereau), *Danton*, *Vergniaud*
2e division:	*Voltaire* (CA Amet), *Mirabeau*, *Condorcet*
3e escadre de ligne:	
1re division:	*Justice* (VA de Gueydon), *Vérité*, *Démocratie*
2e division:	*Patrie* (CA Marliève), *République*
1re escadre légère:	
1re division légère:	*Edgar Quinet* (CA Biard), *Waldeck-Rousseau*, *Ernest Renan*
2e division légère:	*Jules Michelet* (CA Charlier), *Victor Hugo*, *Jules Ferry*

refit, escorted by a single torpedo boat, *Massue*. As she passed south of Sardinia she was struck by two torpedoes from the German submarine *U64*, and sank with the loss of 290 men. She was the first of the modern French battleships to be sunk, and it was subsequently decreed that battleships sailing independently were to be escorted by three or four torpedo boats.

The other ongoing issue was a severe shortage of coal. Coal for the battle fleet was brought from Bizerte but could not be stocked ashore, so ships had to replenish directly from the colliers. By January the situation in was Corfu was concerning: only 6000 tons remained, and the cruisers had sufficient for only 48 hours of steaming. Gauchet estimated the monthly requirements at 22,000 tons for Corfu, 6,000 tons for Argostoli, 18,000 tons for Salonika, and 10,000 tons for Salamina and Milos.

In March the Minister allocated 45,000 tons of shipping to the transport of coal, to operate from Algiers, Bône and Bizerte. It was estimated that this would deliver the required 56,000 tons per month with a 25-day turnaround. However, three colliers were sunk by U-boats during July and August, others in November and December, and the coal supply problems were exacerbated by a miners' strike in October. The bunkers of the battleships were raided for the smaller patrol craft. The *Armée Navale* was able to conduct regular exercises from March to July, but after the conclusion of the operations against Greece (see below) the big ships remained at their moorings in Corfu. This reduced training opportunities for new personnel (particularly stokers and engineers), so readiness deteriorated further.

Following a conference in London it was decided to

Left: *Edgar Quinet* docked at Sidi-Abdallah (Bizerte) in August 1917. The single white band on the first funnel marks her out as the flagship of the 1st Light Division. Rear Admiral Biard had replaced Rear Admiral de Gueydon as flag officer commanding the elite 1st Light Division on 7 July of the previous year. *(Private collection)*

reduce Allied forces in the Aegean. The battleships *Patrie* (CA Salaün) and *République* were placed at the disposal of Vice Admiral Thursby; they arrived in Mudros and Salonika on 1 and 8 August respectively. Together with the old armoured cruisers *Bruix* and *Latouche-Tréville* they constituted a new *Division navale d'Orient*. On 7 August the 3rd Battle Squadron was dissolved. The three remaining battleships formed the *Division de complément* under Rear Admiral de Marliave in *Justice*; they were immobilised all year due to the shortage of coal. The old battleships *Saint Louis* and *Charlemagne* were decommissioned, and on 12 August the 2nd Light Division was dissolved: *Jules Michelet* was reassigned as the fourth ship of the 1st Light Division, *Jules Ferry* was assigned to the transport service, and *Victor Hugo* was placed in reserve at Bizerte

The Stand-off with Greece

Coercive measures against the Greeks continued into the first half of 1917. The French insisted that the Greek army be concentrated on the Peloponnese, so that it was isolated from the capital by the bridge over the Corinth Canal. Gauchet left Vice Admiral de Gueydon (3rd Squadron) in command of Allied forces on Salamina Island to blockade the Gulf of Athens (Saronic Gulf) and to be ready to intervene against the capital and the port of Piraeus.

On 26 February the provisional government at Salonika mobilised the troops in the local area. Protests in Athens led the French consul to embark in the cruiser *Bruix*. De Gueydon and Salaün, with the older battleships, were instructed to take possession of the Greek battleships and cruisers at Piraeus if there was further trouble, and to be prepared to bombard and land troops.

On 28 April *Jules Michelet* (CA Charlier) arrived at Argostoli with *Victor Hugo*, with orders to seal off the western end of the Corinth Canal and, if necessary, prevent the passage of Greek troops over the bridge. Incidents ashore finally convinced the British that regime change was necessary, and a combined operation was planned to land troops at Piraeus on either side of the Isthmus of Corinth. The 1st Light Division (*Waldeck-Rousseau* and *Ernest Renan*, with the old cruiser *Latouche-Tréville*) was sent to reinforce the 3rd Battle Squadron in Salamina Bay, and 13,300 troops were assembled at Salonika, to be transported in fourteen steamers.

On 11 June a 3500-strong detachment of troops, escorted by the battleship *République* and the cruiser *Latouche-Tréville*, was landed to secure the bridge over the Corinth Canal. At the other end of the Canal the 2nd Light Division put ashore a company of Senegalese infantry embarked at Corfu, reinforced by naval machine-gun parties. The cruiser *Bruix* was at Piraeus. On 11 June the troops from Salonika arrived

Below: *Bruix* at her moorings at Salonika on 6 December 1915. On 26 February 1917, during the Greek crisis she embarked the French consul in the port of Piraeus. *(DR)*

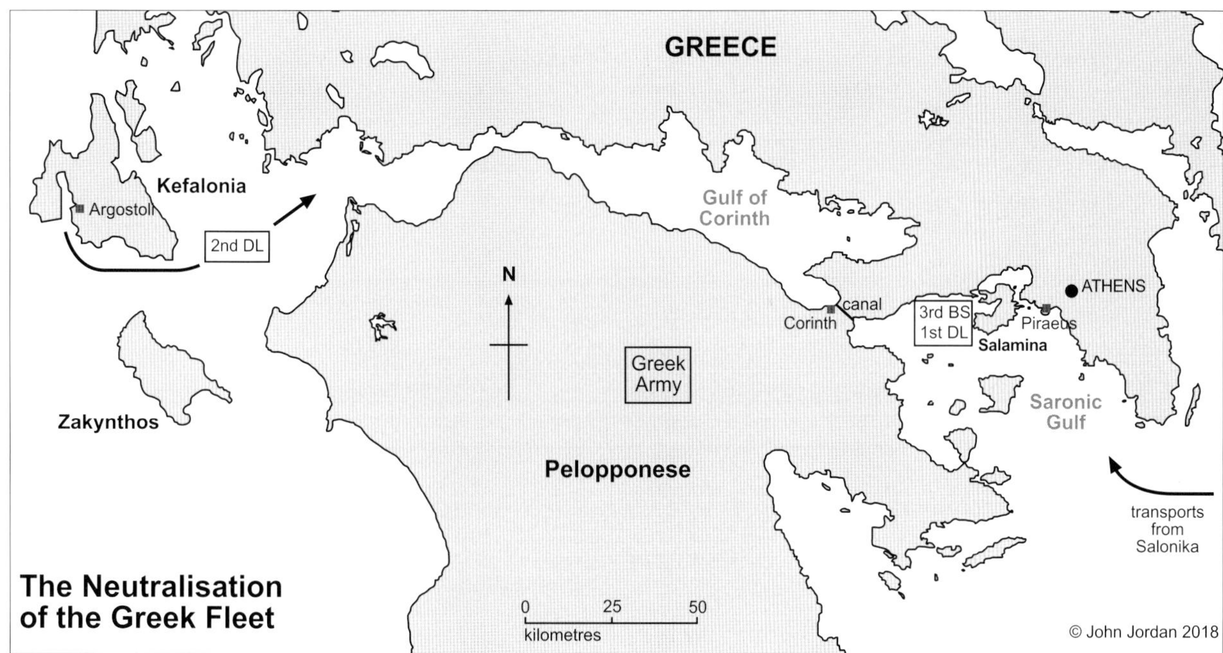

in Salamina Bay, and the battleships prepared to conduct a bombardment. *Ernest Renan* and *Waldeck-Rousseau* cruised off Piraeus, keeping watch over the Greek cruisers and torpedo boats, and an ultimatum was delivered to Constantine. On the morning of 12 June the King abdicated, nominating his son Alexander as his successor. He subsequently went into exile in Italy

On 16 June the blockade was lifted. Five days later Athens was occupied, and former First Minister Venizelos arrived from Salonika on the cruiser *Jurien de la Gravière* to form a new government. On 29 June Greece declared war on Germany and her allies.

The Atlantic

From early 1917 there was renewed activity by German surface raiders. The converted merchantmen *Möwe*, *Wolf* and *Seeadler* left Wilhelmshaven and Kiel during the last two months of 1916 and evaded the British blockade in the North Sea. *Möwe* operated off Brazil and south-west Africa, sinking twenty-five ships; she returned to Kiel on 22 March. *Wolf* crossed the Atlantic and headed for the Indian Ocean via the Cape of Good Hope; she would not return until February 1918. The sailing ship *Seeadler* operated in the South Atlantic and the Indian Ocean, sinking sixteen ships in seven months; she was wrecked on the Mopelia Atoll in French Polynesia on 2 August.

Gloire left Brest in late December 1916 to try to intercept *Möwe* off Halifax; she returned on 14 January 1917. The armoured cruisers of the French 3rd and 4th Light Divisions continued to be based at Fort-de-France in the French West Indies.

The entry of the USA into the war on 6 April 1917 made heavy demands on personnel to man patrol craft operating out of Brest, and only a single light division could be maintained in the West Indies with a second in West Africa. On 18 May it was decided to decommission the 3rd Light Division with effect from 1 June: *Gueydon*, *Montcalm*, and *Dupetit-Thouars* returned to Brest to form a reserve division under Rear Admiral Etienne-Aubry. The four cruisers remaining in the West Indies became the 4th Light Division, now renamed the *Division navale de l'Atlantique et des Antilles*. Initially the division comprised: *Jeanne d'Arc* (CA Grasset), *Marseillaise*, *Amiral Aube* and *Gloire*; *Jeanne d'Arc* returned to Brest on 21 November, to be replaced by *Condé*, and Grasset transferred his flag to *Gloire*.

On 16 August *Marseillaise* left Brazil for Agadir to escort nine tugs purchased by the French government. During a visit to Dakar in late September the ship was infested with mosquitoes, leading to an outbreak of malaria that affected 420 crew members out of 597. *Marseillaise* returned to Fort-de-France on 12 November with only the outer two engine rooms manned and speed reduced to 4 knots, and the epidemic subsided only in December.

On 18 May the 6th Light Division at Dakar was reduced from three to two ships and renamed the *Division navale de la côte d'Afrique*. *Kléber* was to return to Brest to reserve, and Rear Admiral Jaurès transferred his flag to *Dupleix*. At 06.00 on 27 June *Kléber* struck a mine laid by *UC61* in the approaches to Brest. The mine exploded to starboard abreast the bridge; Boiler

Below: *Kléber* at Brest before the war. She would be sunk by a mine laid by the submarine *UC61* off the Pierres Noires, Molène Peninsula, on 27 June 1917. *(Private collection)*

Rooms 1 and 2 and the forward auxiliary machinery room were flooded, putting the order transmitters, steering and telephones out of action. The forward part of the ship was isolated, and pressure in the after boilers maintained for 20 minutes. *Kléber*'s CO tried to ground the stricken cruiser, but the list increased rapidly and he was compelled to reverse engines. Help then arrived in the shape of trawlers, a French torpedo boat and a British steamer. At 06.30 the bulkheads began to give way, the ship starting to sink rapidly, and the order to abandon ship was given; some of the boats could not be launched because of list. The ship then rolled over and sank; thirty-eight men were lost, including fifteen from the forward boiler rooms.

Left: *Waldeck-Rousseau* quayside during the second half of 1917. The crew's washing has been hung to dry on the stays for the foremast. The paint has been scraped from the turrets and replaced with a mix of soot and grease informally known as *bouchon gras*, and the original 4ft 6in (1.37m) rangefinders have been replaced by three 15ft (4.57m) models on a Triplex pedestal mounting. *(Private collection)*

On 14 September the *Division de la côte d'Afrique* was dissolved: *Dupleix* decommissioned, leaving only *Desaix* to patrol the zone.

The Red Sea

During 1916 the British encouraged the Arabs to rise up against the Turks, but towards the end of the year they suffered reverses, and Jeddah and Rabegh were threatened. Vice Admiral Wemyss, commanding the East Indies and Egyptian Squadron, requested the assistance of *Pothuau* and *D'Entrecasteaux* to provide fire support and to re-embark troops if required. Until February one of these two ships was off Jeddah or Rabegh while the other replenished at Suez. The situation on land stabilised, and on 11 February 1917 the French cruisers (which now included *D'Estrées*) were ordered to reinforce the British naval presence in the Gulf of Aden; the division, under the command of Captain de la Fournière in *Pothuau*, was renamed *Groupe détaché en océan Indien* and based at Djibouti; *Pothuau* spent only a short time on station before being sent to refit at Saigon. *D'Entrecasteaux* and *D'Estrées* escorted convoys from Madagascar to Djibouti until the end of May; the liners proceeded through the Red Sea unescorted.

D'Entrecasteaux returned to France in late July; she would be replaced by the protected cruiser *Du Chayla*, which arrived in October. Meanwhile *Pothuau* was refitting at Saigon. In September the presence of the German raider *Wolf* was signalled, and *Pothuau* patrolled the Bay of Bengal from 22 September to 4 December. However, having laid mines in the Indian Ocean, *Wolf* moved on to the South Pacific; she would return to her home port of Kiel on 24 February 1918 after a record cruise of 451 days; during that time she had sunk thirty-five steamers and sailing ships, and two warships.

THE YEAR 1918

The Mediterranean

On 20 January 1918 the ex-German battle cruiser *Sultan Yavuz Selim* and her consort *Midilli*, now commanded by the German Vice Admiral von Rebeur-Paschwitz, sortied from the Dardanelles and headed for Mudros. The battleship *Patrie*, the only major French unit currently based at Mudros, prepared for action, and the *Justice* division of Rear Admiral Fatou, reinforced by the armoured cruiser *Jules Michelet*, was ordered to depart Corfu and Salamina for the Aegean. However, the operation was cancelled when both the enemy ships struck mines; *Midilli* was sunk, and *Sultan Yavuz Selim* grounded in the Sea of Marmara before being towed back to Constantinople.

On 3 March the Russians signed the Treaty of Brest-Litovsk, which stipulated that all Russian warships were to be decommissioned. On 4 April intelligence sources reported that *Sultan Yavuz Selim* had been repaired, and an inter-Allied conference took place on 12 April to consider the overall situation. The British were concerned that the Germans would seize the Russian Black Sea Squadron, which included two recently-completed dreadnought battleships, and then sortie in strength from the Dardanelles. They proposed a joint Anglo-French Aegean naval squadron comprising the two *Lord Nelson*s, three French dreadnoughts of the *Courbet* class and two French armoured cruisers; the remainder of the French fleet was to be joined at Corfu by an Italian battle squadron to guard against a sortie by the Austro-Hungarian fleet. The French preferred to send ships of the *Danton* class, which following modification to their main guns were capable of ranging to 17,000m. These were duly despatched to Mudros, arriving in early July. However, in the face of Italian delaying tactics, the

French withdrew from discussions about a joint force at Corfu, and the elite squadrons of the *Armée Navale*, the 1st Battle Squadron[9] and the 1st Light Division, spent the rest of the conflict at their moorings.

The reorganisation of late June also saw the *Division navale d'Orient* dissolved and replaced by a combined-arms formation designated the *Division navale de Salonique*; this included the old armoured cruisers *Latouche-Tréville* and *Bruix*.

The Atlantic

Following the appearance off the US east coast of German cruiser submarines, an Allied conference was held at Kingston on 15 February to determine how best to protect merchant shipping in the West Indies zone. It was decided that convoys leaving Saint Thomas (Virgin Islands) for Europe were to be escorted by the French cruisers of the *Division des Antilles*. This was, however, only a temporary measure, and on 21 April Rear Admiral Grasset met with the US authorities in Washington to agree the participation of the French cruisers in a more comprehensive arrangement for the escort of convoys to Europe. Of the four cruisers in the *Division des Antilles*, three were to be assigned to the US 'Cruiser Force', tasked with the protection of convoys of cargo ships that were scheduled to leave New York every two weeks – the troop convoys were escorted exclusively by US ships. *Desaix* continued to be based at Dakar and assigned to the South Atlantic zone.

On 1 March *Dupetit-Thouars* replaced *Condé* in the *Division des Antilles* and was integrated into the Cruiser Force. She returned to France with a convoy, and left again for New York, this time to replace *Gloire*, which had been damaged in a collision with the US liner *City of Athens* on 1 May; she arrived on 17 May. On 21 May Rear Admiral Grasset embarked with his staff to return to France, arriving in Brest with the convoy on 6 June. He handed over his command to Rear Admiral Grout the next day. On 15 June Grout sailed with *Dupetit-Thouars* for the USA, arriving ten days later. On his arrival he took command of the division, now renamed *Division de l'Atlantique*, hoisting his flag in *Gloire*; the other ships in the division were *Marseillaise*, *Montcalm* and *Dupetit-Thouars*

On 7 July the British proposed a new organisation for the Atlantic convoys. Convoys between Gibraltar and the USA were to be escorted by US ships (nine cruisers), convoys from Hampton Roads to Britain and from New York to France were to be escorted by the Royal Navy, and convoys from New York to the Bay of Biscay by the French (nine cruisers). The Minister[10] agreed in principle but pointed out that only six

[9] The 1st Battle Squadron now comprised the seven dreadnoughts of the *Courbet* and *Bretagne* classes plus the 'semi-dreadnought' *Condorcet*.

[10] Georges Leygues had been Minister of Marine since 16 November 1917.

Below: *Jules Michelet* was one of the ships ordered to the Aegean to contain a reported sortie by the ex-German battle cruiser *Goeben*. She is seen here at Toulon shortly after the war. *(Marius Bar)*

Left: An unusual aerial view of *Edgar Quinet* with her mainmast cut down to enable her to operate a tethered balloon for reconnaissance and anti-submarine work. Note the Triplex rangefinder at the forward end of the bridge. *(Private collection)*

French cruisers were available,[11] so the other three would have to be provided by Britain or the USA. In reality even these six cruisers were worn out, and generally operated on only two shafts when on escort and patrol duties.

On 24 July *Dupetit-Thouars* left New York with a convoy of twenty-eight ships. At 21.00 on 7 August, when 400nm from Brest, she was struck abreast the bridge by a torpedo from *U62*; a second torpedo struck to starboard 10 seconds later. Boiler Rooms 1 and 2 and the dynamo room were flooded, and the ship lost all power. A small emergency radio was used to transmit an SOS and the captain prepared to abandon ship; *Dupetit-Thouars* sank in 50 minutes.

11 Three ships of the *Gloire* class – *Amiral Aube* had been deployed to the Arctic – and three of the *Gueydon* class. *Jeanne d'Arc* was under repair at Brest.

Left: *Dupetit-Thouars* moored beneath the transporter bridge at Brest, She would be sunk on 7 August 1918 by *U62*, 400 nautical miles from Brest, while escorting a transatlantic convoy. *(Private collection)*

US destroyers from Brest rescued the survivors on 8 August; only twelve men were lost, most of whom were stokers in the forward boiler rooms. With the loss of *Dupetit-Thouars* the *Division de l'Atlantique* was reinforced by *Condé* in August.

The Arctic

Following the signing of the Treaty of Brest-Litovsk, the French despatched *Amiral Aube* to Murmansk to protect and repatriate French nationals, including the military missions; she arrived on 18 March. On 23 March 1918 an Allied conference discussed the resupply of Allied troops through Murmansk.

On 10 August the British took Arkhangelsk with the help of French troops and support from *Amiral Aube*. The latter ship was replaced by *Gueydon*, which left France on 12 October, arriving six days later; she moored for the winter on 27 November.

On 21 April 1919 *Montcalm* arrived at Murmansk to embark 176 mutineers from the French colonial infantry. She left on 20 May, arriving in Brest eight days later; the mutineers were then transferred to *Condé*, which took them to Casablanca for court martial. *Condé* subsequently relieved *Gueydon* on 25 June, and covered the withdrawal of French troops from Arkhangelsk to Murmansk, which in turn was evacuated by the Allies on 12 October.

Aftermath in the Black Sea

On 13 November an Allied naval squadron entered the Dardanelles and moored off Constantinople. The French Premier Georges Clemenceau, who along with his British allies wished to push back against the Bolsheviks, planned to occupy the ports in southern Ukraine and seize the coal basin of Donetsk; the French and Greek armies in the Balkans were to operate in conjunction with the 'White Russians'. The battleships of the 2nd Battle Squadron at Constantinople were reinforced with the dreadnoughts *France* and *Jean Bart*, which arrived from Corfu on 11 December and 10 January respectively; Vice Admiral Jean-François-Charles Amet was appointed to command the naval squadron, now designated the 2nd Squadron, and hoisted his flag in *Jean Bart* on 15 January.

The winter of 1918–19 was cold, and the French colonial troops were neither accustomed to nor equipped for these conditions, leading to mutinies ashore. The local population was generally hostile, so the naval personnel had to do the work of dockers, and there was growing discontent among the crews regarding this unwanted (and, many believed, unwarranted) extension of their military service and the continued separation from their families in metropolitan France. Moreover, the land campaign did not go well. The White Russian forces were poorly organised and led, and there were repeated military reverses. Red Army forces under General Grigoriev took first Kherson, then Nikolayev, which was evacuated on 12–14 March. On 19 March Mariupol was attacked, and on 7 April Odessa fell. Only Crimea, with its key port of Sevastopol, remained. The French attempted to hold on to the peninsula, but Sevastopol itself was immobilised by strikes and demonstrations, which had a major psychological impact on the French seamen when ashore on leave. On 12 April the French decided to evacuate. An attack launched by the Red Army on 16 April would probably have succeeded without the intervention of the battleships.

Right: The cruiser *Condé* at Arkhangelsk in the summer of 1919, when she provided cover for the withdrawal of French troops to Murmansk. *(Courtesy of Jean-Marie Gall)*

Above: *Ernest Renan* at the end of the Great War. The mainmast was cut down to enable the ship to operate a tethered observation balloon. In March 1919 *Ernest Renan* was assigned, together with *Jules Michelet* and *Waldeck-Rousseau*, to the 2nd Division of the 2nd Squadron, which operated against the Bolsheviks in the Black Sea. *(Private collection)*

On 16 April there was a mutiny on the torpedo boat *Protet*, led by engineering officer André Marty. Three days later the agitation spread to the battleships *Jean Bart* and *France*: groups of seamen gathered on deck and sang the Internationale; equipment on board was vandalised and prisoners released from the cells. Amet assembled the crew of *Jean Bart* on the quarterdeck and offered a return to France without sanctions, but the reception was so hostile that he was compelled to leave the ship. On 20 April the red flag was raised on the two battleships. The mutiny now spread to the battleships *Vergniaud*, *Mirabeau* and *Justice*. However, a division opened up between the small number of radicals and the vast majority of the crews who simply wanted to return to France, and this was exploited by the officers of the ships to restore a degree of order. The 2nd Squadron left Sevastopol on 23 April, and *France* arrived at Bizerte on the 29th.

Meanwhile, on 2 March the armoured cruiser *Waldeck-Rousseau*, flagship of Rear Admiral Louis Caubet, had left Toulon to join the 2nd Squadron, in which she was to form a 2nd Division with *Ernest Renan* and *Jules Michelet*. She joined the old cruiser *Bruix* off Odessa on 4 April, and participated in the evacuation on 9 April. On 25 April news arrived of the events off Sevastopol, and the crew learned that Marty was imprisoned on board their ship. This provoked a further mutiny. Caubert assembled the crew to make the same offer as Amet, but his words were drowned by whistles and booing, and he even feared that the ship might be delivered to the Bolsheviks. Order was briefly restored, but the mutiny broke out again when sixty men arrived from Sevastopol. The mutineers gathered on the forecastle, but the officers, CPOs and senior ratings formed an armed guard on the quarter-deck and advanced to the bow. Most of the crew opted to rally behind them, leaving only a hard core who were arrested. *Waldeck-Rousseau* left the Black Sea on 28 April, and arrived back in Toulon on 31 July after a detour to Cattaro.

The situation initially returned to normal, but there would be a second wave of mutinies in the summer that carried on into the autumn and infected the ports and naval bases. At Toulon the crew of the battleship *Provence* mutinied and the red flag was raised. The Minister responded by sending the classes of 1909–1911 on leave, and order was eventually restored.

Despite the promises made by the ships' officers, courts martial followed and 100 seamen were convicted, of whom six had served in *Waldeck-Rousseau*. The sentences handed out were draconian: death (subsequently commuted to 20 years), 10–20 years hard labour, 15–20 years in prison or 6–8 years of community service. However, these sentences were subsequently reduced, and by the end of 1920 only twenty-one men were still detained. The *Parti communiste français* (PCF) was founded in 1920 and lobbied for a general amnesty, which was accorded in July 1922 except for Marty, who was finally released in 1923; the following year he was elected to the National Assembly.

CHAPTER 12:

POSTSCRIPT

Nineteen French armoured cruisers survived the war out of the total of twenty-three which had been in service on 2 August 1914:

2 x *Amiral Charner* class [*Amiral Charner* torpedoed by *U21* 8 Feb 1916]
Pothuau
D'Entrecasteaux
Jeanne d'Arc
2 x *Dupleix* class [*Kléber* lost to mine laid by *UC61* 27 Jun 1917]
2 x *Gueydon* class [*Dupetit-Thouars* torpedoed by *U62* 7 Aug 1918]
4 x *Gloire* class
2 x *Léon Gambetta* class [*Léon Gambetta* torpedoed by AH *U5* 27 Apr 1915]
Jules Michelet
Ernest Renan
2 x *Edgar Quinet* class

Like their foreign counterparts, they had rarely been employed as intended; they performed patrol and escort duties, for which their seakeeping qualities – principally a function of their size – and their economical reciprocating engines made them well-suited. Their elaborate protection systems, which were responsible for a substantial proportion of their cost, were tested only by shore batteries; not a single shot was fired in anger against them by an enemy surface vessel. They proved particularly vulnerable to torpedoes and mines, which not only accounted for the four wartime losses but imposed increasing constraints on their employment for patrol close to land. Their powerful gun batteries proved valuable for fire-support missions in the eastern Mediterranean, and the big, modern cruisers of the 1st and 2nd Light Divisions were frequently deployed as fast transports for troops, but they were never used for the high-speed missions for which their advanced propulsion systems were designed.

Of the major naval powers, France was the only one which failed to build modern light cruisers. When the war ended, the other navies generally decommissioned their armoured cruisers, except for a handful of ships used for training; the French ships, on the other hand, had to be retained *faute de mieux*, at least until the ex-German light cruisers allocated as 'prizes' could be refurbished.[1] The latest French armoured cruisers

[1] The former German ships were: *Mulhouse* (ex-*Stralsund*), *Strasbourg* (ex-*Regensburg*), *Metz* (ex-*Königsberg*) and *Colmar* (ex-*Colbert*). *Colmar* was deployed to the Far East (DNEO) on 19 June 1922, returning on 11 February 1924. She decommissioned in November of the same year; the other three ships decommissioned 1929–30, when the newly-built cruisers of the *Duguay-Trouin* class entered service. The former Austrian cruiser *Novara*, rechristened *Thionville*, became a training ship for the torpedo school (*Ecole d'application de lancement à la mer*, or EALM).

Right: *Pothuau* off the coast of Provence. From 1919 until 1926 she would resume her pre-war role as a gunnery training ship. The mainmast had already been landed in order to accommodate a tethered balloon. The two main 194mm turrets were disembarked and replaced by four single 75mm HA guns. Note the Triplex rangefinder forward of the bridge. *(DR)*

were only seven years old; most were less than 15 years old, having been completed in 1903–04. However, the war had shortened their service lives considerably. In the pre-war period the ships were generally active only during the spring and summer months, and some spent long periods in reserve for maintenance and repair. During 1914–1919, on the other hand, they had been driven hard, often in difficult winter conditions and with little respite; many were worn out and needed serious refurbishment of their boilers and engines.

THE OLDER CRUISERS

The older ships completed during the 1890s were quickly decommissioned at the end of the war with the exception of *Pothuau*, which resumed her pre-war role as a gunnery training ship (*Ecole d'application du tir à la mer*, or EATM); she was decommissioned in June 1926 and replaced by the more recent *Gueydon* (see below).

THE ATLANTIC

The six surviving cruisers of the *Gueydon* and *Gloire* classes continued to serve in the *Division navale de l'Atlantique*[2] until 1920–1, when the four *Gloire*s were placed in reserve. The machinery of *Gueydon* and *Montcalm* was in slightly better condition, and both ships continued in service. *Montcalm* deployed to the Far East as flagship of the DNEO in 1921–2, and in 1923 *Gueydon* underwent a three-year reconstruction at Brest to equip her as a gunnery training ship (EATM); she replaced *Pothuau* in this role in 1927.

Jeanne d'Arc was refurbished and resumed her role as school ship for officer cadets, undertaking no fewer than nine world cruises, the last of which took place in 1927–8. Worn out, she was replaced by *Edgar Quinet* in 1928, pending the entry into service of a new purpose-built ship, also to be named *Jeanne d'Arc*. Unfortunately *Edgar Quinet* ran aground off Algeria in January 1930, and the role of school ship for officer cadets had to be shared between three of the newly-completed treaty cruisers for the annual training cruise of 1930–1.

THE MEDITERRANEAN

Following the abortive interventions in the Black Sea, French attention from 1919 to 1921 was focused on the Eastern Mediterranean. In accordance with the Sykes–Picot Agreement secretly signed by Britain and France in 1916, the British assumed control of most of Ottoman Mesopotamia and the southern part of Ottoman Syria (Palestine and Transjordan), while the French controlled the rest of Ottoman Syria, including Lebanon, Alexandretta and other areas of south-eastern Turkey. In 1923 British and French control of these territories would be formalised by a mandate from the League of Nations.

The French Navy responded to this new situation by dissolving the *Armée Navale* on 10 February 1920 and replacing it by two formations: the Western Mediterranean Squadron (*Escadre de la Méditerranée occidentale*), and the Eastern Mediterranean Squadron (*Escadre de la Méditerranée orientale*) – see accompanying table. The latter force had a single modern battleship as flagship: *Provence* flew the flag of Vice Admiral Ferdinand-Jean-Jacques de Bon. It also included the 1st Light Division of Rear Admiral Charles-Henri Dumesnil, comprising the armoured cruisers *Edgar Quinet*, *Ernest Renan* and *Waldeck-Rousseau*. On 20 July 1921 the Western and Eastern Mediterranean Squadrons were dissolved; in their place there was a single squadron, the *Escadre de la Méditerranée*, and the 1st Light Division became the *Division du Levant*.

MEDITERRANEAN SQUADRONS: MARCH 1920

Escadre de la Méditerranée occidentale	
1re Escadre de ligne:	
1re Division de ligne:	*Courbet* (VA Charlier), *Jean Bart*, *Paris*
2e Division de ligne:	*France* (CA Violette), *Lorraine*
1re Escadrille de CT:	*Casque* (CF), *Bouclier*, *Capitaine Mehl*, *Bisson*, *EV Roux*, *Mangini*
2e Escadrille de CT: (replacements)	*Magon*, *Cimeterre*, *Cdt Bory*, *Cdt Lucas*, *Protet*, *Francis Garnier*
transports:	*Duguay-Trouin*, *Bien-Hoa*
oiler:	*Csar Nicolas II*
minelayer:	*Pluton*
Escadre de la Méditerranée orientale	
flagship:	*Provence* (VA de Bon)
1re Division légère:	*E Quinet* (CA Dumesnil), *E Renan*, *W-Rousseau*
2re Escadrille de torpilleurs:	*Algérien* (CF), *Bambara*, *Kabyle*, *Sakalave*, *Sénégalais*, *Somali*
3e Escadrille de torpilleurs:	*Touareg* (CF), *Annamite*, *Arabe*, *Hova*, *Marocain*, *Tonkinois*
gunboats:	*Aigle*, *Espiègle*, *Tapageuse*, *Capricieuse*
sloops:	*Dunkerque*, *Yser*, *La Suippe*, *Tahure*, *Toul*, *Bar-le-Duc*, *Duchaffault*, *Duperré*
Division de Syrie:	*Jurien de la Gravière* (CA Mornet), *Algol* yacht *Albatros*

OVERSEAS DEPLOYMENTS

Desaix deployed to the Far East in 1919–21. In 1921 the *Division navale de l'Atlantique* was dissolved and replaced by the 'Flying Division' (*Division volante de l'Atlantique*). The armoured cruisers of the *Gloire* class were paid off, and the new division was formed with *Montcalm*, *Jules Michelet* and the two surviving units of the *Gambetta* class, *Jules Ferry* and *Victor Hugo*, which had been in reserve at Bizerte at the end of the war. The Flying Division was intended to provide the ships for overseas deployment, notably to the Far East. *Montcalm* deployed as flagship of the DNEO in 1921–2, *Jules Michelet* (flag) and *Victor Hugo* in 1922–3, *Jules Ferry* in 1923–5, and *Jules Michelet* again in 1925–7 (see accompanying table). All of these ships were decommissioned following their last deployment, and the final deployment to the Far East by an armoured cruiser was by *Waldeck-Rousseau* in 1929–32.

[2] The official designation of the squadron at Brest was initially the *Escadre du Ponant* (Western Squadron). From 15 September 1921 it was designated the *Division navale de la Manche et de la Mer du Nord* (Naval Division of the Channel and North Sea).

DEPLOYMENTS TO INDOCHINA 1919–1927

	Left France	Arrived Saigon	Left Saigon	Returned France
Desaix	Nov 1919	??	??	31 Mar 1921
Montcalm	15 Jan 1921	22 Mar 1921	27 Jun 1922	16 Aug 1922
Colmar	19 Jun 1922	07 Sep 1922	?? Nov 1924	11 Feb 1925
Jules Michelet	12 Oct 1922	19 Apr 1923	10 May 1923	11 Jul 1923
Victor Hugo	[as *Jules Michelet*]		[as *Jules Michelet*]	
Jules Ferry	27 Sep 1923	21 Nov 1923	21 Sep 1925	10 Nov 1925
Jules Michelet	15 Jun 1925	?? Jul 1925	?? May 1929	10 Jul 1929
Primauguet	20 Apr 1927	09 Aug 1927	07 Oct 1927	22 Dec 1927
Waldeck-Rousseau	10 May 1929	22 Jun 1929	?? May 1932	03 Jul 1932
Duguay-Trouin	05 Sep 1931	16 Oct 1931	14 Nov 1931	22 Dec 1931

Note:
From 1930 all deployments made to the Far East were by modern cruisers.

THE POST-WAR CAREERS OF THE FRENCH ARMOURED CRUISERS

The following information should be treated with caution; it has been compiled from a variety of French secondary sources that often disagree and occasionally contradict themselves. The dates of deployments and events are generally reliable, but the dates of assignment to a particular formation are complicated, as always, by the time-lag between the original ministerial directive (DM) and its implementation.

Amiral Charner class

Latouche-Tréville

18 Dec 1918 Reserve Corfu; used to train gunlayers.
31 Dec 1918 Returned to Toulon.
1 May 1919 Decommissioned; stricken 21 Jun 1920; hulked by company refloating battleship *Liberté* and sold for BU 1926.

Bruix

31 Jan 1918 Reserve Salonika until end of war.
29 Nov 1918 Recommissioned and sailed to Constantinople; assigned Armoured Cruiser Division of 2nd Squadron; March–May Black Sea; evacuations Nikolayev and Odessa; not involved in mutinies but some unrest; to Constantinople 5 May.
22 May 1919 Left for Toulon; placed in reserve.
21 Jun 1920 Stricken; sold for BU 21 Jun 1921.

Below: *D'Entrecasteaux* lying disarmed at Zeebrugge during the 1920s. *(DR)*

Left: *Baltyk*, ex-*D'Entrecasteaux*, at Gdynia during the 1930s. Her turrets and boat-handling equipment have been removed, and she has now been reduced to a training hulk. *(Private collection)*

Below: *Jeanne d'Arc* on a visit to Antwerp during one of her world training cruises. The 138mm QF sponson guns have been disembarked. *(Leo van Ginderen)*

Pothuau

1919	Gunnery training ship (EATM): *Ecole de canonnage*, Toulon.
12 Jun 1926	Decommissioned; stricken 3 Nov 1927.
25 Sep 1929	Sold for scrap.

D'Entrecasteaux

10 Jul 1918	Repairs Bizerte.
25 Jan 1919	Durazzo and Cattaro; monitored handover of Austro-Hungarian ships to Italy; repatriated troops of *Armée d'Orient*.
2 Jul 1919	Reserve Brest; decommissioned 1 Jun 1921.
24 May 1923	Towed to Zeebrugge; depot ship for Belgian torpedo boats.
4 Feb 1926	Returned to Cherbourg; sold to Poland.
28 Jul 1927	Sailed from Cherbourg for Gdynia; renamed *Karl Wladislaw IV*, then *Baltyk* 13 Aug.
Sep 1939	Survived German bombing of Gdynia; utilised as hulk by Germans.
Jun 1942	Broken up.

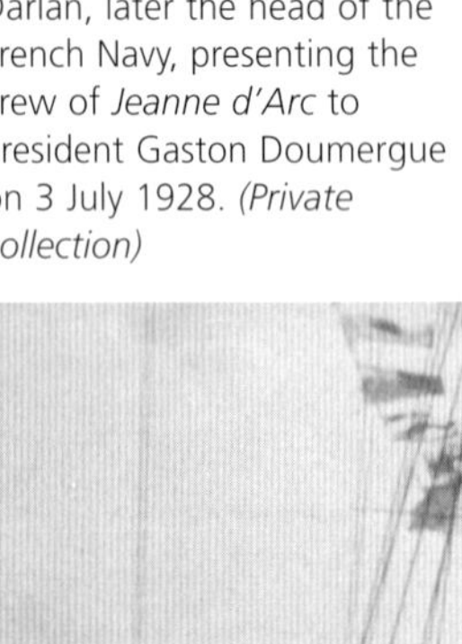

Below: Captain François Darlan, later the head of the French Navy, presenting the crew of *Jeanne d'Arc* to President Gaston Doumergue on 3 July 1928. *(Private collection)*

Jeanne d'Arc

1919	Refitted Brest to resume role as school ship for officer cadets; recommissioned August.
Aug 1919	School ship for officer cadets, *Division des écoles de l'Océan*; nine world cruises.
1928	Decommissioned; renamed *Jeanne d'Arc II* 1930.
15 Feb 1933	Stricken and laid up Landévennec.
9 Jul 1934	Sold for BU; towed to La Seyne August.

***Dupleix* class**

Dupleix

15 Oct 1917	Reserve Brest.
1 May 1919	Decommissioned; stricken 27 Sep.
1920	Laid up Landévennec.
1922	Sold for BU.

Desaix

[11 Nov 1918]	Dakar.
Nov 1919	*Division navale de l'Extrême Orient* (DNEO).
31 Mar 1921	Returned Toulon, decommissioned; stricken 27 Jul.
1927	Sold for BU.

***Gueydon* class**

Gueydon

12 Oct 1918	Arctic (replaced *Amiral Aube*): Murmansk and Arkangelsk.
20 Jun 1919	Left for Cherbourg.
Nov 1919	*Division de la Baltique* (replaced *Marseillaise*).
15 Mar 1920	*Division navale de l'Atlantique* (replaced *Condé*).
Nov 1921	*Division volante de l'Atlantique.*
21 Nov 1922	Reserve Brest.
1923	Refit Brest to serve as gunnery training ship (EATM).
1927	*Ecole de canonnage*, Toulon (replaced *Pothuau*).
24 Jul 1931	Stricken and hulk Brest.
1932	EATM Toulon.
Jul 1935	Hulk Brest until Armistice Jun 1940.
1941	Used as dummy for *Prinz Eugen*.
1942	Destroyed during occupation; BU after war.

Montcalm

27 Nov 1918	Returned Brest.
19 Dec 1918	*Division de la Baltique.*
Apr 1919	Murmansk.
28 May 1919	Returned Brest; *Division de l'Atlantique.*
15 Jan 1921	*Division navale de l'Extrême Orient* (DNEO) as flagship; embarked Marshal Joffre Singapore 6 Dec for visit to Japan Feb 1922.
16 Aug 1922	Returned Brest; reserve Landévennec; repairs Lorient.
20 Sep 1923	Assigned *Division volante*; in poor condition, did not leave; to reserve.
28 Oct 1926	Stricken and became hulk Brest.
1 Oct 1934	Renamed *Trémintin* to free up name for new cruiser; hulk Brest until Armistice Jun 1940.

1943	Destroyed during occupation; BU after war.

Gloire class

Gloire

11 Nov 1918	*Division de l'Atlantique* with *Marseillaise, Condé*; 1 Sep 1919 escorted liner *Leviathan* returning General Pershing to USA.
7 Jul 1922	Stricken; sold for BU 1923.

Marseillaise

11 Nov 1918	*Division de l'Atlantique* with *Gloire, Condé.*
18 Dec 1918	*Division de la Baltique.*
Mar 1920	*Division de l'Atlantique* with *Gloire, Condé*; 29 Jun 1920 escorted liner *George Washington* carrying President Wilson back to USA.
1921	Reserve Brest.
1925	Training ship: *Ecole de canonnage*, Toulon.
1929	Stricken.
13 Feb 1932	Renamed *Marseillaise II*; condemned and BU Brégaillon.

Amiral Aube

Mar 1918	Arctic.
early 1919	*Division de l'Atlantique* with *Gloire, Marseillaise, Condé.*
Mar 1920	Decommissioned Mar 1920; special reserve Lorient.
7 Jul 1922	Stricken; sold for BU 1924.

Condé

11 Nov 1918	*Division de l'Atlantique* with *Gloire, Marseillaise.*
15 Mar 1920	Special reserve Brest (replaced by *Gueydon*).
1922	Barracks for *fusiliers marins*, Lorient.
1928	*Ecole des fusiliers*, Lorient.
15 Feb 1933	Stricken, but continued to serve as hulk.
1940	Seized by Germans Lorient; depot ship for submarines.
1944	Target, sunk by aerial bombs; BU 1954.

Below: *Gueydon* following her 1926 reconstruction, after which she served as a training ship for the Gunnery School at Toulon. The two main turrets were disembarked, the bridge structure rebuilt, and the ventilation trunking amidships received a platform for two searchlight projectors. The foremost turret was replaced by a single open mounting for a 138.6mm gun, the after turret by two 75mm HA guns; the guns may have been transferred from *Gueydon*'s predecessor as EATM ship, *Pothuau*. Note the multiple rangefinders installed atop the bridge. *(Private collection)*

Above: *Gueydon* at Brest after 1935, when she became an accommodation ship for the Navy's initial training establishment. To starboard, the old transport *Armorique* and the disarmed cruiser *Trémintin* (formerly *Montcalm*), also hulked and serving for boys' training. *(Private collection)*

Right: A sad end for *Gueydon*, disguised in 1942 as the German cruiser *Prinz Eugen* in order to deceive the RAF. *(Private collection)*

Above: In June 1920 *Marseillaise* escorted the liner *George Washington*, with President Woodrow Wilson embarked, back to the United States. *(Marius Bar)*

***Léon Gambetta* class**

Jules Ferry

Jul 1918	Reserve Bizerte.
19??	Returned Toulon.
27 Sep 1923	*Division navale de l'Extrême Orient* (DNEO).
10 Nov 1925	Returned Toulon; reserve.
19 Jan 1927	Stricken.
1928	Sold for BU.

Victor Hugo

11 Nov 1918	Reserve Bizerte.
May 1922	*Division volante de l'Atlantique.*
12 Oct 1922	*Division navale de l'Extrême Orient* (DNEO) with *Jules Michelet.*
11 Jul 1923	Returned Toulon; reserve.
20 Jan 1928	Stricken.
26 Nov 1930	Sold for BU.

Jules Michelet

12 Dec 1918	*Escadre de l'Entente* (Constantinople).
2 Mar 1919	*2e Division, 2e Escadre* (Black Sea).
Jul 1919	Returned to Toulon; reserve.
Nov 1921	*Division volante de l'Atlantique* (flag).
12 Oct 1922	*Division navale de l'Extrême Orient* (DNEO) as flagship, with *Victor Hugo.*
11 Jul 1923	Returned Toulon; reserve.
15 Jun 1925	*Division navale de l'Extrême Orient* (DNEO) as flagship.
10 Jul 1929	Returned Toulon; decommissioned.
1931	Converted as target for *Ecole de canonnage*; stricken 3 May 1936; sunk 8 May 1937 by submarine *Thétis* during manoeuvres.

Ernest Renan

2 Mar 1919	*2e Division, 2e Escadre* (Black Sea)
Mar 1920	*Division légère de la Méditerranée orientale*; evacuated Georgian political class from Batoumi, together with national treasure (fleeing Soviets).
20 Jul 1921	*Division navale du Levant*; Sep 1922

Left: *Condé* was used as a target in the Bay of Verdon during the Second World War. *(Private collection)*

	brought back refugees from Smyrna following Turkish occupation.
Jun 1924	Reserve Toulon.
1927	Training ship: *Ecole de canonnage*, Toulon.
1931	Converted to target vessel.
3 May 1936	Stricken; sold for BU 1937.

Edgar Quinet class

Edgar Quinet

1 Jul 1919	Reserve Bizerte.
Mar 1920	*Division légère de la Méditerranée orientale* (CA Dumesnil).
20 Jul 1921	*Division navale du Levant*; Apr 1922 embarked President Millerand for visits to Portugal, Morocco and Algeria; Sep 1922 brought back refugees from Smyrna following Turkish occupation.
1 Oct 1923	*Escadre de la Méditerranée.*
1924	Reserve Toulon.
1927–8	Converted as school ship for officer cadets, *Division des écoles de l'Océan* (replaced *Jeanne d'Arc*).
12 Oct 1928	First world cruise.
10 Oct 1929	Second world cruise; 4 Jan 1930 grounded Cap Blanc, Algeria; 8–9 Jan broke back and sank.

Waldeck-Rousseau

2 Mar 1919	*2e Division, 2e Escadre* (Black Sea); involved in mutinies.
31 Jul	Returned Toulon.
Mar 1920	*Division légère de la Méditerranée orientale*; evacuated Wrangel army from Novorossiysk, Black Sea.
20 Jul 1921	*Division navale du Levant.*
Sep 1923	Returned Toulon; reserve.
10 May 1929	*Division navale de l'Extrême Orient* (DNEO) as flagship.
3 Jul 1932	Returned Toulon.
1932	Reserve Brest.
14 Jun 1936	Stricken; hulked Landévennec, destroyed during Occupation.

Below: In April 1922 President Alexandre Millerand embarked on *Edgar Quinet* for visits to the French colonies in North Africa which took in Tunisia, Morocco and Algeria. *(Marius Bar)*

Above: *Ernest Renan* is seen here during the early/mid-1920s. She has a uniform overall light grey paint scheme. A Triplex rangefinder has been fitted atop the bridge and a 75/50 HA gun (Mle 1897 G) atop the forward turret. In 1927 *Renan* was assigned to the Gunnery Training School at Toulon. *(Private collection)*

Left: *Jeanne d'Arc* at the end of her career. All except the main 194mm guns have been removed, and the masts and superstructures have been stripped of equipment. The photo may have been taken shortly before she was towed to the 'ships' graveyard' at Landévennec in 1933. *(Private collection)*

Jules Michelet during a visit to Melbourne in January 1923. She is flying the flag of Rear Admiral Eugène Gilly, C-in-C of the DNEO. *(Allan C Green collection, State Library of Victoria, H91_325_22)*

Above: *Ernest Renan* as a target in 1931. *(Private collection)*

Right: *Edgar Quinet* visiting an unidentified port during her first deployment as a school ship for officer cadets in 1928–9. During her conversion, the centre boilers and their corresponding funnels were suppressed and the 194mm casemate guns disembarked. *(Private collection)*

Left: The wreck of *Edgar Quinet*, which grounded on a rock off Cape Blanc in Algeria during her second world cruise. The ship broke her back on the night of 8/9 January 1930, making salvage out of the question. *(Private collection)*

Below: *Waldeck-Rousseau* at her moorings in the midst of an international fleet during her deployment to the Far East from 1929 to 1932. *(Private collection)*

Waldeck-Rousseau (left), USS *Rochester* (CA 2) (centre), and a Japanese armoured cruiser, probably *Tokiwa* (right), moored in the Whangpoo River, Shanghai, China, April/May 1932. *(Courtesy of Conrad Waters)*

SOURCES

PUBLICATIONS

Bertin, Louis-Emile and Robertson, Leslie S (translator and editor), *Marine Boilers: Their Construction and Working*, 2nd revised/enlarged edition (New York: Van Nostrand, 1906).

Brown, David K, *Warrior to Dreadnought: Warship Development 1860-1905* (London: Chatham Publishing, 1997).

Dumas, Robert, and Prévoteaux, Gérard, *Les cuirassés de 18 000 tonnes* (Outreau: Lela Presse, 2011).

Feron, Luc, 'The Cruiser *Dupuy-de-Lôme*', *Warship 2011* (London: Conway, 2011).

Feron, Luc, 'The Armoured Cruisers of the *Amiral Charner* Class', *Warship 2014* (London: Conway, 2014).

Feron, Luc, 'The Armoured Cruiser *Jeanne d'Arc*', *Warship 2018* (Oxford: Osprey Publishing, 2018).

Feron, Luc, 'Le Croiseur *D'Entrecasteaux*', *Marines*, nos 46–48 (Rennes: Marines Editions, 2006–07).

Feron, Luc, '*Dupleix* Croiseur Cuirassé', *Marines & Forces Navales*, no 168 (Rennes: Marines Editions, 2017).

Feron, Luc, *Cent ans de Marine Française: Les Croiseurs* (*hors série*) (Rennes: Marines Editions, 2002).

Friedman, Norman, *Naval Weapons of World War One* (Barnsley: Seaforth Publishing, 2011).

Friedman, Norman, *British Cruisers of the Victorian Era* (Barnsley: Seaforth Publishing, 2012).

Gardiner, Robert (ed), *Conway's All the World's Fighting Ships 1860-1905* (London: Conway Maritime Press, 1979).

Gardiner, Robert (ed), *Conway's All the World's Fighting Ships 1905-1922* (London: Conway Maritime Press, 1985).

Guiglini, Jean, *Les marques particulières des navires de guerre français 1900-1950* (Vincennes: Service Historique de la Marine, 2002).

Jordan, John, and Caresse, Philippe, *French Battleships of World War One* (Barnsley: Seaforth Publishing, 2017).

Jordan, John, and Moulin, Jean, *French Cruisers 1922-1956* (Barnsley: Seaforth Publishing, 2013).

Le Guilcher, J-M, *Traité Pratique des Chaudières & Machines de la Marine de Commerce*, 3rd edition (Paris: Société d'Editions Géographiques, Maritimes et Coloniales, 1923).

Prévoteaux, Gérard, *Les cuirassés de 15 000 tonnes* (Outreau: Lela Presse, 2006).

Prévoteaux, Gérard (completed Dumas, Robert), *La Marine Française dans la Grande Guerre*, Vols I and II (Le Vigen: Lela Presse, 2017).

Roberts, John, *Battlecruisers* (London: Chatham Publishing, 1997).

Ropp, Theodore (ed Roberts, S), *The Development of a Modern Navy: French Naval Policy 1871–1904* (Annapolis: Naval Institute Press, 1987).

Seligmann, Matthew, 'Britain's Great Security Mirage: The Royal Navy and the Franco-Russian Naval Threat, 1898–1906', *Journal of Strategic Studies*, Vol 35, No 6 (December 2012), pp 861–86.

Spencer, John, '*Conduite du Tir*: The Birth of Centralised Fire Control', and '*Conduite du Tir* Part 2: 1900 to 1913', *Warship 2010* and *2012*, (London: Conway 2010 and 2012).

Taillemite, Etienne, *Dictionnaire des Marins Français* (Paris: Editions Maritimes et d'Outre-mer, 1982).

Selected pages and reports from *Journal de la Marine, Le Yacht:* (1898–1908), and from *Triton* and *La Revue Maritime* (1950s).

ARCHIVES

Plans and other documentation from the Centre d'Archives de l'Armement (CAA), Châtellerault, and from the Service Historique de la Défense, département marine (http://www.servicehistorique.sga.defense.gouv.fr/02fonds-collections/banquedocuments/planbato/planbato/central.php)

Service historique de la défense – Département Marine at Toulon.

Service historique de la défense – Département Marine at Vincennes, Paris: Boxes BB4 2541 (documentation on policy debates), 2546 (cruisers 1895–1919), and 2547 (armoured cruisers); BB8 (proceedings of *Conseil des Travaux*),

Admiralty Library, Portsmouth: Reports on Foreign Naval Affairs (RFNA) 1901 to 1908.

The National Archives, London: *Bouches à Feu de l'Artillerie Navale de tous Calibres & Modèles.*

INDEX

NOTE ABOUT THE INDEX

The main body of the index consists predominantly of names of ships, people and places. For ships the type of vessel, together with nationality for non-French vessels, are given are in parentheses. Due to the broad scope of the historical section, the only place names included in the index are major ports and those associated with significant actions or campaigns. With regard to French naval officers, only those of flag officers feature in the index. There are 'thematic' entries for the following: **formations, guns, marine boilers, rangefinders** and **underwater weapons**. Sections of the book which focus on a particular system, or on a particular aspect of a ship (or class of ship) are in **bold** type; *italics* are used for photographs.